SAVING
SAN ANTONIO

The Fairmount Hotel's six-day, six-block escape from destruction in 1985 made the Guinness Book of World Records. *Here the 1,600-ton hotel makes a nearly four-hour turn from Bowie Street onto Market Street just before its perilous crossing of a bridge over the San Antonio River. C. Thomas Wright.*

SAVING
SAN ANTONIO

The Preservation
of a Heritage

SECOND
EDITION

Lewis F. Fisher

Foreword by
T. R. Fehrenbach

MAVERICK BOOKS
TRINITY UNIVERSITY PRESS
San Antonio

Published by Maverick Books, an imprint of Trinity University Press
San Antonio, Texas 78212

Cover design by Neeta Verma, designNV, Albuquerque, New Mexico
Cover illustrations: front, istock / James Anderson; back, istock / Glenn Nagel
Book design by Barbara Whitehead

ISBN-13 978-1-59534-777-0 paper
ISBN-13 978-1-59534-781-7 ebook

Trinity University Press strives to produce its books using methods and
materials in an environmentally sensitive manner. We favor working with
manufacturers that practice sustainable management of all natural resources,
produce paper using recycled stock, and manage forests with the best possible
practices for people, biodiversity, and sustainability. The press is a member
of the Green Press Initiative, a nonprofit program dedicated to supporting
publishers in their efforts to reduce their impacts on endangered forests, climate
change, and forest-dependent communities.

The paper used in this publication meets the minimum requirements of the
American National Standard for Information Sciences—Permanence of Paper
for Printed Library Materials, ANSI 39.48–1992.

CIP data on file at the Library of Congress

20 19 18 17 16 | 5 4 3 2 1

Contents

Foreword

San Antonio is a unique city in many senses. Perhaps the most important of these is that it is a city where much of the past still seems alive.

This has fostered a mystique rare in America, a feeling of living on historic, even sacred ground. San Antonio is not just a place in time but part of a continuum that stretches back to primitive Amerindian settlements beside its springs, to Spaniards discovering an oasis rising from the dusty plain, to a struggling frontier outpost flying the royal banners of Castile, to a town, many times destroyed—the most fought-over city in North America—which somehow survived and moved majestically into the Victorian era. San Antonio's past is more than "the Alamo and all that;" it is a complex mix of European and native American, of Spanish royalist and Mexican insurgent, of sober German, civilizing French, and brash Anglo, all of whom have left both their blood and mark upon the city.

In San Antonio each era built upon the old, and somehow in its ambiance and architecture, glass towers rising beside adobe walls, something of the past has always been preserved. Some of this saved heritage came about by accident, some by grace, but much in modern times was due to the heroic efforts of many citizens.

This book, I think, is also unique, because it is the first I have read whose theme is an American city's cultural and architectural soul, and whose heroes are those who strove, and are still striving, to save it. It is also history in the best sense of the word, a telling of the past, meticulously researched and documented, cutting through the accretions of myth and fable that have surrounded each preservation effort. While a history of historic preservation may seem dull to some, a tempest in a teapot, it is a story worth telling, both for what it reveals about our past and what it may presage for our future.

Historic preservation today is big business. Much tourism, an industry of the future, depends upon it. Every state, most major cities, have their historic preservation agencies; the federal government has recognized its importance through legislation and incentives. Yet it is still controversial. Many believe preservation stands in the way of progress. Civic governments have not advanced much beyond the mindset that demolished historic structures to create parking lots for the tourists who came to see them. While preservation provides obvious economic as well as aesthetic and cultural benefits, there is still more money to be made and there are many jobs created by tearing down and building anew.

Many Americans still agree with Henry Ford that "history is bunk" and we should be well rid of it. However, some San Antonians have always understood that our history, both the heroic and the now-unpalatable, has made us what we are and we can't escape it. Destroying the artifacts of our past will not change us; it would merely leave a gaping hole and a sense of loss for future generations.

The San Antonio Conservation Society, this unique historical gathering of concerned women (and men, to be sure) has won some, lost some, in its struggles for sensible preservation. It will go on doing so, in a war that if not quite lost, is never won. The Society represents a certain sort of civic responsibility at its best. And it itself has become "historic," part of the city's past, present and future.

This book, filled with follies as well as famous preservation fights, provides a wonderful perspective of how and why so much of today's San Antonio still stands. Some passages, trampling on cherished mythology, will raise hackles. But it should be read for that very reason: to set the record straight.

May it inspire others around the land to go and do likewise.

T.R. Fehrenbach

Preface

S*aving San Antonio* is the previously untold story of how embattled residents directed swirling forces of growth and change, however partially and inefficiently, along a course which salvaged much of their city's heritage. As a result of this hard-won achievement, San Antonio retains a charm which causes it to be routinely listed among the nation's top travel destinations. By 1992 the city was beginning to appear among the top ten travel destinations of the world as well.[1] Tourism and conventions have grown to become San Antonio's second-largest industry, drawing seven million visitors and injecting $3 billion annually into the city's economy.

To get to the real story of how this occurred requires stripping away layers of familiar but often conflicting fables and of subsidized hyperbole long repeated and embellished upon by those who should have known better. San Antonio's hired publicists, for example, a few years back solemnly invoked Will Rogers as the source for their pitch, "San Antonio is One of America's Four Unique Cities."[2] But Will Rogers was a humorist. Was he just pulling our leg?

Will Rogers was not, the evidence shows, pulling our leg. The publicists were.

In 1926 Will Rogers began one of his newspaper columns by observing, "I have run into a good many pleasant things on my jaunts but the other day I hit San Antonio, what used to be before Progress hit it one of the three unique Cities of America."[3] Not one of "Four Unique Cities." One of three. And not even one of three, although "it used to be before Progress hit it." To the boosters: Close, but no cigar.

Will Rogers continued: "It's a great old Town, is San Antonio, even if they have got a filling station in connection with the Alamo. You have to sacrifice something to Progress, but I never thought it would be the Alamo."[4]

The gasoline filling station and Hertz car rental agency beside the Alamo are gone now. In any event, the Alamo had already been saved. But by whom? A statewide magazine was only reflecting the confusion of oft-told tales when it reported in 1994, "the Alamo wouldn't be here to argue over if the Daughters [of the Republic of Texas] hadn't stopped the state from selling it."[5]

The State of Texas, however, never tried to sell the Alamo. The state bought the Alamo—in 1883, eight years before the Daughters of the Republic of Texas was organized and when Clara Driscoll, who gets personal credit for saving it, was only two years old. Latter-day adulation of Miss Driscoll's courageous advance of funds to purchase remains of the Alamo's adjoining convento and the Daughters' assumption of its care in 1905 have caused that date to be used instead, distracting national writers to this day into missing the fact that the original purchase occurred twenty-two years earlier and was the first time a building was purchased for historic preservation in the nation west of the Mississippi.

In 1993, a San Antonio guidebook tried to deal with traditional garblings of the saving of the downtown River Bend. But it only made things worse: "A small group of women, who were determined to save the river, formed what is today the San Antonio Conservation Society. With a puppet show whose characters resembled members of the city council, they convinced the city to adopt the plan of local architect Robert H.H. Hugman, who proposed a plan to beautify the banks of the river with a bypass channel and floodgates to control the water coming into what has become known as the Big Bend."[6]

The San Antonio Conservation Society was indeed formed by a small group of women who did present a show of puppets which resembled the appearances of members of the city council, then actually called the city commission. But there the facts end. The purpose of the puppet show was to boost efforts of a now-forgotten men's club to save unique aspects of San Antonio. The river was as incidental to the puppet show as it was to the founding of the Conservation Society, which did not champion the cause of the river until a few years later. Nor did the puppet show convince the city to adopt the plans of Robert Hugman, who was living in New Orleans at the time and, as yet, had advanced no plan at all for the San Antonio River. The bypass channel and floodgates were planned long before Hugman returned and presented his ideas for what has become known as the River Bend, or the Paseo del Rio.

Continuing the ongoing and errant stream of what too often has passed in San Antonio for history, the sound track of the orientation show at San Antonio Missions National Historic Park as late as 1995 was crediting anonymously "many individuals and organizations" for saving the San José Mission compound. In truth, the complex was put back together and rebuilt around its church primarily through the leadership of a single effective organization—the San Antonio Conservation Society, founded in 1924 with the sickening realization of what was happening to the city's heritage, as confirmed by Will Rogers two years later. In its scope and continuing achievement in saving not only historic landmarks but also much of the city's cultural tradition and natural environment as well, the San Antonio Conservation Society has carved a record unique in the nation.

The Conservation Society picked up an ongoing preservation tradition. After the Alamo Monument Association engineered the saving of the Alamo church, the mantle of preservation activism fell more or less in succession on four groups—two chapters of the Daughters of the Republic of Texas and the Texas Historical and Landmarks Association, and, finally, on the San Antonio Conservation Society. All helped generate an awareness of the subject but achieved little beyond adding the old convento to the preserved Alamo and making temporary repairs at San José Mission.

Much of the problem in understanding what has actually been going on in San Antonio all these years is nurtured by a pervasive civic self-deception. There exists, for example, a fierce local pride in San Antonio's census rank among the ten largest cities in the United States, a ranking relevant in some respects but one misused as a rationale for having such big-city amenities as professional sports teams. In the more meaningful ranking by broad metropolitan area, adding suburban populations to the totals of suburb-choked central cities outside Texas regularly knocks suburb-shy San Antonio's rank down into the thirties. When San Antonio's National Basketball Association team foresaw financial difficulties, its president acknowledged, "Because we're a small market, we have to chase dollars more than most teams do."[7] But the reality doesn't seem to sink in. When San Antonio found itself listed by a national business magazine as a mid-sized city, one local chamber of commerce leader huffed, "What do you mean, *mid-sized* city?"[8]

Mythology, likewise, commonly substitutes for reality in San Antonio's understanding of its past. Perhaps due to the city's historic location on the frontier, books like *Glamorous Days and Roaring Nights in Old San Antonio* and *San Antonio-City of Flaming Adventure* have gone on the market in the absence of more authoritative accounts, although a number of fine scholarly works on certain aspects of the city's past have appeared in recent years.[9] The first general history of San Antonio was not published until the Scotsman William Corner put out his *San Antonio de Bexar* in 1890, when San Antonio was nearly 175 years old. By contrast, a much larger general history was published of Rochester, New York a half-century earlier, in 1837, when Rochester, its metropolitan area now not far in the listings from San Antonio's, was only twenty-five years old. Continuing the disparity, Rochester's history has since been the subject of dozens of authoritative historical volumes.[10]

Saving San Antonio was begun with the expectation of gathering and documenting familiar but scattered accounts of how the city's distinctive character was preserved. This seemingly simple pursuit, however, was quickly complicated by a labyrinth of false paths, dead ends and hidden passages winding through what William Corner even in 1890 termed "a history inexhaustible in interest," a resource since proven vital to San Antonio's ongoing economic health and stability.

Notes

1. The designation came from *Condé Nast Traveler* magazine, which surveyed 24,000 readers and reported in October of 1992 that San Antonio ranked ninth, between Paris and Venice and, in the United States, behind only Santa Fe and San Francisco.

2. Lewis Fisher, "S.A. Becomes One of Nation's Top Contenders for Giant Conventions," *San Antonio Express-News*, Aug. 24, 1969, 4-B. In a not-unprecedented case of governmental amnesia, one recent city publication attributes "this marvelous designation" instead to Mark Twain. ("Market Square," Market Square Department, City of San Antonio, 1994, 1.) When asked, department officials could not provide the source.

3. James M. Smallwood, ed., *Will Rogers' Weekly Articles: Vol. 2, The Coolidge Years 1925–1927,* Oklahoma State University Press (Stillwater: 1980), 265–69.

4. Ibid.

5. "We Will Never Surrender Or Retreat," *Texas Monthly*, May 1994, 142.

6. *San Antonio On Foot,* Texas Tech University Press, 1993, 29.

7. Charlotte-Anne Lucas, "Team releases private finances predicting loss of $3.3 million," *San Antonio Express-News*, Sept. 21, 1995, 1.

8. Lesli Hicks, "City ranking lofty, but via downsizing," *San Antonio Express-News*, Sept. 21, 1995, 1-E.

9. In delving into the city's earliest history, these scholars have not allowed themselves to be overcome by challenges of gaps in the archival record caused by loss during the city's often violent past. Also, documents written in Castilian Spanish and documents inconsistently translated or mistranslated in Spanish, German and English are seen as problems which characterize "any research [that] must be conducted in San Antonio." (Joseph H. Labadie, *La Villita Earthworks* [San Antonio: Center for Archaeological Research, The University of Texas at San Antonio, Archaeological Survey Report No. 139, 1986], 11–12.)

10. Blake McKelvey, *A Panoramic History of Rochester and Monroe County, New York* (Woodland Hills, Calif.: Windsor Publications Inc., 1979), 5.

Acknowledgments

In commissioning this book, the San Antonio Conservation Society placed me under no constraints except, "Tell the truth." I benefited from encouragement through the initial writing from an attentive ad-hoc society committee chaired by Beverly Blount-Hemphill and including Peggy Penshorn, Sally Eckhoff, Glory Felder, Marie McGonagle, Camille Rosengren, then-president Marianna Jones and Executive Director Bruce MacDougal. That support has continued in the final phase with President Sally Buchanan, Lynn Osborne Bobbitt and Maria Watson Pfeiffer. Johanna Williams and other chairmen and members of the Oral History Committee performed their difficult tasks well. I have had full access to the Conservation Society's three linear feet of minutes and to all files in the library in its Wulff House headquarters, where the entire staff has provided aid, as have many members and past presidents of the Conservation Society itself.

Among others providing valuable assistance were Dr. Félix D. Almaráz, Jr., University of Texas at San Antonio professor of history; Trinity University Professor Emeritus of History Dr. Donald E. Everett; Texas historian T.R. Fehrenbach; Anne L. (Bebe) Fenstermaker, who gave special access to the papers of her grandmother, Rena Maverick Green; San José Mission art tile authority Susan Toomey Frost; architectural historians Mary Carolyn and Eugene George; Dr. William E. Green, curator of history at the Panhandle-Plains Historical Museum in Canyon and former assistant curator of history at the Witte Museum in San Antonio; Rebecca Huffstutler and Cecelia Steinfeldt at the Witte Museum; Ron Jones at Photo Arts; Trinity University's Maddux Library Assistant Director Craig Likness; Danielle Matusic, assistant for the Schwimmer-Lloyd Collection in the Rare Books and Manuscripts Division of the New York Public Library; University of the Incarnate Word St. Pius X Library Director Mendell D. Morgan, Jr.; San Antonio Missions National Park Historian Dr. Rosalind Rock; Trinity University Maddux Library Special Collections Director Janice Sabec; Tom Shelton, San Antonio's photo archivist extraordinaire, at the University of Texas at San Antonio's Institute of Texan Cultures, and the Institute's librarian, Diane Bruce; Bill

Simmons at the Texas State Archives in Austin; Martha Utterback, assistant director of the Daughters of the Republic of Texas Texas History Research Library at the Alamo; Nelle Lee Weincek, Barbara Santella and Eva Milstead at the San Antonio Conservation Society Library; and *San Antonio Express-News* Librarian Judy Zipp.

My wife, Mary, proved, as always, an invaluable critic. Our sons, William and Maverick, provided critiques and research backup while in graduate and undergraduate programs at the University of Texas at Austin. Perceptive and supportive throughout have been Texas Tech University Press Editor Judith Keeling, Production Supervisor Marilyn Steinborn and Editorial Assistant Fran Kennedy in Lubbock, four hundred miles but, fortunately, only one phone call away.

Twenty years later, this second edition—published by Trinity University Press, ably directed by Tom Payton—replaces the original book's final chapter with four new ones and an afterword. I have been aided by a new ad hoc committee composed of Conservation Society President Janet Dietel and former presidents Nancy Avellar, Janet Francis and Sue Ann Pemberton, plus Bruce MacDougal, preparing to retire after twenty-five eventful years as the society's executive director. Also of particular assistance have been Beth Standifird, since 2001 the society's fulltime librarian; cartographer John Culp, for the map of San Antonio preservation districts; and Shanon Miller, director of the City of San Antonio's Office of Historic Preservation, and her staff.

"Without the aid of original records and authentic documents, history will be nothing more than a well-combined series of ingenious conjectures and amusing fables. The cause of truth is interesting to all . . . and those who possess the means . . . of preventing error, or of elucidating obscure facts, will confer a benefit by communicating them to the world."

—Founders of The New-York Historical Society, 1805

Introduction:
The Goose
With the Golden Eggs

It was the 1920s. A building boom was transforming San Antonio into a metropolis. Rising in downtown San Antonio were twice as many skyscrapers as in downtown Dallas, as subdivisions spread into the semi-arid South Texas countryside. Newly-paved highways brought new waves of ground traffic as air travel cut the city's isolation even more. San Antonio was playing cultural catch-up with the rest of the world as well. A philharmonic orchestra was organized. A new auditorium provided a home for the state's first civic grand opera. A larger public library was built, and the city's first true museum. One of downtown's new movie palaces hosted the world premiere of a locally-filmed movie that won the first Academy Award for Best Picture.

But in all the excitement, San Antonio was devouring its soul.

Fifty years earlier, the railroad ended San Antonio's century and a half of isolated evolution. San Antonio's "antiquated foreignness" charmed nineteenth-century travelers even if it embarrassed many San Antonians themselves. Now that fast-growing automobile traffic provided an excuse to widen downtown streets in the manner of other major cities, most businessmen gave little thought to the consequences of destroying the old city.

There was one notable exception. In 1883, the Alamo had become the first landmark west of the Mississippi River purchased by a public body and saved in the nation's growing historic preservation movement. Like Mount Vernon, Independence Hall and Fort Ticonderoga, it was a place where great men had lived or died. As a shrine, it was to honor martyrs and inspire future generations of Americans. Beyond Alamo Plaza, San José and San Antonio's other Spanish missions were interesting. But, as with the city's other less-hallowed landmarks, decline and decay could generate only passing sentiment. Their role in history had been played. Progress meant accommodating the future, not the past.

Not so, thought a few San Antonio women. Unlike most women elsewhere in a nation whose preservation efforts were motivated by patriotism and by remembering deeds of ancestors, these preservation-minded women were artists. They had grown up in San Antonio, and traveled abroad. They knew their picturesque home city was different from anyplace else, and that its cultural heritage was fast disappearing. Women had gained the right to vote and were no longer confined to keeping the hearth. Now they could go out and defend it.

In February of 1924 came news that San Antonio's old Market House was doomed by still another downtown street-widening. Its Greek Revival style made it among the city's few fine examples of classic architecture. But the Market House was not even a hundred years old, and held no association with anyone or anything of any particular historical significance. Elsewhere in the nation no one would yet think of saving such a purely commercial building.

Emily Edwards, however, had just returned from studying art in Province-town, Massachusetts, and was seeing San Antonio with a fresh eye. She found San Antonio "just such a relief" after visiting other cities that she thought it a shame to change anything, especially such landmarks as the Market House.[1] Another artist, civic activist Rena Maverick Green, came to the same conclusion. In a fateful chance meeting near the Market House, the two decided to form the San Antonio Conservation Society and do something about it. As new members' concerns grew, the new society apparently became the first in America to seek preservation of both the historic built environment and the natural environment.

Two other proposals were on the table at the time. For nearly ten years, pioneer preservationist Adina De Zavala had been trying to have the Spanish Governor's Palace preserved. Also, as chairman of a local Daughters of the Republic of Texas committee, Rena Green had been trying to get four of the city's ruined Spanish missions restored and preserved in a state park. With the growing awareness of the city's endangered heritage, the men's Technical Club proposed a landmarks management program called S.O.S.—Save Old San Antonio. The Governor's Palace would be purchased and run by the state as the city's long-sought public museum. The Catholic Daughters of America would oversee the missions. The Market House would get financial backing from the city and be in the charge of the new Conservation Society.

Some group was always asking the city for money, and city hall had seen many schemes come and go. But city commissioners soon found that they had never reckoned with the likes of the San Antonio Conservation Society. First, the three-month-old society took City Commissioner for Parks Ray Lambert with them on a bus tour to inspect the city's parks and landmarks and made him Honorary President. Then, to get across to all commissioners the idea of saving landmarks like the Market House, the artists of the

Conservation Society came up with not just another resolution or a formal visit to city hall. They took an unconventional approach unprecedented, and no doubt unduplicated, in the cause of historic and environmental preservation.

Emily Edwards had taught drama in San Antonio's Brackenridge High School before a stint as a stage designer in New York City. In Provincetown she made puppets and staged puppet shows for an experimental theater.[2] To dramatize issues involved in the S.O.S. effort, Miss Edwards proposed a puppet show for city commissioners, a show to urge preservation of the uniqueness of the city "on the principle that 'a word to the wise is sufficient.'"[3] The script, in loosely-written verse, was entitled "The Goose With the Golden Eggs," the eggs being unique characteristics of the city—in some cases representing literal gold, in the form of tourist dollars.[4] In a performance lasting less than ten minutes, Mr. and Mrs. San Antonio would quarrel over the goose's fate. Mr. San Antonio would want the goose killed immediately to get all the gold. Mrs. San Antonio would want it spared to keep laying golden eggs. City commissioners themselves would be the court hearing the case.

At a midsummer meeting of city commissioners, Emily Edwards, Rena Green and other member artists sat in the back row sketching the men for the puppets' design.[5] "We had [already] been going to their meetings, so they didn't know anything was up," Miss Edwards recalled. The puppets were made of cloth, with button eyes. Mr. and Mrs. San Antonio and the Stage Manager were manipulated by inserted hands and held on the stage above the puppeteers' heads. The five commissioner puppets were placed on bottles along a shelf, as if they were seated in chairs. Their few gestures were made by helpers behind a curtain.[6]

By August, the puppets were ready. A basket held five golden eggs labeled Heart of Texas, Missions, History, Tourists and Beauty. The chance for a dress rehearsal came when the men of the Technical Club and the Scientific Society invited ladies of the Conservation Society to a joint luncheon.[7] The opportunity to present the show to city commissioners came in September of 1924 in the city hall meeting room after the close of a regular commissioners session.[8] The Stage Manager puppet made the introductions:

Your Honor, Commissioners, Ladies, gentlemen,
I have come to crave an audience
For an old, old tale made new again,
For foolishness mixed up with sense.

I am the "Spirit of Yesterday"
The hero and heroine be pleased to know—
I introduce the actors of today
Mr. (enter) and Mrs. (enter) San Antonio.   (They bow.)

Local peculiarities for our present use
Will be represented by this fetching Goose.   (She enters and bows.)
"The Goose With the Golden Eggs" is the play
The place is here, the time today.   (Bows and exits.)

As the first scene opened, Mr. and Mrs. San Antonio were on stage with
the goose. Mr. San Antonio went to the right to bring in the basket of golden
eggs, "which he places center with great care."[9] Then Mrs. San Antonio
individually held up each egg, with comments as, in the case of the second
egg, "Beauty:"

Yes they loved you for your beauty,
For your winding stream and trees,
For your skies of deepest azure,
And your ever-welcome breeze.

San Antonio Conservation Society members in 1924 sketched city commissioners unawares during a session in city hall, then made life-like puppets to present commissioners a play entitled "The Goose With the Golden Eggs." The play stressed the need to save the city's landmarks and character in order to produce civic pride and the gold of tourists' dollars. These original puppets, first seated on bottles which could be jiggled from below, represent from left, Fire and Police Commissioner Phil Wright, Park Commissioner Ray Lambert, Mayor John W. Tobin, Street Commissioner Paul Steffler and Tax Commissioner Frank Bushick. Quarreling Mr. and Mrs. San Antonio, on bottles at right, are next to the mustachioed Stage Manager. Only the goose, which represented "local peculiarities," is not original. The original goose was smaller, but, like the impact of the show itself, the new goose was made larger in later years. San Antonio Conservation Society.

So each built strong to hold you,
First the missions, grand and bold,
Then a city of unequaled beauty,
And this gift, too, was gold.

At the end of Scene One, the impatient Mr. San Antonio declared:

But wife—there is no telling
What she withholds from me
This income is too slow,
I want more Prosperity.

The couple tussled as Mr. San Antonio went for his knife to kill the goose. As the curtain fell, Mrs. San Antonio proposed that the city fathers decide the goose's fate. As the curtain rose on Scene Two, the mayor and commissioners were seated at the council table. They began with some remarks about the incoming Texas governor, "Ma" Ferguson:

Mayor Tobin: Hurrah for Ma!
Commissioner Steffler: Our Governor!
Commissioner Lambert: Boys can you beat it,
A *petticoat* seated!

Commissioner Wright: But now we'll have the surprise of your lives
If we find we have to listen to our *wives*.

The wife of Mr. San Antonio entered and was welcomed by Mayor Tobin, whereupon Commissioner Lambert suggested:

Now that we've flooded the city with bonds
To bind the floods with a dam,
Are making more parks out of ponds
And have gotten all out of the jam
Since this is a good time for wishing
I move we adjourn and go fishing.

The vote to adjourn for another of the commissioners' well-known fishing trips to the Texas coast was unanimous. But, after a few sobs from Mrs. San Antonio, the mayor let the couple speak. He rapped for order. Mr. San Antonio complained about the crooked streets and then about the goose itself:

Now I'd have only Broadways
And cut out her lanes
And make this a speedway
For autos and trains.

She waddles and she winds
When she swims on the river
And takes up more land
Than I'm willing to give her.

Her home is old buildings
That simply won't fall down
And keep us from looking
Just like every other town—

She has her own customs
(Wife:) Yes and this is the truth   (sarcastic)
She even eats chili
Not served in Duluth.

After more give-and-take, Mrs. San Antonio pleaded:

Ah spare this goose for future use
The voice of culture begs,
Your reward will come, for this precious goose
Will lay *more golden eggs*.

The mayor, rapping for order, put the question to the audience: "Shall we kill the goose or not?" The audience, stacked with Conservation Society members, responded, loudly, "No!" The curtain fell as Mrs. San Antonio clutched the goose. The stage manager stood before the curtain with a shiny new egg:

See the egg laid on the way
Civic Pride—You'll win the day!   (turns it over, showing S.O.S.)
S.O.S. 'Tis the danger cry—
Save Old San Antonio—ere she die.

As the stage manager exited, the goose took a final bow.

The city commissioners weren't sure how to take it. Remembered Rena Green's daughter, Rowena, who was in the audience: "The men turned scarlet, Steffler particularly. The women enjoyed it more than the men, but the men had to laugh. . . . And it was very successful."[10]

Two months after the puppet show, the Conservation Society took Mayor John W. Tobin, Parks Commissioner Ray Lambert and the city's new flood control engineer, S.E. Crecelius, on a two-hour rowboat ride through downtown to impress them with the natural beauty of the San Antonio River and with a practical use for an attractive river—as a site for a Fiesta boat parade. Spectators were stationed above bridges to cheer as the rowboats passed below, as spectators would cheer for a large parade.

It was not long, however, before the imaginative ladies of the Conservation Society realized that "a word to the wise" through bus tours, puppet shows and river rides was not sufficient. The Technical Club abandoned the Save Old San Antonio campaign. City hall likewise dropped its support of the

Market House project, and removed the building to widen the street. The city then cut through the Market House site for a new river course, part of a flood control project which brought years of uproar from the ladies over concrete channels and cantilevered streets. Mr. and Mrs. San Antonio's quarrel over killing the golden goose resumed as if there had been no verdict.

But when it came to Saving Old San Antonio, the women proved they had more staying power than the men. The Conservation Society elicited enough guilt from city commissioners that the facade of the Market House was replicated as that of the new San Pedro Playhouse. With no state funds forthcoming to save the Spanish Governor's Palace, the City Federation of Women's Clubs successfully encouraged a city bond issue to buy the building. The Conservation Society took up the cause of locating the city's long-over-due museum in the Market House, and, with that gone, saw the effort to completion in the form of the Witte Memorial Museum in Brackenridge Park. With still little being done about saving the Spanish missions, the Conserva-tion Society boldly set about buying up old mission lands and buildings, even in the depths of the Depression.

So the goose lives, and the original golden eggs are still with us—Heart of Texas, Missions, History, Tourists and Beauty, plus Civic Pride. Their survival is not accidental. The oftimes frustrating, always continuing and not infre-quently heroic efforts led by the San Antonio Conservation Society to save San Antonio's cultural heritage have transcended the dramatic individual struggles and left a truly golden legacy. The record shows that as a direct result of the hard-won preservation of what is left of Old San Antonio, San Antonio has become, as the city's earliest preservationists knew it could, one of the most-visited cities in the nation and in the world. San Antonio's $3 billion annual tourism industry is second only to the military as the city's largest.

The record also shows that this impact on the economic health of a major city is unequaled among the works of private preservation groups elsewhere in America.

Notes

"Minutes" in endnote entries refer to minutes of the San Antonio Conservation Society, which as the organization grew were divided into separate sections in minutes books. The following abbreviations are used for minutes of later years: G—General membership meetings, D—Directors meetings, F—Conservation Society Foundation meetings, E—Executive Committee meetings and A—Associate Members meetings. Unless other-wise noted, the reference is on the first page. The abbreviation OHT is for Oral History Transcript. Minutes and Oral History Transcripts referenced are kept at the San Antonio Conservation Society's Wulff House headquarters.

1. Emily Edwards, Oral History Transcript (OHT), Jul. 24, 1971, 4. Emily Edwards was interviewed by Charles B. Hosmer, Jr. in preparation for his definitive two-volume work *Preservation Comes of Age, From Williamsburg to the National Trust, 1926–1949*, published in 1981.

2. Cecelia Steinfeldt, *Art for History's Sake: The Texas Collection Of The Witte Museum* (San Antonio: The Texas State Historical Association for the Witte Museum, 1993), 65.

3. Minutes, Jul. 5, 1924.

4. The title written on the original script and referred to within is "The Goose With the Golden Eggs." The show was referred to in Conservation Society minutes as "The Goose That Laid the Golden Egg," one of several minor name variations which appear through the years as the script was revised and presented on other occasions. Quotations herein are from the original version. As myths regarding the puppet show grew in later years, the goose and/or the eggs became credited with representing the San Antonio River. The play then came to be believed responsible for saving the River Bend. The goose and the eggs in fact represented less specific concepts, and the river was mentioned in the play only in passing. Like the society's subsequent rowboat journey, the play helped create only a general awareness of questions not resolved until coming to boiling points years later.

5. Rowena Green Fenstermaker OHT, Feb. 2, 1984, 28–29.

6. Emily Edwards OHT, 6; Description appended to the original script in San Antonio Conservation Society (SACS) files with the note, "Information from Miss Emily Edwards, April, 1977."

7. "Society," *San Antonio Express*, Aug. 31, 1924, 8-B. The men assured the ladies that they "were in thorough accord with the aims of the Conservation Society."

8. Emily Edwards, "The San Antonio Conservation Society and the River," *San Antonio Conservation Society Newsletter*, Sept., 1966. The presentation is not recorded in the City Commissioners Minutes.

9. Behind the scenes, Lucretia Van Horn was the voice and puppeteer for Mr. San Antonio, and also the voices of the mayor and commissioners. Emily Edwards was the voice and puppeteer for Mrs. San Antonio. Charlotte Reeves was the puppeteer for the goose. Helpers were Margaret Van Horn and Henry Wedemeyer, who at the appropriate times jiggled the bottles on which the "commissioners" were placed.

10. Fenstermaker OHT, 30.

I

Preservation West
of the
Mississippi
Begins in San Antonio
(1879–1924)

1

A City of "Odd and Antiquated Foreignness"

San Antonio's cultural kaleidoscope has intrigued travelers for more than two centuries. Born where a sandy plain and shallow valley meet gently rolling hills, and fed by a narrow, meandering river, San Antonio in its formative years was whipsawed by divergent cultures clashing over rights to hold a vast area from the Gulf of Mexico to the Chihuahan Desert, from the outposts of colonial France to the north and east to those of New Spain to the south and west. By the time the various empires and newly independent countries and their challengers were done in 1865 and San Antonio could finally begin to enjoy long-term peace, the town had become in appearance and culture a curious amalgam of all that it had met. Its ambiance yet evokes an almost mystical sense of past and present.

When its isolation ended with the arrival of the railroad in 1877, San Antonio welcomed an era of prosperity and exuberance that threatened to sweep all before it. Travelers, who once claimed to think they were in Italy rather than in Texas and who marveled over the mix of cultures and "confusion of unknown tongues," now began to warn local residents about the value of what San Antonio had to lose by becoming a modern city.

Admonishments fell at first on deaf ears. But as a new generation of San Antonians traveled elsewhere and returned with new perspectives, attitudes began to change—slowly, at first, then with new thrust and direction. A century after the railroad arrived, San Antonio was unmistakably a modern metropolis. But there was also no mistaking that San Antonio was not totally up-to-date and faceless in the mold of other places. Efforts of several generations of aroused citizens had overcome many, but not all, seemingly insurmountable odds to keep the city charmingly cloaked in the partly torn but still vibrantly colored mantle of distant times and nearly forgotten peoples.

Among the half-dozen major American cities founded as outposts of the Spanish Empire, San Antonio has uniquely maintained its Spanish heritage. The tie may not appear as dominant as in smaller American cities also established by Spain—St. Augustine, Santa Fe, Santa Barbara. But nor have the ravages of time and unthinking development swept away the cultural remnants of the Spanish Empire to the same extent as in the other major American cities with comparable roots—San Francisco, Los Angeles, San Diego, Tucson and Albuquerque.

San Antonio, to be sure, started with—and kept—the nation's largest grouping of Spanish missions. Four, stretching along the San Antonio River in southern San Antonio, are now linked by the San Antonio Missions National Historical Park. The church of the fifth, downtown, is revered as the Alamo. But even in downtown San Antonio, the heart of city and county government still beats within the still-visible confines of a city plan decreed by the King of Spain in 1573. San Antonio's city hall is literally within a stone's throw of two landmarks from the days of Spanish rule—the Spanish Governor's Palace (1749) and the apse of the parish church of San Fernando (1738).[1]

As in the case of other communities on the arid northern frontier of New Spain, San Antonio's beginnings were modest. Its site was identified in mid-1691, when a group of Spanish soldiers and priests came to the head-waters of a shaded stream at the edge of the plains they called the New Philippines in an area known by native Indians as Yanaguana. It happened to be June 13, the day of St. Anthony of Padua—a good enough reason to name the spot San Antonio de Padua.

By then the French were entrenched in Louisiana, between Spanish Florida to the east and Spanish Mexico to the west. LaSalle had landed on the Texas coast in 1685. Although the Frenchman's expedition failed, Spain realized it needed a buffer north of the Rio Grande to protect its colonies and silver

Uniquely among the nation's largest cities established under Spanish rule, San Antonio's downtown still functions in large measure as directed by the King of Spain. Facing the original civilian Main Plaza, or Plaza de las Islas, is the enlarged parish church of San Fernando, now a cathedral and still a central place of worship for the Catholic community. The tip of its mid-1700s apse can be glimpsed at the rear of the roof. The civil government building of the county faces Main Plaza—the county courthouse, off the picture at left foreground. The city's civilian council meeting place, which in Spanish times looked out to Main Plaza from the foreground below, is now housed in the tall Municipal Plaza building at right, still Frost National Bank when this picture was taken toward the west in the 1940s. San Antonio's second major Spanish plaza, Military Plaza, or Plaza de Armas, where soldiers of the Spanish presidio once were stationed, now accommodates a four-story city hall in its center. Still facing Military Plaza is the home of the presidio commander—the restored Spanish Governor's Palace, which extends slightly past city hall on the far side of the plaza. San Antonio Conservation Society.

Colorful patterns originally decorated the walls of San Antonio's San Jóse mission church to attract the nomadic Indians whom Spanish Franciscans wished to convert. Ernst Schuchard Collection, Daughters of the Republic of Texas Library at the Alamo.

mines in Mexico to the south. In 1716, Spain approved a plan for eight missions and forts, some in east Texas near the Louisiana border and others farther inland. The Texas missions were to be established by competing Franciscan colleges deeper in Spanish Mexico, in Zacatecas and in Querétaro. Lacking settlers for the new area, the Spanish planned to make allies of the Indians by converting them to Christianity at the missions. Not far from each mission would be a presidio, or fort, where Spanish soldiers could keep an eye on things.

Father Antonio Olivares of the Franciscan College at Querétaro visited the site of San Antonio in 1709 and saw its potential. Nine years later, on May 1, 1718, he returned to establish a mission. There was a ready source of Indian converts in the nomadic bands of Coahuiltecans, more primitive than the Tejas of central and eastern Texas but wishing protection from their enemies, the Apaches.[2] At the headwaters of San Pedro Creek Father Olivares dedicated the site of a mission he named San Antonio de Valero, substituting for Padua the name of the viceroy of New Spain, the Marques de Valero. Four days later the new governor, Martín de Alarcón, picked a site nearby for the presidio of

San Antonio de Béjar, which he named by substituting for Padua the name of the viceroy's late brother, the Duque de Béjar (Bexar), a Spanish hero who died fighting Turks in Hungary. Within three years, both mission and presidio were moved farther south, the presidio to the Plaza de Armas and the mission across the river to the east.

In 1720, the Franciscan College of Zacatecas established Mission San José y San Miguel de Aguayo, named after the new governor of New Spain, two miles downstream from the Queréterian Mission San Antonio de Valero. A mission named San Francisco Xavier de Nájera was begun by Queréterians north of San José two years later, but merged with San Antonio de Valero in 1726 when it failed to attract Indian residents.

As operating missions near the French colonial frontier became more difficult for the Spaniards, the river plain south of San Antonio appeared an increasingly attractive haven. In 1731, three East Texas missions of the Querétaro Franciscans were reestablished along the San Antonio River nearby— Nuestra Señora de la Purisma Concepción de Acuña, San Francisco de la Espada and San Juan Capistrano. A few priests at each mission worked with converts to build fortified compounds for a church and monastic buildings, quarters for the converts, a granary and workshops. Buildings were of plastered rubble with dressed stone trim, compared to the plastered adobe construction of California missions.[3]

The five San Antonio missions were at their height for a quarter century, beginning in the 1740s. San José, the largest and most consistently prosperous, was housing between 106 and 350 Indians from 1740 to 1793.[4] By 1745, more than two thousand had been baptized at all four Queréterian missions. Another 141 of the 885 then living at the four were preparing for baptism. They had 5,115 head of cattle, 3,325 sheep and goats, 257 horses and 86 yoke of oxen to help raise corn, beans and cotton.[5]

Critical to the entire Spanish presence around San Antonio was the water provided by the San Antonio River. The water and land rights distribution system, brought to Spain by the Moors, was established at San Antonio in 1718 with the first of a system of eight engineered acequias, hand-dug ditches which diverted water from the river for nearly two hundred years. For the missions and for civilians as well, the irrigation opened surrounding land for farming and pastures.[6]

Priests could count on mission architects in Mexico for help in designing mission churches. Civilians and military personnel got no such architectural assistance, but were required to follow specific planning guidelines. After the American Revolution, most settlers moving west from the Atlantic seaboard voluntarily planned their towns in the gridiron pattern predominant in the east, with straight streets intersecting at right angles to form rectangular blocks. In New Spain, however, this was not left to chance. Rediscovered

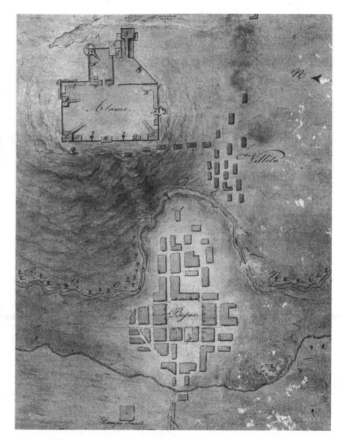

The general layout of Spanish San Antonio, looking eastward in this map of 1836, shows at the top the walls of Mission San Antonio de Valero, later known as the Alamo, enclosing the mission church and other buildings. In La Villita, to its right above a bend in the San Antonio River, lived soldiers and families of the Alamo's latter-day garrison. In the main town below, "Bejar" marks Main Plaza, site of the civilian Villa. The military presidio was around Military Plaza, the open square below Bejar on the map and past a group of buildings which include the parish church of San Fernando. Map Collection, The Center For American History, The University of Texas at Austin, copy negative 01625.

architectural principles of the Roman planner Vitruvius evolved into the town planning sections of the Laws of the Indies, codified and promulgated by Spain's Philip II in 1573. They became the standard planning principles for new towns throughout the empire, including those on the northern frontier of New Spain.[7]

For civilian communities, the Laws of the Indies prescribed the Vitruvian principle orienting plazas so that diverging streets were protected from what was believed to be the four principal winds. Proportions of the medium-size main plaza were to be "the best for festivals in which horses are used and any other celebrations which have to be held," or four hundred by six hundred Spanish feet—the precise original measurements of San Antonio's Main Plaza. Ideally, twelve straight streets were to lead from the plazas, two from each of the four corners and one from the middle of each side. Streets were to be wide in cold climates but narrow in hot ones, to minimize exposure to direct sun. There were other directives for placing churches, homes, hospitals and businesses and for towns' geographical limits. Town boundaries were typically square, with each side five and a quarter miles in length for a total territory of some twenty-eight square miles.[8] San Antonio de Béjar's boundaries were six miles on each side, covering thirty-six square miles. The geographical center was the cross atop the apse cupola of the parish church on Main Plaza.[9]

In addition to utilizing established formats for the civilian community and for the mission communities, the Spanish in San Antonio used their third form of colonization—the presidio, a walled compound for defense.[10] In San Antonio the presidio took the form of the Plaza de Armas, its name later Anglicized to Military Plaza before being changed back again. The Plaza de Armas became a twin to the civilian Main Plaza. The two were separated only by the church and its adjoining buildings, which faced Main Plaza. Main Plaza was also designated Plaza de las Islas in honor of fifty-six Spanish settlers who arrived in San Antonio on March 9, 1731. The only large group of Spanish civilians to settle in San Antonio, they were recruited in Spain's Canary Islands and formed the core of San Antonio's civilian community, named the Villa de San Fernando de Béxar in honor of the heir to the Spanish throne who became Ferdinand VI.

To build homes, the first settlers used what was readily available—sticks and mud. Pioneers in heavily wooded areas of the New World could build cabins of large, horizontal logs. In the semi-arid countryside of San Antonio, pioneers used *palisado* construction to erect cabins of vertical logs—*jacales,* most commonly built of closely spaced narrow cedar posts set into a continuous trench and covered with adobe mud or lime plaster. Attached at the top of the posts was a framework of timbers supporting a roof of thatched grass. Canary Islanders favored a more substantial type of construction, baking mud into adobe blocks before adding flat or pitched flat roofs or, instead of adobe, sawing large blocks of the abundant soft caliche limestone for walls.[11]

San Antonio became the most important settlement in the entire province of Texas—"an almost empty honor," noted frontier urban historian John W. Reps, "for there existed few competitors."[12] Dominating San Antonio's Spanish skyline was the stone parish church of San Fernando, begun in 1738 and completed twenty years later in time for the visiting Bishop of Guadalajara to confirm the first communion class.[13] Three other substantial buildings were constructed during the Spanish period, all flat-roofed, one-story plastered stone homes: the Gironimo de la Garza House (1734), where Spanish coins were later minted, on the northern edge of the town; the residence of the captain of the presidio, later known as the Spanish Governor's Palace (1749), on the western side of the Plaza de Armas; and the home of Juan Martín Veramendi, known as the Veramendi Palace by the early 1800s, off Main Plaza on the street leading north from its northeast corner. An unimposing government building, the Casa Real, faced the east side of Main Plaza.

East Texas lost its strategic importance for New Spain after the French and Indian War, when the Louisiana territory was transferred to Spain and its administration assigned to Cuba rather than to New Spain.[14] As part of the

San Antonio's finest Spanish colonial residence was that of Juan Martín Veramendi. Its large doors, now on display in the Alamo, opened onto a courtyard. Raba Collection, San Antonio Conservation Society.

consolidation and fall-back to the Rio Grande as New Spain's true northern frontier, an inspector sent to the region by King Charles III even considered recommending abandonment of San Antonio and its five "wealthy" missions. He "reluctantly concluded," however, that too much money and effort were invested in San Antonio to justify such a move.[15] Also, compared with conditions he had seen elsewhere, the inspector found San Antonio functioning rather well, although he thought the twenty-two man presidio, which posted three guards at each of the five missions, was undermanned.[16] In 1772 east Texas was abandoned, and the capital of Texas moved westward from Los Adaes to San Antonio. Since Apaches then had fewer places to attack to the east, more troops were stationed at the presidio to cope with an expected increase in Apache attacks around San Antonio.[17]

San Antonio eventually became home to two thousand persons, less than one-fourth of them Spanish. In 1778, Father Juan Agustín Morfi, visiting with new provincial Commandante General Teodoro de Croix, found "fifty-nine houses of stone and mud and seventy-nine of wood, but all poorly built, without any preconceived plan, so that the whole resembles more a poor village than a villa . . . . The streets are tortuous and are filled with mud when it rains."[18] Croix described a scene of "huts and little wooden houses which a wind and rain storm largely destroyed last year. They have neither walls nor stockade to protect them from the attacks of the Indians."[19] He also complained of illiterate citizens who "live in wretched poverty to this day because

This group of homes which once stood on Laredo Street reflects San Antonio's early architecture. At the far left is a home of plastered adobe or caliche blocks. In the center home, flaking plaster shows the underlying caliche blocks. Mud and plaster have fallen away from walls of the home at the right to reveal indigenous palisado, or vertical log construction. Courtesy of the Witte Museum, San Antonio, Texas.

of their laziness, trifling ways and lack of steadiness."[20] The situation, however, may have been caused more by chronic difficulties in transportation to distant markets and lack of mineral resources or cash crops. With a limited number of livestock the only export, San Antonio's economy remained marginal throughout the eighteenth century.[21]

After several decades the missions were failing, their Indian inhabitants apathetic and decimated by periodic epidemics. In 1773 the Quéreterian missionaries left Texas, turning their four San Antonio missions over to their Franciscan brothers of the College of Zacatecas, which had founded San José.[22] Between 1793 and 1824, during reforms throughout Mexico, all missions were gradually closed and their lands secularized. A cavalry troop transferred from the Mexican post of San José y Santiago del Alamo de Parras arrived at the turn of the century and stationed itself in the deserted mission of San Antonio de Valero, where it became known as "the Alamo troop." Some of those with families joined former mission land workers along a nearby bend in the San Antonio River in a neighborhood of flimsy homes known as La Villita.

The parish church of San Fernando, built in 1749, was the dominant feature of Spanish San Antonio's Main Plaza. On Military Plaza behind it, past the two-story shuttered building at the right, can be glimpsed part of the Spanish Governor's Palace. The University of Texas Institute of Texan Cultures, San Antonio, Texas, courtesy Mary Ann Noonan Guerra.

Helping to bind inhabitants into a community and elevate their attention from the hardships of daily life was the parish church of San Fernando, which faced the public plaza designed to permit festivals. The clergy organized a calendar of festivals of patron saints and such traditional feasts as Christmas and Holy Week, while civil leaders organized celebrations there for new monarchs, peace treaties and installation of new town council members. The calendar yielded a combination of religious and secular festivals unique in New Spain.[23] The color they added to the city is reflected in the description of the festival day of the Virgin of Guadalupe by Mary Adams (Mrs. Samuel A.) Maverick in 1840, less than twenty years since the time of Spanish rule:

> Twelve young girls dressed in spotless white bore a platform on which stood a figure representing the saint, very richly and gorgeously dressed. First came the priests in procession, then the twelve girls bearing the platform and each carrying in her free hand a lighted wax candle, then came fiddlers behind them playing on their violins, and following the fiddlers the devout population generally, firing off guns and pistols and showing their devotion in various ways. They proceeded through the squares and some of the principal streets, and every now and then they all knelt and repeated a short prayer . . . . Finally the procession stopped at the Cathedral of San Fernando on the Main Plaza, where a long ceremony was had[,] afterwards the more prominent families taking the

Patroness along with them [and] adjourning to Mr. José Flores' house on [the] west side of Military Plaza, where they danced most of the night.[24]

Of the residents of Spanish San Antonio, concluded T.R. Fehrenbach, "at the far end of the empire, untrained and unequipped, beset by hostile savages, and living in an isolated outpost lacking economic outlets, they could only adopt the common stockraising way of life and culture of the northern regions of Spanish Mexico, a hardy life that put down roots and Spanish seeds in Texas soil but produced no manifestations of superior culture. The Spanish stock survived, and that is tribute enough."[25]

Soon, San Antonio was involved in the struggle for Mexican independence from Spain. In 1813 a Mexican Republican army moved on San Antonio from the east, defeated nearby Royalists in the Battle of Salado and took over the town. But the Republican army, split by dissension between Mexican Republicans and American volunteers, was in turn wiped out by a Spanish Royalist army sent up from Mexico. Several hundred San Antonians were summarily executed for aiding the rebels. Mexico finally achieved independence from Spain in 1821.

At the end of 1820, shortly before his death, Moses Austin arrived in San Antonio and received Spanish permission to bring American colonists into Texas as a buffer against the Indians. In 1822 the new Mexican government gave Austin's son Stephen the same authority. Soon the new colonists, who began to call themselves "Texians," had "felled more trees, planted more fields and built more settlements along the river bottoms of East Texas than the Spanish had in three hundred years."[26] Like the first English colonists in America, the new American immigrants grew used to being left alone by government. They soon outnumbered Hispanic Texans ten to one, but stayed primarily in east Texas. Among the few who drifted to San Antonio was James Bowie, who married a daughter of Juan Martín Veramendi.[27]

In 1824, Mexico adopted a federalist constitution. Texas was made part of the Mexican state of Coahuila and the capital was moved from San Antonio to Saltillo, south of the Rio Grande. But in 1835, the Mexican government under its new president, Antonio López de Santa Anna, replaced the 1824 constitution with one greatly increasing centralized authority. Like the American colonists in 1776, the Texians felt their freedoms betrayed. They rebelled, and on October 2 won a fight southeast of San Antonio at Gonzales. Santa Anna's brother-in-law, General Martín Perfecto de Cós, arrived in San Antonio to take command of the Mexican troops. He met a Texian force under James Bowie near Mission Concepción, then retreated into San Antonio. The Texians laid siege to the town.

By the end of November, 1835, the Texians were preparing to forget the siege and go home when Ben Milam rallied some three hundred men—most of the force—and led a charge on the city. On the third day of house-to-house fighting, Milam was shot by a sniper hiding in a tall cypress tree along the San Antonio River. Milam was buried in a Masonic ceremony in the courtyard of the Veramendi house. Finally, on December 10, General Cós personally met his attackers in a house in La Villita to sign articles of capitulation. He was released after promising that he and his 1,100 men would never again oppose the original constitution or the Texians. The Texians left a hundred-man garrison in San Antonio.

Back in Mexico, President/General Santa Anna, livid, decided to ignore his brother-in-law's promises and to strike back at the insurgents. When the Mexican Congress agreed that colonists who participated in the uprising would be executed or exiled, and all others would be resettled in the Mexican interior, Santa Anna and his troops began a forced march toward San Antonio. They arrived on February 23 to find the Texians fortified within the walls of the old Alamo mission. Overall command was shared by William Barret Travis and James Bowie, until Travis took charge when Bowie fell ill.

Travis, Bowie, former United States Congressman David Crockett, James Bonham and some one hundred and fifty others who determined to stand their ground were finally overcome in the third Mexican assault on the Alamo compound, on March 6, 1836. Santa Anna led his battered Army east, where, on April 21, he was outwitted and defeated at San Jacinto by the main Texian army, under Sam Houston. The victors, however, were now more than insurgents, they were defenders of a new country. On March 2, 1836, while the Alamo still lay under siege, delegates to a convention at Washington-on-the-Brazos, including delegations from Bexar and from the Alamo, approved the Declaration of Independence of the Republic of Texas.[28]

Despite the formal end of hostilities and creation of the new republic, there was little relaxation in San Antonio. A dozen Comanche chieftains arrived in 1840 seeking peace. But Texan soldiers, angry that only two white captives were returned instead of the two hundred promised, killed most of the chiefs and their families in a massacre that began in the Council House on Main Plaza and spread to the rest of the town. In addition to danger of retaliation from the Comanches there was still a constant threat from Mexico, which refused to recognize the new republic. In 1842, a Mexican force of 1,200 men seized and looted San Antonio, then marched fifty of the town's officials and leading citizens off to Perote Prison in Mexico.[29]

Three years later, the United States agreed to annex the struggling nation, with Texans' concurrence. In 1845 the United States Army checked out San Antonio, posted a detachment in the old Spanish barracks on Military Plaza and established a supply depot in the ruins of the Alamo. When annexation was finalized in 1846, it sparked a two-year war with Mexico over the question of who owned Texas. The toll on San Antonio can be measured by its population, which four years before Santa Anna's invasion had fallen to 1,634, making it the thirteenth city in size in the province of Coahuila y Texas.[30] At the end of the war it had dwindled to 800. Future president Rutherford B. Hayes, passing through on horseback, described San Antonio simply as an "old, ruined Spanish town."[31]

With the United States Army on hand to assure peace, and with new links to the vibrant economy of a young nation, a decade began which would redefine San Antonio. From its nadir at the time of the Mexican War, San Antonio's population grew to more than 8,000 by the time of the Civil War, fifteen years later. Immigrants poured in, forming their own communities in the shadow of the surviving Spanish culture and adding to what one visitor in 1828 described as the town's "confusion of unknown tongues."[32] Unrest in Germany in particular drew disenchanted intellectuals accustomed to an urban environment, and German superseded Spanish as San Antonio's dominant language.

Supplying the growing town with water were the Spanish acequias, still fed by San Pedro Creek and by the San Antonio River, which one visitor found "winds through and across the city in so many tortuous courses and deflections that no stranger can tell which way it runs or how many rivers there are."[33] New thoroughfares tended to follow the acequias' meandering gravitational course as, among other nationalities, Mexicans gathered to the west of downtown San Antonio, Germans to the east and then south, Anglo-Americans to the north and east, Irish to the northeast, Italians to the northwest, blacks to the eastern edge and, toward the end of the century, Chinese to the near west. "Only in frontier San Antonio," observed Donald E. Everett, "did such a conglomerate group of diverse nationalities settle in a single community."[34]

Although Southern sympathizers forced the surrender of Union troops in San Antonio in 1861, and gained the valuable quartermaster stores in the city, secessionist fervor was not as strong as in less isolated east Texas. San Antonio played no significant part in the war, even gaining a measure of prosperity from the mercantile trade stimulated from Mexico. In 1865 the United States Army returned to San Antonio and to the Alamo, less an army of occupation than a defending force back to man the forts of the Indian frontier. Radical Republicans led by the Texas governor and by James Pearson Newcomb of the *San Antonio Express* launched an ill-fated drive to establish a breakaway state of West Texas, with San Antonio its capital.[35] Selected chairman for the movement's local committee was banker George Washington Brackenridge, an anti-secessionist from east Texas who served in the Union occupation government of New Orleans and grew wealthy in the cotton trade, but chose the less polarized San Antonio as his new home.[36] Brackenridge

Above and beyond the Mill Bridge crossing of the San Antonio River rises the steeple of the first St. John's Lutheran Church. A short distance below and to its left in this 1860s view can be seen the twin houses on South Presa Street which were later restored in the original La Villita project. Institute of Texan Cultures.

expanded his wealth and became San Antonio's only major local philanthropist during the late nineteenth and early twentieth centuries.

Arrival at last of long-term political stability and removal of the threat of raiding Indians finally brought prosperity to surrounding ranchlands, with San Antonio their natural market center for cattle and sheep. In the 1870s San Antonio's population continued the growth rate of fifty percent which had brought it to more than 12,000 at the start of the decade. In 1876, a group of cattlemen gathered at Alamo Plaza, then "a mudhole," and watched a makeshift corral of barbed wire contain a herd of range cattle, the first demonstration of the fence wire which would soon transform the frontier.[37]

With the changing ethnic makeup of the city, by the early 1850s San Antonio's built environment was going in new directions as well. The German architect John Fries designed a variety of new landmarks contrasting with native styles, such as the Greek Revival City Market House (1859) and James Vance House (1859), the classic Menger Hotel (1859) and the Gothic-style First Presbyterian Church (1860), as well as the now-famous parapet on the Alamo (1850). Too, Germans brought in breweries (Degan's, 1853), mills (C.H. Guenther, 1859) and other industry (Menger's soap works, 1850).

They encouraged education (German-English School, 1858) and culture (Casino Hall, 1857). A distinctive style came to the river at the north end of town with Jules Poinsard's first building (1851) of the Ursuline Academy and Convent, home to a French-based order of nuns newly arrived from New Orleans. Additions went up under the direction of the French-born architect brothers François and T.E. Giraud. François, a future mayor, designed the first St. Mary's School (1857) and in 1868 began the Gothic Revival front portion of San Fernando Cathedral, its Spanish-era apse retained but its other walls and single tower replaced. San Antonio also imported architectural talent, as in the design by Richard Upjohn, who designed Trinity Church at the head of New York City's Wall Street, of the limestone-block, Gothic Revival St. Mark's Episcopal Church (1859, completed 1875).

Despite the new styles and numbers of new buildings, their usually creamy limestone walls and pitched roofs blended well with the low Spanish and Mexican era structures, not totally altering San Antonio's appearance as a town of low native buildings spreading from two Spanish plazas separated by a parish church.[38]

San Antonio's location as a crossroads of Texas guaranteed that it would be visited by travelers. The first were charmed by San Antonio's Spanish style, in particular the style reflected by the missions. In 1767, Father Gaspar José Solís found San José "so pretty and so well arranged both in a material and in a spiritual way" that he was left with "no voice, words or figures with which to describe its beauty," and that was a year before construction of its church, for which Solís blessed the foundation and laid the cornerstone.[39] Josiah Gregg in 1846 thought the completed San José church "the best piece of ancient architecture in the country."[40]

San Antonio's missions led another traveler to fantasize, in 1837, that he was in Italy rather than in Texas.[41] In 1807, Lt. Zebulon Pike was surprised to discover a fiesta spirit which had the governor dancing in the plaza with his people.[42] San Antonio was even found more pleasing than other towns in Texas. Despite the "bizarre" atmosphere produced by "the rushing conflux of Americans, Mexicans, Germans, Frenchmen, Swedes, Norwegians, Italians and negroes," wrote Sidney Lanier, in San Antonio "things are more decently done, life is less crude, civilization is less new than at Austin, and this variety, which was there grotesque, is here picturesque."[43]

San Antonio's exotic appeal was heightened by its isolation. As the third quarter of the nineteenth century ended, a railroad had still not arrived. San Antonio's connections with the outside world were only by horseback or stagecoach for passengers and, for supplies, by freight wagon from the Texas coast. Pioneer landscape architect Frederick Law Olmsted wrote for most travelers on his visit in 1856, two years before he designed New York City's Central Park, that San Antonio's remote "jumble of races, costumes, languages

Two-story buildings were already replacing older structures by the time of this view looking southwest to Main Plaza in the 1870s. A long adobe building remained at the far side of the plaza on the future site of the Bexar County Courthouse, and beyond it can be seen columns of the Vance House. Raba Collection, San Antonio Conservation Society.

and buildings, its religious ruins" so combined with its heroic history that only New Orleans could vie with San Antonio in picturesque "odd and antiquated foreignness."

As Olmsted's party approached on horseback from the east, the riders crested a hill to gaze down upon San Antonio's white clustered dwellings. To the north was a gradual sweep upward to high, rolling hills, to the west and south open prairies. The few trees to be seen formed a thin edging along the narrow river winding through the town. The remote, vibrant place which Olmsted's group reached was the San Antonio which later generations most sought to recall in restorations of its remaining buildings, and in festivals inspired by the multi-cultural flair and flavor of this particular time.

As Olmsted entered San Antonio, his trained eye caught Germans' neatly roofed and finished homes built "of fresh square-cut blocks of creamy white limestone, mostly of a single story and humble proportions . . . . Some were furnished with the luxuries of little bow-windows, balconies or galleries. From these we enter the square of the Alamo. This is all Mexican [with] windowless

Crockett Street Looking West *was painted by Karl Friedrich Hermann Lungkwitz in 1857. This view from the east shows the tower of the church of San Fernando in the center skyline, to its right the spire of the new St. Mary's Catholic Church. Near right center is the rear of the Alamo church. Courtesy of the Witte Museum, San Antonio, Texas.*

cabins of stakes, plastered with mud and roofed with river-grass . . . or low, windowless but better thatched houses of adobes (gray, unburnt bricks). . . ."

Crossing the narrow Commerce Street bridge across the river and entering the main part of town, he found signs to be "German by all odds, and perhaps the houses, trim-built with pink window-blinds. The American dwellings stand back, with galleries and jalousies and a garden picket-fence against the walk, or rise next door in three-story brick to respectable city fronts. The Mexican buildings . . . are all low, of adobe or stone washed blue and yellow, with flat roofs close down upon their single story. Windows have been knocked in their blank walls . . . and most of them are stored with dry goods and groceries, which overflow around the door. Around the plaza are American hotels and new glass-fronted stores, alternating with sturdy battlemented Spanish walls and confronted by the dirty, grim old stuccoed stone cathedral, whose cracked bell is now clunking for vespers . . . ."

By moonlight, Olmsted strolled through streets "laid out with tolerable regularity, parallel with the sides of the main plaza, and . . . pretty distinctly shared among the nations that use them. On the plaza and the busiest streets, a surprising number of old Mexican buildings are converted by trowel, paintbrush and gaudy carpentry into drinking-places, always labeled 'Exchange' and conducted on the New Orleans model. About these loitered a set of customers, sometimes rough, sometimes affecting an 'exquisite' dress. . . . Here and there was a restaurant of a quieter look, where the traditions of Paris are preserved under difficulties by the exiled Gaul. The doors of the cabins of the real natives stood open wide, if indeed they exist at all, and many were the family pictures of jollity or sleepy comfort they displayed to us as we sauntered curious about . . . ."

By day, he watched customers of various nationalities do business at a dozen stores offering the same wide variety of wares, the only specialized shops being those of druggists, saddlers, watchmakers and gunsmiths. Olmsted was entertained by the street life. "Hardly a day passes without some noise. If there be no personal affray to arouse talk, there is some Government train to be seen with its hundreds of mules on its way from the coast to a fort above; or a Mexican ox-train from the coast with an interesting supply of ice or flour or matches, or of whatever the shops find themselves short. A Government express clatters off, or news arrives from some exposed outpost, or from New Mexico. An Indian in his finery appears on a shaggy horse in search of blankets, powder and ball. Or, at the least, a stagecoach with the 'States' or the Austin mail rolls into the plaza and discharges its load of passengers and newspapers.

"The street affrays are numerous and characteristic. I have seen for a year or more a San Antonio weekly, and hardly a number fails to have its fight or murder. More often than otherwise, the parties meet upon the plaza by chance and each, on catching sight of his enemy, draws a revolver and fires away . . . . It is not seldom the passers-by who suffer. Sometimes it is a young man at a quiet dinner in a restaurant who receives a ball in the head, sometimes an old negro woman returning from market who gets winged . . . . If neither [antagonist] is seriously injured they . . . drink together on the following day, and the town waits for the next excitement. Where borderers and idle soldiers are hanging about drinking-places, and where different races mingle on unequal terms, assassinations must be expected. Murders, from avarice or revenge, are common here."

Olmsted found other "amusements" much less exciting. Performances of a poor local theater company were "death on horrors and despair," while "a permanent company of Mexican mountebanks [gives] performances of agility and buffoonery two or three times a week, parading before night in their spangled tights with drum and trombone through the principal streets . . . ." The nighttime crowds attracted vendors of whiskey, tortillas and tamales selling their wares "all by the light of torches, making a ruddily picturesque evening group."

On Sunday, "a scanty congregation attends the services of the battered old cathedral. The Protestant church attendance can almost be counted upon the fingers. Sunday is pretty rigidly devoted to rest, though most of the stores are open to all practical purposes and the exchanges keep up a brisk distribution

Outdoor food vendors, as these on Military Plaza, provided color, and nourishment, on San Antonio's plazas day and night for more than a century. The University of Texas, The Institute of Texan Cultures, courtesy Robert M. Ayres Estate.

of stimulants. The Germans and Mexicans have their dances. The Americans resort to fast horses for their principal recreation . . . ."

The old Alamo mission church Olmsted thought to be "a mere wreck of its former grandeur. It consists of a few irregular stuccoed buildings, huddled against the old church in a large courtyard surrounded by a rude wall, the whole used as an arsenal by the U.S. quartermaster. The church-door opens on the square and is meagerly decorated by stucco mouldings, all hacked and battered in the battles it has seen. Since the heroic defense of Travis and his handful of men in '36, it has been a monument not so much to faith as to courage." The four missions south of town he found "in different stages of decay but all . . . real ruins, beyond any connection with the present—weird remains out of the silent past . . . . One of the missions is a complete ruin, the others afford shelter to Mexican occupants who ply their trades and herd their cattle and sheep in the old cells and courts."[44]

Two years later, in 1858, another keen observer, Richard Everett, was with a mule train of the Santa Rita Silver Mining Company bound for Arizona. Twelve days after leaving the Texas coast the caravan found itself in San Antonio. He wrote his perspectives, and a prescient conclusion, for *Frank Leslie's Illustrated Newspaper*:

Military Plaza was a major gathering place for wagons which kept San Antonio supplied with goods before arrival of the railroad. Raba Collection, San Antonio Conservation Society.

"San Antonio is like Quebec, a city of the olden time, jostled and crowded by modern enterprise . . . . Walking about the city and its environs, you may well fancy yourself in some strange land . . . . The narrow streets, the stout old walls which seem determined not to crumble away, the aqueducts, . . . the dark, banditti-like figures that gaze at you from the low doorways—everything, in the Mexican quarter of the city especially, bespeaks a condition widely different from what you are accustomed to behold in any American town . . . ."

Everett's observations were aided, no doubt, by being in the company of muleteers. He wrote that every Sunday after mass at San Fernando, "there is

Fandango, *set in the Spanish Governor's Palace, was painted by Theodore Gentilz in 1848. Yanaguana Society gift, DRT Library at the Alamo.*

a cock-fight, generally numerously attended . . . . The pit is located in the rear of the church, about one square distant. On [the] last Sabbath, going past the church door about the time of service I observed a couple of Mexicans kneeling near the door in a pious attitude, which would doubtless have appeared very sober and Christianlike had not each one held a smart gamecock beneath his arms . . . .

"The fandangoes take place every evening, and are patronized by the lower orders of people . . . . A large hall or square room, lighted by a few lamps hung from the walls or lanterns suspended from the ceiling, a pair of negro fiddlers and twenty or thirty couples in the full enjoyment of a 'bolero' or the Mexican polka, help make up the scene. In the corners of the room are refreshment tables, under the charge of old women, where coffee, frijoles, tortillas, boiled rice and other eatables may be obtained, whiskey being nominally not sold . . . . At these fandangoes may be seen the muleteer, fresh from the coast or the Pass, with gay clothes and a dozen or so of silver dollars; the United States soldiers just from the barracks, abounding in oaths and tobacco; the herdsman, with his blanket and the long knife, which seems a portion of every Mexican; the disbanded ranger, rough, bearded and armed with his huge holster pistol and long bowie-knife, dancing, eating, drinking, swearing and carousing like a party of Captain Kidd's men just in from a long voyage. Among the women may be seen all colors and ages from ten to forty; the Creole, the Poblano, the Mexican, and rarely the American or German—generally, in some cases, the dissipated widow or discarded mistress of some soldier or follower of the army.

"San Antonio is rapidly improving. Near the Alamo a fine hotel of stone is being erected by an enterprising German [William Menger]. The new [St. Mary's] Catholic Church is a grand edifice for Texas . . . . Some fine warehouses have just been completed; one is rented by the United States for a storehouse and barrack . . . . A building of any pretensions to style and finish is a remarkable and costly affair. Everything but the stone must be imported, iron from Cincinnati, window frames from Boston and pine lumber from Florida. Even shingles are brought from Michigan, and glass from Pittsburgh. A railway from some point on the coast is needed to develop and improve the country, and until one is constructed, San Antonio will be a peculiar and isolated city.[45]

Notes

1. Outside its central city core San Francisco has its 1776 Mission San Francisco de Asis and the Spanish presidio commandante's headquarters, converted into the Officer's Club of the Presidio military reservation. Los Angeles preserves 44 acres in its elusive downtown as the El Pueblo de Los Angeles Historic Monument, its oldest surviving major landmark built in 1822. San Diego has its Old Town (oldest major surviving landmark: 1824) as does Albuquerque with its San Felipe de Neri Church (1706). Tucson has its El Presidio Historic District (oldest home: 1850). (*American Automobile Association Tourbooks* (Heathrow, FL: 1994–95), *Arizona-New Mexico*, 80, 98; *California-Nevada*, 97–98, 147, 163, 164.)

2. Marion A. Habig, *The Alamo Chain of Missions* (Chicago: Franciscan Herald Press, 1968), 25, 80.

3. Jay C. Henry, *Architecture in Texas 1895–1945* (Austin: University of Texas Press, 1993), 144.

4. Ibid., 270.

5. Ibid., 25–26.

6. Joseph E. Minor and Malcolm L. Steinberg, *The Acequias of San Antonio,* (San Antonio: San Antonio Branch of the Texas Section of the American Society of Civil Engineers, 1968), iii, 8, 25.

7. John W. Reps, *Cities of the American West, A History of Frontier Urban Planning* (Princeton: Princeton University Press, 1979), 3, 35–37.

8. Ibid., 40.

9. Ibid., 37–40, 66. San Antonio graduated to the status of a *villa*, a rank among America's six largest cities with Spanish origins shared only with Albuquerque. Smaller, less important communities were designated *pueblos*. Both were outranked by the *ciudad*, a designation not made within the boundaries of the present-day United States. (Ibid., 48, 68, 99, 108, 110, 122, 698.)

10. Ibid., 42.

11. Eugene George, "The Hispanic Touch," *Discovery*, Summer 1984, 8–10.

12. Reps, *Cities of the American West*, 71. Other principal settlements were around the short-lived presidio of Los Adaes in east Texas and at the presidio of La Bahía at present-day Goliad on the Guadalupe River. By the mid-nineteenth century, notes the leading authority on early Texas travelers, "Only Nacogdoches and Goliad compared with San Antonio in age or endurance. All others were characterized by newness, rapid growth, a certain impermanence—and sometimes even nonexistence." (Marilyn McAdams Sibley, *Travelers in Texas, 1761–1860* (Austin, University of Texas Press, 1967), 65.)

13. Charles Ramsdell, *San Antonio, A Historical and Pictorial Guide*, 106.

14. Donald E. Chipman, *Spanish Texas, 1519–1821* (Austin: University of Texas Press, 1992), 182.

15. Reps, *Cities of the American West*, 78.

16. Chipman, *Spanish Texas*, 179.

17. Ibid., 181, 184.

18. Juan Agustín Morfi, *History of Texas, 1673–1779*, 2 vols. (Albuquerque: Quivera Society, 1935), I, 92.

19. Alfred Barnaby Thomas, ed. and trans., *Teodoro de Croix and the Northern Frontier of New Spain, 1776–1783*, 77.

20. Ibid.

21. Jesús de la Teja, *San Antonio de Béxar: A Community on New Spain's Northern Frontier* (Albuquerque: University of New Mexico Press, 1995), 137.

22. Habig, *The Alamo Chain of Missions*, 26.

23. Timothy M. Matovina, *Tejano Religion and Ethnicity, San Antonio, 1821–1860*, (Austin, University of Texas Press, 1995), 6.

24. Rena Maverick Green, ed., *Memoirs of Mary A. Maverick* (San Antonio: Alamo Printing Co., 1921), 53–54.

25. T.R. Fehrenbach, *The San Antonio Story* (Tulsa: Continental Heritage Press, 1978), 37.

26. Ibid., 49.

27. "James Bowie," *The Handbook of Texas* I, Walter Prescott Webb and Eldon Stephen Branda, eds., 3 vols., (Austin: The Texas State Historical Association, 1952–1976), 197.

28. Paula Mitchell Marks, *Turn Your Eyes Toward Texas: Pioneers Sam and Mary Maverick* (College Station: Texas A&M University Press, 1989), 53–54, 57, 58.

29. "Perote Prison and Prisoners," *The Handbook of Texas* I, 362–63. Most Bexar prisoners and other Texans captured were released in stages after nearly two years, in large part through the influence of the U.S. Ambassador to Mexico, who was instructed by President John Tyler to help.

30. Jesús de la Teja and John Wheat in *Tejano Origins In Eighteenth-Century San Antonio*, Gerald E. Poyo and Gilberto M. Hinojosa, eds. (Austin: University of Texas Press, 1991), 4–5.

31. Claude M. Greuner, "Rutherford B. Hayes's Horseback Ride Through Texas," *Southwestern Historical Quarterly* 68 (Jan., 1965), 359, in Everett, *San Antonio: The Flavor Of Its Past*, 4.

32. "J.C. Clopper's Journal and Book of Memoranda for 1828," *Quarterly of the Texas State Historical Association* 13 (Jul., 1909), 71, in Everett, *San Antonio: The Flavor Of Its Past*, 4.

33. Memphis (Tenn.) *Leader*, quoted in *San Antonio Express*, Jun. 10, 1877, in Everett, *San Antonio: The Flavor Of Its Past*, 4.

34. Everett, *San Antonio: The Flavor of its Past, 1845–1898*, 10.

35. Marilyn McAdams Sibley, *George W. Brackenridge: Maverick Philanthropist* (Austin: University of Texas Press, 1973), 86.

36. Ibid., 5.

37. W.D. Hornaday, "Pioneer Barbed Wire Man Tells of Early Texas Days," *San Antonio Daily Express*, Feb. 27, 1910, 33. Although an historical marker on Military Plaza states the demonstration occurred there, Hornaday's interview with Gates associate and eyewitness Pete McManus places the demonstration on Alamo Plaza, a more likely location in any event since it was then away from the center of town and more conducive to such a demonstration.

38. Reps, *Cities of the American West*, 151.

39. Fray Gaspar Jose Solís, *Diary of a Visit*, 50, in Sibley, *Travelers in Texas*, 63.

40. Josiah Gregg, *Commerce on the Prairies; or the Journal of a Santa Fe Trader*, 2 vols. (New York, 1844), I, 234, in Everett, *San Antonio: The Flavor Of Its Past* , 4.

41. Andrew Forest Muir, ed., *Texas in 1837*, (Austin, 1958), 94, in Everett, *San Antonio: The Flavor Of Its Past*, 4.

42. Elliot Cones, ed., *The Expeditions of Zebulon Montgomery Pike, to the Headwaters of the Mississippi River, through Louisiana Territory, and in New Spain, during the years 1805–6–7*, 3 vols. (New York, 1895), II, 698, in Everett, *San Antonio: The Flavor Of Its Past* , 7.

43. Charles R. Anderson and Audrey H. Starke, eds., *The Centennial Edition of the Works of Sidney Lanier*, 10 vols. Baltimore, 1945) 8, 277, in Everett, *San Antonio: The Flavor Of Its Past*, 3.

44. Frederick Law Olmsted, *A Journey Through Texas*, (New York, 1857), 148–59.

45. Richard Everett, "Things In and About San Antonio," *Frank Leslie's Illustrated Newspaper* 7 (Jan. 15, 1859), 1.

2

Preservation
Becomes a Cause

Virtually every important city in the United States was already connected with the rest of the nation by rail when the Galveston, Harrisburg and San Antonio Railway reached San Antonio in 1877. The city's isolation was over. The full fury of the homogenizing process would now descend. In the last two decades of the nineteenth century San Antonio's population more than doubled, to 53,000. In the first two decades of the twentieth century it tripled beyond that, to more than 160,000.

San Antonians were well aware of the potential impact of the railroad. Indeed, they had been actively seeking one for twenty-five years.[1] When the Sunset Route's first train pulled in from Houston on the afternoon of February 19, 1877, a crowd of eight thousand was on hand to welcome the governor and a host of other state and railway officials, the mayors of Austin and Galveston and two hundred representatives of other Texas communities. The celebration lasted two days.[2]

Ironically, the only cautionary note at the time on the pitfalls of unbridled progress was sounded by the railroad's president, Col. Thomas W. Pierce. In an interview with James P. Newcomb of the *San Antonio Daily Express*, Pierce suggested that there be both an old and a new city of San Antonio. The old city would be "left undisturbed with all its ancient quaintness, and the modern growth kept out of the old confines."[3] Newcomb picked up on the idea. In competition with the fast-growing "so-called genuine business city, San Antonio may have a hard time keeping in the race," he wrote. "But with some of our old-time charming customs still preserved, some of our old buildings still standing, some of our old, narrow, crooked streets still left, we might still be, with our incomparable climate, the Mecca of the traveler."[4]

Most San Antonians were unfazed. Their attitude remained that of the *San Antonio Herald*, which casually reported that the destruction on Flores Street of "one of the old landmarks of the Spanish era" was noticed only by

Arrival of the railroad in 1877 ended San Antonio's isolation and brought rapid change. The Institute of Texan Cultures.

"disappointed candidates and other persons of that character," who, the paper said, hoped that some Spanish doubloons would turn up among the debris.[5]

San Antonians seemed self-conscious and even embarrassed about the antique appearance of their city, so long removed from the modern world. A newspaper in the rival, smaller city of Houston reported that of the travelers brought to San Antonio by rail the first year, "many came on pleasure only for a day to peep at the old town, and then go away to tell how queer it looked."[6] Journalist Richard Harding Davis confirmed after he passed through on the train: "The citizens of San Antonio do not, as a rule, appreciate the historical values of their city; they are rather tired of them."[7] Yet praise from beyond Texas continued. Wrote a visiting *New York Post* reporter: "There is something in the air of this quaint old city of San Antonio, this child of Spanish faith and missionary zeal, that throws a spell upon the passing visitor . . . . The past and present seem to have joined hands here; the seventeenth and the nineteenth centuries are both looking you in the face."[8]

Railroad magnate Thomas Pierce, who brought up the issue of historic San Antonio's preservation, was, significantly, from Boston, which already recognized the need for saving its own landmarks and historic sites. The notion that history was not just what happened in ancient Greece and Rome had caught on in the northeast, where it was not yet a hundred years since the end of the

American Revolution.[9] A sense of pride in America's Revolutionary War origins led to development of the historic preservation movement in the United States.[10] In 1816, the Philadelphia city government was convinced to save its Old State House—Independence Hall—due to its association with the Revolution.[11] In 1828 its missing steeple was replaced with one in the original style, apparently the first time in America that a landmark was repaired in a style earlier than that of the time in which the repair was made.[12]

In 1850, the New York State legislature became the first public body in America to buy a landmark simply to save it. Legislators came up with nearly $9,000 for Newburgh's Hasbrouck House, George Washington's headquarters during the last two years of the Revolution. In Philadelphia, Carpenters' Hall, site of the first meeting of the First Continental Congress, was soon restored.[13] In 1853, South Carolinian Ann Pamela Cunningham decided that Washington's home should be preserved. The Virginia Legislature chartered her Mount Vernon Ladies' Association of the Union. Miss Cunningham organized subsidiary fund-raising groups in every state and signed up the noted orator Edward Everett for fund-raising addresses along the entire east coast. His appeal was so non-partisan that, even on the brink of civil war, the New Englander was given free passage on the railroads of South Carolina.[14]

Across the Appalachians, the Tennessee legislature in 1856 came up with $48,000 to purchase Andrew Jackson's Nashville home, The Hermitage.[15] It was later turned over to the Ladies' Hermitage Association, responsible to a board of nine male trustees just as the Mount Vernon Ladies' Association reported to an all-male Board of Visitors. That showed, wrote preservation historian Charles B. Hosmer, Jr., that "women were not yet trusted to run their affairs unassisted."[16]

Boston preservationists in 1863, however, could not prevent the razing of John Hancock's home. In 1876, as the Centennial Exposition in Philadelphia was making Americans more aware of their heritage, Boston's Old South Meeting House of 1729 was also to be torn down. Workmen began removing the clock from its tower. But Old South was the setting for such Revolutionary meetings as that which planned the Boston Tea Party. Preservationists dug in their heels, and a series of campaigns and legal maneuvers culminated with its purchase. A Citizens' Committee raised $75,000, one lady contributed $100,000 and the New England Mutual Life Insurance Company took on a $225,000 mortgage. Fund-raising events gained the support of the city's intellectual elite, including James Russell Lowell, Ralph Waldo Emerson, Julia Ward Howe, Oliver Wendell Holmes and Harvard President Charles W. Eliot.[17]

In Texas, bitter memories of the defeated Confederacy were transcended by remembering an earlier war, one with a glorious ending. Recognition on the east coast of the importance of landmarks of the American Revolution began the historic preservation movement in the United States. Recognition in Texas of the importance of landmarks of the Texas Revolution launched the historic preservation movement in the United States west of the Mississippi River—in San Antonio. The New York State Legislature in 1850 made the first purchase of an historic landmark by a public body in the United States, a Revolutionary War headquarters of George Washington. The Texas Legislature in 1883 made the first purchase of an historic landmark by a public body in the United States west of the Mississippi River—the Alamo, symbol of Texas independence.[18]

The saving of no other landmark in America can surpass the preservation of the Alamo in depth of symbolism, in breadth and characterization of players and in sheer drama, on which the curtain did not drop after the first two public purchases of Alamo land. More than a century later, the oft-debated appearance of the old Alamo compound remains an unresolved problem in historic preservation.

The Alamo had been ingrained in the Texas psyche since its defenders died in 1836. A monument made from the Alamo's stones was purchased by the Texas Legislature two decades later and placed on the front portico of the state Capitol. After the Capitol burned in 1881, the legislature built another monument near the new statehouse.[19] Finally a group of San Antonians, having decided that the remains of the Alamo itself should be purchased and a monument put up nearby, in 1879 organized the Alamo Monument Association.

When the subject of actually saving the Alamo came up, San Antonio could still be reached only by stagecoach or on horseback. But progress of historic preservation efforts elsewhere was not unknown on the distant frontier. "The 'Old South Church' of Boston, with all its hallowed memories that belong to it, is yet not crowded with the sad glory that surrounds the Alamo," editorialized the *San Antonio Express* early in 1877. "The proposition we suggest regarding the Alamo has been or is about to be done by the citizens of Boston, with the difference that, in their case, it is through private enterprise and liberality that the old monument of Revolutionary fame is to be preserved. It would be too much to ask of this city to bear all the expense that the suggestion incurs, but it is not too much to ask that that duty be performed by the State .... We hope that the proper authorities may move in the matter, and the Alamo, the glory of Texas, will be insured from what will in time otherwise befall it, absolute decay."[20]

The need for action became immediate when the Alamo's tenant, the United States Army, began moving out. To the north the Army was building Post San Antonio, later renamed Fort Sam Houston. The Alamo was vacated in early 1877, leaving its future up to its landlord, the Catholic Church.[21] The Rt. Rev. Anthony Pellicer, first Catholic Bishop of San Antonio, kept the

Preservation of no landmark in America can equal that of the Alamo in depth of symbolism, breadth of players and sheer drama. The first landmark publicly preserved west of the Mississippi River, the Alamo undergoes periodic restorations. The Alamo church got a new roof to mark the centennial of its fall in 1836. DRT Library at the Alamo, copied from Eugene A. Duke.

Alamo church but not the adjoining convento, the much-altered onetime dormitory, cloisters and work area of the mission priests. The church sold the convento to merchant Honoré Grenet, who set up a wholesale grocery in the building and leased the Alamo church for a warehouse. Capitalizing on memory of the battle, he built false wooden parapets above the convento's second floor and set wooden cannons atop its old stone walls.

Once the Catholic Church had sold some of the Alamo real estate, it was thought that the "remainder can of course be obtained at a reasonable figure."[22] No restoration was envisioned. The *Express* believed the state should simply "purchase the dear old structure, erect an appropriate monument in front of it, encircle it with a neat and substantial fence and shield it from the hands of visitors disposed to mar its original aspect."[23] The Alamo was like a loved but "dying relative" and it "should be preserved; it is sacred to us, and although it is bound to be leveled with the dust some day, we should protect and guard it."[24]

Wooden parapets and battlements were added to the building to the left of the Alamo church when it was used as a wholesale grocery warehouse. They covered stones from the building's days as the Alamo mission convento, and became the subject of a bitter preservation dispute early in the twentieth century. Raba Collection, San Antonio Conservation Society.

In 1879, San Antonians began urging the state to purchase the Alamo church. To provide a monument for the site, the *Express* urged that a fund-raising memorial association be formed. That turned out to be the Alamo Monument Association.[25] Elected president by the twenty-six charter members was pioneer San Antonian Mary Adams Maverick, widow of Samuel Augustus Maverick, one of two delegates sent from the Alamo to sign the Texas Declaration of Independence at Washington-on-the-Brazos only days before the Alamo fell.[26] The group planned not only to erect a monument but, according to the charter approved by the legislature on April 23, 1879, "to otherwise preserve and mark the spot upon which this great historic event transpired."[27] The Alamo Monument Association asked the legislature to buy the Alamo, a request endorsed in 1880 by the Texas Veterans' Association.[28]

The next year, merchant Honoré Grenet died unexpectedly. His heirs sold the convento property to merchants Charles Hugo and Gustav Schmeltzer. The Alamo church reverted to the Catholic Church, which informed the legislature it could buy the Alamo for $20,000. The San Antonio City Council promised that the city would then assume its care. In January of 1883, six legislators coming from Austin to investigate were welcomed by a delegation including Mayor J.H. French and a male representative of the Alamo Monument Association. Legislators decided the price was reasonable.[29] Purchase of the Alamo was approved, as was purchase of ten acres of the San Jacinto battlefield near Houston.[30] The Alamo was assigned to the Commissioner of Insurance, Statistics and History to arrange "its proper preservation and maintenance, free of cost to the state."

On May 12, 1883, the French-born Rt. Rev. Jean C. Neraz, new Catholic Bishop of San Antonio, transfered the Alamo to the State of Texas.[31] At once came calls for "restoring the Alamo, placing it in proper condition and . . . making it a museum worthy of the wealth and importance of the city." Major

Joseph E. Dwyer was ready to contribute "a large collection of animals and birds which will make a handsome nucleus for the museum."[32]

Six months later, the doors of the newly rescued and cleaned Alamo opened to an incongruous scene—a two-day bazaar held by ladies of the St. Mark's Episcopal Cathedral Altar Society, raising funds for a parsonage. "Every pillar is now entwined with evergreens, and the American, German and Mexican flags festoon alcove and hall," noted one reporter. To the music of the Eighth Cavalry Band, within the sacred walls visitors could buy popcorn and candy, eat oysters and find "goods of every style and price," to say nothing of discovering the Gypsey Encampment where two young ladies foretold "secrets of love and riches."[33]

The City of San Antonio kept its end of the bargain by hiring a caretaker. The first Alamo custodian was Captain Tom Rife, 60, a Texas War of Independence veteran and former San Antonio policeman. In 1887 he caught Iqnatius Coyle smashing the Alamo's image of St. Theresa. Shortly before Rife's death in 1894 he was succeeded by Captain McMasters, "the well-known veteran of San Jacinto." There were many complaints when the third custodian chosen, former Missouri River steamboat captain Samuel Bennett, was not "a Texan."[34]

As time passed, the Alamo remained unrestored. Major Dwyer's stuffed animals and birds were nowhere to be seen. San Antonio's Belknap Rifles sent two officers to ask the governor's permission to use the Alamo as an armory, but were told that was up to the legislature.[35] In 1887, the Alamo Monument Association accepted architect Alfred Giles's design for a 165-foot monument enclosing an elevator rising one hundred feet to a balcony overlooking the Alamo. Boosted by pledges of Association President Mary A. Maverick's four sons, the fund soon reached $25,000 of the $150,000 goal.[36] While fund-raising remained short, the condition of the Alamo, also being used as a police station and, during elections, as a polling place, was becoming an embarrassment.[37] In 1893 the Alamo Monument Association sent architect Alfred Giles over along with Hamilton P. Bee, a former Confederate general and onetime speaker of the Texas House, to study the Alamo and come up with a restoration plan and cost estimates. The plan was sent to the legislature and duly referred to "appropriate committees."[38]

But no funds were forthcoming, and complaints continued: "Hundreds of strangers visit the Alamo during the year, and what do they see? A very untidy, dirty, negligently kept old building, in one room a crazy, smoky old stove, sticking its pipe out of one of the front windows to begrime the walls. Old lumber, rickety old floors and unsightly furniture greet the eyes."[39] Weighed in Episcopal clergyman George Q.A. Rose: "Of all the public delinquencies of San Antonians the one, it seems to me, for which there is the least excuse is that of the present discreditable condition of the Alamo . . . . One of the qualities whose cultivation Americans are inclined to forget in this eminently practical age is that of veneration—love for the aged, the beautiful and the historic . . . . I, for one, see something interesting beyond measure, venerable and majestic in the place where Crockett, Travis and Bowie fell in defense of their honor, but I withhold my homage from old lumber and dirt having nothing to do with the cause for which a noble band went down to a man before Santa Anna's legions."[40]

In the face of such broadsides, the City of San Antonio appointed a committee which promised to remove the rickety flooring and the loft and to make other repairs, including fixing the old wooden roof which the custodian complained was "little more than a sieve."[41] There was no shortage of other ideas. Rather than restoring the Alamo to its appearance after the battle, which would require removing both the roof and supporting stone work, the ever-helpful James P. Newcomb suggested cleaning it up, placing explanatory tablets on the walls and constructing an iron and glass roof to capture some feel of the roofless building during the siege.[42]

The direction of historic preservation in America, too, was evolving. Throughout the nineteenth century it was "a thoroughly romantic movement." Before the Civil War, believers thought restored Revolutionary era landmarks would bring greater regard for sacrifices of the founding fathers and cure disunion. After the Civil War, backers hoped it would foster a new sense of national dedication, and that "a willingness to pause inside a historic house and reflect upon the simple, rugged life of the past would provide an antidote for the materialistic ills of the present."[43] By the 1890s, urbanization, the fast-growing economy and increased leisure caused the nation's new women's club movement to branch into the hereditary society, producing "an epidemic of Sons, Daughters and Dames."[44] The concept was picked up immediately in Texas, and the Daughters of the Republic of Texas organized in Houston at the end of 1891.[45]

By this time, a new historical activism was arising in San Antonio. Its leader was a young schoolteacher named Adina Emilia De Zavala, eldest child of a Confederate blockade runner and granddaughter of the first vice president of the Republic of Texas, Lorenzo de Zavala.[46] She returned to San Antonio to teach in 1886, at the age of 24, and the next year began gathering a group of local "patriotic women" to discuss ways to arouse interest in Texas history.[47] In 1893, Adina De Zavala's group was invited to join the new Daughters of the Republic of Texas. Members organized the De Zavala Chapter, honoring Lorenzo de Zavala, and elected Miss De Zavala president.[48]

Traditional historical societies were struggling to get organized in Texas, where there was still no museum of any significance and the only historic building purchased for preservation in the entire nineteenth century had been the Alamo.[49] Yet the De Zavala Chapter's by-laws specified that the chapter

Symbolizing a goal of America's romantic early historic preservation movement is this scene at the Alamo about 1908. Simply seeing "the door through which some noble man or woman passed" would fill children with "high ideals, the desire to emulate" was a belief, typical of early preservationists, expressed by San Antonio's outspoken Adina De Zavala, sponsor of this group of young boys called the Alamo Defenders. They were officially organized by the elderly Dr. James L. Davis, standing beside the Texas flag, to inspire patriotism. Their young commander, directly in front of Miss De Zavala (center), was the aptly named J. Crockett Snider. The policeman at the right guided them as they marched in Fiesta parades. To be doubly certain the Alamo's mystique would rub off, pairs of boys were placed in niches which once held statues of saints on either side of the door. Adina De Zavala Papers, The Center For American History, The University of Texas at Austin, CN08640.

would dedicate itself to "especially the marking out of historic spots in San Antonio and the preservation and recording of the true history" of those locations.[50] It was a manifesto which would guide its young president in her checkered quest for more than six decades. Adina De Zavala's determined pursuit would not be derailed by controversy or insurmountable obstacles, as she single-mindedly sought to instruct all Texans on the nobility of the character and sacrifices of the Texas patriots who had gone before.[51] "I consider historic shrines of inestimable worth," she once said, placing herself squarely in the romantic mainstream of American preservationists of the era. "If people—especially children—could actually see the door through which some noble man or woman passed . . . they'll remember . . . . Inevitably they'll be filled with high ideals, the desire to emulate."[52]

Number One on her list of unrecognized Texas patriots was Ben Milam, the fighter killed while leading the successful attack on the Mexican army besieging San Antonio in 1835. The De Zavala Chapter placed a granite monument at his grave in the old cemetery which had become Milam Square, and on March 6, 1897, the anniversary of the fall of the Alamo, organized an annual Texas Heroes Day observance at the spot.[53] Its second marker, in 1901, was a marble tablet placed at the Alamo.[54] The next year Miss De Zavala persuaded her employer, the San Antonio Board of Education, to change the designation of schools from numbers to the names of Texas heroes.[55]

The historic preservation movement stirring elsewhere in the state looked to San Antonio for guidance. Early in 1902, the editor of the *Nacogdoches Plaindealer* asked Adina De Zavala to come help save the Old Stone Fort, built by Spaniards in 1779.[56] The concept of historic preservation may have been having difficulty being understood in San Antonio, but it was in even deeper trouble in East Texas. "I had to stay overnight in some small-town hotel enroute," Miss De Zavala recalled of her journey to Nacogdoches, "and found myself of great curiosity to the natives. From time to time one would saunter in, have a look, then say, 'What be your business?' I'd answer, 'I have no business exactly. I just came from San Antonio to look up some historic sites and try to save the Old Stone Fort.' No matter how much I explained, pretty soon another would be sent in to find out what my business really was, what I had for sale." [57]

Back in San Antonio, Miss De Zavala's group turned its attention to the state of the crumbling Spanish missions. Even the names of the missions were forgotten by the general public. Mission San Antonio de Valero was known by its nickname, the Alamo. The others were popularly identified only by number, in order of their distance from downtown. Closest was the church of Concepción, thus the "First Mission." It was in relatively good condition by the turn of the century, having been repaired and rededicated by local Society of Mary community superior Brother Andrew Edel in 1861 and again by Bishop Neraz in 1887.[58] Deserted San José was the "Second Mission," its church's north wall, dome and most of the roof having collapsed in 1868 and 1874.[59] The chapel of San Juan, the "Third Mission," was roofless, its frescoes nearly obliterated. All walls but the original facade of the chapel of Espada, the "Fourth Mission," were rebuilt during the last half of the century largely at the personal expense of its parish priest, the French-born Rev. François Bouchu, who served there from 1858 until his death in 1907.[60]

Some damage at Concepción was caused in the 1840s by soldiers who were garrisoned at San José and used Concepción as a supply depot after the Battle of Concepción, fought a quarter-mile away in 1835.[61] Some destruction was due to public policy. In 1885 Bexar County commissioners sought to raise funds by selling Concepción's "Public Rock belonging to the County" to the highest bidder.[62] Most damage to the missions, however, was done by increasing numbers of tourists, who were arriving on the railroad and making San Antonio a winter resort. William Corner in 1890 railed against "the wanton mutilation of the sculptures of the Missions by thoughtless relic hunters . . . . At San José whole figures have been stolen and others made headless; the fine old cedar paneled doors of this Mission were entirely wrecked and carried away piecemeal."[63]

Adina De Zavala, a devout Catholic, was frustrated at the steady decline of the historic missions despite efforts of the church. She led her chapter of the Daughters of the Republic of Texas in the first historic preservation effort to save them, and gained the endorsement of the state Daughters organization for purchase of the missions by the State of Texas.[64]

Preservation work began at San José in the spring of 1902.[65] Adina De Zavala herself made the rounds of San Antonio businesses with Elizabeth (Mrs. Pompeo) Coppini in the Coppinis' horse-drawn buggy, collecting contributions of "bricks, lumber, cedar posts or wire to repair fences."[66] Lumberman Albert Steves was persuaded to donate seventy-five fence posts and the Alamo Cement Company gave sixteen sacks of cement. Another businessman gave twenty-five more fence posts, another four barrels of lime, another four barrels of sand. Workmen were paid for up to fifty-four days of labor. Some spent three days bracing the arch of the mission's front door.[67] Crevices were filled in San José's decaying walls, and falling stones were replaced. Three coils of fence wire were purchased to enclose the mission and adjacent square with a six-foot fence, "thus protecting graves which were being tramped down and keeping out those bent on destroying the beautiful carving." Ignacio Salcedo, who lived nearby with his family, was paid to keep an eye on the grounds.[68]

At the state level, fund-raising efforts were backed by Daughters of the Republic of Texas co-founder Adele B. Looscan of Houston and by the president of the Texas Federation of Women's Clubs, Texas history textbook writer and Chautauqua Institution trustee Anna J. Pennybacker of Austin.[69] The biggest fund-raising effort was a flurry of form letters which went out in mid-1902 under the signature of Bettie T. (Mrs. John J.) Stevens, chairman of the De Zavala Chapter's Committee on Missions and wife of the manager of the Hot Sulphur Wells Hotel. Recipients were asked to contribute and to send "the names of five people whom you know have enough appreciation of art and history to do likewise."[70]

The largest contributions were twenty-five dollars from the Texas Chapter of the Colonial Dames of America and fifty dollars from Helen Gould, daughter of the late railroad magnate Jay Gould. Otherwise, response was light.[71] Bishop John Anthony Forest became concerned enough to ask how repairs were being paid for. Based on Adina de Zavala's recollections, Bishop

First Mission South View

By the close of the nineteenth century, the four Spanish mission churches and chapels south of downtown San Antonio were in various stages of disarray, not even their names remembered by the general public. Concepción, the "First Mission," was in excellent repair, and its ruined outbuildings useful for sheltering farm animals. Courtesy of the Witte Museum, San Antonio, Texas.

The roof of the "Third Mission," San Juan, seemed in constant need of repair. Courtesy of the Witte Museum, San Antonio, Texas.

San José, the "Second Mission," was in an advancing stage of collapse, its dome and stone roof already fallen by the mid-1870s. Courtesy of the Witte Museum, San Antonio, Texas.

Espada, the "Fourth Mission," was maintained by an immigrant French priest for nearly fifty years. Courtesy of the Witte Museum, San Antonio, Texas.

At the end of the nineteenth century, only the headless statue of one saint guarded the disintegrating baroque doorway of the San José mission church, its original doors already carried off. Adina De Zavala Papers, The Center For American History, The University of Texas at Austin, CN08643.

Lighting a candle rather than cursing the darkness, in 1902 Adina De Zavala led San Antonio's Daughters of the Republic of Texas in an effort to stabilize the walls and baroque doorway at San José's mission church, including construction of this wooden brace as seen from inside the roofless sanctuary. Adina De Zavala Papers, The Center For American History, The University of Texas at Austin, CN08644.

Forest calculated the cost of repairs to San José at $318.38, including forty-five dollars of donated materials.[72] Two-thirds of that—$207.88— remained unpaid.[73] When Bishop Forest made his next deal with the Daughters that fall, he was careful to be specific about consequences of debts.

In October of 1902, Bishop Forest gave the De Zavala Chapter of the Daughters of the Republic of Texas a five-year lease on the mission complex in poorest repair—San Juan. The agreement, which he and Adina De Zavala both signed, specified that the Church would not be responsible for debts incurred during the Daughters' restoration work and that mission property could not be subjected to any liens from suppliers. Otherwise, as long as the Bishop approved the plan and the mission remained available for public worship, the Daughters were free to restore San Juan, hire a custodian, charge admission and keep the fees.[74]

Terms of the lease of San Juan are strikingly similar to those of leases being negotiated that same year between the Catholic Bishop of the Diocese of Monterey and Los Angeles and the young Landmarks Club of California, then undertaking its highly successful private historic preservation of four of California's Spanish missions.[75] Landmarks Club of California founder

Charles F. Lummis—journalist, adventurer, pioneer conservationist and founder of the Southwest Museum in Los Angeles—was himself a contributor in 1903 to a preservation project of San Antonio's Daughters of the Republic of Texas. That project superseded the San Juan restoration effort and led to a melee that drew national attention and caused aftershocks still being felt nearly a century later.[76]

If the influx of tourists brought increasing destruction to San Antonio's Spanish missions, the dynamic growth of the city was causing immediate destruction of much of the city's historic downtown core, as earlier observers had feared would happen. In 1900 San Antonio regained its long-lost position as largest city in the state from Dallas, which only ten years before had outstripped Galveston for the title. San Antonio's population was growing each decade at rates sometimes exceeding eighty percent.[77]

To accommodate the new rush of people, wholesale street widening stripped away historic streetscapes and created sites for downtown to spread upward as well as outward. At one corner of Alamo Plaza rose the five-story Maverick Bank Building (1885), its elaborate balcony grillwork rendering it a transplant from New Orleans. It was considered San Antonio's first sky-scraper and the tallest building west of the Mississippi.[78] Alfred Giles and James Riely Gordon were among local architects flourishing as they designed new homes and commercial buildings in variations of the popular Richardson Romanesque. George W. Brackenridge brought in New York's Cyrus L.W. Eidlitz, designer of the New York Times Building, to design the Moorish-style San Antonio National Bank Building (1886).

The railroads not only brought prosperity, they literally brought style to the city as well. Spanish missions were established in Texas before they were in California. But Mission Revival architecture, with its "simplified repertoire of vaguely Spanish motifs," developed first on the west coast and spread eastward as the signature style for buildings of the two major southwestern railroads, the Southern Pacific and the Atchison, Topeka and Santa Fe.[79] Between the Spanish Baroque towers of San Antonio's elaborate Mission Revival Southern Pacific station (1902), San Francisco architects J.D. Isaacs and D.J. Patterson placed the Alamo's familiar curved gable parapet design. Local architect Harvey L. Page used it in San Antonio's International & Great Northern Railway Station (1907). With the Alamo motif soon widespread in such commercial buildings as J. Flood Walker's St. Anthony Hotel (1910) and in places beyond San Antonio, it became a distinctive regional branch of Mission Revival known as the Alamo Revival or Texian Style.[80]

Forces of growth and development, however, found themselves on a collision course with a rising generation of San Antonians better-traveled than their forebears. They cared more for the subtleties of their surroundings and were attentive to what generations of travelers to San Antonio had been

The Alamo Revival branch of the Mission Revival architectural style is reflected in the curved gable parapet design borrowed from the Alamo for San Antonio's Southern Pacific Railroad depot, designed by San Francisco architects in 1902. The San Antonio Express-News *Collection, The Institute of Texan Cultures.*

saying. They were quite unhappy over the harvesting of the city's past. Their concern focused on the old Alamo mission, where an impending storm brewed as ominously as when Santa Anna's forces surrounded the compound in the previous century. This time, challengers at the ramparts were fed by the city's vibrant economy and spread up Houston Street toward the Alamo from Main and Military plazas along the route of Santa Anna's army itself. Multistory sentinels gathered south of the Alamo: the Menger Hotel (1859) with its new iron grillwork, beyond it the Joske Brothers Store (1888). On the Alamo's western flank were the three-story Crockett Block (1882), the Opera House (1886) and the Maverick Bank, with the Richardson Romanesque Federal Building and Post Office (1890) looming from the north.

The final assault would be launched by men sweeping in not from south of the border but from the north. The target would again be the stone walls of the old mission convento, now cloaked in a frame exterior and scorned by one observer as "a grotesque half-stone, half-gingerbread lumber misfit construction of a country wholesale merchandise store and warehouse, certainly not fit to be in the most prominent location of the town."[81] Its leading defender this time was not a Travis or a Crockett but the petite Adina De Zavala, her defense no cannon or sword but an agreement on the old building. A decade before, merchants Hugo and Schmeltzer promised her "not to sell or offer the property to anyone else without . . . giving the [Daughters of the Republic of Texas] Chapter the opportunity to acquire it."[82] She was steadfast in believing that the Spanish mission convento building must be restored.

Others agreed that the convento property needed to be reunited with the mission church, but thought the old building was not the original convento and should be removed for a park. The view was summarized in the romantic verbiage of the times by nineteen year-old Clara Driscoll, who fired off a salvo to the *Daily Express* in 1900:

> We travel to European countries and do a great deal of wearisome sightseeing. We visit their churches, and gaze in awe and wonder at their monuments. We are not allowed to lay a finger hardly on one of the cherished stones, so carefully are these places guarded. We uncover our heads and speak in hushed voices in their pantheons, where are buried their famous heroes . . . . And yet there is standing today right in our very home an old ruin, a silent monument of the dark and stormy days of Texas, when her sons were sacrificing their lives and shedding their blood for her independence, when men whose names will live forever in the history of the ages were dying like martyrs to free this glorious State from the tyrannical Mexican rule, a monument that any city, state or country would feel the deepest pride in possessing.
>
> It is our Alamo, and how do we treat it? We leave it hemmed in on one side by a hideous barracks-like looking building, and on the other by two saloons. Listen to what strangers say upon seeing the Alamo amid such surroundings: 'Is that the Alamo? . . . . ' Today the Alamo should stand out free and clear. All the unsightly obstructions that hide it away should be torn down and the space utilized for a park . . . . Every Texan would willingly give his little mite to see the Alamo placed amid surroundings where it would stand out for what it is—the grandest monument in the history of the world.[83]

With the rising commercial value of the convento property, Adina De Zavala knew an effort to save it would require tactics more widely reaching than those that tried to save remains of the four other missions. In 1902, the De Zavala Chapter of the Daughters of the Republic of Texas organized a Congress of Patriotism, its purpose no less grandiose than its name: to assist the Daughters in repairing and maintaining both the Alamo church, still cared for by the city, and the Hugo & Schmeltzer building, in which would be established a "Texas Hall of Fame—a Museum of History, Art, Literature, and Relics." Membership was open to "anyone of good moral standing interested in the objects of this organization."[84]

Shortly thereafter, sculptor Pompeo Coppini was offered a commission for a ten-foot marble statue of David Crockett for the lobby of a major tourist hotel to face the rear of the Alamo convento. Coppini learned that hotel investors wanted the convento removed for a park, and at once alerted Adina De Zavala. Together they went to the Menger Hotel, whose owners they thought might want to block a new competitor. Instead, they were introducted to the visiting Clara Driscoll.[85] Intrigued, Miss Driscoll went with Miss De Zavala to see building owner Charles Hugo, who put his price at $75,000, the 1990 equivalent of $1.1 million. On March 18, 1903, Miss Driscoll gave Hugo $500 for a thirty-day option. When it expired, the Daughters could come up with only $1,000. Miss Driscoll contributed the remaining $3,500 to extend the option until February 10, 1904.[86]

Fund-raising, a difficult effort in most places, has been particularly vexing in San Antonio, for historic preservation or for anything else. Lacking the strong industrial community and the private fortunes on which an eastern city like Boston could draw to save its Old South Meeting House, San Antonio even at the beginning of the twentieth century was handicapped by an economic base little changed from the hardscrabble times of Spanish rule—an Army post, commercial activity and some beef shipping for the outlying ranch country, to which had been added mainly brewing and tourism. This base was sufficient to support rapid population growth, "but not for substantial, independent and self-sustaining capital accumulation."[87]

To finance expansion of the Alamo property, Clara Driscoll, new treasurer of the De Zavala Chapter of the Daughters of the Republic of Texas, helped mount a nationwide fund-raising campaign based on the previous year's fund-raising technique for San José Mission. This time several thousand letters went out, each asking for a donation and the names of five more potential donors. One fund-raiser in the statewide network, San Saba's District Judge Clarence Martin—a former legislator helping lobby in Austin for the Alamo Purchase Bill—gathered $160.95 in public meetings.[88] Noted the local newspaper: "The tale he told about the solitary individual who forsook his comrades during the battle of the Alamo kept anyone from leaving while the collection was being taken."[89]

By early 1904, nearly $7,000 was in from some five hundred individuals throughout the nation and from three foreign countries. But that was far short of the $20,000 needed for the down payment, and a legislative appropriation to cover even option payments had already been vetoed by the governor.[90]

So Miss Driscoll paid the balance of $65,000 herself and purchased the property in her name. As the search for funds to repay her continued, the Shrine of Texas Liberty once again opened its doors to a fund-raising bazaar, this one held by the De Zavala Chapter of the Daughters of the Republic of Texas for the Alamo Mission Fund.[91]

The state Democratic Party defied its recalcitrant governor with a requirement in the party's platform that Miss Driscoll be reimbursed by the state.[92] In January of 1905 the governor signed a bill to reimburse her and put title to the property in the name of the State of Texas.[93] The legislature turned custody of the property over to the Daughters of the Republic of Texas state organization and transferred custody of the adjacent Alamo church from the City of San Antonio to the Daughters as well, with "all of said property being subject to future legislation by the Legislature of the State of Texas."[94]

Harmony among the Daughters, however, foundered on the rocks of a debate which remains unresolved in the historic preservation movement: Should a landmark be restored to its original appearance or to the period in history with which it is most identified? Should the newly acquired Alamo building be restored as a Spanish mission convento or, instead, reflect exclusively its role in the Battle of the Alamo?

The issue was arising independently on the east coast at the same time. In 1904, the Sons of the American Revolution in New York City began restoring Fraunces Tavern not to its original appearance in 1719 but to how it was thought to have looked at its most famous time in history—in 1783, when it was the scene of Washington's farewell to his troops.[95] In 1905, pioneer New England preservationist William Sumner Appleton helped raise funds to restore a Boston home built in 1680 that in the next century was the home of Paul Revere. Architectural merit, perhaps for the first time in America, was given precedence over patriotic impulses.[96] Revere's home was restored not to its appearance at the time of its most famous occupant, but rather to the time of its original construction.

In the northeast, both climate and emotions were cooler than in South Texas, and no battle lines seem to have been drawn there over the matter. But in San Antonio, the single-minded Adina De Zavala was determined that beneath the Hugo & Schmeltzer facade stood "a large part" of the original convento, significant to both mission and battle, and still advocated its reincarnation as a Texas Hall of Fame. The high-spirited Clara Driscoll was equally determined that "the monastery fell to pieces long ago." She first agreed that some walls may have stood during the battle and, therefore, a replica of the convento could "serve as a Valhalla for Texas."[97] Before long, however, she declared the matter to be of no consequence. Whether or not walls pre-dated the battle, "the idea . . . is to lend more prominence to the chapel, which, of course, is the main feature in the Alamo mission." The convento

A bitter debate over how or whether to restore remains of the Alamo mission's Spanish convento building arose in 1905. Partisans led by Adina De Zavala thought its ruins should be restored, perhaps as a two-story Texas Hall of Fame, as shown. Adina De Zavala Papers, The Center For American History, The University of Texas at Austin, CN08641.

walls overshadowed the Alamo church, and must therefore be removed for a dignified park—the very goal sought by the the hotel developers.[98]

The state Daughters of the Republic of Texas organization, and many San Antonians and Texans as well, divided into De Zavalans and Driscollites. For the next eight years blow followed counter-blow, as newspaper readers read in wonder. Local custody of the Alamo was given to the De Zavala Chapter, then held back and given to Clara Driscoll. When Miss Driscoll left town before picking up the keys, Miss De Zavala went to city hall and picked them up herself. She shooed away a locksmith hired to change the lock and returned the keys only after a lawsuit. Driscollite Daughters of the Republic of Texas in San Antonio seceded from the De Zavala Chapter and formed the Alamo Mission Chapter. By the next year each faction was holding its own state convention.[99]

Then, in 1908, someone told Adina De Zavala that the Driscollites planned to rent the vacant Hugo & Schmeltzer building for vaudeville shows. That was too much. She hired three men to protect the building, but the sheriff, armed with an injunction, ordered them away. Miss De Zavala reported what followed: "The agents of the syndicate threw my men out bodily, expecting to take possession. They did not know I was in an inner room, and when I hurried out to confront them, demanding by what right they invaded the historic building, consternation reigned. They withdrew outside the building for whispered consultation. The instant they stepped out, I closed the doors and barred them. That's all. There was nothing else for me to do but hold the fort. So I did."[100]

Miss de Zavala remained barricaded inside for three days and three nights, as reporters stood by. Deputies on guard denied her food and water, but a

Partisans including Clara Driscoll agreed with businessmen that remains of the Alamo's convento should be cleared away for a park, which could feature a monument to Alamo heroes and leave an open vista for the high-rise hotel proposed behind it. Neither restoration nor open park resulted. The convento remains were reduced to a one-story shell, and the hotel proposed behind it was never built. Shown at the far left of the Alfred Giles drawing is San Antonio's 1890 Federal Building, to its right an imagined building on the site of the future Medical Arts Building/Emily Morgan Hotel.
Greater San Antonio, the City of Destiny and of Your Destination, *78, DRT Library at the Alamo.*

friend managed to pass in a few oranges. Finally she surrendered to the state superintendent of public buildings, sent from Austin by the governor, and the Driscollites were back in charge.[101]

The *Light* was already demanding the building's immediate clearance for the park in front of the proposed hotel, declaring "The interests of San Antonio are far superior to the interests of any firm or individual."[102] The majority in an *Express* poll favored tearing down the convento's walls rather than restoring it. Banker Franz Groos was more hesitant, suggesting that enough be left for a low wall "covered with ivy, with an arch here and there" so as "to satisfy our wish for something beautiful without entirely doing away with something historic."[103] Alfred Giles brought up his earlier design for a 163-foot monument with an observation platform two-thirds of the way up, an edifice the *Express* declared "would draw to San Antonio tourists from all over the world."[104]

Driscollites in 1910 were at last preparing to clear away the building for the park when Governor Oscar Colquitt sided with the De Zavalans and concluded that many walls did indeed pre-date the Texas Revolution.[105] He took title to the Alamo back for the state and ordered the convento's restoration.[106] As the modern roof and wooden walls began to come off in January of 1912,

ALFRED GILES CO.

the governor was on hand to watch second-story arches and other Spanish stone work revealed, confirming Miss De Zavala's belief.[107] The Texas Supreme Court soon reentrusted the Alamo property to the Daughters, but permitted restoration to continue. Money ran out before it was finished, and in 1913, while the governor was out of the state, the lieutenant governor allowed removal of the upper story walls.[108] The lower walls remained un-roofed until covered for a museum in time for San Antonio's world's fair fifty-five years later.

Confusion over what was saved and by whom has remained for generations. Two women are variously given credit for the feat of saving the Alamo. Leadership of the initial effort was actually by a third, Mary Adams Maverick. But, as in the case of the first property purchased for historic preservation in the United States, in the northeast, credit for saving the Alamo may go instead to a group of men.

In the public mind, the Alamo is the stone building with the rounded entrance and the curved gable parapet that has appeared in countless drawings, paintings, photographs, movies and on postage stamps for more than a hundred years. When people come to San Antonio to see the Alamo, that is the building they expect to see. In their zeal to gain maximum support for expanding the publicly owned Alamo property, however, the Daughters tried defining the old convento building itself as the Alamo, with the justification that more of the fighting occurred in the convento than in the church.[109] Consequently, Clara Driscoll became widely known as the "Savior of the Alamo."[110] So, to a lesser extent, did Adina De Zavala.[111]

The more common image of the Alamo, however, was in the mind of one writer when he praised a group of men as the Savior of the Alamo. Joseph E. Dwyer represented the Catholic Church in its sale of the Alamo church to the state in 1883, when Adina De Zavala was twenty-one and Clara Driscoll had just turned two. Shortly after the state's purchase, Dwyer wrote Kingsville's State Senator Rudolph Kleberg: "God bless the noble and patriotic legislators who saved for Texas the Alamo."[112]

Notes

1. Donald E. Everett, "San Antonio Welcomes the 'Sunset'—1877," *Southwestern Historical Quarterly* 65 (July 1961), 47–48.

2. *San Antonio Express*, Feb. 19, 1877 in Everett, "San Antonio Welcomes the 'Sunset,'" 49–50.

3. "Passing of the Chili Stands," *San Antonio Daily Express*, Jun. 9, 1901.

4. James Newcomb, unpublished typescript, 982 in Everett, *San Antonio, The Flavor of its Past,* 9.

5. *San Antonio Herald,* Jan. 23, 1875.

6. *Texas Sun*, Feb. 1878, in Everett, "San Antonio Welcomes the Sunset," 56.

7. Richard Harding Davis, *The West from a Car-Window*, (New York, 1892) in Everett, *San Antonio, The Flavor of its Past*, 2.

8. *New York Post* in *San Antonio Express*, Oct. 21, 1885 in Everett, *San Antonio, The Flavor of its Past*, 2.

9. The roots of historic preservation ran deeper in the Old World. Sweden had a Director General of Antiquities in 1630 and passed the world's first legislation to protect monuments in 1666. France created a Commission des Monuments Historiques in 1837. An Ancient Monuments Protection Act was passed for England and Wales in 1882. (Robert R. Garvey, Jr. in *With Heritage So Rich* (New York: Random House, 1966), 151.)

10. Charles B. Hosmer, Jr., *Presence of the Past, A History of the Preservation Movement in the United States Before Williamsburg* (New York: G.P. Putman's Sons, 1965), 299.

11. Ibid., 30–31. The effort to save Independence Hall was not, reports Hosmer, totally enlightened. The original wing buildings were torn down to make room for new "fireproof" buildings, and someone removed the original woodwork from the room in which the Declaration of Independence was signed and the Constitution written.

12. William J. Murtagh, *Keeping Time, The History and Theory of Preservation in America* (Pittstown, N.J.: The Main Street Press, 1988), 27.

13. Hosmer, *Presence of the Past,* 36–37.

14. Ibid., 43–47.

15. Ibid., 37.

16. Ibid., 70.

17. Ibid., 103–05.

18. Purchase of buildings for historic preservation west of the Mississippi next occurred in California, where the Native Sons of the Golden West organized in 1888 and by 1891 had purchased and donated to the state the last remaining building at Sutter's Fort. In 1894 the Landmarks Club of California organized to preserve the state's Spanish missions. New Mexico was still a territory in 1898 when local preservationists got Congress to award title of the territory's best-known landmark, Santa Fe's Palace of the Governors (1610), to the future state. (Hosmer, *Presence of the Past,* 124–27.) In New Orleans, a landmarks society was suggested in 1895, resulting in a city ordinance preserving as a museum the Cabildo, the Spanish government building dating from 1795. (Charles B. Hosmer, Jr., *Preservation Comes of Age, From Williamsburg to the National Trust, 1926–1949,* [Charlottesville: The University Press of Virginia, 1981], 290.) The U.S. government purchased its first prehistoric ruin in 1889, with a Congressional appropriation for Casa Grande in Arizona. Preservation of the natural environment by the United States government began in 1872 with establishment of Yellowstone National Park, but U.S. national policy—unlike England's—still kept natural preservation separate from historic preservation. (Murtagh, *Keeping Time,* 51–52.)

19. "Alamo Monument," *The Handbook of Texas.* I, 23–24.

20. "The Alamo," *San Antonio Daily Express,* Jan. 16, 1877.

21. Ownership of the Alamo, its lands secularized in 1793, was returned to the church, along with properties of other former missions, by the Republic of Texas in 1841. (Habig, *The Alamo Chain of Missions,* 70–71.)

22. "Sale of a Portion of the Alamo Property," *San Antonio Daily Express,* Dec. 1, 1877.

23. Ibid.

24. *San Antonio Daily Express,* Jan. 17, 1876, in Everett, *San Antonio, The Flavor of its Past,* 5.

25. William Elton Green, "Remembering the Alamo," unpublished manuscript, 9. The Alamo Monument Association absorbed the membership of the Irving Literary Society-turned-Alamo Literary Society, formed in 1869 under the presidency of William H. Maverick. (Ibid., 30–31.)

26. Marks, *Turn Your Eyes Toward Texas: Pioneers Sam and Mary Maverick,* 51–52, 258. The last name of Samuel Augustus Maverick, a Yale-educated lawyer and landowner, entered the English language after some of his cattle on the Texas coast were allowed to wander unbranded. (Ibid., 161.) Nineteen of the 26 members listed in the Alamo Monument Association charter were men. (Green, "Remembering the Alamo," 12–13.)

27. Quoted in "Memorial to The Legislature of Texas for the Purchase of the Alamo Church" in the Texas State Archives.

28. Ibid.; Green, "Remembering the Alamo," 14–15. Grenet continued to capitalize on his property's history. In 1881 he sponsored an exhibition of loaned

historical materials upstairs in the former convento. "Every bit of space" was filled by the exhibition, which the *San Antonio Light* reported "met with astonishing success." Items displayed ranged from a peach seed basket made by Sam Houston to a piece of lava from Mount Vesuvius to a drinking gourd used by Samuel Maverick while held by the Mexicans in Perote Prison. As an added attraction, "an elegant lunch will be spread in the building, and the rooms brilliantly lighted up." (*San Antonio Light,* Nov. 1, 1881.)

29. House Concurrent Resolution Number V, Jan. 22, 1883, recorded in the 18th Legislature's House Journal 53 and Senate Journal 84; "Thermopylae of Texas," *San Antonio Daily Express,* Feb. 20, 1883.

30. "San Jacinto State Park," *The Handbook of Texas* II, 556.

31. "The Transfer of the Alamo," *San Antonio Light,* May 17, 1883, 1.

32. "The Alamo," *San Antonio Light,* May 16, 1883, 1.

33. "The Alamo Metamorphosed by the good Ladies of the St. Mark's Altar Society," *San Antonio Daily Express,* Nov. 27, 1883, 4; "The Alamo," unattributed clipping in Daughters of the Republic of Texas Library at the Alamo, Nov. 27, 1883.

34. "The Alamo," *San Antonio Daily Express,* Jan. 6, 1887; "Capt. Rife Passes Away," *San Antonio Daily Express,* Dec. 28, 1894, 8; "Death of the Alamo Custodian," *San Antonio Daily Express,* Jan. 16, 1900; *DRT Proceedings,* 1903, 3, 21 in L. Robert Ables, *The Second Battle for the Alamo, The Southwestern Historical Quarterly* 70 (Jan., 1967), 378.

35. "The Alamo," *San Antonio Daily Express,* Jan. 17, 1885.

36. William Buckey, "Would Honor Heroes of the Alamo," *San Antonio Daily Express,* Dec. 12, 1909, 3A. Fund-raising events included, in mid-1889, Alamo Day in San Marcos, sponsored by the local Chautauqua Association. Mrs. Maverick and several Monument Association members took the train to San Marcos, where they heard former State Senator Seth Shepard of Dallas deliver an oration entitled "The Fall of the Alamo" and R.M. Potter's "Hymn of the Alamo" sung "in magnificent voice and tone" by the Chautauqua's choir. (Hon. Seth Shephard [sic], *The Fall of the Alamo* (San Antonio: Maverick Printing House, 1889.)

37. "The Alamo," *San Antonio Daily Express,* Jun. 17, 1895, 4.

38. "To Remodel the Alamo," *San Antonio Daily Express,* Jan. 31, 1893, 6; "Remember the Alamo," *San Antonio Daily Express,* Feb. 4, 1893, 4.

39. *San Antonio Express,* May 19, 1903. The writer continued: "Then there is a picture of a proposed monument and a contribution box nearby to which the attention of visitors is called. How many dollars have been dropped into that contribution box has never been divulged. Many complaints have been made of the treatment of visitors, but the matter was thought too delicate to be commented upon. The fact is, the Alamo needs a through looking into."

40. G.Q.A. Rose, "Condition of the Alamo," *San Antonio Daily Express,* May 19, 1895, 6.

41. To Repair the Alamo," *San Antonio Daily Express,* Jun. 13, 1895, 8.

42. "The Restoration of the Alamo," *San Antonio Daily Express,* Jul. 28, 1895.

43. Hosmer, *Presence of the Past,* 299. At the turn of the century, preservation was also seen as a tool for Americanizing immigrant children.

44. Wallace Evan Davies, *Patriotism On Parade, The Story of Veterans' and Hereditary Organizations in America, 1783–1900* (Cambridge: Harvard University Press, 1955), 353. Synthesizing the women's club movement was organization of the General Federation of Women's Clubs in 1889. First of the women's hereditary organizations was the Colonial Dames of America in 1890. The Daughters of the American Revolution was formed later that year, followed by the breakaway National Society of Colonial Dames of America in 1891. (Ibid., 56–58.)

45. National patriotic women's groups did not begin organizing in Texas for another five years. The Texas Chapter of the United Daughters of the Confederacy organized in 1896, a National Society of the Colonial Dames of America chapter formed in 1898 and a Daughters of the American Revolution chapter in 1899. (William Elton Green, "Historical Preservation in Texas: A Chronology" (unpublished manuscript), 3.)

46. The "D" in the family name began being capitalized by Miss De Zavala's father, Augustine. (Luther Robert Ables, "The Work of Adina De Zavala," unpublished master's thesis at the Centro de Estudios Universitarios of Mexico City College (1955), 17.)

47. Although Miss De Zavala gives the date of this informal group's organization as "about 1889" in her *History and Legends of the Alamo* (San Antonio, 1917, 212), the specific year 1887 is given in *The Handbook of Texas* (II, 741), in an item which lists Miss De Zavala as one of two contributors. Born not far from the San Jacinto battlefield in east Texas, Miss De Zavala spent her early childhood in Galveston and later moved with the family to a ranch near the northern Bexar County community of Shavano, near the future intersection of Fredericksburg and De Zavala roads. (Ables, "The Work of Adina De Zavala," 4, 8–11.) "I [can]not remember when I could not read," she once said. "My favorite story books were about history; myths came next. My sister and I produced 'plays'—always scenes from history." (Pearl Howard, "Southern Personalities—Adina De Zavala, Patriot-Historian," *Holland's Magazine* 64 (Dec., 1935), 36, in Ables, "The Work of Adina De Zavala," 6.)

48. "Texas Historical and Landmarks Association," *The Handbook of Texas* II, 741–42. The Auxiliary, De Zavala Chapter, Daughters of the Republic of Texas was formed in 1900 for those not qualified by sex or ancestry to be Daughters.

49. The first Texas historical societies appeared briefly in Houston in 1870 and the next year in Galveston, where a more permanent group formed in 1894. The Texas State Historical Association was organized in 1897. (Green, "Historical Preservation in Texas," 2–4.

50. The full text of Article 2: "Its objects in general shall be the same as those of the State Association, but especially the marking out of historic spots in San Antonio and the preservation and recording of the true history pertaining to same in order to prevent their being forgotten when old landmarks are demolished and the old inhabitants shall have passed away." ("Constitution and By-Laws of the De Zavala Chapter, Daughters of the Republic of Texas," Adina De Zavala Papers Box 2M164, The Center For American History, The University of Texas at Austin).

51. As Holly Beachley Brear reports in *Inherit The Alamo: Myth and Ritual at an American Shrine* (Austin: University of Texas Press, 1995), 93–94, some latter-day observers suggest that ethnic discrimination because of her Hispanic background

caused Adina De Zavala the difficulties she faced in her struggles through the years. But there is no indication that such an idea ever occurred to anyone else at the time nor that it even occurred to Adina De Zavala, who openly spoke with pride of her distinguished Hispanic heritage, although three of her four grandparents were Anglo-Americans. She was accepted early on by founders of the Daughters of the Republic of Texas—some of the leading ladies in the state—and was elected to the DRT's state executive committee in 1902 and later to the executive council of the Texas State Historical Association and to membership in other leading statewide organizations.

Miss De Zavala's difficulties appear to have been, instead, largely self-inflicted— "her forthrightness, her tendency toward stubbornness which bordered upon intractableness if she thought she was right, a quick tongue . . . ." Further noted L. Robert Ables: "It is an anomaly in the history of the State of Texas that a woman of Spanish-Mexican ancestry should have such an intense desire to preserve and illuminate Texas history while many of her Anglo contemporaries did little or nothing." (Ables, "The Work of Adina De Zavala," 1–5, 12, 131; Ables, "The Second Battle for the Alamo," 378; "Adina De Zavala," *The Handbook of Texas* III, 243.)

52. Ables, "The Work of Adina De Zavala," 6–7.

53. "Benjamin Rush Milam," *The Handbook of Texas* II, 191; Ables, "The Work of Adina De Zavala," 25.

54. "17 Tablets," *San Antonio Express,* Aug. 3, 1924, 26. The Alamo marker later disappeared.

55. Ables, "The Work of Adina De Zavala," 28–29.

56. Henry Fuller to Adina De Zavala, Jan. 15, 1902, Adina De Zavala Papers Box 2M138, The Center for American History, The University of Texas at Austin.

57. Howard, "Southern Personalities," in Ables, "The Work of Adina De Zavala," 82. The effort failed and the old fort was torn down shortly afterward, only to be reconstructed during the Texas Centennial in 1936 on the campus of Stephen F. Austin University. ("Old Stone Fort," *The Handbook of Texas* II, 310.) The De Zavala Chapter passed a resolution "extending sympathy to the patriotic women of Nacogdoches." ("Preservation Of Missions," *San Antonio Daily Express,* Feb. 5, 1902, 7.)

58. Condition of the missions is described in William Corner, *San Antonio de Bexar: A Guide and History* (San Antonio: Bainbridge & Corner, 1890), 14–22; Habig, *The Alamo Chain of Missions,* 110–11; and in Félix D. Almaráz, Jr., *The San Antonio Missions After Secularization, 1800–1983*; (San Antonio: San Antonio Missions National Park, photocopy), 69, 97–98, 116–17, 119, 122, 163–64. Adina De Zavala futilely attempted to set the numbering straight by identifying the Alamo instead of Concepción as the "First Mission." (Letterheads in Adina De Zavala Papers Box 2M136, The Center For American History, The University of Texas at Austin.)

59. Arches for a monastery were added at the rear of the San José church by Benedictines based in Latrobe, Pennsylvania, at San José from 1859 to 1868. From 1872 until title was returned to the Diocese of San Antonio in 1885, San José was owned by the Holy Cross religious order in Indiana which sought unsuccessfully to make it a summer faculty residence for Notre Dame University. (Ibid.)

60. Father Bouchu was living in one of Espada's old mission buildings when he was visited by Adina De Zavala and Adele Looscan in the summer of 1903. He offered

to share with them "his midday meal, which consisted of fried onions, cream cheese and bread." The ladies gratefully declined. (Adele B. Looscan, "Old Spanish Missions of San Antonio," *San Antonio Daily Express,* Oct. 25, 1903.)

61. Habig, *The Alamo Chain of Missions,* 111, 148.

62. Commissioners Court Minutes, Oct. 12, 1885, in Almaráz, *The San Antonio Missions After Secularization,* 32–33. Almaráz suggested that "the rock-pickers in all probability viewed the mission rubble as strenuous labor and turned to other enterprises." Forty-five years earlier, the City of San Antonio sold stones from walls of the Alamo. (San Antonio City Council Minutes, Apr. 2, 1840 in Everett, *San Antonio, The Flavor of its Past,* 18.)

63. Corner, *San Antonio de Bexar,* 13.

64. *DRT Proceedings, 1903,* 3, in Ables, "The Second Battle for the Alamo," 378. Such repairs as those of Army workmen renovating the Alamo in 1850 or Father François Bouchu's later repairs at Espada were incidental to the primary project or were done largely for religious purposes, rather than being intended to return those buildings to their appearance at a particular point in time.

65. "Women Will Preserve The Old Spanish Missions," *Sulphur Springs (Tex.) Democrat,* Dec. 12, 1902. The first project was to be restoration of the tower's circular staircase, its original wooden steps strewn about the area. But the $300 estimate was too high "and the matter was laid aside, pending the negotiations of the committee appointed to visit the church authorities." ("Preservation Of Missions," *San Antonio Daily Express,* Feb. 5, 1902, 7.)

66. Pompeo Coppini, *From Dawn to Sunset* (San Antonio: The Naylor Co., 1949), 106.

67. "Bill for the Work and Material for repairing St. José Mission, San Antonio, Texas," in Adina De Zavala Papers Box 2M164, The Center for American History, The University of Texas at Austin.

68. Ibid.; "Women Will Preserve," *Sulphur Springs Democrat,* Dec. 12, 1902; Adele B. Looscan, "Old Spanish Missions of San Antonio," *San Antonio Daily Express,* Oct. 25, 1903. Salcedo's wife was a descendant of Pedro Huizar, traditionally credited with carving the "Rose Window" at San José. ("Old Spanish Missions, *San Antonio Daily Express,* Oct. 25, 1903.) Four years later, the county attorney ordered him to remove the fence when nearby residents complained that it blocked their access to the public square, which was owned by the county. (T.J. Newton to Ignacio Salcedo, Dec. 29, 1906, in Adina De Zavala Papers, St. Pius X Library, University of the Incarnate Word.)

69. "Women Will Preserve," *Sulphur Springs Democrat,* Dec. 12, 1902; Anna J. Pennybacker to Adina De Zavala, Jul. 30, 1902, in Adina De Zavala Papers Box 2M138, The Center for American History, The University of Texas at Austin.

70. Solicitation letters in Adina De Zavala Papers Box 2M138, The Center for American History, The University of Texas at Austin.

71. "Preservation Of Missions," *San Antonio Daily Express,* Feb. 5, 1902, 2; "Women Will Preserve," *Sulphur Springs Democrat,* Dec. 12, 1902.

72. The equivalent amount of $318 in 1990 was $4,831.34, determined through Composite Consumer Price Index tables devised by John J. McCusker in *How Much*

Is That in Real Money/ A Historical Price Index for Use as a Deflator of Money Values in the Economy of the United States (Worcester, American Antiquarian Society, 1992).

73. "Bill for the Work and Material for repairing St. José Mission." In a burst of self-righteousness at the bottom of her copy, Miss De Zavala penciled her umbrage at the very idea of being asked to account for her selfless efforts: "I furnished *all* the *material* mentioned and itemized herein. I *personally paid* all the workmen and attended to the entire matter . . . . I spent much more than accounted for here because I could not remember the items when he [the bishop] was questioning me, and besides I could see no sense in putting it down as it did not cost the *Bishop* nor the *Church* a cent."

74. "Agreement between J.A. Forest, Bishop of San Antonio, and Adina De Zavala, president, De Zavala Chapter DRT, Oct. 29, 1902" in Adina De Zavala Papers Box 2M138, The Center for American History, The University of Texas at Austin.

75. Indentures between George Montgomery, Roman Catholic Bishop of the Diocese of Monterey, and the Landmarks Club, 1902, in Rena Maverick Green Papers, copies in San Antonio Conservation Society Library; Hosmer, *Presence of the Past*, 126. According to its letterhead, since its formation in 1894 the club had saved "all that remains of the Missions San Diego, Pala, San Juan Capistrano and San Fernando." (The Landmarks Club of California, Inc. letters in Rena Maverick Green Papers.)

76. "Chain Letters, Alamo Mission Fund, Clara Driscoll, San Antonio, Tex.," account book in Adina De Zavala Papers Box 2M164, The Center for American History, The University of Texas at Austin.

77. From a level of 8,235 in 1860, San Antonio's population rose to 12,256 in 1870 (+49%), to 20,550 in 1880 (+68%), to 37,673 in 1890 (+83%), to 53,321 in 1900 (+42%), to 96,614 in 1910 (+81%) and to 161,379 in 1920 (+67%). Only after hitting 231,542 (+44%) in 1930 did the city's growth percentage drop significantly, to enjoy major growth again in the 1950s (+61%) and '60s (+44%) before tapering off to relatively sedate decade increases of no more than 20%.

78. "Maverick Bank," *San Antonio Express*, Sept. 10, 1926, 2-A.

79. Henry, *Architecture in Texas 1895–1945*, 144.

80. Ibid., 144–45.

81. Coppini, *From Dawn to Sunset*, 106.

82. Ables, "The Second Battle for the Alamo," 378.

83. "A Plea For The Old Landmarks," *San Antonio Daily Express*, Apr. 29, 1900. Signed only "A Texas Girl," the writer is identified as Miss Driscoll in Ables, "The Second Battle for the Alamo."

84. "Constitution, 'Congress of Patriotism,'" Adina De Zavala Papers Box 2M164, The Center for American History, The University of Texas at Austin.

85. This series of incidents is recounted by Coppini in *From Dawn to Sunset*, 105–08.

86. *DRT Report*, 1906, 44 in Ables, "The Second Battle for the Alamo," 381.

87. John A. Booth and David R. Johnson, *The Politics of San Antonio* (Lincoln & London: University of Nebraska Press, 1983), 8.

88. Clarence Martin to Adina De Zavala, Nov. 19, 1903, Adina De Zavala Papers Box 2M138, The Center for American History, The University of Texas at Austin.

89. *San Saba County News,* undated clipping in Adina De Zavala Papers Box 2M138, The Center for American History, The University of Texas at Austin.

90. "Chain Letters, Alamo Mission Fund, Clara Driscoll, San Antonio, Tex." Contributions ranged from the suggested 50 cents from Mrs. Walter Gresham in Galveston to $50 from Robert J. Kleberg in Kingsville to $100 from Uriah Lott, president of the Brownsville & St. Louis Railroad. Railroad heiress Helen Gould, who had contributed $50 to the group's mission fund-raising drive the previous year, sent a like amout to the Alamo Mission Fund. Landmarks Club of California founder Charles Lummis sent $1, and is the only person active in historic preservation elsewhere in the nation at that time who can be identified among the contributors.

91. Flier in Adina De Zavala Papers Box 2M138, The Center for American History, The University of Texas at Austin.

92. Ables, "The Second Battle for the Alamo," 382.

93. The bill did not reimburse the DRT for the $10,000 it had already collected and paid. (*DRT Report,* 1905, 34 in Ables, "The Second Battle for the Alamo," 382.)

94. *General Laws of the State of Texas,* 29th Leg., Reg. Sess., 7–8 in Ables, "The Second Battle for the Alamo," 382.

95. Laurie Beckelman and Anthony Robins, "Coping With History," *Historic Preservation Forum* (May/June 1994), 12.

96. Murtagh, *Keeping Time,* 31.

97. *San Antonio Express,* Jan. 22, 1905.

98. *Fort Worth Record,* Jan. 22, 1905 in Ables, "The Second Battle for the Alamo," 383–84. The Alamo shrine is, correctly, a church, rather than a chapel.

99. Ables, "The Second Battle for the Alamo," 384–403.

100. "Adina De Zavala, 'Savior of the Alamo,' Dead at 93," *San Antonio News,* Mar. 2, 1955, 1-C.

101. Ables, "Second Battle," 403–405.

102. "Are Anxious to Have Park," *San Antonio Light,* Sept. 9, 1906.

103. "How Alamo Would Look," *San Antonio Express,* Apr. 21, 1912, 27-B.

104. "Would Honor Heroes," *San Antonio Daily Express,* Dec. 19, 1909.

105. Ables, "The Second Battle for the Alamo," 406–07. After Clara Driscoll offered to finance "the immediate removal of the unsightly modern structure now known as the Hugo-Schmeltzer building," a DRT official urged members to "have the Alamo protected from the intrusion of other buildings. Insist that it must stand there alone . . . and that the Hugo-Schmeltzer building be removed at once . . . . The stones of that building should be placed in a wall . . . with Texas vines gracefully twining over its rugged points . . . . The Alamo must stand there alone . . . ramparts . . . washed with the blood of heroes . . . . Any other building . . . would detract . . . and would be an insult to those blood stained walls . . . ." (*DRT Report,* 1909, 11 in Ables, "The Second Battle for the Alamo," 407.)

106. Ables, "The Second Battle for the Alamo," 407–11.

107. "Falling Stones Reveal the Alamo Santa Anna Stormed," *San Antonio Express,* Feb. 4, 1912, 25-B.

108. Ables, "The Second Battle for the Alamo," 411–12.

109. Miss De Zavala wrote that she sought to "make plain . . . that the chief struggle was in the monastery, . . . a large part of which to-day is still standing . . . . It was long

one of my dreams . . . to restore the Alamo and make of it a Texas Hall of Fame and a Museum of Historic Art, Relics and Literature." (Adina De Zavala, "Texas History—Written and Unwritten," *Texas Talks I (Jun. 1904),* 5 in Ables, "The Second Battle for the Alamo," 383.) A later pamphlet of Clara Driscoll's Alamo Mission Chapter agreed: "The greatest battle . . . was fought in the convento . . . and in the courtyard . . . . Historically, the church of the Alamo was of very little consequence. The convento was the real 'Alamo' . . . ." (Jack Butterfield, *Clara Driscoll Rescued the Alamo* (San Antonio, 1961, n.p.) in Ables, "The Second Battle for the Alamo," 413.)

110. "Clara Driscoll," *The Handbook of Texas* I, 519.

111. "Adina De Zavala, 'Savior of the Alamo,' Dead at 93," *San Antonio News,* Mar. 2, 1955, 1-C. Indicative of the chronic and continuing confusion over who did what and where were the published reasons for selection of both Adina De Zavala and Clara Driscoll among 27 women to have new river barges named in their honor. In a public contest administered by the *San Antonio Express-News,* Miss De Zavala was selected in part "for saving the Alamo's Long Barracks," or convento. Clara Driscoll, however, was chosen "as the 'savior of the Alamo' for purchasing the land where the Alamo stands and donating it to the state . . . ," a common if convoluted belief. (Terry Scott Bertling, *San Antonio Express-News,* Aug. 27, 1995, 1-B.)

112. Joseph E. Dwyer to Rudolph Kleberg, quoted in partial typescript by Kleberg dated April 26, 1923 in Alamo file, DRT Library at the Alamo. A misconception persists that the "Alamo"—either or both buildings—was once to be torn down for a hotel. The hotel, however, was to be built across the street behind the convento area. Developers were quite specific on their desire to retain the Alamo church. A form letter signed by Miss De Zavala stated the situation: "A St. Louis syndicate proposes to erect a hotel back of the Alamo and wishes to tear it down and make a park in its place for their own benefit." To be sure the recipient understood what was to be removed, above the word "it" in "tear it down" she wrote by hand "the Alamo," meaning the convento. (Undated form letter in Adina De Zavala Papers Box 2M129, The Center For American History, The University of Texas at Austin.)

3

The "March of Progress" Quickens

 While San Antonio's thin ranks of preservationists wrangled over whatever was called the Alamo, increasing numbers of disappearing landmarks were mourned only by headlines which typically sighed, "Passing of a Landmark of Other Days."[1]

Two homes associated with Robert E. Lee vanished—the adobe house on South St. Mary's Street, where both Lee and Albert Sidney Johnston had lived, and the Howard House on South Alamo Street, where San Antonians believed Lee wrote his resignation from the U.S. Army.[2] One casualty in the widening of North Flores Street was the old Chavez House, "Bullet-Ridden and Tomahawk-Scarred."[3] The widening of Dwyer Avenue claimed the adobe Spanish-era La Quinta, built in 1761, which quartered Spanish soldiers and later was San Antonio's first post office. It would "Give Way in the March of Progress, and No One Offers an Objection."[4] In 1909, the *Light* matter-of-factly reported under the headline "Passing of the Adobe at Hand in San Antonio" the disappearance during the previous five years of most of the city's adobe buildings, "almost unnoticed in the hurry of events of city building."[5]

Taking the biggest single toll of landmarks was the widening of Commerce Street, which lasted three years. Mule-drawn street cars had been barred from traveling on the city's main commercial street so that "the ringing of bells and clanking of the chains" would not disturb the conduct of business. Electric street cars were later banned as well.[6] But as new buildings sprang up along Houston Street two blocks north instead of along Commerce Street, businessmen realized the mistake. Also, Commerce Street had an irregular width, no important cross streets and sidewalks were too narrow. To correct the situation, an improvement district bond issue in 1912 raised $240,000. The city added $100,000 and businesses along the north side another $100,000, to balance private losses suffered along the south side as fronts of buildings

Commerce Street, shown looking east from Main Plaza in the late 1890s, was crowded even before arrival of the automobile. Shown in its original location is the Hertzberg Jewlery Company's clock, later moved with the firm to the corner of Houston and Navarro streets where it was turned over, in 1982, to the care of the San Antonio Conservation Society. Historic facades on the right side of the street were removed in 1913–15 in San Antonio's largest single street widening project. Zintgraff Collection, The Institute of Texan Cultures.

came off in the widening. By 1915, Commerce was a street uniformly sixty-five-feet wide and extended nearly six miles east from Santa Rosa Avenue, past Main and Military plazas and across the San Antonio River.[7]

As antique facades on the south side were sheared off or the buildings leveled altogether—with the notable exception of the new five-story Alamo National Bank Building, jacked up and moved slowly back on rollers while business was conducted as usual inside—the last remains of Spanish military garrisons on Military Plaza were cleared away. West of the "Bloody Corner" at Soledad and Commerce streets, once the site of frequent shootings, was the doomed Silver King Saloon. J.C. Roberson, bartender or proprietor for the previous twenty-six years, pointed out holes made by bullets in the floor and in the transom. "Sometimes the smoke has been so thick I could not see through it," he told a reporter, "but somehow I have come out without a scratch."[8] More tangible relics came to light during excavations for the new Commerce Street bridge over the San Antonio River, where the contractor

Rescued in the widening of Commerce Street was the new Alamo National Bank, then five stories tall, which was raised and moved back on rollers while business inside continued. San Antonio Express-News *Collection, The Institute of Texan Cultures.*

Relics often surfaced as buildings were torn down during downtown San Antonio's rapid growth following arrival of the railroad. When Fischer's Drug Store on Houston Street at Alamo Plaza made way for the 1912 Gibbs Building, these old cannons came to light beneath the floor. Adina De Zavala Papers, The Center For American History, The University of Texas at Austin, CN08639.

The Dullnig Building did not have its Commerce Street facade torn off for the widening of Commerce Street, since that fate befell buildings on the opposite side of the street. It did, however, have the misfortune of also facing on the west side of South Alamo Street, and lost sixteen feet of its original east side and one of its towers about 1913 when that street was widened. The Institute of Texan Cultures, courtesy of John Kellogg Kight.

The historic Veramendi Palace was already protruding into the widened east side of Soledad Street in the mid-1880s, a situation which finally led to its destruction in 1910. Western History Collections, University of Oklahoma Library.

gathered a collection of rusted small arms, bullet molds, bayonets, cannon balls and part of a brass cannon.[9]

Except for the two-story Frost National Bank, nearly an entire block of buildings on the south side of Commerce Street between Main and Military plazas was demolished after the Frost family sold a twenty-foot strip for the widening. First to go was an adobe "containing numerous rooms, most of which have quaint arched fireplaces." The spectators included "an aged Mexican" who pointed out the room in which he was born.[10] Another victim was the Trevino House, its "old walls . . . very thick and in all respects substantial, and the wrecking crew had hard work."[11]

The widening worked, although Commerce Street never regained its retail pre-eminence. Three years later, the National Bank of Commerce tore down the historic buildings facing Main Plaza across Soledad Street from its four-story home and began construction of a seven-story headquarters. Three years after that, Frost National Bank removed remaining old commercial buildings, including its own, and built a twelve-story building. The National Bank of Commerce added five more stories and called things even. By the time Alamo National Bank began its twenty-two story building down the

Promoters left their sign against the wall as the Veramendi Palace's demise drew near. Raba Collection, San Antonio Conservation Society.

street to the east, Commerce Street, which also had four smaller banks, was being touted as the "Wall Street of San Antonio."[12]

Another street widening caused the demise of the city's finest Spanish-era residence, the so-called Veramendi Palace. Its removal completed the widening of Soledad Street, a matter of "Transforming the 'Street of Solitude' into the Street of Business."[13] The flat-roofed, single-story limestone and adobe home built by Don Fernando Veramendi became known as the Veramendi Palace after his son, Don Juan Martín Veramendi, was appointed Vice-Governor of the Province de Bexar in 1830. It was of typical Spanish construction, with barred windows facing the street and tall, heavy doors opening to an inner court. The structure was "the scene of more picturesque events than any private residence in the history of San Antonio," including the death of Ben Milam and the formal surrender of local Union forces to commissioners of the Confederacy.[14]

"See the massive 12 ft. doors that have been swinging on their wooden pivots for nearly 200 years," beckoned—inaccurately—the elaborate sign promising free admission at the turn of the century. In 1901 the structure received a more decorous marker, the third historical tablet placed by the De Zavala Chapter of the Daughters of the Republic of Texas.[15] Half saloon and half "museum" and curio shop, the building's sentence had already been pronounced once, by Mayor George Paschal, who said in 1893 that "the old Veramendi building . . . will soon have to come down and give place to a more modern structure."[16]

In 1897 the city council, told that the city engineer "reported the building to be in an unsafe condition," passed a resolution declaring "the walls and roof of the Veramendi palace . . . to be a nuisance and liable to fall, and directing the city marshal to proceed to have said building removed in accordance with the city ordinance governing such cases."[17] Three days later the Veramendi Palace owners were in district court seeking an injunction. This was, no doubt, the first time the City of San Antonio faced legal action concerning the razing of an historic building. But historical significance was not the issue. The owners successfully complained, rather, that they had not been given "the opportunity of placing the building in a safe condition as they were ready and willing to do," and that through condemnation the city was simply trying to widen the street and "avoid liability to compensate the petitioners for their property."[18]

The east side of Soledad Street was, indeed, already being widened on either side of the Veramendi Palace, which, with its sidewalk, protruded ten feet farther than adjacent buildings. Pedestrians walking around it on the narrow sidewalk were directly in the path of traffic. Someone had the bright idea simply to leave the Veramendi's front wall in place and cut arches through the walls at either end of the building so pedestrians could pass through and the building would not have to be torn down, but the proposal had no takers.[19]

In 1909 the Veramendi property was sold to L.B. Clegg and Adolph Groos, who announced they would tear down the rear of the Veramendi Palace for a printing company but would leave the front "intact for the present."[20] The Alamo Mission Chapter of the Daughters of the Republic of Texas protested the razing, but it was too late.[21] Clegg and Groos began "a bitterly fought contest" with the city over the price of the strip of land for the widened street. They started at $6,000, but settled in 1910 for $1,250 when the city insisted that the value of the property would be greatly enhanced with "the removal of the historic wall."[22] The city immediately began to level the remains of the palace, while the woodwork, materials and what relics were found reverted to previous owners John H. James and F. F. Collins, who promised to hold them in case the palace could be rebuilt on another site.[23]

Mayor Bryan Callaghan, who as a young man was among those hosting legislators investigating the Alamo purchase twenty-seven years earlier, was no doubt only half kidding when he remarked, "It may be that the opposing factions of the Daughters of the Republic will enter into a fight for the possession of the doors, as I believe they would like to have them placed on exhibition."[24] The Veramendi's massive, hand-carved cedar doors were stored in the Collins home for sixteen years, when they were presented to the Alamo Mission Chapter of the Daughters for display at the Alamo—three years before the Collins home, with all its contents, burned to the ground.[25]

A second significant Spanish-era residence disappeared two years later across Soledad Street, a victim not of street widening but of clearance for a new "skyscraper" on Houston Street—the eight-story Rand Building, built in 1913 to house the Wolff & Marx department store.[26] This was the Garza House, a thick-walled stone complex which once covered practically an entire city block just north of Main Plaza, facing Houston Street between Soledad Street and Main Avenue. Built in 1734 by Gironomo de la Garza, it housed a Spanish mint in the early 1800s, was the first house captured by Ben Milam in the lifting of the siege of the city and later was used, in part, for county offices.[27] Its history not approaching the drama of the Veramendi Palace's past, the Garza House seems to have disappeared without a murmur.

As the second decade of the new century began, however, the epidemic of demolitions was requiring some justification. Under the headline "Passing of the Old; Era of the New," the business-boosting *San Antonio Light* explained in 1912: "The old and obsolete must give way for the march of progress, and when the modern necessity demands, the historic and otherwise memorable must pass to give room for the modern and commercial."[28] On the other hand, two months later the arch-rival *San Antonio Express* listed historic preservation among wider streets, civic centers and other public conveniences to be considered in future city improvements. The issue was presented across the front of the Sunday real estate section under the headline, "Tending the Goose That Lays Golden Eggs Feeding the City of Tomorrow."

"In everything human, to obtain the perfect balance the spiritual growth must keep pace with the physical," the *Express* editorialized. "If you feed a man on meat alone he sickens; if you build a city of stone and brick and concrete and steel and give no thought to the streets or the parks, if you are insensible to beauty, your work is undone, for the spiritual is lacking—your city sickens, its greatness, not fortified with the soul-food, does not abide . . . . Every storm that batters on San José and its fellow missions, every wind that still further crumbles these venerable piles comes as a rebuke that the work of ruin is going on unheeded . . . . Monument after monument of the

The rambling Garza House, which in its last days housed a saloon in one corner, became the second major Spanish-era residence to disappear in San Antonio in two years when it made way in 1912 for the eight-story Rand Building on Houston Street between Soledad Street and Main Avenue. The San Antonio Light *Collection, The Institute of Texan Cultures.*

past is falling . . . . The storm of progress is leveling them to be replaced by modern structures, but let us keep what we have. No longer let us be careless custodians of the goose that lays our golden egg. The tourist comes because he has heard of San Antonio's fame as a picturesque, historically interesting city. He brings millions of dollars annually . . . . In the San Antonio River we have another asset, if it was only made a thing of beauty . . . . The moral of the fable is that greed oft o'erreaches itself. In San Antonio's case it may well be paraphrased that neglect of the goose will result in the loss of the golden eggs that are helping to build the big city of tomorrow."[29]

As these words were being written, Adina De Zavala was re-assembling her allies. What the affair's historian L. Robert Ables aptly termed "the second battle for the Alamo" was over, and the defeated De Zavala Chapter of the Daughters of the Republic of Texas had ceased to exist. In 1912 Miss De Zavala organized ten women into a counter-organization most often known as the Daughters and Sons of the Heroes of Texas. More importantly, with her penchant for overlapping and interlocking Chapters, Congresses and Auxiliaries, she formed at the same time the Texas Historical and Landmarks Association.[30] By 1915, the association could welcome at its annual convention in the St. Anthony Hotel both male and female representatives from ten chapters, from Houston to Menard to Sanderson to Fort Worth as well as from "Founder's Chapter No. 1 of San Antonio," also known, predictably, as the De Zavala Chapter.[31]

During the few years that San Antonio's only preservation activist outspoken enough to cause a commotion was re-grouping, new construction creeping westward toward the less-prosperous heart of the old Spanish town had claimed two of the city's best-known Spanish residences, with only a hint of protest. Now that she was back in business, Adina De Zavala set out to defend another moldering structure in the path of development. She identified a row of low-rent shops and cantinas on Military Plaza as the last remaining Spanish aristocratic residence in the State of Texas—the "Spanish Governor's Palace."[32] A week after the close of her new association's 1915 convention, Miss De Zavala was recounting that landmark's history to readers of the *Express*, and hoping "that this old relic of imperial Spain will be saved from the vandals."[33] Its keystone bore the Hapsburg coat of arms and the date 1749, which may only have marked the last stage of a series of constructions and rebuildings.[34] Built facing the west side of Military Plaza for the captain of the Spanish presidio, the decaying building had been owned primarily by two families since 1763. Its three-foot thick, lime-plastered single-story walls enclosed ten rooms and a loft, with a walled patio at the rear, but by the turn of the century its original roof and flagstone floor were both gone.[35]

Miss De Zavala's strategy to save the Governor's Palace mirrored her plan for saving the old Alamo convento. She decided that, like the convento, the Governor's Palace had once been two stories. But, with the convento now out of reach, it was a two-story Governor's Palace which should become the Texas Hall of Fame. As she had done with the Alamo convento, she obtained a purchase option on the Governor's Palace, launched a public appeal for large numbers of small contributions and created a subsidiary organization to focus on the project.[36]

In 1917, World War I provided a patriotic wrinkle for fund-raising: the Governor's Palace would be purchased and turned into a sort of USO for the soldier, "a school, a recreation place and a home where he will meet many persons interested in his welfare." The "rearranged" interior would feature a patio with a fountain, around which would be rooms for reading, writing, the teaching of French and Spanish and for music and games. Then, "the old walls of the palace will ring again with laughter as in the old days when the representatives of the Court of Spain held their entertainments."[37] This concept of adaptive reuse did not, however, bring the Purchase Fund close to its down payment goal of $10,000.[38] The prestigious Woman's Club did pass a resolution supporting it. Capt. John E. Elgin, president of the Texas Historical and Landmarks Association and one of the four men and sixty-six women listed as actively supporting the project, supplied the *Express* with testimonials from a number of persons, including the commander of Fort Sam Houston. "There is probably in the United States no monument so international in its character as this old building," Capt. Elgin declared. "Its

Identity of the Spanish Governor's Palace at the beginning of the twentieth century could be guessed at only by its keystone, barely visible in the shade above what had become the entrance to L. Moglia's saloon. Adina De Zavala Papers, The Center For American History, The University of Texas at Austin, CN08645.

In the absence of documentary evidence, Adina De Zavala thought the Spanish Governor's Palace originally had a second floor. Her efforts to restore the Alamo's convento having failed, she used this drawing to show how she would rescue and restore the Governor's Palace, instead, as a Texas Hall of Fame. Adina De Zavala Papers, The Center For American History, The University of Texas at Austin, CN02139.

architecture harks back to the distant period with the hosts of Mohammed, when he swept westward and carried his empire to the western confines of Europe."[39]

The Governor's Palace effort, however, still could not approach the might of the "hosts of Mohammed," and no Clara Driscoll could be found to take up the slack. In 1919 the only classes held in the old building were in English and the Bible, taught by missionaries who had established the Chinese Gospel Hall, forerunner of San Antonio's First Chinese Baptist Church.[40] In mid-1920, the tenacious Adina De Zavala was at the Gunter Hotel exhorting the Lions' Club to help the stalled project. She won the club's endorsement and three pledges of $100 each.[41] Two years later, reporting on activities of the

Daughters of the Heroes of Texas to the City Federation of Women's Clubs, she urged "all women of the city to come to the rescue."[42] One civic leader suggested that the city acquire the Governor's Palace and let the Board of Education use it for offices.[43]

Nor was the Texas Historical and Landmarks Association having much luck in the pursuit of another of its goals, "restoration and conservation of all the missions of Texas along the lines of such work in California."[44] In this case the Catholic Church itself was trying to restore what was left of the mission churches and chapels. After the death of Espada's long-time resident parish priest, the Rev. François Bouchu, architect Leo M.J. Dielmann was hired in 1908 by the Spanish Claretian missionary order to estimate the cost of restoring the mission chapels at both Espada and San Juan.[45] Services were held in the restored San Juan Capistrano chapel in 1909.[46]

Two years later, new Catholic Diocese of San Antonio Bishop John William Shaw committed his administration to the restoration of the Spanish missions and to their re-occupation by the Franciscans.[47] Bishop Shaw had the encouragement of his chancellor, the English-born Rev. William Wheeler Hume, who had gained an appreciation for historical architecture while studying in Europe and who sang High Mass at the re-dedication of the Espada mission chapel in 1911.[48] Two years later, the Mission Concepción church was once again repaired and reopened.[49] Under Father Hume's direction in 1917, a program at San José largely funded by Ethel Tunstall (Mrs. Henry P.) Drought stabilized the church ruins, cleared fallen debris from the interior of the church and used stone from the fallen dome to rebuild the collapsed north wall. In 1918 the sacristy was opened for services.[50]

Mission restoration efforts of the Catholic Church focused only on the specific places of worship, the mission churches and chapels, since the surrounding complexes which first supported them were of less religious than historical significance. Traces of the once-walled enclosures, long split into separately owned tracts and criss-crossed by public roads, were slowly vanishing. The few outlying mission buildings not totally reduced to rubble were housing multiple families, many of them descended from the original mission Indians. They managed an existence on land still watered by the ancient San Juan and Espada mission acequias.

With the Texas Historical and Landmarks Association increasingly perceived as an autocracy unable to achieve its ambitious goals, there seemed to be little hope for the old mission complexes, even as publicity generated by the Landmarks Association was aiding dialogue on such subjects.[51] The *Express* in 1921 compared San Antonio to New Orleans in an editorial headlined, "Save the Landmarks That Made San Antonio First."[52] The *Light* reported that the Chamber of Commerce, the Old Spanish Trail Association and the Real Estate Board of San Antonio were jointly working "to prevent the destruction of . . . places of historical interest that set San Antonio apart from other cities in the state, making it a . . . favorite destination of tourists," but nothing substantive was emerging.[53] The only local organization actively engaged in some form of historic preservation was the Alamo Mission Chapter of the Daughters of the Republic of Texas, which had organized its own Missions Committee. Chairman of that committee was Rena Maverick Green, granddaughter of pioneer San Antonio preservationist Mary Adams Maverick and widow of Robert B. Green, a onetime county judge and district judge who was serving in the Texas Senate at the time of his death. She was one of the first women elected to the San Antonio Board of Education, had been instrumental in getting women appointed to the San Antonio Police Department and campaigned for woman suffrage as state chairman of the National Woman's Party.[54] She was accustomed to getting things done.

Mrs. Green became concerned as the rapid growth of San Antonio spread within blocks of the once isolated San José mission. As the Daughters' missions committee chairman she proposed purchase by the state of one thousand acres around San José, San Juan and Espada missions for a state park. Next, restoring the acequia system would not only permit the property to be rented out as productive farmland, it "would make one of the most unique surroundings imaginable for the missions." She had support from New York's Reginald Pelham Bolton, a leader of the American Scenic and Historic Preservation Society, who "often deplored the condition of the several missions around San Antonio;" from Charles F. Lummis of Los Angeles, the landmarks pioneer who engineered preservation of several California missions; and from neighboring Congressman John Nance Garner.[55]

Beyond mere expressions of support, Mrs. Green was able to draw Governor Pat Neff and the entire Texas State Parks Board to San Antonio one afternoon in the spring of 1924 to view the San José property firsthand. At a dinner sponsored by the Alamo Mission Chapter that evening at the Gunter Hotel, remarks were delivered by persons including Governor Neff, Rena Green, Clara Driscoll Sevier, County Judge Augustus McClosky and the San Diego, California, Chamber of Commerce vice president, who was in town to help promote the revived Old Spanish Trail from California to Florida. His topic was, "What California would do with the San Antonio Missions if they were located there."[56]

But for those hoping to preserve what remained of old San Antonio, there were more challenges to face than the threat to the Governor's Palace and encroaching development at the Spanish missions. As growth downtown continued unabated, there were still old streets not yet widened and also the flood situation to deal with. In 1921, a deluge swept up to twelve feet of water over the downtown banks of the San Antonio River, wrecking bridges and buildings before it. Fifty persons drowned. One measure to prevent such

Most downtown bridges over the San Antonio River had to be replaced after they were battered by debris during the 1921 flood. San Antonio Conservation Society.

The historic St. Mary's Catholic Church on North St. Mary's Street suffered such damage from the 1921 flood, as suggested by the water line, that it was torn down and replaced. San Antonio Conservation Society.

disaster in the future was construction upstream of Olmos Dam. Another was to straighten much of the river channel itself and to dig a new cutoff channel to eliminate the flow of future floodwaters around the downtown River Bend.

Decked by a one-two street-widening, cutoff-channel punch was to be the city's 1859 Market House, considered one of the finest examples of Greek Revival architecture in Texas. It was in the path of both the widening of Market Street and of the new river cutoff channel. Much earlier the Market House lost its usefulness as the major place for the butchering, inspection and sale of meat when state inspection laws changed in 1893 and meat could also be inspected at smaller markets throughout the city. The Market House turned first into an overflow area for the jail and then was sold to Heusinger Hardware.[57] As news of its impending demolition spread, the hardware store prepared to move out.[58]

In a fateful meeting near the Market House early in 1924, two ladies chanced to greet each other—Rena Maverick Green, 50, and Emily Edwards, 35, a schoolteacher and social worker who had just returned to San Antonio. Each had come to look over the building after reading the news.

"When I came back to San Antonio it was just beautiful," Miss Edwards later recalled. "It was such a relief, you know, after other cities. And it seemed that it would be a pity to change anything about it." She was "seeing everything freshly, and the old Market House was just a perfect specimen of its kind, neo-classic. And Mrs. Green . . . was also worried. Finally, Mrs. Green said, 'Well, we can just protest all we wish as individuals, and no one will pay any attention to us. But if we organize, they will.' I said, 'Then let's organize.'"[59]

Notes

1. *San Antonio Express*, Jul. 24, 1905.

2. *San Antonio Express*, Nov. 4, 1906; "Where Lee Lived," *San Antonio Express*, Jul. 12, 1907.

3. *San Antonio Daily Express*, May 19, 1914. The Odet House, removed "because it was unsafe and menaced the lives of passers by," was recalled only as the site of the fatal stabbing by a "jealous senorita" of a female "American rival" during a fandango. The señorita fled to Mexico but had recently returned, although, like the house itself, she "has lost all trace of the beauty that was once her glory." ("Old Buildings To Be Doomed," *San Antonio Daily Express*, Jul. 26, 1893, 5.)

4. "Historical Landmarks Go As San Antonio Expands," *San Antonio Light*, Jun. 27, 1920, 9-D; "Widening of Dwyer Avenue Removes More Old Landmarks," *San Antonio Express*, Feb. 27, 1921, 1-A.

5. *San Antonio Light,* Aug. 1, 1909, 19. In 1979, a Trinity University student identified 29 adobe buildings, plus perhaps an additional 5, still existing in the city. (Dabney Bassel, "Adobe Project," list copy in SACS Library.)

6. *Report of the Widening of Commerce Street* (San Antonio: "Published under the direction of the Committee," 1915), 19.

7. Ibid., 29, 36–37, 40.

8. Ibid., 46; "Historic Block To Be Demolished," *San Antonio Express,* Jan. 13, 1915, 14.

9. "Dig Up Many Old Relics," *San Antonio Express,* Jul. 5, 1914, 3-B.

10. "Historic Block To Be Demolished," *San Antonio Express,* Jan. 13, 1915, 14.

11. "Wreckers Remove Landmarks Where Tragedies, Romance And War Were Staged," *San Antonio Express,* Jan. 17, 1915, 28-B. A selection of copies of newspaper articles on such landmarks just before and after the turn of the century is in the Donald E. Everett Collection of the Special Collections at Trinity University's Maddux Library.

12. "Commerce Street Is Assembling Its Banking Houses," *San Antonio Express,* Apr. 7, 1929, 1-C; John M. Bennett, *Those Who Made It: The Story of the Men and Women of National Bank of Commerce of San Antonio* (San Antonio: 1978, n.p.), 25. The other banks were San Antonio National Bank, Groos National Bank, D&A Oppenheimer and D. Sullivan & Co.

13. *San Antonio Express,* Dec. 9, 1917, 1-A. Continued the headline: "March of Time and Progress Wipes Out Homes of the First Families of the Old San Antonio, Quaint Buildings That Long Were Hedged About With Romance."

14. Bartlett Cocke, "Veramendi Palace," Historic American Buildings Survey No. Tex-3128.

15. "17 Tablets Mark City's Historic Spots," *San Antonio Express,* Aug. 3, 1924, 26.

16. "Old Buildings To Be Doomed," *San Antonio Daily Express,* Jul. 26, 1893, 5.

17. "Meeting of City Council," *San Antonio Daily Express,* Apr. 13, 1897, 3.

18. "Want the City Restrained," *San Antonio Daily Express,"* Apr. 17, 1897, 6.

19. "Save Veramendi House and Widen the Street," *San Antonio Daily Express,* Oct. 31, 1905, 5.

20. "Old Veramendi Place Sells," *San Antonio Express,* Mar. 7, 1909, 52.

21. "Men Capitulate; Women Win; No Alamo Fall Act," *San Antonio Daily Express,* Mar. 11, 1909.

22. "Veramendi Palace To Be Leveled," *San Antonio Light and Gazette,* Feb. 25, 1910, 2.

23. Ibid., "Part Of Veramendi House Will Be Torn Down Monday," *San Antonio Daily Express,* Apr. 30, 1909, 3.

24. Ibid.

25. "Doors of Old Veramendi Palace Presented to Museum of Alamo," *San Antonio Express,* May 15, 1926, 2; "Historic Collins Home Destroyed," *San Antonio Express,* Dec. 2, 1929, 18. The doors remain on display at the Alamo.

26. "Walls Showing Bullet Marks of Battle When Ben Milam Led Men to Come Down," *San Antonio Express,* Feb. 4, 1912, 1-A; "Plans For Rand Building Received," *San Antonio Express,* Apr. 11, 1912, 4.

27. Charles Merritt Barnes, "Historic Garza House," *San Antonio Daily Express,* Jan. 26, 1908, 32.

28. *San Antonio Light,* May 26, 1912, 35. That sense of inevitability was echoed by none other than the noted architect James Riely Gordon on his first visit to San Antonio after an absence of twenty-five years. Observed Gordon, whose own buildings would become successful targets of San Antonio preservationists: "I found the city has lost some of its old-time charm which I once loved . . . . The street widening program and the many new buildings have necessitated tearing down some of the picturesque old structures, but this must be to make way for progress." ("Architect for Federal Building, Old Court House Back After 25 Years, Amazed at City's Growth," *San Antonio Express,* Feb. 10, 1927, 8.)

29. *San Antonio Express,* Jul. 28, 1912. The image of the golden goose seems not uncommon in these years. Developers headlined advertisements of the Alamo Heights subdivision of Montclair "The Goose That Lays the Golden Eggs," complete with the drawing of a bespectacled goose which produced many advantages, among them cool breezes, healthy atmosphere, no malaria, no mosquitoes and "no railroads to cross." ("Montclair," *San Antonio Daily Express* advertisement, Mar. 22, 1908.)

30. Ables, "The Work of Adina De Zavala," 31; "Hope to Preserve Landmarks That Tell Of History," *San Antonio Express,* Mar. 14, 1915, 1-A; "Daughters of the Heroes and Pioneers of the Republic of Texas," papers in Adina De Zavala Papers Box 2M138, The Center For American History, The University of Texas at Austin. Origins of the Texas Historical and Landmarks Association were traced to the De Zavala DRT chapter's auxiliary of 1900. Its purpose was preservation of landmarks to keep alive "the history of Texas and the memory of the great deeds of the fathers . . . and love for the Lone Star flag and the lessons it teaches." First officers of the organization were Hal C. King, Jr., president; Miss Ann Sullivan, treasurer; and Charles Boelhauwe, secretary. The Landmarks Association later got its own auxiliary, the Young Patriots Society, "circles" which school teachers and principals were encouraged to organize at their schools. ("Young Patriots Society," papers in Adina De Zavala Papers Box 2M138, The Center For American History, The University of Texas at Austin.)

31. "Hope to Preserve Landmarks That Tell Of History," *San Antonio Express,* Mar. 14, 1915, 1-A. Establishing a statewide landmarks organization was not easy, as Adina De Zavala once implied to a Houstonian who had returned from a visit to Austin: "We have not an organized chapter in Austin, and while our members there are patriotic they have been ill a great part of the time and are very timid, so have not always made themselves known to you on your visits." (Adina De Zavala to L.W. Kemp, undated letter copy in Adina De Zavala Papers Box 2M138, The Center for American History, The University of Texas at Austin.)

32. Ables, "The Work of Adina De Zavala," 86.

33. *San Antonio Express,* Mar. 21, 1915.

34. Anne A. Fox, "The Archaeology and History of the Spanish Governor's Palace Park," Archaeological Survey Report No. 31 (San Antonio: Center for Archaeological Research, The University of Texas at San Antonio, 1977), 2.

35. "Spanish Governor's Palace," National Register Nomination.

36. Ables, "The Work of Adina De Zavala," 86–88; "Charter of The Association for the Preservation of the Historic Landmarks in Texas," 1922, in Adina De Zavala Papers Box 2M138, The Center For American History, The University of Texas at Austin. The charter specified its purpose of "preservation of the ancient Governor's Palace of Texas" as well as establishing a museum and other intents, but, like the Congress of Patriotism organized to preserve the Alamo convento nineteen years earlier, there is no indication that the newly chartered Association for the Preservation of the Historic Landmarks in Texas ever actually functioned.

37. "Thousand Dollar Contribution to Saving of Venerable Palace," *San Antonio Express,* Jul. 22, 1917.

38. Of the "substantial donations and many individual $1 contributions" reported, the largest were one for $1,000, one for $500 and one for $100. (Ibid.)

39. Ibid.; "Women Active To Save Old Palace," *San Antonio Express,* Jun. 17, 1917; "Old Government Palace International Monument," *San Antonio Express,* Jul. 15, 1917.

40. Steve Schlather, "Chinese church has flourished," *San Antonio Light,* undated clipping of Sept., 1983 in SACS Library.

41. "Old Landmark is Now Only a Ruin," *San Antonio Express,* Jun. 3, 1920, 18.

42. Ables, "The Work of Adina De Zavala," 89.

43. *San Antonio Express,* Oct. 12, 1922. The suggestion was made in an address to the San Antonio Traffic Club on landmarks by Dr. Frank Paschal.

44. "Hope To Preserve Landmarks That Tell Of History," *San Antonio Express,* Mar. 14, 1915, 1-A.

45. Leo M.J. Dielmann to Adeline (sic.) de Zavala, Sept. 12, 1908, in Adina De Zavala Papers Box 2M129, The Center For American History, The University of Texas at Austin.

46. Habig, *The Alamo Chain of Missions,* 185; Thurber et. al., *Of Various Magnificence* II, 8.

47. Thurber et. al., *Of Various Magnificence* II, 2.

48. Almaráz, "The San Antonio Missions After Secularization," 244; "Mission Used Again After Two Centuries," *San Antonio Light,* Oct. 15, 1911. After further work, the Espada chapel was again re-dedicated four years later. ("To Hold Services In Old Mission Of San Francisco," *San Antonio Express,* Sept. 18, 1916, 12; Habig, *The Alamo Chain of Missions,* 231.)

49. "To Hold Services In Old Mission Of San Francisco," *San Antonio Express,* Sept. 18, 1916, 12.

50. "Saving From Total Ruin Most Beautiful Mission," *San Antonio Express,* Oct. 14, 1917; Habig, *The Alamo Chain of Missions,* 111; Habig, *San Antonio's Mission San José,* 175; Thurber et. al., *Of Various Magnificence* II, 16.

51. Although the Texas Historical and Landmarks Association regularly changed officers, Adina De Zavala alone was "the unchallenged leader of the group and . . . regardless of title, it was never in doubt that she was the *de facto* president." (Ables, "The Work of Adina De Zavala," 32.)

52. *San Antonio Express,* Nov. 20, 1921, 1-A.

53. "Historical Landmarks Go," *San Antonio Light,* Jun. 27, 1920, 9-D.

54. Mary Vance Green OHT, Feb. 2, 1984, 46.

55. "Daughters of Texas Republic to Co-Operate With Catholics in Preserving Old Missions," *San Antonio Express,* Jun. 15, 1924. When in San Antonio earlier in the year, Bolton also visited with Adina De Zavala. ("Landmark Association Marks Navarro House," *San Antonio Express,* Mar. 20, 1924, 9.)

56. "Mission Parks Idea for Board," *San Antonio Express,* Mar. 19, 1924, 22; "Neff Announces Donation of 13 New State Parks in Southwest Texas," *San Antonio Express,* Mar. 20, 1924, 17. The chamber official, Stanley Hale, said San Diego officials had sent a telegram instructing him, "Bring the missions home with you."

57. "Old City Market House," *San Antonio Daily Express,* Jul. 31, 1893, 5. The De Zavala DRT chapter secured a lease on the Market House from the city after the turn of the century and cleaned it up for a school of art to be headed by sculptor Pompeo Coppini. The Board of Education, however, won a title lawsuit with the city in 1905 and sold the building for the hardware store. (Adina De Zavala, *History and Legends of the Alamo and Other Missions* (San Antonio, n.p., 1917), 214.)

58. "Market House," *San Antonio Express,* Jan. 1, 1925.

59. Emily Edwards OHT, Jul. 24, 1971, 3–4, 7.

II

Feeding

the

Golden

Goose

1924–1971

4
Artistic Activists Organize

 As San Antonio was no conventional American city, neither was the group that sprang from the chance meeting of two ladies on a San Antonio street the type of group which typically formed elsewhere to combat the threatened loss of a landmark. Its organizers were, as customary elsewhere, women. But there the general comparisons end. The newly forming San Antonians did not represent, as in other cities, an extension of the old elite, although many of its members were from San Antonio's old families. Nor were the women drawn by a common passion to preserve patriotic memories of their ancestors, though many in the new group had impeccable credentials to do so if they chose.

The first generation raised amidst San Antonio's new-found prosperity of the late nineteenth century had come to maturity. Many of its women were well-educated and well-traveled, and with the right to vote had gained new self-respect. They were ready for more than such traditional women's activities as teaching or art, a field which thrived in San Antonio's vibrant, multi-cultural ambiance. Art was a discipline shared, in fact, by Rena Maverick Green and Emily Edwards, who were at the point of taking bold new steps to save San Antonio. In addition to her civic accomplishments, Mrs. Green, her four children nearly grown, was a watercolorist and sculptress who had studied art in Provincetown, Massachusetts, and in San Francisco.[1] Miss Edwards, who also studied in Provincetown, left San Antonio as a teenager to live with her aunt in Jane Addams's Hull House, where she did social work while attending the Chicago Art Institute, then taught art in private schools in Chicago and at Brackenridge High School in San Antonio.[2]

Vigorous and imaginative, these women and their future compatriots did not need more admonitions on the uniqueness of their city from cosmopolitan travelers, warnings which in the previous century fell on deaf ears locally anyway. They felt its charm instinctively. The entire mix of cultures was their birthright, the soul of their home city, and it was not to be taken away. Their goal became the saving not only of landmarks but of traditions and ambiance and natural features as well, the preservation of no less than San Antonio's entire historic cultural and natural environment.

Their inspiration blended with general enthusiasm abroad in the city. It would be hard to pinpoint a more exuberant, progressive time in the history of San Antonio, the largest city in the largest state, than the 1920s. By the summer of 1928 there were fifteen downtown construction projects costing $10 million under way or about to be in the downtown area alone. New projects were expected to double the total by the end of the year.[3] People kept count as skyscrapers went up. By the end of the decade downtown San Antonio had four skyscrapers taller than twenty stories, compared with five in Houston and two each in Dallas and Fort Worth.[4] Other buildings in the south may have been taller than San Antonio's thirty-story Smith-Young Tower, but status-conscious San Antonians took comfort in believing that the one hundred-foot flagpole atop the Smith-Young building made it the highest flagpole on any building in the south.[5] Retail business was booming as well, and the usual summer slump was declared "nonexistent."[6]

New streets spread in every direction to reach new subdivisions. A new air base was under construction in the northeast corner of the county, and an airplane manufacturing plant was planned.[7] Civic works included five new fire stations and a $1 million sewage disposal plant, plus a major river flood prevention project.[8] A resort hotel was planned for the booming winter tourist trade.[9] Filmmakers flocked in, and a motion picture studio was on the drawing boards. One of San Antonio's grand new downtown movie houses—the Texas—hosted the first major motion picture world premiere staged outside New York City or Los Angeles, for the locally filmed *Wings,* winner of the first Academy Award for Best Picture.[10] As San Antonio aggressively played cultural catch-up with the rest of the nation, the new Municipal Auditorium provided a facility for the state's first Civic Grand Opera, and the new San Pedro Playhouse provided space for a major local theater company.[11] A philharmonic orchestra was organized; a new public library was built.[12] Not only did San Antonio at last get a real municipal museum, a two-story wing was added to it.[13] The zoo in Brackenridge Park was becoming "one of the best in the country" with new bear pits and a monkey island.[14]

San Antonio's rampant growth was still not landmark-friendly. But in the exuberance of 1924, Rena Green and Emily Edwards were not at first trying to save the type of landmark of concern to preservationists elsewhere in the nation—a grand old home or meeting hall or fortress recalling the days of some famous patriot or heroic struggle. These San Antonio ladies focused on saving something yet unknown to be worth saving—a commercial building. And one not yet a hundred years old, a market house of the common people holding no association whatever with anyone or anything of any particular significance. But it was a major Greek Revival architectural presence in a city of equally memorable-if-fast-disappearing Spanish, Moorish, Mexican, French and varying shades of other European and American architecture. Its Doric columns and classical facade spoke of order and harmony and dignity. In this colorful city, the Market House offered the sort of contrast that was especially appealing to artists.

Not ones to waste time dreaming, once the two ladies had met near the Market House and decided to organize, they marched around the corner to the office of attorney Thomas Franklin, a friend of Mrs. Green's, to get some advice on exactly how to proceed. "I was just amazed [at] how simple it was," Miss Edwards recalled. "All we had to do was to get people who were like-minded together and work out a slate between us—who should be what—and have a meeting, go through the regular formalities of nominating and seconding and so forth, and . . . then we would be organized."[15]

Emily Edwards was using as her studio the small two-story stone home of one of Rena Green's sisters, Lucy Maverick, who was away studying art in New York City. It was on the upper level of this home, off San Pedro Avenue at 220 Belvin Street just north of downtown, that thirteen women gathered on Saturday, March 22, 1924, to organize the San Antonio Conservation Society.[16] Rena Green pled too many activities and Emily Edwards was elected president. Six vice chairmen were selected: Lucretia (Mrs. R.O.) Van Horn, an artist and Army wife, records; Rena Green, program; Josephine Tobin (Mrs. W.P.) Rote, sister of Mayor John W. Tobin, membership; Amanda Cartwright (Mrs. Lane) Taylor, member of a pioneer ranching family, publicity; Ethel Tunstall (Mrs. Henry P.) Drought, social leader, president of the San Antonio Art League and recent benefactress of San José Mission, historian; and Esther Perez (Mrs. G.C.) Carvajal, director of Spanish for the San Antonio school district, Spanish records. Fannie Grayson Applewhite, recently retired as custodian of the Alamo, was elected treasurer and Anna Ellis, a history teacher, secretary. Completing the list of founders present were Mrs. E. C. Branch, Mrs. Conrad Schasse, Emily Edwards' sister Floy (Mrs. Jules) Fontaine and Eleanor Onderdonk, painter, daughter of artist Robert J. Onderdonk and, later, art curator at the Witte Museum.[17]

The ladies set their sights far beyond trying to save a single building. Minutes record that those present comprised no less than "a group of women interested in the preservation of all those things characteristic of San Antonio, things of historic as well as aesthetic value—losing which, San Antonio loses local color and atmosphere."[18] They decided: "The object of this Society is to co-operate in the preservation of the Missions, to conserve Old Buildings, Documents, Pictures, Names, Natural Beauty, and anything admirably distinctive of San Antonio."[19] The goal was "cultural conservation."[20] Members

Emily Edwards struck an artistic pose at the Spanish Governor's Palace during a return visit to San Antonio in 1933, when she lectured on the work of one of her instructors in Mexico, muralist Diego Rivera. The San Antonio Light *Collection, The Institute of Texan Cultures.*

The seal of the Conservation Society, adopted in 1931, reflects its pioneering concern with both the historic built environment, symbolized by the tower of the then-endangered San José Mission, and the natural environment, represented by a branch of wild olive. Both are under the watchful gaze of the society's "all-seeing eye." San Antonio Conservation Society.

liked the broad name San Antonio Conservation Society better than San Antonio Preservation Society.[21]

Until organization of the San Antonio Conservation Society, American women preservationists' concerns were generally limited to history and patriotism.[22] In England, however, organizations preserving the historic built environment were saving the natural environment as well.[23] Britain's National Trust for Places of Historic Interest or Natural Beauty was formed in 1895 by three social reformers concerned about the effect of industrial development on the English countryside.[24] It was precisely the danger of industrial encroachment spoiling the "naturally beautiful setting" of San José Mission which worried Conservation Society co-founder Rena Maverick Green, a frequent visitor to England.[25]

Once San Antonio's newly united conservationists tended to organizational details at their first meeting, nine subjects were assigned for reports: "Twohig House; Adobe Home on Villita Street occupied by Augusta J. Evans while writing *Inez, Child of the Alamo*; Pecan Trees and Playgrounds in Parks; Governor's Palace and San Antonio Legends; Old Spanish Nomenclature; *Jacales* in Brackenridge Park and Old Spanish Art; Selective Study of Special Buildings; Old Doors and Entrances; and, Old Adobe Houses and Vance Home."[26] Suddenly, here was a group framing its goals with an artist's eye. Three of the nine reports were, indeed, about specific landmarks. But the free association of old Mexican *jacales* as Spanish artistry in the rambling Brackenridge Park or of pecan trees with playgrounds seems more to reflect the viewpoint of an artist selecting the subject while preparing the paints.

Members did not stand on formality. A future president was signed up in a bookstore. "I didn't know Mrs. [Perry] Lewis, so we hadn't invited her," recalled Emily Edwards. "I was in a bookstore and Mrs. Lewis came over and said, 'Emily Edwards, what is the society you're organizing? I want to belong to it.' And I said, 'Well, you belong.' That's all! The way we got our members was, everyone who had any ideas and would be interested [could join]. We had the idea of not making it one group, but to reach into the different parts of the city . . . . We would try to reach all groups to make it a true city-community thing."[27] As a result, the Conservation Society gained "a richly varied membership." [28] The society tried to recruit men, who spoke at meetings and often supported the society's goals but did not accept invitations to become regular members.[29]

Unfazed, the women continued alone, coping with strictures of the time. The identity of married women was subordinate to that of their husbands, a custom continued by Emily Edwards herself nearly fifty years later when she repeatedly referred to, simply, "Mrs. Lewis," the wife of Perry Lewis. Mrs. Perry Lewis was not referred to by her friends as "Margaret" any more than Mrs. H.P. Drought was then called "Ethel" or Mrs. Lane Taylor was

"Amanda." Emily Edwards could keep her own name, properly preceded by "Miss," as long as she remained unmarried. A widow kept her husband's surname but reemerged with her own given name and married surname, as, after her husband's death, Mrs. Robert B. Green officially became Mrs. Rena Maverick Green. There were legal distinctions to contend with as well. One of Mrs. Green's daughters recalled with amusement "how jealous" some women were of her mother. "She, being a widow, could sign a legal paper herself, you see. They had to get their husbands to sign with them. They were indignant that she could go right in and sign."[30]

But they did not allow such affronts to bother them for long. The women went about ignoring convention by holding a mobile meeting three months after they organized. The White Sight-Seeing Company had offered to take the new conservationists on a bus tour so they could see their city through the eyes of a tourist. At 10 AM on a Saturday in mid-June, assembling in front of the Alamo were twenty-seven persons, including six men, two of them husbands of members. Rather than just boarding the bus and listening to a guide, Emily Edwards called an official meeting to order on the spot. Routine business was dispensed with and City Commissioner Ray Lambert, whose responsibilities included parks the group was about to visit, was asked to say a few words. Members then enthusiastically and unanimously made Lambert the Honorary President of the Conservation Society.[31] The meeting was not adjourned, but remained in session as the bus drove on.

Resolutions of protest spontaneously passed condemning changes of street names and the condition of Mexican *jacales* and campsites in Brackenridge Park. In front of the Market House, "an interesting and convincing paper" on saving the building was read. At Mission Espada, the Rev. M.S. Garriga of the nearby school gave a history of the ruin. At the Spanish aqueduct, resolutions asked the county judge to build a bridge across the creek there and have the aqueduct made a state park. Remarks about O. Henry were made in front of his old home on South Presa Street. Not forgetting their manners, members closed the trip/meeting with a vote of thanks to their guide and to her company.[32]

Flaunting convention simply for the sake of doing so, however, was not the aim of the new society. In many ways it was behaving like a traditional women's club. There were picnics with children and grandchildren in San Pedro Park and meetings in members' homes, where older residents shared reminiscences.[33] Its first social meeting was in mid-July of 1924 northwest of San Antonio at Sunshine Ranch, home of the Albert Maverick family.[34] Three months later the society met in Kendall County at the Maverick Ranch, owned by Rena Green's branch of the family, where family members served "a real feast."[35] There were events at Mrs. Gus Mauermann's Mitchell Ranch on Pleasanton Road and at Miss Alice O'Grady's Argyle Hotel in Alamo Heights, and a Christmas party in Mrs. Adolph Wagner's home on Guenther Street. Six months after the society's formation, Miss Marin B. Fenwick, longtime society editor of the *San Antonio Express* and the city's arbiter in such matters, could pronounce, "Socially, the Conservation Society is proving a success."[36]

There were some rough spots. Emily Edwards picked up her *San Antonio Light* to see the announcement of the new officers headlined, "Emily Edwards And Her Battleaxes." The choice of words did not please her. "Well, I hit the ceiling," Miss Edwards remembered. "We had quite good, impressive officers, and I showed [the editor] the list . . . and I said, 'I don't think those ladies would like to be called battleaxes.' He was as mad, and for a while he didn't give us any publicity."[37]

And when word of the new society got out, Adina De Zavala, accustomed to her heretofore-unchallenged role as chief guardian of San Antonio's past, became highly agitated. "Miss De Zavala," recalled Emily Edwards, "called me up and told me that that was her field . . . there was just room for nobody else. She was just furious." Adina De Zavala headed for Emily Edwards' studio on Belvin Street, but when she got there Miss Edwards was gone. "Well, I found she had been there, she had made herself at home," Miss Edwards added. "Someone was with her, I think, but I didn't meet her. But when I reported to our board what had happened—that I'd been told to clear out and had been visited in my absence—Mrs. Lewis said, 'I know her, and I will take care of this.' And she did. [Mrs. Lewis] came back and she said, 'We will be permitted to exist. There were many tears, but we will be permitted to exist.'"[38]

Miss De Zavala's Texas Historical and Landmarks Association then launched a burst of activity. During the previous eleven years it had placed a total of five historical tablets. Suddenly, six more were placed during just a few months in 1924, which became "the banner year in the work of the organization."[39] There were headlines and speeches by civic leaders and descendants of old families as markers were donated by the Texas Historical and Landmarks Association, then accepted on behalf of the Daughters of the Heroes of Texas, Miss De Zavala's counter-organization to the Daughters of the Republic of Texas, from which she remained in exile.[40] At one Conservation Society meeting a member moved that joint meetings be held with the Landmarks Association, since both "stand practically for the same things." From the thirty Conservation Society members attending, however, there came no second. They did pass a resolution "extending the Landmarks Association hearty appreciation and encouragement in the work they are doing and have done."[41] Conservation Society directors later called a special meeting with Landmarks Association representatives to try setting up jointly a committee of businessmen to conduct a single fund-raising drive to buy both the Market House and the Spanish Governor's Palace.[42]

An effort to preserve San Antonio's 1859 Greek Revival Market House on Market Street just east of Main Plaza caused the San Antonio Conservation Society to organize in 1924. The Market House, however, was razed by the city to widen the street. Its site disappeared altogether when the River Bend cutoff channel came through. Adina De Zavala Papers, The Center For American History, The University of Texas at Austin, CN02181.

Even as they made enthusiastic plans about preserving the ambiance of San Antonio, the ladies of the Conservation Society did not lose sight of short-term goals. A committee appointed at their second meeting presented city commissioners with a petition to save the Market House.[43] A ten-dollar donation to the cause came from City Clerk Fred Fries, whose father designed the building.[44] Hardware magnate Edward W. Heusinger, who still owned the Market House, first declined an invitation to speak to the society on the subject until "after hearing from the city," then came to outline the "uses and practical methods of utilizing the building." He was accompanied by J.H. Briggs, chairman of the City-Different Committee of the men's Technical Club, which was about to unveil a landmarks management plan called S.O.S.—Save Old San Antonio.[45]

Briggs called S.O.S. "a co-operative plan of conservation, . . . a sort of division of labor scheme whereby various organizations will be grouped to look after given landmarks."[46] To purchase the Market House from Heusinger, the city would be asked to pledge $12,000 if the Conservation Society

To placate the Conservation Society, the City of San Antonio directed that the facade of the city's San Pedro Playhouse, built in San Pedro Park in 1929, replicate that of the lost Greek Revival Market House downtown. In 1994 the society returned the favor with a $300,000 grant for the theater facade's restoration. Zintgraff Collection, The Institute of Texan Cultures.

could raise an additional $18,000 and take charge of the facility. The state would be asked to buy the Governor's Palace for a state museum, or it would be purchased with locally raised funds if the state did not come through. Asked to oversee the Spanish missions would be the Catholic Daughters of America, assisted by the Knights of Columbus and with "the financial assistance of all San Antonio." The effort would also remove signs immediately adjacent to the Alamo.[47]

The plan generated the Conservation Society's first major resolution, a seven-part measure terming the endangered Market House "a building of great beauty." Since "it is next to impossible to reconstruct a building so as to retain the original unity of design and the quality which time alone can give," members asked the city to purchase the Market House for a museum and sent a committee with the resolution to city hall.[48] The closest thing to a real museum San Antonio had yet seen was the twenty year-old Scientific Society's natural history collection, open to the public two afternoons a week

San Antonio Conservation Society co-founder Rena Maverick (Mrs. Robert B.) Green, left, and Meta (Mrs. Raymond) Russell display one of the touches of artistry lent to the society's early activities, a poster done by noted local artist Mary Bonner advertising the society's fund-raising bus tour of historic sites in 1929. San Antonio Express.

in showcases on the second floor of the Stevens Building on Commerce Street.[49] A city museum in the Market House seemed a fine place to house the Attwater Collection, a wide-ranging natural history collection newly purchased under the leadership of Main Avenue High School botany teacher Ellen Schulz (Quillin), who displayed it in two Main Avenue classrooms.[50] During these years, many Texas historical societies were organizing to open museums.[51] San Antonio was not to be left behind.

The mayor and city commissioners promised the Conservation Society their "hearty cooperation." Commissioner Ray Lambert, a former stone mason, offered his personal help in moving back the stone facade to accommodate the widened street. Mayor John W. Tobin agreed that the Conservation Society would then own the Market House, and the society voted to study incorporation so it could own property.[52] Rena Green and Emily Edwards sought a purchase option on the Market House, while others met with Heusinger about transfering the Attwater Collection to the Market House.[53] Soon the Conservation Society accepted its first gift for the museum, a collection of Indian idols gathered in Mexico.[54] The Technical Club and the Scientific Society invited the Conservation Society to a joint luncheon. For entertainment, the Conservation Society presented a dress rehearsal of "The

Goose With The Golden Eggs," a puppet show by Emily Edwards featuring a disagreement between Mr. and Mrs. San Antonio over whether San Antonio's unique charms should be killed to achieve prosperity more quickly. Hearing formal arguments were five newly made puppets closely resembling San Antonio's city commissioners, who were given the performance in city hall following a commissioners meeting the next month.[55]

But soon word came from the Technical Club that the S.O.S. campaign was being abandoned "at least temporarily, it being deemed an inauspicious time for putting on such a campaign." The ladies turned for help on the Market House museum to the Scientific Society.[56] The Scientific Society decided to buy the Market House itself to house its own collection as well, and fund-raising plans began.[57] The Conservation Society considered the Market House saved at last.[58] In December, the new museum was promoted with an exhibit of borrowed art and antiques in the ballroom of the St. Anthony Hotel, organized according to the six flags which had flown over Texas.[59] Editorialized the *Express*: "Until the San Antonio Conservation Society's excellent comprehensive exhibit this week, only a few persons here realized the great wealth of historical material to be found in this city and region."[60]

By spring, however, the Market House was doomed. "We trusted them and we weren't watching," said Emily Edwards of the city hall politicians. Plans for an open flood channel directly through the Market House site were changed to a tunnel at the Conservation Society's request so the Market House, its depth shortened by the street widening, could be preserved, according to Miss Edwards. "But then there were property interests involved that owned buildings they wanted to sell, or something of that sort. At any rate, all of a sudden that was all off." When Emily Edwards went back to Edward Heusinger for the option on the building, "he was very interested and very willing, and all of a sudden he wasn't. And that was my first suspicion . . . . I thought well, . . . maybe he was going up in his price or something. And it was then [we] discovered . . . what was in the air. They were going to have to destroy it because . . . the Market House was exactly in the cut."[61]

By the end of 1927, Market Street was widened from thirty-five to seventy feet, with a "white way lighting system" along its entire length.[62] The city took the stonework of the Market House facade to an old quarry on the future site of Trinity University.[63] The city promised to use it as the facade of a fine arts auditorium for events not large enough for the new Municipal Auditorium.[64] When architect Bartlett Cocke went looking for the old Market House stonework, however, he found it badly damaged, "not carefully salvaged nor properly stored . . . [but] dumped, along with parts of other structures," unable to be reused.[65] Cocke and fellow project architect Marvin Eickenroht traced profiles, calculated dimensions of broken pieces and, with the aid of photographs, duplicated the Market House facade entirely with new stone for the 700-seat San Pedro Playhouse, which opened in 1930 as the home of the San Antonio Little Theater.[66]

San Pedro Playhouse was built at the San Pedro Park site selected for a city museum to replace the museum intended for the Market House, until the unexpected $65,000 bequest of the reclusive Alfred Witte specified that a museum in memory of his parents be located in Brackenridge Park. The location was dutifully moved to a brush-covered site facing Broadway in Brackenridge Park.[67] Mayor Tobin named a board to represent four groups: the San Antonio Museum Association, the San Antonio Art League, the Scientific Society and the San Antonio Conservation Society, represented by Amanda Taylor, who was elected chairman.[68] It was considered the Conservation Society's "first recognition as a factor in public affairs."[69]

The museum building's north wing went to the Museum Association and the second floor to the Art League. When the Scientific Society declined exhibit space, the Conservation Society ended up with the entire south wing, and began collecting Texas history material.[70] Appeals went out for donations of family heirlooms to join the bequest of items collected on their travels by the late Congressman James L. Slayden and his wife, Ellen Maury Slayden.[71] The San Antonio Conservation Society was put in charge of laying the cornerstone, later changed to a tablet, for the Witte Memorial Museum, which opened in October of 1926.[72]

Important though the Conservation Society's role may have been in establishing San Antonio's first significant museum, the young group did not make memorabilia an overwhelming concern but maintained its original wide-ranging interests, still with an artist's perspective.[73] Early in 1925, local artist Sybil Browne was hired to give a series of fund-raising lectures on art appreciation. Mary Bonner designed postcards for sale by the society. Emily Edwards did a large two-color pictorial map of San Antonio, also sold for the society's benefit.[74] An exhibit of old portraits was held in the Gunter Hotel ballroom in 1926 and the next year a "Tableaux Vivants" [Living Picture] exhibit, in which many artists participated, was held in Municipal Auditorium.[75] Lavish vistas of Texas wildflowers, a favorite subject for regional artists, were promoted to transform the Olmos Dam construction area and flood basin "into a preserve for Texas flowers and trees." Prizes were promised for the largest amount and greatest variety of wildflower seeds collected to sow there.[76] Fearing that unchecked springtime picking of bluebonnets and other native flowers and plants along the highways might cause them to become extinct, the Conservation Society joined with the Izaak Walton League in a luncheon at the St. Anthony Hotel to publicize the problem.[77]

As the San Antonio Conservation Society mingled artistic perspectives and concern for the natural environment with efforts to preserve the historic built

Opening in 1926 of San Antonio's first bona fide public museum, the Witte Memorial Museum in Brackenridge Park, was a major goal of the San Antonio Conservation Society. It was originally designed in the Spanish Colonial Revival style by Robert M. Ayres. The Institute of Texan Cultures, courtesy Ann Russell.

environment and relics of the past, and as it quietly sought approval of a master plan to save the fast-decaying four Spanish missions south of downtown, members also determined to put their energies behind some unfinished business at San Antonio's first mission and the state's most hallowed landmark, the Alamo. Many Conservation Society members were also longtime members of the Alamo Chapter of the Daughters of the Republic of Texas, and the Daughters needed some help.

Once the dust had settled over who was in charge at the Alamo and what would and would not be left standing, the Alamo church remained little changed from its earlier decades of management by the City of San Antonio. Visitors' donations and a steady sale of souvenirs paid the custodian and gardeners, with enough left over to put a new roof on the Alamo church.[78] Still, in 1922, remembered Leita Applewhite Small, its custodian for twenty-four years, "the Alamo had a dirt floor, a few second-hand showcases and some relics. Electricity and a new roof had but recently been installed, and there was an old wood stove that threw off such fumes [that] we had to keep the doors open no matter how inclement the weather."[79] In 1924, a three-year accumulation of $558 in excess revenues bought seven long oak-framed display cases for relics and two smaller cases to show letters and documents.[80] Gas lines were laid into the building so stoves could be installed for the first time to warm winter visitors.[81]

The setting of the Alamo continued to be a civic embarrassment, as it had been in 1895 and would still be, for some, in 1995. Five parcels of privately owned property plus the city's new main fire station took up nearly two-thirds of the block adjoining the two pieces of state-owned property maintained by the Daughters.[82] The two-story brick building a few feet south seemed bigger than the Alamo itself. Early in 1926 it became a branch of the Travis Driverless Company's Hertz Drivurself System, a twenty-four-hour operation with full service station facilities.[83] Even Will Rogers, visiting San Antonio a short time later, joked in his syndicated newspaper column, "It's a great old Town, is San Antonio, even if they have got a filling station in connection with the Alamo."[84] Nevertheless, the Alamo continued to draw other distinguished visitors as well. Mrs. Small, the custodian, remembered that Calvin Coolidge and his wife just "walked in one day," accompanied by Governor and Mrs. Dan Moody.[85] Vaudeville comedian Al Jolson dropped by before his appearance in Municipal Auditorium.[86] The list went on.

The Conservation Society decided that something had to be done. In the fall of 1925 it co-sponsored with the Alamo Mission Chapter of the Daughters of the Republic of Texas a public meeting in the Menger Hotel. Those present passed a resolution asking for a city bond issue to buy at least the land immediately south of the Alamo church to improve the setting. Representatives of "virtually every civic organization in San Antonio" were present— the City Federation of Women's Clubs, the City Plans Commission, the Technical Club, Council of Jewish Women, even the San Antonio Typographical Union.[87] Said the Alamo Chapter's vice president, Mrs. Alexander Boynton, who presided: "We are fifty years late in starting this movement, but I hope we are not too late." Amanda Taylor, chairman of the Conservation Society's committee on the project, introduced the speakers. Future Mount Rushmore sculptor Gutzon Borglum, in town to do a sculpture of Texas trail drivers, declared, "Where the Alamo stands is probably the most precious spot in the United States. Weigh the amount of martyrdom represented by the Alamo and you cannot equal it anywhere in history." Mayor John Tobin supported the overall effort "heart and soul" and thought the city did too, but hedged on city funding by asking those present "to wait a while, as we have a great many irons in the fire at this time."[88]

Two months later, Mayor Tobin backed a different plan for the Alamo—a Court of Honor in the plaza directly across from the Alamo church, with statues of three Alamo heroes and tablets bearing names of all of San Antonio's war dead. He disapproved the Fiesta de San Jacinto Association's plan, prepared by Atlee B. Ayres, for a sixty-foot-high white limestone triumphal arch across Crockett Street south of the Alamo on the grounds it would make the street too narrow for traffic.[89] The Conservation Society asked the city to forget both ideas and just buy the land next to the Alamo.[90] Six months later, the Conservation Society and the Daughters sent a joint resolution to City Commissioners and held "an enthusiastic joint session" in Mrs. Taylor's

The Conservation Society and the Alamo Mission Chapter of the Daughters of the Republic of Texas joined forces to lead a drive for public funding to purchase remaining buildings around the Alamo church, shown looking northeast from a blimp in 1931. All were removed except part of the fire station with the narrow gabled roof at right, much of its framework used for a DRT meeting hall after its donation by the city. At left is the unroofed remain of the Alamo convento. The San Antonio Light *Collection, The Institute of Texan Cultures.*

home, but Mayor Tobin still said the purchase would cost a "whole lot of money" and would have to wait.[91] The mayor finally gave in, however, and the city set aside $75,000, half of a recent bond issue's parks allocation, to buy the offending service station building.[92]

It would be nearly a decade before the rest of the block was purchased. First the Conservation Society took San Antonio's legislative delegation to lunch to discuss state purchase.[93] Then, as before its purchase of the Alamo church in 1883, the state sent a committee to San Antonio to investigate. Its chairman was none other than Mrs. Clara Driscoll Sevier, who found that completing purchase of the block would cost six times the amount she advanced for the convent property, adjusted for inflation.[94] Nevertheless, a $1 million dollar purchase bill went forward, only to be gradually cut back as the Depression worsened to $250,000.[95]

Progress was slow until the Texas Centennial of 1936 provided a catalyst. Although land purchase was not completed by the precise centennial of the fall of the Alamo, the shrine was still the focus of San Antonio's Centennial observance. It began at sunup on March 5, 1936 and continued past sundown in a rapid succession of speeches, concerts, parades, presentations and a Pontifical High Mass. A late afternoon flyover by nine Kelly Field bombers, flying in a T-for-Texas-and-Travis formation, from an altitude of 3,000 feet showered the Alamo with blue paper stars.[96] That fall, once the City of San Antonio agreed to donate its fire station property, the state's $250,000 bought the rest of the land.[97] The Alamo's share of federally appropriated centennial funds ended up at $75,000, which went for a new roof and a new floor.[98]

With the entire block around the Alamo church under single management, there was no shortage of ideas on what to do with it. Frank H. Bushick, in his capacity as president of the State Association of Texas Pioneers, urged that it become a "beautiful park, with the sacred Alamo its crown jewel."[99] An update of the Alamo Plaza portion of his 1929 Conservation Society city plan entry came from landscape architect Robert Hugman, a graduate of Brackenridge High School, where he had been an art student of Emily Edwards.[100] Hugman sent it to Clara Driscoll Sevier's board. He recommended razing all newly acquired buildings in the Alamo block to create an open park, providing "simple treatment to emphasize the Alamo in a true Texas setting," with buildings facing the Alamo from the rear having arched arcades for a harmonious backdrop.[101] On the other hand, several existing buildings on the new property "were splendidly built and . . . historic and perfect examples of typical adobe buildings, and as old as any in San Antonio," thought Rena Maverick Green.[102] One of them, the Probandt House, was a feature of Karl Friedrich Hermann Lungwitz's painting "Crockett Street Looking West" in 1857, when it was the home of Mayor W.C.A. Thielepape, thought to be shown standing in the doorway.[103]

"I decided to go to the state meeting the Daughters held in Corpus Christi," wrote Rena Green, "and try to persuade Mrs. [Clara Driscoll] Sevier to at least retain the adobes which curved with Nacogdoches Street—the former home of one of the best mayors of San Antonio, also the handsome stone home of Peter Gallagher, the excellent builder and contractor . . . . This building could well be used as a museum, was simple, cool and handsome . . . . Mrs. Sevier was thoughtful about the suggestions . . . . She invited me to a luncheon she gave, but let me know in no uncertain terms that her mind was already made up and an architect selected. She could not change."[104]

Quiet diplomacy having failed to avoid straining the close relationship of the Conservation Society and the Daughters of the Republic of Texas, a public meeting was called at Municipal Auditorium in December of 1936 by Rena Green, then chairman of the society's natural beauty committee, and by Mrs. Edwin Leighton, its old buildings committee chairman. Purpose of the meeting was to protest any development "not in harmony with the original outline of the Alamo mission" and to oppose construction of a museum on the property and the building of a stone wall around the entire area.

At the public meeting, architect Harvey Smith quoted from an early description of the Alamo.[105] Adina De Zavala, who already suspected her old adversaries of plotting to finish tearing down the convento, read a long description of the mission's construction and of the battle.[106] Mrs. Green presented a parchment petition ornately lettered by Robert Hugman. It protested a new museum building and asked, instead, that either remains of the old convent or the Probandt House be restored for that purpose. Mrs. Green declared that a voice vote to submit the petition to the state was unanimous, but, at the prompting of the Alamo custodian, two women, including the president of the Daughters' Alamo Mission Chapter, disagreed. Things went downhill from there.[107]

During the ensuing discussion of the Probandt House, Conservation Society President Elizabeth Graham rose to report that she passed the Alamo ten minutes before and had seen that the Probandt House was already torn down. "Several times she gave this information," the *Express* reported, "but it served as no deterrent to discussions of ways to preserve it. Someone suggested the petition include a demand that it be restored, but no notice was paid to the remark."[108] Herman H. Ochs, San Antonio's representative on the nine-member Texas Centennial Commission, pleaded, "Let's not get excited." He said that there had been argument and controversy during the entire centennial. Ochs favored a wall around the property but urged that no new building be put up and that the convento be restored instead as a museum so that all exhibits could be removed from the Alamo church.[109]

At that point, Sara Roach (Mrs. O.M.) Farnsworth, past Daughters of the Republic of Texas state president and a member of the San Antonio Centennial Committee, rose to defend the plans. Mrs. Green had said anything built before 1850 should be preserved, said Mrs. Farnsworth, but the Probandt House was not built until 1852. In any event, Mrs. Farnsworth added, the program ahead was "preservation, not restoration." She stated flatly that "it was the purpose of the centennial celebrations to observe the one hundredth anniversary of the independence of Texas, not the Spanish period, the Civil War period or any other era."[110]

That seemed to end the discussion, and the petition had no subsequent effect. All the historic buildings were removed, and a museum/gift shop was built northeast of the Alamo church. In 1939 the Daughters began using the partly razed former city fire station as the framework for an auditorium. The Junior Chamber of Commerce, its beautification committee chaired by Robert Hugman, protested that the Daughters had said they would tear down all pre-existing buildings on the new land to prevent that very thing from happening—to keep the grounds "free from buildings which clutter the site

and mar the beauty of the Alamo."[111] Nonsense, replied the Daughters'
Alamo Committee chairman, the new auditorium would be very much in
harmony with the site. As far as breach of faith went, she said, "This is a state
project, approved by the State Board of Control, the Daughters of the
Republic of Texas [and] the City Commissioners, and I fail to see what the
Junior Chamber of Commerce can do about it."[112]

Three days after New Year's Day, 1936, Conservation Society board
members looked forward to establish priorities. All projects were eventually
accomplished practically in the order of total votes received. First was completion of the San José Granary and the Espada Aqueduct effort, with
seventeen votes. Second was "to bring back past interest" of historic Villita
Street, ten votes. Tied with three votes each were beautification of the San
Antonio River and acquisition of property adjoining the Spanish Governors'
Palace on the north.[113] One major accomplishment had already been
achieved: restoration of the Spanish Governor's Palace itself. Although conceived by others, it was San Antonio Conservation Society members who
successfully concluded the Governor's Palace project, foreshadowing their
crucial role in preserving San Antonio's distinctiveness.

Notes

1. Mary Vance Green OHT, Feb. 2, 1984, 46; Irvin Frazier, *The Family of John Lewis, Pioneer* (San Antonio: Fisher Publications Inc., 1985), 166, 174.

2. Floy Fontaine Jordan to Sherry A. Smith, Jul. 29, 1981, letter copy in SACS Library.

3. $10,000,000 Buildings Under Construction," *San Antonio Express*, Aug. 12, 1928, 1-C. Largest projects were the Smith-Young Tower, Majestic Theater and the Nix, Alamo National Bank and Express Publishing Company buildings.

4. "San Antonio Has 17 of 135 Skyscrapers In State Of Texas," *San Antonio Express*, Nov. 10, 1929, 15-C. A "skyscraper" was designated as having more than 10 stories.

5. "Tower Flag Pole Highest In South," *San Antonio Express*, Nov. 25, 1928, 15-C. Its thirty-inch golden ball perched precisely 405 feet above street level. The flag flying from the pole measured 20 feet wide by 38 feet long.

6. "'Summer Slump' Period Is Nonexistent in San Antonio," *San Antonio Express*, Jul. 14, 1929.

7. *San Antonio Express*, Jun. 7, 1929, 13.

8. "Municipal Projects Keeping San Antonio 'In Step With Itself,'" *San Antonio Express*, Jul. 21, 1929.

9. "650 Acres in North Side Tourist Hotel Development," *San Antonio Express*, Dec. 18, 1927, 1-C.

10. "Capacity House to See 'Wings,'" *San Antonio Express*, May 18, 1927, 24; "$50,000 Studio to Be Built on South Presa," *San Antonio Express*, Feb. 26, 1928, 5-C.

11. "San Antonio First Texas City To Launch Civic Grand Opera," *San Antonio Express*, Feb. 20, 1927, 17.

12. "New Orchestra In First Concert," *San Antonio Express*, Feb. 14, 1929, 13; "Municipal Projects Keeping San Antonio 'In Step With Itself,'" *San Antonio Express*, Jul. 21, 1929; *San Antonio Express*, Jan. 16, 1930, 6.

13. "Municipal Projects Keeping San Antonio 'In Step With Itself,'" *San Antonio Express*, Jul. 21, 1929.

14. Ibid.

15. Emily Edwards OHT, 4.

16. When Interstate 10, San Antonio's first expressway, wiped that part of Belvin Street off the map, Lucy Maverick had the home moved to Castroville, where it stands, enlarged, at the edge of a plain above the east bank of the Medina River.

17. Minutes, Mar. 22, 1924. Also present were Emily Edwards's and Floy Edwards Fontaine's father Frank Edwards, who had driven them there and brought along a granddaughter, Floy Fontaine (Jordan). Henry Wedemeyer, who drove Lucretia Van Horn, remained after Frank Edwards asked him "to stay and give me courage here." (Floy Fontaine Jordan OHT, May 22, 1991, 13.) The incidental presence of the two men was not recorded in the minutes.

18. Minutes, Mar. 22, 1924.

19. This appears on the society's earliest letterhead. The motto "The greatest good to the greatest number for the longest time" was suggested, but was tabled along with a proposal to use the facade of the Market House as the society's insignia. (Minutes, Apr. 19, 1924.) The official motto came up unexpectedly. A form letter written by Anna Ellis to raise funds for the granary project in 1931 ended with the flourish, "The question is, will San Antonio sit idly by and see this gem of San Antonio's earliest architecture pass without offering to help? Will they sometime show their friends a photograph and say, 'Yes, we remember it' or will they say, 'Come and see it, we helped to save it.'" When the letter was read to the seventh anniversary meeting of the society, Mrs. J.B. Lewright suggested that the final words become the society's motto. They were slightly reworded: "Shall I say, 'Yes, I remember it,' or 'Here it is, I helped to save it'?" (Minutes, Mar. 27, 1931, 2.)

Five months later Amanda Taylor designed the seal "to meet the emergency" of imprinting official documents. The name of the society formed a circle enclosing the simplified San José mission tower symbolizing preservation of landmarks, an olive branch symbolizing the natural environment and "an all-seeing eye" symbolizing the society's watchfulness. Official colors of senisa (also known as cenizo) lavender and senisa green having already been picked, in 1936 the club backed them up by naming the senisa its official flower. (Minutes, March, 1936.) An official statement of purpose was adopted later: "The purpose for which it is formed is to preserve and to encourage the preservation of historic buildings, objects, places and customs relating to the history of Texas, its natural beauty and all that is admirably distinctive to our State; and by such physical and cultural preservation to keep the history of Texas legible and intact to educate the public, especially the youth of today and tomorrow with knowledge of our inherited regional values."

20. "A Message from Emily Edwards," undated typescript in SACS Library.

21. Minutes, Apr. 19, 1924.

22. Hosmer, *Presence of the Past,* 300–01. Charles Hosmer reports that women's preservation groups at this time were shifting, if anywhere, to a greater concern "with battling subversion and furthering Americanism." Otherwise, they were still preoccupied with only "history and patriotic inspiration." The San Antonio Conservation Society did conform socially and economically: ". . . The core of preservationist support was middle-class in character. With very few exceptions philanthropic foundations and people of great wealth did not take a deep interest in historic sites until John D. Rockefeller, Jr.'s transformation of Virginia's colonial capital in 1926. Middle-class enthusiasts, motivated by a desire to enrich the lives of their fellow men, bore the financial burden."

23. Murtagh, *Keeping Time,* 51.

24. Sarah Lyall, *The New York Times,* May 28, 1995, 8 xx.

25. "Daughters of Texas Republic to Co-Operate With Catholics in Preserving Old Missions," *San Antonio Express,* Jun. 15, 1924.

26. Minutes, Mar. 22, 1924.

27. Emily Edwards OHT, 14.

28. Miss Edwards credited the society's emphasis on diversity as having come from Rena Maverick Green. (Emily Edwards, " A Backwards Glance," *SACS Newsletter* 13, 8 (Mar. 1974), 16.)

29. Two men who spoke to the group in July were invited to join, but did not. (Minutes, Jul. 5, 1924.)

30. Mary Vance Green OHT, Feb. 2, 1984, 62. When their given names could be found, women are referred to herein as they would be after such barriers fell.

31. Minutes, Jun. 21, 1924. Other commissioners, the mayor and the chamber of commerce president did not accept invitations to attend but "sent words of encouragement."

32. Ibid.

33. At a meeting in the home of Mrs. John James, personal recollections of Robert E. Lee were given by Mrs. Florida Tunstall Sharpe, in whose parents' home Lee visited, and by the aged Aunt Tillie Brackenridge, a former slave and servant in the James Vance home when Lee visited there. ("Conservation Society To Hear Tales Of Lee," *San Antonio Express,* Mar. 8, 1928, 28.)

34. Minutes, Jul. 19, 1924. Speaker on "the historic and artistic value of old San Antonio buildings" at the society's third meeting was Rena Green's first cousin Maury Maverick, youngest son of the Albert Mavericks and later one of the six men on the bus tour, who was beginning his nationally recognized political career. (Minutes, Apr. 5, 1924.) At the same meeting the society received its first financial donation, five dollars from Rena Green's sister Lola Maverick (Mrs. William B.) Lloyd of Chicago, a leader of the National Woman's Party and daughter-in-law of nineteenth-century social reformer Henry Demarest Lloyd.

35. Minutes, Oct. 18, 1924. The next year Rena Green's mother, Mary Vance (Mrs. George) Maverick, and brother, George Vance Maverick, provided the

Conservation Society with its first business office, Room 404 of the Maverick Building on Houston Street. (Minutes, Oct. 3, 1925.)

36. Marin B. Fenwick, "Facts and Fancies About People at Home and Abroad," *San Antonio Express*, Sept. 28, 1924, 10-B. For the society's second anniversary, Josephine Tobin Rote arranged a Mexican supper for members, families and friends on the lawn of the French Place home of Margaret and Perry Lewis. Rather than marking the anniversary of the end of two years, the event was to celebrate the beginning of a third. (Minutes, Mar. 27, 1926.)

37. Emily Edwards OHT, 6. Press coverage hadn't improved sufficiently by the fall of 1925, when a committee of three was appointed to visit the president of the Chamber of Commerce to see if he could be of help in "securing more discerning and intelligent publicity for those features of San Antonio which are of historic and artistic value." (Minutes, Oct. 3, 1925.)

38. Emily Edwards OHT, 2–3. Added Miss Edwards: "I had protested to [Miss De Zavala] over the phone, you know, 'We are not an historic society.' Then it was just our fate, when we went to incorporate there was no category except the historic society in which we could enter without a great deal of trouble, so we had to incorporate [as an historical society]. Made out liars!" The desired Cultural Conservation category did not exist. ("A Message from Emily Edwards," undated typescript in SACS Library.)

39. "17 Tablets Mark City's Historic Spots," *San Antonio Express*, Aug. 3, 1924, 26. Although the headline says there were 17 tablets, only 16 are listed.

40. Ibid.; "Bronze Tablet to John Twohig," *San Antonio Express*, Jul. 10, 1924, 10.

41. Minutes, Aug. 23, 1924.

42. Minutes, Sept. 5, 1924.

43. Minutes, Apr. 5, 1924; City Commissioners Minutes, Jun. 9, 1924, Book F, 186.

44. Minutes, May 3, 1924.

45. Minutes, Jun. 7, 1924.

46. "Technical Club Sponsors City-Wide Plan to Save San Antonio Landmarks," *San Antonio Express*, Jun. 12, 1924, 11.

47. Ibid. Rena Maverick Green, still chairman of the Alamo Mission Chapter of the Daughters of the Republic of Texas Mission Committee, pledged cooperation "with the Catholic Daughters of America, the Knights of Columbus or whatever Catholic organization takes up the work." ("Daughters of Texas Republic to Co-Operate With Catholics in Preserving Old Missions," *San Antonio Express*, Jun. 15, 1924.)

48. Minutes, Jun. 7, 1924.

49. "Opening the Treasure Vault of Science," *San Antonio Express*, Sept. 16, 1917, 25; "Rare Lizard Specimen is Given to Scientists," *San Antonio Express*, Dec. 4, 1925, 7. The Scientific Society also housed its 4,000-volume library in the Stevens Building. Beginning in 1869 with the Alamo Literary and Scientific Society, several short-lived groups sought to establish a science or natural history museum in San Antonio. ("Scientific Society to Celebrate 500th Meeting," *San Antonio Express*, Feb. 5, 1933, 1-D.) In 1914, at the urging of the Scientific Society, San Antonio City Commissioners

set aside twelve acres in Brackenridge Park for a zoological garden—the present-day San Antonio Zoo—and the Scientific Society announced plans for a building near the future Witte Museum site. ("Ideal Site Selected for City's Zoological Garden and Museum," *San Antonio Express,* May 19, 1914, 7.)

50. Ibid.; Bess Carroll Woolford and Ellen Schulz Quillin, *The Story of the Witte Memorial Museum* (San Antonio: n.p., 1926), 23–29.

51. Green, *Historical Preservation in Texas,* 5. In 1923, the legislature created the Texas Historical Board to advise legislators on historic places and markers.

52. Minutes, Jun. 14, 1924. The price of $30,000 was considered a bargain, since the Real Estate Board's appraisal requested by the Conservation Society put value of the land at $33,000 and improvements at $5,000.

53. Minutes, Jun. 14, 1924.

54. Minutes, Jul. 5, 1924. Collector and donor was G.H. Gage, Jr.

55. The puppet show is described in more detail in the Introduction.

56. Minutes, Aug. 2, 1924.

57. "Society To Buy Old City Market," *San Antonio Express,* Sept. 26, 1924, 22.

58. Minutes, Oct. 4, 1924; "Market House to be Preserved," *San Antonio Express,* Jan. 1, 1925, 8-B.

59. Minutes, Nov. 22, 1924.

60. *San Antonio Express,* Dec. 18, 1924.

61. Emily Edwards OHT, 8–9; Minutes, May 2, 1925.

62. "Market St. Widening Project Completed," *San Antonio Express,* Nov. 6, 1927, 13. Only 15 feet, however, were to have been cut from the front of the Market House property, which supporters believed would have still permitted its use as a museum. ("Society To Buy Old City Market," *San Antonio Express,* Sept. 26, 1924, 22.)

63. Bill Parrish to Gen. Billy Harris, undated memo in SACS Library. Architect Parrish interviewed Cocke on the subject on Jun. 26, 1979.

64. "Fine Arts Auditorium in San Pedro Park Preserves Landmark," *San Antonio Express,* Jul. 14, 1929, 10.

65. Parrish to Harris, undated memo.

66. Ibid.; "Little Theatre, San Pedro Park, Opens Wednesday Next," *San Antonio Express,* Jan. 19, 1930, 1-D. Diehard society members five years later were still urging that remains of the original columns be preserved. (Minutes, Feb. 27, 1935.)

67. Woolford and Quillin, *The Story of the Witte Memorial Museum,* 40–44. Witte apparently based his choice of Brackenridge Park on the site picked there by the Scientific Society eleven years earlier for a museum building. ("Ideal Site Selected for City's Zoological Garden and Museum," *San Antonio Express,* May 19, 1914, 7.)

68. Ibid., 32, 45. The Museum Association, formed in 1922 to handle fund-raising for the Attwater Collection, was represented by school principal Emma Gutzeit, the Art League by Ethel Drought and the Scientific Society by Henry B. Dielmann.

69. Anna Ellis, "Conservation Society Rounds Out Eight Years," *San Antonio Express,* Mar. 13, 1932.

70. Woolford and Quillin, *The Story of the Witte Memorial Museum,* 45; Minutes, Jan. 16, 1926.

71. "Appeal Made for Museum Articles," *San Antonio Express*, Sept. 22, 1926, 6; "Slayden Curios to Be Shown at Museum Opening," *San Antonio Express*, May 9, 1926, 19.

72. Minutes, Jan. 16, Mar. 27, 1926; Woolford and Quillin, *The Story of the Witte Memorial Museum*, 45.

73. The Conservation Society decided to work jointly with the Alamo Chapter of the Daughters of the Republic of Texas in collecting "historical relics," giving donors the choice between their display in the new municipal museum or in the Alamo museum. ("Bill For Alamo Park Property Purchase to Be Discussed at Luncheon For Legislators," *San Antonio Express*, Sept. 18, 1926, 22.) In 1927 the Witte had the first Texas showing of Mexican artist Diego Rivera, arranged through former Conservation Society President Emily Edwards, who was studying under him in Mexico. ("Mexican Artist To Exhibit Here," *San Antonio Express*, Sept. 23, 1927, 9.) In 1930 the society's South Hall at the museum was made an Early Texas Room, with appropriate exhibits set up. (Minutes, Sept. 25, 1930, 2.)

74. Minutes, Oct. 17, 1925; "Block Prints to Advertise City," *San Antonio Express*, Oct. 3, 1928, 17. A Federal Writers Project's San Antonio guidebook was sponsored and marketed by the Conservation Society. (Minutes, Jan. 13, 1938.) A book review of *The Yearling* at San Pedro Playhouse cleared $101. (Minutes, Feb. 25, 1939; Mar. 3, 1939.) The society sponsored a monthly tea to benefit a cooperative art studio owned by artists, and at least one tea in conjunction with an Art League exhibit opening. (Minutes, Feb. 5, 1931; Jan. 23, 1934.)

75. "Miss Anna Ellis Named Head of Conservationists," *San Antonio Express*, Mar. 8, 1927, 6; Ellis, "Conservation Society Rounds Out Eight Years in Civic Work." Proceeds from the Tableaux Vivants went toward new display cases for the Witte Museum. By mid-1931, membership increased to 275. Directors set a limit of 300, with those in good standing permitted to bring in two members per year, subject to approval of the membership committee. As impact of the Depression increased, two dozen delinquent members were allowed a grace period of three years before being dropped. With meeting attendance ranging up to 75, general meetings were scheduled quarterly in various public locations while directors continued to meet monthly. (Minutes, Jun. 17, 1930, 2; Jun. 23, 1931, 2; Oct. 25, 1933.)

76. "Society Offers Prizes for Wild Flower Seed," *San Antonio Express*, Jul. 16, 1926, 6. Native plantings were encouraged along highways and at the missions, including a proposed White Garden complete with underground pipes and rock construction. The Park and Tree Chairman extracted a promise from city hall that trees in Travis Park would not be cut down, even though diseased. Members petitioned the city to hire a tree surgeon and complained to county commissioners and the State Highway Department of "incorrect cutting" of trees on Fredericksburg Road. One member was so carried away by discussion of the subject that she suggested "someone sing the beautiful song 'Trees.'" (Minutes, Oct. 29, 1931, 3; Feb. 8, 1934; Feb. 22, 1934; January, 1936; Feb. 27, 1936, 2; Apr. 16, 1936; Nov. 23, 1939.)

77. "Students to Aid In Conservation Of Wildflowers," *San Antonio Express*, Mar. 27, 1929, 12; "Izaak Walton League Joins Conservation Society in Move To Save Texas Wildflowers," *San Antonio Express*, Apr. 2, 1929, 11. Conservation Society President Margaret Lewis said that on a Sunday drive through the country she saw

"at least 100 automobiles filled with wildflowers" and thought a public campaign should be started in the schools with "teachers daily informing the children that it is wrong to pick these flowers." Several years later, picking wildflowers along Texas highways became illegal.

78. "Alamo Will Get New Relic Cases," *San Antonio Express*, Sept. 13, 1924, 6.

79. "Mrs. Small Leaves Alamo," *San Antonio Light,* Jul. 14, 1946, 3-B. Mrs. Small retired in 1946, having succeeded her mother, Fannie Grayson Applewhite, who took the job in 1915. Mrs. Applewhite, the Conservation Society's first treasurer, was the daughter of Capt. Thomas W. Grayson, Texas Revolution veteran and master of the Texas steamboat *Yellow Stone.* ("Two San Antonio Authorities on Local and Texas History," *San Antonio Express*, Oct. 25, 1925, 10.)

80. "Alamo Will Get New Relic Cases," *San Antonio Express*, Sept. 13, 1924, 6.

81. "Alamo Brought Up to Date, Gas Stoves in Use," *San Antonio Express*, Nov. 22, 1928, 11. A gas stove was already used in the small front room used as an office.

82. "Agreement Near On $75,000 Price To Close Purchase Of Property Back Of Alamo," *San Antonio Express*, Feb. 20, 1936, 7.

83. "Travis Driverless Company Open New Drivurself Station on Alamo Plaza," *San Antonio Express*, Feb. 14, 1926, 4-C.

84. James M. Smallwood, ed., *Will Rogers' Weekly Articles: Vol. 2, The Coolidge Years 1925–1927,* Oklahoma State University Press (Stillwater: 1980), 265–69.

85. "Mrs. Small Leaves Alamo," *San Antonio Light,* Jul. 14, 1946, 3-B.

86. "Jolson Sees Passing of Vaudeville Stage," *San Antonio Express*, Jan. 27, 1930, 18.

87. "City Commission Asked by Civic Organizations to Provide Funds," *San Antonio Express,* Oct. 27, 1925, 5.

88. Ibid. Borglum's assigned topic was on a proper setting for the Alamo. Judge Sidney J. Brooks told what the Alamo meant to the city and Conservation Society Vice Chairman Lucretia Van Horn showed lantern slides of improvements proposed in a plan by architect Henry Steinbomer. A resolution seeking the purchase was introduced by Mrs. J.K. Beretta, chairman of the City Beautiful Committee of the City Plans Commission. ("How the Alamo Would Look With Elbow Room," *San Antonio Express*, Oct. 25, 1925, 6.)

89. "Mayor Will Approve Triumphal Arch Plans," *San Antonio Express*, Dec. 9, 1925, 10; "Triumphal Arch Idea Disapproved," *San Antonio Express*, Dec. 10, 1925, 10.

90. Minutes, Jan. 16, 1926.

91. "Bond Issue to Purchase Land For Memorial Park Near Alamo to Be Requested," *San Antonio Express*, Jun. 5, 1926, 6; City Commissioners Minutes, Jun. 7, 1926, Book G, 317; "Mayor Shelves Alamo Park Idea," *San Antonio Express*, Jun. 8, 1926, 24.

92. "Appeal Renewed For Alamo Park," *San Antonio Express*, Jan. 6, 1927, 7; "City Sets Aside $75,000 For Purchase of Property Near Alamo For Park Purposes," *San Antonio Express*, Jan. 12, 1927, 7; "Alamo Property Too High, Claim," *San Antonio Express*, Feb. 24, 1927, 7. Heading the appeal were the Conservation Society's Amanda Taylor and Margaret Lewis.

93. "Bill For Alamo Park Property Purchase to Be Discussed at Luncheon For Legislators," *San Antonio Express*, Sept. 18, 1926, 22.

94. "Alamo Property Too High," *San Antonio Express,* Feb. 24, 1927, 7; "State Purchase of Alamo Block for $829,500 is Asked," *San Antonio Express,* Mar. 10, 1927, 1–2.

95. "Alamo Purchase Board Is Named," *San Antonio Express,* Aug. 14, 1929, 4; "City Ready To Aid Alamo Purchase," *San Antonio Express,* Apr. 12, 1930, 22; "City Asked To Do Its Share Toward Alamo State Park," *San Antonio Express,* Mar. 8, 1936, 1-A; "First Alamo Park Contracts To Be Awarded Tuesday," *San Antonio Express,* Nov. 23, 1936, 1-A. The Daughters' primary backup—from lobbying to motorcades to Austin—continued to be the Conservation Society, with other organizations assisting. (Mrs. P.J. Lewis and Anna Ellis to Hon. P.L. Anderson, Jan. 19, 1929, copy in SACS Library; "Alamo Caravan Ready For Start," *San Antonio Express,* Feb. 4, 1930, 8.) The Daughters and the Conservation Society honored Clara Driscoll Sevier in her latest Alamo role with a dinner at the Menger Hotel. (Minutes, Jan. 28, 1932, 2.) The service station building was owned by Mrs. Johanna Steves, widow of immigrant Edward Steves. The corner property was owned by O.M. Farnsworth. Behind those parcels, facing Crockett Street, were the new city fire station and the Probandt property. To the north were those of the Catholic Women's Association—headquartered in the onetime Gallagher House—and the former Clifton George Ford Co. ("Agreement Near on $75,000 Price To Close Purchase Of Property Back Of Alamo," *San Antonio Express,* Feb. 20, 1936, 7.)

96. "100th Anniversary of Fall of Alamo," *San Antonio Express,* Mar. 6, 1936, 1. The main Centennial Exposition was held in Dallas, even though it was generally acknowledged that San Antonio was "the city with the most to offer historically." San Antonio leadership, concluded the Centennial's historian, was "either unable or unwilling to compete with other Texas cities." San Antonio's Centennial Committee proposal "exuded an aura of negative self-righteousness while tendering a financial proposal that was minimal, if not ludicrous . . . ." (Kenneth B. Ragsdale, *Centennial '36, The Year America Discovered Texas* (College Station: Texas A&M University Press, 1987), xviii–xix, 47–48.)

97. "City Asked To Do Its Share Toward Alamo State Park," *San Antonio Express,* Mar. 8, 1936, 1-A; "Alamo Park Deal Left Up To Quin," *San Antonio Express,* Oct. 9, 1936, 6.

98. Ragsdale, *Centennial '36,* 113; "U.S. Fund To Give Alamo New Roof," *San Antonio Express,* Sept. 8, 1936; "Alamo Custodian Refuses To Close Doors For Repairs," *San Antonio Express,* Dec. 6, 1936. Of the $3 million in federal funds, as provided to major expositions in the past, $1.9 million was divided among 31 projects for historical sites, monuments, museums and restorations. In addition to the $75,000 for the Alamo, major San Antonio allocations were $98,000 to the Texas Trail Drivers Memorial, $20,000 to San José Mission repairs and $100,000 for, at last, a monument at the Alamo, the controversial cenotaph designed by Pompeo Coppini and begun in 1939. (Ragsdale, *Centennial '36,* 77, 113; "First Dirt Turned For Memorial," *San Antonio Express,* Mar. 11, 1939, 8-A.)

99. "Alamo Park Plan Pleases Pioneers," *San Antonio Express,* Apr. 23, 1929, 15.

100. Floy Fontaine Jordan OHT, May 22, 1991, 8.

101. "Hugman Scheme for Alamo Park Changes Street," *San Antonio Express,* Aug. 16, 1931, 1-A.

102. Rena Maverick Green's notes read by Rowena Green Fenstermaker in OHT, Feb. 2, 1984, 39.

103. Cecilia Steinfeldt, *Art For History's Sake* (San Antonio: Witte Museum, 1993), 161–63. The painting is reproduced on page 29.

104. Green's notes in Fenstermaker OHT, 39–40.

105. "Daughters of Republic Refuse to Join Conservation Society in Protest on Alamo Park Plans," *San Antonio Express,* Dec. 5, 1936, 18.

106. Ibid.; "Battle of Alamo Again Under Way," *San Antonio Express,* Oct. 11, 1936, 13. Miss De Zavala had previously announced plans to speak out anew on the cause throughout the state, and already, according to the Associated Press, had obtained the support of the Houston Pen Women's Club.

107. Ibid.

108. Ibid.

109. Ibid.; Ragsdale, *Centennial '36,* 36.

110. Ibid.; Ragsdale, *Centennial '36,* 48.

111. "State Asked to Stop Construction of Alamo Park Auditorium," *San Antonio Express,* Mar. 24, 1939, 10-A.

112. "D.R.T. Ignores Protest Against Alamo Building," *San Antonio Express,* Mar. 25, 1939, 10-A.

113. Minutes, Jan. 4, 1936. The property adjoining the Governor's Palace, however, would not be purchased until 1969, when the retail structure to the north was purchased by the city and razed for a small park.

5

The Spanish Revival

Every Sunday for twenty-eight years, Otto Blumenthal walked the seven blocks from his home to city hall to help San Antonians mark the passage of time.

He went up the stairs to the third floor and unlocked the steel door to the roof, then entered the rococo clock tower and climbed its steep steps. As caretaker of the city clock, Blumenthal slowly wound a crank 160 times to raise a 1,200-pound weight so a bell would strike each hour during the week ahead. The strike weight for the smaller quarter-hour bell was lighter, but took as many turns. The weight that powered the running mechanism was only 500 pounds, and wound too easily for him to bother counting.

Otto Blumenthal's weekly ritual came to an abrupt end in the spring of 1927. San Antonio's explosive growth of recent years was straining the entire downtown infrastructure, and the thirty-five-year-old city hall had become too small to handle all its new business. As in the rest of the crowded downtown, the obvious direction to expand was up. The tops of the turrets were taken off the four corners of city hall, the clock tower came off the roof and another floor of offices was added on in their place.[1] The style of city hall was transformed from the ornate Second Empire to the smoother lines of Spanish Revival.

At the very time that San Antonio's development was accelerating to new levels, it was apparent that the conservation camel was at last getting its head under the city hall tent. In these frenetic years, a city commissioner himself articulated the problem. "San Antonio is one of only six or seven cities in the United States which really have individual atmosphere," stated Commissioner Frank Bushick, "and that atmosphere is one of the things—and not climate alone—that brings us our annual thousands of tourists. Kill that atmosphere by abolishing the old landmarks and names, and so far as individuality goes we might as well be Kansas City, Dallas, Houston or any other bustling

San Antonio's ornate Second Empire-style city hall, completed in 1891 in the center of Military Plaza, was crowned by a central 135-foot octagonal tower with a clock cupola. The Institute of Texan Cultures, courtesy Ann Russell.

western town. We shall not only make the city ordinary where it is now unique, but also . . . we shall kill one of the geese that lays the golden eggs."[2]

Climate was the major point being used by the Chamber of Commerce to sell visitors on San Antonio. In 1923 the chamber focused a $60,000 Winter Tourist Program on golf, tennis and polo, more than a third of that budget spent on a nationwide newspaper campaign.[3] The Conopus Club opened a tourist headquarters in the Texas Hotel at Navarro and Martin streets, with croquet and quoits courts on the grounds and horseshoe-pitching courts in Travis Park across the way.[4] The club's third annual Tourist Day celebration in 1926 drew more than 2,000 visitors to San Pedro Park.[5] The Salesmanship Club offered tourists identifying buttons and windshield stickers along with a guidebook to the city.[6] Adina De Zavala pitched in to provide Sunday afternoon tours for the historically minded.[7] By 1928, the rate of visitors to the Alamo rose from as many as 1,000 a day in the winter to 1,400 a day in

Faced with burgeoning administrative needs of a fast-growing city, in 1927 city hall was renovated in a Spanish Colonial Revival style, the clock tower and tops of the round turrets at one end and square turrets of the other all removed for a fourth floor. The San Antonio Light Collection, The Institute of Texan Cultures.

the summer, and San Antonio's tourist industry was adding more than $5 million annually to the city's economy.[8]

With railroads joined by a rapidly developing highway network, it was becoming easier for tourists to get to San Antonio. A new theme across the south appeared as part of revived interest in the region's Spanish heritage: the Old Spanish Trail highway from San Diego, California to St. Augustine, Florida, a route which would become the basic path of Interstate 10. Completion of the first ten years of building concrete bridges and paving the route, or at least improving it, was celebrated in San Antonio in 1929. That spring, seven automobiles that left San Diego in an inaugural motorcade five days earlier arrived on the outskirts of San Antonio. They were ceremoniously escorted down Fredericksburg Road for a round of speeches and festivities before they departed for Florida.[9] Another celebration came that fall when an Old Spanish Trail motorcade passed through in the opposite direction, first

Tours for historically minded visitors to San Antonio were conducted on Sunday afternoons by Adina De Zavala, shown pointing to the keystone over the door of the yet unrestored Spanish Governor's Palace in 1926 beside her long-time preservation associates Nellie Lytle, center, and Frances Donecker. The San Antonio Light *Collection, The Institute of Texan Cultures.*

pausing near Houston to celebrate the newly laid concrete pavement between Rosenberg and East Bernard.[10]

But while warm winters might be the hook to get tourists to San Antonio, it was the city's other-worldly atmosphere which charmed them once they arrived. Although the few remaining original Spanish landmarks were neglected and crumbling, their spirit was being renewed in the regional building boom's popular Spanish Colonial Revival. Variations in San Antonio ran the gamut from the "vaguely Spanish Renaissance-inspired ornament" of the twenty-one story Milam Building (1928) to the traditional Plaza Hotel (1927) to the "extreme" Spanish Baroque of the Southwestern Bell Building (1931).[11] A cockle-shell doorway at Mission San José inspired two front windows of the Spanish Colonial Revival Municipal Auditorium (1926).[12]

A traditional Spanish Colonial Revival style was chosen for the Plaza Hotel, opened in 1927 at the southern St. Mary's Street bridge over the San Antonio River. In the right background is the framework for the expanding Bexar County Courthouse. The Institute of Texan Cultures, courtesy Florence Collett Ayres.

Spurred by visitors' "delight in the Latin atmosphere of San Antonio," the St. Anthony Hotel's roof garden was done over into "a typical village of Old Spain, with tables for dining placed on the sidewalks before the houses as in the streets of Spanish villages of today."[13]

Broad towers roofed with glazed ceramic-tiled domes punctuate the facade of San Antonio's Spanish Colonial Revival Municipal Auditorium, shown as completion neared in 1926. San Antonio Conservation Society.

The style swept outward from downtown in the design of homes in subdivisions like Spanish Acres in Woodlawn Hills, and in dozens of commercial buildings such as those of the new Handy-Andy chain, which made Spanish Revival its official architectural style when its first San Antonio grocery opened in 1927.[14] One of the surburban resort hotels planned for tourists was the eight-story, 306-room El Conquistador, not completed after its groundbreaking in Spanish Acres.[15] The Atkinson-McNay residence, "the largest home in Texas," which became the McNay Art Museum, was built the same year on the northern outskirts of the city "of true Spanish design," in stucco with stone trim, wrought iron grills and balconies.[16] The Spanish Colonial Revival style of San Diego's Naval air base inspired a similar construction program at Fort Sam Houston.[17] Where eight hundred buildings were to go up at Randolph Field, "from a mesquite-covered plain will spring, as if at the magic touch of Aladdin, a Spanish village in which will center America's air activities."[18]

As popularity of the Spanish Colonial Revival grew, the newly formed Conservation Society was ready to drive home the point that San Antonio's original Spanish landmarks themselves gave the city's charm a rare authenticity of inestimable economic benefit, as was already being shown in California. Santa Barbara was a good example. The case of Santa Barbara was presented by the Conservation Society in a "landmark rally" at the Gunter Hotel in the

The Spanish Colonial Revival also included distinctive interiors, as in the home at 202 Bushnell Avenue—now in the Monte Vista Historic District—built for Thomas E. Hogg, son of Texas Governor James Hogg. Finished in 1924, it was the first major Spanish Colonial Revival local work of architect Atlee B. Ayres, one of San Antonio's great practitioners of that style. The Institute of Texan Cultures, courtesy Florence Collett Ayres.

fall of 1924. The speaker, a native of Santa Barbara introduced by Maury Maverick, told how efforts of businessmen in her home city had not only preserved many old adobe buildings, but even achieved remodeling of the city hall to permit a new Spanish-style plaza around it. The replica of a Spanish street was built, a community art center was established and tourism soon became a major factor in Santa Barbara's economy. The speaker noted, however, that "San Antonio has more beautiful missions and more historic landmarks and relics of its past than does Santa Barbara."[19]

A prime example was the only major Spanish-era secular building remaining in San Antonio—the crumbling Spanish Governor's Palace, for which Adina De Zavala's Texas Historical and Landmarks Association had been appealing for funds to save since 1915. Despite support from the new Conservation Society, the effort remained stalled.

The largest planned complex of Spanish Colonial Revival buildings in Texas is San Antonio's Randolph Air Force Base. The baroque tower of its headquarters building conceals a water tower. Zintgraff Collection, The Institute of Texan Cultures.

While Miss De Zavala created widespread awareness of the Governor's Palace's existence, its continuing survival may have had more to do with the accident of its location on the far side of Military Plaza, away from impending development. But in mid-1924, as downtown growth appeared ready to leapfrog Military Plaza, Governor's Palace owners got an offer of $57,000 for the property from New York City. As had happened two decades before when eastern developers sought removal of the old Alamo convento, futile appeals went out to the state legislature to purchase the Spanish landmark as a Texas

Hall of Fame, and Miss De Zavala pleaded with city commissioners for funds.[20]

Into the breech this time stepped not a Clara Driscoll but the City Federation of Women's Clubs. Alarmed by news of the impending sale, three Federation representatives—including the president, Mrs. J.K. Beretta—went to Mayor Tobin to urge the city to buy the building.[21] Noted the *Express* of the simultaneous appeals of the Landmarks Association and the Federation of Women's Clubs, "The two movements are independent of each other."[22]

While the fate of the Governor's Palace was on the line, historic preservation efforts in San Antonio were undergoing a transition from an old-style Preservation by Petition to a more broadly based Preservation By Consensus. Miss De Zavala's Sons and Daughters of the Heroes of Texas formally petitioned city commissioners for funds to save the palace in 1924 and again two years later, while buttonholing passersby for small donations to the cause in a Tag Day downtown.[23] At a city commissioners meeting Miss De Zavala tried scolding: "You are spending hundreds of thousands of dollars for what we might term industrial and commercial development of San Antonio," she said to commissioners, "so why should you deny us the few paltry dollars we are asking? You are doing nothing to preserve the spiritual and historical side of San Antonio."[24]

As other organizations working together made commissioners aware of the breadth of support for the Governor's Palace, however, things began to advance. Purchase funds were included in a $5 million bond issue in 1926, then cut out when the bond package was trimmed by nearly a third.[25] But with the added weight of more than 5,000 voting women in all forty-three member clubs of the City Federation of Women's Clubs behind it, Mayor C.M. Chambers backed a $55,000 Governor's Palace purchase item in a $4.8 million bond issue in the boom year of 1928. Voters approved.[26]

To oversee restoration and administration of the Governor's Palace, Mayor Chambers sought consensus. He asked six local historical organizations to each select three of their members to make up an advisory board: the Daughters of the Republic of Texas, the Daughters of the American Revolution, the History Club, the Pioneer Association, the San Antonio Conservation Society, the Texas Historical and Landmarks Association and the Daughters and Sons of the Heroes of the Republic of Texas. As its chairman he appointed a representative of the Conservation Society—Rena Maverick Green, who had known Mayor Chambers when he and her late husband were state senators together in Austin.[27]

On the eve of the palace board's first meeting, Adina De Zavala presented the mayor with a petition signed by sixty persons saying that it wasn't fair. Administration of the palace she thought should be directed, rather, by only

Purchased with funds from a city bond issue approved in 1928, the vacant Spanish Governor's Palace awaits restoration. The San Antonio Light *Collection, The Institute of Texan Cultures.*

two organizations—her Texas Historical and Landmarks Association and her Sons and Daughters of the Heroes of Texas, who "started the movement."[28]

With Miss De Zavala's acerbity diluted by the number of organizations represented on the new palace board, the San Antonio Conservation Society turned out to be its unifying force. Due to member crossover, half of the representatives were also active Conservation Society members, including the advisory board's entire leadership: General Chairman Rena Green, Vice Chairman Mrs. J.B. Lewright and Secretary Anna Ellis.[29] In June the board successfully recommended that commissioners choose Harvey P. Smith as the architect.[30] Commissioners picked Guy C. Holder as contractor at the request of Rena Green, who admired his local work under the California architect George Washington Smith, whom she considered the best Spanish-period architect in the nation.[31]

Harvey Smith's task was formidable. Research took nearly a year, but interviews of descendants of early families and library searches did not turn up

The Spanish Governor's Palace restoration was completed in 1931 in time for a celebration of the two hundredth anniversary of the arrival of Spanish colonists from the Canary Islands. A building rising one story above the palace at the left was blanked out by the photographer. DRT Library at the Alamo, Harvey Patteson photographer.

plans or detailed descriptions as hoped. The earliest interior illustration that could be found was of a fandango painted from memory by Theodore Gentilz a year after his visit in 1847.[32] Excavations revealed foundations of a rear wing.[33] On the keystone below the Hapsburg coat of arms, chipping away a putty-like filling with a pen knife revealed the date 1749.[34] Believing that sufficient records would still turn up in San Antonio or could be obtained by writing, the mayor refused to approve funds for Smith's travel to Santa Fe to study its Palace of the Governors or to Saltillo, Mexico, to study records there.[35] Smith ended up going to Santa Fe on his own, and found what he learned to be "most helpful."[36]

As reconstruction began, ceiling beams were made from old telephone poles and railroad ties to replicate the original roof. Worn flagstones from old sidewalks went down for the missing floor. Period plastering was applied to the walls. New front doors were made from solid black walnut by Austin woodcarver Peter Mansbendel. The patio was designed by landscape architect Homer Fry and paved with pebbles from the San Antonio River under the supervision of artist Georgia Maverick (Mrs. Eugene) Harris.[37] Among those answering an appeal for interior furnishings was arts patron Marion Koogler McNay.[38]

The process of restoration was, however, fraught with the same types of frustrations and inter-personal conflicts which the Spanish governors themselves had faced in dealing with the surrounding territory. As successful governing required the patience of Job and the wisdom of Solomon, so did it take a skillful chairman to successfully maneuver through the toils and snares which accompany any major effort involving large numbers of volunteers. To help herself get through the project, Rena Green kept a "Diary of Insults." In it, "she wrote down the insults she received . . . from the other women," a daughter recalled. "And in that way she was no longer frustrated. If she was, why then she'd write it down and she could laugh about it." For the women "didn't agree about . . . anything."[39]

Some feared the result would look too much like the Palace of the Governors in Santa Fe. There was disagreement over whether to have the floor of rock or of tile—which was not available in any event. There was no indication of a well ever having been in the patio, but some board members talked about "how much the tourists would like a well." Over Rena Green's objections it was finally built. University of Texas librarian Carlos Castañeda sent Rena Green a letter from an early Spanish notable in San Antonio. When she went on vacation another person copyrighted the letter in her own name, which put Mrs. Green "in a terrible position."[40]

Then there was the problem of Frederick C. Chabot. The local historian had discovered critical new information but believed the fruits of his research labors were just as valuable as the work of architects, stone masons or electricians. His price was $500. He would apply the money to printing one thousand copies of his history of the palace, which the advisory board had earlier approved for exclusive sale in the restored building but which the mayor had not.[41] Now the advisory board could sell the pamphlet for fifty cents apiece and recover the costs. "In other words," Chabot said, "my offer . . . is to do the research work free if nobody else is paid, or to get $500 from the sale of historical pamphlets if any fees are paid to others."[42]

The idea of holding history for ransom threw the palace advisory board into an uproar. Adina De Zavala personally objected to Mayor Chambers in a conference she maneuvered just as the mayor was to meet with Rena Green and a committee on the subject.[43] "Even Miss Ellis joined for once with Miss De Zavala in voting against Fred's proposition," Rena Green wrote her sister. "I don't like Fred's ways either, . . . but I do think that before we begin building we should get his . . . [material] and have a look at it." She added that a Conservation Society leader "criticized Fred so bitterly that of course I had to say that I had found him and his historic facts very dependable. I could speak against the whole room of them—including [a cousin] who was speaking against the deal. And then I went home and Mama gave me quite a lecture about holding to one's friends!—etc., and how I must now be very *patient.*"[44]

Calmed by the lecture from her 74–year-old mother, Rena Green came up with a minority compromise recommendation which the mayor approved: raise the $500 by voluntary subscription and let Chabot publish the pamphlet on his own. She promised to contribute personally.[45] The matter resolved, Chabot turned over to the mayor the copy of an 1804 will he had found in the courthouse which gave the only known interior description of the palace, and which indicated that it was always a one-story building rather than the two stories Adina De Zavala had imagined.[46] Chabot felt sufficiently shaken by the experience to devote his pamphlet's entire five-page introduction to a blow-by-blow defense of his role in the affray.[47]

By mid-1930, the $30,000 restoration paid for with city funds was sufficiently complete for an informal twelve-hour "housewarming." Spanish music was furnished by the contractor.[48] As the formal dedication in 1931 approached, however, the advisory committee had to deal with one more contretemps.

The Conservation Society made plans for a pageant marking arrival of San Antonio's main group of Spanish settlers from the Canary Islands as the feature of the Governors' Palace dedication on March 4, four days short of the arrival's two hundredth anniversary. His Eminence Patrick Cardinal Hayes of New York would be the featured guest.[49]

Esther Carvajal, Elizabeth Orynski Graham and Anna Ellis wrote "The Coming of the Canary Islanders," its production financed by sale of bicentennial coins and of eight hundred grandstand seats, at fifty cents each. The city built the platforms and advanced expense money.[50] Rena Green found a way to make up to a young architect they liked but who had not been selected for the restoration. She happened to sit next to him at a *Los Pastores* presentation at Christmas and found that "he sang beautifully," as well as being "very tall and handsome, too."[51] He was picked for the role of Captain Alarcon, leader of the Spanish soldiers.

"Sounds simple," Rena Green wrote her sister. "But next, all the descendants of the . . . Islanders demanded the right to act the Islanders—and [said] that we agreed to through [a member and her brother, who] were very ugly about it, quite horrid. But I did stop their idea of putting out all the other members of the Conservation Society . . . . All are behaving well now."[52] And at the dedication, she wrote, "With a few minor exceptions our 'pageant' went off beautifully. They tell me it was the most effective thing in that line ever put on—had so many interesting people helping, such nice costumes, etc. Only criticisms—no one looking after seating, and Mrs. Castanola evidently

His Eminence Patrick Cardinal Hayes of New York holds an ornate coin box during dedication ceremonies for the Spanish Governor's Palace on March 4, 1931. Standing beside him is Texas Governor Ross Sterling. Before the microphone at far right is Republican leader R.B. Creager, with San Antonio Mayor C.M. Chambers seated at his right. The San Antonio Light *Collection, The Institute of Texan Cultures.*

sold too many. Then, no policing the huge crowd when we marched into the Palace! But fortunately no one was hurt."[53] After expenses there was a surplus of $175, forwarded to the city. But "the mayor, with warm words of praise for the pageant and surprise at our little expense account, very generously returned the check to Mrs. Taylor for the Conservation Society treasury."[54]

The check was especially welcome, for by now the full effects of the Great Depression were hitting San Antonio. As the city's building and development boom ended, fund-raising efforts were becoming even more difficult. The city had given the Conservation Society custodianship of the Governor's Palace. Its first custodian, Josephine Tobin Rote, the Conservation Society's third vice president, came up with a scheme of asking fifteen well-known artists to paint scenes in and about the palace. They would donate their works to be sold at $15 apiece, which would finance the printing of postcards.[55] A contest to write a palace guidebook was judged by a trio of college professors.[56] In September the Conservation Society held its "first rousing meeting . . . in [the] old Palace yard. Hot as the devil, but [we] had a grand review of our main efforts of the past seven years and [a] sort of memorial of Josie Rote, who worked hard for the garden and who died in June."[57]

Elizabeth Graham was named the new custodian, and very soon had a real crisis to face. The deepening Depression brought the city's worst bank failure, that of City Central Bank and Trust. Lost were deposits of more than $500,000 in municipal funds, nearly twenty percent of the entire city budget. The city went into deficit operations. Sixty parks workers and twenty office employees were eliminated. Street department workers, their force already reduced by 250, were used only on alternate weeks. City unemployment relief efforts were ended.[58] The beleaguered city government now obviously saw the expense of keeping open the Governor's Palace as unessential.

So Elizabeth Graham and Georgia Maverick Harris went to city commissioners with a proposal: they would keep the Governor's Palace open from nine to five daily, hire a maintenance man/gardener and charge ten cents admission for adults and five cents for children. Admission fees would be their compensation. The city accepted.[59] A Conservation Society committee met with city commissioners to outline palace policies and the custodian's duties.[60] The job was not lucrative. Remembered Elizabeth Graham's son: "Sometimes they'd come home and Mother'd say, 'Well, we took in fifty cents today.' That'd be five grown-ups."[61] As times improved, admissions began to average ten dollars a day. Now that it was profitable, and San Antonio itself was recovering, the city took back palace operations and put Elizabeth Graham on a salary.[62]

Saving the Spanish Governor's Palace was, for San Antonio, a relatively uncomplicated, focused goal. Smaller places like Santa Barbara could gather a consensus more quickly. They could move with greater singleness of purpose and fewer distractions toward such a general goal than, in the 1920s, could San Antonio, larger and growing at a far faster rate. It was not only much harder to manage San Antonio's "atmosphere," it seemed almost impossible to get any consensus on just exactly what that term meant and on how procedures to preserve and expand it should be implemented. But the San Antonio Conservation Society was ready to try. There were Spanish customs to be preserved, names to be defended and an education effort to be undertaken for the public and, seemingly as always, for city hall.

The Conservation Society picked up sponsorship of one unusual custom, the traditional Spanish-language Christmas miracle play *Los Pastores*, which could last from three to five hours and was usually held in a patio on San Antonio's predominantly Mexican-American west side, where the previous

Old telephone poles were used as ceiling beams during restoration of the Spanish Governor's Palace, as shown in this view of the palace's family room which opens onto the patio. San Antonio Conservation Society.

year more than five hundred spectators overflowed the area.[63] The lengthy re-enactment of hazards confronting shepherds making their way to the manger and using archaic language made the play so confusing that, wrote one translator with pen in cheek, "The fame of the play lies in the fact that, when it is enacted, very few understand what it is all about."[64]

To recreate the authentic flavor of a Mexican Market in Haymarket Plaza for the 1928 convention of the National Federation of Women's Clubs, the Conservation Society sponsored a design contest for an electric lantern best resembling the original candle-lit tin lanterns.[65] Prizes went to the chili stand with the best food, the best Mexican music and the girl with the best costume, all "in keeping with the society's policy of encouraging any form of attractive individuality in San Antonio."[66] Keeping the colorful chili stands on San

Elaborate costumes and regalia used in the Spanish Christmas miracle play Los Pastores, *which can last up to five hours, are shown in 1957 by this cast of players, workers from the San Antonio Portland Cement Company. San Antonio Conservation Society.*

Antonio's plazas and streets was vigorously defended in the mid-1930s, when some stands' lack of sanitation in preparation and serving of food was blamed for causing yellow fever, malaria and other diseases.[67] Rena Green was delegated to take the matter up with city hall, but no number of resolutions or meetings was able to prevent their being banned.[68]

Traditional names were under assault from every direction. When the telephone company announced that Crockett and Travis would no longer designate telephone exchanges, the Conservation Society sent over a delegation to "save the names of our heroes" and encourage use of even more such names.[69] The San Antonio River after it met the Guadalupe River downstream still must remain the San Antonio River, not the Guadalupe River, as it had suddenly appeared on highway maps.[70] San Jacinto Street was not to become St. Ann Street, although some unspecified street name should be changed to honor Mexico.[71] Losoya Street was not to be changed to Broadway, nor Zarzamora Street to Aviation Boulevard.[72] When North St. Mary's Street was joined at its north with Oakland Street, it was all right to name the entire street North St. Mary's, as it was when, to the south, Garden Street was extended and renamed South St. Mary's.[73]

But when the name of Roosevelt Avenue, which stretched up from southern San Antonio, was to replace the names of the newly connecting Navarro and Romana streets through downtown, alarms went off.[74] In May of 1924, the City Federation of Women's Clubs formally protested the change to city commissioners.[75] Three months later the fledgling Conservation Society, holding a Mexican supper in a pecan grove near the pool at San Pedro Park, adopted a resolution "condemning change of street names having historical or other interesting significance," and sent a delegation to formally protest to city commissioners.[76]

The larger problem was the lack of any official concept of how San Antonio was supposed to be growing, which kept landmarks and parks at constant risk. The iron-balconied J.P. Garcia House on East Commerce Street, an increasingly rare example of the New Orleans French style, went down in 1926 for the extension of Bonham Street.[77] Lexington Avenue was allowed to bisect Madison Square under the guise of facilitating traffic flow to and from Municipal Auditorium. Market Street cut off one side of Main Plaza and East Crockett Street was cut through Alamo Plaza, over the protest of Commissioner of Parks Ray Lambert.[78] When Main Avenue bisected Crockett Park and caused the park's remains to start being known as "Twin Parks," the Conservation Society, State Association of Texas Pioneers and Daughters of the Republic of Texas joined to extract a promise from the city to clearly mark the area as Crockett Square.[79]

To reduce traffic on Broadway by connecting it with North Alamo Street, City Commissioner Paul Steffler supported a proposal to diagonally bisect Maverick Park. Where Broadway bent southwest as it crossed what became Jones Avenue at one corner of the park, a connecting leg would cater-corner through Maverick Park to meet North Alamo at Tenth Street. The cost to the city would be small, as no private land would have to be purchased. "The park would not be destroyed," proponents had the temerity to contend, "as there would remain two triangular strips of land on either side of the new street." The scheme was not approved.[80]

What made it all so frustrating was that the process was not bringing long-term solutions. Despite the eternal street widenings and straightenings, a survey directed by the National Safety Council concluded that San Antonio's downtown traffic was "approaching the saturation point," and a traffic loop around the downtown area was necessary.[81] But that would not correct the "regular hodge-podge" being built around the downtown perimeter without some sort of city planning, businessmen were beginning to point out.[82] Had these "improvements" really accomplished anything?

To help the public articulate for itself San Antonio's unique spirit, and understand the scope of the problem, the Conservation Society decided upon essay contests. One was to increase appreciation of the San Antonio River, with a prize substantial enough "to obtain worthwhile articles." Another topic was added: "Why Are Adobe Houses Beautiful?"[83] Sculptor Gutzon Borglum convinced members in 1926 that a third topic, on the need for a city master plan, was important enough to be an entirely separate contest with major prizes—such as a first prize of $500. When he volunteered to contribute toward it, he was made an honorary member of the Conservation Society.[84] With encouragement from the City Plans Commission, the society solicited donations from the Technical Club and other groups so a $300 second prize and a $100 third prize could be included as well.[85]

But when the City Plans Commission chairman, architect John M. Marriott, asked city commissioners to help with money for prizes, reaction was swift and sharp. Commissioners unanimously rejected not just the request for money but the entire concept of the contest. Mayor Tobin declared "it would be useless to get up a city plan unless we knew first that it would be legal, feasible and that we could carry it into effect." Commissioners thought that not even $500 would attract high-caliber talent. The city attorney ruled that a plan requiring zoning was unconstitutional, according to his interpretation of property rights guaranteed in state and federal constitutions.[86]

When a City Plan Contest was held anyway, prizes of fifty, twenty-five and fifteen dollars were offered. Rena Maverick Green, chairman of the contest committee, explained in the rules: "We do not expect technical details nor scientific solutions of the problems of traffic, drainage, water supply, etc. What we want is to call attention to the possibility of comfortable and beautiful growth in our modern city without sacrificing the good points of old San Antonio."[87] It would have been hard for preservationists anywhere to come up with a more constructive orientation. Seeking to bring widespread order out of chaos was a far-reaching goal few preservation groups of the time even articulated, much less seriously tried to address in a time of unbridled prosperity. Ongoing city planning and zoning was, after all, a relatively new concept, and it needed all the boosting it could get.[88]

Gradually, the rising level of city-planning dialogue and civic dismay over patchwork changes led to interviews with professional city planner Harland Bartholomew of St. Louis.[89] In the fall of 1929, Planning Commission Chairman N.H. White spoke optimistically about his possible hiring to Conservation Society directors at their luncheon meeting at the Argyle Hotel in Alamo Heights. The ladies liked the sound of things so much that the next day seven of them went to see Mayor Chambers and Commissioner Paul Steffler, who complained that "he could make [a] plan for less money." Nevertheless, "two days after [a] hard session," Bartholomew was hired, for a three-year period. Anna Ellis and Rena Green got a letter of thanks from White for their help. Rena Green believed, "I really think we put it over."[90]

Saving the Spanish Governor's Palace and addressing the larger problem of saving the city's distinctiveness by a plan of coherent municipal development required preservationists' full repertoire of persistence, compromise, inventiveness and vision. But until a city plan was pulled together that could weather economic downturns, or until preservationists could develop a broad and effective strategy of their own, preservation of all but the most unusual landmarks would remain a haphazard affair.

Rena Green, for example, was walking down Villita Street one day when she saw workmen with pick-axes knocking down a wall of the Spanish-era Cós House, La Villita's most historic building, where Santa Anna's brother-in-law capitulated to Texans two months before the Battle of the Alamo, and which even bore a marker from the Texas Historical and Landmarks Association. A daughter recalled that Mrs. Green, horrified, "said, 'Stop, right now. Just stop. I'm going to call Mr. Goeth, who's head of the Water Board [which owned the building]. And they looked at her like, 'Well, this crazy woman.' And she made them stop, and she called Mr. Goeth and he came right over and he stopped them."[91]

City government's approach to issues of the natural and built environments at the time might best be described as schizophrenic. In 1927 the city purchased, commendably, a block of land on the city's east side for a park. It included the deteriorating two-story stone home built in 1853 by Anthony Michael Dignowity, pioneer San Antonio physician and perhaps the first Czech to immigrate to Texas.[92] In one of the more bizarre cases of landmark abuse in San Antonio's history, a pile of shingles in an upstairs room of the Dignowity House was saturated with kerosene. At six o'clock one August morning the pile of shingles was ceremoniously lit by Acting Mayor Phil Wright, "and the old place slowly burned to the ground" while three companies of city firemen stood by. The burning saved the city "from tearing it down and carting off the lumber, rock and adobe." Debris was swept into two deep wells on the property.[93]

If Spanish or any other landmarks in San Antonio were to be saved, preservationists were going to have to continue to provide the leadership themselves.

Notes

1. "Official Clock Winder Regrets Passing of City Hall 'Friend' Visited Weekly for 28 Years," *San Antonio Express*, May 22, 1927, 8. "I should have been allowed to supervise the work," the aging Blumenthal complained of the clock's removal. He

estimated the clock in 1927 would cost nearly four times the $2,800 the city paid for it in 1892, but nobody seemed to care. "They had men working on it who knew nothing about clocks," he said. "In taking it down they harmed it to such an extent that it cannot be used again."

2. "Street Name Stand Wins Bushick Praise," *San Antonio Express*, Mar. 22, 1928, 9. Heritage-minded Frank Bushick was also the author of *Glamorous San Antonio* and served as president of the State Association of Texas Pioneers.

3. "The Chamber," *San Antonio Express-News*, May 1, 1994, 2-G. In the fall of 1926, the Chamber of Commerce dispatched its highway department director on a four-week, 3,500-mile journey to determine the best two routes and to log facilities between San Antonio and St. Louis, where San Antonio had a tourist bureau in the Missouri Hotel. ("Map Showing Two Routes Between S.A. and St. Louis to Be Logged by Furlong," *San Antonio Express*, Oct. 3, 1926, 6-C.)

4. "Tourists To Have Club Rooms In Hotels Here," *San Antonio Express*, Dec. 5, 1925, 3. Originally a chapter of the now defunct Conopus International, a service organization in the mold of Rotary, Kiwanis, and Lions clubs, San Antonio Conopians later severed their ties with the larger organization, dropped their mission of service and still continue weekly luncheon meetings, but under the motto "We do nothing, and we do it well."

5. "2,000 Tourists Attend Barbecue," *San Antonio Express*, Feb. 27, 1926, 5. A Charleston contest and "bathing girl view" were followed by prizes for the best decorated automobiles, won by drivers from California, Kentucky and New York. The farthest car came from Toronto.

6. "City's Tourists to Advertise Themselves," *San Antonio Express*, Oct. 20, 1926, 22.

7. "Four Historic Points Visited in First Tour," *San Antonio Express*, Nov. 22, 1926, 18. Miss De Zavala, assisted by Frances Donecker, picked up tourists at Travis Park Methodist Church and took them to the Seymour Thomas House on North Flores Street, Chapel of the Miracles on Ruiz Street and Ben Milam's grave in Milam Square, ending up at the Governor's Palace. Later the Texas Historical and Landmarks Association was conducting its "pilgrimage . . . to historic shrines" on a monthly basis. ("Historical Society To Conduct Tour," *San Antonio Express*, Mar. 17, 1929, 15.) A more ambitious effort was that of the Conservation Society in 1929 to raise prize money for its City Plan competition, which sought to create awareness of the need for municipal planning. A police motorcycle escort led a Saturday afternoon procession of 56 cars with 200 persons from the Alamo to an exhibit of Gentilz paintings and on to stops at the Des Mazieres House on South Alamo Street, O. Henry House on South Presa Street, Twohig House on the river, Vance House, Governor's Palace, Chapel of the Miracles and to a basket maker. The tour disbanded after coffee, tamales, chocolate and pan dulce at a cafe on South Santa Rosa Avenue. ("Historic Places To Be On Tour," *San Antonio Express*, Mar. 6, 1929, 10; "Conservation Society Pilgrimage To Historic Landmarks of City Saturday Attracts 200 Persons," *San Antonio Express*, Mar. 17, 1929, 10-A.)

8. "1,000 Persons In Single Day Pay Alamo Visit," *San Antonio Express*, Jan. 24, 1928, 9; "Alamo Visitors 1,400 Each Day," *San Antonio Express*, Aug. 16, 1928, 10; "Tourist Big Benefit To San Antonio," *San Antonio Express*, Aug. 21, 1928, 10-D.

9. "OST Motorcade Delayed By Bad Roads Arrives in City," *San Antonio Express*, Mar. 29, 1929, 11.

10. "O.S.T. Motorcade Arrives Monday," *San Antonio Express*, Oct. 6, 1929, 7-B.

11. Chris Carson and William McDonald, eds., *A Guide To San Antonio Architecture* (San Antonio: San Antonio Chapter, American Institute of Architects, 1986), 50. Jay C. Henry terms the Southwestern Bell Building's design "an extreme case of the use of Spanish Baroque ornament to define a skyscraper." (Henry, *Architecture in Texas 1895–1945*, 182–83.)

12. "Mission Sets Style," *San Antonio Express*, Mar. 21, 1926, 1. Auditorium architects were Atlee B. Ayres, Robert M. Ayres, George Willis and Emmett Jackson.

13. "Public Evinces Spanish Taste," *San Antonio Express*, Dec. 13, 1925, 15-A.

14. "Handy-Andy Store," *San Antonio Express*, Mar. 2, 1927, 5-A; "Spanish Acres," *San Antonio Express*, Mar. 6, 1927, 6-A.

15. "Work Begins on $2,000,000 Hotel," *San Antonio Express*, Oct. 20, 1926, 7.

16. "S.A. To Have Largest Private Home In State," *San Antonio Express*, May 15, 1927, 5-A.

17. "U.S. Army Urged To Adopt Spanish Type Architecture For New Buildings At Post," *San Antonio Express*, Aug. 6, 1926, 6.

18. "Spanish Mission Type To Prevail In Construction," *San Antonio Express*, Apr. 14, 1929, 1-A. Atlee B. Ayres and Robert M. Ayres designed the Atkinson-McNay residence, the Fort Sam Houston project and the headquarters building at Randolph Field, a complex considered "perhaps the greatest single planned ensemble in the Spanish Colonial Revival in Texas." (Henry, *Architecture In Texas 1895–1895*, 192.)

19. "Landmark Rally To Be Saturday," *San Antonio Express*, Sept. 9, 1924, 4; "How Santa Barbara Utilizes Spanish Atmosphere For Profit Told to Conservation Society," *San Antonio Express*, Sept. 14, 1924, 20. The speaker was Gail Harrison of Columbia University, in San Antonio to lecture at a teachers' meeting.

20. "City Again Asked to Buy Palace," *San Antonio Express*, Aug. 3, 1924, 26; City Commissioners Minutes, Aug. 25, 1924, Book F, 238. "Our organization . . . through many trials and much labor have saved it for the people of San Antonio thus far," Miss De Zavala told the *Express*. Mary Walsh, speaking for her father, Governor's Palace owner Frank T. Walsh, did not mention any preservationists' purchase option when she said of a sale, "Unless one individual or private organization takes the matter up without delay, we do not feel that we can wait any longer." ("Mayor Asked For Finances To Forestall Old Palace Sale For Business Building," *San Antonio Express*, Aug. 2, 1924, 16.)

21. "Mayor Asked For Finances To Forestall Old Palace Sale For Business Building," *San Antonio Express*, Aug. 2, 1924, 16; "City Again Asked to Buy Palace," *San Antonio Express*, Aug. 3, 1924, 26. The two other women were Mrs. J.C. Griswold and Laura Maverick (Mrs. Amos) Graves, another first cousin of Rena Maverick Green.

22. "City Again Asked to Buy Palace," *San Antonio Express*, Aug. 3, 1924, 26.

23. Ibid.; "City Asked Again to Purchase Old Spanish Palace," *San Antonio Express*, Nov. 5, 1926, 22; "Paintings To Be Given For Most Tags Sold," *San Antonio Express*, Apr. 5, 1927, 11; "Tags Will Be Sold For Landmarks Body," *San Antonio Express*, Apr. 9, 1927, 7. A Tag Day sought donations to a cause from passersby who, in return,

The Spanish Revival : 139

received donor tags on their lapels acknowledging the support. One downtown Tag Day raised $580 for the Milk and Ice Fund of San Antonio schools, another raised nearly $800 for Mississippi River flood victims.

24. "Mayor Endorses Old Palace Bonds," *San Antonio Express,* Mar. 27, 1928, 10.

25. *San Antonio Express,* Oct. 1, 1926, 1.

26. "Mayor Endorses Old Palace Bonds," *San Antonio Express,* Mar. 27, 1928, 10; "All Proposed Bond Issues Carry Safely," *San Antonio Express,* May 20, 1928, 1.

27. "Old Painting Depicts Dance in Spanish Palace," *San Antonio Express,* Feb. 4, 1929, 4; "Size of Palace Board Criticized," *San Antonio Express,* Feb. 8, 1929, 7; Rowena Green Fenstermaker OHT, Feb. 2, 1984, 33–34.

28. "Society Denied Exclusive Custody of Spanish Palace," *San Antonio Express,* Feb. 6, 1929, 6; "Size of Palace Board Criticized," *San Antonio Express,* Feb. 8, 1929, 7.

29. "Old Governor's Palace Restored," *San Antonio Express,* Jun. 29, 1930, 1-A. Adina De Zavala did not take the perceived affront sitting down. "I think that the mayor has made a mistake," she complained to the press on the eve of the advisory committee's first meeting in February of 1929. She said the two groups had "worked together before the World War, and they started the movement," and while she was glad that the city had bought the palace, she was sorry they were not chosen to manage it. ("Size of Palace Board Criticized," *San Antonio Express,* Feb. 8, 1929, 7.)

30. "Old Palace Plan Pushed," *San Antonio Light,* Jun. 18, 1929, 5-A.

31. Rowena Green Fenstermaker OHT, 34. George Washington Smith had designed the Robert Mavericks' Alamo Heights home at 401 Torcido Drive, later the home of the H.B. Zachrys. Smith, who returned to California, was black, indicating a level of tolerance among local preservationists not shared by all their contemporaries.

32. Harvey Smith, "Architect Who Restored Palace Appeals to San Antonio to Keep Individuality All Its Own," *San Antonio Express,* Mar. 1, 1931, 4-A. That painting is shown on page 33.

33. "Foundation of Wall Long Buried Beneath Earth Found by Architect," *San Antonio Express,* Aug. 18, 1929, 1-A.

34. "Data in Regard to Governor's Palace Here Gathered From Many Widely Scattered Sources," *San Antonio Express,* Jul. 21, 1929, 1-A.

35. "Mayor Vetoes Trip For Palace Data," *San Antonio Express,* Jul. 25, 1929, 15.

36. Smith, "Architect Who Restored Palace Appeals."

37. Ibid.; Mary Green OHT, 23.

38. "Furniture Requested For Spanish Palace," *San Antonio Express,* Oct. 15, 1929, 8. The Conservation Society honored Mrs. McNay and other donors at a Governor's Palace open house in 1944. (Minutes, G-Oct. 26, 1944.).

39. Mary Green and Rowena Green Fenstermaker OHT, 21–22. Mrs. Green's "Diary of Insults" cannot be located by her descendants.

40. Ibid., 21–23, 45.

41. "Book Concession At Palace Okehed," *San Antonio Express,* Mar. 22, 1929, 15; "Mayor to Study Palace Board's Recommendations," *San Antonio Express,* Mar. 30, 1929, 22.

42. "Palace Plan Fee Not Understood, Says Fred Chabot," *San Antonio Express,* Nov. 17, 1929, 10.

43. *San Antonio Evening News,* Nov. 12, 1929.

44. Rena Maverick Green to Lola Maverick Lloyd, Nov. 30, 1929 in Schwimmer-Lloyd Collection, New York Public Library.

45. "Palace History Research Hunt is Independent," *San Antonio Express,* Nov. 26, 1929; Frederick Chabot, *Presidio de Texas at the Place Called San Antonio* (San Antonio: Naylor Printing, 1929), xvii.

46. "Mayor Gets Data On Old Palace," *San Antonio Express,* Dec. 3, 1929, 7.

47. In 1933, Chabot and others chartered the Yanaguana Society, its name derived from the original Indian designation for San Antonio. The society encouraged local historical research and published several authoritative books before dissolving in 1947, four years after Chabot's death at the age of 51. ("Yanaguana Society," *The Handbook of Texas* II, 941; III, 1135.)

48. "Old Governor's Palace Restored for $30,000 To Be Opened July 7," *San Antonio Express,* Jun. 29, 1930, 1-A. Including the purchase price, the total cost to the city was $85,000—approximately $655,000 in 1990 dollars.

49. Minutes, Jan. 12, 1931.

50. Minutes, Feb. 5, Feb. 26, Mar. 7, 1931.

51. Rena Maverick Green to Lola Maverick Lloyd, Jan. 24, 1931 in Schwimmer-Lloyd Collection, New York Public Library.

52. Ibid., Mar. 3, 1931.

53. Ibid., Mar. 9, 1931. José Arpa was on hand to paint the scene and capture "the vivid motion and exotic beauty of this spectacle." (Elizabeth Graham, "A History of the San Antonio Conservation Society," 1953, 8, manuscript in SACS Library.)

54. Minutes, Mar. 7, 1931.

55. Minutes, D-April, 1931; G-Sept. 24, 1931.

56. Minutes, Oct. 29, 1931, 1–2.

57. Rena Maverick Green to Lola Maverick Lloyd, Sept. 24, 1931 in Schwimmer-Lloyd Collection, New York Public Library.

58. Mary Maverick McMillan Fisher, "San Antonio—The Hoover Era" in *Texas Cities and the Great Depression,* Robert C. Cotner, ed. (Austin: The Texas Memorial Museum, 1973), 56–57.

59. Henry J. Graham OHT, Dec. 15, 1983, 70–71.

60. Minutes, Oct. 31, 1935, 2.

61. Ibid., 72.

62. Wanda Graham (Mrs. O'Neil) Ford OHT, Dec. 15, 1983, 74.

63. *Los Pastores* program in Schwimmer-Lloyd Collection, New York Public Library; "Large Crowd Sees *Los Pastores,*" *San Antonio Express,* Dec. 29, 1928, 4. Scripts of *Los Pastores,* also adapted as a Christmas pageant in San Antonio schools, were placed on sale by the Conservation Society in local bookstores. (Minutes, Dec. 19, 1930, 1–2.) That version was arranged by Conservation Society member Esther Perez Carvajal, director of Spanish in city schools and author of *Language, Literature and Life of the Spanish People.* (Minutes, Sept. 25, 1930, 3.)

64. Rev. Carmelo Tranchese, S.J., musical notation by Carmela Montalvo, O.S.B., *Los Pastores,* (San Antonio: n.p., 1949, second printing 1976), 4. Playing the role of Madrina, or godmother, in 1929 was the visiting Emily Edwards, who resigned as Conservation Society president at the end of 1926 and left to study art in Mexico

City. (Program in Schwimmer-Lloyd Collection, New York Public Library; "Conservation Society President Resigns," *San Antonio Express*, Jan. 27, 1927, 6.)

65. "Plaza Chili Stands To Be Illuminated," *San Antonio Express*, Jan. 7, 1928, 6. The contest, chaired by Rena Maverick Green, was won by Sybil Browne. ("Old Type Lanterns To Light Chili Stands," *San Antonio Express*, Mar. 20, 1928, 7.)

66. "Best Chili Stands Will Get Prizes," *San Antonio Express*, Apr. 21, 1928, 8; "Fiesta De Biennial, June 1, 1928," flier in Rena Maverick Green Papers.

67. "Chili Stands to be Removed," *San Antonio Express*, Mar. 5, 1936, 20.

68. Minutes, Dec. 2, 1937; Jan. 13, 1938; Jun. 6, 1939, 2. A temporary reprieve was won for the Texas Centennial in 1936, when the Conservation Society was joined by the Centennial Association's Arts and Atmosphere Committee and by the League of United Latin-American Citizens to gain permission for the chili stands to remain at Haymarket Plaza to create "a typical Mexican atmosphere project of chili stands, arts and crafts shops and a flower mart." ("Chili Stands to be Removed," *San Antonio Express*, Mar. 5, 1936, 20.)

69. Minutes, Mar. 31, 1932, 2. The news came back that the changes had to be made since "certain names with special letters" were needed in the conversion to dial telephones. (Minutes, May 26, 1932.)

70. Minutes, May 25, 1933.

71. Minutes, Jun. 17, 1930, 2; May 9, 1940, 2; Nov. 14, 1940, 2.

72. "Society Asks Street Name Be Unchanged," *San Antonio Express*, Dec. 25, 1929, 6; "Steffler Opposes Losoya St. Change," *San Antonio Express*, Jan. 25, 1930, 22.

73. "Garden St. Now Named St. Mary's," *San Antonio Express*, Mar. 6, 1928, 8.

74. Ibid.; "Street Name Stand Wins Bushick Praise," *San Antonio Express*, Mar. 22, 1928, 9.

75. City Commissioners Minutes, May 12, 1924, Book F, 167. The federation objected to "the theory that property owners on these streets have sole rights in such matters as these."

76. Minutes, Aug. 9, 1924, Aug. 23, 1924.

77. "Old Landmark Being Razed," *San Antonio Express*, Aug. 22, 1926, 12.

78. "Street Extensions Would Cut Two Parks," *San Antonio Express*, Jun. 14, 1925; "Street To Cut Through Plaza," *San Antonio Express*, Jun. 16, 1927, 7. At the time of his death in 1927 at the age of 57, Lambert was praised for "his belief that San Antonio could not have too many parks." During his twelve-year tenure as Commissioner of Parks, Sanitation and Public Property, Lambert improved existing parks and was responsible for creating Brackenridge Park's Japanese Sunken Gardens, Roosevelt Park, Pittman-Sullivan Park and Dignowity Park. ("Body of Commissioner Lambert to Lie in State in Auditorium Two Hours Wednesday Morning," *San Antonio Express*, Dec. 20, 1927, 18.)

79. "Crockett Square Urged as Name For Twin Parks," *San Antonio Express*, Nov. 17, 1929, 3; "Crockett Square To Be Marked," *San Antonio Express*, Nov. 16, 1929, 24.

80. "Street Through Park Advocated," *San Antonio Express*, Feb. 14, 1929, 15. Instead, the city overcame objections of property owners farther north and extended

North Alamo Street diagonally across one commercial block to meet Broadway at Cunningham Avenue.

81. "Street Layout In San Antonio Called Problem," *San Antonio Express*, May 26, 1929, 1-A.

82. "City Plan Expert To Be Employed," *San Antonio Express*, Jul. 19, 1924, 24.

83. Minutes, Nov. 15, 1924. "By adobe buildings," Mrs. Green explained, "the contest committee members mean adobe in the more general sense as it is used in San Antonio. They do not refer to adobe in the strict sense of a sun-baked brick." ("San Antonio Charm Contest to End Soon," *San Antonio Express*, Dec. 1, 1925, 9.) Two $25 prizes were awarded in 1926, one on the topic "What is the Charm of Our Adobe Buildings?" and the other on "What the Alamo and the Missions Mean to San Antonio." (Minutes, Oct. 17, 1925; Jan. 16, 1926.) Members were not above a touch of whimsy in such a sober undertaking. Rena Green thought of an additional prize—a Mexican hairless dog she had been given but didn't want. "We said, 'Mama, you can't do that,'" remembered one of her daughters. "Didn't faze her at all . . . . Well, so came the day, we all wanted to hide. And she gave it. And it was to some Army woman who was simply delighted. Happy as a lark about it." (Mary Green OHT, 70–71.)

84. Minutes, Oct. 17, 1925, 1–2.

85. "City Plan to be Essay Subject," *San Antonio Express*, Dec. 8, 1925, 22.

86. "City Rejects Plan Contest," *San Antonio Express*, Dec. 22, 1925, 11.

87. "San Antonio City Plan," contest rules in Schwimmer-Lloyd Collection, New York Public Library. Names of entrants were in sealed envelopes separate from the entries. Contest Chairman Rena Green took first place overall, Robert Hugman second and Elizabeth Graham third. Mrs. Green, who returned half of her $50 prize to the society's San José granary project, urged, among other things, preservation of characteristic homes, establishment of farmers' markets in each section of the city, preservation of parks and landmarks and a Spanish-style public laundry on the west side. Hugman suggested re-making Alamo Plaza, beautifying the San Antonio River, replacing streetcars with buses, preserving landmarks and having businesses advertise San Antonio on flaps of envelopes they mailed. ("San Antonio Offers to Tourists," *San Antonio Express*, Feb. 2, 1930, 4-A; "Hugman Scheme for Alamo Park Changes Street," *San Antonio Express*, Aug. 16, 1931, 1-A.)

88. The first school of city planning in the United States was not established until 1929. ("Harvard To Have First School Of City Planning In U.S.," *San Antonio Express*, Oct. 21, 1929, 3.)

89. "Mayor Names City Plan Body," *San Antonio Express*, Dec. 7, 1928, 10; "H. Bartholomew Planners' Choice," *San Antonio Express*, Jan. 15, 1929, 24; "City Plan Survey Contract Okehed," *San Antonio Express*, Mar. 22, 1929, 16.

90. "City Heads Praised For River Plans," *San Antonio Express*, Oct. 26, 1929, 24; Rena Green to Lola Lloyd, Oct., 30, 1929, in Schwimmer-Lloyd Collection, New York Public Library. Art had its place in planning too, members believed as they considered sponsoring a committee on civic art "to the end that public buildings in spirit with the city's established charm be recommended, and those out of tune be condemned." (Minutes, Jan. 12, 1931.)

91. Mary Green OHT, 48–49.

92. "Anthony Michael Dignowity," *The Handbook of Texas* I, 502.

93. "City Burns Old Dignowity Home," *San Antonio Express*, Aug. 5, 1927, 8. Wright's cavalier attitude surfaced again in 1938, when the ornate two-story brick Municipal Market House, designed near Milam Park by Alfred Giles in 1899 and topped by an elaborate two-tiered columned cupola, came down to little protest. "It has no historical significance," then-Commissioner Phil Wright declared, "because it was built since I've been working for the city, and I'm still a young man." ("Chili Stands To Be Removed," *San Antonio Express*, Mar. 5, 1936, 20; Minutes, D-Sept. 25, 1941, 2; Jutson, *Alfred Giles*, 124.)

6

Putting San José
Mission Back Together

A mighty roar echoed through the early morning darkness at San José Mission on Friday, March 9, 1928, as the mission church's Spanish Baroque tower split down the middle and half of it crashed to the ground in a heap of broken rock. A new crevice slowly widened as the remaining half leaned away from the west wall of the church. The San José mission church, which a traveler once called San Antonio's "crowning glory," was now merely a jagged shell—minus dome, minus roof, minus much of one wall and, now, minus tower.

Shock waves spread throughout the city with the news. By afternoon a steady stream of cars was arriving. Most spectators "were content to gaze at the ruined pile for a moment and then turn away, sadly shaking their heads."[1]

Unlike the times of the other elements' collapse in the previous century, however, a rescue network was in place. Early on the scene was the Roman Catholic Archbishop of San Antonio, the Most Rev. Arthur Jerome Drossaerts, who ordered the tower rebuilt immediately.[2] And there was the San Antonio Conservation Society, which during its brief four years of existence had been trying several approaches toward putting the entire San José Mission complex back together. The Conservation Society was holding a scheduled meeting that afternoon.

"With the falling of the belfry of San José Mission a crisis faces us," a Conservation Society spokeswoman told the *Express*. "Citizens of San Antonio ought to feel that they should long ago have taken concerted action to save our historic, romantic and artistic monuments . . . . May it spur us on to re-double our efforts . . . ."[3]

Rebuilding the tower of the San José mission church, however, would take eight years. This interval spanned a global economic upheaval, which caused a shift in funding the preservation of the city's historic built environment.

Collapse of the tower of the San José Mission Church in 1928 followed sixty years of disasters in which the church gradually also lost its dome, its roof and much of its north wall. The San Antonio Light *Collection, The Institute of Texan Cultures.*

Final reconstruction of the tower was finished only after an infusion of public funds, which also helped accomplish the long-sought restoration of the San José Mission compound, enlargement of public land around the Alamo, restoration of La Villita and development of the San Antonio River Bend.[4]

These improvements came in a time when not only San Antonio's economic health but its civic pride was low. With the Depression, the building boom ended abruptly, and with the 1930 census San Antonio's coveted crown of Largest City in Texas slipped inexorably away to Dallas, which, in turn, lost it to Houston ten years later. Local newspapers had tried to head it off with a strenuous "Keep San Antonio First" campaign, which took on the trappings of a moral imperative: "The greater number of citizens there are who will think of this city's welfare before their own personal interests," the *Express* intoned, "the faster San Antonio will grow and the more surely will it remain in the first position among Texas cities."[5]

Population estimates at the beginning of 1928 showed San Antonio still ahead, with a lead of one hundred persons over Dallas. Annexation of all adjoining incorporated and unincorporated suburbs was seen as the salvation.[6] That would nearly triple the city's territory, from thirty-six to eighty-one square miles, and, by counting Army families, 75,000 persons could be added to San Antonio's population.[7] As commissioners discussed the shape of the new city limits, in a square since Spanish times, citizens divided into straight-liners, zig-zaggers and "square parallelogrammers," the latter faction favoring a pattern of extension proposed by Commissioner Frank Bushick.[8] San Antonians chuckled when Dallas was unable to annex Highland Park to increase its own population to gain on San Antonio.[9] But San Antonio's efforts at annexing incorporated suburbs were also unsuccessful. Once final 1930 results were in, San Antonio could only count its own suburban population anyway, and ask, lamely, for a recount.[10]

The nearly forty-year funk into which San Antonio development would slip was, however, less a result of losing face to Dallas than a natural outcome of an economic shift which had already occurred, though clouded by bursts of local civic cheerleading. San Antonio's position in the boom years of the late 1920s was never as secure as some boosters would have had it. True, San Antonio's four buildings taller than twenty stories might be within one skyscraper of Houston and twice the number of Dallas or Fort Worth. But among more numerous lesser buildings between fifteen and twenty stories, Dallas had twelve, Fort Worth seven, Houston six, and San Antonio, two. Of buildings from ten to fourteen stories, Dallas had twenty, Houston fifteen, San Antonio eleven and Fort Worth eight.[11] In one significant area, public parks and playgrounds, San Antonio had already fallen hopelessly behind—to thirteenth in acreage per capita in the state. In 1928, Fort Worth had one acre of parkland for every thirty residents. Dallas had one acre for every forty-one residents, Houston one acre for every fifty-six. San Antonio had one acre for every one hundred and eighteen.[12]

One of the few areas the slowdown would benefit was one that would ultimately be responsible for much of the reborn city's economic prosperity: historic preservation. For almost forty years, remaining landmarks were little threatened by street widenings or new construction. The primary threat was simply decay. Thanks to national efforts to cure the Depression, some of that could be remedied with the help of new public funds and federally subsidized workers. Despite its overwhelmingly negative impact, the Great Depression gave San Antonio preservationists some breathing room.

The New Deal's Civic Works Administration came immediately to the rescue of the Conservation Society's project to restore the ancient mission granary at San José, the society's consolation prize to itself after four years of efforts seeking to supervise restoration of the four crumbling missions' churches and chapels and reunite the mission lands had failed.[13] With the Market House effort over, other than making a pass at saving the antebellum Vance House the Conservation Society kept its landmark focus on what physically remained of the city's Spanish missions.[14]

As chairman of the Missions Committee of San Antonio's Daughters of the Republic of Texas before shifting her activities to the Conservation Society, Rena Maverick Green significantly raised the visibility of the cause when the governor and the Texas State Parks Board came to consider San José as a state park.[15] When her friend Congressman John Nance Garner wrote that Congressional support for a National Mission Park was doubtful and that a state park was more attainable, she proposed the four-month-old Conservation Society's second major resolution, which urged just that.[16] As a first step, county officers and state legislators were asked to purchase as future parkland the property around the missions, since "one of their chief attractions is the open natural country surrounding them." As founders of Great Britain's National Trust had long feared of the English countryside, "at any time factories may spread in their neighborhood."[17] The Conservation Society named Mrs. Green chairman of a committee to obtain purchase options on former mission lands.[18]

By August of 1924, the tax assessor's office, at the request of the county judge, prepared maps showing land ownership around the missions. Commissioner Ray Lambert, who had visited the area with the society committee, recommended purchase of at least twenty-five acres around each mission.[19] Next came the report that almost thirteen acres near the aqueduct could be purchased for $4,000.[20]

As San Antonio's architects and builders introducing the Mission Revival and Spanish Colonial Revival styles looked to California for inspiration, so did San Antonio preservationists look to the Landmarks Club of California for guidance on how to save San Antonio's missions. Its founder, the noted Charles F. Lummis, had visited San Antonio's missions long before. Thirty years after his group began saving four California missions, Lummis had many pointers for Rena Maverick Green when she contacted him early in 1924.[21]

"Broadly speaking," Charles Lummis wrote Mrs. Green, "the Catholic Church has no authority to use its own funds for the preservation of deserted temples of worship as historic monuments," unless the mission churches supported active congregations which could support restoration costs. As that had not been the case in California—nor was it in San Antonio—the Landmarks Club leased each of the four missions from the local bishop for ten years at one dollar per year, which gave the group the legal right to make necessary repairs to the mission churches.[22] The landmarks group for its part agreed "to do nothing which will injure the Sacred character of the buildings," and to be guided by authenticity in its work.[23] The Landmarks Club was run by

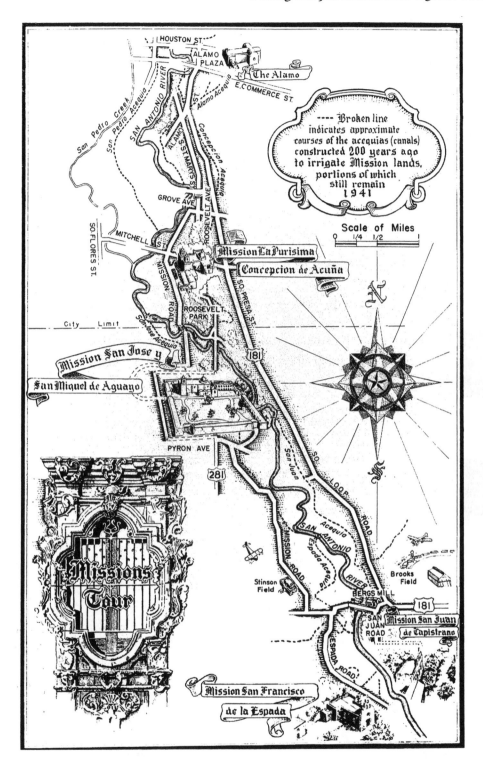

Relative locations of San Antonio's five Spanish missions are shown in this map published in the Conservation Society-sponsored WPA guidebook to San Antonio. San Antonio Conservation Society.

non-Catholics who realized that the history of the missions was based in their use by churches, Lummis explained, and who therefore were pleased that two of the restored missions were being used again as Catholic houses of worship.[24]

For the next four years, the San Antonio Conservation Society sought to duplicate the works of the Landmarks Club of California. Rena Green reported Lummis's approach to Conservation Society members in an artist's terms, remarking that he viewed them "both as examples of art and as historical relics, as the expression of the artist's vision and the embodiment of a great spiritual idea."[25] In January of 1925 she also reported that the Rt. Rev. Arthur Jerome Drossaerts, the Dutch-born Roman Catholic Bishop of San Antonio, had met with her committee and "appeared to consider favorably the plan of leasing the Missions to a chartered organization for a period of years." He wanted to know more about the arrangements between the Landmarks Club of California and the Bishop of Los Angeles.[26]

Mrs. Green quickly wrote Charles Lummis who, in turn, contacted the Rt. Rev. John J. Cantwell, Bishop of Los Angeles and San Diego.[27] Bishop Cantwell sent a letter to Bishop Drossaerts highly praising the work of the Landmarks Club. "The Bishops here were obliged to look after the living stones, and had not much time, and less money, for the rehabilitation of the Missions," Bishop Cantwell wrote his San Antonio colleague. "The arrangement entered into with Mr. Lummis was eminently satisfactory." If a San Antonio group "accomplishes as much for San Antonio Missions as [the Landmarks Club] did for the Spanish landmarks of California, you will have no regrets in giving them your hearty support."[28]

The Conservation Society immediately began work for a state charter which would permit it to hold property, following Lummis's earlier advice.[29] The charter's provisions were to be "best fitted to meet conditions existing in regard to the San Antonio Missions."[30] Within five months the charter was approved by the membership and by the Texas secretary of state.[31] Adoption of a final constitution and by-laws took a little longer, one adjustment being addition of a parliamentarian, a move the secretary wrote was taken "with a little trepidation by our somewhat recklessly unparliamentary organization."[32]

The day after Rena Green and her committee met with Bishop Drossaerts, he expressed to her "fullest and undivided support in your noble efforts."[33] After the matter was considered by the Diocesan Board in June, the aim of the Conservation Society "won the admiration and undivided applause of all those present." Its members' "zeal and enthusiasm" on behalf of preserving the missions was still highly valued. However, "for various and weighty reasons all thought it better not to give any lease to these buildings and properties."[34] Rena Green tried again. Her youngest brother, Lewis Adams Maverick, and two Conservation Society members met that summer with Charles Lummis in California and returned with copies of the Landmark

Society's mission leases.[35] Mrs. Green and her committee took them to Bishop Drossaerts, who advised her to send them to the church's mission committee and to meet with that group.[36]

Finally, in April of 1927, the Conservation Society was reduced to pleading with Bishop Drossaerts by petition. Signatures of nineteen society members included Ethel Drought, who subsidized the Catholic Church's own mission repairs ten years earlier. Even the diocesan attorney, R.J. Boyle, handwrote at the bottom, "I earnestly recommend that you grant this petition. I have examined the California leases and believe that with a few slight changes to meet local conditions they would be satisfactory."[37] But it was to no avail. Collapse of the San José tower eleven months later could only have confirmed preservationists' worst fears.

Rena Maverick Green remained pleasantly persistent, apparently never aware that twenty-five years earlier one of the bishop's predecessors had granted the De Zavala Chapter of the Daughters of the Republic of Texas precisely the sort of lease on San Juan which the Conservation Society was seeking on all four missions. In mid-1928 she was still trying to discuss the previous year's petition with the now-Archbishop Drossaerts, even though when word of the proposal leaked to the press he openly stated that the church would not lease any of its mission property.[38]

But by now it was obvious, after four years of effort and cross-country trips and communiques, that San Antonio's mission churches could not be leased, and that they would not be soon restored by the Catholic Church itself. Amanda Taylor recalled that "on more than one occasion" Archbishop Drossaerts told her that "the church has no funds for preservation or restoration, but only for saving souls."[39] Likewise, despite visits from county and state officials as high as the governor, it was clear that neither county nor state was about to purchase any of the old mission lands for parks, whether they were threatened by development or not. Any measure like California's 1928 state bond issue that appropriated matching funds and established parks at two California missions was simply not going to come up in Texas.[40] If any action was to be taken, members of the San Antonio Conservation Society were going to have to take it themselves. They would begin at San José.

"Our first step was to buy pieces of land—a few feet at a time—surrounding the mission and granary and save the buildings from threatened encroachments of little homes, stores, filling stations . . . and factories," recalled Amanda Taylor. "Our lawyer without fee, Mr. Perry J. Lewis, thought we were just a little crazy to buy the land without being able to get a clear title, but we said, 'If we couldn't get title nobody else could,' and went right ahead. The joke of it was that Mrs. Perry Lewis, our then-president, made him buy the very first piece at $500 for a birthday present for her. And so it went. Elizabeth Graham got one strip of fifty feet by using her charm on the owner,

By 1932 the San José Mission Church's tower was mostly rebuilt, but otherwise the famous landmark remained a roofless shell. The old mission compound likewise was still in disarray, no longer enclosed by walls and criss-crossed by county roads. The roof of the granary at left center had collapsed. A sign of hope was the new friary of the just-returned Franciscans, outside the original mission compound at right center. San Antonio Conservation Society.

and I picked up several pieces from the Mexican owners. And what I couldn't buy, we just fenced, since nobody seemed to own it."[41] By the end of November, 1929, the Conservation Society owned land on three sides of the granary—the county owned the land on the fourth—and had borrowed $2,000 to buy one-third of the granary itself from several joint owners.[42]

To casual observers, the old granary seemed hardly worth the effort. It once formed the northwest corner of the old mission compound across the courtyard from the San José church. Now it stood isolated by a county road and driveways, its walls no longer part of the compound's walls, which were mostly gone. Most of its high barrel vault roof had fallen long before when the north wall collapsed after some buttresses were removed. Trees, grass and cactus grew from its crumbling walls. "It presents the appearance," the *Express* noted in 1929, "of a somewhat disorderly rock pile."[43]

As the Depression tightened its grip on the city, funds to pay the granary property loan became hard to come by. Some money was raised with a "shabby shop sale" in a West Houston Street storefront.[44] Emily Edwards's two-color pictorial San Antonio map project, however, was running a deficit of nearly $300 by mid-1930, with less than 450 sold of the 2,000 printed. Jack Beretta was asked to buy some for souvenirs at the dedication dinner for the Army's Randolph Field northeast of the city.[45] Cost of decorating the society's Battle of Flowers parade float came to only ten of the allotted twenty-five dollars, putting fifteen dollars back in the treasury.[46] A silver tea brought in $131 in June, reducing the $2,000 granary note to $500.[47] One member offered to put the society in charge of sales at her Oriental Specialty Shop for a week.[48] By November of 1930 the note was down to $400, although the treasurer had to report that the entire Conservation Society treasury then totaled fifty-five cents.[49] But by mid-December the granary note was paid off, thanks to $565.92 from a rummage sale run by thirty-two members. President Amanda Taylor's announcement that the society was not only free of debt but also owned $4,500 worth of San José mission property was met with "loud and prolonged cheering."[50]

The remaining two-thirds of the granary was owned by Ignacio Salcedo, no doubt the same Ignacio Salcedo hired twenty-two years earlier by Adina De Zavala to guard, repair and fence the San José church, and four years earlier the seller to the Conservation Society of the last original granary doors.[51] For his part of the granary, recalled Mrs. Taylor, "Old Salcedo said, '$10,000, not a cent less,' which floored us. Can't you just hear our husbands saying, '$10,000 for that old pile of rocks?'"[52] Salcedo's price rose, on occasion, to as high as $25,000.[53] His "false and stubborn ideas as to the value of the land" frustrated the Conservation Society to the point that, finally, "it was decided to let the matter rest for a while."[54]

On March 7, 1931, as twenty-one Conservation Society directors prepared to meet in Amanda Taylor's home, Ignacio Salcedo phoned.[55] "Thanks to Prohibition, our friend Salcedo got arrested for bootlegging and gambling, and had to have $2,500 in three days' time to keep out of jail," said Mrs. Taylor. "If we would give him $2,500 pronto, we could have the granary for $5,000. All excited . . . we took a vote. Of course, we didn't have a cent in the treasury, but we voted unanimously to buy it. There was nothing to do but to borrow the money.

"So Mrs. Rena Green, Mrs. Perry Lewis and I went to the National Bank of Commerce and asked them to lend us $2,500. We would sign the note. They explained to us very gently and politely that husbands had to sign a note with wives. We were terribly crestfallen as we had to confess to our husbands and beg them to sign. They did, under duress, calling us the most impractical women of their acquaintance. But we believed in miracles, and before we had finished with the transaction the president of the bank, Mr. J.K. Beretta, and the chairman of the board, Mr. John Bennett, joined us and our husbands in 'signing a note whose collateral was a pile of rocks.' Needless to say it was a very good note, so acknowledged by the bank."[56]

Adding to the repayment potential was the society's chance to sell a lot outside the mission compound just behind the church. It went for $2,500 cash to the returning Franciscan order, which finished its retreat center and regional headquarters on the site in the fall of 1931.[57] The Franciscans agreed to keep the building and its purpose "strictly within character of the atmosphere of Mission San José."[58] Then the ladies bought another parcel from Louisa Salcedo for $500. The secretary recorded what, to the women, may have been the ultimate compliment: "The entire transaction has been commented on by business men as a very good piece of work."[59]

A gift of $250 bought more land which was for sale directly behind the mission for unpaid county taxes. Yet another cousin of Rena Maverick Green, County Commissioner Albert Maverick, Jr., promised to see about canceling that tax indebtedness altogether, a move accomplished by his younger brother, Maury Maverick, by then the county tax collector.[60] As far as future taxation went, the Conservation Society did not clearly qualify for an exemption on its mission lands. But, the county attorney concluded, the Conservation Society in a public-spirited, unselfish manner was "perpetuating for the benefit of future generations the artistic and architectural beauty of the old Missions and other historic buildings. If government itself has not seen fit to do these acts, it can, and should, further their doing by others to the extent of a tax exemption."[61]

Next, for $1,700 the Conservation Society bought the last privately owned tract adjoining the mission. Its owner agreed to drop his title suit against Ignacio Salcedo over land Salcedo had already sold the society.[62] By August of 1931, the San Antonio Conservation Society's purchases totaled some $15,000.[63] It had accomplished what earlier generations of preservationists could only dream about: ownership of all private land surrounding the San José Mission church.[64]

Paying for it, in a city by then in the depths of the Depression, would require all the wits members could muster. One inspiration was Pig Bank Day. Margaret Lewis happened to have "dozens" of Mexican clay pig banks, which she gave members to take home and fill with pennies.[65] With them went a society poet's seven-stanza "A Pig With a Purpose," including:

But our little pig has a purpose,
A purpose you'll wisely condone:
The mission lands must be paid for,
Those rare mission lands we must own.

So feed 'Piggie' all of your pennies,
That troublesome coin in your purse.

He will gobble them up without blinking,
His diet could really be worse.[66]

One hundred members attended Pig Bank Day, a basket picnic held at the end of June, 1931, at "Willow Way," Elizabeth Graham's self-designed Spanish-style home in a pecan grove between San José Mission and the San Antonio River. Tribute was paid Margaret Lewis, the imaginative president who had donated the banks shortly before her unexpected death the previous fall. At the end of the meeting the Pig Bank Chairman stepped up to the iron pot, which hung from a tripod. There she presided as members with full banks came up to break them and spill the contents into the pot. It was made an annual event, and in 1932 brought in $42.55.[67]

More funds came through direct appeals to the membership. Donations of supplies sent the entire twenty-five dollars budgeted for the society's Battle of Flowers parade float back to the treasury, along with sixty dollars from two first-place prizes.[68] The superintendent of schools permitted junior and senior high school students and teachers to help the society solicit donations at a Tag Day downtown.[69] A Mexican Supper in Brackenridge Park's Sunken Gardens brought in $489, and was a true community event—music was by the Municipal Band, the Army furnished three field kitchens and their three-men staffs, firemen set up the Recreation Department's tables and the Witte Museum staff did posters and table cards. Conservation Society members served the food.[70] The bank loan was whittled to $100 after another rummage sale netted $200.50.[71] The debt was wiped out altogether when a card party at the Governor's Palace in March of 1932 brought in $276.[72]

Concurrently, the Conservation Society was working to upgrade the San José area. In 1931 Missions Chairman Rena Green got the city to put twenty-six copies of oil lamps once used on city plazas on cedar posts beside San José and along the entire road past all four missions.[73] The Southside Improvement League had already enlisted the City Federation of Women's Clubs, Conservation Society and Chamber of Commerce in an effort to rename the three-mile South Loop Road as Mission Road.[74] Two county commissioners promised at a public meeting that planning to widen the road to eighty feet would begin at once, and a city commissioner offered the city's cooperation.[75]

Then the Conservation Society discovered that a new north-south national highway was planned over a newly discovered mission compound wall and across part of the original mission compound. The route was moved.[76] Highway Beautification Chairman Anna Ellis was put in charge of making certain that supervising engineers nearby kept highway construction workers from unnecessarily damaging or destroying native trees and shrubbery.[77] A

The San Antonio Conservation Society's remaining debt on its purchase of the San José granary was paid with proceeds from this card party held in the courtyard of the recently restored Spanish Governor's Palace in March of 1932. A.L. Fenstermaker.

society committee met with county officials to be sure that the $25,000 highway beautification budget was being properly spent.[78]

With the bank loan to purchase the granary paid off, the Conservation Society was ready to think about restoration.[79] How to finance it was another matter. "By then I had followed Mrs. Lewis into the presidency," recalled Amanda Cartwright Taylor, "and after her sad and untimely death we were wondering how we could go on when one Sunday afternoon Jack Beretta and Ward Orsinger called on Mrs. John Bennett and me." They suggested that the "hundreds of men" reduced to chopping weeds for the county to earn food and shelter be used to rebuild the granary. Beretta offered to donate the engineering work and said Harvey Smith would donate his services as architect if the society furnished material. "Again with high hopes and strong faith in miracles, which we have never lost, we voted to 'go ahead,' with $12.50 in the treasury."[80]

Once unemployed workers were hired through the Central Relief Committee and paid by the county, "we began our search for help," the well-connected

Old walls of the Conservation Society's San José granary were removed for rebuilding, revealing a view of the mission church and its mostly rebuilt tower. The San Antonio Light Collection, The Institute of Texan Cultures.

Mrs. Taylor continued. "Miss Ellis wrote such a wonderful letter that money began to roll in. I went to the Public Service Company and they gave us an old truck with a telephone pole strapped on it with a pulley to help lift rocks. Then, not having any gasoline, I phoned Mr. Raymond Russell [and] got a drum of it sent out as a gift. I went to Mr. [San Antonio Portland Cement Company President Charles] Baumberger and asked for some cement. He gave us three hundred sacks, delivered. The fire commissioner, Mr. Phil Wright, gave me ropes to use on our pulleys. He looked as though I was demented when I asked for it, but finally gave in. Then I called the County Judge and asked to borrow his wheelbarrows, spades, hoes, pick-axes, etc. Frost Woodhull was overcome with surprise but said, 'Well, if you will return them.'"[81] A landscape gardener offered his services. Others offered to help translate Spanish or German documents that might need to be deciphered.[82] Noted the secretary: "Mrs. Taylor's list each month of donations and assistance given reads like the Conservation Society had some Aladdin's Lamp to make wishes come true."[83]

Civil Works Administration-paid workers reconstructed the Conservation Society's newly purchased barrel-roofed San José mission granary in 1932–33. The San Antonio Express-News Collection, The Institute of Texan Cultures.

There were other details. Some workers had to be gotten out of jail. A soda stand operator who wouldn't get out of the way had to be evicted by court order. "I think Mrs. Green made her son George do the legal work," said Mrs. Taylor.[84] While President Amanda Taylor gathered supplies, First Vice President and Missions Chairman Rena Green was in charge of overseeing archeology.[85]

President Taylor checked on things every morning, often in the company of Rena Green or Anna Ellis, and found the excavations brought "thrilling discoveries."[86] Footings of the original mission walls were located, a covered ditch was discovered leading out from the mission, a skeleton with a cross was found and numerous relics were sifted from debris.[87] Most surprising was uncovering along the old acequia just outside the mission's north wall of "a vaulted, plastered room with stone steps leading down," which turned out to belong to the original mission mill.[88] A one-acre land swap was arranged to

Onetime Indian barracks along the walls of the San José mission compound are reconstructed by federally funded workers in the mid-1930s. The San Antonio Light Collection, The Institute of Texan Cultures.

bring it within the Conservation Society's property line.[89] With the aid of donations to the Conservation Society from the National Society of the Colonial Dames in the State of Texas, the contribution of reconstructed machinery from Pioneer Flour Mills and the assistance of Pioneer Flour's engineer Ernst Schuchard and of architect Harvey Smith, the mill was rebuilt.[90]

Thrilling though the discoveries were, the scope of her responsibility thoroughly frustrated Mrs. Green. While CWA crews finished the granary, workmen began lesser improvements on the grounds of San José, Espada and San Juan all at the same time. "Nobody could control the work or watch it," her daughters recalled. There was no archeologist or authority available at the University of Texas to assist, she was told, and a plea to the Smithsonian Institution brought the reply that they had no funds to permit one of their archeologists to help.[91] Consequently, there were incidents like the time "the call came that they had found a seven-foot skeleton in an octagonal foundation at San Juan . . . . And we went out, and when we got there the skeleton was in a bushel basket," her daughters remembered, with no photographs taken or drawings made. Too, "Mother insisted that the men sift the soil that they were taking away from the granary . . . . There were shards of china and coins and even Spanish bridle bits . . , . [But] they didn't have enough money to buy cases to put the things in." As a result, many of the artifacts were picked up by tourists. "That just drove Mama crazy."[92]

A week before Thanksgiving, 1933, the granary nearly completed, Conservation Society members gathered for their first meeting inside. "Nothing could have been more thrilling," recorded the secretary, "than to step over the threshold of the granary doorway into that great expanse of walled-in, arch-roofed space and know it was ours—all ours! As we took our places in the old chapel benches, we felt the reverence of the cathedral atmosphere, which was so in keeping with the spirit of dedication which was to follow. The front north window was beautifully and simply dedicated to our beloved past president, the late Mrs. Perry J. Lewis . . . . The original doors, salvaged from a trash heap and bought by the Conservation Society many years ago, were dedicated by Miss Anna Ellis to the memory of Mrs. Essie Crawford Castanola . . . . Ernst Schuchard told how . . . he found the old colors on the interior of the granary, how he had chemically analyzed and then reproduced [them] . . . in redecorating the walls. Maury Maverick told of . . . the necessity for vigilance by people of understanding, . . . that the work be well and correctly done. He said that more funds would be made available through the public works department of the federal government."[93]

When it was finished, Amanda Taylor told Conservation Society members years later, "from a period of 'blood, sweat and tears' we finally emerged into the light of triumphant fulfillment. The stone work was done, with [flagstones for] floors given by Frank Palfrey and decorations by Ernst Schuchard [and] marvelous work by Mr. Harvey Smith, who was cited by the National Society of Architects for one of the finest pieces of restoration in the country. Girls, never say the men were not with us; they were. The Centennial Committee of eleven men and me—the lone woman—allocated $20,000 to complete the restoration of the entire project."[94] On June 14, 1936, the San Antonio Conservation Society held a "Night in Spain," featuring a Mexican supper, to honor officials who had helped complete the work and also to celebrate opening of the newly designated Fiesta Plaza beside the mission church.[95] When Amanda Taylor asked the county judge to say a few words, she recalled, "he arose and said, 'Madam President, where are my tools?' I told him they were 'plumb wore out.'"[96]

Within a few weeks, hard-pressed Bexar County commissioners, who maintained the county-owned plaza around San José, informed the society that they could no longer afford the upkeep. Members volunteered to maintain Fiesta Plaza themselves. Soon the Conservation Society was contracting for weed clearing, and bought a lawnmower.[97]

The prime tenant of Fiesta Plaza—and housed in the granary, no less—was the shop of Mexican Arts and Crafts, an enterprise that could hardly have been more compatible with the artistic and historic instincts of San Antonio Conservation Society members. The company had been founded in the late 1920s by Ethel Wilson (Mrs. Arthur) Harris, daughter of a lumberyard owner who also sold tile. Using the abundant clay deposits south of San Antonio and local artisans for whom pottery was a native craft, Ethel Harris was the major force in making San Antonio the state's center of the Mexican decorative art tile craze which was sweeping the nation.[98] The aim was to "conserve the Mexican art and local color in San Antonio," keeping in San Antonio those artisans "fast leaving for work in the fields and the mills of the north, . . . turning away from the skill and talent inherited through generations past."[99] At her request, in 1931 the Conservation Society endorsed the project.[100] Two years later, Mrs. Harris proposed that her shop, located in the landmark Nat Lewis stone barn near the river on South St. Mary's Street, be moved closer to her San José Potteries kiln near the mission and occupy the restored San José granary, where artisans could ply their native trades and sell the work to tourists.[101] She got a two-year option to lease the granary when mission restoration work was complete.[102] The move was finally approved for August of 1935.[103]

In the first five months of Mexican Arts and Crafts operation in the granary, the society's ten percent commission on gross sales brought $53.40 into the treasury. As Mexican decorative motifs became ever more popular, purchases by increased numbers of tourists arriving in Public Service Company buses helped boost the society's share of sales to more than $200 in August and September of 1936.[104] To add life to the area, rooms in the row of restored Indian apartments were put up for rent to sponsored artists and clubs or organizations, as long as rooms were furnished in the style of the mission period and nothing was sold but paintings or pictures.[105] Eventually, Ethel Harris fixed up an apartment for herself along the north wall of the granary and moved in.[106]

With the granary restored and occupied and the old mission plaza cleared, society members lost little time in moving beyond the practical realities of buying land, raising money, cutting weeds and leasing space. Since the Night in Spain was such a success in June, members planned another fiesta five months later, to be "in the nature of an Indian Festival on the plaza" the Sunday evening before Thanksgiving.[107] This would be a sort of Southwestern answer to the Pilgrim Thanksgiving, a revival, as a newspaper described it, of "the harvest festival custom observed by Indians of this area even before the San Antonio missions were established," when they gorged on pecans in the forests. The Conservation Society had pecan trees on the mission grounds

Once the Conservation Society's granary restoration was completed, the building was leased to society member Ethel Harris for her Mexican Arts and Crafts shop, which featured work of local artisans. Susan Toomey Frost.

threshed, and members gathered in the restored Indian quarters of San José to shell the nuts.[108]

The Indian Harvest Festival was conducted with the society's customary élan. To replicate the missions' farmlike environment, Elizabeth Graham brought ducks, turkeys, chickens and other animals from her nearby home.[109] A pageant, too, was de rigueur. It portrayed the imagined life of Indians at the missions and featured an Indian dance called the Matachin. It was, explained the society's publicity chairman, "originally a heathen dance celebrated by the Aztec Indians, but after the arrival of the Spaniards in Mexico the dance was gradually changed to a religious one" still performed along the Mexican border.[110] The first Indian Harvest Festival in 1936 led to another the next year, with "a massed chorus in costume, Spanish dance numbers, orchestra selections and some of the best vocalists in the city."[111] But a norther blew in with rain, sleet and hail. Temperatures dropped to near freezing, and attendance was light.

In 1938, the event was moved up to mid-October, with more success. Ticket sales alone brought in more than $260. Profits ranged from $17.74

The restored Indian Barracks were put up for lease to artisans whose work was in keeping with the mission environment. Susan Toomey Frost.

from the booth selling member-made candy to lesser amounts from bottled beer, silhouette cutting, gypsy numerology readings, archery, and soft drinks down to 85 cents from the fish supper served by Indian maidens in a canoe.[112] The next year, the chairman of the Teepees Committee thought all Conservation Society members should attend in costume.[113] That festival netted $181.87 after supper was provided to the eighty-one-member cast of the pageant. The pageant was presented just beyond the mission's north wall in the natural sloping area graded the previous year by Works Progress Administration employees, who also built the stage. It was designated the Huisache Bowl.[114]

While the drama of the Spanish missions' restoration was featuring in San Antonio the reconstruction of long-neglected outbuildings, sale of Mexican curios in the restored granary and costumed Harvest Festivals with Indian maidens serving fish suppers from canoes, another and quite different missions scenario was being acted out between church and state in a setting that extended to the halls of government more than a thousand miles away, in Washington, D.C.

Federal Civic Works Administration funds funneled through the Bexar County Board of Welfare and Employment had been paying labor costs for rebuilding San José mission walls and for other mission restoration work, while a Conservation Society committee headed by Mrs. Frost Woodhull, wife of the county judge, furnished supplies and materials.[115] Further clearing of interior debris from the San José church began as Catholics supported the restoration by organizing the Margil Mission Society, headed by Archbishop Drossaerts and named in honor of San José founder Rev. Antonio Margil de Jesús.[116] The newly formed San José parish first held its own bazaar on the mission plaza that summer, and by fall the church was wired for electricity.[117] High Mass was celebrated in the partially completed church the next spring.[118]

But when the Civic Works Administration was replaced by the Works Progress Administration, requirements changed. Neither the Conservation Society nor the church could qualify for federally paid workers. The WPA could conduct restoration programs only on property owned by a political subdivision. Mission work could proceed on land owned by the county, but the only way to continue work on Conservation Society or church property, new Conservation Society President Elizabeth Graham was told, would be if it were leased to the county for ninety-nine years.[119]

However, the Conservation Society had a friend in Washington—its long-time supporter Maury Maverick, who burst onto the national stage as a first-term congressman in January of 1935.[120] Only eleven days after he took office, Maverick asked the National Park Service to get San José Mission into the National Park System. He began lobbying Congressional delegations from New Mexico, Arizona and California to support a study of all southwestern Spanish missions.[121] In March, Congressman Maverick introduced the Historic Sites Act in the House of Representatives, two weeks after it was introduced in the Senate by Virginia Senator Harry F. Byrd. The bill, which President Franklin Roosevelt signed in August, provided for a national survey of historic sites and cooperative public-private agreements for their maintenance. It permitted the secretary of the interior to accept properties as part of a national system of historic sites with approval of an advisory board.[122] Until this time, the United States had been "the only major nation in the western world" without a formal national policy on historic preservation.[123]

Maverick was piqued over the work stoppage at San José, especially since full-blown federally funded reconstruction was going on at the Espíritu Santo Mission in nearby Goliad. But the work in Goliad was directly for the State of Texas, since the Catholic Church long before abandoned the site. At San José, the Park Service could not authorize further spending on buildings owned by the church. Moreover, the National Park Service was becoming more particular in restoration matters. Personnel sent to San Antonio found architect Harvey Smith and his assistants working with the best information and material available to them, but since the Park Service had not been involved initially it would not accept responsibility for work already done without itself doing further careful study.[124]

As the Conservation Society's San José mission work expanded, federally funded workers prepared to rebuild the mission church, seen through its front doorway. The San Antonio Light Collection, The Institute of Texan Cultures.

To help satisfy Maverick and preserve the momentum at San José, planners in Washington drafted a pioneering agreement to permit the state of Texas, the Catholic Church and the National Park Service to play equal roles in mission work while allowing the Catholic Church to keep title to the church. The Park Service would provide Harvey Smith backup in history and archeology. But it would require the San Antonio Conservation Society and Bexar County to transfer their property to the Park Service. It was a chancy proposal, for the Conservation Society had already voted not to release its property to either state or federal authorities.[125]

Underlying all assumptions, sufficient funding for the San José project was expected from the $3 million Congressional appropriation for the upcoming Texas Centennial. Apportionment was to be made by the Texas Centennial Commission. But when the allotment for San José dwindled to $20,000, the National Park Service staff realized that its role could be only minor. Although it acknowledged that San José was of national significance, the Park Service's new advisory board refused to allow the service to be subordinated to supervisors unable to afford required Park Service procedures. By the end of 1935 it was clear that involvement of the National Park Service at the San Antonio missions would have to wait.[126]

The Catholic Church, with a partly restored mission church on its hands, then reversed its position on funding historic preservation. The Church decided that "every soul with a living faith" would "be glad to see this monument to religion restored to some at least of its past glory and dedicated anew to its original sacred purpose, the praise of God and the salvation of souls," and resumed work on its own in October of 1936.[127] The $20,000 from the Texas Centennial helped complete restoration of the church's dome and tower.[128] A new flagstone floor was laid in the San José church, gates of the walnut communion rail were carved and oak pews were installed, "a necessary compromise with the modern age." An old photograph enabled original doors to be duplicated in black walnut by Peter Mansbendel, the Austin woodcarver who had carved the new doors to the Governor's Palace. The mutilated statues on either side of the entrance were left for future repair.

Formal re-dedication of the San José church was scheduled, appropriately, on April 18, 1937, a "Sunday within the Octave of the Solemnity of St. Joseph, Patron of the Universal Church."[129] A procession from the nearby Franciscan friary was followed by a Solemn Pontifical Mass celebrated by Archbishop Drossaerts. The sermon was by the Most Rev. Mariano S. Garriga, Coadjutor to the Bishop of Corpus Christi, until his recent elevation and transfer the Custodian of the Missions and, as a young priest thirteen years earlier, the speaker on the missions' history to the three-month-old San Antonio Conservation Society on its bus tour.[130]

As dedication of the mission took place, a suit filed by the Catholic Church against the Conservation Society and Bexar County was pending in district court. It was "a friendly suit," intended to determine legal title to who owned what around San José.[131] Limits of Bexar County's right-of-way through the mission plaza, for example, were undelineated.[132] Amanda Taylor pleaded with Archbishop Drossaerts to withdraw the suit before it came to trial, "not

By the end of the 1930s, restoration work at San José had returned the mission complex to its original configuration. San Antonio Conservation Society.

in any fear of your recovering any property from us, for we went into that matter pretty thoroughly before we purchased it, . . . but, what is vastly more important, to prevent a fight in the courts which will cause bitter feelings."[133] Mrs. Taylor dismissed rumors that the society claimed the small square in front of the church, and offered to concede the "few inches or feet" that new walls on old foundations may have encroached on church property. Regarding an accusation taken very seriously in those years, she added that "the other gossip, that we are a group of Communists trying to injure the Church or usurp its rights, is too absurd to be even considered, since so many of our members are good Catholics."[134]

The suit was settled at the end of 1937. County and church got an undivided half interest in the plaza through which ran the county's Pyron Road, rerouted around the mission compound six years later. The Conservation Society was to maintain the plaza and be reimbursed by the county.[135] The society retained title to the granary, quarters and land to the north, including the mill and theater. The Catholic Church held title to the church and small plaza and cemetery in front. Also, the Church could use one of the society's restored Indian barracks rooms for five years.[136] A six-foot-high chain-link fence the church then erected along its new property line came down during the war years.[137]

Despite the intense activity at San José, preservationists were not ignoring San Juan and Espada, the smallest missions. Tracts of twelve private property owners around San Juan were mapped, in apparent hopes of a purchase campaign like that around San José.[138] Rena Green warned in 1931 that stones were being hauled away from Espada and, later, that roofs of the Espada and San Juan mission chapels were gone and the walls were crumbling.[139] During Prohibition, federal agents discovered a one hundred-gallon still, quantities of mash and a small amount of whiskey in an old stone house beside the acequia only 350 yards from the Espada mission chapel. The resident of the house swore the still was not his, but he was arrested anyway.[140]

In 1937, retiring Conservation Society President Elizabeth Graham offered the society the six and a half-acre tract near Espada Mission including the aqueduct, a rock house and a well, which she had just purchased for $1,500 with her "burying money." The deal was approved by acclamation, and the Conservation Society became the owner of the only Spanish structure of its type still in use in the United States.[141] The old aqueduct "was leaking badly, and we had to have many repairs made to keep the water from just seeping out of the sides of it," recalled one society member. While nearby farmers depended on it for watering their fields and feeding their animals, they "didn't care very much whether it leaked or not if they just got enough down at their end. But we were afraid it was going to wash out, and so we spent a great deal of time out there trying to keep it bolstered up."[142]

Even with the San José mission complex restored, the idea of some relationship between San José and the National Park Service continued to come up. Early in 1940, San Antonio's Plaza Hotel Manager Jack White, whose wife was a Conservation Society member, got Dallas oilman George C. Gibbons to contact mission custodian-turned-bishop Mariano Garriga in Corpus Christi and put him in touch with the National Park Service. In July, Undersecretary of the Interior Alvin Wirtz chanced to be in Austin, where he met with Aubrey Neasham, the department's regional supervisor of historic sites. Wirtz proposed to Neasham that the State of Texas administer San José mission land not belonging to the Catholic Church. The two found Texas State Parks Board Chairman Frank D. Quinn agreeable. All came to San Antonio to meet with Amanda Taylor, then serving a second term as president of the Conservation Society.[143]

Only four months earlier the Conservation Society had re-affirmed its intent to maintain ownership of its San José property, believing that the society's rights should equal those of the Catholic Church.[144] But Mrs. Taylor thought the new proposal might work. Title of the properties would go to the Texas State Parks Board. The Conservation Society would retain certain rights of use at the granary, and the state would assume Ethel Harris's lease.[145] The National Park Service would have no administration or maintenance costs but would furnish plans, supervision and funds for further restoration, assuring "sound principles of preservation development."[146] The Conservation Society

In mid-1941, the restored Mission San José became a state-operated park and a National Historic Site following consent of its three property owners—the Catholic Church, Bexar County and the San Antonio Conservation Society. Shown presenting the agreement to the Most Rev. Robert E. Lucey for his signature are, from left, standing, Dr. Aubrey Neashan, National Park Service historic section director, and Frank Quinn, director of the Texas State Parks Board. Seated are Bexar County Judge Charles W. Anderson and Conservation Society President Amanda (Mrs. Lane) Taylor. San Antonio Express-News.

considered the proposal at a special general meeting. It was approved unanimously.[147]

With Bexar County's approval under the leadership of County Judge Charles W. Anderson, final execution of documents followed with the signatures of newly installed Archbishop Robert E. Lucey, state officials and Secretary of the Interior Harold Ickes.[148] Formal ceremonies were held at San José on June 1, 1941.[149] It was named a national historic site. The Park Service's Aubrey Neasham told the Conservation Society that the donations of property set a precedent which he hoped would be followed in similar programs planned in St. Augustine, Monterey and Tucson.[150]

Notes

1. "San José Tower Ruined By Sudden Collapse To Be Rebuilt At Once," *San Antonio Express,* Mar. 10, 1928.

2. Ibid.; *San Antonio Express,* Mar. 11, 1928. The engineering firm of L. Diver, which recently built Municipal Auditorium, was put in charge of the engineering work to aid Fred B. Gaenslen, the church's longtime architect in charge of mission repairs, which only two months previously had included the tower itself.

3. "San José Tower Ruined," *San Antonio Express,* Mar. 10, 1928.

4. "U.S. Funds To Give Alamo New Roof," *San Antonio Express,* Sept. 8, 1936.

5. "Keep San Antonio First by Unselfish Citizenship," *San Antonio Express,* Aug. 12, 1928, 1-C. The *Express* thought it the duty of citizens, for example, to render their properties "fully and at fair value" for tax assessments, to sell land wanted by the city for less than market value and even to avoid such corner-cutting as driving through an amber traffic light. A citizen would thereby have a code of conduct in relation to the city "just as he has a code for his business or his luncheon club or his lodge."

6. "Unofficial Figures as of Jan. 1, 1928 Give San Antonio Population Lead of 100;" *San Antonio Express,* Dec. 30, 1927, 3.

7. "Suburb Annexation to Boost Population 75,000," *San Antonio Express,* May 26, 1929, 1-A.

8. "Annexation War Over-Chambers," *San Antonio Express,* Aug. 15, 1929, 28.

9. "Effort To Take In Suburb Is Abandoned," *San Antonio Express,* Dec. 31, 1929, 3.

10. "Enumerators Find 263,613 in San Antonio and Suburbs," *San Antonio Express,* May 22, 1930, 1.

11. "San Antonio Has 17 of 135 Skyscrapers In State Of Texas," *San Antonio Express,* Nov. 10, 1929, 15-C.

12. "San Antonio Is 13th In Parks," *San Antonio Express,* Aug. 20, 1928, 5.

13. Minutes, Mar. 3, 1926. The Conservation Society's first properties were the San José granary's last two original doors, bought off a scrap heap in 1926 for $50. They were stored in the Alamo, awaiting completion of the new city museum.

14. "Conservation Society Would Save Old Vance Residence," *San Antonio Express,* May 2, 1926.

15. Leaders of the DRT Missions Committee were Mrs. Green, Essie Castanola and Anna Ellis, all among the first members of the Conservation Society and at least two of them also having later leadership roles in the DRT. A lengthy list of DRT committees in 1929 no longer included a Missions Committee. ("Mission Parks Idea for Board," *San Antonio Express,* Mar. 19, 1924, 22; "Daughters of Texas Republic to Co-Operate With Catholics in Preserving Old Missions," *San Antonio Express,* Jun. 15, 1924; "Alamo Chapter, D.R.T., Installs Officers," *San Antonio Express,* Mar. 13, 1929, 17.) Joining the three in Conservation Society membership was Ethel Drought, the first major private benefactress of mission restoration, who was named the Conservation Society's historian. (Minutes, Apr. 5, 1924.)

16. Jno. N. Garner to Mrs. Rena Maverick Green, May 31, 1924, in Rena Maverick Green Papers; Minutes, Jul. 5, 1924, 1–2. The idea of a San Antonio missions national park also caught the imaginations of California missions preservationist Charles F. Lummis and the American Scenic and Historic Preservation Society's Reginald Bolton, with whom Mrs. Green continued to keep in touch. (Charles F. Lummis to Rena Maverick Green, Apr. 7, 1924 in Rena Maverick Green Papers; Minutes, Jun. 14, 1924; May 2, 1925.)

17. Minutes, Jul. 5, 1924, 2.

18. Ibid.

19. Minutes, Aug. 2, 1924.

20. Minutes, Sept. 20, 1924.

21. Charles F. Lummis to Rena Maverick Green, Mar. 21, 1924 and Jan. 24, 1925, 2, in Rena Maverick Green Papers.

22. Charles F. Lummis to Rena Maverick Green, March 21, 1924 in Rena Maverick Green Papers.

23. Charles F. Lummis to Rena Maverick Green, Jan. 24, 1925, in Rena Maverick Green Papers.

24. Charles F. Lummis to Rena Maverick Green, March 21, 1924 in Rena Maverick Green Papers. In a year when Alfred E. Smith was denied the Democratic nomination for the Presidency largely because of his Catholic faith, Lummis stressed to Mrs. Green that it was "absolutely vital that you keep the control in the hands of those whose heads and hearts can be trusted to do the right historic things without selfish coloration or aims. And if you should allow religious bigotry to creep in, your whole crusade would be ruined. It makes no odds whether the Old Missions were Catholic or Mohammedan or Christian Science. The only point for decent Americans to count is that they are Landmarks and Monuments, of History and Faith and Romance; and therefore to be saved for a Future so intelligent that there will be no bigots left at all!" (Charles F. Lummis to Rena Maverick Green, Sept. 13, 1924, in Rena Maverick Green Papers.)

25. Minutes, Oct. 4, 1924. At the same meeting Mrs. Green reported she had been in touch with Samuel E. Gideon, who had come from Massachusetts Institute of Technology in 1913 to teach architectural history at the University of Texas, and whose early leadership in historic preservation in Texas would include the presidency of the state chapter of the National Committee on the Preservation of Historic Buildings. ("Samuel Edward Gideon," *The Handbook of Texas* I, 687–88.)

26. Minutes, Jan. 10, 1925.

27. Charles F. Lummis to Rena Maverick Green, Jan. 24, 1925, in Rena Maverick Green Papers.

28. John J. Cantwell to Rt. Rev. A.J. Drossaerts, Jan. 30, 1925 (two letters), copies in Rena Maverick Green Papers.

29. Charles F. Lummis to Rena Maverick Green, Apr. 7, 1924 in Rena Maverick Green Papers; Minutes, Jan. 10, 1925.

30. Minutes, Feb. 7, 1925.

31. Minutes, May 2, 1925. The charter, officially approved on July 8, 1925, was signed by Rena Maverick Green, Anna Ellis, Amanda G. Taylor, Margaret Wilson

Lewis and Emily Edwards. Charter members were Amanda C. Taylor, Anna Ellis, Rena M. Green, Florida Tunstall Sharp, Lucretia Van Horn, Margaret Lewis, Josephine Tobin Rote, Flora Beach Stout, Susan Negley, Mary V. Maverick, Ethel T. Drought, Mary Frances Norton, Esther Perez Carvajal, Emily Edwards, Ella Mauermann, Sallie Ward Beretta, Sadie C. Hinkle, Essie C. Castanola, Jessie D. Oppenheimer, John M. Bennett, Lewis J. Hart, Charlotte N. (Mrs. William) Cassin, Jessie Beeson (Mrs. E.C.) Branch and Mary Vance (Mrs. A.B.) Spencer.

32. Minutes, Oct. 17, 1925. The by-laws, approved in December, preserved the original structure of vice presidents, chairmanship duties now being: first vice president, records; second, programs; third, membership; fourth, press and publicity; fifth, house; sixth, Spanish records. (Minutes, Dec. 5, 1925.)

33. Minutes, May 2, 1925; Arthur J. Drossaerts to Rena Maverick Green, May 7, 1925, in Rena Maverick Green Papers.

34. Arthur J. Drossaerts to Rena Maverick Green, Jun. 12, 1925, copy in Rena Maverick Green Papers.

35. Minutes, Oct. 3, Dec. 5, 1925.

36. Minutes, Nov. 7, 1925.

37. Most Reverend Arthur J. Drossaerts from Rena Maverick Green, Chairman of Committee, et. al., Apr. 30, 1927, copy in Rena Maverick Green Papers.

38. "Church To Hold Mission Sites," *San Antonio Express*, Apr. 5, 1928, 7; Rena Maverick Green to Archbishop Arthur J. Drossaerts, Jul. 3, 1928, copy in Rena Maverick Green Papers. Both Mrs. Green and the archbishop ducked the true nature of the proposal when approached by a reporter, who reported that, according to Mrs. Green, the Conservation Society was "merely seeking to improve the immediate grounds." The story added that the archbishop knew nothing about the society's plans "other than at one time the members considered purchase of private property adjacent to the missions to transform it into gardens," a beautification plan of which he heartily approved. In her latest letter asking for a lease on the mission churches Mrs. Green took an ecumenical tack: "Please remember . . . that our organization which is non-sectarian is an ideal one to undertake this work, for, being composed of members of various faiths, it can best allay the unreasonable prejudices which have followed the war."

39. Mrs. Lane Taylor to Most Rev. A.J. Drossaerts, Feb. 12, 1937, copy in SACS Library.

40. Elizabeth D. Mulloy, *The History of the National Trust For Historic Preservation 1963–1973* (Washington: The Preservation Press, 1976), 7. The California parks were developed in the 1930s at La Purisima and San Juan Bautista missions.

41. Remarks by Mrs. Lane Taylor to San Antonio Conservation Society meeting at San José Granary, Dec. 5, 1955, 1, in SACS Library.

42. Rena Maverick Green to Lola Maverick Lloyd, Nov. 30, 1929, 2, in Schwimmer-Lloyd Collection, New York Public Library; "Granary Built About 1720," *San Antonio Express*, Dec. 8, 1929, 1-A. The deal was put together by Frederick Chabot and a friend.

43. "Granary Built About 1720 To Be Made Into Curio Shop," *San Antonio Express*, Dec. 8, 1929, 1-A; Almaráz, "The San Antonio Missions After Secularization" II, 298.

44. "Old Granary At San José To Be Bought," *San Antonio Express*, Dec. 3, 1929, 22.

45. Minutes, Jun. 17, 1930, 1–2.

46. Minutes, May 22, 1930.

47. Minutes, Jun. 17, 1930, 2.

48. Minutes, Oct. 23, 1930, 3.

49. Minutes, Nov. 20, 1930.

50. Minutes, Dec. 19, 1930.

51. Minutes, Aug. 2, 1924; Rena Maverick Green to Lola Lloyd, Nov. 10, 1930, 5, in Schwimmer-Lloyd Collection, New York Public Library.

52. Remarks by Mrs. Lane Taylor, 1–2.

53. Minutes, Mar. 7, 1931, 2.

54. Minutes, Dec. 19, 1930.

55. Minutes, Mar. 7, 1931, 2.

56. Remarks by Mrs. Lane Taylor, 1–2. Members volunteering to sign the note were Mrs. A.G. Castanola, Mrs. Rena Maverick Green, Mrs. H.D. Thompson and Mrs. Lane Taylor. (Minutes, Mar. 7, Mar. 27, 1931.)

57. "Franciscans Start Work Reconstructing Ancient Site of San José Mission," *San Antonio Express*, Aug. 16, 1931, 1-A. The sale price was $100 less than the Conservation Society paid for the property. The minutes add: "The several tracts of land bought by the Conservation Society and Mrs. Perry J. Lewis to be held for the prevention of filling stations and cold drink stands, etc., seemed to be the ideal land for the Franciscans' purpose." (Minutes, Mar. 7, 1931, 3.)

58. Minutes, Mar. 7, 1931, 3; Aug. 18, 1931; Mrs. Lane Taylor to The Most Rev. A.J. Drossaerts, Feb. 12, 1937, copy in SACS Library. To assure the Conservation Society would be pleased by appearance of the building, dedicated that fall, Franciscans put two society members on the building committee. (Minutes, Mar. 7, 1931, 2; Oct. 15, 1931, 5.)

59. Minutes, Mar. 27, 1931.

60. Minutes, Jun. 23, 1931; Conservation Society to Maury Maverick, July, 1931, partial copy in SACS minute book.

61. Leo C. Huth to Mrs. Lane Taylor citing opinion reported by Arthur V. Wright to County Judge W.A. Wurzbach, quoted in Minutes, Aug. 18, 1931, 1–2.

62. Minutes, Jun. 23, 1931.

63. Mrs. Lane Taylor to The Most Rev. A.J. Drossaerts, Feb. 12, 1937, copy in SACS Library.

64. Minutes, Aug. 18, 1931.

65. Minutes, Oct. 23, 1930, 1–2.

66. Ibid., 4.

67. Minutes, Jun. 27, 1931, 1–2; Feb. 25, 1932, 2; Oct. 27, 1932.

68. Minutes, Mar. 27, 1931, 5.

69. Supt. B.M. Hartley to Mrs. Lane Taylor, Apr. 4, 1931, copy with Minutes, April, 1931.

70. Minutes, Sept. 1, 1931, 1–2; Sept. 24, 1931, 1–2.

71. Minutes, Nov. 24, 1931.

72. Minutes, May 26, 1932, 2.

73. "Mission Road Lighting is Planned," *San Antonio Light,* Jan. 26, 1931.

74. "Mission Drive Improvement Plan Advanced," *San Antonio Express,* Dec. 13, 1929, 3; "Beautification South Loop Aim," *San Antonio Express,* Jan. 7, 1930, 8; "It's Mission Road Now," *San Antonio Express,* Jan. 19, 1930, 1-A; "New Name Asked For Loop Road," *San Antonio Express,* Mar. 18, 1930, 8.

75. "South Loop To Be Renamed Mission Road And Widened," *San Antonio Express,* Jan. 8, 1930, 3. There was "no doubt the county will build the boulevard," said County Commissioner A.G. Trawalter. He explained the route "would have to be rebuilt entirely because the present type of road is what is known as a 'turtle back,' which has a high crown and [is] very dangerous to the present traffic." For beautifying the route Rena Maverick Green volunteered the help of Archbishop Drossaerts, who was "delighted" with the plans when she explained them to him.

76. Minutes, Jan. 27, 1932.

77. Minutes, Oct. 27, 1932, 1, 4.

78. Minutes, Jan. 27, 1934, 2

79. The society borrowed half of the $5,000 from the bank for the cash to pay Ignacio Salcedo, who took the other half in a note from the Conservation Society. Salcedo later sold his $2,500 note for $2,000 in cash to Conservation Society member Mary Jewett (Mrs. E.A.) Wilson. At the start of 1932 its balance was $1,650 and five years later was down to $750, when a dinner the society put on for visiting bankers netted $1,015 and allowed it to be paid off. Mrs. Wilson refused to accept interest. (Minutes, Jan. 28, 1932; Mar. 31, 1932; May 27, 1937.) The granary thus cost approximately $40,000 in 1990 dollars.

80. Remarks by Mrs. Lane Taylor at SACS Meeting at San José Granary, Dec. 5, 1955, 1–3, copy in SACS Library. Fund-raising efforts included a downtown Tag Day during Mrs. Taylor's presidency. ("Funds To Restore Granary Donated," undated clipping in SACS files.) Harvey Smith was well aware of California's head start in restoring its missions, noting that "although they are at distances apart and [there is] only one mission to a city, . . . San Antonio has five missions all her very own more ancient and more beautiful than any in California, San José being the queen of all missions in the United States [and] the finest piece of Spanish colonial architecture existing in the United States today." (Minutes, Jan. 27, 1932.)

81. Remarks by Mrs. Lane Taylor, Dec. 5, 1955.

82. Ibid., 2.

83. Minutes, Jan. 27, 1932, 2.

84. Minutes, Mar. 31, 1932, 2; Remarks by Mrs. Lane Taylor, Dec. 5, 1955.

85. Minutes, Dec. 20, 1932, 2.

86. Remarks by Mrs. Lane Taylor, Dec. 5, 1955.

87. Minutes, Dec. 20, 1932; Rena Green to Lola Lloyd, Feb. 22, 1933, 2, in Schwimmer-Lloyd Collection, New York Public Library.

88. Rena Green to Lola Lloyd, Feb. 22, 1933, 2, in Schwimmer-Lloyd Collection, New York Public Library; "Underground Chamber At Mission San José Found," *San Antonio Light,* Mar. 19, 1933.

89. Minutes, Jan. 30, 1935.

90. Minutes, Oct. 31, 1935; Feb. 27, 1936. In 1935 the local Colonial Dames, headed by Mrs. J.K. Beretta, gave $600—the 1990 equivalent of $5,700—to restore

the mill as their Texas Centennial project, and gave another $300 the next year to finish the building. (Minutes, Nov. 21, 1935; May 14, 1936.) The group earlier contributed $25 for an iron grill for the granary gate. (Minutes, Nov. 22, 1934, 2.) Reconstruction was completed in 1938. ("Long Forgotten Mill Restored," *San Antonio Light*, Mar. 18, 1938, 1-C.)

91. Smithsonian Institution Assistant Secretary A. Wetmore to Rena Maverick Green, Mar. 16, 1934 in Rena Maverick Green Papers; Rowena Green Fenstermaker and Mary Green OHT, 55–56. The Smithsonian held out hope that one of its archeologists might be free after completing a project in Macon, Georgia, but he probably "would not be available without some compensation."

92. Rowena Green Fenstermaker and Mary Green OHT, 55–56. Ernst Schuchard was eventually placed in charge of displaying artifacts, some of them in a showcase later donated to the granary by the Witte Museum. (Minutes, Jan. 27, 1932; Jan. 23, 1934, 2; January, 1936.)

93. Minutes, Nov. 23, 1933. While additional money was certainly welcome, Maury Maverick's rapid-fire manner unsettled many San Antonians, including his cousin Rena Green. She wrote her sister the day of the society's first meeting in the granary: "Maury has jumped in [this] past week and reached out for government money to reconstruct all the missions, and I tremble! (Don't get worried. I'll be barking around, and our architect [is] in charge.)" (Rena Green to Lola Lloyd, Nov. 23, 1933, 2, in Schwimmer-Lloyd Collection, New York Public Library.)

94. Remarks by Mrs. Lane Taylor, Dec. 5, 1955, 1–3. Given the scarcity of local records and the unavailability of outside authorities to help out, some questions were raised about authenticity of the work. A Conservation Society board meeting at the home of Rena Green to discuss "to what extent restoration was being guided and controlled by proper authorities" brought the response from Harvey Smith that "only authentic records were being followed in all work." He said he would meet with members at the mission five days later to discuss it. (Minutes, Apr. 25, 1934.)

95. Minutes, May 14, May 26, 1936. The event also netted the society $167.90 toward restoration work. (Minutes, Aug. 25, 1936.)

96. Remarks by Mrs. Lane Taylor, Dec. 5, 1955.

97. Minutes, Jul. 7, Aug. 25, 1936.

98. Susan Toomey Frost, "San José and Miz Harrie: Texas Tile With a Mission," *Tile Heritage II* (Fall 1995), 19–22. An evidence of the trend was popularity of the brightly colored Fiesta dinnerware, made in Ohio.

99. Minutes, Nov. 11, 1931; Nov. 24, 1931, 1–2. Artisans would include the potter, wood-carver, glass-blower, weaver, silversmith and workers in iron and tulle reed.

100. Minutes, Nov. 24, 1931, 2.

101. Ethel Wilson Harris to Conservation Society, Feb. 8, 1933, copy in SACS minutes; Frost, "San José and Miz Harrie." Mexican Arts and Crafts maintained a separate company identity from San José Potteries, of which Mrs. Harris was also president. Its work is often confused with pottery produced in San José, California.

102. Minutes, Jul. 17, 1934.

103. Minutes, Nov. 22, 1934, 1–2; D-June, 1935; G-Jun. 27, 1935; Jul. 25, 1935. A bathroom was installed and a porch screened.

104. Minutes, G-Jan. 1936; Sept. 24, 1936; Frost, "San José and Miz Harrie." To cover the cost of entertainment when the society's 1939 annual Mission Tour reached San José—tourists were solicited from local hotels and charged $1 for the trip—Ethel Harris got the nationally known Spanish dance team of Carla and Fernando Ramos to perform in exchange for a table on sale in her shop. (Minutes, Mar. 9, 1939; "Society to Buy Mission Aqueduct," *San Antonio Express,* Mar. 12, 1939, 2-A.)

105. Minutes, Dec. 2, 1937, 1–2.

106. Minutes, Apr. 4, 1940, 2; Sept. 26, 1940. Conservation Society members supported a Good Neighbor program to see that medical needs of area residents were tended to and urged the county and the WPA establish a neighborhood playground, completed as a recreation center by mid-1940. (Minutes, May 27, 1937, 2; Mar. 5, 1940, 2; May 30, 1940, 4.)

107. Minutes, Sept. 24, 1936, 2; Oct. 14, 1936.

108. "Mission to Hold Ancient Fiesta," unattributed 1937 newspaper clipping in SACS Library.

109. Glory Felder OHT, Oct. 15, 1992, 5.

110. "Indian Dance Part of Mission Pageant," unattributed 1936 newspaper clipping in SACS Library. Among the dozen or more characters were Malinche, the Indian wife of Hernando Cortez, leader of the Conquistadors; Cortez; and Montezuma, last of the Aztec rulers.

111. Minutes, Nov. 23, 1937.

112. Minutes, Oct. 28, 1938, 1–2. Chairman of the early festivals was Mrs. Edward Leighton.

113. Minutes, Sept. 28, 1939, 2.

114. Minutes, Mar. 16, 1938; Oct. 28, 1938; Oct. 26, 1939, 2.

115. "Board Endorses Mission Program," *San Antonio Express,* Nov. 9, 1933; Minutes, May 31, 1934. The county used its permanent improvement fund to move houses off the mission plaza and to build replacement roads—other than the main road beside the church—around the mission. Property for the roads was donated by the Conservation Society. ("Dream For San José Coming True," *San Antonio Light,* Mar. 25, 1934; Rena Maverick Green to Most Rev. A.J. Drossaerts, Feb. 25, 1938, copy in SACS Library.) There was some competition for services of the federally paid workers. Complaints to Conservation Society President Rena Green that workers spent too much time on the granary rather than on the San José church led society directors to release workers to the church. Eight months later, unable to give Ethel Harris's shop promised possession of the granary and thus begin receiving rent for the space, directors moved the federally paid workers back to complete the granary, thus costing the society only $150 for supplies instead of some $2,000 for both supplies and labor. ("Board Endorses Mission Program," *San Antonio Express,* Nov. 9, 1933; Minutes, May 9, 1934; Nov. 22, 1934, 1–2.)

116. "Mission San José Chronicle," Nov. 26, 1933, 86–87 in Almaráz, "The San Antonio Missions After Secularization" II, 299. Initial funds for supplies were donated by Ethel Drought.

117. "Mission San José Chronicle," Oct. 1, 1934, 112 in Almaráz, "The San Antonio Missions After Secularization" II, 301.

118. Ibid., 117.

119. Elizabeth O. Graham to E.A. Baugh, Aug. 5, 1935; E.A. Baugh to Elizabeth O. Graham, Aug. 15, 1935. Copies in SACS Library.

120. "Few freshman members of Congress have equaled his performance," noted Maverick's biographer. "His unmatched candor and audacity, even when dealing with the president, became the talk of Washington . . . . In a matter of months the name and appearance of Maury Maverick was known throughout the United States . . . . In his first year, Maverick was the primary subject of sixteen items in the *New York Times* as compared with nine items concerning the majority leader, William B. Bankhead." (Richard B. Henderson, *Maury Maverick: A Political Biography* (Austin & London: University of Texas Press, 1970), 74–75.)

121. Hosmer, *Preservation Comes of Age,* 281, 688.

122. Ibid., 572–75.

123. Mulloy, *The History of the National Trust for Historic Preservation 1963–1973,* 8. The bill passed with the enthusiastic support of Secretary of the Interior Harold Ickes, who noted, "In the past few years the American people have displayed a sharply increased awareness of its historic past. This growing interest and pride in both local and national history is a healthy and encouraging phenomenon which is reflected in the ever-increasing number of bills being introduced in both Houses of Congress, providing for the marketing, preservation or restoration of historic sites or structures throughout the country. More than sixty such bills have been introduced during the present session." (Hosmer, *Preservation Comes of Age,* 573.)

124. Hosmer, *Preservation Comes of Age,* 689–93.

125. Ibid; Minutes, Nov. 21, 1935.

126. Hosmer, *Preservation Comes of Age,* 287, 689–93.

127. "The Restored San José Mission Church Re-Dedicated," Apr. 18, 1937 program in SACS Library; "San José Doors Restored From Old Photograph," *San Antonio Express,* Jul. 11, 1937, 1-A.

128. "U.S. Funds To Give Alamo New Roof," *San Antonio Express,* Sept. 8, 1936.

129. "The Restored San José Mission Church Re-Dedicated." An earlier re-dedication was held on April 18, 1934, and priests began celebrating Mass once again in the church building. (Almaráz, "The San Antonio Missions After Secularization" II, 306–07.)

130. Ibid.

131. "Title to San José Plaza is Settled," *San Antonio Express,* Nov. 9, 1937, 16.

132. The county already had 2.88 acres beyond the San José acequia from an equal land swap for a road around the mission. (Minutes, Mar. 27, 1935.)

133. Taylor to Drossaerts, 2. Some members also wondered why the church waited to file the suit until after the defendants had paid for so much of the work. (Rena Green to Lola Lloyd, Jan. 16, 1937, 3–4 in Schwimmer-Lloyd Collection, New York Public Library.)

134. Taylor to Drossaerts, 2. When Mayor Maury Maverick cited freedom of speech as his reason for granting a permit for 100 Communists to gather in Municipal Auditorium in 1939, the meeting was broken up by a rioting crowd of 5,000. Maverick received editorial support from newspapers throughout the country, but locally the permit was condemned by groups from the American Legion to the Catholic Church, with Archbishop Drossaerts himself leading the criticism. (Henderson,

Maury Maverick, 214–17.) Times change. The local Communist Party leader granted the permit that sparked the riot—Emma Tenayuca—was honored by having a San Antonio River barge named in her honor in 1995 for her work in local labor organizations. (Becky Schmidt, "The Right to Boat," *San Antonio Express-News*, Sept. 11, 1995, 6-C.)

135. The county, however, was slow in paying the plaza's $250 annual maintenance cost. Finally the caretaker's plaza work was eliminated and his salary cut to cover granary upkeep only, and Amanda Taylor went before Commissioner's Court to appeal for the arrears and for future payments. (Minutes, Aug. 17, 1939.)

136. "Title to San José Plaza is Settled," *San Antonio Express,* Nov. 9, 1937, 16; Minutes, Jan. 27, 1938; Mar. 2, 1939. Judge Sidney J. Brooks and E.P. Arneson, who represented the Conservation Society, were made honorary members by a grateful society at the conclusion. (Minutes, May 13, Sept. 23, 1937.)

137. The fence went up despite complaints and suggested substitution of a low rock wall. ("Mission San José House Chronicle," Jan. 18 and Feb. 28, 1938, 158–59 in Almaráz, "The San Antonio Missions After Secularization" II, 309; "Fence Causes New Dispute," *San Antonio Light*, Mar. 20, 1938, 2.) The Conservation Society complained it would "detract immensely" from its granary property and from mission surroundings, and would block passage of tourists between the church and the granary's Mexican Arts and Crafts shop. (Rena Maverick Green to Most Rev. A.J. Drossaerts, Feb. 25, 1938, copy in Rena Maverick Green Papers.) Two years later, the church tentatively agreed to allow visitors to pass through a gate into the granary property, but not to enter church premises from the granary. Mrs. Harris was to collect admission fees of ten cents per adult and five cents per child, returning twenty percent of the fees to the church caretaker, holder of the only key to the gate. (Agreement signed by Rev. Alois J. Morkovsky and Ethel W. Harris, Apr. 26, 1940, copy in SACS Library.)

138. "San Juan," undated hand-drawn map in Rena Maverick Green Papers.

139. Minutes, Mar. 4, 1941, 2.

140. "Distillery Found In Historic House Near Old Mission," *San Antonio Express,* Aug. 22, 1928, 11; Minutes, Feb. 26, 1931. Mrs. Green had just been placed in charge of saving the Espada aqueduct.

141. Minutes, May 27, 1937, 2. The paperwork was drawn up in October of 1937. Within three years $400 was paid on the note. In 1941 the society was ready to spend $180 on a bargain purchase of an additional two and a half acres across the road. (Minutes, Oct. 28, 1937; May 30, 1940; Jan. 9, 1941, 2; Jan. 23, 1941, 2.)

142. Virginia Tapp OHT, May, 1987, 7.

143. Hosmer, *Preservation Comes of Age,* 287.

144. Minutes, Mar. 5, 1940, 2.

145. Ibid., 287–88.

146. John White to Arno B. Cammerer, Jul. 30, 1940, in Hosmer, *Preservation Comes of Age,* 287.

147. Minutes, Nov. 14, 1940, 2.

148. Minutes, Dec. 19, 1940.

149. "San José Mission Due Designation," *San Antonio Express,* Apr. 5, 1941.

150. Minutes, Feb. 7, 1941, 1–2; "Society Hears Speaker on Missions," *San Antonio Express,* Mar. 2, 1941. It was widely stated at the time that San José was the first Spanish mission to be named a national historic site, which may be true. Thirty-three years earlier, however, in 1908, ruins of the Spanish mission founded in 1691 at Tumacacori, 45 miles south of Tucson, Arizona, were named a National Monument. Tumacacori got an adobe visitor's center and museum four years before San José received its lesser designation and is now also operated as a national historical park. (Judith Anderson, "Markers of Arizona History," *The New York Times,* Jan. 21, 1996, xx–9.)

7

Showdowns
on the River

The San Antonio River along its original course took thirteen miles to find its way through a city a crow could fly in six. Rather than providing rushing water to power the large mills which turned other river cities into industrial giants, the meandering San Antonio River's more languid flow through a gentle South Texas valley could mainly support life in the homes and missions near its banks. The "beautiful stream is so crooked it almost crosses itself," one writer observed, "and is a constant puzzle to tourists and strangers in the city who meet it every few blocks."[1] Within the city it was spanned in the 1920s by no fewer than thirty-two bridges.[2]

Both the river and the city happened to be having one of their periodic bursts of energy at the same time in the spring of 1921, when San Antonio's fast-growing downtown was inundated by floodwaters as high as twelve feet that caused fifty casualties. Debris piling up at the numerous bends impeded the flow and made flooding worse. This sort of thing had happened before, most seriously in 1819, when floodwaters reached Military Plaza. A 1920 study for the city by the Boston engineering firm of Metcalf and Eddy predicted it would occur again. By the 1920s, developers had an eye on the efficiencies of a straight line, not just to get floodwaters through downtown more quickly and safely but also to free choice land from the occupation of crooked bends. The straightened course of a convoluted double bend downtown provided the site of Municipal Auditorium.[3] To control future flooding on the San Antonio River and on San Pedro and Alazan creeks, voters in 1924 passed a $2.8 million bond issue to build a new dam and straighten the streams.[4]

Beautification was not the issue, nor was it a new topic. In 1912 the city had appointed a committee of architects to study improvements along a southern section of the River Bend near South St. Mary's Street.[5] Five years later, part of City Commissioner Ray Lambert's beautification plan was carried

The San Antonio River flowed slowly through downtown in this view from the St. Mary's Street bridge of a segment of the River Bend about 1900. San Antonio Conservation Society.

out by stringing lights in trees along the banks, although the 1921 flood swept the lights away.[6] Later, riverbank property owners proposed an ornamental fountain in the River Bend between St. Mary's and Navarro streets, where it could be seen from Crockett Street. It would consist of a submerged center ring and four outer rings, each two feet in diameter, with jets shooting water twenty-five feet into the air. Beneath each ring would be six searchlights, each of a different color, for a total of thirty automatic or manually controlled lights which could display any combination of colors. "The beauty of this fountain cannot be described in words," thought one businessman. Mayor Tobin was so enthusiastic over the idea that he wanted the city to place five more fountains so "one could be visible from every bridge spanning the river on principal streets."[7]

But it was natural beauty rather than contrived attempts to be beautiful which concerned members of the San Antonio Conservation Society. Rather than basing their case on aesthetics alone, they wanted to present a practical reason to preserve the river's natural banks and trees. As with the puppet show which dramatized conflicts involving the overall charm of the city, members opted against pleading letters or entreaties across a conference table. Their message would be delivered personally, as with the puppet show, in an unconventional way—on a tour by rowboat.

The society's Chairman of Natural Beauty was Margaret Lewis, who also happened to be president of the Battle of Flowers Association which sponsored the Fiesta parade each spring. Why not hold the next parade in boats on a still-beautiful San Antonio River? "There would be ample room along the river banks for spectators," Mrs. Lewis reasoned, and "the numerous bridges under which the pageant would pass could afford a very choice view of the parade. It is not only something different from the . . . commonplace procession through the streets, but we can boast of being the only city in the country introducing an innovation of this kind."[8]

So it was that on Wednesday morning, November 12, 1924, four rowboats were put in the water just north of downtown. Oarsmen provided by the city waited in the middle seats. Boarding the first boat for a two-hour trip to the Market Street bridge were Conservation Society President Emily Edwards and Col. S.E. Crecelius, the city's newly chosen flood control engineer. In the next were Margaret Lewis and City Commissioner Ray Lambert, the society's honorary president for the past five months. Amanda Taylor followed with member husband Col. R.O. Van Horn, apparently substituting for a city commissioner. Into the last boat went Mayor John W. Tobin with Lucretia Van Horn, perhaps picked to ride with the mayor because she was "very attractive and very enthusiastic."[9]

"People were on every bridge to cheer us," remembered Emily Edwards. "As we came down, everything looked so lovely." As the flotilla approached a large cottonwood tree near the Houston Street bridge, Col. Crecelius declared to Emily Edwards that anything blocking the river channel would be taken out. Recalled Emily Edwards, "That [tree] was so near it . . . I said, 'Would that have to go?' And he said, 'Oh, yes, that would have to go.' And so I turned to Mrs. Lewis [in the next boat] and I said, 'Mrs. Lewis, that has to go.' And Mrs. Lewis said—she was very excitable—'That does NOT have to go!' And [her] boat began to rock!" Mrs. Lewis's fellow passenger, Ray Lambert, was "a great big man." No doubt clutching the sides of his rocking

Mayor John W. Tobin and Conservation Society member Lucretia Van Horn share one of the four rowboats on a tour to show city officials practical reasons to save the river's natural beauty during the upcoming flood control program.
San Antonio Express-News.

boat, he quickly replied, "No, no, no!" The tree did not go.[10] Emily Edwards said that saving that cottonwood tree was the first victory of the San Antonio Conservation Society.[11]

Six months after the boat trip, the Conservation Society recommended to the mayor that a committee of architects be appointed to assure that all new bridges would be designed "with a view to their beauty as well as usefulness."[12] By January of 1926 work on Olmos Dam was well under way, and flood prevention planning was ready to begin downstream. The first work began that month with excavation south of the city to drain a 2,400-foot river bend and replace it with a cutoff channel of 545 feet.[13] Two other major southern bends were designated for elimination. One of them, a 1,200-foot bend to be replaced with a 300-foot channel near the U.S. Arsenal, required destruction of the mill built by Carl Guenther in 1859, the predecessor of Pioneer Flour Mills. Several small bends north of downtown would disappear as well.[14]

The obstacle for floodwaters most dangerous to property and life was, however, an almost perfectly shaped sideways horseshoe bend which curved 2,640 feet through downtown until it resumed a southerly course. An overflow channel cut from one end of the horseshoe to the other could be only 650 feet in length, shortening the course of floodwaters by nearly half a mile.[15] Gates to the new channel were to remain closed under normal conditions.[16] Unlike the bends in uncongested areas north and south of downtown, the downtown River Bend was not intended to be filled in but to carry the normal flow of the river.[17] The Conservation Society's Natural Beauty Chairman, Margaret Lewis, and her committee enlisted the aid of property owners in convincing the city to build the overflow channel underground.[18]

The overflow channel offered some intriguing opportunities for recouping costs of the project. The city came up with a plan to build the fifty-foot wide channel with concrete walls with foundations capable of supporting eight-story buildings, then to cover the overflow channel with concrete and rent the frontages on Commerce, Market and Dolorosa streets to developers. But commissioners decided instead to pave over the cutoff channel to create a new street between Commerce and Dolorosa streets, only to reverse themselves five months later. The new street, they decided, would be too close to existing streets, while rent for the new building spaces could generate up to $200,000, which could be used for flood work downstream.[19]

With the Market House already removed in the widening of Market Street, the only major downtown landmark in the way of the overflow channel project was the two-story French Building, built in 1855, which faced the southeast corner of Main Plaza. Rocks from its walls were used to build walls of the river channel from Travis Street north to Municipal Auditorium.[20] A new health department and police headquarters was built on the front portion of the French Building site.[21]

Meanwhile, the city also went forward with plans to beautify the river. In addition to backing a network of ornamental fountains along the northern section of the River Bend, Mayor Tobin in mid-1926 announced that beautification would include the immediate stringing of lights for more than a half-mile along the main course of the river from Travis Street to Commerce Street. Four owners of a property fronting on 125 feet of Houston Street beginning at the west bank of the river donated two feet of their property to

Position of the north-south cutoff channel to carry floodwaters past the downtown River Bend is shown in this map on the cover of Robert H.H. Hugman's river plan for the Shops of Aragon and Romula in 1929. The east-west street north of Houston Street below the map's title is Travis Street. San Antonio Conservation Society.

the city to permit widening of the sidewalk to improve visibility of the river. They also planned to eliminate a gallery which protruded over the river's west bank. Soon city officials and a four-man citizens' committee studied plans for the illumination, and the Public Service Company organized a lighting demonstration.[22] It was so successful that multicolored lights were strung across the river from Martin Street on the northern edge of downtown south to the bend and around half of the bend, to Market Street, in time for Fiesta in 1927.[23]

"The river is one of San Antonio's real assets, and we are to develop plans that will make it a thing of real beauty and something visitors will remember and comment on long after they leave the city," Mayor Tobin said.

By mid-1927, clubwomen of San Antonio were mobilizing for an epic event—the General Federation of Women's Clubs' biennial convention, expected to bring more than 5,000 delegates for ten days of meetings and social activities the following May. The event was too large even for the new convention facilities in Municipal Auditorium and would spill into nearby churches. As the city's hotel rooms would be overwhelmed, room for visiting delegates had to be found in local members' homes. The San Antonio Federation of Women's Clubs, under the chairmanship of Ethel Drought, raised $25,000 from clubwomen throughout the state to cover costs. It also organized forty-nine committees to make arrangements and to make the city as beautiful as possible.[24]

The San Antonio Conservation Society was assigned to prepare a Mexican Market in Haymarket Square and to plan tours to the Spanish missions and Espada Aqueduct. The Old Spanish Trail Association, designated to oversee beautification of the river, planted shrubbery and flowers along the riverbank, asked adjacent property owners to clean things up and got the city to promise to build a flagstone walk along one side of the river between Commerce and Houston streets.[25]

Backing up the Old Spanish Trail Association's committee was the Conservation Society's own river lighting committee, chaired by Amanda Taylor, which had enlisted the aid of sculptor and honorary Conservation Society member Gutzon Borglum on the ornamental lighting of the river.[26] After the Public Service Company's trial of new lighting on a segment of the northern leg of the River Bend, the city decided to replace strings of ornamental lights with permanent reflective floodlights on fixed posts, a system which city officials thought "will throw light onto the water and illuminate the flower beds on the banks . . . [and] be much more artistic."[27] The lights would also require "cleaning out of all the trash in the river," noted City Commissioner Phil Wright. "The huge lights shining on the river make the trash stand out."[28] Completion of the project, which might also include lights beneath all

While construction of a flood-control cutoff channel was under way to relieve the danger of flooding from the San Antonio River, the River Bend was the subject of many proposals, from constructing an elaborate system of mid-river fountains to filling it in for development. Prior to the flood, City Park Commissioner Ray Lambert beautified the river at night by stringing lights, shown above about 1917. The San Antonio Express-News *Collection, The Institute of Texan Cultures.*

downtown bridges, was promised before the Federation of Women's Clubs convention opened.[29]

As city hall and women's groups planned beautification of the downtown river and its bend, a group of businessmen became uneasy over the planned fifty-foot width of the cutoff channel and urged it be widened to seventy feet.[30] The ailing Mayor Tobin opposed the widening on the grounds that it would require another bond issue and that Col. Crecelius, the project engineer, had found that twin conduits beneath the covered cutoff channel would be quite sufficient to handle floodwaters.[31] But the businessmen feared that a covered channel might block debris during a flood.[32] After Mayor Tobin's death, his successor, C.M. Chambers, agreed that an outside expert could be brought for a second opinion, although excavation for a fifty-foot channel had already begun.[33] Two engineers from Dallas detected a miscalculation in flood velocity by Col. Crecelius. Commissioners unanimously voted for an expanded, uncovered seventy-foot channel, and planned a new bond election.[34]

Now the overflow channel became as wide as the River Bend itself. This meant that it could also handle the normal flow of water previously intended to continue around the bend. The city obtained an estimate that the River Bend encompassed 294,000 square feet of land. All could be reclaimed for development if the entire river flow went through the widened cutoff channel and the bend was drained and filled. Estimated value of the reclaimed land ranged from $2 million to more than $14 million.[35]

One week after the wider, uncovered channel was approved, "rumors of a well-defined movement headed by at least three real estate promoters" to drain and fill the River Bend swept the city. "Alarm has become so wide-spread," reported the *Express*, "that a well-defined counter-movement to the plans to reclaim the river bed was being organized, particularly among women's clubs of the city."[36]

Politicians scrambled for cover. City commissioners came out "unequivo-cally in opposition" to any such scheme. Mayor Chambers declared that he was "absolutely against abandoning the river," which he termed "one of the biggest assets of this city." He promised that the River Bend would never be filled as long as he was mayor. Commissioner Frank Bushick said that the matter had never been presented to him and he had not been called upon to vote on it, but if he had he "would never vote for it under any circumstances." Commissioner Phil Wright assured constituents that "there is nothing to any rumor that we are considering its abandonment." He and Commissioner Paul Steffler warned that filling in the bend would require all storm sewers emptying into the River Bend to be realigned to empty into the new cutoff channel, a project which would require "the whole downtown section to be torn up" and would "cost a fortune, almost as much as the reclaimed land would be worth."[37] The idea was dropped, and work went forward on a channel for overflow purposes only.[38]

A year later, downtown developers modified their approach.

Had the River Bend been filled, new streets could have opened new properties to development. One logical move would have been to extend Losoya Street, which at that time did not cross Commerce Street, on south over the filled-in vertical leg of the River Bend. Early in 1929 the East Side Improvement League proposed just such a move, in what must have been a fall-back plan: since the bend's vertical leg was to remain, they wished to simply cantilever Losoya Street above the river's course until land was reached, then connect Losoya with Villita Street. Even though the businessmen had to give up their plan to fill the River Bend, development would thus still have an easy path to expand into the rundown district of La Villita.

San Antonio city commissioners thought that was a wonderful idea. The river, after all, would not be completely covered over, for the new, cantilevered street would be only forty-five feet wide. The river channel was seventy feet wide, which they recognized would leave twenty-five feet of riverbed still visible from above. Commissioners appropriated $100,000 for the "improvement."[39] While city engineers prepared surveys for the new street, real estate agent Ernest J. Altgelt, Jr. went about paying $11,000 for purchase options on property along the new route.[40]

Two weeks later, city commissioners did an about-face. Mayor C.M. Chambers declared that his administration would "not tolerate any such plans." What he meant was that city hall could not take the heat. Two commissioners acknowledged that the project had unleashed "a storm of protests from all sections of the city."[41] The mayor was also besieged with requests for ninety-nine year permits to obstruct the river with other projections and balconies, even though the city had just spent several thousand dollars in settling private land claims to clear city title to riverbed property.[42] Moreover, flood prevention engineers warned that, cutoff channel aside, the cantilevered street could still become a blockage for debris in flood times.[43]

Businessmen were most displeased with the turn of events. Ernest Altgelt complained about losing the money he had paid for property options. The street would not have had to go over much of the river at all, he said, except for the stubbornness of the City Water Board in refusing to part with some of its property along the river south of Market Street. Altgelt claimed that strip did not even belong to the Water Board. The Water Board had merely filled in part of the river bed and claimed it as its own property although it really still belonged to the city, he said.[44] But when an East Side Improvement League committee appeared before city commissioners, its members were stopped before they could present their arguments. Mayor Chambers told committee members he wanted to be frank with them. The city was "spending nearly $1 million to retain the charm of the river," he said, "and to ask them to spend money to destroy it was ridiculous."[45] The San Antonio Conservation Society must have been behind much of the protest, for the next day Conservation Society President Margaret Lewis and River Committee Chairman Amanda Taylor paid a visit to city officials "to congratulate them on their stand in the matter."[46]

That fall, a group of two dozen firms and individuals got Losoya Street extended to the southeast, rather than to the southwest. Taking the $100,000 appropriation still offered by the city, the group contributed a like amount to complete the purchase of the block across Commerce Street from the Dullnig Building and donate a thirty-foot right of way diagonally southeast through the block to extend Losoya to meet South Alamo at its intersection with Market Street.[47]

Also in the fall of 1929, construction work on the flood prevention project got under way after the year's hiatus which followed the resignation of the city's project engineer, Col. Crecelius, and his replacement with engineers from Dallas. Since the construction of Olmos Dam and subsequent work downstream, the $8.9 million raised in three bond issues since 1924 had dwindled to $150,000. City commissioners were in no mood to spend more money than they had to, yet controversy had erupted on four fronts: on the river channel south from the cutoff channel; on the channel north from the cutoff channel; on the cutoff channel itself; and on the River Bend, saved but with its beautification still undecided.[48]

The southern channel from Nueva Street south to Guenther Street was to be completed first so it would be large enough to hold floodwaters once upstream channels were improved. The issue in this section was whether to accept bids for the 120-foot deep concrete channel pushed by Hawley and Freese, the Dallas engineers, instead of digging a 150-foot earthen channel. Mayor Chambers believed the earthen channel would be more attractive and less expensive. Bids for the concrete channel were returned to the bidders and Hawley and Freese were fired. City commissioners and engineers took direct charge of the entire river project, including an earthen southern channel, with the input of newly hired city planner Harland Bartholomew.[49]

To ease passage of floodwaters through the northern channel, from Ninth Street south to Commerce Street, Hawley and Freese had recommended removing all trees and shrubbery along the banks. Discussion of this segment was complicated by the Swiss Plaza Hotel Corporation's proposal to donate twelve acres for a river cutoff between Fifth and Seventh streets and then to loan the city funds for its construction—$215,000—if the city would, in return, deed over the old meandering river channel for Swiss Plaza to build a high-rise apartment hotel complex on it.[50]

By now, city hall was under no misconception about women being a force to reckon with. City Commissioner Paul Steffler, whose department at the time was still overseeing the project in conjunction with Hawley and Freese, tried to appease opponents with an address to the City Federation of Women's Clubs, which had 64 member clubs. He explained the proposal for the northern channel and then announced that a new bond issue would be required to raise $2 million to finish the entire flood program. The women greeted this "with lack of enthusiasm," then began attacking both removal of trees and the land swap. Their position was soon buttressed by a new resolution from the Conservation Society.[51] Shortly before the dismissal of Hawley and Freese, the company's local engineer, H.R.F. Helland, reminded commissioners that if they were not going to build a concrete channel or remove the trees and grass to make the northern channel wider, it would have to be dug deeper.[52] "Dig to Hades!" retorted the beleaguered mayor. "I had rather spend a half million dollars beautifying this river than a million dollars making it a concrete-lined sewer."[53] The vegetation remained and a deeper channel was dug.[54]

In the case of the River Bend's concrete-lined cutoff channel, widening from fifty to seventy feet required slicing fifteen feet from the rear of the Health and Police Department building, newly constructed on the site of the French Building.[55] As work progressed, Mayor Chambers became exasperated with the controversy over appearance of the channel, its concrete perpendicular walls extending twenty to twenty-six feet below street level. He stormed that he was unalterably opposed to "another foot" of the river being lined with cement, and wanted "to forget about spending large sums of money and quit worrying about flood prevention." The mayor finally swore that the cutoff channel was "one of the biggest eyesores in the city, and should be filled up."[56]

To mute the stark appearance of the deep concrete walls, within the wider channel a sixteen-foot channel was dug and dirt banks were created on either side for plantings of grass, flowers and shrubbery.[57] The City Federation of Women's Clubs, annoyed that the cutoff channel's concrete wall extended a bit northward from the bend, declared that the river was "being constantly menaced by the selfishness and greed of promoters and politicians." Just in case the subject ever came up again, they pledged eternal opposition to straightening the River Bend or diverting its water into the cutoff channel.[58]

C.M. Chambers indeed had no easy job navigating his administration through the treacherous decisions of whether the northern and southern channels should be concrete or earthen, or whether a meander of the northern channel should be swapped for a hotel. The mayor was also embarrassed at having to slice the back off a new municipal building to permit a wider River Bend cutoff only to have the cutoff channel's appearance roundly criticized. He clearly would end up in no mood to take on a matter irrelevant to the goal of flood prevention: beautification of the River Bend.

As the River Bend was being rescued first from being filled in and then from being partly covered by a cantilevered street, a young architect named Robert Harvey Harold Hugman was taking it all in. Hugman had studied architecture at the University of Texas at Austin after graduating in 1920 from San Antonio's Brackenridge High School, where he was an art student of Conservation Society co-founder Emily Edwards.[59] After three years in New Orleans, Hugman returned to begin his architectural practice in San Antonio in 1927. He was impressed with the similar charms of New Orleans and San Antonio, and saw a unique future for the San Antonio River.

"The river is sometimes looked upon with disfavor, as taking too much room in its vagabondish winding through the valuable downtown area," thought Hugman. "This, I believe, is an entirely wrong slant on the situation.

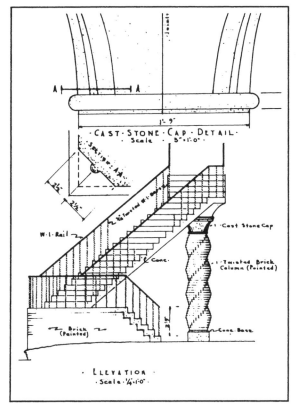

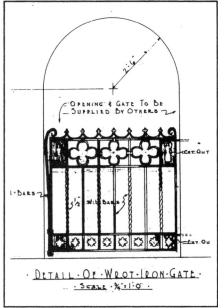

A decorative iron gate for an entrance to the river is one of the elements designed by Robert Hugman but not carried out. San Antonio Conservation Society.

A twisting column of brick was designed by Robert Hugman to support the stairway from the Crockett Street Bridge to the San Antonio River. San Antonio Conservation Society.

To me, the river is one of nature's greatest gifts to San Antonio and should be appreciated and developed as such . . . ."[60] He took his thoughts to the San Antonio Conservation Society's Amanda Taylor, who was encouraging.[61] In May, Hugman took a concept to Mayor Chambers. The mayor "heartily" endorsed it as one "that will do much to preserve and enhance the distinctiveness of San Antonio," and was reasonably sure that the city would adopt it.[62]

Armed with his endorsement from the mayor, Hugman prepared a brochure outlining his plan and obtained other endorsements from "about one hundred prominent people" in the city. At the end of June, thirty persons— among them the Mayor and two city commissioners plus property owners— met at Chamber of Commerce headquarters to hear Hugman propose the Shops of Aragon and Romula.[63]

"Wedged in behind the pretentious business houses on Houston, Soledad, Commerce and St. Mary's, why not a quaint old cobblestoned street rambling lazily along the river?" he asked those present. "On this little street of my imagination, the shops would be built of old stone and brick of very simple architecture, creating maximum charm at minimum expense. They . . . would be called 'The Shops of Aragon' . . . . Upon leaving Aragon with its shadowed charm, we come to a foot-bridge which crosses the new channel in one graceful span, bringing us to Romula, . . . in fact . . . no more than an interesting flagstone walk along the river bank with shops similar to those of Aragon on the one side—both banks of the river being treated in like manner. Beginning at the new [cutoff] channel, Romula would follow the river's meanderings around the horseshoe bend to the Plaza Hotel, presenting an opportunity for unlimited development of beauty and interest . . . . A fitting climax to the whole scheme will be gaily colored boats fashioned after the gondolas of Venice, though of Spanish design, to take pleasure seekers over the picturesque route from Travis Street to the Plaza Hotel . . . .

"Think what a wealth of advertising material the city would have in the Shops of Aragon and Romula, lending themselves, as they would, to the most colorful descriptions . . . . Like a stage setting designed and directed by one mind to produce the proper unity of thought and feeling, so must this scheme be treated as a whole and not as separate units. The shops, lighting effects, advertising—everything—must be designed to create the right atmosphere . . . . Will you work with me to this end?" Nearly all present said they would.[64]

Shortly thereafter, Hugman annoyed officials when he suggested the city conduct a national design competition for the River Bend rather than relying on input from city planner Harland Bartholomew. The City Plans Commission chairman, stung by what he apparently took as a swipe at the hard-earned hiring of Bartholomew, countered that Hugman's plan was an "idle dream." Others followed suit.[65] Nevertheless, the City Federation of Women's Clubs sent its endorsement of Hugman's plan to city commissioners.[66] Partisans lobbying for Hugman's plans were finally told by Mayor Chambers, at the end of 1929, that any decision to employ Hugman would have to wait until completion of the flood control work. Until then, he didn't want to be bothered about it any more.[67]

When most of the flood control work was finished, however, the River Bend's beautification had to wait once more, until the Depression could be overcome. Hugman nevertheless continued to carry his concept of Aragon and Romula to organizations from the Conservation Society to the Daughters of the American Revolution.[68] Interest in the River Bend picked up in the spring of 1936 when two boats making regular trips on the river, the Alamo and the Flora, were christened.[69]

Two years later, a group of businessmen led by Plaza Hotel manager Jack White was turned down by the city for funds to implement Hugman's project. So White instead formed an Improvement District of River Bend residents and property owners, who approved a bond issue.[70] The district issued $75,000 in bonds, which cleared the way for $450,000 in federal Works Progress Administration funds. Those were secured largely through efforts of

The friendship between San Antonio's Congressman and, later, Mayor Maury Maverick and President Franklin D. Roosevelt was helpful in accomplishing the city's river and La Villita projects. Here Maverick shows the President a point of interest during Roosevelt's visit to the Alamo during the Texas Centennial in 1936. Jane M. McMillan.

WPA engineer Edwin P. Arneson, State WPA Director H.P. Drought and, at the national level, Congressman Maury Maverick.[71] "Harold," Franklin Roosevelt is reported to have said to Secretary of the Interior Harold Ickes, "give Maury the money for his damn rivah so he will stop bothering me."

On Friday, March 24, 1939, nearly three hundred San Antonians gathered for the groundbreaking on the river level near the Market Street bridge, where a WPA orchestra was playing. Jack White wielded a golden shovel and declared, "Let us begin now to make San Antonio once again the first city in the state." That afternoon, a WPA workforce ultimately numbering some one thousand men began work under Construction Superintendent Robert Turk.[72] Robert Hugman, hired as project architect and assisted by Arneson, estimated that private investment would swell riverbank improvement expenditures to $5 million.[73]

Workmen prepare forms for the stairway from the Navarro Street bridge down to the San Antonio River in mid-1939. The Institute of Texan Cultures, courtesy Robert H. Turk.

Walkways were built, fresh limestone retaining walls were constructed and fanciful new bridges arched the river, but San Antonians were not altogether pleased with the look of Hugman's work. While Emily Edwards was visiting from Chicago, she discussed the project with her former student on behalf of the Conservation Society. Miss Edwards later suggested that the board declare that it "did not endorse one hundred percent of all the work now in progress on the San Antonio River." A resolution passed "protesting the desecration of the beauties of San Antonio."[74]

Then Rena Maverick Green sent a letter to the editor of the *Light* entitled "A Plea for Simplicity in Further Landscaping of the River." Approved by Conservation Society members, it observed that "San Antonio is surrounded by rock quarries and our last two park commissioners were formerly stone masons, so the temptation to excessive stone work was great." Amanda Taylor suggested that the "extremes in rock work" might mellow in time, but Mrs. Jack White suggested a copy of the critique be sent to Robert Hugman.[75] Architect Atlee B. Ayres wrote Mrs. Green to express his opinion "that the work was not done in a simple manner," and that, "with few exceptions, it is a most unwise expenditure and will be a source of ridicule to our tourist friends and others."[76] Mayor Maury Maverick wrote Mrs. Green that there may indeed have been too much stone used, and "in line with your ideas I have eliminated a large amount that they originally planned to use."[77] Hugman responded politely to Mrs. Green that the softening effects of planting then getting under way would remove most objections, although, he realized, "this is hard to visualize at the present time."[78]

Both Rena Green and Amanda Taylor then met with Hugman, who the next month reported his assurances that the work was being finished "in a manner that preserves more of the simple and natural beauty of the river and its surroundings." Members were by then so pleased with the river work that they planned their March Founders' Day luncheon in honor of project instigator and member husband Jack White.[79] By that time, however, Robert Hugman was no longer in charge of the project he conceived, having just been dismissed by Mayor Maverick. According to city officials, it was because he did not hire a particular landscape architect and had irregularities in cost estimates. According to Hugman, it was because he had proof that materials ordered for the river were being improperly diverted to the La Villita project. Hugman's job went to another local architect, J. Fred Buenz.[80]

The Works Progress Administration turned the completed river project over to the City of San Antonio on March 13, 1941. The area improved stretched through 21 blocks and 8,500 feet of riverbank from South St. Mary's Street around the River Bend and on north to Fourth Street and then jumped to Brackenridge Park, where stone channel walls were built. There were 17,000 feet of new riverwalks and sidewalks, 11,000 cubic yards of masonry, 31 stairways and 3 dams, plus numerous benches of stone, cement and cedar. In addition to new sod, landscaping included planting of 4,000 trees, shrubs and plants.[81] "We believe," wrote Mayor Maverick in his final report, "that in all the United States of America there is no city in which a river has been made a more attractive resort for all people."[82]

One of the unique features of the River Bend project was the Arneson River Theater, named in memory of the recently deceased engineer who helped it get approved and who worked on its early phase. Built into the natural curving slope of the south riverbank on the southern leg of the bend, on a site which would have been obliterated by the earlier plan to extend Losoya Street, its stage is separated from the seating by the river itself.[83] Original plans called for a spray of water to act as a curtain between acts.[84] The theater was designed to seat one thousand persons. It links the river with a sidewalk through an archway at the top row of seats past the Cós House to Villita Street and a major concurrent Depression-era program, the redevelopment of La Villita.

Villita Street extends generally eastward from the Bexar County Courthouse above the southern side of the south leg of the San Antonio River Bend. Like the Spanish Governor's Palace, it had avoided destruction during the downtown building boom of the '20s by being away from the path of development. La Villita has since been romantically referred to as "the restored

The San Antonio River separates the audience and stage in the Arneson River Theater below La Villita. Lewis F. Fisher.

little Spanish village" and as the site of San Antonio's original settlement, though it is neither. Very little remains from its undistinguished days under the Spanish crown, and the credit of being the site of the city's first settlement goes properly to the Villa of San Fernando de Bexar around Main Plaza, the Plaza de las Islas.

La Villita was originally the site of a Coahuiltecan Indian village and later the location of huts of Spanish soldiers assigned to the presidio and, then, to the Alamo. La Villita did not take the form of a permanent settlement until after the flood of 1819, when San Antonians moved onto its high ground and built more substantial homes than had stood there before. German immigrants arrived in the 1840s, joined by immigrants from France and Switzerland and, later, Mexico.[85] By the time of the Depression, the small homes of Villita and adjoining streets had become a slum. However, its colorful mix of picturesque, decaying old buildings was the very type of setting to appeal to the heritage-minded artists who organized the San Antonio Conservation Society in 1924.[86] Restoration of Villita Street and of its most historic home, where General Cós surrendered to Texans in 1835, was recommended to the society in 1935 by the chairman of its planning committee.[87] Three years later, the Conservation Society held its first meeting in La Villita in the Villita Street Arts Gallery, at number 511. The speaker described as a model for La Villita the downtown Los Angeles Olvera Street. Still a center for Mexican handicrafts, Olvera Street's thriving artistic activities and crafts were "of great interest to tourists and lovers of the quaint and picturesque."[88]

La Villita was a ready-made cause for the historic and social activism of Maury Maverick, defeated for a third term in Congress in 1938 but elected mayor of San Antonio the next year.[89] He promptly began a thorough housecleaning at city hall. Administrative procedures were tightened, the police department was reorganized and a new health department established. As Maverick had begun working for the preservation of San José Mission on his eleventh day as a Congressman, so as mayor did he focus quickly on the restoration and rehabilitation of La Villita. He saw it as nothing less than a project which could restore an historic neighborhood, provide jobs for the unemployed, unite the Western Hemisphere and promote world peace.[90]

Targeted was the block at the southeast corner of Villita and South Presa streets. It incorporated seven historic houses, generally hidden by vines and debris. Also included in the concept were the Cós House, the nearby Villita Art Gallery and, across the street, a former church which was to become a puppet theater.[91]

Headlines about La Villita would not chronicle the agonies of gradual acquisition of small parcels of land at high prices that had plagued preservationists at the Alamo and at San José Mission. Scarcely three months after he was sworn in, Mayor Maverick announced that by trading plots of land with the City Water Board and the San Antonio Public Service Company, which had a power plant across the street, he had completed most land acquisition for the project.[92] Never given to understatement, Maverick declared that not only was the land-swapping deal "the best any city administration has made in fifty years," he also thought La Villita was "superior in its historical value" even to the newly restored Williamsburg, Virginia, where he said the Rockefellers had just spent $15 million.[93]

Within two weeks of the final property acquisition, twenty-five youths paid by the National Youth Administration began the clean-up. Maury Maverick retained the friendship of Franklin Roosevelt, and on October 2, 1939 the President's approval of a $53,174 appropriation for La Villita was announced.[94] Ten days later, city commissioners adopted the Villita Ordinance. The Plaza would be named Plaza Juarez in honor of Benito Juarez, former president of Mexico, to promote "peace, friendship and justice between the United States of America and all other nations of the Western Hemisphere, as well as of nations of the world." The museum-library-forum-community building would be the Bolivar Building, after the South American patriot Simón

La Villita's most historic building, the house where the Mexican General Martín Perfecto de Cós surrendered to a Texan army in 1835, languished for more than a century, remembered only through a marker from Adina De Zavala's Texas Historical and Landmarks Association. San Antonio Conservation Society.

The Cós House was restored beside an entrance to the Arneson River Theater during the 1939-41 La Villita project. San Antonio Conservation Society.

La Villita homes were in an advanced state of decay when all these but the one in the foreground were rescued in 1939. They faced the new Juarez Plaza to the north. *Grandjean Collection, A-95, DRT Library at the Alamo.*

National Youth Association workers construct walls around Juarez Plaza at a corner of the La Villita project. *Zintgraff Collection, The Institute of Texan Cultures.*

La Villita looking southeast during initial restoration shows the newly finished Juarez Plaza in left foreground, with Bolivar Hall under construction and in need of a roof past houses facing the plaza. At lower left is the old City Public Service Company power plant, used as a workshop by project artisans, on the future site of Villita Assembly Hall. To the right of the building at top left is the Schultze Hardware Store, later restored at the HemisFair entrance which replaced the street it faces. Buildings along the near side of South Alamo Street above Bolivar Hall occupy the future site of Maverick Plaza. At upper right is the future site of the Fairmount Hotel. The San Antonio Light *Collection, The Institute of Texan Cultures.*

Bolívar. A new interior street would be Calle Hidalgo, after Father Miguel Hidalgo y Castillo, who proclaimed the independence of Mexico. Activities would preserve the arts and crafts of early Texas and Spain and study the Great Southwest. One of the restored homes would become a Societies Building, for historical, literary, scientific and conservation societies.[95]

When Conservation Society directors met in mid-1939, "with the word 'Villita' enthusiasm took the meeting." Members were ready to raise funds for a Conservation House, and empowered newly elected President Amanda Taylor to act for the society on all Villita matters.[96] Blanding Sloan, National Youth Administration supervisor of arts and crafts for the Villita project, described the concept to society members. His wife predicted that Villita

The young architect O'Neil Ford explains his plans for La Villita to Conservation Society members at "Willow Way," home of his wife's mother Elizabeth Graham, standing at far left. Past the unidentified woman to her left are, from left, Mary Aubrey Keating, Amanda Cartwright Taylor, Eleanor Onderdonk (hidden), Ford, Mrs. J.B. Lewright (seated) and Ethel Wilson Harris. Courtesy of the Witte Museum, San Antonio, Texas.

Street would become "the center of culture for Pan-American art" due to San Antonio's geographic location and historic setting.[97]

Architect and NYA Assistant Administrator David R. Williams recommended that Maverick hire as La Villita's project supervisor his young Dallas protégé, O'Neil Ford. Ford took the job and moved to San Antonio. "Exciting, eccentric and paradoxical," wrote his biographer, Mary Carolyn George, "San Antonio and O'Neil Ford were a good match."[98] Ford had lengthy discussions with the mayor and conservationists, assessed what had to be done and jumped in with characteristic energy. He saw La Villita as having distinct styles "infinitely more varied and original than are those of Charleston and New Orleans and Cape Cod." The project was to provide "a sensitive and carefully restored group of little houses that show clearly that our own culture has produced, from a varied source, an architecture not based on any 'style' but definitely establishing character that is native."[99]

Workmen replaster one of the seven early houses in the original La Villita project. Courtesy of the Witte Museum, San Antonio, Texas.

Ford decided that La Villita should ultimately create a mood rather than be a museum-style restoration to a specific period in time, since the meager evidence of the buildings' original and subsequent appearance gave "no end of confusion . . . . For instance: One of the most interesting houses . . . shows evidence of having been rebuilt as many as three definite times. It began as adobe blocks, then a clear line in the wall shows where it had fallen down; next is a superimposed wall of rocks and mud joints where the first upper area had fallen; and last, another area of adobe was placed on top. This last adobe is entirely different in manufacture and system of laying from the first adobe. Certainly this house could have had a flat adobe roof over large timbers . . . or it could have had a thatched roof . . . or it could have been built just as it stands, with a roof of split cypress shakes . . . . All the refinements of [the houses' original] sound design are lost. Therefore most everyone has considered that we should make every effort to turn far back instead of leaving details and appendages that are comparatively recent additions."[100]

The indigenous architecture of La Villita, therefore, would be restored to show how sophisticated architectural styles were adapted by San Antonio's varied national cultures to yield a style "far more fresh and stimulating than those houses in New Orleans, the old South and around the Gulf Coast to Virginia," even transformed "in a warm and free manner unlike the use of the same influence in [nearby] Anglo-Saxon Austin, in German Fredericksburg, in Alsatian Castroville or in the coast towns where a different climate prevailed." Various styles of doors, windows, mantles, cabinetry and hardware made by NYA workers on the premises were to enhance such lessons of evolution. Picturesqueness was never to replace "good sense and structural honesty." The overall result was to be "one general atmosphere of cool shady places of profuse banks of blossoming native trees and shrubs . . . [with] no sharp separation of the things that make houses and grounds and furniture one fine whole."[101]

As work proceeded, rooms in the old city power plant became workshops of the arts and crafts training program. Ford's office and the ceramics, weaving and design studios were in old houses that could be used. A cabinetmaker supervised making furniture for restored houses. A blacksmith set up a forge to make door handles, latches and hinges. Tiles were made by potter Harding Black. Landscape architect Stewart King supervised native plantings. Rena Green's daughter Mary was among artists on the teaching staff.[102] However, "with so many creative people working together on a tight schedule with limited funds and unskilled workers," as Ford's biographer put it, "tensions were naturally generated . . . . Ford felt free to disagree, and Mayor Maverick was not accustomed to being crossed."[103] Finally, as had been the case with creative River Walk architect Robert Hugman, there came a parting of the ways.

Onetime Conservation Society President Floy Edwards Fontaine explained Ford's dismissal by describing "the Tuesday factor." It was caused by Maverick's national prominence as a congressman casting attention on his subsequent creative reform in San Antonio, bringing to the city and the La Villita project a host of notables, among them Eleanor Roosevelt, Sherwood Anderson, Thomas Mann and H.G. Wells.[104] Acknowledging that while the Conservation Society knew that with Maverick involved the La Villita project "would be done well," Mrs. Fontaine explained that the mayor, on the other hand, "was not so easy to work with . . . . He had a way of saying it had to be ready next Tuesday, Tuesday somebody was coming. And it got to be a saying—'Well, it just has to be ready by Tuesday.' Well, O'Neil Ford is an artist, and O'Neil Ford is a perfectionist, and somehow you can't be a perfectionist and have it ready by Tuesday. You have to take the necessary time and research. And so Maury and he clashed on that, and Maury was rather unreasonable and called in somebody else who would do it [by] Tuesday."[105]

Transferring the spirit of the Conservation Society's Indian Harvest Festival to the River Jubilee which promoted the San Antonio River beautification project in 1940 are these Conservation Society daughters, gathered in front of a teepee on the banks of the San Antonio River Bend. The annual event, originally held at San José mission, stayed on the river and evolved into A Night In Old San Antonio. San Antonio Conservation Society.

After his dismissal, O'Neil Ford stayed in San Antonio to continue his architectural career. One enticement to stay was Wanda Graham, daughter of recent Conservation Society President and Governor's Palace Custodian Elizabeth Graham. In the summer of 1940 the two were married in an afternoon ceremony at the restored San José Mission granary. A reception followed at the bride's nearby home, "Willow Way," where the young couple moved.[106]

Maverick firmly believed that La Villita, like San José, should be declared a National Historic Site, and wasted no time in calling his old friends in Washington to press the point. Maverick asked the National Park Service to send experts to help while work was under way. But the Park Service was less into creating moods and more into strict historical accuracy. Maverick asked the Park Service to send down an archeologist. But the Park Service told the city to hire its own archeologist, an option Maverick dismissed as a waste of money. The Park Service's advisory board ultimately rejected the national historic site proposal.[107]

The original La Villita project was completed by the time Maverick's term as mayor ended in 1941 with his defeat by C.K. Quin. La Villita was one of Maverick's proudest accomplishments, "one of the few achievements of which he would boast."[108]

To celebrate the San Antonio River project, which ultimately had even more impact on the city than did La Villita, in the fall of 1940 the Conservation Society replaced its traditional Indian Harvest Festival at San José with a River Jubilee, featuring a parade of boats. The Conservation Society and the Daughters of the Republic of Texas co-sponsored a turkey supper which yielded a profit of $800, half of which was sent to Mayor Maverick to help the city "to carry on conservation work."[109] With restoration work at San José Mission basically completed and the state poised to operate the complex, the Conservation Society's principal focus of activity began to shift permanently from San José to downtown. In 1940, the society moved its Christmastime *Los Pastores* pageant from San José to La Villita as well.[110] The society's fall event remained on the river in 1941. Re-named the River Festival, it netted nearly $375. One-third was given to the city for additional lighting of the River Bend.[111]

By the time of American involvement in World War II, San Antonians had completed a host of pioneering projects which put the city in the forefront of the national historic preservation movement. In less than two decades, the San Antonio Conservation Society had become a primary factor in seeing that the unique amenities which yet define San Antonio to the rest of the world were in place—the enlarged grounds of the Alamo, the restoration of San José Mission and the Spanish Governor's Palace, La Villita and the River Walk. In his two-volume *Preservation Comes of Age,* which focuses primarily on the years prior to World War II, Charles B. Hosmer, Jr. noted that the artistic perspectives of San Antonio Conservation Society members enabled them to put on "imaginative entertainments, festivals and displays on a scale that would have been unthinkable in Charleston or Boston . . . . Men (with the exception of a few harried husbands and Maury Maverick) did not contribute much to the local preservation movement. Harvey Smith and O'Neil Ford were almost the only professionals involved. It was a woman's world with a pleasant admixture of Latin culture . . . .

"When one compares the writings of Mayor Maverick and the statements of the founders of the Conservation Society, it is clear that Maverick was in the mainstream of San Antonio thinking—long on inspiration and short on research, with a highly developed sense of historical reality but little appreciation of the need for professional assistance. These same amateurish characteristics, however, gave San Antonio preservationists great strengths. The women were years ahead of the men because they viewed their city as a total environment; they wanted to save the things that went into making the community lively and beautiful . . . . No visitor to San Antonio can ignore the river bend, the charm of La Villita or the awesome power of the Conservation Society. If the artists of 1924 set out to preserve a setting, they certainly succeeded."[112]

Notes

1. "San Antonio River Flows 13 Miles to Get to a Point Only Six Miles Distant," *San Antonio Light*, Jan. 29, 1911, 34.

2. "San Antonio—City of Bridges—Claims Nearly 100," *San Antonio Express*, Feb. 5, 1928, 1-A.

3. "City Designates Auditorium Site," *San Antonio Express*, Jun. 1, 1920.

4. "Flood Prevention Underway," *San Antonio Express*, Sept. 26, 1924, 6.

5. "Refuse In River Retards Efforts for Cleaner City," *San Antonio Express*, Sept. 20, 1912.

6. "River Lighting Ordered By City," *San Antonio Express*, Jun. 9, 1926, 24.

7. "Ornamental Fountains Between Every Bridge Pictured By Mayor Tobin," *San Antonio Express*, Oct. 26, 1924, 2; "River Lighting Ordered By City," *San Antonio Express*, Jun. 9, 1926, 24.

8. "Queen's Pageant on River Likely," *San Antonio Express*, Nov. 13, 1924, 11. The Conservation Society also considered organizing a Canoe Club "as a factor in advertising . . . the natural beauty of our river, . . . keeping before our people the real obligation . . . to future generations." (Minutes, Nov. 1, 1924.)

9. Ibid.; "Committee Finds River Practicable for Parade of San Jacinto Gondolas," *San Antonio Light*, Nov. 12, 1924, 1; "Clubwomen On Trip With Mayor Tobin Inspecting Stream," *San Antonio News*, Nov. 12, 1924; Emily Edwards OHT, 16–17; Mrs. Jules Fontaine OHT, Jun. 29, 1971, 4. Miss Edwards later thought Commissioner Phil Wright was in one of the boats, but the city's three daily newspapers all list Col. Van Horn instead.

10. Description of the voyage is from Emily Edwards OHT, 16–17. Despite the enthusiasm of its president, the Battle of Flowers Association did not hold its next parade on the river.

11. Emily Edwards, "The San Antonio Conservation Society and the River," *San Antonio Conservation Society Newsletter*, Sept., 1966.

12. Minutes, May 2, 1925.

13. "River Channel Work To Begin," *San Antonio Express*, Jan. 9, 1926, 1.

14. "Two Bends In River Will Be Eliminated," *San Antonio Express*, Jun. 8, 1926, 8; "$175,000 Voted For New Channel," *San Antonio Express*, Jun. 15, 1926, 1; "Old Mill Wrecked to Straighten River," *San Antonio Express*, Aug. 19, 1926, 5.

15. "Proposed Overflow Channel Cuts Flood Flow Half-Mile," *San Antonio Express*, Jun. 15, 1926, 3.

16. "$175,000 Voted For New Channel," *San Antonio Express*, Jun. 15, 1926, 1.

17. Ibid.

18. Minutes, Jan. 15, 1926.

19. "Street Will Top Overflow Tunnel," *San Antonio Express*, Jul. 2, 1927, 6; "City Will Rent Channel Lots," *San Antonio Express*, Nov. 20, 1927, 11.

20. "River Wall Extended," *San Antonio Express*, Apr. 6, 1927, 9. Several cast iron urns from the top of the building are preserved at the Witte Museum.

21. "Famous Old Lawyers' Office Building to Be Torn Down," *San Antonio Express*, Jan. 20, 1927, 6.

22. "River Lighting Ordered By City," *San Antonio Express*, Jun. 9, 1926, 24; "Three Plans For Lighting River," *San Antonio Express*, Jun. 16, 1926, 9; "River Lighting Demonstration Will Be Made," *San Antonio Express*, Jul. 3, 1926.

23. "River Will Be Lighted Through Business District," *San Antonio Express*, Mar. 25, 1927, 9; "A Night Scene on San Antonio River," *San Antonio Express*, Mar. 30, 1927, 8.

24. "Committees Report Ready For Federated Clubs Meeting," *San Antonio Express*, May 15, 1928, 10.

25. "Walk To Be Built Along River Bank," *San Antonio Express*, Jan. 27, 1928, 9. The Conservation Society sought such donations as cacti and Texas plants for a fund-raising sale on Alamo Plaza during the convention. (Marin B. Fenwick, "Facts and Fancies About People at Home and Abroad," *San Antonio Express*, May 28, 1928, 14-D.)

26. "River Lighting Conferences to Be Held Thursday," *San Antonio Express*, Jan. 25, 1928, 8. Borglum's wife was a member of the Old Spanish Trail Association's river improvement committee, chaired by Mrs. John L. Browne. ("Walk To Be Built Along River Bank," *San Antonio Express*, Jan. 27, 1928, 9.)

27. "New River Lights to Be Tried Out Wednesday Night," *San Antonio Express*, Feb., 15, 1928, 15; "River Lighting To Be Changed," *San Antonio Express*, Mar. 22, 1928, 9.

28. "Flood Lights for Illumination of River Approved," *San Antonio Express*, Mar. 24, 1928, 2.

29. Ibid.; "River Lighting To Be Changed," *San Antonio Express*, Mar. 22, 1928, 9.

30. "City Will Not Change Plans for 70-Foot Overflow Channel, Mayor Tobin Answers Protests," *San Antonio Express*, Oct. 11, 1927, 8. Protest committee chairman and real estate broker Ernest J. Altgelt, accompanied by L.J. Hart and Franz Groos, presented commissioners with a petition signed by two dozen other business-men seeking the widening. (Ibid.; "Bond Issue For Library Planned," *San Antonio Express*, Jan. 17, 1928, 8.) The group was later headed by T.B. Baker and Altgelt was secretary. ("Cut-Off Channel Decision Expected," *San Antonio Express*, Jan. 26, 1928, 7; "Channel Width Will Be 70 Feet," *San Antonio Express*, Feb. 9, 1928, 9.)

31. "City Will Not Change Plans for 70-Foot Overflow Channel, Mayor Tobin Answers Protests," *San Antonio Express*, Oct. 11, 1927, 8.

32. "Cut-Off Channel Decision Expected," *San Antonio Express*, Jan. 26, 1928, 7.

33. "Bond Issue For Library Planned," *San Antonio Express*, Jan. 17, 1928, 8; "Work On Cut-Off Channel Gets Under Way," *San Antonio Express*, Jan. 24, 1928, 10.

34. "$500,000 Bond Issue Needed," *San Antonio Express*, Feb. 10, 1928, 7. The channel eliminated the site of the 1840 Council House Fight between San Antonians

and Comanches. It took place behind the Casa Real, the Spanish-era government building facing Main Plaza. ("New River Channel Blots Out Site of Council-House Fight," *San Antonio Express-News*, Jan. 5, 1930, 1-D.)

35. "River Land To Be Reclaimed By City," *San Antonio Light*, Feb. 15, 1928, 2-A. The figures were prepared by Ernest J. Altgelt, Jr.

36. "'Big Bend' Not To Be Eliminated," *San Antonio Express*, Feb. 16, 1928, 9. Few pivotal events in San Antonio's history are as shrouded in myth and misinformation as the defeat of developers' efforts to destroy or deface the downtown River Bend. Although early 1928 is the only time local newspapers in that era can be found to have reported any plan to fill the River Bend, accounts in recent years have stated that such a plan was permanently defeated at various times between 1924 and 1929. Such accounts give no specifics, other than to blame city hall and refer to a public protest meeting allegedly called at the Menger Hotel by the Conservation Society.

The most authoritative treatment of the subject has been considered that written four decades later by Emily Edwards, first president of the Conservation Society. She wrote that a plan "to drain and pave" the River Bend was abandoned after it was denounced at a public meeting called by the Conservation Society at the Menger Hotel, where Amanda Taylor introduced Judge Sidney Brooks, who backed the society's position. She implies in this and subsequent writings that the meeting and defeat of the proposal occurred in early 1926. (Emily Edwards, "The San Antonio Conservation Society and the River," *San Antonio Conservation Society Newsletter*, September, 1966; [Emily Edwards], *A Review By The San Antonio Conservation Society* (San Antonio: San Antonio Conservation Society, 1970), 10.)

Miss Edwards, who did not live in San Antonio in the 33 years between late 1926 and 1959, wrote her article in 1966, shortly after river beautification designer Robert Hugman complained to Conservation Society President Peggy Tobin that he had "never read one correct writing on the history of this project." (Robert H.H. Hugman to Mrs. Don Tobin, Apr. 11, 1966, in SACS Library.) Miss Edwards consulted with Mrs. Taylor, but apparently not with Hugman, and was handicapped by the four-year gap after March of 1926 in Conservation Society minutes, which previously make no reference to any plot to drain and pave the River Bend. She explained that her article "does not pretend to be a complete one, but [is] just to suggest continuity of interest." (Emily Edwards to Mrs. Don F. Tobin, May 25, 1966, in SACS Library.)

Hugman, in his letter cited above, stated that the River Bend was saved in 1929. He did not mention a public meeting, nor had newspapers when they reported in 1928 that the River Bend had just been saved. No report of any public meeting opposing a River Bend-filling proposal could be found in San Antonio newspapers between 1924 and 1930, nor in any of the Conservation Society's own accounts of its history written as late as 1953. Other early writings of Conservation Society members mention the river only in general terms of beautification, if at all. (Rena Maverick Green to Lola Maverick Lloyd, 1925–1938, letters in Schwimmer-Lloyd Collection, New York Public Library; Anna Ellis, "Conservation Society Rounds Out Eight Years in Civic Work," *San Antonio Express*, Mar. 13, 1932; "San Antonio Conservation Society" in "A Survey of Historical Records of Bexar County," 1934, research by Clara Dunn, supervised by Frederick C. Chabot in Frederick Charles Chabot Papers Box 2L281, The Center For American History, The University of

Texas at Austin; "History of San Antonio Conservation Society," *San Antonio Conservation Society Handbook*, 1935; "Story of the San Antonio Conservation Society," *The Yearbook of the San Antonio Conservation Society 1924–1936*, 19–24; Elizabeth Graham, script of untitled WOAI radio play, 1940, in Rena Maverick Green Papers; Elizabeth Graham, addendum by Amanda Taylor, "History of the San Antonio Conservation Society," 1953, manuscript in SACS Library.)

Frequent public meetings on other, often lesser subjects were, however, regularly reported in the press at the time. One was a public meeting in 1925 called by the Conservation Society at the Menger Hotel at which Mrs. Taylor introduced speakers including Judge Sidney Brooks, who backed a Conservation Society position—the need to purchase additional land at the Alamo, the purpose of the meeting. ("City Commission Asked by Civic Organizations to Provide Funds to Purchase Ground Near Alamo," *San Antonio Express*, Oct. 27, 1925, 5.)

37. "'Big Bend' Not To Be Eliminated," *San Antonio Express*, Feb. 16, 1928, 9. No complaints on official handling of the River Bend appear in City Commissioners minutes during these years. In the five years prior to 1929, river beautification was formally brought up to commissioners only by the Woman's Club, which in March of 1928 petitioned for further beautification of the river banks prior to the National Federation of Women's Clubs convention. (City Commissioners Minutes, March 26, 1928, Book H, 404.)

38. "Dam to Deepen River in Business Section of City," *San Antonio Express*, Feb. 24, 1928, 22.

39. "Street Will Be Built Over River," *San Antonio Express*, Mar. 29, 1929, 28. President of the East Side Improvement League was J.H. Kirkpatrick.

40. "Suspended Street Project 'Ditched,'" *San Antonio Express*, Apr. 13, 1929, 24.

41. Ibid. Also, Conservation Society representative Anna Ellis introduced a successful City Federation of Women's Club resolution praising city commissioners for these actions. (City Federation of Women's Clubs Minutes 1927–30, 99—Mar. 21, 1929, minute book in San Antonio Public Library.)

42. City officials were refusing to part with any of the city's river channel property, and were investigating encroachments and marking the property line, all of those steps endorsed in a Conservation Society resolution to city commissioners. (City Federation of Women's Clubs Minutes 1927–30, 99—Mar 21, 1929; "Society Approves City River Resurvey Stand," *San Antonio Express*, Mar. 21, 1929, 10; "City To Establish River Bed Width," *San Antonio Express*, Apr. 20, 1929, 24; "City Will Mark Banks of River," *San Antonio Express*, Apr. 23, 1929, 15.)

43. "Suspended Street Project 'Ditched,'" *San Antonio Express*, Apr. 13, 1929, 24.

44. "Losoya Extension Plan Abandoned," *San Antonio Express*, Apr. 14, 1929, 1-A. Altgelt's complaint did not mention that running a street across the land the Water Board claimed would also require the Water Board to cut off part of its main building.

45. "Suspended Street Project 'Ditched,'" *San Antonio Express*, Apr. 13, 1929, 24. Members of the East Side Improvement League committee were C.W. Fenstermaker, E.J. Altgelt, Marshall Terrell and Dr. John Herff. City officials agreed to inspect the area to see if the street could be built without touching the river, but, said Mayor Chambers, "We might just as well not have met." City officials did promise to use

the $100,000 set aside for an appropriate area project, as they believed "this portion of the city is entitled to this amount of improvements." ("Losoya Extension Plan Abandoned," *San Antonio Express*, Apr. 14, 1929, 1-A.)

46. "Losoya Extension Plan Abandoned," *San Antonio Express*, Apr. 14, 1929, 1-A. The City Federation of Women's Clubs made a "hearty endorsement" of the decision in a resolution introduced by its Civic Chairman, Mrs. John L. Browne. (City Federation of Women's Clubs Minutes 1927–30, 106—Apr. 18, 1929.)

47. "Losoya Street Extension to South Alamo at Market Street Arranged," *San Antonio Express*, Oct. 4, 1929, 1-C.

48. "Wider River Channel From Nueva To Guenther Street Favored," *San Antonio Express*, Sept. 10, 1929, 7.

49. "City To Reject Engineers' Plans," *San Antonio Express*, Sept. 13, 1929, 8; "Channel Project Checks Returned," *San Antonio Express*, Oct. 23, 1929, 15; "Plans For River Ready Saturday," *San Antonio Express*, Oct. 26, 1929, 24; "City Heads Praised For River Plans," *San Antonio Express*, Nov. 16, 1929, 24. The move brought a favorable resolution to the mayor from the Woman's Club, its civic committee headed by Mrs. Roscoe Hauser. Bartholomew acknowledged the need for careful planning for the downtown San Antonio River, the sort of issue he said he had already encountered in his work for the city of Rochester, New York, which also had a river through its downtown. However, Rochester's Genesee, like rivers through other major American cities, is wide and deep, its rushing waters responsible for extensive industrial growth along its banks.

50. "S.A. Clubwomen Unite To Fight River Project," *San Antonio Light*, Sept. 8, 1929, 1; "Club Women Fight Cut-Off," *San Antonio Express*, Oct. 4, 1929, 28. The City Federation of Women's Clubs favored construction of the hotel, but feared that the straightened channel would be built of concrete. ("New River Plan Offered For Channel," *San Antonio Light*, Oct. 18, 1929, 2-A.)

51. Ibid.; "Women's Clubs to Oppose Removing River Parkway," *San Antonio Express*, Sept. 8, 1929, 1-A; "Second Protest Against River Marring Filed," *San Antonio Express*, Oct. 5, 1929, 10. Leading the charge were Mrs. J.L. Browne, chairman of the Federation's civic committee, and Mrs. H.A. Moos, chairman of the Old Spanish Trail Association's beautification committee.

52. "Wider River Channel From Nueva To Guenther Street Favored," *San Antonio Express*, Sept. 10, 1929, 7.

53. Ibid.

54. What clearing of native growth was done along the riverbank upstream drew a blast from Witte Museum Director Ellen Quillin, who complained that "ruthless destruction has been wrought by ignorant workmen on relief payrolls." (Minutes, Jan. 24, 1935.) Elizabeth Graham reported later for the society's river committee that filling in of part of the river near the Elmira Street tourist camp "seems to be of no real damage to the river." (Minutes, Oct. 31, 1935.) Closer to downtown, Ethel Tunstall Drought spoke of the "ugliness of big signs" along the riverbank, which the river committee was trying to get removed. (Minutes, Jan. 4, 1936.) The old Tunstall Bend below Ninth Street, where Conservation Society founders and city officials departed on their 1924 boat tour, was not removed until the river there was finally straightened twenty-five years later, long after the Swiss Plaza Hotel Corporation's

plans evaporated with the Depression. (Dick Balmos, "Placid S.A. River Became Unpredictable as City Grew," *San Antonio Light*, Jan. 2, 1961.)

55. "3 Major Changes Made In Design Of Flood Channel," *San Antonio Express*, Feb. 17, 1929, 1-A; "Home Firm Given Channel Work," *San Antonio Express*, Mar. 20, 1929, 28.

56. "Mayor Is Opposed To Using More Cement In Lining River Banks," *San Antonio Express*, Oct. 20, 1929, 1-A. Mrs. F.W. Sorell, speaking for herself rather than any club, predicted that in 20 years San Antonians would so regret the "ugliness" of the cutoff that the cement would be dug out and the area beautified. Street Commissioner Paul Steffler tried to tone things down by promising to change the label "flood prevention program" to "river beautification," observing, "this city has been receiving far too much publicity on flood prevention. People [all] over the country must think that we have a flood every week." ("New Plan Offered for Channel," *San Antonio Light,* Oct. 18, 1929, 2-A.)

57. "Half Million-Dollar Cut-Off Eliminates Big Bend," *San Antonio Express*, Jul. 21, 1929, 1-C; "City Starts Big Bend Beautification Plan," *San Antonio Express*, Apr. 9, 1930, 13.

58. "Mrs. W.E. Pyne Federation Head," *San Antonio Express*, Feb. 21, 1930, 5.

59. Floy Fontaine Jordan OHT, 8.

60. Vernon Zunker, *A Dream Come True: Robert Hugman and San Antonio's River Walk* (San Antonio, n.p., 1994), 97.

61. Zunker, *A Dream Come True*, 3, 139. The book includes Hugman's own account of the preservation of the River Walk, written in 1978. President of the Conservation Society in 1929 was Margaret Lewis rather than Mrs. Taylor, as Hugman states.

62. C.M. Chambers to To Whom It May Concern, May 29, 1929, in SACS Library.

63. "Preliminary Steps Toward Creation Of Miniature 'Old World Street' Along Big Bend Taken at Meeting," *San Antonio Express*, Jun. 29, 1929, 8.

64. Ibid; Zunker, *A Dream Come True*, 95–99. Among those favoring Hugman's plan at the gathering were conservationists John M. Bennett and Rena Maverick Green. In an earlier speech to a convention of the Southern States Art League, Gutzon Borglum encouraged using canoes and gondolas on the river. ("Monks Lauded As Architects," *San Antonio Express*, Apr. 5, 1929, 10.)

65. "Prize City Plan Idea Condemned," *San Antonio Express*, Jul. 16, 1929.

66. "Women's Club Members to Urge City to Hire Landscape Architect To Develop River Beautification," *San Antonio Express*, Oct. 18, 1929, 8. At the same meeting, women expressing their organizations' support of river widening without sacrificing the river's beauty were Mrs. F.W. Sorrell and Mrs. Alex Adams of the Federation and Amanda Taylor of the Conservation Society.

67. "Landscape Architect Employment To Wait," *San Antonio Express*, Nov. 16, 1929, 24.

68. "Architect Tells Of River Beauty," *San Antonio Express*, Oct. 11, 1935, 18; Minutes, Jan. 4, 1936.

69. Minutes, Apr. 16, 1936.

70. "City Rejects River Plans," *San Antonio Light*, Apr. 28, 1938, 10-B; "Bonds Approved For River Work," *San Antonio Express*, Oct. 26, 1938, 1.

71. "Ceremony Starts $265,000 River Beautification Project," *San Antonio Express*, Mar. 25, 1939, 10-A; Henderson, *Maury Maverick*, 201.

72. "Ceremony Starts $265,000 River Beautification Project," *San Antonio Express*, Mar. 25, 1939, 10-A.

73. "Business Group Looks Ahead," *San Antonio Express*, Oct. 30, 1938, 1-A.

74. Minutes, Sept. 28, 1939, 2; Jan. 3, 1940, 2. The board was also displeased with plans for "walling the river" in Brackenridge Park, and sent a committee to discuss the whole river project with the Chamber of Commerce president. (Minutes, Mar. 5, 1940.)

75. Minutes, Jan. 25, 1940; copy of letter to the editor in SACS Library.

76. Atlee B. Ayres to Mrs. Rena M. Green, Jan. 31, 1940 in Rena Maverick Green Papers.

77. Maury Maverick to Mrs. Rena Maverick Green, Feb. 19, 1940 in Rena Maverick Green Papers. Referring to the River Bend channel walls which supported sidewalks the mayor wrote, "I do think that a large amount of rock is necessary if people are to walk in a more or less confined area. If walls were not placed there walks could not be placed either, because they would be continually washed over." He added that, in line with her other suggestions, he had informed City Forester Stewart King to plant magnolia and pecan trees along the banks of San Pedro Creek.

78. R.H.H. Hugman to Mrs. Rena M. Green, Feb. 1, 1940 in Rena Maverick Green Papers.

79. Minutes, Feb. 22, 1940, 2. The river walk plan offered an excuse for the Conservation Society to swing support behind one of its lesser pet projects, one with a direct tie to the Spanish era. That effort involved conversion of the alley beside the Solo Serve store to a river walk access passage to Main Plaza. The endangered strip—first referred to by members as "the old cattle trail" and then simply as "the cow path"—was the historic public watering route to the river from Main Plaza, between the old Veramendi Palace and the old county court house. In 1936 the county planned to sell the alley to the adjoining Solo Serve store, but the Conservation Society protested on the grounds of its history and of Hugman's proposed plan for it. (Minutes, Sept. 24, 1936, 2; Oct. 14, 1936.) With the river walk plan approved, the Conservation Society through its attorney first got the alley reopened and then got the county to agree to lease the land to the city for beautification. (Minutes, Jun. 8, 1939; Aug. 17, 1939, Sept. 28, 1939.) Solo Serve itself agreed to make $12,000 in improvements on the passageway, including "lovely iron gates" to keep it closed nights and Sundays. The Conservation Society voted that it be named "Paseo de Veramendi." (Minutes, Apr. 4, 1940, 2; May 9, 1940, 2; May 30, 1940.) Keeping the entry open continued to be a problem, however, as Solo Serve within a few years closed it and sometimes used it to display nursery items. (Minutes, D-Mar. 22, 1945, 2; D-Nov. 25, 1952, 3.)

80. Zunker, *A Dream Come True*, 116.

81. "River Beautification Project Turned Over to City by WPA," *San Antonio Express*, Mar. 14, 1941, 1-A.

82. Zunker, *A Dream Come True*, 120.

83. Some have traced Hugman's inspiration for the riverbank theater to his student days at Brackenridge High School, when Emily Edwards—who taught drama as well as art—had Hugman's class build seats and staging beside the river as it passed the school for a performance of "Ali Baba and the Forty Thieves." (Floy Fontaine Jordan OHT, 8.)

84. "Business Group Looks Ahead to $5,000,000 River Street," *San Antonio Express,* Oct. 30, 1938, A-1.

85. "La Villita," *Handbook of Texas* II, 38; Mary Carolyn Hollers George, *O'Neil Ford, Architect* (College Station: Texas A&M University Press, 1992), 62.

86. Minutes, Mar. 22, 1924.

87. Minutes, Oct. 31, 1935. Chairman of the Committee was Mrs. J.B. Lewright, who had the endorsement of President Elizabeth Graham.

88. Minutes, Jan. 27, 1938.

89. Maury Maverick was sworn in by his father, Albert Maverick, on May 13, 1939, one hundred years to the day since his grandfather, Samuel Augustus Maverick, became mayor of San Antonio. (Henderson, *Maury Maverick,* 193.)

90. Ibid., 195–200. See also note 94.

91. "Colorful Spanish Village to be Restored," *San Antonio Light,* Jul. 18, 1939, 1; "La Villita," a report of progress with statement of aims, methods and historic significance of the Villita restoration published by the City of San Antonio, page excerpts in SACS Library.

92. "Colorful Spanish Village to be Restored," *San Antonio Light,* Jul. 18, 1939, 1.

93. Ibid.

94. The NYA, which employed 110 youths at La Villita, ultimately contributed $100,000 and the City of San Antonio $10,000. One example of creative funding was the $15,000 obtained from the Carnegie Corporation, persuaded to fund construction of Bolivar Hall as "an Hispanic-American Library and Art Museum and Community Center . . . for the promotion of world peace . . . ." and as an extension of the San Antonio Public Library, to which Andrew Carnegie contributed $50,000 in 1900. ("An Ordinance Accepting a $15,000 Grant From the Carnegie Corporation of New York for La Villita, Dec. 28, 1939," copy in SACS files.) Helping obtain the grant was Maverick's cousin-in-law, Carnegie board member Nicholas Kelley, a Chrysler Corp. vice president and a former Assistant U.S. Secretary of the Treasury who married Rena Maverick Green's youngest sister, Augusta. (Rowena Green Fenstermaker OHT, 81–82.)

95. "The Villita Ordinance," adopted Oct. 12, 1939 by the City of San Antonio, "enacted in Lively Narrative form, with illustrations."

96. Minutes, Aug. 17, 1939, 2.

97. Minutes, Sept. 28, 1939, 2.

98. George, *O'Neil Ford, Architect,* 72.

99. O'Neil Ford to J.C. Kellam, Aug. 30, 1939, copy in SACS Library.

100. Ford to Kellam, Aug. 30, 1939. Sixteen months later Ford reiterated many of these points to Conservation Society members, who had already heard from Mayor Maverick on the subject on Washington's Birthday, when he spoke to members meeting in the old La Villita church. Afterwards, all went outside for the planting of a frijolilla tree. (Minutes, Feb. 22, 1940, 1–2; Dec. 19, 1940.)

101. Ibid.

102. George, *O'Neil Ford,* 68.

103. Ibid.

104. George, *O'Neil Ford,* 69.

105. Mrs. Jules Fontaine OHT, Jun. 29, 1971, 11.

106. George, *O'Neil Ford,* 76–77.

107. Hosmer, *Preservation Comes of Age,* 285–86.

108. Henderson, *Maury Maverick,* 199.

109. Minutes, Sept. 26, 1940; Oct. 24, 1940. The city used the funds to buy chairs for the Cós House. (Minutes, G-Oct. 22, 1942.)

110. Minutes, Jan. 9, 1941.

111. Minutes, Nov. 21, 1941. Amanda Taylor was pleased to help direct the city contract for running boats on the river not to a person who would run noisy motor boats, but to another who would use "a gondola-type of boat with boatmen dressed in Mexican costumes and providing Mexican music."

112. Hosmer, *Preservation Comes of Age,* 288–90.

III

Clashing

Over

Urban

Redevelopment

(1941–1971)

8

Conservationists
Enter a New Era

 Completion of the La Villita and the San Antonio River beautification projects, and of Mayor Maury Maverick's administration itself, coincided with entry of the United States into World War II. As energies refocused once the war was over, San Antonio's preservationists faced an array of challenges which could not have been predicted before the war.

At the beginning of the post-war era, most structural remains of San Antonio's Spanish heritage were saved, or were at least out of danger. The risk then was to what remained of the old environment of shaded plazas and unusual streetscapes, a built environment which evolved in its most distinctive form up to the arrival of the railroad in the 1870s. Lethargic downtown development gave preservationists a grace period of sorts shortly after the war. But soon they would have to mount heroic defensive measures to combat the post-war onslaughts of development and redevelopment about to be unleashed in every major American city as the nation coped with its renewed prosperity. The San Antonio Conservation Society still had an imaginative and enthusiastic membership, and the means to build a war chest to meet its opponents head-on.

Preservationists' strength to use these advantages was being fashioned even as the Conservation Society dealt, in characteristic fashion, with the distractions of world war. Never fazed by the enormity of a challenge when it could be reduced to the purview of a committee, the society named Amanda Taylor its Chairman of Defense. She urged members to take courses in first aid and to donate cots and mattresses for the bomb shelters being planned.[1] "With so much being destroyed in the world today," noted President Martha (Mrs. John F.) Camp, "it is more than ever necessary to conserve."[2] Funds were donated to the city for additional lighting of the river, due to "all the soldiers in the city," which members hoped would also gain the society "better cooperation with city officials and the police."[3] A host of efforts on behalf of servicemen based in San Antonio continued throughout the war.[4] It took the USO to suggest that the Conservation Society give Sunday afternoon historical tours for the soldiers; they continued for the war's duration.[5]

Evolution of the Conservation Society's fall fund-raising festival accelerated during the war. Flush with the success of the festival's move from San José Mission to celebrate the redesigned River Walk in 1940, the next year's festival stayed on the river, with the theme "Patriotism." The theme of the river parade, a "Water Pageant," was "The Defense of Democracy."[6] The festival was divided around the River Bend, beginning with an Indian section on the northern bank between the cutoff channel and St. Mary's Street. Next, between St. Mary's and Navarro streets, came the Spanish section, followed around to the river theater by the Mexican, Western, Southern, Gay Nineties, Artists, International and Patriotic sections.[7] Past the theater, on either side of the river waited the Carnival of Nations.[8] When the street-level gates opened at 6 PM, each chairman and her committee members, all dressed in period costumes, held receptions for ticket purchasers at the foot of their section's stairway. At 8 PM, the first boat headed downstream toward the river theater, followed in turn by the others, each escorted along the River Walk by the sections' costumed participants who gathered on the theater stage. By 8:30, participants began a mummer's parade onward to the Carnival of Nations, open to all guests in costume, with prizes for the best. At 9:30 the focus shifted up to La Villita's Juarez Plaza, where Delphian Club festivities included an orchestra playing for dancing until midnight.[9]

"Sounds simple," one can imagine Festival Chairman Elizabeth Graham saying, as had Rena Green ten years earlier before carefully laid plans for dedication of the Spanish Governor's Palace went temporarily awry. This time the complications were triggered by a Saturday night downpour just as the festival began. A vote to postpone the event until the next Friday night immediately drew a host of complaints from both visitors and members. The Daughters of the Republic of Texas already had their turkey dinners set up and had to go ahead and serve the food that night anyway.[10]

There were dry skies six nights later when the Water Pageant at last began—but the Trail Drivers discovered that no one had decorated their boat. The Western Section chairman assured them that their "colorful costumes did not make this noticeable." Placating the Texas Pioneers was more difficult. They were assigned to the Western section, too, but wanted no part of trail drivers or cowboys—those came in the years after the original Texas pioneers had done their work. The chairman moved the Texas Pioneers as far from the Western section as she could, and suggested that the next year there be both a Western and a Pioneer section. Then a small boy who stowed away on a boat in the Artists Section "caused great confusion by getting seasick." He was finally put ashore. Some of the Boy Scouts rowing the boats were thought to be too young. Sure enough, two of them fell overboard from the Mexican boat. Fortunately, "as this was after the parade, few people noticed."[11]

On revenues of nearly $800 the Conservation Society salvaged a profit of more than $400, half the previous year's but still more than at any of the Indian Harvest Festivals at San José.[12] The fall festival had found its niche and struck a chord of interest with the city and the rest of the nation as well. At the 1942 fall festival, known as the La Villita River Carnival, a photographer for *Time* and *Life* magazines and a newsreel cameraman from Paramount shot the Conservation Society's river parade and activities on Villita Plaza. For the first time, profits rose above the $1,000 mark.[13] The impact of future festival profits was foreshadowed when most of the 1942 profits provided the down payment on the society's first purchase of property away from the missions—the Villita Art Gallery building at 511 Villita Street, bought that summer for $7,000 since the city would not buy it for the La Villita project.[14] The one-story limestone home with a raised basement was built for Jeremiah Dashiell about 1850. It was named Casa Villita.[15]

Buying a slightly run-down, century-old home in the heart of San Antonio brought a quite different set of challenges than had the purchase of a derelict two-century-old stone mission granary at the edge of town. Restoration procedures would be different, as would the upkeep. Fire, hail and tornado insurance had to be negotiated; the society took out a $3,000 policy, but the noteholder thought it should be $5,000.[16] Tenants had to be located, and rents had to be collected.[17]

In addition to her duties as Chairman of Defense, Amanda Taylor was made chairman of the Casa Villita Committee. She had to oversee repainting, replastering, laying a new floor downstairs, putting in new plumbing and adding a bathroom.[18] One of the home's charms was its backyard along the San Antonio River below. A new retaining wall reclaimed 1,000 square feet of land, with the help of several loads of rock which the city donated along with iron grills and gates.[19] Providing advice was former La Villita project architect and now member husband O'Neil Ford, who offered his services at no charge but who, nevertheless, was sent a check from a grateful society.[20] With interest and renovation costs coming to just over $2,600, wartime efforts were not allowed to get in the way of fund-raising.[21] One suggestion was to hold a book review as of old, but the idea was rejected as now having too little profit potential.[22] A card party at the Witte Museum was approved along with a "Guadalajara Tea" at the Governors' Palace. In addition, each member was assessed one dollar.[23] By mid-1946, rental income and fund-raising activities enabled the remaining indebtedness of $750 to be paid off with profits from the River Festival.[24]

As the post-war era began, the San Antonio Conservation Society was firmly anchored in the center of an historic downtown neighborhood which also

Above: The mid-nineteenth century Jeremiah Dashiell House at 511 Villita Street was purchased by the San Antonio Conservation Society in 1942, when the city would not buy it to add to its La Villita property. Grandjean Collection, LVA-52, DRT Library at the Alamo. Below: Restored as Casa Villita and initially rented out, the old home at 511 Villita Street served as Conservation Society headquarters from 1953 until 1974, when headquarters moved to King William Street and Casa Villita became offices for A Night In Old San Antonio. San Antonio Conservation Society.

provided the setting for its major annual fund-raising event. Only one change was needed to complete the formula for future success: the timing of the festival. San Antonio's Fiesta Association saw the value of adding the Conservation Society's Indian Harvest Festival-turned-River Festival to generate more downtown activity around the traditional parades and ceremonies of April's Fiesta Week.[25] As an enticement to move the River Festival to the spring, the Fiesta Association promised to begin underwriting entertainment for the event if the society would agree to take out rain insurance. The River Festival joined Fiesta Week in April of 1946, and profits rose above $1,200.[26]

There had been no festival the previous fall. A Victory Fiesta was proposed at San José in November of 1945 by Ethel Harris, who had been named curator of the San José Historic Site by its new board and who continued to run her pottery operation nearby. That festival was canceled, however, due to conflicting activities for the Texas statehood centennial. Mrs. Harris then held a Fiesta Day during Christmas week.[27] In 1946 she got a fall festival approved by declaring, "in her enthusiastic manner," that since the Conservation Society was responsible for bringing the San José complex to the status of a National Historic Site it was the society's "inherent right" to have an annual festival on the mission grounds.[28] The event was scheduled for Columbus Day, 1946 as an observance of the statehood centennial. It drew a throng of 3,000.[29] The Conservation Society got half of the $2,164 in proceeds, the remainder being split for work on the granary and on the mission church.[30] A San José Fiesta Association was formed to stage an annual fall San José fiesta as a counterpart to the spring fiesta downtown, but the San José fiesta was not repeated.[31]

In 1947, the society's spring festival moved from the riverbanks up to Villita Street. Roped off, its sidewalks were lined with concession stands. Under the chairmanship of Rena Green's daughter Mary Vance Green in 1948, when its theme was San Antonio during the Texas Republic, the event was first referred to as "A Night in Old San Antonio." The designation was picked up by the press, although internally the society still referred to it more frequently as Fiesta at La Villita.[32] The name change was universally accepted the next year. As the event grew, so did efforts of volunteers intensify. In 1947, Chairman Mrs. Ed Leighton, who had run the Indian Harvest Festivals at San José, announced that she would put replicas of the old-time chili stands on Juarez Plaza and serve Mexican food.[33] Two months before, volunteers began meeting Friday mornings to make paper flowers.[34] When profits between 1949 and 1951 more than tripled to $6,500, discussions began on holding the event two nights a week.[35] When profits two years later exceeded $9,000, a second night was approved for 1954.[36] Two years later profits were above $16,700, and, not surprisingly, a third night was suggested.[37]

Wearing her Texas State Parks Board uniform as she rings the mission church bell at San José in the 1940s is Ethel Wilson Harris, who maintained her activity in the San Antonio Conservation Society—and served as president—while also manager of the San José state park. San Antonio Conservation Society.

Rising profits were fortuitous, for another La Villita property came on the market during the summer of 1949. The one and two-story limestone building at the northwest corner of Villita and South Alamo streets, built about 1855 by Otto Bombach and occupied by a bar known as O'Con's Place, was to be torn down for a parking lot.[38] Society directors voted to take a purchase option.[39] Architects O'Neil Ford and Harvey Smith, sent to look the building over, estimated that repairs and improvements would cost $5,000. Directors voted to proceed if the city would not buy it for La Villita.[40] Despite angling by society members, the city would not.[41] By the end of 1949 the terms of the purchase by the Conservation Society were set at $35,000, of which Walter W. McAllister's San Antonio Building and Loan Association would lend $20,000 over fifteen years without requiring the society to mortgage its 511 Villita Street property. Another $5,000 was donated by Mrs. Ted James, chairman of the society's Old Buildings Committee.[42] The new property was dubbed Conservation Corner.

When news of the deal came out, the proprietor called to invite some of the ladies to come by the bar to receive a donation. Ella Daggett (Mrs. Franz) Stumpf, Floy Fontaine and Helen Witte accepted. "Those were the days when 'the ladies' were white-gloved and wore beautiful flowered hats in the spring," Ella Stumpf wrote later. "That afternoon, we three formally presented ourselves

"Conservation Corner," the mid-nineteenth century building at the corner of Villita and South Alamo streets, was purchased in 1949 by the San Antonio Conservation Society. First used in part to house its Old San Antonio Exhibit, with the rest of the building rented, in 1967 it was leased to become the Little Rhein Steakhouse. San Antonio Conservation Society.

at the bar and rotund, smiling Mr. O'Con handed us a check for one hundred dollars. 'Ladies,' he said, 'I was sorry when you bought the building. I have to move. It will be bad for business, but I like what you are doing.' . . . Then he added, 'Won't you ladies have a drink?'

"This was indeed our moment of truth. It's an understatement to say that we were uncomfortable in the dark and dingy bar, half-filled with habitués and their ladies of the downstairs-upstairs. But to refuse the invitation of our donor and make a precipitous exit seemed downright ungracious and unbecoming. We looked at each other. Noblesse oblige. 'Yes, thank you. We will.'

"I doubt if Mrs. Fontaine or Helen Witte at that time ever sipped anything stronger than sherry at Thanksgiving. But having gone that far, each of us put our little foot on the brass rail and sipped three beers at Mr. O'Con's bar. I wish I had the picture."[43]

With the transaction complete, new society member Henry Steinbomer was named project architect, and work began.[44] The drill had become familiar. The Lumbermen's Association gave wood for rafters and floors.[45] Jack Beretta drew instructions for City Street Commissioner James Knight, who volunteered to excavate and remove dirt at the rear. A cistern was uncovered plus a basement room previously filled with silt from the flooding river and with other debris, including an enormous pile of beer bottle caps dropped through a knothole in the floor above.[46] Stone was donated for the rear wall.[47] The

San Antonio River Authority helped get the stone steps down to the river at the rear completed. A stairway was given from the George Brackenridge mansion being torn down for the Bel Meade subdivision and Amanda Taylor's landscaping committee got a check for grass and donations of shrubs, which Mrs. Lutcher Brown and Eleanor Bennett were helping to plant.[48]

As expenses mounted, there was the usual scramble for more funds. The Committee on the Opening Tea was directed to work with the Committee on White Elephant Sales.[49] A fund-raising review was set of Elizabeth Graham's new mission play. Mrs. Graham agreed to loan the society $2,000 if need be.[50] Mrs. Ted James loaned another $1,000.[51] A Canasta Party was held in the Corral Building of the Pearl Brewery.[52] Mrs. Victor Braunig, the "Chairman of Patios" and of the new building as well, arranged four hundred chairs on the building's riverbank to rent at two dollars each for the Texas Cavaliers' Fiesta river parade.[53] The rummage sale was revived, and netted $638.[54] To boost admissions at A Night in Old San Antonio, each member was sent ten tickets to sell.[55] An anonymous restoration loan of $3,000 came in. The city, however, still had to be asked to help out on the "immediate financial difficulties."[56]

The pressure began to ease by the spring of 1951. Leases for the two ground-floor shops and the upstairs apartment were signed in January. Only the basement remained to be finished and leased.[57] Dues were raised.[58] When the $3,000 loan came due in May, it could be paid off with less than half of the proceeds from that year's A Night in Old San Antonio.[59] By the end of the year the building's monthly rental income was more than twice the amount of the monthly debt payments.[60]

While La Villita was absorbing the Conservation Society's energies, members kept aware of situations in other parts of the city. In 1941 the society supported the city's purchase of the Guilbeau House on South Main Avenue and counted on its becoming a museum after the war. It hoped for preservation of the picturesque small limestone block houses on what was known as the Irish Flat on the northern edge of downtown.[61] Rena Green wanted the society to help preserve the old stone Leon Springs stagecoach inn, about to be sold.[62] In 1944 two members went to Austin to urge the governor to free dormant Confederate veterans benefit funds so the Daughters of the Confederacy could purchase the antebellum Vance House just south of the Bexar County Courthouse.[63] When that effort failed, four years later the Conservation Society tried to buy the home itself.[64]

Chance, however, was still playing the major role for landmarks. In 1940 the number came up for the historic Menger Hotel on Alamo Plaza. At a party in 1940, a banker friend told Ella Stumpf that Joske's Department Store across Blum Street from the Menger had a purchase option on the hotel and intended to tear it down for parking. Mrs. Stumpf went to Conservation

Society President Amanda Taylor, who "refused to take any action" because she was a friend of one of the owners trying to sell the hotel. Next Mrs. Stumpf went to the editor of the *San Antonio Express.* He "wouldn't touch" the story "because Joske's was one of their largest advertisers." So she spread the alarm to her friend J. Frank Dobie, the University of Texas folklorist who also wrote a syndicated newspaper column. Much to her surprise, the following Sunday a nearly full-page article with a picture of the Menger patio appeared in the *San Antonio Light.*[65]

"Every Texan, paraphrasing what Macaulay once said of Paris, has two homes, his own and San Antonio," wrote Dobie. "San Antonio, the city of the Alamo, where Travis and Bowie and Crockett and Bonham and 180-odd other Texans will live, despite death, as long as liberty is a word in the human language. San Antonio of the twisted river, of plazas and of much else that made Lord Bryce reckon it as one of the three or four cities of atmosphere and individuality in the whole United States. James H. Cook, who came to San Antonio not long after the Civil War and hired to a cowman who was returning to a ranch with his Mexican vaqueros who had driven up a herd of cattle, says as they rode down the trail they kept singing 'Mi San Antonio Querido,' 'My Loved San Antonio.' It is an old song, its words and tune perhaps lost; but its burden will go on echoing for generations yet to come in the hearts of people all over the land.

"And now rumor comes that one of the most signal of all of San Antonio's landmarks is on the verge of being destroyed to make room for something that will make more money. This landmark is the Menger Hotel. It is hard by the Alamo, on Alamo Plaza . . . . No, I am not writing an advertisement. I am writing with the hope of preservation for something beautiful and more valuable than money, something rich in memories, something that seems to belong to 'Mi San Antonio Querido,' to Alamo Plaza and to Texans every-where—belongs as quietly and as rightly as the evening star belongs to after-twilight, something settled and in harmony with itself in this screeching world of ceaseless change. I hear a lovely singer, but she has a little money in her purse. Who would kill her and kill her voice to get that money? If any reader wants to add his voice to saving the Menger, let him write to Mrs. Ella Daggett Stumpf, 602 Augusta Street, San Antonio. Voices will count."[66]

Mrs. Stumpf took the responses to Joske's President James Calvert. He decided not to exercise his option to buy the Menger. And the banker friend who unwittingly tipped her off, she said, "never spoke to me again."[67]

After having had to go it alone to save the Menger Hotel, the next year Ella Stumpf led organization of the Historic Buildings Foundation, which saw itself not as having the wide-ranging goals of the Conservation Society but simply as "a society for the preservation of Texas antiquities." The group

When Joske's Department Store considered buying the historic Menger Hotel and razing it for a parking lot, J. Frank Dobie wrote that the Menger Hotel belongs to San Antonians and Texans everywhere "as quietly and as rightly as the evening star belongs to after-twilight, something settled and in harmony with itself in this screeching world of ceaseless change." Joske's backed off, the Menger was later restored and the store leveled the nearby Blum Street neighborhood for parking instead. Zintgraff Collection, The Institute of Texan Cultures.

included local architects Marvin Eickenroht, J. Fred Buenz and Henry Steinbomer, who was elected the first president.[68]

Two years earlier, Steinbomer had designed the replica Texas pioneer log cabin built behind the Witte Museum with National Youth Administration labor.[69] In 1941, the two-story, century-old stone home of Irish merchant and banker John Twohig on the banks of the San Antonio River was to be torn down by the San Antonio Public Service Company. The Historic Buildings Foundation furnished three architects and an engineer to oversee its disassembling and reconstruction far upstream, on the banks of the river behind the Witte Museum. The City Public Service Company donated the building and paid for the move, and the Conservation Society gathered furnishings. The last of 430 sacks of cement donated by the Portland Cement Company arrived just before a wartime freeze on use of cement went into effect. Used as the shared headquarters of the Historic Buildings Foundation and the San Antonio Garden Center, the Twohig House was the last project completed in Texas by WPA workers.[70]

The Twohig house was joined in 1943 by the reconstructed home of native Texas Declaration of Independence signer José Francisco Ruiz. Severely damaged by a hurricane, the one-story home had been built of plastered rubble stone about a century before. It faced north on Military Plaza on Dolorosa Street, and at the turn of the nineteenth century housed the city's first public school.[71] Technical assistance was provided by the Historic Buildings Foundation as it was again in 1947 for the third reconstructed building funded through the museum—the small, limestone block home built on Camaron Street about 1835 by Celso Navarro, father of Texas Declaration of Independence signer José Antonio Navarro and uncle of José Francisco Ruiz. The Celso Navarro house lay in the path of Fox Tech High School's athletic field expansion. It was saved purely by chance. When Museum Director Ellen Schulz Quillin first called the San Antonio Board of Education and asked if the house was still standing, she was told, "It is, but only because a bulldozer has broken down."[72]

The Historic Buildings Foundation focused on architectural assistance during its decade of existence; most of its members ultimately joined the Conservation Society. The Texas Historical and Landmarks Association still did not venture beyond placing historical markers. But the Conservation Society continued to broaden its support and seek bigger things. From a full complement in 1942 of 300 members, more than half of whom were behind on their dues, membership requirements were changed and by mid-1953 membership had more than doubled to 787. Nearly half were in the recently created category of associate members, from which active members were selected. Dues payment rules and attendance records were tightened. Within eight months another 159 associate members joined, bringing total membership close to the 1,000 mark.[73]

Older members were honored, but youth was also prized as a means of maintaining the society's vitality. One member went on the board to replace her mother, one of the first directors to retire in line with "an announced decision of placing more youthful members on the board and in all offices."[74] In 1950 the society recognized as its oldest member Frank Edwards, 94, the father of Emily Edwards and Floy Edwards Fontaine who was present at the first meeting. Members then drank a toast to the youngest person present—Mitchell Robin, two and a half, the grandson of Mrs. George Wurzbach.[75] In 1949, Agnes Virginia Temple became the society's first president to become a mother while in office. With word of the arrival, members interrupted their meeting at the home of Mrs. Marion Koogler McNay to send the newborn Susanna Virginia Temple a telegram of welcome.[76] Christmas parties were made annual mother-daughter events, and the promotion

Above: The 1835 José Francisco Ruiz House was sandwiched between commercial buildings facing north on Military Plaza by the end of the nineteenth century. Courtesy of the Witte Museum, San Antonio, Texas. Below: Damaged by a hurricane and about to be razed, the José Francisco Ruiz House was rescued in 1947 with help from the Historic Buildings Foundation, reconstructed on the grounds behind the Witte Museum and first used as a pottery shop by Harding Black. Courtesy of the Witte Museum, San Antonio, Texas.

worked. Of twenty-three new members admitted in May of 1947, eleven were daughters of current members.[77]

After the Conservation Society turned its San José Mission property over to the state, in five years its financial assets grew from $2,400—two-thirds of it the aqueduct property and the rest the cash value of two United States Defense Bonds—to $16,900 with the addition of Casa Villita.[78] In 1948 Ethel Harris became chairman of the new Committee of Properties.[79] A telephone chairman was named in 1951 to notify board members of the "numerous emergency meetings."[80] A part-time secretary was hired in 1952, and within four years there were several part-time employees.[81] An office was opened in two rooms of Casa Villita early in 1953, when the River Art Group agreed to reduce the amount of space it was renting.[82] A Night In Old San Antonio so dependably replenished the treasury by annually netting in the vicinity of $10,000, barring bad weather, that in 1955 directors decided to protect the name by registering it.[83]

Beyond the burden of administrative concerns, the San Antonio Conservation Society continued to broaden its outlook in the city and state. Annual awards, first presented at the Texas Independence Day reception at the Spanish Governor's Palace in 1948, recognized not only San Antonians for preservation work but persons in nearby towns as well.[84] Annual tours went to nearby historic communities—Castroville, Fredericksburg, Boerne, Comfort, New Braunfels and Bandera, as well as to Guerrero across the border in Mexico.[85]

When the legislature created the Texas State Historical Survey Committee in 1953 to coordinate historical information and preservation throughout the state, appointees included Conservation Society members Amanda Cartwright Taylor and Meta (Mrs. Raymond) Russell.[86] Several other members were named two years later to the state committee's new subsidiary, the Bexar County Historical Survey Committee.[87] As the historic preservation movement began coalescing nationwide, in 1952 the Conservation Society joined the National Council for Historic Sites and Buildings, soon to be merged with the National Trust for Historic Preservation.[88] The Conservation Society backed preservation of Savannah's old Market House in Georgia, and formed a committee to aid New Mexico's Pueblo Indians in protesting the building of dams on their land.[89] Texas Senator Price Daniel was urged to introduce a bill establishing a Fine Arts Commission to aid in preserving historical sites throughout the nation.[90]

As the Conservation Society entered the post-war era, however, members did not lose sight of the challenges in San Antonio itself. For whatever threats to preservation were removed by the lack of new downtown construction were made up for by a seemingly insatiable demand for new parking lots. One of the first customers for more parking was San Antonio's largest department store, Joske's, which prior to World War II had been dissuaded from putting a parking lot to its north in place of the Menger Hotel. With the war over, Joske's looked instead across Bonham Street to its east, to the Blum Street neighborhood of quaint adobe homes dating back a century and a half.

Ella Stumpf and company went back on alert. Early in 1947, Historic Buildings Foundation President Henry Steinbomer approached the Conservation Society to help form a joint delegation of members from the Conservation Society, Historic Buildings Foundation, Texas Historical and Landmarks Association, Yanaguana Society and Texas Pioneers. The group went to meet with Joske's President James Calvert to urge that at least some of the homes be saved and used for individual shops. Calvert replied that "nothing could be done" to save the homes, but held out hope that one could be used as a plant nursery.[91]

Presenting to a leading businessman the case of a well-known and thoroughly documented landmark like the Menger Hotel was one thing. Presenting to the same businessman, however, the case of a group of small houses that looked charming but about which little specific information was known was considerably less compelling. It only underscored the dangers inherent of being, as Charles Hosmer had observed of early San Antonio preservationists, "long on inspiration and short on research." The neighborhood disappeared for a huge parking lot.

The loss of the Blum Street neighborhood points out a dichotomy between the inspired San Antonio preservationists and more traditional preservationists elsewhere. While San Antonio preservationists were gathering a vibrant membership, saving landmarks and preserving a mood, preservationists in Charleston were gaining the nation's first local legislation to establish an historic district.[92] In 1939, San Antonio preservationists won a Carnegie grant to help build Bolivar Hall to encourage harmony in the western hemisphere and promote world peace. Two years before, preservationists in Monterey, California obtained an historic preservation master plan and zoning ordinance using an earlier Carnegie Institution study done on the subject for St. Augustine, Florida.[93] Charlestonians also lowered their sights to less than hemispheric idealism and got a Carnegie grant to help survey the historic resources of their city. A fifteen-month study produced a report with documentation and photographs of 1,168 historic buildings, summarized in 1944 in *This Is Charleston* and credited with awakening public support to save the old city.[94]

Local preservationists knew something like that should happen in San Antonio, at least through a study if not a book. But the commitment to undertake such a vast and dull effort was lacking. After most Blum Street houses were cleared for parking, Conservation Society President Mary (Mrs. Nat) Kenney did seek to gather a data base of San Antonio landmarks so the society would at least know what it was defending when the time came. In late 1947 she asked that each member make a list of "the interesting houses and buildings in San Antonio" as a reference list for the society.[95] A year later two members began taking pictures of the city's old buildings and putting them in the society's scrapbook.[96] Four years after she assigned the project, as a past president Mrs. Kenney was again asking members to submit lists—in two months—of buildings they thought should be saved.[97] It was another six months before a listing was prepared.[98] Then, nearly a year after that, someone remembered that the Texas Historical and Landmarks Association's list of landmarks should be checked over.[99] It took nearly another year to obtain that list and get copies passed around.[100]

Until some sort of professional inventory was undertaken, San Antonio preservationists were going to have to over-compensate with enthusiasm. But that was still more than preservationists in most American cities could count on in these years.

Notes

1. Minutes, G-Jan. 22, 1942, 2. In mid-1941 the society began to purchase United States savings bonds. Shortly after Pearl Harbor the society began meetings by singing "The Star-Spangled Banner," voted to continue meeting during the war and donated $25 to the Red Cross. Members vowed to engage individually in some kind of defense work and also named a Chairman of Nutrition in National Defense. (Minutes; D-Jul. 23, 1941; D&G-Dec. 18, 1941; G-Aug. 6, 1942.)

2. Minutes, G-Dec. 18, 1941, 1, 2. In the spring of 1942, members marked the anniversary of the society's founding with a Victory Tea, its proceeds helping buy another war bond. In December, officers bought a $25 savings bond instead of refreshments for the Christmas meeting. ("Victory Tea Fund Buys War Bond," *San Antonio Express*, Apr. 26, 1942; Minutes, G-Dec. 17, 1942, 2.)

3. Minutes, D-Sept. 25, 1941

4. Minutes, D-Jun. 18, 1941, 2. Soldiers without furloughs were invited by society members to their homes for Christmas in 1941. The next spring, members served 50 Kelly Field cadets an Easter Sunday Mexican dinner at the Cós House and the Brooks Field Glee Club presented a program. Members gathered books for servicemen and sewed handkerchiefs. High school bands were scheduled for a series of Sunday concerts for soldiers at the Arneson River Theater, the society's only cost being five dollars to rent a piano. As the war continued, a party for convalescents was held at Brooke General Hospital and others were entertained with a party at the River Carnival. (Minutes, G-Dec. 18, 1941, 2; G-Mar. 26, 1942; D-Apr. 24, 1942; G-May 28, 1942, 2; G-Dec. 17, 1942, 2; G-Jan. 28, 1943; D-Apr. 27, 1944; G-May 25, 1944; G-Oct. 26, 1944; "Conservation Society to Entertain Cadets," *San Antonio Express*, Apr. 6, 1942.)

5. Minutes, G-Sept. 21, 1944. To conserve paper, no new yearbooks were printed in 1944 and general membership meetings were at last suspended.

6. Minutes, G-Sept. 25, 1941.

7. "Fall Festival Along River," *San Antonio Express,* Sept. 28, 1941, 12-D; "Fall Festival Set for Today," *San Antonio Express,* Oct. 11, 1941; Minutes, G-Oct. 23, 1941, 1–2. In the River Festivals, each section chairman, "the mainspring of a coordinated group," was to complete a "living picture" of an assigned time in San Antonio history, including appropriate entertainment and finding clubs and/or merchants to pay for decorating boats anchored at each section. In 1941, for example, Solo-Serve sponsored the Selene Club's boat with a Spanish theme; Fomby Clothing Store, the Woman's Club's boat featuring the Old South; Frost Brothers, the Red Cross entry; Stowers Furniture, the Liberty Belles with a USO theme; Frank Brothers, the San Antonio Academy boat with its Future Home Guards. Among others were the City Water Board Social Club, "Texas Gives the World the Homesteading Law;" White Star Laundry, "Buy A Defense Bond;" Delaware Punch, "Keep 'Em Flying;" and Our Lady of the Lake College, "Victory." ("River Festival is Major Event Tonight," *San Antonio Evening News,* Oct. 11, 1941, 6; "Conservation Society River Festival Instructions to Section Chairmen, 1944" in Conservation Society Scrapbook for 1924–1964 in SACS Library.)

8. In 1944, a "grand march" led to the carnival section, termed "a mammoth masquerado." ("Instructions to Section Chairmen.")

9. Ibid.; "Fall Festival Set for Today," *San Antonio Express,* Oct. 11, 1941; Minutes, G-Sept. 25, 1941, 2. Concessionnaires gave the Conservation Society ten percent of sales.

10. Minutes, G-Oct. 23, 1941, 1–2. Their losses, however, ended up at only about eight dollars.

11. Ibid.

12. Ibid.

13. Minutes, Jan. 23, 1941, 1–2; G-Oct. 22, 1942. Wartime kept the festival from being held in 1943 but there was one again in 1944, yielding another $1,000-plus profit.

14. Ibid; G-Aug. 6, 1942. The 1990 equivalent price is $56,000. The house was purchased the previous year by Society President Martha Camp and held for the society to buy from her. (Josephine H. Henning OHT, Dec. 8, 1983.)

15. Minutes, G-Oct. 28, 1943, 2.

16. Minutes, D-Oct. 22, 1942; D-Dec. 17, 1942.

17. Once furniture was donated, in April of 1943 the downstairs apartment was rented to "a defense worker," who also began helping with the furnishings. In 1947 upstairs tenants left for the renovation to society meeting rooms. But within two years the space was leased to the River Arts Group, and members went back to meeting in other locations. Continuing festivities included the patriotic reception held since 1943 at the Spanish Governors' Palace on March 2—Texas Independence Day—which replaced the traditional March Founders' Day; the May picnic, held sometimes at the Governor's Palace and other times at the Ford family's "Willow Way;" and the Christmas party, which followed each December meeting. (Minutes, G-Mar. 25, 1943; G-Apr. 19, 1943; D-Jan. 12, 1944; D-Mar. 15, 1944; G-May 25, 1944; D-Jan.

23, 1947; D-Feb. 25, 1947; G-Nov. 20, 1947; D-Sept. 22, 1949; G-Mar. 23, 1950; G-May 24, 1955.)

18. Minutes, G-Dec. 17, 1942; G-Mar. 25, 1943; G-Apr. 29, 1943; D&G-May 27, 1943; D-May 25, 1944.

19. Minutes, G-Mar. 25, 1943.

20. Minutes, D-Sept. 4, 1947, 2.

21. Minutes, D-Oct. 22, 1942; G-Oct. 23, 1947.

22. Minutes, Feb. 25, 1943.

23. Minutes, G-Feb. 25, 1943, 2; G-Sept. 23, 1943, 2; D-Oct. 28, 1943.

24. Minutes, D-Jun. 6, 1946.

25. Minutes, D-Dec. 6, 1945; G-Dec. 20, 1945; D-Jun. 6, 1946; G-Sept. 19, 1946; D-Sept. 4, 1947.

26. Minutes, G-Sept. 16, 1946, 2. Entertainment underwriting by the Fiesta Association ceased after 1951. (G-Jan. 25, 1951.)

27. Minutes, G-Jun. 4, 1941, 1–2; D-Aug. 22, 1945; D-Sept. 27, 1945; D-Dec. 6, 1945.

28. Minutes, G-Sept. 19, 1946, 2.

29. "San José Centennial Fiesta Attracts 3,000," *San Antonio Express,* Oct. 14, 1946, 1-A.

30. Minutes, D-Dec. 5, 1946.

31. "Annual Fiesta for Fall at San José Planned," *San Antonio Light,* Sept. 22, 1946, 1-C. In 1947 the Conservation Society discovered it still owned two tracts of mission land thought to have been given to the state. The Huisache Bowl was given to the state and the strip of land near the granary was sold for $400 to Ethel Harris, who built her home on the land. (Minutes, D-May 20, 1947; D-Oct. 25, 1949; G-Dec. 15, 1949; D-Jan. 23, 1950, 2.) Mrs. Harris specified that her property go to the state after her death. (Glory Felder OHT, 7.)

32. Minutes, D-Feb. 24, 1948; D-May 25, 1948.

33. Minutes, G-Feb. 27, 1947.

34. Minutes, D-Feb. 25, 1954.

35. Minutes, D-May 3, 1949; G-May 24, 1951; D-Jan. 16, 1952; G-Feb. 28, 1952.

36. Minutes, G-May 28, 1953; G-Jun. 24, 1953. The 1990 equivalent of 1953 profits was $44,000. Rewarding volunteers gave another excuse for regular parties. Mary Green held a thank-you party for her 1948 committee in San Pedro Park and in 1954 Elizabeth Graham and daughter Wanda Graham Ford held both a pre-Fiesta party for the new NIOSA committee and a post-Fiesta party for workers. (Minutes, May 25, 1948; D-Apr. 15, 1954; D-May 24, 1954; D-Jun. 22, 1954.)

37. Minutes, D-Jun. 25, 1956, 3; G-Sept. 27, 1956.

38. Minutes, D-Jul. 27, 1949; Agnes Virginia Temple OHT, Mar. 10, 1986, 6.

39. Minutes, D-Jul. 27, 1949.

40. Minutes, D-Oct. 25, 1949, 2–4. Former Mayor Maury Maverick helped the society seek eligibility for property tax exemption.

41. Floy Edwards Fontaine OHT, 1.

42. Minutes, G-Dec. 15, 1949. The 1990 equivalent of the purchase price was $192,000.

43. Ella Stumpf, "Three Beers at O'Con's Bar," *The San Antonio Conservation Society News*, 30 (March, 1994), 9. The story was the Memory Lane Contest anecdote winner years earlier.

44. Minutes, D-Sept. 22, 1949; D-Jan. 23, 1950. Steinbomer and the rest of the Historic Buildings Foundation membership were apparently absorbed into the Conservation Society by this time.

45. Minutes, D-Sept. 12, 1950.

46. Minutes, D-Jan. 16, 1951; Fontaine OHT, 2; Temple OHT, 7.

47. Minutes, D-Mar. 20, 1951.

48. Minutes, G-Mar. 22, 1951, 2.

49. Minutes, D-Sept. 12, 1950.

50. Minutes, D-Jan. 16, 1951.

51. Minutes, D-Apr. 3, 1951.

52. Minutes, G-Jan. 25, 1951.

53. Minutes, D-Apr. 3, 1951.

54. Minutes, G-Mar. 23, 1950.

55. Minutes, G-Feb. 23, 1950.

56. Minutes, G-Dec. 21, 1950, 1, 3.

57. Minutes, D-Jan. 23, 1951.

58. Minutes, D-May 22, 1951, 2.

59. Ibid., 1.

60. Minutes, G-Nov., 1951.

61. Minutes, G-Jun. 5, 1941, 2. The term Irish Flat refers to the level area settled by Irish immigrants. The designation is often corrupted to Irish "Flats" and mistakenly interpreted to identify Irish immigrants' homes themselves as "flats," or apartments.

62. Minutes, D-Apr. 24, 1942; G-May 28, 1942.

63. Minutes, G-Oct. 26, 1944, 1–2.

64. Minutes, D-Dec. 14, 1948.

65. Mrs. Franz (Ella) Stumpf OHT, Feb. 4, 1976, 4–5.

66. J. Frank Dobie, "Save Old Menger Hotel, Dobie Pleads," *San Antonio Light*, Jul. 21, 1940, 10. Lord Bryce was the British historian James Bryce (1838–1922), who also served as British ambassador to the United States.

67. Stumpf OHT, 6–7. The Menger was eventually purchased and refurbished by National Hotel chain owner W.L. Moody of Galveston. At its formal reopening in 1950, the Conservation Society arranged for antique Texas garb to be worn by owners' descendants. (Minutes, D-Oct. 24, 1950.)

68. Ella K. Daggett Stumpf to Samuel Gideon, Apr. 10, 1941, in Samuel Gideon Papers, The Center for American History, The University of Texas at Austin. Tapping into the growing numbers of preservation organizations not only nationwide but, by then, within the state as well, the Historic Buildings Foundation was in touch with both veteran preservationist William Sumner Appleton of the Society for the Preservation of New England Antiquities and Texas preservationist Samuel E. Gideon at the University of Texas in Austin.

69. Woolford and Quillin, *The Story of the Witte Memorial Museum*, 79–80. A replica of a Hill Country log cabin was built nearby in 1947–48.

70. Ibid., 98–101; "Twohig Home to be Moved, *San Antonio Express,* Nov. 22, 1941; Minutes, G-Dec. 17, 1942, 2; "The Story of the Twohig House," brochure in SACS Library.

71. Ibid., 85–86, 89.

72. Ibid., 90–92.

73. Minutes, D-Mar. 25, 1942, 2; D-Mar. 21, 1950; D-Jun. 17, 1952, 2; D-May 22, 1953; G-Jan. 28, 1954; G-May 27, 1954; G-Jun. 22, 1954. The active membership allotment was increased to 450 in 1954. In 1952, a five-tier associate membership plan with dues running from $2 to $100 brought in 47 new business members. (Minutes, D-Sept. 10, 1952, 2; D-Nov. 25, 1952, 2; D-Jan. 14, 1953.)

74. Minutes, Feb. 27, 1941, 4-5. Mrs. Bruce Brough replaced her mother, Mrs. E.A. Holmgreen.

75. Minutes, D-Jan. 23, 1950, 2.

76. Minutes, G-Mar. 24, 1949. Susanna, later Mrs. John Stiles, was given a cup and a life membership in the society, and in a burst of enthusiasm was voted the society mascot. (Minutes, May 3, 1949, 2.)

77. Minutes, D-May 20, 1947; G-Dec. 21, 1951. Mrs. Elizabeth Graham read a paper on the inheritance the society was passing on and her daughter, Wanda Graham Ford, responded with a paper of her own. Mrs. Ford later was the first president to be the daughter of a former president. (Minutes, G-Dec. 14, 1944; D-Apr. 12, 1955.)

78. Minutes, D-May 28, 1942, 2; D-May 20, 1947. Savings ran from a few hundred to a thousand dollars during the war years to above $3,000 during the following decade except during the Conservation Corner pinch, when savings dipped to $124.83 just before A Night in Old San Antonio in 1951. (Minutes, G-Mar. 22, 1951.)

79. Minutes, D-Jul. 27, 1948, 2. Reports of all committees had to be made with "brevity and clarity;" it was suggested that a sergeant at arms stop each report after five minutes. (Minutes, D-Dec. 6, 1954, 2.)

80. Minutes, D-Oct. 25, 1951. The next year, a newsletter was first planned and speakers prepared slides for outside presentations. A part-time "publicity agent" was first hired to promote to the newspapers the fall River Jubilee in 1940. In 1950, two months after a proposed contract was rejected, an anonymous donation of $50 covered half of a two-month fee to *San Antonio Express* writer Charles Ramsdell for publicizing the purchase of Conservation Corner. (Minutes, G-Sept. 25, 1941; D-Nov. 15, 1949; D-Jan. 23, 1950, 2; D-Nov. 25, 1952, 3.)

81. Minutes, D-Jan. 16, 1952; D-May 21, 1956, 2.

82. Minutes, D-Jan. 14, 1953; G-Jan. 22, 1953; D-Feb. 26, 1953, 2.

83. Minutes, D-May 16, 1955. The society broke even on its $4,200 sponsorship of Ramsey Yelvington's play "A Cloud of Witnesses," which had a cast of 65 performing at the newly renovated Huisache Bowl at San José Mission on six July nights in 1955. (Minutes, D-Jun. 6, 1955; D-Sept. 19, 1955.)

84. Minutes, D-Feb. 26, 1948; D-Jan. 25, 1949, 2.

85. Minutes, D-Jul. 23, 1941; G-Jan. 22, 1942, 2; G-Oct. 28, 1948, 2; D-Feb. 17, 1953, 2; D-Apr. 15, 1954; D-Feb. 24, 1955; D-Feb. 20, 1956.

86. Minutes, G-Nov. 11, 1953, 1-2. Nominated the next year by the Conservation Society to serve on the state committee were Eleanor Bennett and Ethel Harris, plus, if a third member were authorized, Wanda Ford. (Minutes, D-Nov. 22, 1954.)

87. Minutes, G-Dec. 8, 1955.

88. Minutes, D-Jan. 16, 1952, 2.

89. Minutes, G-Jan. 27, 1944, 1–2; D-Mar. 15, 1944; D-Apr. 27, 1944; D-Sept. 16, 1953.

90. Minutes, D-Jan. 14, 1953; D-Feb. 17, 1953.

91. Minutes, D-Feb. 25, 1947; G-Feb. 27, 1947 1-2; D-Mar. 27, 1947; G-Mar. 27, 1947, 2; D-May 20, 1947.

92. Hosmer, *Preservation Comes of Age*, 1065. The Charleston legislation passed in 1931. Five years later the Louisiana constitution was amended to establish the Vieux Carré Commission in New Orleans.

93. Ibid. Soon after the war, historic district ordinances were passed in Alexandria, Va., Williamsburg, Va. and Winston-Salem, N.C.

94. Helen Duprey Bullock, Chief of Historical Research, National Council for Historic Sites and Buildings, to SACS Corresponding Secretary Mrs. Jack Watts, Mar. 28, 1952, in SACS Library.

95. Minutes, G-Nov. 20, 1947.

96. Minutes, D-Nov. 16, 1948; G-Dec. 18, 1948. The scrapbook has long since disappeared.

97. Minutes, G-Nov., 1951.

98. Minutes, D-May 22, 1952.

99. Minutes, G-Jan. 22, 1953, 3.

100. Minutes, D-Dec. 3, 1953.

9

Six Flags
Over San Antonio

The end of World War II brought no military stand-down to San Antonio. The Cold War kept San Antonio's five military bases thriving, their new civilian employees helping boost the city's population during the 1940s by sixty percent, to 400,000, and keeping San Antonio's industry-short economy over-whelmingly service-based. As was the case in other American cities, most of these new residents joined former residents of the central city in San Antonio's fast-spreading outskirts.[1]

The political machine which wrested control back from Maury Maverick in 1941, however, had trouble providing services to newly annexed areas of the city. In the spring of 1951, hotelier and San Antonio River beautification proponent Jack White led reformers to a clean sweep of city hall. Banker Walter W. McAllister was put in charge of a commission to revise the city charter.[2] The new charter set up a council-manager form of municipal government. No longer was each elected city commissioner responsible for a specific sector of city government. To elimi-nate cronyism and create a more impersonal and objective governmental process, city councilmen were now to perform advisory roles for an appointed city manager, who, rather than a strong mayor, would implement council policy.

Dealing with this city government called for a new sophistication on the part of civic interest groups like the San Antonio Conservation Society, and develop-ing a new approach would take time. But unlike so many American cities where preservation organizations were only beginning, in San Antonio the Conser-vation Society was well seasoned, having survived its first flush of enthusiasm, kept its sense of purpose and continued to grow. It was still composed of well-connected members with broad-ranging goals who could anticipate many problems and who were flexible enough to adapt to new challenges.[3]

As San Antonio's municipal reformers plunged headlong into planning change throughout the spring and summer of 1951, leaders of the San

Antonio Conservation Society were wary of some of the new proposals, in particular of proposed charter provisions calling for creation of a city planning commission and for redevelopment of blighted neighborhoods. If the character of San Antonio's distinctive historic built environment was not to be bled to death by a thousand cuts, Conservation Society leaders realized, the society had to make good on its declaration to develop an overall plan and an effective preservation strategy. And that had to be compatible with members' insistence that landmarks be preserved in place to reflect the neighborhood's original character, rather than being carted off to an artificial grouping of restored buildings as that behind the Witte Museum. A suggestion by the Highland Park Lions Club that rescued landmarks be gathered at the Southside Lions Park was politely rejected.[4]

At a pivotal meeting on September 18, 1951, Conservation Society directors gathered at "Willow Way" to address the situation. Immediate concerns were nearly as wide-ranging as those of the society's first meeting twenty-seven years before. Three of the founders were, in fact, still playing leadership roles at this meeting. Like the first, it dealt in no uncertain terms with the need to restore landmarks, to preserve the environment and to continue San Antonio's cultural traditions. It even acknowledged faith in the ability of women to achieve change on their own. Featured speaker on this Tuesday morning was Sam Zisman, urban planning specialist and associate of O'Neil Ford, who discussed implications of new city planning and downtown redevelopment.

Following Zisman's remarks, Amanda Cartwright Taylor proposed a successful resolution asking that a Conservation Plan be included in whatever master plan the city adopted. It recommended full consideration of "the preservation and conservation of significant historical public and private buildings and places." The resolution expressed concern with planning for the San Antonio River and its tributaries and for parks and other open spaces. It promised that the society would cooperate in setting up the Conservation Plan and forming a Planning Commission.[5]

Elizabeth Graham formally presented to directors "a plan dear to the heart of all Conservation members" as the Conservation Plan: Texas Under Six Flags. The concept had been around since the nineteenth century.[6] In this incarnation, it would feature one San Antonio landmark for each of the six nations which once controlled Texas land. The Spanish Governor's Palace would represent Spain; the Guilbeau House, France; Haymarket Plaza, later substituted by the José Antonio Navarro House, Mexico; the Alamo, Texas; the Vance House, the Confederacy; and the Arsenal, the United States.[7] It was no coincidence that two of these were currently in great danger: the Guilbeau House and the Vance House. The plan was later described by President Ethel Harris as "a sort of battle cry to spur interest in history and conservation work."[8]

The time-honored theme of the six flags of Texas, here presented to Amelia Earhart, left, during her visit to the Alamo in 1936, was picked up by the Conservation Society in 1951 as the basis of a plan for historic preservation in San Antonio. Looking on is City Commissioner Phil Wright. The San Antonio Light *Collection, The Institute of Texan Cultures.*

To deal with specifics, a committee was named to entreat with the new also owner of the Guilbeau House. Directors zeroed in on another endangered landmark—the old German-English School complex newly vacated on South Alamo Street by San Antonio Junior College. The San Antonio Board of Education was asked for and granted custody of the complex to the Conservation Society to the Conservation Society for one year.[9] To be ready to protect landmarks in general, Mary Kenney suggested that the Old Buildings Committee present in two months "a complete list" of buildings which had to be preserved, the task she had tried to get accomplished as president four years before.[10] At the end of the meeting, one member decided that her own earlier motion asking that a Men's Advisory Committee be formed to aid the Conservation Society was not such a good idea after all, implying that the women could still do just fine on their own. Other directors agreed that the motion should be withdrawn, and all adjourned for lunch.[11]

Conservation Society relations with city hall were cordial in the coming months. A committee visited the first city manager, C.A. Harrell.[12] Harrell, in turn, came to a Conservation Society general membership meeting, observing that, as a Virginian, he was well aware of the value of historic preservation.[13] Amanda Taylor and Eleanor Bennett were appointed to the San Antonio River Authority Board. Representation was urged on the San Antonio Housing Authority board, to "show the society's interest in all civic movements."[14] Two members were named to the Fine Arts Commission established to advise the Planning Board.[15]

While the Conservation Society fine-tuned its Six Flags plan, Ethel Harris invited city officials and community-minded men to join society directors for a two-hour lunch at the Governor's Palace in May. Forty-five persons attended. After outlining circumstances involving the two most endangered landmarks—the Guilbeau and Vance houses—Sam Zisman stated the importance of the Conservation Society and the city working together and of the need to preserve adequate park land.[16] City Manager Harrell, in response, said that groups like the Conservation Society "are necessary," and that it was up to them to say what should be done. The society's scribe thought Harrell "willing and ready to help the society." O'Neil Ford said such matters should be thought through "in a studious attitude rather than in an emotional one."[17]

Two months later, the Conservation Society's board of directors and its city planning committee, chaired by Wanda Graham Ford, was ready to formally unveil the Texas Under Six Flags plan to new City Planning Board members and their spouses at a dinner at "Willow Way," making every effort to conduct the affair in a "studious" rather than an "emotional" attitude. After dinner, Mrs. Ford told of the history of the Conservation Society and its view that city planning should combine "the old with the new, resulting in a unique city of outstanding value and charm, a well-rounded community attractive to

The French-style Guilbeau House in the 1920s retained much of its pre-Civil War charm. It was built in 1847 by François Guilbeau, French consul in San Antonio, who is credited with saving the blighted French wine industry by shipping hardy Texas mustang grape roots onto which French vines could be grafted. San Antonio Express-News.

outsiders as well as those who live in it." In outlining the Six Flags plan, she urged that parks be preserved and that San Pedro Park be restored to its former elegance, and that encroaching commercialism in La Villita be reversed.[18]

A series of speakers then outlined circumstances involving each of the Six Flags landmarks. Of the Spanish Governor's Palace, former Mayor Gus Mauermann told how prices increased when it was perceived that a landmark was valuable and property next door became too expensive. Daughters of the Republic of Texas Alamo Mission Chapter President Josephine Henning promised cooperation with the Alamo. Attorney Stanley Banks outlined the history of the Arsenal.[19]

Main Avenue was cut directly in front of the Guilbeau House in 1929. By 1945, above, its original casement windows had been replaced, two of its three front entry doors were blocked and it served as a military police station. Its owner, the City of San Antonio, promised it would be preserved, but in 1952 the Guilbeau House was sold and razed for a postal substation. The San Antonio Light *Collection, The Institute of Texan Cultures.*

In 1941, Helen Witte related, the city purchased the 1847 Guilbeau House for a military police headquarters. Located on South Flores Street, it was the last remaining French-style early home in San Antonio, and city hall had promised it would become a museum after the war. But it was sold instead to developer Morris Kallison, who resold it for a Post Office parcel post station. Kallison offered the house to the society to be moved away. But it was in poor condition, and was razed not long before the "Willow Way" meeting. A likely candidate for restoration now was the home's smaller "slave quarters." Kallison, who was present at the dinner, announced that if the city would give the Conservation Society some surplus property he, in turn, would trade the city some nearby property he had under option. The Conservation Society could rebuild the "slave quarters" on the new property, and he would contribute toward the rebuilding.[20]

Elizabeth Graham spoke on the José Antonio Navarro home, to represent Texas under Mexico. Navarro signed the Texas Declaration of Independence. When imprisoned by Santa Anna he refused to accept release if he would recant his signing, "and suffered untold agony."[21] Lastly, Stanley Banks spoke again, this time on the Vance House. Completed on the block behind the present-day Bexar County Courthouse in 1859, it was visited by Col. Robert E. Lee, who was stationed in San Antonio in 1861 "and reportedly paced the gardens behind the house while trying to decide whether to remain with the Union or join the Confederate forces." The Vance House had been purchased for a Federal Reserve Bank of Dallas branch, but Ethel Harris said the local vice president promised it would not be torn down for another month, providing a last chance to save it.[22] It may have been structurally inadequate for banking purposes, but O'Neil Ford thought the property allowed "plenty of room for another building," even though much of the grounds had been taken by a street extension twenty-five years before.[23]

In response to the Conservation Society's presentation, City Planning Director William O. Parker promised to do "everything in his power" to carry out the society's recommendations. City Councilwoman Eloise Gerhardt said the council would be "glad to cooperate with the society." Reagan Houston noted the "outstanding power" of the Conservation Society in the community. O'Neil Ford called attention to the value of other, smaller houses. After a slide show of city landmarks, the event was adjourned.[24] Ultimately, the Conservation Society asked the city to include $150,000 in an upcoming proposed bond issue to buy threatened Six Flags landmarks.[25]

In the meantime, the City Attorney's office ruled that sale of the Guilbeau House by the city was legal.[26] Postmaster Dan Quill was asked to name the parcel post station on the site the Guilbeau Station, as he did, while hope remained that at least the presumed slave quarters could be moved elsewhere.[27]

Although the Guilbeau House went quietly, the Vance House went down only after the greatest pitched battle over an historic San Antonio landmark since the Alamo convento affray a half-century earlier.

The Vance House was a worthy cause. The two-story limestone Greek Revival house with its flat roof, six square columns and ornamental iron railings on galleries at the front and also at the rear spoke well of San Antonio's antebellum taste and prosperity.[28] It was well-situated across the street to the south of the Bexar County Courthouse, which it faced. The association with Robert E. Lee cemented its appeal to devotees of the Old South. Its builder, James Vance, was a member of a prominent local banking and hotel family. Its architecture was attributed to John Fries, designer of the 1859 Market House and the "new" Alamo parapet. The Vance House suffered from no

The Vance House, built in 1859 across Nueva Street from the future location of the Bexar County courthouse, was considered to be one of the finest homes ever built in the state. In 1939 it was an office of the State Employment Service. The San Antonio Light Collection, The Institute of Texan Cultures.

shortage of documentation. In 1934 it was one of the first structures in the state to be thoroughly measured and drawn and included in the Historic American Buildings Survey. It was, thought architectural historian Ernest Allen Connally, "not only the paradigm of the antebellum mansions in Texas, but intrinsically one of the best domestic buildings ever erected in the state."[29]

The battle was joined on June 11, 1952, when six San Antonio Conservation Society members led by President Ethel Harris filed into a special afternoon meeting of the Building Committee of the San Antonio Branch of the Federal Reserve Bank of Dallas.[30] After society members presented their views, W.E. Eagle, the vice president in charge, explained that when the local federal reserve district was created in 1914, it ranked eleventh out of twelve districts in volume of reserve deposits. It now ranked fifth, and its old building at Villita and Presa streets was no longer adequate. Harry P. Drought, acting chairman of the building committee, told of the "numerous difficulties" encountered in finding a suitable new downtown location, and said that the Nueva Street site "was finally decided upon as practically our last resort," short of moving to Austin. The Federal Reserve paid $400,000 for the site and planned to erect a $1 million building.[31]

Of society members' suggestions for including the Vance House in the plans, Federal Reserve minutes record, "Each question was given due consideration, and in their answers [Federal Reserve Representatives] explained the reasons why the suggestions would hardly be practical. In each instance the matter was not positively rejected, but little encouragement, if any, was given that the Vance House could be preserved or incorporated as a part of the new bank building," this in spite of the admission that plans for the new building had not yet been drawn.[32]

Wanda Ford, the Conservation Society's City Planning Committee chairman, followed up the meeting with a three-page lesson in architecture to the building committee. She had learned much from her architect husband, she said, concluding, "Save the Vance House as an example of the respect the Federal Reserve Bank (or any agency so concerned with national well-being) has for the socially created intangible values that have been held by communities over long periods."[33] Two months of gentle persuasion, however, produced no more than promises to delay its demolition. So Society President Ethel Harris opened up a new front, in Washington, D.C.

Not long before this time, preservationists throughout the nation were largely on their own. It was not until San José Mission was saved that the National Park Service began official government involvement in historic preservation, a role being defined even as San Antonio preservationists worked on La Villita. In 1947, a variety of independent regional and national preservation groups sent delegates to Washington, D.C., to organize the National Council for Historic Sites and Buildings, under the initial presidency of Maj. Gen. U.S. Grant III. Two years later, the Council obtained a congressional charter establishing the National Trust for Historic Preservation to acquire and operate historic properties. The Council became its educational arm.[34]

In midsummer of 1952, Ethel Harris took advantage of the San Antonio Conservation Society's new membership in the National Council for Historic Sites and Buildings to enlist the aid of its director, Frederick L. Rath, Jr. He telegraphed a reply that although appropriations for land purchases for the Federal Reserve's site were made in Washington, locations were at the discretion of individual banks. Federal landmark safeguards applying to the Army's San Antonio Arsenal did not apply to the Federal Reserve System. Rath pledged the Council's support of the Vance House effort and agreed to help by contacting the Federal Reserve's Dallas office directly.[35]

The Federal Reserve Bank of Dallas had, however, just replied to Mrs. Harris that "it would be impracticable" to leave the Vance House on the property.[36] Rath's letter to Dallas stating that the Council was "impressed by the logic and good economic sense of the San Antonio Conservation Society in its approach to the problem," and that "careful planning" on the bank's part would not necessitate demolition of the Vance House, would fall on deaf ears.[37] Never one to be deterred, Ethel Harris went to Washington herself. She met with Ronald F. Lee, chief historian of the National Park Service and secretary of the National Council. She met with Frederick Rath, who got her an appointment with the assistant general counsel of the Federal Reserve Bank. After he investigated, the assistant counsel replied that there was in fact "nothing they could do from Washington."[38]

Meanwhile, things in San Antonio heated up. In early August, the City Planning Commission passed a resolution asking the Federal Reserve to save the Vance House. The Vance House became the keynote for news stories on the Six Flags plan.[39] But September dragged on without progress, and the end of the stay of execution drew near. Shortly after 4 PM on Monday, September 29, the Federal Reserve branch obtained a demolition permit from city hall. A wrecking crew began work less than an hour later.[40] Before long the front railing was gone, and the roof was torn off.[41] Preservationists instantly cried foul.

Ethel Harris said she would get the demolition permit rescinded. "The Federal Reserve Bank has been very rude in this matter," Mrs. Harris declared. Fiesta Association President Reynolds Andricks, whose board was meeting that night, said his association would help. City Planning Commission Chairman Albert Steves III complained that the Federal Reserve Bank "should have gone along with the planning commission on its request" that demolition be deferred for six months.[42] On the other side, the Federal Reserve's Harry Drought said he had "only second-hand knowledge of the demolition project, and that the contract 'probably' was signed in Dallas," the *Express* reported. Branch Vice President W.E. Eagle was nowhere to be found.[43]

The Conservation Society sent out a blizzard of protest telegrams to local city officials, Federal Reserve officials, Governor Allen Shivers, U.S. Treasury Secretary John Snyder and President Harry Truman, among others.[44] They replied with little or no encouragement, except for Truman, who was in Montana campaigning for Adlai Stevenson and who made no response at all. Governor Shivers, who was backing Republican presidential candidate Dwight D. Eisenhower at the time, took the opportunity to fire off a shot at Truman. "I'm not surprised at the Truman administration doing it," Shivers told the *Express*. "They have seized the lands around Texas' borders [the tidelands rich with offshore oil] and now they're trying to tear down our landmarks."[45]

Acting City Manager J.L. Dickson was more immediately helpful. The time of day that demolition work began was, he said, "most unusual." On Tuesday morning he served a suspension notice on the wrecking crew.[46] But the stop-work order did not hold. The city attorney ruled it illegal. Preservationists,

In one of San Antonio's most bitterly fought preservation battles, the Vance House was torn down in 1952 for a Federal Reserve branch bank, the distinctive architectural elements promised to the Conservation Society instead hacked to pieces. The San Antonio Light Collection, The Institute of Texan Cultures.

"We clear the path for progress as Texas marches on" was the motto of the wrecking company shown salvaging materials from the rear of the Vance House. The San Antonio Light Collection, The Institute of Texan Cultures.

fuming, were reduced to hoping to save enough original materials to reconstruct the house on another site.[47] W.E. Eagle surfaced in Dallas long enough to ask Conservation Society members to list items they wanted saved, but he made no reply when the chairman of the Chamber of Commerce's beautification committee asked that "millwork, hardware, doorframes, trim and doors and the celebrated stairway complete with cornice mouldings" be preserved.[48]

When the city engineer and others arrived at the site the next Monday morning to supervise salvage efforts, they found the demolition work that was to have been postponed to allow salvage had actually continued, and that everything was wrecked "beyond restoration."[49] Local Federal Reserve officials said they had nothing to do with that, the property was leased to a parking lot company which hired the wrecking company. The owner of the wrecking company, whose motto was "We clear the path for progress as Texas marches on," said it wasn't his fault; Federal Reserve attorneys ordered him to finish the job.[50] When Ethel Harris called the beleaguered Harry Drought one more time, "he stated he had nothing further to say about the whole thing."[51] Declared Mrs. Harris: "We have been thoroughly double-crossed. They deliberately mangled" the house.[52]

Drought explained to the press that "the bank's intention to purchase the property . . . was known for a considerable time before the deal was closed last July 1, and no protest was received until after that date. The local board then gave the Conservation Society until August 31 to submit a plan before beginning demolition, and did not actually begin to demolish the structure until . . . thirty days after this deadline."[53]

All that was left for San Antonio Conservation Society members to salvage was their dignity. On October 21, with the arrival from Washington of the National Trust's Frederick L. Rath, Jr., flags went up at six historic San Antonio sites, hindered though the series of events was "by delayed hostesses, misplaced flags and a great deal of general confusion."[54] The rumble of wrecking equipment at the Vance House site prevented a scheduled speech from being delivered, and limited the ceremony to the raising of a Confederate flag, draped with black crepe, to half-mast.[55]

Once the mournful flag ceremonies were over, participants opened a new door. They adjourned to the tea opening the San Antonio Conservation Society's latest acquisition, the yet-to-be-restored Steves Homestead on King William Street.[56]

The moldering three-story Victorian mansion near the western end of King William Street was built in 1874 by German immigrant lumberman Edward Steves. Its acquisition by the Conservation Society had been considered for several years when, in 1952, Mrs. Louis Gordon offered to buy it for the society. Ethel Harris and Mrs. Gordon broached the idea to Steves's granddaughter, Mrs. Curtis Vaughan, and within a few days heard back that Mrs.

The Victorian 1874 Edward Steves home on King William Street was donated in 1952 to the San Antonio Conservation Society, which restored and opened the home as a house museum. San Antonio Conservation Society.

Vaughan would be happy to give the home to the society over a period of five years if the current tenants would be retained as caretakers.[57] The offer was accepted with enthusiasm. It was seen as an ideal Victorian house museum of San Antonio's German community. Mr. and Mrs. Vaughan and their attorney, Ben Foster, were made honorary members of the society. Mrs. Gordon and Mrs. Ernst Schuchard, who lived across the street, were named co-chairmen of the property.[58]

As work got under way, the caretakers moved to the upper floor and the attic and began repairs to the roof. Grounds were cleaned up, grass was planted and a garden plan formulated. With the artesian well on the property

William Sydney Porter was using the pen name O. Henry when he lived for a short time in this house, shown on its original site at 904 South Presa Street. In 1959 the Conservation Society preserved the home by buying it for one dollar and getting it moved to the Lone Star Brewery, which bought the home for the same price and keeps it open to visitors on brewery grounds. A Texas Historical and Landmarks Association marker is at the left of the door. The Institute of Texan Cultures, courtesy Bartlett Cocke, Sr.

temporarily dry, a city water connection was made. Gravel was donated for the driveway, and fixtures for the kitchen. New period furnishings included an 1857 Chickering grand piano given by Yale University. By spring the home was ready for the annual King William Street tour. At Christmas in 1953 an open house and bazaar raised $715.[59] On April 4, 1954, the Steves Homestead was formally opened to the general public, and was the occasion for the society's first press party. More than 200 persons came, and admissions totaled $105.[60] Admission revenues increased when the house was added to the Gray Line Bus Tours itinerary.[61]

As yet another indication of the broadening horizons of the San Antonio Conservation Society, the final meeting presided over by President Ethel Harris was moved from the San José Mission Granary to a permanent meeting place—River House, in the back yard between the Steves Homestead and the San Antonio River. The building had enclosed San Antonio's first indoor swimming pool. A new floor built over the pool allowed seating for 270 persons.[62]

While the successful Steves Homestead project took some edge off the loss of the Vance House, the Conservation Society continued to focus on the Six Flags theme. First choice to replace the Vance House to represent the Confederacy was the Sarah Eagar home at 434 South Alamo Street. At the end of 1955, with the help of attorney C. Stanley Banks, the society voted to offer $18,000, all but $4,500 of that from a fifteen-year loan at Walter McAllister's San Antonio Savings and Loan. But the Eagar home was sold to someone else, and the Devine House on South Flores Street was the next choice.[63] Saving the U.S. Arsenal complex on South Flores Street, a designated United States landmark, was not as tenuous a matter. As federally owned property it came under various surplus property regulations, activated once the government was officially made aware of the property's historic value.[64]

The Navarro House compound was more problematic. Once the city agreed not to destroy it to widen Nueva Street, the society got assurances from the property's owner, named Lady Patricia Brady, that it would be kept intact.[65] Then Morris Kallison bought property on the same side of the street for a parking lot, and offered the city a seventeen-foot strip of his property to widen Nueva Street to four lanes as a feeder street for a new expressway. If that widening were extended, the two-story Navarro building on the corner of Nueva and South Laredo streets would project up to eight feet into the street, as the Veramendi Palace had a half century earlier. City Manager Ralph Winton came to discuss the situation with the Conservation Society.[66]

"I am just trying to find some way out," Winton pleaded after directors pointedly asked why letting the Navarro building stick into the street would be any different from what newer buildings had been allowed to do on two other streets; "Those two examples were bad and should not be repeated," he said.[67] Winton was reminded that the Spanish Governors' Palace had been purchased with public funds raised through Conservation Society support of a city bond issue. Why not do the same with the Navarro House? "Do you want wires and letters sent now concerning this?" Society President Eleanor Bennett asked Winton. "Not now," he replied, no doubt hastily.[68] Realizing that the Conservation Society was ready to go to the mat on the Navarro House and would not support moving the structures to another site, Winton promised to see what he could do. He left with directors' good wishes.[69] By May of 1959, within a sixty-four-acre urban renewal district and adjacent to the new county jail, the Navarro House was officially safe.[70]

With the aid of architect Brooks Martin, restoration began. Cypress lumber was used for a rest room and a grape arbor in the rear courtyard. A rock and cypress fence went along the new south property line once a six-foot strip was sold to the city for widening Nueva Street, although it meant trimming the width of the smallest building on the property.[71] The corner building was

The 1850s limestone home and law office of Texas Declaration of Independence signer José Antonio Navarro was endangered by urban renewal in the 1950s. San Antonio Conservation Society.

Purchased by the San Antonio Conservation Society in 1960 and saved after extended negotiations with the city, the José Antonio Navarro complex was opened to the public as a house museum in 1964. Eleven years later it was deeded to the Texas Parks and Wildlife Department to be maintained as a State Historic Site. San Antonio Conservation Society.

restored as Navarro's law office, complete with family document copies donated by County Clerk James W. Knight. Officials at the new jail provided prisoners to cut into firewood the trees removed by city workers clearing the land and buildings across the street.[72] On October 7, 1964 visitors were greeted at an Open House. The $15,000 note on the property was paid off the next day. On October 30 the complex was toured by members of the National Trust for Historic Preservation, for the first time holding its annual meeting in San Antonio.[73]

As tactics to save the four surviving original Six Flags landmarks continued, the concept of Texas Under Six Flags developed a life of its own. Newspapers picked up on it.[74] The Battle of Flowers Association selected Texas Under Six Flags as the theme of its 1953 Fiesta parade.[75] The Junior Chamber of Commerce substituted its traditional Fiesta commercial parade with one with the same theme.[76] The society's Texas Under Six Flags Committee chairman got the Six Flags theme adopted for a music series at Trinity University.[77] The six flags were alternated on the Milam Building flagpole.[78] The new twenty-story Soledad Street headquarters of the National Bank of Commerce, chaired by Conservation Society ally John M. Bennett, Jr., and the only major downtown building built between 1933 and 1968, featured the six flags with shields at its main entrance.[79]

Beyond the city, on the day of Texas-born President Dwight D. Eisenhower's first inauguration the Conservation Society got San Antonio's National Republican Committeewoman Mrs. Tom Slick and local Republican organizer Joe Sheldon to see that the new president was presented with the flags on a stand of mesquite wood bearing the inscription "Texas Under Six Flags, San Antonio Conservation Society, Mesquite Wood." President Eisenhower promptly acknowledged the gift.[80] Mamie (Mrs. Preston) Dial, head of the state's Good Neighbor delegation, told the society that as her group traveled the world, they presented the six flags to dignitaries and kings, read a poem and sang Texas songs, causing the group to be known as the "Singing Texans."[81]

The Vance House—one of the prime motivations of this Six Flags effort—was, however, fading into memory. Eight months after its rubble was bulldozed into its old basement so the site could be smoothed for a temporary parking lot, its obituary appeared in the *New York Times* in a roundup of major recent preservation wins and losses throughout the nation. "Foresighted planning and preventive zoning legislation," the *Times* observed, "could have averted this destruction."[82]

Four years after the Vance House was razed, the Federal Reserve Bank held an open house at its new facility, on October 8, 1956. Among the form letters of invitation under the mimeographed signature of President Watrous H.

Taking the place of the razed Vance House, mourned by The New York Times *as one of the nation's greatest historic preservation losses of the time, was this Federal Reserve branch bank building, which opened in 1956. San Antonio Conservation Society.*

Irons was one mailed to the San Antonio Conservation Society. "Dear Sir," began the invitation to the ladies.

President of the Conservation Society by then was Wanda Graham Ford, one of the most vocal critics of the demolition. "Put on calendar," she noted at the bottom of the invitation. "Doubt if we'll go."[83]

Notes

1. John A. Booth and David R. Johnson, "Power and Progress in San Antonio Politics," in *The Politics of San Antonio*, 20–22. Another unsettling indication that this was a new age was the subject proposed by sculptor Pompeo Coppini. When Conservation Society members met in his studio in the spring of 1946 he unveiled a model of *The Atom,* a sculpture which he hoped the society would sponsor to help make future generations think about self-destruction. His proposal was politely declined on the grounds that it did not fit in with the society's goals. (Minutes, G-Mar. 24, 1946; D-Apr. 9, 1946.)

2. Booth and Johnson, "Power and Progress" in *The Politics of San Antonio,* 20–22.

3. Minutes, D-Aug. 22, 1945.

4. Minutes, D-Aug. 21, 1953.

5. Minutes, D-Sept. 18, 1951, 3.

6. Mary Evelyn Davis's *Under Six Flags: The Story of Texas* (Boston and London: Ginn & Co., 1897) was a popular state history textbook. The concept was ingrained in San Antonio by the 1930s, when distinguished visitors were presented with miniature six flags and six flagstaffs were ceremoniously dedicated in front of the new friary at San José Mission. (Habig, *San Antonio's Mission San José,* 163–65.)

7. Minutes, D-Sept. 18, 1951.

8. Minutes, G-May 28, 1953, 5.

9. Minutes, D-Sept. 18, 1951, 1–2; Oct. 22, 1951. The Board of Education accepted the society's request and gave an option to continue renting at the end of the term. Seven society members guaranteed a loan for interim repairs. After various rental plans proved too complicated, the city exchanged city land with the Board of Education for the German-English School, and used it as a recreation center. (Minutes, D-Jun. 1, 1951; D-Oct. 22, 1951; D-Dec. 21, 1951; D-Feb. 28, 1951; D-Sept. 10, 1951, 3; G-Dec. 4, 1952, 2; G-May 28, 1953, 5.)

10. Minutes, D-Sept. 18, 1951, 1–2.

11. Ibid.

12. Minutes, D-Dec. 21, 1951.

13. Minutes, G-May 22, 1952, 2.

14. Minutes, D-Jan. 16, 1952; D-Apr. 17, 1952.

15. Minutes, D-Feb. 28, 1952, 2; D-Oct. 2, 1952; G-Oct. 16, 1952, 2; G-Jan. 22, 1953, 2; D-Jun. 24, 1953. Later, the society's Educational Committee Chairman Eloise Gerhardt, then also serving on the city council, was asked to prepare a questionnaire for political candidates on conservation-related issues. (Minutes, D-Feb. 21, 1955.)

16. Minutes, notes of luncheon of May 29, 1952.

17. Ibid., 1–2.

18. Minutes, D-Jul. 28, 1952.

19. Ibid., 1–2.

20. Ibid., 1–3. Postmaster Dan Quill had offered to not purchase the Guilbeau property if the Conservation Society objected, Ethel Harris added, but the society "released Mr. Quill of this obligation."

21. Ibid.

22. Minutes, D-Jul. 28, 1952, 2.

23. Minutes, D-May 22, 1952, 4, 5; "Historic Estate Farm to S.A. Business Site in Few Years," *San Antonio Light,* Oct. 16, 1927, 1-R. The program did not end there. Aline Badger (Mrs. H.C.) Carter spoke on "the need of a spiritual as well as a historical background for San Antonio" and Mrs. Harold Gee discussed parks. Sam Zisman noted the society's desire for preservation of the San Antonio River and for any downtown reconstruction to combine the old with the new, taking into account the need to think in terms of the "maximum rate of safety as well as having breathing spaces," since, he noted, "we are living in the Atomic Age." (Minutes, D-Jul. 28, 1952, 2–3.)

24. Ibid.

25. Minutes, D-Oct. 9, 1953, 2.

26. Minutes, E-Jun. 17, 1952.

27. Minutes, D-Sept. 10, 1952, 2, 3; G-Dec. 4, 1952, 2. During the next summer the society found itself unable to purchase a nearby property offered to the society for $30,000 to be exchanged for Kallison's Guilbeau "slave quarters" property. (Minutes, D-Aug. 21, 1953, 1–2.)

28. Paul Goeldner, comp., *Texas Catalog, Historic American Buildings Survey,* (San Antonio: Trinity University Press, 1974), 208.

29. Ernest Allen Connally, Miami University of Ohio, to Elizabeth O. Graham, Feb. 19, 1953, in SACS Library. A hotel formally named the Vance House was torn down to make way for the Gunter Hotel. James Vance's descendants included granddaughter Rena Maverick Green.

30. "Minutes of the Building Committee of the San Antonio Branch, Federal Reserve Bank of Dallas, Held June 11, 1952 at 3:00 p.m.," copy in SACS Library.

31. Ibid., 2–3; "Truman Asked to Save Historic Vance House," *San Antonio Express,* Oct. 1, 1952, 14-C.

32. "Minutes of Building Committee," 2.

33. Mrs. O'Neil Ford to H.P. Drought, Jun. 25, 1952, copy in SACS Library.

34. Mulloy, *The History of the National Trust for Historic Preservation 1963–1973,* 10–11.

35. Frederick L. Rath, Jr. to Ethel W. Harris, Aug. 1, 1952, telegram in SACS Library.

36. Reference to letter of Jul. 22, 1952 in W.D. Gentry to Ethel W. Harris, Sep. 30, 1952, telegram in SACS Library.

37. Frederick L. Rath, Jr. to R.R. Gilbert, Aug. 11, 1952, 1–2, copy in SACS Library.

38. "Statement from Mrs. Ethel Wilson Harris," undated, in SACS Library.

39. "Conservation Society To Ask City to Help Save Six Landmarks," *San Antonio Express,* Aug. 3, 1952; Director of Planning William O. Parker to Vice President W.E. Eagle, Aug. 8, 1952, copy in SACS Library; "S.A. Conservation Society Outlines Campaign to Preserve Historical Landmarks," *San Antonio Light,* Aug. 24, 1952.

40. "Razing of Historic Vance House Begun Monday," *San Antonio Express,* Sept. 30, 1952.

41. "Wrecking of Historic Old Vance House Suspended," *San Antonio Evening News,* Sept. 30, 1952.

42. Ibid.

43. Ibid.

44. "Razing of Historic Vance House Begun Monday," *San Antonio Express,* Sept. 30, 1952; "Truman Asked to Save Historic Vance House," *San Antonio Express,* Oct. 1, 1952, 14-C; Minutes, D-Sept. 10, 1952; D-Oct. 2, 1952, 2.

45. "Historic House Seems Doomed," *San Antonio Express,* Oct. 3, 1952.

46. "Wrecking of Historic Old Vance House Is Suspended, *San Antonio Evening News,* Sept. 30, 1952.

47. "Restoration on New Site Planned," *San Antonio Light,* Oct. 1, 1952, 1.

48. "Demolition of Old Vance House Stops," *San Antonio Light,* Sept. 30, 1952, 1. The chairman was architect Ralph Cameron.

49. "Vance Home Past Salvage," *San Antonio Light,* Oct. 6, 1952.

50. "Women, Bank Official Clash," *San Antonio Evening News,* Oct. 6, 1952.

51. Minutes, D-Sept. 10, 1952.

52. Ibid.

53. "Truman Asked to Save Historic Vance House," *San Antonio Express,* Oct. 1, 1952, 14-C.

54. "Destruction Noise, Dust Spoil Vance House Rites," *San Antonio Express,* Oct. 22, 1952; Minutes, D-Sept. 10, 1952; D-Oct. 2, 1952, 2.

55. Ibid.; "Vance House Flag to be at Half Mast During Conservation Society Rites," *San Antonio Express,* Oct. 21, 1952. A news release from the Federal Reserve's H.P. Drought tried to discredit reports of Robert E. Lee's association with the Vance House by stating that Lee was never stationed in San Antonio, and that if he had ever stopped at the Vance House, it was called Mrs. Philip's Hotel. The Conservation Society came up with voluminous references to counter the ill-informed allegation. ("Conservation Society Takes Exception to Vance House Remarks," *San Antonio Express,* Oct. 18, 1953, 17-C.)

56. "Destruction Noise, Dust Spoil Vance House Rites," *San Antonio Express,* Oct. 22, 1952.

57. Minutes, D-Apr. 17, 1952.

58. Minutes, G-May 28, 1953, 4.

59. Minutes, D-Jun. 20, 1952; D-Sept. 10, 1952, 2-3; D-Oct. 2, 1952, 2; G-Dec. 4, 1952; D-Jan. 14, 1953, 2–3; D-Feb. 17, 1953, 2; D-Mar. 24, 1953, 2; G-May 28, 1953, 2; D-Dec. 3, 1953, 2.

60. Minutes, D-Jan. 25, 1954, 2; G-Jan. 28, 1954; D-Mar. 22, 1954, 3; D-Apr. 15, 1954, 2.

61. Minutes, D-Jan. 11, 1956.

62. Minutes, G-May 22, 1952; D-Mar. 24, 1953, 3.

63. Minutes, D-Oct. 9, 1953, 2; D-Oct. 24, 1955, 2; G-Nov. 17, 1955; D-Jan. 23, 1956, 2.

64. National Park Service Assistant Director Ronald F. Lee to Ethel Harris, Jun. 3, 1953, in SACS Library.

65. Minutes, D-Aug. 21, 1953.

66. Minutes, D-Mar. 22, 1954, 1–3.

67. Ibid., 1–2.

68. Ibid., 2–3.

69. Ibid. Winton was also impressed to learn that the Texas State Historical Survey Committee had just passed a resolution asking the city not to destroy the site.

70. Minutes, D-Oct. 20, 1958, 3; D-Jan. 19, 1959, 3; D-Feb. 23, 1959, 3; G-May 28, 1959.

71. Minutes, G-Sept. 28, 1961, 2; D-Mar. 19, 1962, 2; D-Oct. 22, 1962; D-Feb. 24, 1964, 2.

72. Minutes, D-Apr. 9, 1962, 2; D-Feb. 25, 1963, 2–3; D-Feb. 24, 1964, 2; G-Feb. 27, 1964; D-May 25, 1964, 1–2; D-Sept. 21, 1964, 2. Ethel Harris brought tile from Mexico for the house itself, and State Senator Adrian Spears brought up some old wrought-iron hardware from Nuevo Laredo. Under the guidance of Stewart King, a dying mulberry tree was replaced by a large live oak in memory of Georgia Maverick Harris, and Mrs. Hugo Elmendorf gave a desert willow in memory of her parents. Mrs. J. Edwin Young was hired as curator.

73. Minutes, D-Sept. 21, 1964, 2.

74. Minutes, D-Sept. 10, 1952, 2.

75. Minutes, G-Mar. 26, 1953, 3.

76. Minutes, D-Mar. 24, 1953, 3.

77. Minutes, G-Oct. 28, 1954.

78. Minutes, D-Mar. 24, 1953, 3; D-May 22, 1953; G-May 20, 1955.

79. Minutes, G-Oct. 24, 1957.

80. Minutes, D-Jan. 14, 1953, 3; D-Feb. 17, 1953.

81. Minutes, G-Oct. 16, 1952, 2. In 1961, the commercial value of the concept was shown with opening of the Six Flags Over Texas theme park between Dallas and Fort Worth. ("Six Flags Over Texas," *The Handbook of Texas* III, 888.)

82. "To Save the Houses of Our Heritage," *The New York Times Magazine*, Jun. 28, 1953, 16. Among other major losses reported were the Grand Union Hotel in Saratoga Springs, N.Y. and the Bell Grove mansion in White Castle, La. The Vance House was described as "the best example of Greek Revival in the region."

83. Federal Reserve Bank invitation in SACS Library.

10

Doomsday for City Parks

As downtown businessmen saw post-war city limits spreading farther and farther into the once lightly-populated county, they knew that suburban shopping malls would not be far behind. Worse, San Antonio's streets could hardly provide sufficient parking for the city's pre-war population, much less for growing numbers of people who would soon have a choice of shopping elsewhere.

Tearing down buildings was messy and expensive, and could generate bad publicity as well. A much easier target for parking lots was land already open. The city's downtown residential parks were no longer lined by the homes of influential citizens; those residents had moved to suburban neighborhoods. Before long, no city park, no matter how small nor sacred, was safe from developers' plans.

Shortly after World War II, city council prepared to uproot three historic parks, including the hallowed Alamo Plaza, for underground parking garages. A fourth park was to be turned into a junior college campus. A city agency wanted to build its headquarters in a fifth. An urban renewal project would eliminate half of another. City council was seriously considering selling a seventh park outright, as it already had an eighth for the branch of a hospital which wanted to turn a ninth park into a parking lot. Another hospital wanted a tenth park not only for surface parking, it wished to build beneath it a nuclear bomb shelter, in which its staff could medically treat 15,000 refugees.

Outside the central city to the south, one of the eternal river straightening projects would shut down a Spanish mission's unique irrigation system and deprive nearby parkland of water. To the north, the city's largest park was threatened by an expressway.

One frustrating, long-standing problem was the forty-acre San Pedro Park, set aside as public land by the King of Spain in 1729, a public park designation many San Antonians consider second in the nation only to that of Boston

During a post-war spate of San Antonio Conservation Society tree sales and plantings to improve the environment, Mrs. Eric Harker and Mrs. Max Goodman plant a tree in memory of their parents at the edge of San Pedro Park across from the new campus of San Antonio College, which the Conservation Society helped keep from being built in San Pedro Park itself. San Antonio Conservation Society.

Common. After the turn of the century, most of San Pedro Park's activities drifted away to Brackenridge Park, ten times larger and less than two miles away. Despite the sentimental value of San Pedro Park and conservationists' planting of memorial trees there, it remained underused, and in a time of growth was an especially tempting target for other purposes. In 1946, San Antonio Junior College was ready to move from the historic German-English School on South Alamo Street. Plans for a new campus centered on San Pedro Park but drew opposition from conservationists, led by Rena Maverick Green.[1] A month after the society's resolution on the subject went to the mayor and city commissioners, San Pedro Park was pronounced "saved." The campus was built to the east, across San Pedro Avenue.[2] The City Water Board planned an office building in Mahncke Park, the site of George Brackenridge's old water works, but ran into an opposing Conservation Society petition and did not build there.[3] The need for new parks in the city's fast-spreading subdivisions was not lost on conservationists. Led by the redoubtable Rena Green, the Conservation Society repeatedly sought a City Park Board with representatives from many organizations to plan what was needed in the new areas.[4] Members, however, still directed most of their energies on the natural environment toward keeping what parks the city already had.

But they did not limit their focus to specific targets. They recognized that trees in general are important in the semi-tropical South Texas environment. On Arbor Day in 1953, the society's Committee on Parks and Natural Beauty planted a cypress tree beside the San Antonio River as a step toward planting several hundred trees in city parks and beautifying the entire city.[5] The idea grew into an annual public sale of pecan, redbud and Arizona ash trees, at cost, in front of Municipal Auditorium, with the help of the Boy Scouts.[6] In 1953, two thousand trees sold in twenty minutes.[7] Over a period of eight years, 75,000 trees and shrubs were sold at wholesale prices. The program ended up a victim of its own success; nursery owners abandoned it after finding too many of their customers buying trees wholesale at the Auditorium and not at retail prices at their nurseries.[8]

An eye still had to be kept on the San Antonio River, which was not realizing the potential of its pre-war plan. In 1946, Casa Rio Restaurant, near the Commerce Street bridge, became the first business to open on the river level. The following winter the River Art Show began, giving the Conservation Society an opportunity for an open house at its newly restored Casa Villita.[9] In 1948 Mayor Alfred Callaghan promised the society he would help prevent encroachments on the river, but two years later general river conditions were still "awful," the River Authority chairman told Conservation Society members.[10] Elizabeth Graham was named head of a committee to assure that work of the River Authority be "in accord as far as possible with ideas of Old San Antonio."[11]

What was considered a serious challenge to the integrity of the river came in 1950, and it had to do with parking. A group of businessmen organized under the umbrella of a corporation called Endowment, Inc. to operate a parking garage north of the river. They planned to build a bridge to connect the garage with Crockett Street between St. Mary's and Navarro streets. It would cross the river near the St. Mary's University Law School and, on the other side, San Antonio Bank and Trust Co.—headed by one of the Conservation Society's longtime supporters, Jack Beretta.

But it was not a personal project of his, Beretta assured Conservation Society directors when he and another shareholder, banker Walter McAllister, were summoned to a meeting at Conservation Corner one October morning in 1951. He was only the engineer. The twelve-foot span would be used for automobiles only in emergencies, and was actually to help the law school increase its endowment by improving access to its facility, he said. Commerce Street businessmen happened to be involved because their customers could park there, which would cause businessmen to beautify the backs of their buildings which faced the river—including Beretta's bank, which would also have a new rear entrance. Houston Street businesses like the Majestic Theater and the Manhattan Cafe would build rear entrances on College Street on the opposite side of the river, he said, adding that the parking garage would never have been planned without the proposed bridge.[12] McAllister thought it too late to stop the project, since it had already been approved by the mayor, the city council and the River Authority. Several society board members, unimpressed, retorted that if the Conservation Society had a seat on the City Planning Board this could all have been discussed ahead of time.[13]

Nevertheless, the specter of a conventional bridge over the middle of one of the River Bend's most picturesque stretches just to provide access to a new parking garage was too much for members to take, even though the Texas Historical and Landmarks Association roused itself to declare that the bridge "will not destroy one single beauty spot."[14] The Conservation Society filed suit on the grounds that the garage would serve a private rather than a public purpose, violating "the public park and recreation area" along the San Antonio River.[15] Society members and friends contributed to the legal fund so that the organization itself bore no expense.[16]

The society took on the cause with its usual fervor. "Ethel Harris was down at city hall waving a banner of the Conservation Society to stop the construction of the bridge across the river," recalled Eleanor (Mrs. John M.) Bennett, who with her husband had just returned to live from the east. "I thought, 'This is the kind of organization that I want to associate myself with.' So I . . . inquired about it, made my wishes known and the next thing I knew I was in the middle of helping Ethel stop the bridge across the river."[17] But the Conservation Society lost its suit for an injunction and also an appeal, leaving it, as the bridge went up, able only to resolve "that this does not change our attitude toward the building of bridges over the river generally."[18]

Parks on the downtown periphery were already targets of nearby institutions. On the north, Baptist Memorial Hospital was eyeing for a parking lot one of the halves of Madison Square, bisected behind the hospital by a street cut through in the 1920s.[19] To compensate, the hospital suggested the city close the street which bisected Romana Plaza in front of the hospital. The Conservation Society's Parks Committee agreed on the Romana Plaza point, but the city did not. Neither suggestion came to pass.[20]

East of downtown, the city had already sold Baptist Hospital the entire Dignowity Park as a hospital site, but repurchased the park in 1951 when the project did not materialize.[21] West of downtown, the Urban Renewal Agency wanted to eliminate half of Columbus Park. Santa Rosa Hospital asked to use Milam Park, already saved from becoming the site of a branch library, for parking.[22] Moreover, in view of the threat of nuclear war, the Santa Rosa staff later asked that a bomb shelter be built beneath the park. Santa Rosa personnel plus those from the nearby Robert B. Green Hospital would provide medical care to the 15,250 refugees it was estimated could be accommodated beneath Milam Park's three and a half acres.[23]

In downtown itself, as city officials looked with more and more frustration on the parking problem they came to a solution which preservationists saw as driving stakes into the very heart of the old Spanish city—underground garages beneath the city's historic downtown parks and plazas. The best underground parking prospect of them all was seen in 1953 to be only a block north of parking-deficient major stores on Houston Street: Travis Park.

The sounds of tourists' dominoes, croquet and pitched horseshoes had long since disappeared from Travis Park, as had its bandstand. Travis was the most southern in feeling of San Antonio's parks. It had served as a campground for Confederate soldiers gathering to go east. Its peaceful, shaded two and a half acres were now crossed by sidewalks meeting symmetrically in the center at a granite memorial shaft topped by the statue of a Confederate soldier. The monument was guarded by two cannon rescued after the Civil War from the site of a Confederate defeat in New Mexico. The park was bordered on the south by the city's most elegant hotel, the St. Anthony. On diagonally opposite corners were St. Mark's Episcopal Church and Travis Park Methodist Church.

This was not the first time underground parking had been suggested for Travis Park. In 1946, at the instigation of both Mayor Gus Mauermann and the owner of the St. Anthony Hotel, contractor H.B. Zachry proposed a two-level, 750-car garage beneath the park. But Mauermann was defeated for reelection, and the deal fell apart in a disagreement over parking rates. In 1947 and again in 1950, voters rejected the idea of revenue bonds to pay for city-operated off-street parking facilities.[24] Beset in its dilemma by parking-starved, tax-paying businesses on the one hand and by a fiscally conservative public on the other, city hall was reluctant to be harried, too, by conservationists, who would only get in the way of "progress." The solution was for City Manager Ralph Winton and his staff to go to work on the underground garage projects quickly and quietly.

In early September of 1953, Winton, apparently only in response to a reporter's question, revealed that the city was about to advertise for bids for construction of parking garages under four city-owned properties—Alamo Plaza, Main Plaza, Travis Park and part of La Villita.[25] A $2.2 million garage beneath Travis Park and a $1.8 million facility beneath Main Plaza had already been unofficially proposed, Winton said. He emphasized that the four garages would be constructed at no cost to the city. Their surfaces "would be restored to a condition 'better' than they are now in," as in similar projects completed or under way in San Francisco, Los Angeles and Chicago, and as in the case of a garage built under a portion of Boston Common.[26]

Conservation Society directors responded to the news by sending a resolution to Winton and to Mayor Jack White, and to the newspapers, stating their concern over the impact of "underground parking lots" on the shade trees and natural beauty of parks and plazas, and requesting further clarification.[27] Then a clandestine telephone call went to the San Antonio Conservation Society's new president, Eleanor Bennett.

Construction bids were being taken by city hall for underground parking garages beneath Travis Park, Main Plaza, Alamo Plaza and part of La Villita when the plot was discovered by the San Antonio Conservation Society. The most advanced proposal was for a garage under Travis Park, shown here looking southwest in a rendering by architects Atlee B. and Robert M. Ayres. In this view showing the St. Anthony Hotel in the background, cars enter and exit the three-level garage from Jefferson Street at the left and Navarro Street at the right. The Confederate monument in the center of the park is placed on a pedestal above escalators providing pedestrian access to the garage. Four feet of topsoil permit plantings on the roof of the garage, also to serve as a bomb shelter. The plan was defeated after four years of lawsuits and a change in city government. The San Antonio Light Collection, The Institute of Texan Cultures.

"Someone called and suggested I attend a city council meeting," Mrs. Bennett related later. "And so I did. Not having any idea of what was up, I ran into Mayor White in the hall, and he said, 'What are you doing up here?' 'I decided to come down,' [I said], but he said, 'We do not have anything on the agenda that is going to concern you.' So I said, 'I'll just stay down here.' I had received a copy of the agenda and there was nothing in there. So, there I was, and suddenly, much to my horror, they stood up and a man unveiled these large pictures, colored pictures of a parking garage under Travis Park, and this was to be—and was—formally presented to the council members, and they had planned to take action on it."[28]

The scope of the city's plans was a conservationist's nightmare. Four firms had submitted proposals to build garages, which would double as bomb shelters, beneath three downtown parks. H.B. Zachry Co. of San Antonio would put in three three-level garages: an 1,100-car garage beneath Travis Park and 500-car garages beneath both Alamo and Main plazas. Parking Inc.

of San Antonio wanted to build three two-level garages: one for 800 to 900 cars beneath Travis Park, another for 600 cars under Alamo Plaza and a third for 400 to 500 cars below Main Plaza. W.&B. Realty Co. of Los Angeles wanted another forty-five days to develop a bid to build the same three. Brown and Root Construction Co. of Houston would build a $3.5 million, 1,000-car garage beneath Travis Park only.[29] Of the four companies, Zachry presented at the council meeting the only detailed, final proposition, for a Travis Park garage. Its construction of the Alamo and Main plaza garages was contingent on acquiring additional capital and was not discussed further. There were plans for a fourth garage beneath part of La Villita.[30]

Under Zachry's proposals, one-fourth of the surface of Travis Park would be used for garage purposes. Public sidewalks around the perimeter would be removed to permit entrance and exit ramps on the east and west sides and for associated tire, repair and other underground shops. A loading ramp would be built at the southwest corner. Two exhaust pipes projecting two feet above the surface at the east and west would blow out air from the subsurface. The Confederate monument would be put back in the center but on a pedestal, to allow for escalators beside it enter the garage below. The city would lease the garage to Zachry free of encumbrances for forty years, with the city retaining an option to buy it at specific intervals at a decreasing price.[31]

"I jumped up, went up to the podium and introduced myself," remembered Eleanor Bennett. "[I] said I was not on the agenda, but neither was this project. I formally protested in the name of the San Antonio Conservation Society the thought of destroying our parks and plazas in San Antonio." She quoted from an *Architectural Forum* article she had with her. It reported that in a national survey of authorities on traffic and parking problems, not one recommended underground parking as a viable solution.[32] And, she asked Zachry, what about the trees? How large would they be?

"As large as possible in the four feet of topsoil," Zachry himself replied, elaborating after further questioning, "From six to eight inches in diameter, but the trees will grow larger."[33] That wouldn't do, Mrs. Bennett replied. She told the council that the Conservation Society had already gathered five tree experts at Travis Park. They agreed that the type of trees now growing there would require a minimum of five feet of earth over the center of the park, increasing to ten feet on the sides.[34] Mrs. Bennett had brought along the Conservation Society's chairman of Parks and Natural Beauty, Anita Pereida (Mrs. Eric) Harker, who also grilled Zachry on the shade trees and on parking fees as well.[35]

The two Conservation Society members were the only ones at the meeting to oppose the plan. But council members, caught off guard, decided to postpone for five days a decision on selecting a contractor.[36] "Of course the press picked it right up immediately," Mrs. Bennett remembered. "From then on we were off and running."[37]

In November of 1953, H.B. Zachry Co. prepared to carry out its construction contract for an 1,100-car parking garage beneath Travis Park by drilling fifty-foot test holes at each corner of the park. On the far side of St. Mark's Episcopal Church in the background, construction cranes prepare for a multi-story addition to the Southwestern Bell Building. The San Antonio Light *Collection,* The Institute of Texan Cultures.

After the delay, the city granted two contracts. One for $3 million went to Zachry for a garage beneath Travis Park. A $1.5 million contract for a 550-car garage beneath Main Plaza went to the Los Angeles firm, subject to its California contractors securing financing.[38] But Conservation Society directors resolved to "take all possible action for the preservation of Travis Park as it now stands—its trees, historic monument and its complete function as a true park—and [to] uphold the provisions and spirit of the city charter."[39] The mayor was invited to the society's general membership meeting at River House, behind the Steves Homestead on King William Street. It was, the press reported, "a tumultuous, three-hour meeting," with more than one hundred women present.[40]

Following a program on one of the six flags, Mayor White was introduced by President Eleanor Bennett. She concluded by reading a pledge he had signed two years earlier: "With San Antonio's unprecedented growth in population, we need more parks instead of fewer. I am opposed to the use of any part of the park area of the City of San Antonio for any purpose except as now used. They are our rightful and lawful places of recreation, rest and play. Furthermore, I will work for and support a city ordinance to effect the above." Just how, Mrs. Bennett asked the mayor, could he reconcile that statement with his action favoring destroying the trees in Travis Park for an underground parking lot?

Because, Mayor White replied, the site would be more beautiful once the garage was built. As it was, grass would not grow under the trees. He had gone by the park that morning and could find no flowers.[41] "No grass will grow there very well, no flowers will grow and it is not a pretty park," he declared.[42] "If I didn't think that the park would be more beautiful, I would not want to change it." The mayor, who "remained courteously unyielding on the stand he had taken," closed by noting that he was also working to save the very declining King William neighborhood they were meeting in.[43] "If *you* don't get busy," he warned the members, "it will be lost."[44]

But the mayor was not successful in redirecting members' thoughts. After he left, Rena Maverick Green, then 79, "rose and sounded the battle cry: 'It's an old story with us, saving parks and public monuments. We have saved them before. We shall save them again. If we must assess ourselves to start a campaign fund, let's start assessing.'"[45] Then, "Somebody passed a plate, and by the time it circulated through the room one time it had $204.05 in it."[46] Mrs. Bennett read the resolution passed by the board three days earlier declaring that "all possible action" would be taken by the society to preserve Travis Park as it stood. On a motion by Mrs. Lutcher Brown and second by Rena Green, it was endorsed unanimously.[47] It was a declaration of war.

The Zachry company hired an engineering survey firm and announced plans to begin construction on January 1.[48] On November 4, drilling crews sank fifty-foot test holes at each corner of the park.[49] Zachry vowed that the new Travis Park "will be no naked square of concrete," since the soil on the $3 million garage roof would nourish grass and trees.[50] Two prominent landscape firms were found to agree that the project could make Travis Park "much, much more beautiful, more interesting that it is today."[51]

Meanwhile, in a six-to-three vote San Antonio City Council declined to support the idea of Councilman—later Congressman—Henry B. Gonzalez and Councilman Emil O. Scherlin to submit the Travis Park project to a public referendum.[52] The denial so enraged some opponents of the project that they rallied around a Voters Recall Movement aimed at removing from office all six council members who voted against a referendum.[53]

Mary Vance Green, daughter of Rena Green and great-granddaughter of Samuel and Mary Adams Maverick, who were credited with having donated

As the Travis Park controversy wore on, City Manager Ralph Winton and construction magnate H.B. Zachry were portrayed accusing each other of causing the affray while conservationists continued on the attack. San Antonio Express-News.

Travis Park to the city in the first place, resigned as Conservation Society secretary so she could lead a recall movement against the city council.[54] "If the use of this land as a public park is abandoned . . . then the right of possession will revert to the heirs of Mrs. Mary A. Maverick, deceased," stated recall movement attorney Charles M. Dickson. "Under no theory can it be actually said that the city has ever acquired the right to use the sub-surface of Travis Park for commercial purposes." City Attorney Jack Davis shrugged off the contention.[55] Sixty "avid" recall proponents picked up petitions at a public meeting in Municipal Auditorium, nearly doubling the number of petitions in circulation.[56]

Within the Conservation Society itself, the Travis Park cause was cloaked in the mantle of what amounted to a national holy war for historic preservation. Landmarks defining the character of not just San Antonio but also of cities across the nation were in danger, Eleanor Bennett declared at a special meeting of associate members. The open-air theater behind the Lincoln Memorial in Washington, D.C., was in danger of being filled in. The Cumberland Canal outside that city was at risk. In Philadelphia, an underground parking project beneath Independence Mall had only recently been halted. Moreover, San Antonio's climate called for shade trees in its parks.[57] Get a copy of the Travis Park ordinance and have your lawyers tell you how illegal it is, Mrs. Bennett challenged Conservation Society members. Read the new city charter, see if you think San Antonio is getting what it is due. Write the newspapers, "create public opinion against the confiscation of Travis Park." The final draft of a lawsuit against the city was being prepared. When it was completed, an appeal for funds would begin; a businessman had already promised to sponsor ten commercials a day on one radio station.[58]

Two weeks later, the suit was filed in District Court on behalf of the Maverick heirs, styled "Mrs. Rena Maverick Green et. al." They were seeking a declaratory judgment that the City of San Antonio's right to use Travis Park was due only to what amounted to an easement granted to the city by Samuel and Mary A. Maverick for park purposes only. The contract with Zachry nullified the agreement and title must therefore revert to the Maverick heirs. After that, construction of a parking garage would constitute trespass. The heirs sought an injunction against both the city and Zachry to prevent this from happening.[59] Although an injunction was not immediately issued, Zachry decided to hold off on construction and let the announced construction starting date pass. The company asked the city that "all salvageable greenery be removed as soon as possible" from the park, but City Manager Ralph Winton replied that he also would delay until the legal situation was settled.[60]

With construction work on Travis Park at a standstill as litigation went forward, the case began to draw national attention. The editor of *Progressive Architecture* magazine came to San Antonio to do an article.[61] The American Civic Planning Association, which held as one of its tenets "that areas once dedicated as parks should not be appropriated for unrelated uses," covered it in its magazine.[62] Eleanor Bennett, attending that group's annual meeting in New Orleans, reported back that planners' cutting-edge thinking on municipal parking woes now rejected "tearing up parks" in favor of multi-story parking garages on the perimeters of congested areas.[63]

The publicity came not without a price. Conservation Society President Eleanor Bennett's husband, John M. Bennett, Jr., was chairman of the National Bank of Commerce, the city's second largest bank, and her father-in-law was one of its founders. "We were well into the case, and my picture was on the front page of the paper," Eleanor Bennett recalled. One afternoon, "I drove in the driveway and John's father was waiting for me. He was standing there with a copy of the newspaper in his hand. He said, 'Eleanor, I am very embarrassed over this. We Bennetts do not appear on the front page of the paper in a protest of such a nature. These people are large stockholders in the National Bank of Commerce and your husband is a prominent banker, and we cannot afford this type of publicity. What will happen if they withdraw their accounts?'

"I said, 'Gramps, that is what I have to do. I'll resign tomorrow if that is your command, but I am president of an organization that has around two thousand members. I am at the will of the desire of the board of directors and this is what they asked me to do. I represent them.'" Her father-in-law replied, "'I don't know what we can do about that, but it's up to you.' He was just very, very upset . . . and did not want any type of publicity. But, luckily, through the whole thing the National Bank of Commerce did not lose a single account. As a matter of fact, I think we picked up some good people [who] felt the same way that we did."[64]

Fourteen months after its filing, district court decision time came on the afternoon of January 27, 1955. Conservation Society members were holding their general meeting at that hour in River House. All present bowed their heads in silent prayer that the judge would, according to the minutes, "use his moral facilities to render a decision to not allow the confiscation of a beautiful park for an underground parking garage."[65]

The judge, however, ruled against the Maverick heirs. Circumstantial evidence may have been convincing that Samuel Maverick originally owned Travis Park. But, amid rumors of recently pilfered records in the courthouse basement, no documents had been found to confirm any conveyance of Travis Park by Maverick to the city, most importantly any which spelled out intent for its use for park purposes only and also showed that the city accepted such terms.[66] The Maverick heirs and the Conservation Society appealed the decision, in the meantime using a little showmanship to draw further attention to the park: the society replaced its annual Texas Independence Day ceremonies at the Spanish Governor's Palace with a band concert in Travis Park, with the Daughters of the Republic of Texas furnishing the six flags of Texas.[67] In mid-September, the Court of Civil Appeals upheld the lower court's decision. A rehearing was denied.[68]

At this point, the course of events was changed dramatically by another transformation at San Antonio City Hall. Many residents thought that Jack White, like earlier reform mayors, had "grown fond of his power and tried to enhance it," at the expense of the city manager. Defeated machine politicians, in fact, were now supporting White. The machine's old opponents saw an immediate need for a permanent political organization to get things back on track and to keep watch over city hall.[69] To achieve this, the Good Government League was organized under the leadership of Chamber of Commerce President Tom L. Powell. Its entire slate swept to victory over the People's Ticket in April, 1955.

Initially, the impact on the Conservation Society's Travis Park position seemed to be negative. The society had sent a questionnaire to all candidates, asking if they would "oppose any infringement or encroachment of our parks and plazas by private and any other interests," support both "extension and beautification of the San Antonio River" and also back "a program to save the historical, cultural and architectural landmarks of the city." Ironically, all incumbent People's Ticket candidates, and most independents, had answered favorably.[70] No Good Government League candidates, however, had responded. The only incoming councilman with any prior city hall experience was Ralph Winton, the former city manager who had backed the Travis Park garage, and the Good Government League had resolved to take no stand on the Conservation Society's questions.[71]

By now the question of legality of the proposed underground garages had gained the attention of other groups as well. The League of Women Voters took no stand on the merits of the issue, but tried in vain to get the old city administration to provide "a written statement as to the basis for the city attorney's opinion."[72] New City Attorney Carlos Cadena promised to come up with a prompt opinion. In the meantime, the council gave a ninety-day extension to the California contractors to complete its financial proposal for the Main Plaza garage.[73]

Two weeks later, Cadena reported that under the city charter both garage contracts could be illegal, the Travis Park contract "more probably illegal" than the other.[74] Since the fundamental issues in the Main Plaza contract were also present in the Travis Park agreement, city council voided the Travis Park contract with Zachry and filed suit in District Court to test its validity.[75] Zachry, in turn, sued the city for breach of contract. In December, District Court Judge C.K. Quin declared the lease invalid. Nine months later, the Court of Civil Appeals upheld Quin's ruling, agreeing that the San Antonio city charter allowed the city to maintain a parking facility but not to delegate such public power to a private company, as it had to Zachry.[76] Zachry appealed to the Texas Supreme Court. Two years later, in 1957, that court upheld the two lower courts, and also ruled against Zachry's contention that in making the lease the city had in effect abandoned Travis Park.[77]

Even as the Travis Park case was lingering in the Texas Supreme Court, the new regime at city hall moved ahead with less disruptive plans for the other downtown parks. Main Plaza was re-landscaped and new one-way traffic patterns adopted.[78] Parking at businesses in the River Road area of Brackenridge Park was curtailed.[79] There was some handwringing over removal of the bandstand and over decreasing green space on Alamo Plaza.[80] When city council revealed its plans to build a multi-story tourist center on the site of the Alamo Plaza bandstand, agitated society directors responded with a resolution on the same day. The tourist center was not built.[81]

What to do about the San Antonio Garden Center's proposed building on the crest of Mahncke Park was more of a puzzle. The seventy-nine garden clubs and thirteen junior garden clubs in the city needed a central meeting place, auditorium and library, but putting any building in a park was counter to Conservation Society goals, especially in view of its opposition to a tourist building on Alamo Plaza. Restoring the Devine House downtown as a Garden Center was thought to be more in keeping with society aims.[82] Planning consultant Sam Zisman reported back from the National City Planning Board meeting that such garden centers were not inconsistent with park activities elsewhere, but in this case, he said, it should be studied with great care.[83] After "much deliberation" directors agreed not to oppose the building, which was built.[84]

Not far down Broadway from Mahncke Park, city council at the same time seemed to be up to its old tricks. Lions Field adjacent to Brackenridge Park created a long green space bracketed by businesses along the west side of Broadway. Nearly fifty years before, the San Antonio Conservation Society's predecessor in parks activism, the City Federation of Women's Clubs, had successfully protested the San Antonio Water Company's proposed sale of the land for building lots and caused the city to buy the land instead for parkland. Now one councilman estimated the city could get $2 million for the property.[85] The Conservation Society was upset with the idea, but the city's thirteen Lions Clubs were especially offended. The downtown Founder's Lions Club had been entrusted with operation of the park. With the aid of city operating subsidies, in the park's early years the club conducted a wide range of public recreational activities there, including operation of what it believed was the first supervised playground west of the Mississippi.[86] Lions Club representatives objected strenuously before city council; the Conservation Society added its opposition and the matter was dropped.[87]

Having been to the courthouse to defend the San Antonio River and Travis Park, the Conservation Society found itself back in court to defend the ancient mission irrigation system south of downtown. The Conservation Society had not given up the challenge of putting together all four missions south of downtown as a park. Society President Ethel Harris and Elizabeth Graham used the occasion of the National Conference of State Parks in Ohio in 1951 to work with the National Parks director and other officials on the subject and get pointers for the project, while Rena Maverick Green once more sought consolidation of all four missions south of the city into a national park.[88] The post-war straightening and widening of the San Antonio River channel for flood control provided a chance for a straight parallel stretch of a coherent Mission Road.[89] With support of the San Antonio Chamber of Commerce, a Mission Area Planning Committee was created.[90]

The Conservation Society's aqueduct property was isolated from San José and the other mission sites, and had become somewhat of a nuisance.[91] But it could not be properly given away, although in 1955 the society tried to give it to the San José Mission Historic Site.[92] So it remained a regular target of weed and undergrowth clean-up efforts. The adjacent rock house seemed to stay in a constant state of disrepair, which aggravated the task of keeping tenants.[93] But when adjoining property became available, the Conservation Society lost little time in acquiring it, as the Catholic Church was by then purchasing property within the original mission compounds themselves.

In the summer of 1957 the Conservation Society purchased twenty-five key pecan-shaded acres of original mission farmland. The site lay east of Espada Dam between the Espada and San Juan acequias and contained an estimated five hundred pecan trees, some as many as two hundred years old, which

San Antonio's two-span Espada aqueduct, first protected in parkland purchased by the San Antonio Conservation Society, remains the only Spanish-era aqueduct in the nation in continuous use. San Antonio Conservation Society.

conservationists feared were about to be smothered by fill dirt from widening of the river channel nearby. The price was $37,500, with $500 down. To raise the money, members decided to add a fourth Night in Old San Antonio and to use the proceeds from the new night for the purchase.[94] Purchase of another four acres near the aqueduct for $2,000 was approved in 1958.[95] The Conservation Society hoped to turn over the park to the State Park Board, which had already agreed to designate it an historic site and to maintain it.[96]

Of the seven acequias built in San Antonio by the Spaniards to irrigate mission lands, only the San Juan and Espada acequias survived. The original two-span Espada aqueduct, the only Spanish aqueduct remaining in the United States, was still in use. The Espada acequia system, operating continuously since its construction between 1731 and 1735, was irrigating some four hundred acres of farmland.[97] Its original dam still raised the level of the river so water could enter the acequia.[98]

During the course of its flood-control widening of the river channel in southern Bexar County in the 1950s, the San Antonio River Authority dug a new channel two hundred feet west of the original San Juan Dam. But that lowered the river, stopping the flow of water into the San Juan acequia. This threatened survival of the five hundred pecan trees on the society's newly purchased park near Espada Dam. Worse, some thirty-five landholders belonging to the San Juan Ditch Company that maintained the acequia and dam were without water.[99] The River Authority began pumping water into the old ditch to accommodate farmers downstream until 1958, when it decided pumping was an expense it could cut. If property owners wanted to pay $2,500 a year for electricity plus whatever would be needed for maintenance and repairs, then the River Authority would be glad to install two pumps and a pumphouse "in six months to a year."[100] Water users—including the Conservation Society—objected. Both sides went for their lawyers.

The River Authority got to the courthouse first. It asked the court to find that none of its actions in diverting water made it liable for compensatory damages to farmers. The Conservation Society responded by invoking an act of the King of Spain as the source of the water rights. The River Authority held that obligation to have been nullified in 1826 and amended its pleadings to file against the Conservation Society too.[101] The Conservation Society got the other adjacent property owners—the "Ditch Group" plus the Catholic Church—to agree to share legal expenses, and all prepared to defend themselves.[102]

Litigation dragged on for six years. The River Authority won in District Court, lost in the Court of Civil Appeals, but won 4-3 in the Texas Supreme Court. The Conservation Society sent attorney Ralph Langley to Mexico City, where further ancient legal authority on water rights was found to buttress the society's position. It was sufficient evidence to merit reconsideration by the Texas Supreme Court, which reversed itself to favor the landowners. The River Authority paid damages to the landowners and by 1967 raised the level of its new dam to allow water to flow back through the San Juan acequia without pumping.[103]

But the outcry over the San Juan acequia, and even the heated opposition to the city's Travis Park proposal, paled in comparison to the emotion about to be unleashed over the sort of project guaranteed to stir things up in any city: an urban expressway, one in this case planned north from downtown past an increasingly busy airport through the only open corridor available—cherished parkland.

Notes

1. Minutes, G-Dec. 18, 1947; D-Jan. 20, 1948; G-Feb. 26, 1948; G-Feb. 26, 1948; D-May 3, 1949; Rena Maverick Green, "Our Parks," *SACS Newsletter*, February, 1961, 2.

2. Minutes, G-Mar. 25, 1948. Planners still got by with locating a junior college tennis court complex in the park.

3. Minutes, D-Jan. 20, 1958.

4. Minutes, D-Jan. 20, 1948; G-Oct. 27, 1949; D-Jun, 20, 1950. For her efforts, in 1954 Rena Green was made Honorary Life Chairman of the society's Parks, Rivers, Creeks and Natural Beauty Committee. (Minutes, D-Apr. 15, 1954, 3.)

5. Minutes, D-Jan. 14, 1953, 2; G-Jan. 22, 1953, 1–2.

6. Minutes, D-Feb. 17, 1953, 2. Trees were also being used as thank-you gifts to institutions which helped the Conservation Society in other efforts. (Minutes, D-Jan. 23, 1956, 2.)

7. Minutes, G-Feb. 26, 1953. Sales totaled $1,132, with a profit of $202 to be used to buy more trees. In 1954, 6,000 trees went on sale at the Auditorium in cooperation with the Nurserymen's Association. Participating organizations ranged from the Chamber of Commerce to the Garden Center to the Council of Churches. (Minutes, G-Jan. 28, 1954, 2.) Mrs. Harker's committee planned to have flowering window boxes outside second-story windows of downtown businesses, and also to have plantings at service stations and parking lots. (Minutes, D-Feb. 25, 1954, 1–2.) The State Highway Department was targeted for reeducation on saving of native trees during highway projects. (Minutes, D-Mar. 19, 1956, 3.)

8. Minutes, D-Jan. 23, 1961, 3.

9. Minutes, D-Oct. 22, 1947, 1–2.

10. Minutes, G-Mar. 25, 1948; D-May 25, 1948; D-Feb. 22, 1949; G-May 25, 1950, 2.

11. Minutes, D-Nov. 14, 1950.

12. Minutes, D-Oct. 2, 1951.

13. Ibid.

14. Minutes, G-Oct. 25, 1951; Martin L. Crimmins to San Antonio City Council, undated note in Box 2M137, Adina De Zavala Papers, The Center For American History, The University of Texas at Austin. Crimmins, then president of the Texas Historical and Landmarks Association's De Zavala Chapter, congratulated the council for its "vision, foresight and wisdom in granting the permit to the 500-car garage owners for an exit over our unique San Antonio River," which he said would relieve crowded conditions and prevent accidents on College Street.

15. "Society Loses Bridge Appeal," *San Antonio Express*, Jun. 4, 1952, 22.

16. Minutes, D-Dec. 21, 1951.

17. Eleanor Bennett OHT, Jun. 4, 1985, 1. She was interviewed by her husband, John M. Bennett, Jr.

18. "City Wins Fight For Bridge, But Losers to Appeal," *San Antonio Express*, Oct. 27, 1950, 1; "Society Loses Bridge Appeal," *San Antonio Express*, Jun. 4, 1952, 22; Minutes, D-Mar. 25, 1957, 3. The bridge was removed in the 1960s.

19. "Fight for Parks," *San Antonio Express,* May 6, 1951.

20. SACS President Mrs. Winfield S. Hamlin to Medical & Surgical Building Corp. Manager Don Tillotson, Nov. 13, 1961, copy in SACS library; "Bagatelles," *San Antonio Light,* Dec. 10, 1961.

21. Ibid.

22. Minutes, G-Mar. 24, 1955; D-Apr. 13, 1966, 1–2; Green, "Our Parks," *SACS Newsletter,* February, 1961, 2.

23. Minutes, D-Oct. 23, 1961, 1–3.

24. "City to Seek Underground Parking Areas," *San Antonio Express,* Sept. 6, 1953, 1; Jon Ford, "Backstage in Politics: Travis Park Garage Slated," *San Antonio Express-News,* Oct. 11, 1953.

25. Downtown's oldest square—Military Plaza—was not an option for underground parking only because it was pre-empted in the previous century as the site of city hall itself.

26. "City to Seek Underground Parking Areas," *San Antonio Express,* Sept. 6, 1953, 1.

27. Minutes, D-Sept. 16, 1953, 2.

28. Eleanor Bennett OHT, 3.

29. "Council Delays Parking Verdict," *San Antonio Express,* Oct. 9, 1953, 14.

30. Ibid.

31. Ibid.; "H.B. Zachry, Trustee vs. City of San Antonio, No. A-6160," Supreme Court of Texas, Jun. 5, 1957, *305 South Western Reporter, 2d Series,* Tex. 562.

32. Minutes, D-Oct. 9, 1953, 5.

33. "Council Delays Parking Verdict," *San Antonio Express,* Oct. 9, 1953, 14.

34. Minutes, D-Oct. 9, 1953, 5.

35. "Council Delays Parking Verdict," *San Antonio Express,* Oct. 9, 1953, 14.

36. Ibid.

37. Eleanor Bennett OHT, 3.

38. "Suit to Test Garage Deals," *San Antonio News,* Jun. 2, 1955.

39. Minutes, D-Oct. 19, 1953.

40. "Downtown Mass Meeting Voted In Garage Fight," *San Antonio Express,* Oct. 23, 1953, 5.

41. Minutes, G-Oct. 22, 1953.

42. "Downtown Mass Meeting Voted In Garage Fight," *San Antonio Express,* Oct. 23, 1953, 5. The paper noted that one member said that the mayor looked at the park at the wrong time, that the flowers were beautiful several weeks earlier.

43. Ibid.

44. Minutes, G-Oct. 22, 1953.

45. "Downtown Mass Meeting Voted In Garage Fight," *San Antonio Express,* Oct. 23, 1953, 5.

46. Minutes, G-Oct. 22, 1953.

47. Ibid.

48. "Garage Won't Mar Beauty of Travis Park," *San Antonio Express,* Oct. 25, 1953.

49. "Drilling Begins For Sub-Parking," *San Antonio Light,* Nov. 4, 1953.

50. "Garage Won't Mar Beauty of Travis Park," *San Antonio Express,* Oct. 25, 1953.

51. "Large Trees Over Garage Held Possible," *San Antonio News,* Nov. 5, 1953, 1.

52. "Council Refuses Vote On Garage," *San Antonio Express,* Oct. 16, 1953.

53. "Recall Group Says City Doesn't Own Travis Park," *San Antonio Express,* Nov. 5, 1953, 16.

54. Ibid., 2–3. Mary Green was back as secretary within a short time, when the recall movement was replaced by a charter revision effort. (Minutes, D-Nov. 24, 1953.)

55. Ibid. Targets of the recall movement were Mayor Jack White and council members R.N. White, Jr., Thelma (Mrs. E.M.) Stevens, H.J. Shearer, Ralph Easley and R.L. Lester. Safe were minority voters Gonzalez, Sherlin and Raymond Russell Jr.

56. "Recall Campaign Picks Up New Punch," *San Antonio Light,* Nov. 10, 1953, 2.

57. Minutes, A-Nov. 10, 1953, 1–3.

58. Ibid.

59. "Mrs. Rena Maverick Green et al. v. City of San Antonio, Appellees, No. 12882," Court of Civil Appeals of Texas, San Antonio, Sept. 14, 1955, *282 South Western Reporter, 2d Series,* Tex. 769–76. While attorneys Hubert Green Senior and Junior were officially employed by the Maverick heirs, legal fees were borne by the Conservation Society, which came up with $1,200 and set up a San Antonio Conservation Society Park Fund to receive additional contributions. Attorney C. Stanley Banks was later retained to assist. (Minutes, D-Nov. 24, 1953, 1–2; D-May 24, 1954, 2.)

60. "City Not To Order Park Shrub Move Until Court Case Settled," *San Antonio Express,* Jan. 5, 1954, 1.

61. Minutes, G-Jan. 28, 1954, 3.

62. Minutes, G-Dec. 3, 1953; D-Mar. 22, 1954, 3.

63. Minutes, G-Feb. 24, 1955, 3.

64. Eleanor Bennett OHT, 4.

65. Minutes, G-Jan. 27, 1955.

66. "Green v. City of San Antonio," 769–76.

67. Minutes, D-Feb. 7, 1955; G-Mar. 24, 1955, 2. Fearing that too many trees were being cut in Travis Park, at the March 2 concert—which featured bands from Harlandale High School and Lackland Air Force Base—the City Parks director approved dedication of several memorial trees, including one in memory of Samuel Maverick. Nine more trees from the Conservation Society and friends were dedicated at another band concert that fall. (Minutes, D-Jan. 11, 1956, 2; G-Feb. 23, 1956; G-Sept. 27, 1956, 2.)

68. "Green v. City of San Antonio," 769–76.

69. Booth and Johnson, "Power and Progress in San Antonio Politics," in *The Politics of San Antonio,* 22–23.

70. "People's Ticket Endorses Conservation Group Aims," *San Antonio Express-News,* Apr. 3, 1955.

71. "League Fails to Take Society Park Policy Stand," *San Antonio Light,* Apr. 3, 1955, 18-A.

72. "League Questions Park Garage Jobs," *San Antonio Express,* May 21, 1955.

73. "Quick Park Garage Opinion Pledged," May 21, 1955.

74. "Suit to Test Garage Deals," *San Antonio News,* Jun. 2, 1955.

75. "Travis Park Garage Text Suit Filed," *San Antonio News,* Jun. 10, 1955.

76. "H.B. Zachry, Trustee, v. City of San Antonio, No. 13031," Court of Civil Appeals of Texas, San Antonio, Sept. 5, 1955, *296 South Western Reporter, 2d Series,* Tex. 299–306.

77. "H.B. Zachry, Trustee v. City of San Antonio, No. A-61610," Supreme Court of Texas, Jun. 5, 1957, *305 South Western Reporter, 2d Series,* Tex. 558–63.

78. "Garage Backers Won't Give Up," *San Antonio News,* Dec. 6, 1955; Minutes, D-Sept. 24, 1956.

79. Minutes, D-Feb. 23, 1959.

80. Minutes, D-Feb. 25, 1957.

81. Minutes, D-Aug. 27, 1959.

82. Minutes, D-May 14, 1959.

83. Minutes, D-Jun. 22, 1959.

84. Minutes, D-Nov. 23, 1959; D-May 21, 1962.

85. "Clubwomen Will Protest Against Ravage of Park," *San Antonio Express,* May 14, 1916; "What Is the Value Of In-Town Parkland?," *San Antonio Express*, Feb. 14, 1962, 4-A.

86. "Lions To Retain Field Supervision," *San Antonio Express,* Jul. 24, 1929, 11; City of San Antonio historical marker at Lions Field.

87. Minutes, D-Feb. 19, 1962; Vivian Hamlin to Louise Briggs, Jan. 26, 1962 and Vivian J. Hamlin to Mrs. R.W. Briggs, Jan. 31, 1962, memos in SACS Library.

88. Minutes, D-Feb. 20, 1951; G-May 28, 1953, 5. In 1958, Society President Helen (Mrs. W. Grant) Bechtel lobbied with the Texas State Parks Board and its longtime member Frank D. Quinn to get $45,000 into the national parks budget for repairs at San José. With the help of Congressman Paul Kilday, Senator Ralph Yarborough and Senator Lyndon B. Johnson, the effort succeeded. "I have visited San José Mission a number of times in the past 30 years," wrote Senator Yarborough, "and will support all efforts to preserve this National Historic Site." (Mrs. W. Grant Bechtel to Paul Kilday, Dec. 10, 1957; Ralph Yarborough to Mrs. W. Grant Bechtel, Jan. 20, 1958; Paul Kilday to Mrs. W. Grant Bechtel, Jan. 28, 1958; Mrs. W. Grant Bechtel to Lyndon B. Johnson, Jun. 2, 1958; letters in SACS Library.)

89. Minutes D-Oct, 22, 1956, 2; G-Oct. 25, 1956. The Conservation Society backed area property owner Thurman Barrett's River Road efforts in 1948. At the recommendation of the society, three years later Bexar County Commissioners' Court again named the proposed artery Mission Road. At the same time, Barrett and Mrs. Elizabeth Graham gave a total of fifteen acres in the flood plain toward a county park, successfully designated by the society as Mission Park. Wanda Ford's committee in early 1953 took three members of the City Planning Board on a tour along the river from Mission Concepcion on to Mission San Juan to plug Mission Road. Eleanor Bennett, the society's representative on the San José Mission Board, also lobbied with that group. While San Juan Mission itself was in poor repair, preservationists were confident that the Catholic Church had the situation in hand and would restore it. (Minutes, G-Feb.26, 1948; G-Feb. 22, 1951; G-Mar. 22, 1951; G-Jan. 25, 1953; D-Feb. 26, 1953; D-May 22, 1953.)

90. Minutes, D-Mar. 19, 1956, 2; G-Sept. 25, 1958, 2.

91. At the end of 1941, Mrs. John Camp donated the remaining principal of $300 plus interest due Elizabeth Graham on the original aqueduct property. The Espada aqueduct was named a National Historic Landmark in 1965. (Minutes, G-Nov. 21, 1941, 2; G-Jan. 22, 1942, 4; D-Mar. 22, 1965.)

92. Minutes, D-Jun. 16, 1955.

93. Minutes, G-Sept. 25, 1941; G-Jan. 22, 1942; G-Apr. 24, 1942; G-Oct. 24, 1946; G-Nov. 20, 1947; D-Oct. 19, 1948; D-Nov. 16, 1948, 23; D-Dec. 3, 1953. A mid-July day in 1956 was made Clean-Up Day for all members, who were to bring their own lunch and beverage. Problems were summed up by O'Neil Ford, who once told members that "there were no directions how to get to it, and . . . once you found it it was difficult to see it properly . . . . There is so much foliage around it that too much of it is covered. A bridge would be helpful also. The house there is a little gem, and has a most unique chimney, but the man who lives there is unable to answer questions intelligently." (Minutes, G-Nov. 21, 1941, 2; D-Jun. 25, 1956, 2.)

94. Minutes, D-Jul. 31, 1957; G-Aug. 22, 1957. It worked. The final balance was paid off the week after NIOSA in 1960. (Minutes, G-Jun, 22, 1961, 2.)

95. Minutes, D-Feb. 24, 1958; D-Mar. 24, 1958, 2; D-May 5, 1958.

96. "Society Fights For New Park," *San Antonio Express,* undated clipping in SACS Library.

97. Arthur R. Gómez, *Espada Dam: A Preliminary Historical Report* (San Antonio: San Antonio Missions National Historic Park, 1990), 14–15.

98. Ibid., 21. The San Juan dam, originally thought to have been destroyed, was later found to exist beneath several feet of dirt and vegetation. (Ibid., 13.)

99. Minutes, G-Jun. 22, 1961, 2.

100. Minutes, D-Nov. 10, 1958; D-Mar. 12, 1962. The River Authority and the U.S. Corps of Engineers had just finished hauling a large amount of dirt fill to the aqueduct area, for which the Conservation Society was grateful. (Minutes, D-Oct. 20, 1958; D-Oct. 5, 1959.)

101. Minutes, D-Nov. 10, 1958; D-Mar. 12, 1962. The suit was styled San Antonio River Authority vs. G. Garett Lewis et. al.

102. Minutes, D-Nov. 24, 1958, 2.

103. Minutes, G-Feb. 22, 1962; D-Mar. 12, 1962; D-Apr. 9, 1962; D-Feb. 24, 1964, 2; D-Apr. 6, 1964; D-May 24, 1965; D-Nov. 22, 1965; D-Nov. 21, 1966, 2; D-Mar. 20, 1967. By 1965 the Conservation Society's trees in Acequia Park were showing damage from lack of water. (Minutes, G-May 27, 1965, 2.)

11

An Urban Expressway
Sparks a Ten-Year War

Leaders in the drive for a North Expressway and, soon, for a
World's Fair, were men of ambition and determination, men
accustomed to overcoming major obstacles in their drive to
achieve. They saw the long-term issues of environment and
quality of life brought up in debate over the expressway as
incidental in the face of the fast-approaching and immovable
deadline for opening the fair. They saw the stakes, correctly, as
a singular opportunity to transform San Antonio into a dynamic
city with more to recommend it than a military-based economy
and the memory of the Alamo.

As the conflict began in 1960 and as skirmishes broadened, those marshaling
the opposing forces of contemporary business and politics—predominantly
male—and of sensitivity and tradition—predominantly female—found themselves locked in a struggle of epic proportions. In San Antonio, as in the rest
of the nation at the time, the "pro-highway juggernaut" included not only
chambers of commerce, developers, businessmen, politicians and national
special interest groups but also the media, much of its advertising revenue
dependent on downtown businesses.[1]

But those leading the charge for an environment which respected the
dynamics of nature and the meaningful trappings of the past had also, in turn,
tasted the fruits of achievement. They found themselves more determined
than ever to prevent what they saw as needless destruction in the single-
minded pursuit of any goal. They viewed the stakes as a final opportunity to
preserve much historic ambiance in what could become a dynamic yet also a
livable city, once the shorter-term goals of urban renewal and a more broadly
based economy were realized sensitively.

The escalating state of war between the City of San Antonio and the San
Antonio Conservation Society created by the proposed expressway would last
for a decade, consuming important resources of energy and money and

By 1960, freeway construction was so pervasive nationwide that few homes were considered sacred. PEANUTS reprinted by permission of United Feature Syndicate, Inc.

goodwill. Hostilities broke out in full scale as the Conservation Society fired a succession of anti-expressway lawsuits at city hall. City officials finally responded in kind with a lawsuit dunning the Conservation Society for alleged back taxes, climaxing with the threat that all of the society's hard-won properties would be sold at a sheriff's sale.

Maneuvering extended all the way to the nation's capital. In one-two lightning strikes from the floor of the United States Senate, Conservation Society ally Senator Ralph Yarborough outflanked legal positions favorable to the city by securing a major amendment to a transportation measure. He next got through a requirement that preservationists, rather than city officials, be the official overseers of landmarks on the site of the upcoming World's Fair, which threw the San Antonio city council into a state of confusion. The expressway matter itself became, in the words of a former Conservation Society president, "undoubtedly the most emotional issue in the history of the society."[2] Long after it was finally built, the subject would still bring muttered imprecations from veterans partial to either side.

The underlying problem was generic, closely tied to the national crisis in downtown parking. Traffic caused by increasing numbers of suburban drivers parking downtown did, after all, have to be carried in and out of downtown. More one-way streets were only a partial solution. Other than wider, faster arterial streets the only solution was more expressways. In San Antonio, as elsewhere, much of the problem was remedied by highway loops around urban perimeters and by spoke thoroughfares through declining neighborhoods near paths of major streets. Such construction was made feasible by Congressional authorization in 1956 of the interstate highway program, a planned $41 billion, 41,000-mile system linking every major metropolitan area in the country, with 90 percent of the costs paid by the federal government. By 1969, its costs had mushroomed to $104 billion.[3] In San Antonio, the designation for U.S. 87, which came from the northwest, was changed from Fredericksburg Road to the path of the new Interstate 10, which also paralleled much of the old U.S. 90 south of downtown. Interstate 35 northeast to Austin followed the general direction of the previous U.S. 81, Austin Highway.

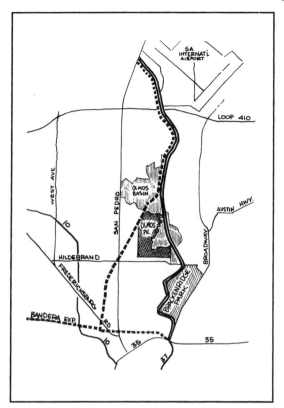

The North Expressway route ultimately selected (solid double lines) skirted Brackenridge Park and the City of Olmos Park, then cut through the Olmos Basin floodplain and crossed Loop 410 beside International Airport. Rejected was an alternate route (dotted line) that skirted the other side of the uncooperative City of Olmos Park and went through a heavily populated area to connect with the proposed Bandera Expressway, which was never built. San Antonio Express-News.

In north central San Antonio, traffic on San Pedro Avenue/U.S. 281 was at near-maximum capacity. Widening or replacement with an expressway would not solve the problem of access to the fast-growing San Antonio International Airport. San Pedro passed too far west. Two blocks east of San Pedro, and only recently cut north through the western edge of the Olmos Basin flood plain, was McCullough Avenue. McCullough, also increasingly congested, was narrower than San Pedro and also passed through high-cost real estate areas, one of which would later be named an historic district. The only other north-south artery near the airport was to the east—Broadway, which passed through other high-cost areas on the far side of Brackenridge Park.

In the mid-1950s, city staff members meeting at the St. Anthony Hotel with Texas State Highway Engineer Dewitt Greer gathered around maps of the city. "When are you going to do something about this?" asked Greer as he pointed to the soon-to-be congested traffic arteries in north central San Antonio.[4] The response was included in the City of San Antonio's first modern comprehensive traffic study, completed in the spring of 1956. It was a newly designated U.S. 281 from downtown due north past International Airport: the North Expressway.

As the only open spaces downtown had been obvious targets for underground parking garages, so now the only open spaces due north of downtown became obvious targets for the path of the North Expressway—the lowlands along the general course of the San Antonio River and its tributary, Olmos Creek, and its flood plain basin, land dubbed Franklin Fields by Mayor Maury Maverick in a 1940 tribute to Franklin Roosevelt.[5] Although the six-mile route north to Loop 410 through the open lands was shown in the city's 1956 traffic report, no one paid much attention for three years, while expressway planning was completed for southern and eastern San Antonio.[6] But urban planner Sam Zisman, the Conservation Society's planning consultant, saw what was up, and raised the subject to Conservation Society members in May of 1959.[7] In early June, the subject of specific northern and western expressways was broached by the editor of the *San Antonio News*. The only part of the North Expressway detailed was that beyond city limits at Basse Road. "Details of the remainder of the route," he reported, "will be revealed later."[8]

At the end of the month, a delegation of city, county and San Antonio Chamber of Commerce officials formally asked the State Highway Commission to study the situation.[9] The San Antonio Conservation Society wired its opposition to the Highway Commission.[10] In August, at the suggestion of Mary Green and "after much discussion," Conservation Society directors ordered drawings to illustrate why the proposed expressway plan would not work.[11]

During the process of preparing a specific plan, the Texas Highway Department concluded that no arterial system of existing streets could meet the anticipated volume of traffic, and that an expressway would indeed be required. Thirteen potential routes were mapped out. In March of 1960, the Highway Department recommended the one north from Interstate 35 which would nick a corner off the Brackenridge Park Golf Course as it swerved to avoid the main portion of the park, then head north between Alamo Stadium and Trinity University. It would cross Hildebrand Avenue through city property and go on straight north across the toe of the City of Olmos Park, exiting into Olmos Basin as it went straight on to Loop 410.[12] While Mayor Walter W. McAllister's Good Government League strongly supported the North Expressway, Good Government League founder Tom Powell in his role as mayor of Olmos Park found himself making the "Not In My Back Yard" response. Texas Highway Department policy was to obtain a city's approval and financial support before planning a highway through its territory. The City of Olmos Park would not agree to such a plan. Another route had to be found.

Both the Texas Highway Department and the City of San Antonio turned to an alternate center section, a third of a mile longer than the preferred route but entirely within San Antonio city limits. Rather than passing by the west

The key center section of the North Expressway was finally planned not between Alamo Stadium and Trinity University and on through a corner of the City of Olmos Park, but through the narrow space between the east side of Alamo Stadium and Brackenridge Park's Sunken Gardens. The San Antonio Light Collection, The Institute of Texan Cultures.

side of Alamo Stadium, it would go by on the east, between the stadium and the cliff above the Sunken Gardens. Then it would traverse an open area once used by the San Antonio Zoo to graze buffalo. It would cross Hildebrand Avenue into an unused stretch of land owned by the Sisters of Charity of the Incarnate Word, physically separating the order's high school and convent up the hill from its mother house and its college down the hill. The highway would pass over Olmos Dam and brush the eastern tip of the City of Olmos Park, then connect with the more favored route in the basin.[13] With property acquisition for more distant alternative routes considered "prohibitively expensive," expressway planners believed they were left with little choice.[14]

City hall set a vote for June 28, 1960 on $9 million in bonds in a single four-project package: turning Highway 90 West into an expressway, constructing a new access road to Kelly Air Force Base, constructing an underpass for Guadalupe Street and building the North Expressway.

Past Alamo Stadium, the North Expressway was to span one end of Olmos Dam past a tip of the City of Olmos Park, then cut through the green spaces of the Olmos Basin floodplain, which conservationists claimed was public parkland. The San Antonio Light *Collection, The Institute of Texan Cultures.*

On June 8, Conservation Society President Lois (Mrs. James V.) Graves called her directors to Oak Hills Country Club for a discussion. Four men were invited to make suggestions: former State Highway Department official and Chamber of Commerce Highway Committee Chairman James W. Francis, past San Antonio Parks Director Stewart King, planner Sam Zisman and architect O'Neil Ford. The upshot was a resolution reaffirming the society's commitment to parks, a measure which also complained that the city had ignored the society's request that the North Expressway be a separate issue in the bond vote. Directors concluded that the idea "to traverse as much of the park area as possible so as to save money" was "false economy." They urged defeat of the bond issue.[15] In addition, Sam Zisman warned the city planning commission in person that the North Expressway as planned would uproot $2.5 million worth of trees, which would cost $3.5 million to replace. He asked whether acreage would be purchased elsewhere to offset parkland taken by the expressway, but got no answer.[16] San Antonio Chamber of Commerce directors unanimously endorsed the bond issue as the business community swung behind the project.[17]

Turning up the intensity of their attack, the Conservation Society adopted a tactic from the Travis Park struggle and passed out shrill fliers headlined "STOP THIEF!" The fliers asserted that the proposed expressway would "Destroy the world famous SUNKEN GARDENS, Wipe out SUNKEN GARDEN THEATRE and ALPINE DRIVE, Destroy the ZOO, . . . Ruin public PICNIC GROUNDS and RECREATION AREAS . . . Make hazardous the use of ALAMO STADIUM, . . . Endanger the City's FLOOD CONTROL" and cause other disasters as well. A coupon for contributions to the Conservation Society was at the bottom.[18]

The outcome stunned city hall. The bond issue was defeated by 331 votes, 18,758 to 18,427. Observed *Life* Magazine: "A new breed of engineers regards concrete, anywhere, as more esthetic than nature, and sometimes need to be put in their places by alert and stubborn conservationists—as San Antonio did . . . ."[19] But the "new breed" was not about to give up. "We knew definitely we were going back to the voters," Chamber of Commerce highway activist James W. Francis later recalled. "We just wanted to wait and work the council and the citizens up to it."[20]

In August, city council told City Manager Lynn Andrews to restudy the route. In early November, Francis led a delegation of civic and business leaders asking the council to reconsider the entire bond issue and to make provision to buy new parkland to "more than offset the small amount of parkland" needed for the expressway. City council set another bond election, for January 10, 1961. Newly elected councilman and onetime Conservation Society ally Walter W. McAllister took charge of the Chamber of Commerce's Committee for Parks and Expressway, which launched a $35,000 media campaign advocating the expressway.[21] The Conservation Society responded with a resolution reaffirming opposition to any expressway that would take land from parks. Wanda Ford outlined further tactics to oppose it. At the same session, a man destined to play a key role in the matter—U.S. Senator Ralph Yarborough—appeared to seek support for his bill to make Padre Island on the Texas coast a National Seashore Recreation Area.[22] Society President Lois Graves took a group to a city council meeting to debate Mayor Edwin Kuykendall on the subject of the expressway, with no effect, except to annoy the mayor.[23]

As the election approached, city fathers got off a warning shot at their adversary. Some thirty years before when the Conservation Society first bought land at San José Mission, members had been able to take advantage of gray areas in the law and, with the help of friends in local government, avoid having to pay property taxes. In 1955 the state legislature specifically exempted nonprofit groups administering landmarks from taxation.[24] But the Conservation Society's properties still remained on the tax rolls, and some were being leased for profit. City and county tax offices periodically sent the Conservation Society notices of delinquent taxes, which the society would seek, unsuccessfully, to settle. The society's back taxes grew into five figures on the books.[25] In the fall of 1960, before the second vote on expressway bonds, city hall raised the tax issue with new force. City Manager Lynn Andrews suggested it could all be solved if the Conservation Society simply deeded its properties over to the city and then leased them back to operate and maintain.[26]

That suggestion prompted an irate three-page resolution from society directors, who cited a dozen grievances against the city—failure to pass an historic preservation ordinance, the reneged promise on preserving the Guilbeau House, recently permitting the Devine House to be razed. Directors declared that a relationship of trust existed between the Conservation Society and the people, "thousands" of whom were counting on the Conservation Society to preserve their heritage and to protect the city's second largest source of income, tourism. The Steves Homestead had been, after all, directors noted archly, "entrusted to us and not to the City of San Antonio."[27] Too, the measure complained, "a few in this city have been obsessed with creating new routes and parking areas even to the extent that they would violate dedicated parks and to the further extent that they would destroy historic buildings, landmarks and sites—our precious heritage." After all that, directors practically commanded city council to exempt promptly all of the society's properties from taxation, to pass an historic zoning ordinance "here and now" and to restore the German-English School as well.[28]

City council held the tax bill in reserve as it faced new ranks of Conservation Society reinforcements. Other expressway opponents organized as the Conserve Our Parks Committee and come up with the battle cry, "Keep off the Grass." A more significant adversary also surfaced—the Sisters of Charity of the Incarnate Word, who announced their intent to file a major damage suit against the city if the expressway were to threaten their property.[29]

In the next bond election, the items were divided into separate bond propositions: one for both U.S. 90 West and the Kelly access road ($5.6 million), the Guadalupe Street underpass ($300,000), the North Expressway ($3.5 million) and a new item, designed to placate expressway opponents: $500,000 for unspecified new parkland, to replace that taken by the North Expressway. By the time polls closed, a record 67,207 voters had approved all four propositions by overwhelming margins. The Highway 90/Kelly access project passed by 83 percent, the Guadalupe underpass by 80 percent, the new parkland by 70 percent and the North Expressway proposition by 63 percent.[30]

San Antonio's first major expressway interchange was between interstates 10 and 35 northwest of downtown, shown looking southeast in the 1960s. Interstate 10 in the foreground of this picture took the site of the home where the San Antonio Conservation Society was organized in 1924—and which, appropriately, was recycled and reconstructed near Castroville. Zintgraff Collection, The Institute of Texan Cultures.

Crestfallen Conservation Society directors responded with a lengthy resolution. It complained that, among other things, "no hearing of interested parties was ever held before the Planning Commission, and our Society was never given the opportunity to bring in competent experts to present their views before the Planning Commission." In the resolution's eleventh "Whereas," directors gathered their composure to declare that "true Americans, true Texans and true Conservationists may lose a battle and their hearts may be heavy, but their determination to continue fighting for their beliefs never falters." Directors then got to their point: "The San Antonio Conservation Society shall vigorously continue its efforts to prevent the appropriation of one said park for other than park purposes, and our stand shall be widely publicized and vigorously carried out before the public, public officials and at all hearings which in any way involve our parks."[31]

The Sisters of Charity of the Incarnate Word, represented by attorney Pat Maloney, responded to the vote with a lawsuit. In June the San Antonio Conservation Society joined them in the suit.[32] The city tax office, in turn, advised the Conservation Society that unless it paid taxes on two of its revenue-producing properties, the city would file suit. Society directors passed another measure which, after a dozen resolves, told the city to study the matter further and then grant an exemption.[33] Two law firms were retained by the Conservation Society to help prosecute the expressway case: the Austin firm of O'Quinn, McDaniel and Randle and the San Antonio firm of Glosserman, Alter and Smith.[34] Attorneys Trueman O'Quinn from Austin and Perry Smith from San Antonio met with the society's executive committee at a mid-July session called by President Vivian (Mrs. Winfield Scott) Hamlin at Casa Villita. Accompanying the attorneys was Roger Busfield, a public relations man from Austin.[35]

"It is a slugging match when you take on the government," Busfield warned the executive committee. "It is a barefisted fight. We cannot be altruistic about it except in our objective." And the objective, O'Quinn stressed, was not to allow the case to be sidetracked on technical points but to "have the case decided on its merits; that is, do they have the power to take a public park away from the people?" Yet, "It is a very critical and complicated case, and does involve some important consideration," O'Quinn counseled. "If the city can prevail on this thing, . . . no park anywhere is safe from the Highway Department." A critical factor was seen to be public opinion, which could obviously be swayed, as the negative vote of the previous summer had been overwhelmingly reversed only six months later.

"The more you make these people villains," said Busfield of the city council and the State Highway Department, the more "you make them see what they are doing, and the less enthusiasm they are going to have . . . . What it is is an effort to get people concerned about the thing." For instance, under the terms of the donation of the park by George Brackenridge, if the land ceased to be used for park purposes it would revert to the University of Texas. "Suppose," Busfield suggested, "there are stories that get into the newspaper properly worded to the effect that the city council is about to give the park away to the University of Texas?"

Strategists believed their strongest point was that the route through the parkland was not even the best route. That, engineers were already on record as stating, was on the other side of Alamo Stadium, on a route that would take homes within the City of Olmos Park. "The Highway Department takes the attitude that we cannot condemn private property," said O'Quinn, "but they do not mind taking the park away from the public." Time should not be sacrificed in developing main points. The city attorney had been cooperative, said O'Quinn, who did not expect the city to send in the bulldozers as long as there was a lawsuit pending.[36]

A hearing on the amended pleadings was delayed until October, and the Conservation Society's attorneys continued seeking an agreement to change the route.[37] Initial victory came as a district court decision blocked any transfer of land from Brackenridge Park to the state for the project. But in the fall of 1962, the Court of Civil Appeals reversed the lower court's ruling. An appeal was authorized to the Texas Supreme Court, which in December denied the motion for rehearing. Attorney O'Quinn suggested that a second motion not be filed.[38] The city now had a legal right to sell parkland to the state. But conservationists were not about to give up. With "the legal approach favored rather than the emotional," O'Quinn was kept to represent the society.[39] Maloney continued to represent the Incarnate Word sisters.

Yet the pull of emotions remained strong, whether in formal hearings or in larger gatherings. Former Conservation Society President Peggy (Mrs. Don F.) Tobin recalled being advised to keep her comments away from traffic counts, exit ramps and other technical areas. "'Just keep on your ground,'" she remembered being told, "which in my case was pure sentiment."[40] Consequently, on a trip to Washington, D.C., "When I testified before this poor old federal highway administrator, I told him that the expressway would never be built because there was a St. Joseph's medal buried in the driveway by one of the sisters I knew at Incarnate Word. So I kept that sort of story line or argument going the entire time . . . . It was most effective. It kept those guys completely off balance. They could not tell me about the traffic count or anything else. As long as the St. Joseph's medal was there, the expressway [could] not go through."[41] Helping her keep perspective were the routines of everyday life. Recalled Mrs. Tobin, a mother of six: "I was always climbing out of the basement . . . while I was running the laundry to talk to the Secretary of Transportation calling from Washington."[42]

Mutual hostility was apparent in October of 1963, when more than five hundred persons gathered in MacArthur Park for a public hearing sponsored by the Texas Highway Department. Presided over by District Highway Engineer R.O. Lytton, it turned into a six-hour marathon, said to be the longest public hearing in Bexar County history, with thirty-one speakers. A "testy" Mayor Walter McAllister responded to planner Sam Zisman and Incarnate Word representative Mother Calixa: Why were the nuns worried about losing sixteen acres of their property when they had already sold far more than that amount at various times to developers? the mayor asked. If their campus was reduced to the point that it could not accommodate growth potential in fifty to one hundred years, "they are the ones who did it."[43] Retorted Incarnate Word attorney Pat Maloney after McAllister left, "He walked in with a closed mind and ran out with a closed mind." The mayor, he charged, had been "prejudiced for seventy years, and it's too late for him to change." The concrete cloverleaf, mused attorney Trueman O'Quinn, was replacing the American Beauty Rose as the national flower. Conservation Society past president Wanda Ford was less philosophical. Should the expressway be built, she promised, she and others opposed to it would "throw themselves in front of the bulldozers."[44]

Despite what might confront the bulldozers, the Highway Department recommended the proposed route. It was approved by the Federal Highway Administration in April of 1964, and acquisition of right-of-way began.[45] But litigation continued.

Notes

1. Richard O. Baumbach, Jr. and William E. Borah, *The Second Battle of New Orleans: A History of the Vieux Carré Riverfront-Expressway Controversy*, (University of Alabama Press for the Preservation Press, University, Ala., 1981), xvi.

2. Pinkie (Mrs. Brooks) Martin to Conservation Society members, Dec. 4, 1970, copy in SACS Library.

3. Baumbach and Borah, *The Second Battle of New Orleans*, xv.

4. Kemper Diehl, "McAllister Expressway," *San Antonio Express-News*, Jan. 29, 1978, 1-7-H.

5. San Antonio already had a Roosevelt Park, named for Theodore. The part of the Olmos Basin flood plain used by the public was devoted to golf courses, picnic areas and playing fields, although the flood plain was not officially considered a dedicated park. An expressway would not be its first northbound violation. In 1952, Anita Harker, the Conservation Society's parks committee chairman, asked city officials that McCullough Avenue not be extended through Olmos Basin north from Olmos Park. Cutting the new route, however, became a city council campaign promise of developer H.J. Shearer, who was elected. The road went through. (Minutes, D-Sept. 10, 1952, 2; D-Dec. 3, 1953, 2–3.)

6. Ed Ray, "North and West Expressways," *San Antonio News*, Jun. 2, 1959, 8-A.

7. Minutes, G-May 28, 1959.

8. Ray, "North and West Expressways."

9. Ibid.

10. Diehl, "McAllister Expressway."

11. Minutes, D-Aug. 27, 1959 (2), 1–2.

12. Gruen Associates, *San Antonio North Expressway Study*, U.S. Dept. of Transportation, Federal Highway Administration (Washington, D.C., 1971), 12–13.

13. Ibid.

14. Ibid., 16, 76–77. Territory of the City of Alamo Heights above the dam on the east did not provide what planners considered a viable alternate route. The Alamo Heights city government refused to take any stand on the expressway.

15. Minutes, D-Jun. 8, 1960, 1–2.

16. "Big Tree Loss Seen," *San Antonio Express*, Jun. 23, 1960.

17. Diehl, "McAllister Expressway."

18. Flier in SACS Library. The format is identical to that of fliers issued by the Conservation Society during the Travis Park struggle.

19. "America—the Beautiful?," *Life* Magazine, Jul. 11, 1960.

20. Diehl, "McAllister Expressway."

21. Diehl, "McAllister Expressway;" "The Chamber," *San Antonio Express-News,* Nov. 13, 1994.

22. Minutes, D-Nov. 21, 1960, 1–2.

23. "Mayor, Ladies Debate Freeway," *San Antonio Light,* Dec. 8, 1960, 1. The *Light* as a matter of policy continued to refer to the road as a "freeway" rather than as an "expressway" so as not to draw inadvertent attention to the name of its primary competitor, the *Express.*

24. "Conservation Group Seeks Tax Pact," *San Antonio Express,* Feb. 11, 1958, 10-A.

25. Ibid.; Minutes, D-Jan. 11, 1956, 2.

26. Minutes, D-Sept. 19, 1960.

27. Ibid., 1–4.

28. Ibid.

29. Diehl, "McAllister Expressway."

30. James McCrory, "All Four Bond Proposals Win," *San Antonio Express,* Jan. 11, 1961, 1.

31. Ibid.

32. Minutes, D-Jun. 5, 1961.

33. Minutes, D-Oct. 23, 1961, 3–4.

34. Ibid.

35. Minutes, E-Jul. 18, 1961.

36. Ibid., 1–7.

37. Minutes, G-Sept. 28, 1961; D-Jan. 22, 1962.

38. Minutes, D-Sept. 24, 1962; D-Jan. 21, 1963.

39. Minutes, D-Sept. 23, 1963, 3.

40. Peggy (Mrs. Don F.) Tobin OHT, Nov. 19, 1990, 10.

41. Ibid.

42. Ibid., 9.

43. James McCrory, "Mayor Assails Foes of Expressway Plan," *San Antonio Express,* Oct. 17, 1963, 1.

44. Ibid.

45. Gruen Associates, *San Antonio North Expressway Study,* 5.

12

A World's Fair Caught in the Cross Fire

As expressway strife simmered, the epidemic urban renewal virus was laying low entire regions of downtowns nationwide. As the malady spread from the western and southern edges of downtown San Antonio, though, it was mutating across town to produce a project which would ultimately transform the development of not just one area, but in a larger sense of the City of San Antonio itself—HemisFair, the first major world's fair to be held in the southern United States.

The idea of a fair expressing relationships between North and South America, first suggested in 1958, was revived four years later by newly elected Congressman Henry B. Gonzalez.[1] To be themed "The Confluence of Civilizations in the Americas," the fair was to be held in 1968, the 250th anniversary of the founding of San Antonio. William R. Sinkin was named president of San Antonio Fair Inc. and Marshall T. Steves the chairman of the underwriting committee, which initially sought $4 million.[2]

Site selection came down to three locations. One was offered by developer Ray Ellison near his Valley-Hi subdivision on U.S. 90 West. Another was the near-downtown area north of Municipal Auditorium. In mid-1963 the Site Selection Committee, chaired by Chairman and Chamber of Commerce President James M. Gaines, instead picked a third site—one hundred and fifty acres just southeast of the immediate downtown area.[3] That site had the potential of tapping into federal urban renewal funds for clearance and new construction, Gaines explained at a mid-1963 press conference at the Menger Hotel. The project could yield, in particular, a badly needed modern convention center. Access to the fair would be aided by completion of the Southeast Expressway, part of Interstate 37; added Gaines, "It would certainly help if a North Expressway has been completed by the time of HemisFair."

Another factor was the site's location near the River Walk. The Chamber of Commerce hoped to see the river developed commercially beyond the two lone businesses on the river level—the Casa Rio Mexican restaurant and, upstream on the other side of the Commerce Street bridge, Lung Jeu, a Chinese restaurant.[4] In 1961, the city and the Chamber of Commerce jointly put up $15,000 to hire California's Marco Engineering Co., designers of Disneyland and of Six Flags Over Texas, to study the River Walk as a potential commercial attraction.[5] The Marco consultants found the River Walk "run down and in need of repainting, improved lighting, better housekeeping, police protection and additional park benches." They prepared a sixty-page report which recommended a River Bend Park incorporating La Villita and creating a "River of Fiestas," with city-owned store buildings built in a colonial Mexican style and leased to private retailers. But shops and restaurants alone would not be sufficient to attract "maximum patronage," they believed, and should be augmented with "considerable show and entertainment." This would attract 700,000 visitors a year—and even more with extension of the park upstream to Brackenridge Park, which was recommended to be finished in three years.[6] In the wake of the plan's rejection as being too commercial, in 1962 under the leadership of David Straus the city established a seven-member River Walk Commission to regulate design plans of future businesses. A local American Institute of Architects committee, chaired by Cyrus Wagner, prepared a development plan. Many of its elements were included in the HemisFair bond issue.[7]

Another long-term goal of both the city and the Conservation Society was realized with expansion of the HemisFair urban renewal area west across South Alamo Street to the La Villita area, to enable La Villita to expand and fill the remainder of the block south to Nueva Street after the fair.[8] The new overall 147-acre urban renewal area—ninety-two acres were for the fair itself—would cause two dozen streets to be altered or disappear completely and force some 1,600 people to move away. Also affected would be manufacturing plants, shops, stores, warehouses, two schools, two parks, the Rodfei Sholom synagogue and four churches. Those included, at 422 South Street, the 1922 Gothic-style St. Michael's Catholic Church, its congregation established in 1866 by Polish immigrants, whose descendants held Mass in Polish until the mid-1950s. The church complex included a rectory, school and convent and was the heart of San Antonio's Polish community, which clustered in the eastern sector of the fair site. German immigrants settled the fair's western area, adjacent to their kinsmen in La Villita and in the King William Street area beyond. Residents of the area had been joined by Mexican immigrants fleeing the revolution of 1910.[9]

Even before the HemisFair site was picked, the San Antonio Conservation Society stressed the importance of having the fair's buildings reflect San Antonio's traditions.[10] As it turned out, the site encompassed dozens of historic buildings, some of them predating the fall of the Alamo. Bexar County

San Antonio's skyline, nearly the same since the Depression, would change dramatically in the wake of HemisFair, the 1968 world's fair on the site of the parially shown neighborhood in the foreground. The Tower of the Americas was built on the site of the Polish community's St. Michael's Catholic Church, toward the lower left in this 1957 view to the northwest. Zintgraff Collection, The Institute of Texan Cultures.

Historical Survey Committee Chairman Marvin Eickenroht, an architect, was puzzled. "It is difficult to comprehend," he wrote Mayor Walter McAllister, "why this area, one of the most compactly historic areas in San Antonio, was chosen."[11] Preservationists were quick to declare that incorporating historic structures into the fairgrounds would give HemisFair a uniqueness heretofore unmatched among world's fairs. At the beginning of 1964, HemisFair Executive Director Ewen C. Dingwall, who two years earlier managed Century 21, the Seattle World's Fair, told Conservation Society members how the historic German-English School would at last be restored to serve as fair headquarters. Conservation Society President Lillian Maverick (Mrs. James T.) Padgitt, Mayor McAllister and Robert Sawtelle jointly officiated in March of 1964 at the start of the restoration, finished three months later.[12]

O'Neil Ford declared that as many as possible of the old buildings and trees on the fair site should be saved, inspiring Mary Green to introduce a society resolution urging Ford's appointment as the fair's coordinating architect.[13]

The historic German-English School on South Alamo Street across from the fairgrounds was restored as HemisFair headquarters, which flew the flags of Western Hemisphere nations. Zintgraff Collection, The Institute of Texan Cultures.

But wounds from the ongoing North Expressway conflict would again handicap other efforts. Mayor McAllister, angered by Ford's opposition to the expressway project, vowed that Ford would get no work from the city and strongly opposed his selection. Ford was, nevertheless, narrowly approved for the job by both city council and the HemisFair executive committee. National media praised the selection of the city's best-known architect.[14] Predictably, Ford became a leading advocate of enlightened regionalism in the fair's design. He and associate Boone Powell successfully argued to change the Convention Center's exterior from aluminum paneling to brick.[15] Ford came up with the idea of extending the San Antonio River channel from the River Bend into the fairgrounds, where it would form a lagoon bordered by the new convention center and the Theater for the Performing Arts.[16]

However, Ford's biographer reported that Marshall Steves "acknowledged that those who supported Ford's selection were unrealistic in their expectation that his boundless supply of energy and enthusiasm could be channeled into realization of the fair's potential." In a management shakeup which included replacement of Ewen Dingwall by Steves as the fair's executive director in May of 1965, O'Neil Ford was demoted to the position of consulting architect.[17]

In another affront, San Antonio River Authority plans to construct an improved river channel past King William Street targeted for removal several historic homes at the end of the street, including Ford's office.[18] Yet Ford's firm under project architect Boone Powell remained designer of the signature HemisFair Tower, some sixty stories high. It was to be the tallest tower in the Western Hemisphere and, like the Space Needle of the 1962 Seattle Fair, would feature a revolving restaurant at the top.[19]

Most of those residing in the HemisFair area had moved out, with the aid of a relocation center run by the Urban Renewal Agency, by April of 1966, when the last recalcitrant couple were removed by the Bexar County sheriff and his deputies, forced to smash through the front door. After that, the lone resident was Florence Eagar Roberts, permitted to stay in her family's historic home for another year, past her one hundredth birthday.[20]

As buildings were boarded up awaiting decisions on their fate, the Conservation Society became increasingly anxious.[21] Architect Henry Steinbomer had already gathered one list of significant buildings in the area.[22] When work began on the HemisFair master plan, the Urban Renewal Agency hired Marvin Eickenroht, who was also chairman of the American Institute of Architects regional Committee on Preservation of Historic Buildings, to prepare another.[23] Eickenroht believed that saving a group of old buildings "would provide HemisFair with a feature attraction that world's fairs of this kind have never before provided."[24] An initial list of 117 significant buildings was pared to 75 in the first published plan.[25]

Action on the North Expressway front, meanwhile, had not been going especially well for the Conservation Society when, in August of 1965, Mayor Walter McAllister made a clandestine visit to the Sisters of Charity of the Incarnate Word's mother superior. They struck a settlement deal, including the promise that the city would close the street separating the rear of the order's Santa Rosa Hospital's main building from others in the complex.[26] To Conservation Society directors, the Rev. Mother Mary Clare's decision was a blow. Hoping the agreement was not final, directors passed a resolution of appreciation to try to shore her up.[27] But a deal went through. For their property on the route the sisters were paid $972,000—$600,000 from the City of San Antonio and the rest from the state—and the state promised to build a $50,000 bridge over the expressway to reconnect the property for pedestrians.[28] Conservation Society President Peggy Tobin scheduled a meeting with Mayor McAllister to discuss options, but the meeting was canceled. Members were urged to write more letters to State Highway Commissioner DeWitt Greer and to Secretary of the Interior Stewart Udall.[29]

There was bad news on the tax front, also. A State Supreme Court decision on a property tax matter in Houston implied that the Conservation Society's position was on shaky ground. To settle some $17,000 in alleged back taxes,

Typical of the historic homes on the HemisFair site were these on Water Street, soon to disappear from the map. San Antonio Conservation Society.

Mrs. Tobin suggested that the city accept the society's donation of Acequia Park.[30] The city declined the offer.

By now there was a Texan in the White House, a Texan with ties to many San Antonians. Conservation Society directors in September of 1965 had noted "the laudable efforts of President and Mrs. Lyndon B. Johnson to focus national concern on the need for parklands and natural beauty, particularly within our increasingly crowded cities." The Conservation Society's third vice president Nancy (Mrs. Alfred) Negley wrote her friend Lady Bird Johnson, who called in Rex Whitton, Chief of the U.S. Bureau of Public Roads, to discuss the expressway matter.[31] Peggy Tobin contacted President Johnson himself.[32] "In the end nothing could be done," directors were told, since the public vote was so decisive, although "Mr. Whitton promised to make it as beautiful as possible."[33] Nevertheless, during a visit to San Antonio in 1966, Mrs. Johnson was presented with a special Conservation Society award "for her contribution to historic conservation and beautification of our land."[34] The interest of the Johnsons was implicitly expressed when the Conservation Society's case was taken over by attorney Barr McClellan, an associate in the prestigious Austin law firm of Clark, Thomas, Harris, Denius and Winters. Headed by Ambassador Edward Clark, the firm was known for its close association with Lyndon Johnson's numerous enterprises.[35]

Back at HemisFair, O'Neil Ford was keeping up the pressure from the sidelines. He praised the "indigenous character and integrity" of the old structures. "All the photographs and books collected or written cannot

Lady Bird Johnson, left, was presented a special San Antonio Conservation Society award in 1966 for her lifelong interest in beautifying the landscape. She is shown being congratulated by former Society President Agnes Virginia Temple, who holds the ceramic award plaque fired by ceramist Mary Green and set in a frame of mesquite heart carved by Lynn Ford. In the center is future Society President Pinkie Martin. San Antonio Conservation Society.

document our westward-moving background in the way the buildings can," he instructed Marshall Steves. "If most of our subdivisions were to burn in one night there would be not one iota of architectural loss, but the careless destruction of a fine old stone house would be the loss of a significant page of our history."[36]

The need to widen South Alamo Street along the fair's western perimeter raised another set of problems, as it would also be made straight and thus take Beethoven Hall and the Eagar House, among other historic buildings. Widening the street on the west side rather than the east side to pass around them would cause a curving street, but what was wrong with that? "A soft curve is far more beautiful than a straight-line street," Ford fumed.[37] The proposed plan was "just drafting-board engineering." It "disregards topographic features, best kinds of land use, character of the area and sensibilities of people," and was an example of "the kind of fuzzy and inconsistent procedure in government offices and agencies." Ford's point was ultimately adopted, and the widened South Alamo Street was allowed to curve. To preserve the German-English School across the street, the once-columned facade of Beethoven Hall was sheared off for the wider street and replaced with a decorative brick wall without doors.[38]

By the end of 1965, the Conservation Society's Old Buildings and Histori-cal Research Chairman Mary (Mrs. Franklyn) Wright won unanimous passage of a resolution calling for twenty-two specific buildings to be preserved and incorporated into the fair site.[39] Her committee met with members of city council, who then inspected the area by bus.[40]

Under Allison Peery, the HemisFair design office executed a concept of a network of triangles centered on the Tower of the Americas. Southeast from the base of the tower would radiate rides and amusements. To the northeast was to be a waterway area, to the northwest was to fan the convention center complex. To the west was planned a grouping of smaller foreign exhibits, shops and restaurants, where historic structures had the best chance of survival. Of the twenty-two historic structures preserved on the HemisFair site, the majority was in this so-called Historic Triangle, bounded by South Alamo and the soon-to-disappear Goliad and Water streets. In this area in the fall of 1966, Humble Oil and Refining Co.—later Exxon—became the first HemisFair exhibitor to announce plans to restore one of the old structures as its pavilion. Humble chose the old Schultze Store, a two-story limestone block structure built in 1891.[41]

As for North Expressway developments, after the Incarnate Word road-block was removed nothing happened. "Then, while we were sitting around," City Attorney Crawford Reeder recalled to *Express-News* political writer Kemper Diehl, "Senator Ralph Yarborough got his amendment."[42] The move caught expressway backers as unawares as opponents had been caught by Mayor McAllister's negotiations with the Incarnate Word sisters.

The Texas Democratic senator's amendment was to the 1966 Congres-sional act which created the U.S. Department of Transportation. As of April 1, 1967, it prevented the new Secretary of Transportation from approving any project using land from a public park unless it was shown that there was no reasonable alternative, and then only if harm to the park was minimized. The purpose was, Yarborough said, to stop those who "would unleash the bulldozer on our public parks, historic sites, wildlife refuges and recreation areas."[43] It seemed the ink was hardly dry on the transportation amendment when Yarborough got another amendment.

Yarborough, a member of the Senate Appropriations Committee and an admirer of O'Neil Ford, successfully appended to the bill designating funds for the United States Pavilion at HemisFair a requirement that "historic structures in the area encompassed by the Fair will be preserved to the maximum extent possible" before United States participation in HemisFair would occur. The Department of Commerce was charged with assuring compliance.[44] To city hall, it was now quite obvious that the San Antonio Conservation Society could pull a lot of strings behind the scenes. Thus, the mountain went to Mohammed.

Workmen place the Humble Pavilion sign on the restored 1891 Schultze Store near the western entrance to HemisFair. At left is the new Hilton Hotel, which rises above Conservation Corner. Zintgraff Collection, The Institute of Texan Cultures.

City Councilwoman Lila Cockrell appealed to Conservation Society directors for help on the 13th of September. She had just left a meeting of city council called to address "a time of crisis for HemisFair." In two days, she explained to the twenty-nine directors present, representatives of twenty-three foreign governments and the Bureau of International Expositions were arriving in San Antonio to discuss participation in the fair, now to open in less than eighteen months. Yet even the United States had not yet officially agreed to participate, and the latest Yarborough amendment muddied the water even more. If the United States did not participate, the council feared, other countries would not either.

City council earlier that morning felt obliged to throw an olive branch to the Conservation Society. The council passed three resolutions, Mrs. Cockrell reported. One repealed its decision of twelve days before not to request the Urban Renewal Agency to relocate the Schultze House. It now made that

As construction of the arena proceeds on HemisFair grounds, two houses await restoration. A third was later moved into the foreground to become, with the 1840s Sam Smith home at the left, the pavilion of India. The framework of the Convention Center Area, razed in 1995-96, rises in the background. The San Antonio Light *Collection, The Institute of Texan Cultures.*

request. Another designated the northwest corner of Alamo and Nueva Streets—in the new area added to La Villita—as the site for the relocated Groos House. And the third resolution went about "expressing and reaffirming" city council's intent to relocate significant buildings whenever possible, and asked Senator Yarborough to withdraw his amendment "in order to expedite Senate action." In return, Conservation Society directors then adopted a reassuring resolution certifying that HemisFair policy "has always stated that historic preservation was a major objective," specifying several of the promises made and expressing "gratitude on behalf of all the people of Texas to the City of San Antonio for its earnest efforts [and] good faith . . . in retaining the character and aesthetic integrity of historic San Antonio in the midst of necessary change." After repledging their support of HemisFair, directors gave Mrs. Cockrell a standing ovation "for her invaluable help in the past."[45]

But if HemisFair management thought that the San Antonio Conservation Society was a nuisance before, soon the society became impossible to ignore. The Department of Commerce chose "to properly assess the assurance" of HemisFair management to preserve all historic structures possible by asking for two independent quarterly reports. One was to be submitted by HemisFair management. The other was to come from the San Antonio Conservation Society.[46] Society directors were aware that there might be a price for their new double expressway-HemisFair victory. The undecided fate of the 114 South Street classical revival home of tinsmith Herman Schultze caused fear that it would become "a target for the mayor's nerves and frustrations."[47]

Nor had location within the Historic Triangle been any guarantee of survival. The picturesque de Bastrop House (1841), by then a bar known as Kinky and Nando's, had disappeared without warning, prompting immediate cries of outrage. A public statement by President Peggy Tobin and Old Buildings Chairman Mary Wright placed the blame on three "mistakes:" the HemisFair area should never have been declared a total demolition zone in the first place, residents should have been allowed to stay longer in their homes to prevent vandalism and "the area should have been researched by a qualified historian before it was turned over to Urban Renewal." Should any additional remaining structures be so blindly destroyed, the two warned, "it will not be just another mistake, it will be a disaster . . . . The tourist industry, recognized by all as San Antonio's largest, is built today on the existence of historic structures and sites," they observed, concluding, "A master plan for the preservation of historic sites in San Antonio, not just those in the HemisFair area, is decades past due."[48]

At the request of the Conservation Society's Historic Index Committee, the Urban Renewal Agency agreed to delay demolition of the Schultze house so that it could be fully documented and so that the Conservation Society could remove its fanciful tinwork, which the city gave to the society.[49] The Conservation Society paid for moving the Heinrich House on Santa Clara Street, the site of the Institute of Texan Cultures, to a temporary location to the north, where it would be used to house maintenance supplies during the fair.[50] Urban Renewal funds paid for dismantling the house of *palisado* construction at 141 South Street and moving it from the site of the Convention Center to await reconstruction in the enlarged area of La Villita.[51] There

Considered the finest home in the HemisFair area was the limestone Greek Revival Frederick Groos House, last used as a hall for St. Joseph's Catholic Church across Commerce Street and which stood in the path of the San Antonio River extension. The Institute of Texan Cultures, courtesy San Antonio Development Agency.

Stones from the Frederick Groos House were to be reassembled in a new corner of La Villita. When many were later found to be missing or broken, the rest were finally hauled away. San Antonio Conservation Society.

the two-story limestone Greek Revival Frederick Groos House was already languishing as a pile of numbered blocks, while officials became increasingly frustrated as reconstruction estimates soared to $250,000. It had been appraised for purchase at only $60,000, and the moving had cost $16,000.[52] The Groos House was considered the finest in the fair area, but it lay in the path of the river extension on East Commerce Street and had to be moved.[53]

Some six months after the second Yarborough amendment, relations between the Conservation Society and HemisFair management suddenly became quite formal. Peggy Tobin expected to be going to a casual conversation with two officials on the subject of saving buildings on the fair site. When she arrived she found herself in the midst of nine, including the Mayor Pro-Tem and city manager, and two members of the HemisFair legal staff.[54] "I remember, vividly, feeling totally alone there as all those dark-suited gentlemen came filing in one by one," Mrs. Tobin recalled nearly thirty years later.[55] She felt she was being mousetrapped into agreeing to demolition of two houses that were in the way of the skyride but which fair management earlier had promised to save.

"I wish to make one major point absolutely clear," she informed HemisFair Executive Vice President Frank Manupelli by registered letter the next day. "It is the responsibility of [the] San Antonio Conservation Society to protect and defend the historic heritage of San Antonio and Texas. It is therefore entirely inconsistent with our basic principles ever to participate in decisions to demolish historic structures or to *agree* to their demolition. As President I follow these principles."[56]

Manupelli responded immediately with a conciliatory letter which thanked the Conservation Society for offering to restore the Sarah Eagar House, which he suggested be used during the fair by the Travelers Aid Society.[57] A few days later Manupelli replied to a telegram from Mrs. Tobin by suggesting that the Conservation Society was overstepping its responsibility in telling the Department of Commerce which structures were to be saved, rather than reporting on recommendations as to what measures the HemisFair staff should take if the staff decided they could in fact be saved. "I sincerely believe that . . . the Conservation Society . . . can forward a report showing substantial progress," Manupelli hinted hopefully.[58] The society's first quarterly report, however, ended up being interpreted by HemisFair staff as "more a polemic than an informative report."[59] Following a subsequent and not entirely diplomatic exchange of letters, the Conservation Society was informed that all responses to society correspondence in the future would come through the HemisFair staff attorney, John A. Watson.[60]

At about the same time, Austin's Barr McClellan, the Conservation Society's new lead counsel on the North Expressway matter, appeared before city council with an alternate center segment proposal from the Conservation

Society. Drafted by architect Boone Powell, the proposal would replace the six-lane expressway with a four-lane parkway which would depart the planned route to go on the west or Trinity University side of Alamo Stadium, as the Texas Highway Department's first recommended route would have. But the Conservation Society was recommending a change in the original route so it would go up Devine Road through a more easterly section of the City of Olmos Park. Less parkland would be jeopardized than along the council's recommended route, and the Incarnate Word property would be avoided altogether. However, citing voter approval and advanced land acquisition on the other route, city council rejected the alternate proposal by a vote of 7-0, with one abstention.[61]

After that decision, Conservation Society President Lorraine "Jake" (Mrs. J.A.) Reaney aired her frustrations on the Allen Dale radio talk show. Society attorney Ralph Langley expressed concern that such comments could cause the city to no longer allow the Conservation Society to use La Villita for A Night in Old San Antonio, block current historic zoning efforts and see that penalties were assessed on top of the alleged back property taxes. Langley asked for a special meeting with the executive committee.[62] But just when, Mrs. Reaney asked Langley at the meeting, was the City of San Antonio ever going to really listen to the society? Would the city send a representative to explain why their plan was more essential than the alternate route? Would the city or the Good Government League rather sit down with the president "and give reasons, other than threats, why we should drop litigation?" Would the city council really answer questions in its citizens-to-be-heard period? The society would certainly be willing to delay its injunction if the city would describe in writing "what we could expect in return." The executive committee gave Mrs. Reaney a standing ovation.[63]

That fall, fearing that North Expressway construction contracts could be let in eight months, society directors evaluated their options. President Reaney reported on her latest lobbying efforts with federal officials, and was again given a standing ovation. Of greatest concern was the danger of an enraged city council preventing the Conservation Society from holding A Night in Old San Antonio in La Villita. NIOSA attendance and profits were increasing dramatically, giving the Conservation Society a measure of financial independence enjoyed by few other such groups in the nation. Total attendance in 1960 passed 50,000, and nearly doubled seven years later. Gross revenues of $100,000 in 1962 more than doubled in five years, causing annual net profits to nearly triple in the same period to more than $110,000. In addition, increasing numbers of individual "NIOSITAs" in La Villita for conventions and gatherings yielded annual profits well into five figures.

In spite of the risk, A Night in Old San Antonio Chairman Betty (Mrs. Neville) Murray declared that if official retaliation caused problems for NIOSA "she would do her best to surmount them." Directors agreed to take "whatever steps that are deemed necessary" to continue the fight. Should those include a lawsuit, it was promised that costs would be paid by four residents of the City of Olmos Park who didn't want the expressway anywhere near their suburb.[64]

In November, the Conservation Society petitioned district court for reconsideration of the expressway's original 1964 federal approval.[65] It was publicly noted that in suing the city on the North Expressway the Conservation Society was spending money on legal fees that could have been used instead to pay the back property taxes.[66] The city gave the society sixty days to formally state its tax case. The society's tax attorney, Harvey L. Hardy, finally recommended that taxes of $1,700 be paid on the Conservation Corner and Ike West properties. The society, however, still did not pay the taxes. The City of San Antonio used the opportunity to make good on its threat and filed suit, declaring, additionally, that the city would not accept the gift of Acequia Park from the Conservation Society until all back taxes on it were paid.[67] This halted action on the city's request for a 60-foot right-of-way through Acequia Park, stalling the recent progress between the Conservation Society, the city and the chamber of commerce on the long-sought Mission Road.[68] There was also a hiatus in efforts to combine the missions into a national park.

Helping sustain Conservation Society members' resoluteness on the North Expressway was awareness of ongoing expressway struggles elsewhere in the nation. The federal interstate highway program had already aroused preservationists in individual cities who were fighting, among others, expressways planned for the neighborhoods of the San Francisco waterfront, the Capitol Mall in Washington, D.C. and Independence Hall in Philadelphia, where San Antonio conservationists backed Philadelphia's Society Hill Civic Association in opposing that expressway project.[69] The Philadelphia group, in return, sent a resolution supporting the San Antonio Conservation Society's North Expressway struggle to Senator Yarborough.[70] An expressway struggle that struck at the heart of the preservation movement was being bitterly waged in New Orleans, where an elevated expressway planned along the Mississippi River past Jackson Square would impact more than a fourth of the entire French Quarter.[71] New Orleans preservationists sought and received endorsements from the San Antonio Conservation Society and from similar groups throughout the nation.[72]

As HemisFair approached, there was a lull in the strife between the Conservation Society and city government, with one exception. Three months before the fair opened, the Conservation Society unanimously passed a resolution, introduced by Wanda Ford, opposing the $1.6 million, six-story garage H.B. Zachry was building over Villita Street west of La Villita. The 600-car facility was, ironically, near the site of one of the four ill-fated

underground garages planned downtown a decade before. The first of the society's half-dozen complaints was that the garage would be "entirely out of scale, inappropriate and unsympathetic with the area, and impede the view of La Villita from the west."[73] Seven weeks later, directors decided there were no legal grounds for an injunction. The garage, termed "brutally ill-conceived" by a *New York Times* writer, went up and harmony prevailed, for the time being.[74]

With the April 6 opening of HemisFair '68 fast approaching, implications of uniqueness for the fair and the future use of the site—including preservation issues—were hardly the greatest challenges facing those seeking to wrest San Antonio from nearly four decades of depression and lethargic growth. The city already had a $12.2 million urban renewal grant for land acquisition and clearance. But in Austin, Governor John Connally was barely able to influence successful funding for the Texas pavilion, to be built as the permanent Institute of Texan Cultures. Opponents said it was unnecessary, since the state had museums in Austin and Dallas, and leveled charges of "HemisFraud." Mayor McAllister outflanked opponents of federal funding of the Tower of the Americas by backing successful passage of a $5.5 million municipal bond issue to fund the project instead. HemisFair Chairman H.B. Zachry had to outmaneuver Senator Ralph Yarborough to get federal funding approved in the fall of 1966.[75]

Zachry pulled off another miracle when the twenty-one story 481-room hotel, critical to success of the fair, seemed hopelessly behind schedule. Nine months before the fair was to open, Zachry's company launched a construction blitz on the Hilton Palacio del Rio, on South Alamo Street across a main fair entrance and backing on the river, only twenty feet from Conservation Corner and its tenant, the Little Rhein Steakhouse. It was so close that when Zachry stopped in once for lunch while pile drivers were preparing the foundations, the intense vibrations caused Zachry's plate to flip from the table into his lap.[76] Modular rooms assembled off-site while the base of the building itself was finished were trucked in and lifted with the aid of a crane and helicopter arrangement into place, completely furnished down to soap and towels, in a total of 202 days. It was the first significant building added to the San Antonio skyline since the 1955 National Bank of Commerce Building, itself the first since the Depression.

Left above: Built in 1852 behind St. Mary's Catholic Church as St. Mary's College, this building later housed the St. Mary's University School of Law until it was sold in 1966. San Antonio Conservation Society.

Left below: The former St. Mary's University School of Law building on College Street was renovated by several St. Mary's graduates led by Patrick Kennedy to become the hotel La Mansion del Rio in time for HemisFair. San Antonio Conservation Society.

An enduring legacy of HemisFair is the city's major convention center, shown shortly after its construction for the fair. Expansion of the original convention center in 1995-96 took the circular HemisFair Arena, a major drawing card for the city's first major-league professional sports team, the National Basketball Association's Spurs. To the Arena's left on the fairground is the Theater for the Performing Arts, in the right foreground the new Hilton Palacio del Rio Hotel. San Antonio Express-News.

Success of the fair itself was mixed. On opening day—Saturday, April 6, 1968—the Tower of the Americas was not finished, and did not open for another month. Five days earlier, in the face of escalating Vietnam War protests President Lyndon Johnson announced he would not seek reelection, and the assassination two nights before of Martin Luther King, Jr. caused violence nationwide. With national attention diverted from San Antonio, attendance suffered. When HemisFair closed on October 6, total attendance of 6.4 million was 800,000 below projections, and the fair lost $6 million.

In spite of the various complications and shortcomings, the downtown world's fair gained San Antonio an enormous worldwide public relations boost and greatly increased its self-confidence. The National Association of Travel Organizations reported that HemisFair was "the most important travel stimulant" in the nation in 1968.[77] There had been thirty-eight government and eighteen industrial and private exhibitions, a skyride, monorail, lake show and amusement park, plus entertainment ranging from Jack Benny to Bob Hope to Louis Armstrong, Herb Alpert, the Grand Ole Opry and the Mormon Tabernacle Choir. And the new convention center, the 10,500-seat

Among historic homes restored for HemisFair was the Solomon Halff House, which became the fair's French Restaurant La Maison Blanche and later the first home of offices for the University of Texas at San Antonio. Zintgraff Collection, The Institute of Texan Cultures.

arena, 2,800-seat theater and the Hilton Hotel were already functioning as the foundation for a vastly increased convention and tourism industry.[78]

As preservationists predicted, the restored buildings on the site charmed visitors. In addition to the Schultze House/Humble Pavilion, the Tynan House (1868) was a restaurant known as Pierre's Interlude, the Acosta House (1890) the Casa San Miguel Philippine restaurant, the Dugosh House (1855) a restaurant called Tipico Tamales, the two-story limestone Meyer-Halff House (1893) the House of Sir John Falstaff, run by the brewery. Among others, the Eagar House (1868) was a pavilion of the Southern Baptist Church. The Czech film and live comedy show *Laterna Magika,* a hit at world's fairs in Brussels in 1958 and Montreal in 1967, was in Beethoven Hall. An uncovered stretch of the Acequia Madre, built in the 1720s to supply water to the Alamo mission, was preserved.[79]

In appraising the fair in *Architectural Forum,* Roger Montgomery, professor of architecture and city planning at the University of California in Berkeley, wrote: "HemisFair's best design lies just inside the main gate . . . . Here the designers took three crucial actions and made them pay off handsomely. They saved all the mature trees existing on the site; they preserved a number of picturesque old buildings and used them for restaurants, shops and a theater; and, to cap it off, they restricted new construction for the foreign exhibit structures . . . ."[80]

"Without their special local flavor," thought *The New York Times*'s Ada Louise Huxtable of the restored buildings, "this would be just another, smaller carbon copy of the flashy commercial formula that has become overly familiar to 20th Century fair hoppers."[81] Later she wrote, "There is no doubt that if more of these characteristic and historic buildings had been saved HemisFair would have been proportionately better, since they would have provided proportionately more genuine local style—which should and could have been the Fair's distinguishing characteristic."[82] Added *Saturday Review* of fair designers' preservation of the old structures: "They are to be commended for this wisdom more than anything else."[83]

Notes

1. The idea of a hemisphere fair is credited to Frank Brothers' Jerome K. Harris, who brought it up at a San Antonio Chamber of Commerce meeting in 1958. Local writer Keith Elliott claimed credit for having coined the term "HemisFair" while writing a headline for *The San Antonian*. (Keith Elliott, "The First Downtown World's Fair," *Saturday Review*, Mar. 9, 1968, 46.)

2. "Downtown HemisFair Site Picked," *San Antonio Express*, Jul. 4, 1963, 10-D.

3. Ibid.

4. Ibid.

5. "River Bend Park Plan Studied," *San Antonio Express*, Jun. 1, 1961, 1.

6. Ibid; Minutes, D-Jun. 5, 1961; D-Apr. 9, 1962. O'Neil Ford, on the outs with the business community due to his opposition to the North Expressway, was not consulted on the river project. He had to write the Chamber of Commerce and ask that a new brochure "printed in such a manner as to infer that I participated in a real way . . . be withdrawn from circulation." (O'Neil Ford to Chamber of Commerce, May 30, 1961, copy in SACS Library.)

7. Sinclair Black, "San Antonio's Linear Paradise," *AIA Journal* July 1979, 30.

8. "Calls for La Villita Expansion," *San Antonio Light*, Apr. 16, 1964.

9. Adolfo Pesquera, "Memories all that remain of many homes, businesses," *San Antonio Express-News*, Mar. 28, 1993, 13-A.

10. Minutes, D-Jan. 21, 1963.

11. Marvin Eickenroht to Walter McAllister, Dec. 21, 1964, letter copy in SACS Library.

12. "Renovation Started on Fair Headquarters," *San Antonio News*, Mar. 25, 1964; "Rites Dedicate Fair Headquarters," *San Antonio News*, Jun. 29, 1964.

13. Minutes, G-Jan. 23, 1964.

14. George, *O'Neil Ford,* 178. Allison Peery was named to direct planning of the site. Ford was not picked as architect for the expanded area of La Villita, which he designed in 1939. He commented: "The city did avoid hiring me to do the new section of La Villita . . . by getting good architects (Eickenroht, Bobby Harris, Jerry Rogers) and that is a satisfactory evasion." (O'Neil Ford to Marshall T. Steves, Jan. 4, 1966, 6, copy in SACS Library.)

15. George, *O'Neil Ford,* 181. The Ford firm's design of Steves's home, completed at 501 Grandview Place in Terrell Hills in 1964, was considered an "inspired contribution" to HemisFair. The 14,000 square-foot, brick-domed Mediterranean style home was seen as favorably interpreting San Antonio to the world as the setting for innumerable parties for official HemisFair visitors. (Ibid., 178, 179.)

16. O'Neil Ford to Marshall T. Steves, Jan. 4, 1966, 7, copy in SACS Library. Ford is also credited with originating the plan in "Calls for La Villita Expansion," *San Antonio Light,* Apr. 16, 1964.

17. George, *O'Neil Ford,* 181.

18. James McCrory, "River Channel OK Sought," *San Antonio Express,* Feb. 10, 1965. After vigorous opposition from preservationists, the plan was modified to avoid re-routing the end of the street and to save the landmarks. The River Authority was unable to negotiate with the Conservation Society over a slice of the Steves Homestead property needed for the river since, during the property tax dispute with the city, title to the property was not clear. (Minutes, D-Feb. 20, 1967, 2.)

19. Ibid.; Adolfo Pesquera, "S.A.'s HemisFair Party," *San Antonio Express-News,* Mar. 28, 1993, 11-A.

20. Adolfo Pesquera, "Memories all that remain of many homes, businesses," *San Antonio Express-News,* Mar. 28, 1993, 13-A.

21. Minutes, D-May 25, 1964, 2; D-Jun. 22, 1964, 2; D-Nov. 23, 1964, 2; D-Feb. 22, 1965, 2.

22. Minutes, G-Jan. 23, 1964.

23. George, *O'Neil Ford, 180.*

24. *San Antonio Light,* Jan. 8, 1965.

25. Mrs. Don F. Tobin et. al. to Marshall T. Steves, Feb. 3, 1966, copy in SACS Library.

26. Diehl, "McAllister Expressway;" Mrs. Don F. Tobin to Bruce MacDougal, Jul. 10, 1995, 2, in SACS Library. Mother Mary Clare's successor, Mother Calixa, nevertheless still helped the society "in all the ways she could under the circumstances." (Tobin to MacDougal.)

27. Minutes, D-Sept. 20, 1965, 2.

28. Diehl, "McAllister Expressway."

29. Minutes, G-Jan. 27, 1966; D-Apr. 13, 1966.

30. Minutes, D-Oct. 31, 1966, 4.

31. Minutes, D-Sept. 20, 1965, 1–2.

32. Minutes, G-Dec. 9, 1965.

33. Minutes, D-Sept. 20, 1965, 1–2.

34. Minutes, D-Jan. 24, 1966; G-Mar. 24, 1966, 2.

35. Tobin to MacDougal, 2.

36. O'Neil Ford to Marshall T. Steves, Jan. 4, 1966, copy in SACS Library. Steves had copied Ford in a four-page letter to Nancy Negley (Dec. 30, 1965, in SACS Library) expressing a litany of problems in saving old structures on the HemisFair site, including one puzzle Steves faced involving the Eagar House: "What we would do with it we don't know, for it faces the wrong direction." Ford shot back in this lengthy letter—a copy is 10 pages typewritten, single-spaced—"I don't understand what you mean . . . as a door could be put in the back . . . . We should do all we can to add or preserve these [historic] features . . . to make the special character of San Antonio entirely evident . . . by actually saving things, instead of destroying them." The bulldozing sentiment he heard expressed by HemisFair officials "is just plain absurd . . . . It is comparable to the deliberate and willful destruction of the Vance House by some members of the Federal Reserve Board . . . [and to] the tragic near-loss of the San Antonio River, the Alamo itself, the Governor's Palace, the San José Quadrangle, etc., which were deemed expendable by decent and practical men who lacked the imagination to see how important these things were . . . to our sensibilities and the economics of our special city."

37. Ibid., 4–5. There were also problems on the west side of South Alamo Street. In the fall of 1965, Conservation Society President Peggy Tobin went to a hearing armed with a lengthy resolution opposing the razing of buildings backing on the river just north of Conservation Corner. Their removal was seen as contrary to the Chamber of Commerce's master plan, against River Walk Commission recommendations, disruptive to La Villita and "injurious to the very image San Antonio seeks to preserve for itself." (Minutes, D-Sept. 20, 1965, 1–2.) The buildings were taken anyway, for the Hilton Palacio del Rio Hotel.

38. Renovated after a fire in 1913, when its original entry columns were removed, Beethoven Hall had been used as a warehouse.

39. Minutes, D-Dec. 9, 1965.

40. Minutes, D-Mar. 21, 1966.

41. "Old Store To Be Humble Pavilion," *San Antonio Express,* Sept. 1, 1966, 8-H. Among the doomed homes outside the Historic Triangle was the stone home at 107 North Street where Otto Blumenthal, the city's onetime official city hall clock winder, had lived and operated his clock shop.

42. Diehl, "McAllister Expressway."

43. Ibid. There were previous but unsuccessful legislative attempts to block the project. State Senator Jake Johnson got a bill passed in 1963 protecting the Incarnate Word property, but it was vetoed by Governor John Connally. In 1965 and 1967 Johnson again tried unsuccessfully to slip in riders to the state budget to block financing for the route. Yarborough's amendment, according to O'Neil Ford, was in large part prepared by Sam Zisman, who worked with local Yarborough staff member Alan Mandel. (George, *O'Neil Ford,* 186.)

44. Section 9 of Public Law 89-284, as amended by Public Law 89-685.

45. Directors passed three more resolutions. One went to Senator Ralph Yarborough, thanking him for "far-sighted efforts" which helped "preserve the historic landmarks and natural beauty of the United States." A second thanked Congressman Henry B. Gonzalez for "appreciation of the necessity to keep the land livable by the preservation of natural beauty," as evidenced by his other efforts such as helping to

save Travis Park. The third resolution thanked Senator John Tower for interest in the cause of conservation. The resolution to city hall reminded the city of its promise to share expenses with the Urban Renewal Agency to move the Gissy palisado house, the Groos House and the Schultze House. (Minutes, Sept. 13, 1966, 1–3.)

46. C.C. Pusey, U.S. Department of Commerce, to Mrs. Don F. Tobin, Dec. 16, 1966, in SACS Library. The Washington office of the Historic American Buildings Survey aided in inventorying the sites. (Minutes, D-Jul. 17, 1967, 2.)

47. Minutes, D-Jan. 23, 1967

48. "Public Statement," Jun. 10, 1966, copy in SACS Library.

49. Minutes, D-Jun. 19, 1967; D-Jul. 17, 1967, 1–2; D-Aug. 1, 1967.

50. "Conservation Society to Move House," *San Antonio Light,* Jan. 12, 1967; Minutes, D-Jan. 23, 1967, 3; D-Feb. 20, 1967, 3. The society had already endorsed the Texas State Historical Survey Committee's formal designation of 29 HemisFair structures as recorded state historic landmarks and asked that the route of the skyride be moved to avoid two historic homes—the Garza and Zork-Sweeney houses—on Goliad Street. The HemisFair executive committee originally agreed, and forwarded the request to city council along with requests that the Koehler and Espinoza houses be preserved on-site on Water Street and that the Heinrich House on the site of the Institute of Texan Cultures be donated to the Conservation Society, to be moved at society expense. (Minutes, D-Oct. 31, 1966, 3; D-Nov. 4, 1966, 1–3.)

51. Minutes, D-Feb. 21, 1966, 2; D-Apr. 4, 1966, 2.

52. Minutes, D-May 23, 1966, 2; D-Jun. 3, 1966; D-Sept. 8, 1966; D-Sept. 13, 1966; Jeff Duffield, "Groos House Plans Hit Another Snag," *San Antonio Express,* Jan. 25, 1968, 12-C.

53. George, *O'Neil Ford,* 180.

54. Frank Manupelli to Peggy Tobin, Apr. 7, 1967, in SACS Library.

55. Tobin to MacDougal, 1.

56. Mrs. Don F. Tobin to Frank Manupelli, Apr. 6, 1967, in SACS Library. Although the letter to Manupelli "could be seen as stiff and unfriendly," notes Mrs. Tobin, she found it "much more effective to carry on with [city officials], at least in conversation, in a very light and airy manner and to insist on the humor in the situation, whatever it might be. The late [City Public Service Board Chairman] Victor Braunig . . . once commented at a public meeting that I was the most difficult person he had to deal with because 'she won't let you get mad at her.' Walter McAllister and I were the best of cocktail party banterers." (Tobin to MacDougal, 2.)

57. Frank Manupelli to Peggy Tobin, Apr. 7, 1967, in SACS Library. The society most recently had tried to purchase the Eagar House in 1962. (Minutes, D-Aug. 24, 1962.)

58. Frank Manupelli to Peggy Tobin, Apr. 13, 1967, in SACS Library.

59. Minutes of Historic Structures Committee, Jun. 30, 1967, copy in SACS Library.

60. John A. Watson to Mrs. V.L. Luckett, Jr., Jun. 30, 1967, in SACS Library.

61. "N. Expressway Restudy Denied," *San Antonio News,* Jun. 16, 1967.

62. Minutes, D-Jun. 19, 1967, 1–2.

63. Ibid.

64. Minutes, D-Oct. 9, 1967, 1–2. Olmos Park residents mentioned were R.W. Briggs, H.H. Dewar and the Arthur Seeligsons senior and junior.

65. Gruen, *San Antonio North Expressway Study,* 5.

66. Jeff Duffield, "Conservationists' Tax Bills Mount," *San Antonio Express,* Nov. 19, 1967.

67. Minutes, G-Dec. 14, 1967; D-Feb. 19, 1968; D-Oct. 28, 1968, 2.

68. Minutes, D-Jun. 3, 1966; D-May 22, 1967, 2; Lloyd Larrabee, "Mission Loop Urged," *San Antonio Light,* Feb. 28, 1969.

69. Minutes, G-May 26, 1966.

70. Minutes, G-Sept. 22, 1966.

71. Baumbach and Borah, *The Second Battle of New Orleans,* 132.

72. Ibid., 101, 131; Minutes, G-Oct. 27, 1966; D-Feb. 20, 1967.

73. Minutes, D-Jan. 3, 1968, 1, 5–8; "Conservationist Hits Garage Plan," *San Antonio Express,* Jan. 34, 1968.

74. Minutes, G-Feb. 22, 1968; Ada Louise Huxtable, "HemisFair, Opening Tomorrow, Isn't Texas-Size, But It's Fun," *The New York Times,* Apr. 5, 1968, 50.

75. Adolfo Pesquera, "Fair stirred community spirit, teamwork," *San Antonio Express-News,* Mar. 22, 1993, 10-A. Steves recalled, "It was embarrassing. We had a Democratic president, a Democratic senator and we had to go to Senator Tower, the Republican."

76. Frank Phelps OHT, Oct. 30, 1986, 9. Workers left their boots outside and walked in for lunch in their stocking feet.

77. Lloyd Larrabee, "Mission Loop Urged," *San Antonio Light,* Feb. 28, 1969.

78. Adolfo Pesquera, "S.A.'s HemisFair party," *San Antonio Express-News,* Mar. 28, 1993, 11-A.

79. A Montreal restaurant group wanted to lease Conservation Society buildings—especially Casa Villita, but also the Navarro House and the old Ursuline Academy—for the duration of the fair. The request was turned down, as was the city's request that A Night in Old San Antonio continue during the fair. (Minutes, D-Nov. 13, 1967, 1–2.)

80. Roger Montgomery, "HemisFair '68, Prologue to Renewal," *Architectural Forum,* October 1968, 86. Montgomery concluded: "As a world's fair it stands no chance of joining the list of great ones. But that was not really what it set out to do. As a catalyst for redevelopment in downtown San Antonio it worked . . . splendidly. Its riches of planting, waterways and artwork; the thoughtful husbanding of old trees and houses; the direct, self-effacing architecture combined to make HemisFair an environment remarkably pleasant to wander in . . . . It makes a fitting addition to the unmatched Paseo del Rio. Where else in America has as much been done to create humane public space in the center of a city? Where has urban renewal done more?"

81. Ada Louise Huxtable, "HemisFair, Opening Tomorrow," *The New York Times,* Apr. 5, 1968, 50.

82. Ada Louise Huxtable, "Remember the Alamo," *The New York Times,* Apr. 14, 1968, 31.

83. Elliott, "The First Downtown World's Fair," *Saturday Review,* 46.

13

Washington Politics and Detente

 By the time HemisFair ended in the fall of 1968, North Expressway strife had dragged on for more than eight years. One element of the city's expressway master planning was the inspired paving of right of way for the Southeast Expressway—Interstate 37—along the eastern edge of the HemisFair site as a giant parking lot for fairgoers, opened to regular traffic only after the fair. But the fate of the northern portion of the planned Interstate 37—the North Expressway—was still in the hands of the Department of Transportation in Washington, where the focus of the struggle had shifted. San Antonio friends had called President and Mrs. Lyndon B. Johnson into play, and Senator Ralph Yarborough had engineered a key legislative amendment which thoroughly muddied the waters for expressway backers.

Alan S. Boyd, the first United States Secretary of Transportation, authorized an analysis of the North Expressway, as required by the Yarborough amendment. The month before HemisFair ended, Boyd announced his conditional approval of federal funding but only if the Highway Department would agree to review key design elements in the center section.[1] The Conservation Society under its new president, Lita (Mrs. E. Humphrey) Price, saw this as an opportunity for all interested groups to create a design team and study the proposals in a spirit of cooperation.[2] However, the society advised the Secretary that his "conditional approval" still did not answer basic objections of the Conservation Society and other interested parties.[3]

Yet the Federal Highway Administration's new highway location and design regulations did reaffirm opinions of the society on the subject. Highways and Highway Beautification Committee Chairman and now past president Peggy Tobin went with her committee and the society's attorney to meet with city officials and the city attorney on the proposed changes. The Conservation Society prepared to file a lawsuit if city, state and federal agencies would not reconsider.[4] In February of 1969, the Texas Highway Department rejected the idea of any change in its plan for the center section.[5]

Expressway backers became more optimistic once the Lyndon Johnson administration was replaced with the Republican administration of Richard Nixon. But their hope was misplaced. "We felt we had a stacked deck with friends of Lyndon Johnson opposing us," City Traffic and Transportation Director Stewart Fischer recalled. "But, so help me, within thirty days we had the same roadblocks in the new administration. I learned these people had friends on both sides of the fence."[6] The "tenacious forces of the San Antonio Conservation Society [had] thrown in the first team," a Washington observer reported. One of the first to retreat was Republican U.S. Senator John Tower, who had helped HemisFair backers counter his Democratic colleague Ralph Yarborough and who had been persuaded by Mayor McAllister to back the city's position. Tower now declared his neutrality on the North Expressway issue.

Working on the Nixon administration, said the *San Antonio Express*, "the Conservation Society has everybody from Ambassador [to El Salvador and national Republican fund-raiser] Henry Catto, Jr. to [Republican activist] Mrs. Nancy Negley in the game now. And they've still got a few reserves. They've still got Gen. John Bennett, Jr."—another major Republican fund-raiser and husband of former Conservation Society president and expressway opponent Eleanor Bennett.[7] In March of 1969, a delegation of San Antonio conservationists went to Washington hoping for assurance from Federal Highway Administrator Francis C. Turner that the North Expressway design would adhere to requirements of the Yarborough amendment.[8] Two months later, new Assistant Secretary of Transportation James D. Braman came to San Antonio to investigate environmental allegations first-hand.

As the year dragged on without a decision from Washington, San Antonio's North Expressway debate became part of what the *Washington Post*'s Wolf Von Eckardt saw as nothing less than a "battle for the heart and mind of Transportation Secretary John A. Volpe." Volpe, before being elected governor of Massachusetts, was a highway contractor and the nation's first Federal Highway Administrator. As the second U.S. Secretary of Transportation he was pulled in one direction by his "uncompromising" Federal Highway Administrator Francis Turner, whom Von Eckardt saw as leading "the militant highway builders" within the Department. Pulling the other way was Volpe's assistant James Braman, the former Seattle mayor and businessman now charged with overseeing the environment and urban systems.[9] The *Christian Science Monitor* termed the San Antonio expressway "nationally significant as a test case."[10]

A major shift in expressway struggles came in July of 1969, when Volpe canceled the proposed Vieux Carré Riverfront Expressway in New Orleans.

Identified by *Business Week* Magazine as the first segment in the interstate highway system to be canceled for environmental reasons, Volpe himself later termed it "the beginning of a new tradition in the Department of Transportation regarding the preservation of the nation's heritage."[11] But the historic preservation issue which made the New Orleans case so compelling was lacking in San Antonio, thus also denying San Antonio the support the National Trust for Historic Preservation had provided in New Orleans.[12] After Braman's report on his visit to San Antonio, Volpe leaned against approving the North Expressway route. But then San Antonio's Republican Mayor Walter McAllister made another of his "unannounced" visits, this time to see Volpe in Washington, D.C., where McAllister had served as director of the Federal Home Loan Bank Board during the Eisenhower administration. McAllister returned thinking he had changed Volpe's mind.[13]

Meanwhile the San Antonio Conservation Society, under new president Pinkie (Mrs. Brooks) Martin, again brought up an alternate center segment up Devine Road through the City of Olmos Park, where it could be a four-lane parkway rather than a six-lane expressway. Design refinements showed that as it passed through the open corner of the Trinity campus it could be covered by a pedestrian mall and fountains. The parkway could cut into the low hill to the north and pass beneath the existing level of Olmos Drive near the western end of Olmos Dam before exiting into Olmos Basin. This would take up to ten Olmos Park homes and three more within San Antonio city limits, but the rest of the neighborhoods would be protected by the depressed and hidden roadway.[14]

Still there was no decision from Washington. "What is it with this man John Volpe, U.S. Secretary of Transportation?" huffed acerbic *San Antonio News* columnist Paul Thompson. "Poop after poop trickles out of his Washington office to the effect that he's all set to rule on the North Expressway here. Then—nothing."[15] Finally, in December, Volpe issued a ruling. If the Texas Highway Department would agree to study alternatives for the route of the center segment, he would approve the start of construction for the segments on either end.[16]

The ruling suggested that the battle for the heart and mind of John Volpe was indeed being won by conservationists. "Freeways that adversely affect our environment cannot be built," Volpe declared in a series of decisions that were, reported *The Wall Street Journal,* "alarming roadbuilders, who expected a clear path when Mr. Volpe joined the Nixon cabinet." Having vetoed the expressway planned through New Orleans' French Quarter, blocked a New Hampshire expressway through Franconia Notch State Park and now held up the San Antonio expressway, Volpe was expected to go even further.[17] The Transportation Secretary seemed to be telling local highway planners "that either they come up with decisions on their own to save the environment and

Construction on the southern leg of the North Expressway in 1971 headed toward a corner of the Brackenridge Park golf course in the yet-unapproved center section. The San Antonio Express-News *Collection, The Institute of Texan Cultures.*

help people, or we might well have to take the project involved off the freeway system." Such a step would eliminate federal funding for the project and, seemingly, halt it altogether.[18]

The Texas Highway Department was working with the Department of Transportation to find a mutually acceptable firm to study the North Expressway's yet-unapproved center section, becoming known as "the Volpe gap."[19] For their part, Conservation Society directors reiterated the "long-standing policy of our society to save Brackenridge Park, Olmos Basin and Franklin Fields" and guaranteed they were ready to file suit if opposed.[20] In June, the society turned Highway Engineer Robert R.O. Lytton's invitation to the board to look at maps and models into a media event. Directors organized a public tour of the proposed route and a bring-your-own "lunch in the park," followed by a bus caravan to the local State Highway Department headquarters to discuss things with the hapless Lytton.[21]

By now, San Antonio's Lone Star Chapter of the Sierra Club had emerged as an active ally. It produced a fifteen-minute film on the North Expressway entitled "Why Pave the Grass?" It was televised in July, followed by equal time for Mayor McAllister.[22] He "came out swinging" with some film clips of his own, and built up to a declaration that "the scenic and dramatic beauty" of the North Expressway route from International Airport to downtown would greet visitors with "the most dramatic entrance of any city in the United States."[23] In August of 1970, the Texas Highway Department agreed with the Department of Transportation's hiring of the Los Angeles consulting firm Gruen Associates and was thus allowed to advertise for construction bids on the end segments.[24] The Conservation Society sought to block granting of the bids, but was rebuffed in both U.S. District Court and in the U.S. Circuit Court of Appeals. On November 19, H.B. Zachry Co. was awarded the bid for the southern section, to be finished within 250 working days, and Killian-House for the northern section, to be done within 300 working days. Work promptly began.[25]

Start of construction on the ends of the expressway changed the equation for the Conservation Society. A final appeal to the U.S. Supreme Court was pending. Should it be granted, President Pinkie Martin told directors on November 23, the Conservation Society might have to post bond to compensate contractors for losses while the case was pending. If it lost, the society would have to pay the bond, perhaps amounting to millions of dollars. On the other hand, if the appeal was not granted and the society continued litigation, not only would legal costs mount but the two ends of the expressway could be finished before a decision was reached.[26] Already, ten years of opposition to the expressway had cost $94,000 in legal fees. Despite "the fact that the Society had been assured by our friends in Olmos Park that its role would never be financial," hardly $32,000 had actually been covered by the promised donations, and not all of that in time to keep the society from being dunned by its attorneys. The society itself had to come up with the remainder, and the end was not in sight.[27]

Too, the human toll was rising. The pressure caused Jake Reaney to resign as Conservation Society president under doctor's orders in mid-1968 and leave town to begin her recovery.[28] Her successor, Lita Price, felt it necessary to ask that no files be taken from the office "without written consent of the president or vice-president." Eleanor Bennett got approval to prohibit original letters from being removed from the office.[29]

But by the end of 1969, suspicion was still growing of disloyalty and of outright sabotage from within the ranks. How could the press have received a copy of the society's resolution and alternate plan within hours of their passage, before the information was officially released? "You are doing a great disservice to the society and its aims and purposes, but most of all to yourself," the unnamed culprit was scolded at a board meeting.[30] A motion was proposed officially stating that only the president was to speak for the society on policy matters, and that "strict adherence" was required "to preserve the unity and dignity of the Society. Therefore, any member of the board not adhering to this policy shall be immediately asked to resign from any official position she holds." One longtime member asked if this meant that "any member who does not agree with the president should resign," for she had not agreed with a president "twice." The motion passed unanimously.[31] Why were there members "who are reticent about our case?" Peggy Tobin asked directors outright. "Who would pay for the litigation?" questioned one member. "Are we going ahead with our suit?" asked another. "Why are all the explosive questions being asked?" wondered a fourth.[32]

The tension was understandable. On top of everything else, the Conservation Society's worst fears were being realized. The staging in city-owned La Villita of A Night In Old San Antonio, the society's phenomenally successful fund-raising event, was now in jeopardy.

In 1968, with the effects of HemisFair looming uncertainly over upcoming Fiesta events, the Fiesta Commission asked the Conservation Society to help underwrite any deficit that year. The society agreed, and ended up paying half of the commission's $8,000 loss. Sensing future opportunity, plus lacking income from not having its carnival that year, the Fiesta Commission decided the Conservation Society should contribute $2,000 a night to use Villita Street plus $500 for each night of NIOSA or ten percent of gross gate receipts, whichever was larger. The Conservation Society, in a toned-down resolution not threatening resignation or an appeal to city council, noted that NIOSA's thousands of volunteers brought world-wide renown to the city, and that no one was covering for it should NIOSA lose money. Therefore, the Conservation Society should pay the Fiesta Commission membership dues only, just like every other member organization.[33] The Conservation Society got through NIOSA in 1969 simply by paying the city $500 a night.[34]

That winter, however, the Fiesta San Antonio Commission tried again. President Pinkie Martin went to Mayor McAllister. "I said, 'Why are you picking on us?' And he said, 'You're the only one that makes any money.' I said, 'The reason we make money is we've got volunteers doing our work. We're not little ladies out there in high-heeled shoes and silk stockings hiring somebody to cook our tamales.'" Next, assembled Fiesta Commission members, Mrs. Martin recalled, "looked me right in the face . . . and said, in so many words, 'pay up or get out.'"[35]

In a meeting beset with concerns over tax problems with the city and over Secretary Volpe's upcoming decision on the North Expressway, Conservation Society directors fumed over the Fiesta Commission's proposed "extortion" in the form of a NIOSA management fee—ten percent of gate receipts—plus an audit of its books. Directors let off some steam about how Fiesta Week would be unsuccessful without NIOSA and how the society should quit the Fiesta Commission, march on city hall and/or move NIOSA elsewhere, then followed their lawyer's advice and send a letter.[36] The letter was carried to the Fiesta Commission the next day and read by Mrs. Martin. "I just hated it, because I had so many personal friends who were members of the commission," she said.[37]

Nevertheless, she read that during the previous five years the Conservation Society had paid more than $50,000 for rent, fees, licenses and police assistance. "Candidly, the San Antonio Conservation Society does not need 'management.' We have all the volunteer help we can use—people serving long hours without pay, people whose contribution not only makes Night in Old San Antonio a financial success, but who lend color and authenticity to the event. It would be difficult, indeed, for us to continue to obtain their services gratuitously while paying your organization a fee for rendering no contribution of value to the Society or Night in Old San Antonio . . . . To assert . . . that [the] Fiesta Commission is rendering a service to us which warrants the payment of a fee is sheer fantasy."[38] As for the notion that the Fiesta Commission could examine and publish results of a NIOSA audit, that idea was "shocking beyond expression and totally unacceptable to the Society." If such nonsense were imposed that day by the Fiesta Commission, the Conservation Society would quit.[39]

The Fiesta Commission passed its proposed changes by a vote of 136–38.[40] But the commission did not yet accept the Conservation Society's resignation.[41] The mayor himself went to visit Pinkie Martin. He "sat in my office and said, 'You can't do this.' And I said, 'We've already done it, Mayor McAllister.'"[42] Next, NIOSA Chairman Beverly Blount formally asked city hall for the use of La Villita during Fiesta in 1970. No doubt fearing a packed and hostile chamber, city council decided to take the matter up in a closed session.[43]

By now, the Fiesta Commission itself was embroiled in turmoil, as long-time commission member Reynolds Andricks publicly resigned with a blast at the commission. Some believed that with the added imbroglio with the Conservation Society the Fiesta Commission could collapse and its role would be taken over by city hall, putting the Conservation Society in a worse position. With less than three months before Fiesta, the Conservation Society's "Plan B" for NIOSA was to hold a scaled-back event on the Conservation Society's 511 Villita Street property and down the street in Villita Assembly Hall, which was rented from the City Public Service Board rather than from city hall.[44]

Soon an Internal Revenue Service agent unexpectedly appeared and spent two days looking through the society's minutes and financial records. In a meeting on the third day, the agent began asking questions: "What about a 109-page brochure sent to a Senate sub-committee? What is the function of our Legislative Committee? What about trips to Washington by Society members; were they for attempting to influence legislation? He asked [for] a letter explaining the Society's position in the expressway suit, etc., etc."[45] Officers huddled in meetings with tax attorneys. Three weeks later, the agent returned to tell the executive committee he was about to recommend that the society's tax-exempt status be revoked, since its expressway activities violated its current non-profit status. However, the society could avoid financial devastation by forming a separate foundation to own and manage historic properties and receive tax-free donations for non-political purposes.[46] Directors took little time establishing the San Antonio Conservation Society Foundation, which met two months later and elected officers mirroring those of the Conservation Society itself.[47]

As the months went on, some directors and members resigned from the Conservation Society.[48] Intrigue was becoming downright Byzantine. "I never did know what was going on," Society President Pinkie Martin recalled. "Meetings would be called. I would be told to come to a meeting, and I would walk in a room and there'd be a big hush. You could tell they'd all been there twenty minutes. They were feeding me information. My mail at the office was being censored. It was an ugly situation, and I thought it was really tearing our board apart."[49]

Such a state of affairs was a far cry from the days when the San Antonio Conservation Society presented a united front against those who would destroy the missions, encroach on the river or uproot parks for underground garages. The expressway fight had become a serious distraction from other goals and a financial drain as well, to say nothing of its being a divisive force in the community. In the ongoing debate, even the noted father-and-son engineering team of Willard E. Simpson, Sr. and Willard E. Simpson, Jr.

publicly held opposing views on the feasibility of an expressway route between Alamo Stadium and the Sunken Gardens.[50]

After an anguished review of the situation to directors on November 23, 1970, Mrs. Martin recommended that the San Antonio Conservation Society dismiss all litigation involving the North Expressway. Nancy Negley put it in the form of a motion. Balloting revealed the motion passed by 31 to 16, one vote shy of a two-thirds majority but still, the parliamentarian ruled, sufficient to carry it.[51] Disenchanted members, not surprisingly, disagreed with the parliamentarian. "But we are not going to waste time and energy pursuing this line," a group of forty-seven members, including four past presidents, wrote in a letter dated December 1.[52] "Much more importantly, we feel that the action violated the spirit and traditions of the Society and failed to reflect the wishes of its membership." Recipients were asked to return a coupon pledging their support.

In a three-page letter to members dated three days after that, Mrs. Martin acknowledged that the North Expressway had been "undoubtedly the most emotional issue in the history of the Society." Summarizing the recent decisive court decisions and deploring a number of "inconsistencies" in communications from the society's lawyers, she asserted, "Further litigation of the case could have meant financial bankruptcy of the Society." The society would continue "the battle to save the parks," but this would now be through working with the U.S. Department of Transportation consultant to seek an alternate route rather than continuing through the courts. The Conservation Society, members were reminded, was not opposed to expressways, it was simply in this case seeking a better route, such as the one that had been blocked by the City of Olmos Park. Noting that the board avoided several opportunities for "name-calling confrontation," Mrs. Martin chastised disaffected members who "have chosen to air the dirty linen of the San Antonio Conservation Society in the press" and urged members to agree, rather, that "the less said about this, the better."[53]

Within a week, the forty-seven dissidents received signed coupons of support from 230 Conservation Society members and associates.[54] The reconstituted opponents hired Washington attorney John Vardaman, who had successfully won a U.S. Supreme Court case blocking the Memphis expressway through Overton Park.[55] U.S. Supreme Court Justice Hugo Black personally granted a temporary stay of construction until a permanent stay could be formally sought before the court. That was unsuccessfully requested a week later. Justices Black, William O. Douglas and William J. Brennan dissented from the majority.[56]

While divisions within the society's ranks had yet to heal, there was one immediate dividend from the matter. Despite their lawyer's advice, by September of 1970 directors had still paid no back taxes even on rent-producing

North Expressway work came to a halt in 1971 when a court barred use of federal funds for construction. The San Antonio Express-News *Collection, The Institute of Texan Cultures.*

properties. City hall had remained adamant against any settlement and had recently threatened to have the sheriff put the Steves Homestead, Casa Villita, the Navarro House, Conservation Corner and all the society's other properties up for sale.[57] The tax situation reached the Texas Supreme Court. But in less than three months after directors dropped the North Expressway litigation, the city and county agreed to settle the entire question of $20,000 in back taxes with the Conservation Society for less than $12,000. Directors, delighted, authorized payment.[58]

When clearing of the expressway route began near Stadium Drive, a young citizens' group called Save Our City joined the Sierra Club and disaffected Conservation Society members in opening a storefront headquarters. Members planted a symbolic "Tree of Hope" near the construction site and began an eleven-day around-the-clock vigil.[59] In May of 1971, the U.S. Circuit Court of Appeals granted a stay of construction, sending the issue back to U.S. District Court and forbidding the City of San Antonio to start work even without federal funds. The next month, Gruen Associates came out with its long-awaited official study. The 120-page printed report recommended avoiding Olmos Dam and following, instead, the Texas Highway Department's initially favored route north through the corner of the Trinity University campus and straight across Olmos Park—or, as an alternate, swerving east to avoid the Trinity property and following the path of Devine Road through Olmos Park.[60] But the City of Olmos Park still refused to grant approval.

As debate dragged on, *Life* magazine ran a two-page spread on the situation, with a large photo of a pensive Wanda Ford whiffing a bouquet of flowers as a half-completed North Expressway ramp loomed behind her. Chronicling the role of the San Antonio Conservation Society, the magazine reported that Mrs. Ford was "leading a ferocious remnant of individual society members and a surprising outcropping of new allies . . . . 'After every legal process has been exhausted,' she promised, 'we can still lie down in front of the bulldozers.'"[61] A year and a half later, Mrs. Ford made opposition to the North Expressway in particular and support of environmental awareness in general the focus of a campaign for city council, issues which had taken her into runoffs in similar campaigns in 1961 and 1969. She was, however, defeated this time by former Councilwoman Lila Cockrell, who later became mayor.[62] In the meantime, the United States Supreme Court let stand the lower court's denial of funding for the project. The North Expressway at last seemed dead.

But this time the phoenix rose from the floors of Congress, as legislation enabling the city and state to construct the highway without federal help passed both houses at the end of 1973.[63] On December 10, a U.S. district judge ruled that the new legislation removed all federal issues. The State of Texas and the City of San Antonio could now legally go it alone. Within twenty-four hours, construction crews were back at work on the end segments, only to be delayed by another court order in 1974, which reopened old wounds. Styling of some litigants as "individual members of the San Antonio Conservation Society" created confusion, thought Society President Beverly Blount. To remove any doubt that the society had dropped the fight nearly four years earlier, the society's attorney was instructed to see that the society's name was removed "from mention in any suit brought before any court concerning the North Expressway."[64]

The final construction stay lasted five months. Then on November 13, 1974, work on the 2.5 mile center section was awarded to the low bidder, at $22.6 million the largest single construction contract in the history of the Texas Highway Department. No opponents appeared in front of the bulldozers. When the route opened as the Walter W. McAllister, Sr. Freeway on February 7, 1978, Walter McAllister, by then 88, was there, smiling broadly.[65]

Longtime opponents felt a certain degree of consolation. Ana Escudero remembered attending a meeting of the Incarnate Word High School Mothers' Club attended by Mayor McAllister. "He stood there and told us, 'I am going to build an expressway whether you want it or not,' pointing his finger," she remembered. "I was mad and everybody was mad, but our president got up and said, 'Very well, Mayor McAllister, you will build it, but let me tell you, we are going to have grandchildren before you do it.' And we did. My youngest daughter was married when they were starting the expressway, so at least we did."[66]

Delay of the North Expressway/McAllister Freeway left a mixed legacy. A long stretch of once-open green space in the heart of a metropolis got noise and a pollution-generating highway through its midst. On the other hand,

When finally completed without federal funds, the newly named McAllister Freeway's narrowest point was betwen Alamo Stadium, left, and the Sunken Gardens, its upper roadway cantilevered over the freeway's northbound lane. The spire of the Incarnate Word Motherhouse is on the skyline. San Antonio Express-News.

vast amounts of fossil fuels were consumed and much time was lost as for more than a decade untold thousands of drivers were denied the efficiency of driving the route. Beginning in 1994 nearly $150 million had to be spent acquiring and clearing twenty acres of land to build an interchange between the McAllister Freeway and Loop 410, when far fewer dollars could have built the interchange as first planned, before construction of buildings that would have to be razed and when property values and construction costs were lower.[67] In 1960, it was estimated that the three segments would cost $11.3 million. Eighteen years later it had cost $40.4 million, or $1,700 per foot.[68]

Exhaust pollution of expressway drivers, however, is now "one-fourth to one-half" of levels that would have been reached by the more frequent starts and stops on alternate non-expressway routes. Gasoline consumption was being reduced by 25,000 gallons daily for the same reasons, highway department officials said at the time of the opening.[69] Park purchase funds from the successful expressway bond issue of January 10, 1961 went for initial purchase of land north of the airport known as Northeast Preserve, later renamed McAllister Park.

Nationally, the Yarborough Amendment remains in place, giving pause to those eyeing parkland as the easiest route for an expressway. Locally, chastened highway designers made heretofore-unusual efforts to blend the expressway

Onetime bitter expressway foes Vivian Hamlin (Terrett), former San Antonio Conservation Society president, and former Mayor Walter McAllister at a social event in 1977, the year before the McAllister Freeway opened. Another former society president and expressway foe, Peggy Tobin, said that she and Mayor McAllister also nevertheless remained "the best of cocktail party banterers." San Antonio Express-News.

as much as possible with the environment. Between the Sunken Gardens and Alamo Stadium, the route of Alpine Drive was preserved by cantilevering the road over the expressway, which cuts into the limestone cliff below, which alone previously supported Alpine Drive. More than two dozen stonemasons took two years to finish mosaic-like stone embankments beneath expressway bridges and on slopes near the Hildebrand Avenue intersection. Where the expressway nears the limits of the City of Olmos Park below Contour Drive, a 153-foot, three-and-a-half-foot high limestone wall went up in place of guard rails, a visual as well as a safety barrier. Arched and pebbled retaining and noise abatement walls of quarry fieldstone from Kerrville and limestone from Austin reduce the sound of traffic in the picnic areas of Olmos Basin Park.[70]

For what it was worth to diehard conservationists, in 1981 the McAllister Freeway was named one of the three most attractive urban expressways in the nation.[71]

Notes

1. Gruen Associates, *Expressway Study,* 5–6. To be reviewed were covering the expressway in the Sunken Gardens-Alamo Stadium area and limiting its height as it crossed Olmos Dam, building a new recreation center in the Olmos Basin Park picnic area and finding fill material elsewhere than Olmos Basin. Boyd afterward became the top executive of Amtrak and, later, chairman of the National Trust for Historic Preservation.

2. Minutes, D-Oct. 28, 1968, 4–5. The resolution with this message listed 19 private and public bodies affected by the expressway route, from incorporated cities to the zoo, Little League, Audubon Society, San Antonio River Authority and the Sierra Club.

3. Ibid. Land to be taken in Olmos Basin had become more than 19 acres. A route fitting existing terrain instead of one on pillars was still thought preferable, but directors thought a route up McCullough Avenue might be cheaper. Too, a newly discovered document showed Olmos Basin land was conveyed to the city in 1925 for park purposes only.

4. Minutes, D-Nov. 18, 1968, 2.

5. Ibid., 6.

6. Diehl, "McAllister Expressway."

7. "Battle Still Rages," *San Antonio Express,* Dec. 14, 1969.

8. *San Antonio Conservation Society Newsletter,* June, 1969.

9. Wolf Von Eckardt, "Paving Our Parks," *The Washington Post,* Nov. 15, 1969.

10. Robert Cahn, "U.S. cities watch skirmish over Texas expressway," *The Christian Science Monitor,* Nov. 15, 1969, 10. Volpe had already "struck a balance," ruling against the elevated expressway through New Orleans' French Quarter but backing Interstate 40's route through Overton Park in Memphis. Neither, thought the *Monitor*'s Cahn, was a good test of the department's true philosophy. The outcome of the San Antonio situation would be far more indicative—as would the next decision, whether Interstate 93 should go through New Hampshire's Franconia Notch State Park.

11. Baumbach and Borah, *The Second Battle of New Orleans,* xviii.

12. Pinkie Martin OHT, Oct. 12, 1988, 14.

13. Ibid.; Minutes, D-Oct. 20, 1969.

14. Minutes, D-Oct. 20, 1969, 1–3, 6–12; Gruen, *San Antonio North Expressway Study,* 107–11. The route was initially sketched by architect Boone Powell, who was commissioned by Olmos Park resident H.H. Dewar.

15. "Paul Thompson," *San Antonio News,* Dec. 18, 1969.

16. Diehl, "McAllister Expressway."

17. Albert R. Karr, "Volpe Stiffens Stand On Roads That Disrupt Housing, Scenic Sites," *The Wall Street Journal,* Apr. 7, 1970, 1.

18. Ibid.

19. Ibid.

20. Minutes, E-Mar. 9, 1970; D-Mar. 23, 1970, 7, 10–11.

21. Minutes, D-May 19, 1969, 1–2.

22. The Conservation Society urged that the film add a tribute in memory of O'Neil Ford's associate Sam Zisman, who had died suddenly of a heart attack at age 62. (Minutes, D-Jun. 22, 1970, 2.)

23. Lewis Fisher, "Mayor defends expressway," *San Antonio News,* Jul. 8, 1970, 9-A.

24. Gruen Associates, *San Antonio North Expressway Study,* 6.

25. Ibid., 6–7.

26. Minutes, D-Nov. 23, 1970, 3.

27. Minutes, D-Oct. 20, 1969, 3; E-Mar. 9, 1970; D-Mar. 23, 1970, 5; D-Apr. 13, 1970, 7; D-Sept. 21, 1970, 6.

28. Minutes, D-Jul. 11, 1968, 1, 3.

29. Minutes, E-Jul. 24, 1968.

30. Minutes, D-Nov. 12, 1969, 4.

31. Minutes, D-Jan. 19, 1970, 2.

32. Ibid.

33. Minutes, D-Jan. 27, 1969, 1–2.

34. Minutes, G-Feb. 27, 1969.

35. Pinkie Martin OHT, 18–19.

36. Minutes, D-Nov. 12, 1969, 3–4, 8–9. Ten percent of the 1969 gate receipts would be $7,200. (Minutes, Jan. 21, 1970, 4.)

37. Pinkie Martin OHT, 19.

38. Conservation Society President Mrs. Brooks Martin to Fiesta San Antonio Commission President Stewart C. Johnson, Nov. 13, 1969, copy in Minutes, D-Nov. 12, 1969, 8–9.

39. Ibid.

40. Minutes, D-Nov. 24, 1969, 5.

41. Ibid.

42. Pinkie Martin OHT, 19.

43. Minutes, D-Nov. 24, 1969, 5.

44. Minutes, D-Jan. 19, 1970, 7. A city council committee chaired by Lila Cockrell, also a Conservation Society member, held a hearing on the matter, with presentations from both the Fiesta Commission and the Conservation Society. Afterward, she suggested a compromise. City council would promise the Fiesta Commission the right to coordinate all Fiesta events, the Conservation Society would rejoin the Fiesta Commission and pay the ten percent of gate receipts and in return would have a ten-year guarantee to use La Villita during Fiesta Week. Conservation Society directors agreed, with the proviso that after the next Fiesta the society could unilaterally cancel the agreement. Discussion at the next board meeting grew so intense that the secretary felt obliged to state in the minutes that she had "tried to get the gist of what was being said, but there were six people talking at the same time." (Minutes, D-Jan. 21, 1970, 1–5.)

45. Minutes, D-Mar. 23, 1970, 2.

46. Minutes, D-Mar. 23, 1970, 2–3.

47. Minutes, D-Mar. 23, 1970, 3; D-Apr. 13, 1970, 2; F-May 21, 1970. The idea of a foundation had been explored in 1968. (Minutes, D-Dec. 16, 1968, 2; D-Feb. 24, 1969, 4.)

48. Minutes, D-Sept. 21, 1970.

49. Pinkie Martin OHT, 11–12.

50. "Father, Son Choose Sides," *San Antonio Light,* Jan. 9, 1961.

51. Minutes, D-Nov. 23, 1970, 1–3.

52. The past presidents were Emily Edwards, Eleanor Bennett, Wanda Ford and Peggy Tobin.

53. Mrs. Brooks Martin to Conservation Society members, Dec. 4, 1970, in SACS Library.

54. James McCrory, "'I Pray We've Learned,'" *San Antonio Express,* Dec. 9, 1970.

55. Diehl, "McAllister Expressway."

56. Gruen, *San Antonio North Expressway Study,* 7.

57. Minutes, D-Mar. 23, 1970; D-Sept. 21, 1970, 2.

58. Minutes, D-Jan. 25, 1971, 3; D-Feb. 22, 1971. The amount covered taxes without penalty or interest on 511 Villita St. for 1943 through 1961, the Old Ursuline Academy for 1966 and on the Steves Homestead property for 1949 through 1966.

59. The Tree of Hope disappeared soon after the vigil ended. A crowd of 200 witnessed the planting of a second tree, then broke up for hikes along the route and within three hours the second tree disappeared, as did a third and, finally, a fourth, its branches spotted protruding from "a late-model, red sports car seen zooming along Stadium Drive." (Deborah Weser, "Anti-Expressway Group Opens Broader Campaign," *San Antonio Express,* Feb. 1, 1971; "N. Expressway foes plant another tree; it's stolen," *San Antonio News,* Mar. 15, 1971.)

60. Gruen, *San Antonio North Expressway Study,* 102, 108, 119.

61. "Some Texas folks suggest where a hated superhighway can go," *Life,* Aug. 27, 1971, 66–67.

62. Fern Chick, "Wanda Ford Opens Drive," *San Antonio Light,* Mar. 5, 1973.

63. The legislation was championed by Texas senators John Tower and Lloyd Bentsen and by representatives Jim Wright and O.C. Fisher. Opposition was led by New York's Senator James Buckley and Representative Bella Abzug and by Houston's Representative Bob Eckhardt.

64. "Freeway Fight Is Denied," *San Antonio Light,* Oct. 25, 1974; Minutes, D-Oct. 16, 1974, 2.

65. "McAllister Freeway midsection opening," *The North San Antonio Times,* Feb. 2, 1978, 1. A plaque beside the artery credits McAllister for having "provided the leadership and determination which was the key to the completion of this long needed facility." Since the highway was built without federal funds, it is not officially part of the federal interstate system and is designated not Interstate 37 but U.S. 281.

66. Ana Escudero OHT, Oct., 1990, 6.

67. "Why you can't get from U.S. 281 to Loop 410," *San Antonio Light,* Mar. 21, 1992; "I-410/U.S. 281 interchange supported," *San Antonio Express-News,* Feb. 18, 1994. Buildings on the original interchange site went up when the city felt obliged to lift restrictions while the expressway was halted by the court.

68. Diehl, "McAllister Expressway."

69. "Highways Aide Hails Freeway," *San Antonio Light.*

70. Ibid.; "Olmos Park given expressway shield," *The North San Antonio Times,* Jul. 29, 1976; Frank Trejo, "Stonework on Freeway Cited," *San Antonio Light,* Feb. 3, 1978.

71. "McAllister Expressway among most attractive," *San Antonio Express,* Jan. 15, 1981. The designation, by the American Association of State Highway and Public Transportation Officials, also went to highways in Charlotte, N.C. and White Plains, N.Y.

The apse of the old Spanish church of San Fernando provided Thomas Allen in 1878–79 with the backdrop for this vivid portrayal of ox carts, covered wagons, hay wagons, animals and diners at chili stands on Military Plaza. Viewing of the painting, titled Market Plaza *by the artist, first occurred at the Paris Salon in 1882. Courtesy of the Witte Museum, San Antonio, Texas.*

Mission San José is the largest of San Antonio's five Spanish missions. Its mission church, begun in 1768, still had its original dome when Seth Eastman, a U.S. Army captain, painted Mission San José *in 1848–49. Courtesy of the Witte Museum, San Antonio, Texas.*

Rising above the southern end of the San Antonio River Bend was La Quinta, one of the city's notable Spanish landmarks. Built in 1761 and named for the Fifth Company of Spanish soldiers quartered there, La Quinta later served as San Antonio's first Republic of Texas post office. La Quinta was painted from the rear by Rolla Sims Taylor in 1918, four years before the building fell victim to the widening of Dwyer Avenue. Courtesy of the Witte Museum, San Antonio, Texas.

The warmth of aged local limestone shows in the walls of the chapel (1867–70) of the restored Ursuline Academy, now the Southwest Craft Center, on the downtown banks of the San Antonio River. Ford, Powell & Carson Inc., photo: Rick Gardner.

Sun and shade set the mood for the old buildings of La Villita, a restoration undertaken as a WPA project in 1939 and since expanded. The Tower of the Americas in HemisFair Plaza rises in the distance. Associated Architects; Saldana Williams & Schubert; Ford, Powell & Carson Inc., photo: Rick Gardner.

Three nineteenth-century homes in the southern half of the La Villita Historic District are incorporated in the courtyard of the Plaza San Antonio Hotel (1979). Among them is the Elmendorf-Taylor/Arciniega House, which serves as the hotel's Restoration Bar and Grill. Ford, Powell & Carson Inc., photo: Rick Gardner.

Its native Texas granite and sandstone is periodically restored to keep the Romanesque Bexar County Courthouse in harmony with its 1892 design. The beehive-topped tower at the left is seven stories tall. Ford, Powell & Carson Inc.; Joneskell Architects; Humberto Saldana & Associates; Joint Venture Architects; photo: Carolyn Peterson, FAIA.

Among King William Street's imposing homes is the San Antonio Conservation Society's Steves Homestead (1875), open to the public as a house museum. San Antonio Convention and Visitors Bureau, photo by Al Rendon.

The fanciful interior of the Majestic Theater (1929), complete with simulated clouds actually moving across the dark blue ceiling, is considered one of the best by prolific theater designer John Eberson, who drew on San Antonio's Spanish and Moorish heritage. The restored theater is owned by the City of San Antonio and operated by Las Casas Foundation, and is the home of the San Antonio Symphony. ©John T. Dyer, 1989.

*Left: Crowding the onetime
Villita Street, shown
transformed into the Mexican
Market area of the
Conservation Society's A Night
In Old San Antonio, are some
of the more than 100,000
celebrants who each year make
NIOSA the nation's largest
single event benefitting historic
preservation.* San Antonio
Express-News.

*Right: The traditional
Christmastime Las Posadas
procession, revived by the San
Antonio Conservation Society
in 1966, is held annually along
the River Walk. It portrays the
search of Mary and Joseph for
shelter.* San Antonio
Convention and Visitors
Bureau, photo by Doug Wilson.

Luminarias *line the banks and strings of lights decorate the trees along San Antonio's River Walk each Christmas. San Antonio Convention and Visitors Bureau, photo by Al Rendon.*

The spirit of San Antonio's Fiesta was captured by Caroline Shelton in her 1983 watercolor of A Night In Old San Antonio festivities in front of Casa Villita, the La Villita home purchased by the Conservation Society in 1942. San Antonio Conservation Society.

IV

Cutting

Deals

(1971–1996)

14

Viva NIOSA!

The end of a decade of bristling hostility between the City of San Antonio and the San Antonio Conservation Society came as a relief to the general public. Non-combatants were tired of endless headlines praising or condemning the North Expressway. They simply wanted to move on, and were tarring conservationists in general with the brush of single-minded obstructionism.

To outward appearances, conservationists had suffered some bitter setbacks. But as wounds from attack and counter-attack began to heal, it became clear that the role of the San Antonio Conservation Society was actually strengthened and transformed, a change perceived perhaps more quickly at city hall than among the populace. True, the North Expressway was built exactly where Mayor Walter McAllister had said it was going to be, and had been renamed the McAllister Freeway to emphasize the point. Yet city hall knew that the price of victory was dear. The cost to city government could be measured in the tens of millions of dollars in increased expressway construction costs due to delays. Cost of untold time and energy spent dealing with a divided citizenry was immeasurable.

Political insiders realized that despite the victory, city hall would have to reckon with a Conservation Society thoroughly tested in battle, its ability to mobilize large numbers of irate citizens well proven. Moreover, it had a track record of effectiveness within the political system stretching to the state capitol and beyond, to the halls of Congress and to the White House itself. Politicians did not have to be reminded that it was now far better to do the reckoning beforehand than after things got out of control. So with the expressway hatchet buried, the Conservation Society was brought into the political process. City council began supporting renewed efforts to establish a San Antonio Missions National Historical Park and appropriated funds to work on a coherent Mission Road. The city even hired its own Historic Preservation Planner—Pat (Mrs. R. Jean) Osborne, a former journalist and a longtime

Conservation Society activist. As time went on there would be numerous breakdowns along the way. But at least the prevailing mood was one of communication and cooperation.[1]

Not the least of the mutual benefits was site security for the Conservation Society's A Night In Old San Antonio (NIOSA), held primarily on city property in La Villita. Renewable five-year rental contracts on La Villita were at last signed, and the society could go forward without worrying about having to move a unique event now taking on mythical proportions not only in its size and benefit to the city, but also within the national historic preservation movement.[2]

As its frequency gradually increased from one to four nights of Fiesta week and its total area was enlarged, attendance rose past 1,000 in 1942, beyond 10,000 in 1955 and leveled off at about 100,000 by 1970. Rising revenues and profits required an armored truck to haul receipts to the bank.[3] A warehouse had to be found to store NIOSA properties and supplies.[4] Crowds spilled into the new two-level Villita Assembly Hall in 1960, then two blocks westward across South Presa Street and to Urban Renewal-purchased land south to Nueva Street.[5] In 1973 over-crowding became so serious that gates at times had to be closed.[6] When society headquarters moved from Casa Villita in 1974, that building became NIOSA's year-round headquarters.[7] By the 1990s, NIOSA needed 4,000 volunteer workers each night and generated some $1.8 million each year. Annual profits in the range of $700,000 went directly to local historic preservation projects, including those benefiting, quite literally, city hall.[8]

NIOSA each year produces far more funds for historic preservation than any other event in the nation. It brings in more than the combined profits of the closest two—the Historic Charleston Foundation's month-long tour of homes and the annual gala of the Landmarks Conservancy of New York City.[9]

Another way to trace NIOSA's growth is to count the cascarones, the egg shells emptied carefully at one end, colored, filled with confetti and sealed by gluing tissue paper over the opening. Collected and saved by members throughout the year, cascarones bring festive surprises to those over whose heads they are cracked, showering the victim with confetti. At the end of March of 1960, NIOSA's Cascarone Committee had finished 900 dozen cascarones, and met its goal of 1,200 dozen two weeks later. In 1986, by comparison, the cascarone committee was dyeing 2,400 dozen.[10] The evolution of NIOSA has occurred through a complex process of additions and subtractions and fine-tuning by thousands of entrepreneurial volunteers adjusting to constant change and growth. Like a crazy quilt of brightly colored patterns snipped in forgotten places, NIOSA is one of a kind.

NIOSA's original intent of dramatizing the varied cultural elements which formed San Antonio and made it distinctive often seems lost in the swirling

In a survival from the earliest Conservation Society festivals, a goat pulling a cart can be spotted near the center of this 1955 view of A Night In Old San Antonio's "Navarro Plaza," its food stands lining the sides of the Arneson River Theater and the old City Public Service Company power plant, now the site of the Villita Assembly Building. Flags in the foreground stretch across Villita Street, which leads to other NIOSA areas. The San Antonio Express-News *Collection, The Institute of Texan Cultures.*

pursuit of exotic foods and live entertainment, and in the greeting of long-lost friends glimpsed somewhere off in the crowd.[11] Volunteers and crowds alike return each year simply because it's fun. Caroline Shelton, who painted watercolors for the first seven NIOSA posters, belonged to a preservation society elsewhere which, she said, "took itself so terribly seriously. They did good work, of course, but they didn't have any fun. San Antonio took its conservation seriously, believe me, but they had fun doing it, and made money so they didn't have to go asking anyone else for it."[12]

Indeed, a preservation-through-entertainment theme runs from the beginnings of the Conservation Society, perhaps stemming from the traditional women's role of planning family entertainment. Even in its first few months organizers did not just exhort, as did traditional preservationists, but rather took officials on a lively bus tour, gave them a puppet show and planned a boat ride to make their points. Repeated festivals with costumes and gala decorations, likewise, were intended to convey a lively spirit of the past, as well as to raise funds.

NIOSA had begun modestly in 1936 as a fall Indian Harvest Festival after the opening of the restored San José Mission. It moved four years later to help dedicate the San Antonio River beautification project and then became a Fiesta week spring river festival before its final incarnation among the landmarks of La Villita. Throughout, NIOSA has maintained its family appeal without taking on a raucous carnival atmosphere. It has always featured colorful ties to San Antonio's historic culture, even though that expression has changed markedly over the years. Elizabeth Graham's pair of donkeys, moved from the Harvest Festivals, no longer compete for space on Villita Street.[13] Keeping the donkeys was "a terrible nuisance" for Mrs. Graham, one society founder remembered, "but she had to have them for Fiesta."[14] Nor can children any longer ride a donkey cart up and down Villita Street for a nickel or a dime nor watch geese being herded down the street, and there are no more prizes for NIOSA-goers wearing the best costumes.

In La Villita, NIOSA at first relied on volunteers to make the items they were selling. When chili stands recalling those in San Antonio's old plazas were revived in Juarez Plaza in 1947, NIOSA volunteers prepared from the beginning the Mexican food they sold.[15] Dolls handmade by society members were the catch for the fish pond.[16] Members baked cakes, cookies and brownies, and cut fresh flowers from their gardens to sell as arrangements and corsages.[17] In 1953, society members were asked to contribute $1 if they were not preparing homemade candy for NIOSA, as only homemade candy would be sold.[18] Bids for pies, however, by then were being taken from "some of the best bakeries in town," and the one thousand dozen tamales offered in 1953 were ordered to go.[19]

The name of one early food-maker has achieved virtual immortality. NIOSA's longest lines are for Maria's Tortillas, even though Maria Luisa Ochoa, the housekeeper for Ethel Harris who was first pressed into service to make them, is no longer living. Booth Chairman Esther (Mrs. Chester) MacMillan recalled, "Every year, Ethel would call me and say, 'Esther, you've got to come out and talk to Maria. She's not going to do it.' And I would say, 'Why don't you do it? She works for you. She's living in your house.' 'You've got to come out and talk to her,' she'd say. I would go out and talk to Maria. And every year we gave her workers just a little more money . . . .

Volunteer Liz Velasquez cooks anticuchos *on a brazier at A Night In Old San Antonio in 1994.* San Antonio Express-News.

Working in the Maria's Tortillas booth at A Night In Old San Antonio in 1990 is Eudalia Morales. San Antonio Express-News.

And I watched . . . what she did. She ordered the maize, a certain percentage of maize made of yellow corn and some with white. And she mixed them and the lime water until she could *feel* when it was right. And, somehow or other, those were the best tortillas that ever were."[20]

Buñuelos, crisp fried Mexican pastry discs dusted with cinnamon and sugar, have been made from an old missions-area recipe by four generations of the same family.[21] Mary Ashley Culp "hired girls around the mission who made them every Christmas," recalled Glory (Mrs. Camp) Felder, who helped. "But there were never enough. Mary asked several members to come to her house and learn how to make buñuelos. We got there . . . and she already had the dough made and the little biscuits ready to roll out . . . .We would slip them into this big twelve-inch skillet filled with hot grease. She would always slip a silver dollar into the middle—which she said kept the grease from burning; I don't know whether it did or not, but it looked pretty down there shining . . . . [The buñuelos] were as big as a big pizza. They would shrink up a little bit, and you would have to break them up with a fork to make them cook."[22]

Anticuchos, specially marinated meat on a shish-kabob stick, made their NIOSA debut in the mid-1950s, when a recipe was brought from Peru by a friend of Ethel Harris.[23] Within twenty-five years the *anticucho* operation went from using two hundred pounds of meat each year to using six tons, requiring three hundred volunteers and bringing in $50,000, making it the top NIOSA seller.[24] But first, the recipe had to be modified "for the general taste." For more than a year, Jane Maverick (Mrs. William B.) McMillan and her husband experimented on their back yard grill with various proportions of vinegar, hot peppers and spices. "One set we made tasted like vinegar sticks," she recalled. "We couldn't eat them, but the neighborhood dogs just loved them." By the time they hit on the winning recipe, the project had "ruined all the family iceboxes. The vinegar smell permeated the freezers."[25]

Anticucho meat chunks are marinated in the sauce for twenty-four hours before being cooked, "but if we forget to brush them with the sauce as they cook, we sure do hear about it," remembered Mrs. McMillan's sister Lillian, who with husband James T. Padgitt co-chaired the *anticucho* booth for its first twenty-five years. The corn husk mops used to spread the basting marinade on the cooking *anticuchos* were handmade by Padgitt himself, who started months before each Fiesta by painstakingly wiring cornhusks onto the sticks. At first bamboo sticks were collected from Brackenridge Park and Mission San José, then wooden dowels and even balloon sticks were tried. The ideal sticks were found to be of hickory and made in Tennessee.[26] At first, *anticuchos* were cooked on inefficient small braziers. But then, "we were out at the ranch," Mrs. Padgitt remembered, "and one of the men was cutting old water heaters in half. I looked at those water heaters and thought, 'Of course, they'd be perfect for cooking the *anticuchos*.' We added legs to the sawed-in-half heaters, filled the hollows with charcoal and put grills on top for the *anticuchos* to rest on. Instant success!"[27]

Louise (Mrs. Robert) Reischling was tapped in the late 1950s as stage manager of the Villita Assembly Building's new Gilded Cage western show based on her background in directing the gridiron show of the old San Antonio Press Club. She soon found herself recruited for society membership and accepting chairmanship of an area which became Frontier Town, a post she kept for twenty years. At that time, she remembered, the only NIOSA area that had its own designation was the Mexican Market, chaired by the indefatigable Ethel Harris.[28]

Frontier Town was added in 1964 when NIOSA expanded to Navarro Street and took in the future site of a parking garage. "We didn't know what to call it," Mrs. Reischling remembered, "so we called it River Plaza." The area had a western band, what onetime NIOSA Chairman Nelle Lee (Mrs. Chester) Weincek called "our pied piper to get people down to that area," and a beer booth named Fast Draw Suds.[29] "Ethel Harris was the one . . . that sat me down and told me I had to have a signature, . . . like her maguey plants," Mrs. Reischling added. "When you were going down Villita Street in a crowd and you saw the maguey plants, you knew you were getting close to the Mexican Market . . . . So my signature was the windmill. I went to Leakey, Texas, and got a model and the Pearl Brewery built my windmill for me," using lumber donated from buildings being torn down that year to make way for HemisFair. "From there I went to the ranch in West Texas and brought back a lot of effects—saddles, trappings that would make it look more western—and that's how Frontier Town got started."[30]

At first, said Mrs. Reischling, "the bar was up against the wall and there were four spigots. People could get to the bar to get their beer, but they couldn't turn back around and get back because of the crowds. So I decided when we moved over to Maverick Plaza that we had to have some way that the people could get served and not be crushed. So I asked the beer people, . . . if I built a circular bar, could they get the beer to it without carrying it through the crowds? They used to have to carry the beer in kegs all the way through the crowds, and it was very difficult.[31] They said, 'You build a circular bar and we'll get the beer there.' And Everett Stephens at the Pearl Brewery designed a little pump. He called it the Sputnik, because it was about the same time the Russians went to space. And so the little Sputnik pumped the beer 240 feet away from the service area, and it went overhead and . . . through the windmill into the bar . . . I had sixteen spigots, and it serviced all of them . . . . So it really worked. In fact, it was the first time the same system had ever been used anywhere in the United States, and now it's used everywhere."[32]

At Frontier Town, now one of NIOSA's largest areas, all food was prepared on site. "We researched most of it," Mrs. Reischling explained. "We had rattlesnake meat, we had calf fries—still have the calf fries, rattlesnake meat priced itself out. We tried a lot of things that didn't go, we moved on to a lot of good food items. I went to New Mexico and found a sopaipilla recipe that is still used."[33]

Four dozen volunteers now belong to NIOSA's Consolidated Food Committee. Its members put out for bid seven pages of food items needed for an upcoming NIOSA—such as, for 1995, 8,410 pounds of chicken, 83 cases of shredded lettuce and 153 cases of 26-ounce containers of salt.[34] Ingredients like 1,500 pounds of guacamole, 2,650 pounds of *masa harina*, 7,300 cocktail chalupa shells, 2,200 pounds of smoked turkey legs and 270 cases of fresh mushrooms go into the annual consumption of more than 200 food items, ranging from 25,000 tacos to 10,000 egg rolls to 18,000 gorditas to 26,000 *anticuchos*.[35] Individual food offerings number as many as 235. New items in 1992 included Quesa Beso, a chipotle chile-flavored chili con carne, and a fruit slush that came about by accident the previous year, when strawberries ordered for fruit kebabs arrived frozen and, instead of being wasted, were incorporated into a frozen strawberry daiquiri recipe concocted on the spot.[36]

NIOSA specialties have become familiar throughout the San Antonio area. Burritos (spiced beef rolled in flour tortillas) were introduced by Juana and Charles Hammer, who had the ingredients special-ordered from California. "We had to tell everybody what [a] 'burrito' was," Mrs. Hammer recalls.[37] Lynn Specia, granddaughter of buñuelo recipe originator Mary Ashley Culp, went into business with a partner at HemisFair in 1968 selling buñuelos made with her grandmother's recipe, a business still operating more than a quarter-century later.[38]

By the mid-1990s, La Villita and parking lots to its west were divided into fifteen NIOSA theme areas, where food and entertainment recall specific sectors of San Antonio's past. A twenty-foot high facade of the Alamo opens to Mission Trail, where, beneath the backdrop of the four other missions' facades and to the music of the Cactus Rose Band, are served Mission Maize (roasted corn-on-the-cob with seasonings), Prairie Chicken (skinless, sautéed chicken with onion and bell pepper in flour tortillas), Pecos Poppies (cored, batter-fried onions which fold open as they cook) and genuine fried cactus strips, dubbed Coahuila Cactus.[39] Nearby, in Maverick Plaza, Frontier Town resembles an early Texas settlement, including a general store with an official U.S. Post Office substation having its own NIOSA cancellation stamp plus a jail and an undertaker, known as Digger O'Dell. To the strains of a country music band are served Shypoke Eggs (crispy corn tortillas with melted white and yellow cheese), Horseshoe Sausage, Cowboy Klopse (a deep-fried meatball with cheese inside a jalapeno pepper, dipped in batter), Texas Caviar, Stagecoach Beef and Apache Coolers (non-alcoholic strawberry daiquiris).

Villa España, decorated in the red and gold of the Spanish flag, serves Paella, Sangria, Taquitos de Puerco and Flan. The Mexican Market area along Paseo de La Villita and around the Villita Assembly Building features, among others, chalupas, bean tacos, burritos, quesadillas (melted Monterey Jack cheese with cilantro and onions in a corn tortilla), sopaipillas and *frijoles borrachos*— literally "drunk beans," Mexican pinto beans cooked in beer.[40] To entertain children, two dozen booths form Clown Alley. Its top-selling item is snow cones, or *raspas*. Long-time clown-costumed snow cone seller Adele Muegge said her barkers preferred to advertise banana-flavored cones "because it's so much fun to bark that name out."[41]

Few volunteers are more exotically dressed than the "gypsy" fortune tellers. Floy Fontaine Jordan was initially "very suspicious" when her aunt, first Conservation Society president Emily Edwards, read palms. But it became a favorite hobby for her, too, and Mrs. Jordan ended up giving hour-long training sessions for several dozen NIOSA volunteer fortune tellers. "We're working on reading cards," she explained one year, "just twenty-eight plain playing cards. And, happily, there are no reverse cards, or cards with double meanings, so we guarantee a happy fortune for everyone."[42] Behind the scenes, professional family entertainment in general became a year-round effort for Margaret (Mrs. Victor) Gallo, who as entertainment chairman in 1985 coordinated performances in each of the dozen-plus NIOSA areas and in the Arneson River Theater by booking thirty-one acts ranging from dancers to bands to jugglers. "Originally, the entertainment started with mariachis and a few bands, but not too many," she recalled. "Now *everyone* wants to get into NIOSA because of the exposure they'll get."[43]

Others not dealing face-to-face with NIOSA-goers include members of such task forces as the Electrical Appliances Committee, which gathers skillets, griddles and warmers for the food booths. Its chairman heard from booth chairmen on NIOSA perimeters that power surges from interior booths near the electrical generators were causing brownouts. Generators were added on the perimeter.[44] To guard against mishaps, longtime NIOSA Fire, Health and Safety Chairman Glory Felder annually made the rounds of the food booths, allocating more than one hundred fire extinguishers and having committee members check them out at the beginning of each evening. Even so, she reported, "We have had a few flash fires with grease and some electrical shortages, but these have been very seldom."[45] Shortages of food can also be distressing, keeping NIOSA chairmen and others roving about to anticipate them. Once, recalled Esther MacMillan, "I sent somebody down to the river to cut cane, river cane, for the sticks for the *anticuchos*."[46]

A variety of crises can occur off premises, as well. Two months before NIOSA in 1992, an unexpected ruling by city council prohibited Fiesta functions from serving beer later than an hour before closing, to address problems at other Fiesta events which closed as late as 1 AM. NIOSA, however, closed at 10:30 PM "We had to go to protest what we felt was an unfair ordinance," said Beverly (Mrs. Milton) Zaiontz, who won an exemption for NIOSA on the grounds that it had no police incidents at all the previous year.[47] Then there was the ticket scam of 1982. Police made five arrests for possession or passing of counterfeit tickets. NIOSA Chairman Loretta (Mrs. William) Huddleston estimated they won entry for at least 4,000 persons, most unsuspecting, representing a loss to the Conservation Society of $14,000.[48]

Chance meetings are not uncommon. One fortune-teller's clients from New Jersey discovered they knew her daughter there.[49] Television weatherman Bill Dante met his future wife, Lisa, near the Maria's Tortillas booth at NIOSA in 1989. They began dating, but a few months later she was offered a job in another city. Bill knew he had to make "a better offer," Lisa remembered, so he invited her to dinner at a Mexican restaurant and hid an engagement ring in the basket of flour tortillas, to symbolize their first meeting at Maria's. "At first, I thought, 'Some poor woman has lost her ring.'" However, Bill convinced Lisa that the ring was meant for her, and they set the wedding date.[50]

NIOSA provides a unifying focus for Conservation Society members as well, often introducing them to the society. "When I first worked in NIOSA," recalled former president Beverly Blount-Hemphill, "we had just moved to town and I didn't even know the organization that put it on. I was working in a barbecue booth, . . . and then my next-door neighbor . . . asked me if I'd like to become a member and put my name up."[51] Former president Janet Francis was introduced at a Texas Bankers Association mini-NIOSA to a friend of her husband. "She put me up for membership in the society . . . [and] it wasn't but a few weeks before I got a call from NIOSA that they needed a treasurer . . . It just so happened that I had worked in accounting and majored in accounting in college, and so I went and talked to them and told them that I would serve as NIOSA treasurer, which, of course, was a much larger job than I anticipated."[52]

NIOSA itself got volunteered to the Smithsonian Institution. Mini-NIOSAs/NIOSITAs had been staged for individual groups since 1959, always in San Antonio.[53] In 1968, the Smithsonian Institution's second Festival of American Folklife on the Capitol Mall on the July Fourth weekend was featuring Texas food, perhaps not coincidentally since there was a Texan in the White House. Invited, incumbent NIOSA chairman Betty (Mrs. Neville) Murray oversaw transporting NIOSA to Washington, D.C.[54] She took thirty-eight society members for the five-day event, which drew 515,000 persons.[55] "There were not very many people who knew how to provision us in Washington, D.C.," she recalled. "The Cornell Restaurant Management Team came down from Cornell [University]. We borrowed the kitchens from George Washington University, and brought our recipes. We brought the recipe for chili. Well, they did a fairly good job of it, except one afternoon it turned out with celery in it."[56] Buñuelos were among the foods airlifted daily. At first they arrived "like Rice Krispies, but we sold them anyway," reported Mrs. Murray, "and [the people] loved them. The other interesting [spectacle], of course, is the traditional response that someone has to a tamale. I remember serving the Deputy Secretary of Health, Education and Welfare [who] was the first to bite into it shuck and all."[57]

Paralleling growth of NIOSA, membership in the San Antonio Conservation Society more than tripled in twenty years, to nearly 2,000 by 1970.[58] Its properties went from three pieces valued at $51,000 to eleven pieces valued at nearly $700,000, the budget from $20,000 to $137,000, full-time employees from zero to seven—eleven by the 1990s—and the number of committees from twenty-seven to forty-five.[59] By 1976 the "bare minimum budget" to operate the society for a year was $200,000.[60] Formation of the San Antonio Conservation Society Foundation in May of 1970 was advantageous not only

Historic Preservation Seminars have been sponsored by the San Antonio Conservation Society since 1971. San Antonio Conservation Society.

for tax reasons, but to help administer the society's increasingly complex assortment of properties, transferred to the foundation.[61] A more difficult transition for the fiercely volunteer organization was accepting the idea of a paid coordinator of operations, and a male one at that, even though the idea had been coming up for years. In 1970 a statement was crafted that an executive director was essential, although to "in no way take over or participate in policy matters of the society" nor "change in any way the great amateur standing of our members."[62]

Once the title was changed to administrative assistant, former Trinity University Alumni Director Conrad True was hired, but only after some directors unsuccessfully rebelled at paying him for more than a three-month trial.[63] Six years later, as True proved an effective aide and conservation advocate, his title was made administrative director.[64] He was followed in 1980 by Louise Cantwell and after that (1982-86) by Ann Maria Watson (Pfeiffer).[65] Historic preservation by then had become a widely taught, formal discipline. Appointed with the new title of executive director was Bruce MacDougal, executive director of the Society for the Preservation of Virginia Antiquities in Richmond, who held a University of Virginia graduate degree in architectural history and had been a staff member of the National Register of Historic Places in Washington, D.C.[66] His credentials matched those of the city's new Historic Preservation Officer, Ann Benson (Mrs. Michael) McGlone, who in 1992 replaced newly retired Pat Osborne. An architect with a Columbia University graduate degree in historic preservation, Mrs. McGlone had done restoration work on New York City's Grand Central Station and the Willard Hotel in Washington, D.C. and, in San Antonio, on the H.E.B. arsenal headquarters and the Fairmount Hotel.[67] Her appointment was not, however, a foregone conclusion.

Five years of public hearings and administrative work had culminated in a strengthened historic preservation ordinance, and duties of the newly redesignated Historic Design and Review Office had grown with the newly combined Historic Review Board, Fine Arts Commission and River Walk Commission.[68] Two years of cuts, however, reduced the Historic Design and Review Office's budget by half. With the top post vacant after Mrs. Osborne's retirement, the city proposed eliminating the office altogether.[69] One assault on the Historic Preservation Office had already been overcome when Conservation Society President Liz (Mrs. Stanley) Davies suggested that the society and the King William Association would help fund computer entry of historic and cultural resource data if the city continued to fund the Historic Design and Review Office. City Manager Lou Fox agreed.[70]

This time the Conservation Society came up with a bigger offer, tied to solving the recurring question of what the society should pay to hold NIOSA in La Villita. The society would guarantee payment to the city of fifteen percent of NIOSA adult admissions, which the previous year came to $67,000. With bad weather the guaranteed minimum would be $30,000. Also, for the next five years the society would contribute $20,000 to the Historic Design and Review Office if the city at least matched that amount. The city would also upgrade the office from a subsidiary of the Building Inspections Department and reassign it with full division level status to the Planning Department, thus meriting a higher salary for the preservation officer. City Manager Alex Briseño approved, city council agreed and, eight months after the post became vacant, Mrs. McGlone was on the job.[71]

Academic training in historic preservation was launched in San Antonio with the Conservation Society's 1995 donation of $100,000 to the University of Texas at San Antonio's new master's degree program in architecture for a professorship in historic preservation named in memory of former Society President Mary Ann (Mrs. James N.) Castleberry.[72] A less formal education program began twenty-four years earlier at the start of the city-society detente, when Nancy Negley (Wellin) chaired the society's first annual Historic Preservation Seminar in conjunction with the City of San Antonio and the Urban Renewal Agency. More than a dozen governmental agencies and local institutions joined as participating organizations in the seminar, its enrollment limited to 350.[73]

A local inspiration with a national impact came during a Conservation Society-hosted reception for local, state and national preservationists on the grounds of Casa Villita, where a spontaneous idea sparked a discussion leading to organization in 1974 of Preservation Action. That national citizens' lobbying group, based in Washington, D.C., continues "to preserve our historic, cultural, architectural and environmental heritage." Any resemblance of its founding goals to those of the San Antonio Conservation Society is not coincidental. Its first president was the Conservation Society president at the time, Beverly Blount (-Hemphill), hostess for the reception.[74]

Shortly after that reception, Conservation Society headquarters got the opportunity to move from its cramped quarters in Casa Villita when the three-story Italianate stone home at the entrance to King William Street came on the market.[75] A decade earlier the society considered purchasing the home, built in 1870 by Anton Wulff, San Antonio's first parks commissioner, but it was purchased instead by the United Brotherhood of Carpenters and Joiners and restored under the direction of O'Neil Ford and Associates.[76] By 1974, vacant and last used by a church youth group as a Halloween spook house, it was up for sale again. [77]

Under the leadership of President Beverly Blount (-Hemphill), and with fund-raising assistance of King William Street neighbor Walter N. Mathis, the Wulff House was purchased for $230,000, nearly half of it a grant from the Sheerin Foundation and more from the Economic Development Administration.[78] Offices went on the lower level, main offices and the Amanda Cartwright Taylor Conference Room on the first floor and a library on the top floor. The Foundation named the lot next door the Pedro Huizar Garden in honor of its original owner and donated it to the city as a park, marking the property boundary with the Wulff House a seven-foot-high wall of limestone blocks recycled from razed landmarks. It was, noted Vivian Hamlin (Terrett), "the first time the Foundation has had the opportunity to make a park out of a parking lot."[79]

Though the scale of San Antonio Conservation Society operations was changing, traditional concerns were not. Place names were still defended. Proposals to change the name of Milam Square and to the change of the name of Brackenridge High School to Wheatley High School were opposed. Returning Eisenhauer Road to Klaus Road and lower Broadway to Losoya Street were supported.[80] The *Las Posadas* Christmas procession representing the search of Mary and Joseph for shelter was reinstituted in 1966.[81] Three years later, police arrived when a passerby mistook the candle-bearing procession at the steps of city hall for a political demonstration; no parade permit had been issued.[82] The *Las Posadas* venue later changed to the River Bend in conjunction with its illumination and lighting of rows of *luminarias* along the banks. With more than 3,000 persons participating each year, the event

Twelve former San Antonio Conservation Society presidents gathered outside the society's recently restored Wulff House headquarters in 1983. They are, from left, back row, Eleanor Bennett, Wanda Ford, Lita Price, Peggy Penshorn, Joanna Parrish, Vivian Hamlin (Terrett) and then-President Lynn Bobbitt; front, Virginia Temple, Helen Bechtel, Beverly Blount (- Hemphill), Mary Ann Castleberry, Lorraine Reaney and Pinkie Martin. San Antonio Conservation Society.

Traditional Las Posadas *processions at Christmas time represent the search of Mary and Joseph for shelter.* San Antonio Express-News.

became a favorite for national magazine coverage.[83] The Christmas miracle play *Los Pastores* at San José Mission was less well-attended, as seated spectators were chilled when weather turned cold and other groups began holding the play elsewhere in the city.[84] Still, *Los Pastores* attendance at the mission in 1973 totaled 1,800. The Guadalupe Players were hired to perform the next year, the twenty-fifth year *Los Pastores* was sponsored by the Conservation Society.[85]

To achieve its traditional environmental conservation goals, the society found itself able to advocate its positions through the host of new specific-interest organizations. The society joined opposition to the proposed Applewhite Reservoir on the basis that more than eighty historic and prehistoric sites would be inundated, and sought National Trust for Historic Preservation involvement in legal action to halt the project.[86] The Sierra Club was given funds to defray legal costs to protect the Edwards Underground Aquifer, sole source of San Antonio's water.[87] The society remained watchful over the San Antonio River, expressing to all boards and commissions concerned the danger to the River Walk of intrusion of "tables, balconies . . . and other business activity."[88]

Even though the Conservation Society maintained "as great an influence in its area as any other organization in the country," it was considered the last major organization of its type maintaining a "first-generation type of organization," without subsequent restructuring.[89] Its by-laws reveal an organizational structure basically unchanged after more than seven decades, still dedicated to volunteer operations and to the ultimate authority of a volunteer president/principal executive officer, whose term does not extend beyond two years.[90] Despite the numbers of women working full-time in salaried positions, in the 1990s its traditionally female president contributes full time to the job. Volunteer directors typically met for a full weekday once a month. The president maintains broad latitude over policy by appointing thirty-two members to the seventy-person board, only thirty of whom are directly elected to rotating three-year terms.[91] As a result the society functions, observed President Sally Matthews (Mrs. Robert) Buchanan, "like a legislature. You have to talk to a lot of people and you have to learn to be very persuasive to get something done."[92]

While the San Antonio Conservation Society defies conventional latter-day wisdom on its organizational structure, it defies other traditional beliefs as well. By mid-1995 it was no longer exclusively a women's organization, as many outsiders believed. Twenty percent of its membership—545—were men, although only three percent of its directors—two out of sixty-seven—were male.[93] Nor was its membership dominated by old families, although their influence may remain strong. A third of its 2,700 members lived in older family zip codes 78209 and 78212. But overall membership lived in virtually every zip code in Bexar County, defying the common traditional dividing line as forty percent of the society's membership lived outside of Loop 410 in newer subdivisions to its north. From the society's more than two hundred Hispanic members was elected, in 1984, its first Hispanic president, Bebe Canales (Mrs. Sherwood) Inkley.[94]

As the new, broad-based era of historic preservation was dawning in San Antonio and the old one passing, the last surviving pioneer conservationists died. Adina De Zavala, the President for Life of her Texas Historical and Landmarks Society, passed away in 1955 at the age of 93, two years after adding her unflinching perspective to the Travis Park struggle by writing a newspaper, "All those who love beauty, all who care for patriotism, should come to the rescue of this unique monument to Travis."[95] At the San Antonio Conservation Society's thirty-eighth anniversary meeting in 1962, five surviving founding members were introduced and honored: Rena Maverick Green, Amanda Cartwright Taylor, Emily Edwards, Eleanor Onderdonk and Floy Edwards Fontaine.[96]

Eight months later, Conservation Society co-founder Rena Maverick Green, the society's Honorary Parks Chairman, died at the age of 88, having summarized the society's parks activities for the society newsletter the previous year and been active throughout the Travis Park controversy.[97] With Eleanor Onderdonk's death two years later at the age of 80, three survivors were left to speak at the forty-first anniversary meeting in 1965.[98] Floy Fontaine died in 1971 and two-time president Amanda Taylor, the society's Honorary Life President, who retired from her twenty-year post on the San José Mission Board in 1964 and was quick to oppose the North Expressway, died in 1977 at the age of 98.[99] In 1980 co-founder Emily Edwards passed away at 91, a conservation activist to the end.

Emily Edwards last lived in the Sarah Roberts French Home in near northwestern San Antonio. From her window she could see the small Woodlawn Lake, which was being neglected by the city. "Why is Woodlawn Lake . . . being abandoned to the water lilies?" she asked in a letter to the editor in 1978.[100] When there were no results, six months before her death she wrote the Conservation Society Parks and Waterways chairman, suggesting she see that the lake be skimmed "and have it returned to usefulness. This is a workers' neighborhood, and the lake has special value for fishing, rowing, sailing, swimming . . . . I think that if the Parks Department knows that the Conservation Society is interested in saving it, they might be more concerned. If we can save a river, maybe a lake can be saved."[101]

Notes

1. To be sure, there was a certain amount of cooperation during the "war years." In 1964, once and future Society President Vivian Hamlin (Terrett) was appointed to the City Planning and Zoning Board. She also served as vice-chairman of the HemisFair Committee, which caused her to resign the Conservation Society directors' Advisory Committee chairmanship when HemisFair officials tried to consider her a society spokesperson. (Minutes, G-Feb. 27, 1964; D-Oct. 31, 1966, 2.)

2. Minutes, D-Apr. 9, 1975, 2; D-Oct., 20, 1976, 3; D-Jan. 19, 1977, 3; D-Mar. 16, 1983, 3. The Conservation Society had dropped its membership in the Fiesta San Jacinto Association, eliminated fee payment to the renamed Fiesta San Antonio Commission and dealt directly with the city, which got essentially $5,000 in rent plus fifteen percent of NIOSA beer and soft drink sales on city-owned property.

3. Minutes, D-Mar. 23, 1970, 4. A Night In Old San Antonio could not begin before Tuesday due to traffic snarls from the Texas Cavaliers' Monday night River Parade, traditionally the week's first major event. It was blocked on Saturday night by the nighttime flambeau parade climaxing Fiesta Week. Nights once had themes. In 1956, Tuesday night was dedicated to the military, Wednesday night to the Conservation Society itself and Thursday night to "International Culture." (Minutes, D-Mar. 19, 1956, 2.)

4. Minutes, D-Aug. 8, 1966; D-Sept. 8, 1966. In 1977, the society borrowed $137,000 to build a new, 10,000 square-foot warehouse on the site, and found the next year that a full-time manager was needed to oversee the warehouse and other properties as well. (Minutes, D-Aug. 31, 1977, 2; D-Oct. 31, 1977; D-Nov. 15, 1978, 3.)

5. Minutes, G-May 28, 1959, 2; D-Mar. 16, 1964; D-Feb. 15, 1973, 2.

6. Minutes, D-Feb. 15, 1973, 2. Presales helped shorten ticket lines, but, to reduce crowds as well as increase revenue, gate tickets went from $1.50 in 1967 to $6 by 1990. (Minutes, D-Feb. 20, 1967, 2; D-Nov. 16, 1983, 2; D-Sept. 19, 1990, 3.)

7. Minutes, D-Jul. 17, 1974.

8. Loydean Thomas, "Fiesta revenues finally made public," *San Antonio Express-News*, May 2, 1995, 1-A.

9. The homes tour nets the South Carolina foundation approximately $325,000 and the annual gala of the Landmarks Conservancy of New York City some $300,000 for historic preservation causes each year. Other groups, however, rely more extensively on private fund-raising than does the Conservation Society. New York's Landmarks Conservancy, for one, raises $2 million annually through smaller fund-raising events (which bring in another $100,000), individual gifts and foundation and corporate grants. (Landmarks Conservancy of New York City President Peg Breen to Lewis F. Fisher, telephone interview, Jun. 12, 1995; Becky Guerard, Historic Charleston Foundation, to Lewis F. Fisher, telephone interview, Jun. 16, 1995.)

10. Minutes, D-Mar. 21, 1960; D-Apr. 4, 1960, 2; D-Apr. 9, 1986, 2. "Flower fluffers" make some 17,000 crepe paper flowers each year, enough to decorate NIOSA an extra time in case of rain.

11. Conveying a feel of the city's multi-cultural heritage remains the event's official purpose. (Minutes, D-Aug. 16, 1978, 3.)

12. Sydney Rubin, "Artist designs NIOSA tribute," *San Antonio Express-News*, Apr. 7, 1983. Mrs. Shelton was also a long-time worker in the NIOSA booth selling hand-painted paper bags.

13. Minutes, D-Feb. 24, 1948.

14. Mrs. Jules Fontaine OHT, Jun. 29, 1971, 13.

15. Minutes, D-Feb. 25, 1947, 2; G-Feb. 27, 1947.

16. Minutes, G-Mar. 26, 1953, 2.

17. Juana Hammer OHT, Sept. 15, 1990, 21.

18. Minutes, G-Mar. 26, 1953, 2.

19. Ibid.

20. Esther MacMillan OHT, Oct. 8, 1992, 12–13.

21. They have been made by Mary Ashley Culp, her daughter Anita Culp Daniel, granddaughter Lynn Daniel Specia and great-granddaughter Arden Specia.

22. Glory Felder OHT, Oct. 15, 1992, 16–17.

23. MacMillan OHT, Oct. 8, 1992, 12–13.

24. Karin Metz, "Anticuchos go on sale for 26th year," *North San Antonio Times Fiesta '79*, Apr. 26, 1979, 7.

25. Mary M. Fisher, "NIOSA anticuchos her claim to fame," *North San Antonio Times*, Apr. 14, 1988, 10.

26. Metz, "Anticuchos go on sale for 26th year."

27. Ibid.

28. Louise Reischling OHT, Jun. 8, 1994, 3–6.

29. Nelle Lee Weincek OHT, Feb. 12, 1987, 15.

30. Reischling OHT, 5.

31. Ibid., 6–7.

32. Ibid.

33. Reischling OHT, 6. A sopaipilla is similar to a French beignet.

34. "Stocking Larders is a Full-Scale Effort," SACS news release, 1995.

35. Mary M. Fisher, "NIOSA chairman hits ground running," *North San Antonio Times*, Apr. 16, 1992, 10; Jacque Crouse, "Stockpile is growing in anticipation of Night In Old San Antonio nibbling," *San Antonio Express-News*, Apr. 19, 1995.

36. Mary M. Fisher, "NIOSA chairman hits ground running."

37. Mrs. Charles R. Hammer OHT, Sept. 15, 1990, 4.

38. Felder OHT, 17.

39. "A Night In Old San Antonio Area Fact Sheet," SACS, 1995.

40. Ibid.; Marlene Gordon, NIOSA glossary, *North San Antonio Times*, Apr. 15, 1982, 5.

41. René Lynn, "Snow cone seller loves her colorful Fiesta job," *Northeast Recorder-Times*, Apr. 14, 1988, 3.

42. Barbara Ryan, "Palm reader finds her task to be a science," *North San Antonio Times Fiesta '86*, Apr. 24, 1986.

43. René Lynn, "Fiesta organizer schedules fun Fiesta entertainment," *Northwest Recorder-Times*, Apr. 11, 1985.

44. Mary M. Fisher, "NIOSA chairman hits ground running."

45. Barbara Ryan, "Fire extinguishers big deal at NIOSA," *North San Antonio Times Fiesta '86*, Apr. 24, 1986, 5.

46. MacMillan OHT, 12–13.

47. Mary M. Fisher, "NIOSA chairman hits ground running."

48. Jacque Crouse, "NIOSA ticket scam loss is at least $14,000," *San Antonio News*, Apr. 27, 1982, 5-A.

49. Minnie Campbell OHT, May 12, 1991, 24.

50. Peggy S. McCaskill (Foerster), "Weatherman, model always under the lights," *Recorder-Times*, Apr. 26, 1990, 4. NBC Today Show weatherman Willard Scott broadcast live from the Arneson River Theater during two days of NIOSA in 1983. (Lynn Osborne Bobbitt, "President's Report," *SACS Newsletter*, May–Jun. 1983, 2.)

51. Beverly Blount (-Hemphill) OHT, Aug. 28, 1990, 2.

52. Janet Francis OHT, Apr. 12, 1993, 2–3.

53. NIOSITA, too, became a registered trademark. NIOSITAs in 1978 included Lloyd's of London (50–75 persons), National Water Resources (1,000), Mission Chevrolet (50–60) and Wholesale Beer Distributors (750). H.B. Zachry Construction was a repeat customer for its more than 1,000 employees. In 1993 the American Waterworks Association guaranteed 5,300 persons at $40 each, plus drinks. By being run by volunteers, NIOSITAs maintained 40 percent profit margins. Profits of nearly $15,000 for a national convention in 1977 boosted NIOSITA profits that fiscal year to more than $45,000. They reached more than twice that amount six years later. (Minutes, D-Jul. 20, 1977, 3; D-Jul. 19, 1978, 4; D-Aug. 16, 1978, 3; D-Nov. 16, 1983, 2; D-Jan. 18, 1984, 3; D-Apr. 14, 1993, 2,4.)

54. Minutes, D-May 20, 1968.

55. Minutes, G-Sept. 28, 1968, 1–2.

56. Betty Murray OHT, 4–5.

57. Ibid. Mrs. Murray credits the American Folklife Festival with inspiring the Texas Folklife Festival, sponsored in San Antonio each August since 1972 by the University of Texas at San Antonio's Institute of Texan Cultures.

58. With the expressway controversy behind it, the society was receiving new associate membership applications at a rate as high as 30 a month. Texas Under Six Flags tours each March grew as well, from 883 students in 1962 to, ten years later, 3,153 students, coming in 51 buses from 28 schools. In 1993, two years after the name of the Six Flags tours was changed to Heritage Education Tours, 4,916 students and teachers from 48 schools were guided by 35 society-trained guides on 92 buses to San Antonio landmarks. (Minutes, D-Feb. 24, 1972; F-Oct. 9, 1991, 1–2; D-Mar. 17, 1993, 2–3.)

59. Minutes, D-Mar. 19, 1962, 4; D-Apr. 7, 1962, 2; D-Mar. 15, 1973, 2. Working with volunteers at Wulff House headquarters are nine paid full-time staff members, including architect Ron Bauml, who serves as properties restoration manager. There are two full-time paid staff members at NIOSA headquarters in La Villita.

60. Minutes, D-May 5, 1976.

61. Minutes, D-Nov. 20, 1969, 7; D-Mar. 23, 1970, 3–4; D-Apr. 13, 1970, 2–3; F-May 21, 1970; G-May 28, 1970; G-Sept. 24, 1970, 2. Properties transferred included the Old San Antonio Exhibit, the society's accumulated memorabilia operated as a museum under the untiring supervision of Kay Hart, its curator. It moved from Casa Villita to Conservation Corner in 1957 and was opened to the public. In 1968 it moved to Bolivar Hall in space rented from the city, but with costs still high and amid continuing complaints of "clutter" it was later closed. The Steves Homestead required constant attention, such as to the ten leaks in the roof discovered one December. In four summer months in 1961 volunteers showed 2,581 persons through the house, which by the next year was open daily. Behind the Steves Homestead, River House, meeting place for directors' and general membership meetings since 1953, got a $40,000-plus renovation beginning in 1969. (Minutes, D-Sept. 25, 1961, 2; E-Jul. 13, 1962; G-Dec. 11, 1969; D-Aug. 24, 1973.)

62. Minutes, D-Jun. 25, 1962, 3; E-Feb. 29, 1968; D-Mar. 23, 1970, 4.

63. Minutes, D-Jul. 11, 1968; D-Mar. 23, 1970, 4–5; D-Apr. 13, 1970, 3; D-Jun. 22, 1970, 2. Three years later the job got a substantial raise, but only by a vote of 15 to 14. (Minutes, D-Jun. 21, 1973.)

64. Minutes, D-Aug. 18, 1976, 3.

65. Minutes, D-Apr. 13, 1970, 3; D-Aug. 18, 1976, 3; D-Feb. 20, 1980, 2; D-Aug. 20, 1980; D-Sept. 16, 1981, 2; D-May 19, 1982, 4; D-Jun. 16, 1982; D-Feb. 18, 1987, 2; D-Mar. 21, 1990, 2; D-Apr. 11, 1990, 5–6.

66. In 1992–93 MacDougal was a member of President-elect Bill Clinton's transition team for preservation and neighborhood issues.

67. "Planning director names new preservation officer," *San Antonio Express-News,* Jun. 10, 1993.

68. Minutes, G-Jan. 27, 1993; Susie Phillips Gonzalez, "Council accepts $100,000 donation," *San Antonio Express-News,* Apr. 9, 1993, 1-D.

69. David Anthony Richelieu, "Waging a historic battle," *San Antonio Express-News,* Apr. 3, 1990, 10-B. During the previous year, the Historic Preservation Office staffed the Historic Review Board's public hearings, committee meetings and regular semi-monthly meetings, handling 452 cases involving 264 commercial properties and

181 residences. The office also oversaw the city's historic properties, as required by terms of several major federal grants.

70. Minutes, D-Mar. 21, 1990, 1–2; D-May 16, 1990, 3–4; D-Jun. 20, 1990, 1–2. The Conservation Society provided $5,000 and the King William Association came up with a like amount. The Conservation Society again gave $5,000 in each of the next two years. Four years earlier the society donated $1,500 so the office could complete a map of the city's original acequias. The Conservation Society had also spent $6,000 for a professional survey of downtown landmarks and the acequia system. (Minutes, D-Sept. 17, 1980, 2; D-Jan. 15, 1986, 2; D-Dec. 11, 1991, 1–2; D-Oct. 21, 1992, 2.)

71. Susie Phillips Gonzalez, "Council accepts $100,000 donation;" Susie Phillips Gonzalez, "Conservation group to beef up preservation office," *San Antonio Express-News*, Apr. 10, 1993, 3-B; Minutes, D-Mar. 17, 1993, 2; D-Jul. 21, 1993, 7. To eliminate any conflict of interest, the Conservation Society agreed the money would be paid even if the historic preservation officer made a recommendation disputed by the society, in a deal that was similar to the recent $500,000 challenge grant accepted by the city from the San Antonio Public Library Foundation toward a new public library. Things did not go as well with Bexar County. In 1992 the Conservation Society offered county commissioners a challenge grant of $15,000 to fill the vacant post of County Archivist. After nearly three years of discussions, the society agreed that the archivist could be shared by district and county clerks, and a job search went forward. (Minutes, D-Nov. 18, 1992, 3; D-Jun. 9, 1993, 2; D-Nov. 17, 1993; D-Jun. 15, 1994, 2; D-Mar. 15, 1995, 5.)

72. Minutes, D-Jun. 21, 1995; "UTSA To Offer Graduate Degree in Architecture," *Ovations*, The University of Texas at San Antonio, September 1995. In other academic efforts, in 1971 the society established a $1,000 Texas Historical Resources Fellowship, soon $1,500, administered by the Texas Architectural Foundation and later renamed in memory of architect Brooks Martin. The first went to University of Texas at Austin architectural student David Hoffman, who measured and prepared drawings of 12 historic buildings in Roma, Texas. In 1993, a UTSA class was given funding to document local historic structures and a planning began for a local public school curriculum on the built environment. Also in 1993, Heritage Tour training for 75 teachers was funded at St. Philip's College. (Minutes, D-Oct. 19, 1970, 3; D-Mar. 22, 1971; D-May 24, 1971; G-Sept. 27, 1973; F-Jun. 9, 1993, 5; D-Jul. 21, 1993, 5; F-Aug. 18, 1993, 2; D-Jan. 19, 1994, 3.)

73. Minutes, D-Jan. 25, 1971, 4–5. The event, during National Historic Preservation Week, was in the newly vacated Vogel Belt Building prior to the society's annual awards dinner, in the chapel of the old Ursuline Academy. Seminar leaders reflected the growing breadth of the preservation movement. The morning session, moderated by Texas Historical Survey Committee Director Truett Lattimer, dealt with adaptive reuse of historic structures. Speakers ranged from Urban Renewal Agency Director Winston Martin to University of Texas School of Business Dean George Kotzmetsky to Robert Stipe of the University of North Carolina Institute of Government. The afternoon session, moderated by Chamber of Commerce President Frank Bennack, was on financing and governmental codes. It featured State Rep. R.B. McAllister, chairman of the Texas House Speaker's Special Committee on Historic Preservation,

followed by a panel with several morning speakers. While preservation awards continued to be an annual feature of Historic Preservation Week, annual Texana publication awards became a Founder's Day event in 1979.

74. "Preservation Action," membership promotion brochure, 1974; Minutes, D-Sept. 21, 1983; D-Feb. 15, 1984. Other founding officers were Arthur Ziegler, president of the Pittsburgh History and Landmarks Foundation; J. Reid Williamson, executive director of the Historic Landmarks Foundation of Indiana; Leopold Adler II of Historic Savannah; and St. Clair Wright, president of Historic Annapolis.

75. Wulff, a commissions merchant, held the parks post from 1875 to 1885 and was responsible for laying out Alamo Plaza. ("Conservation Society finishes new home," *North San Antonio Times*, Oct. 16, 1975, 1.)

76. Minutes, D-May 25, 1964, 2; D-Jun. 22, 1964, 2; D-Sept. 1, 1964, 2; D-Feb. 22, 1965.

77. Minutes, D-Jan. 17, 1974, 3; D-Jun. 19, 1974.

78. Minutes, D-Jan. 17, 1974, 3; D-Feb. 21, 1974, 3; D-May 25, 1975; D-Oct. 20, 1976; "Conservation Society finishes new home," *North San Antonio Times*. An archeological dig was conducted beneath the adjoining parking lot on the site of the Mayer House, razed earlier for the widening of Durango Boulevard and South St. Mary's Street.

79. Minutes, F-May 16, 1974; F-Jun. 19, 1974; D-Jul. 17, 1974; D-Nov. 20, 1974; G-Mar. 26, 1975, 3; F-Jun. 15, 1977; F-Aug. 31, 1977. The library was organized in the 1970s from "corrugated boxes and one wooden shelf" by Alice Louise (Mrs. Eryle G.) Johnson. It was renovated and expanded in 1988 in part through a gift from Floy Fontaine Jordan in memory of her aunt, Emily Edwards. Helping establish the archives was $10,000 from the Ewing Halsell Foundation. In 1994 planning began to locate the library in its own building in the Wulff House vicinity. (Minutes, F-Sept. 16, 1981; F-May 18, 1988; D-Sept. 28, 1988, 2; D-May 18, 1994, 6; "San Antonio memorabilia to have Wulff House home," *North San Antonio Times*, Sept. 12, 1974.)

80. Minutes, D-Mar. 20, 1967; F-Apr. 7, 1972; D-Jul. 17, 1974, 4; D-Jan. 17, 1979; D-May 16, 1979, 4.

81. "Twenty-Seven Years of Society Posadas," *The San Antonio Conservation Society News*, Dec., 1993.

82. Minutes, D-Jan. 19, 1970, 3.

83. Minutes, D-Nov. 18, 1971, 2; D-Jun. 15, 1972, 2; D-Jan. 18, 1973, 3. *Luminarias* are candles placed in small paper sacks weighted with sand.

84. Minutes, D-Jan. 18, 1973, 3; D-Jan. 17, 1974, 2.

85. Minutes, D-Jan. 17, 1974, 2; D-Jul. 17, 1974, 3; D-Nov. 20, 1974, 3.

86. Minutes, D-Jun. 15, 1988, 2; D-Jan. 17, 1990, 2; D-Mar. 21, 1990, 2; D-Apr. 11, 1990, 2. The Conservation Society gained property owner status by accepting a minor percentage ownership in one tract in the ultimately defeated reservoir's area.

87. Minutes, D-May 15, 1991, 2.

88. Minutes, D-Mar. 18, 1992, 3. Design of a new riverfront complex including a Hard Rock Cafe was applauded, but a bridge proposed across the river at that point was not. Among other environmental and parks issues, the society gave $5,000 to the Trust for Public Land to help enlarge the new Government Canyon Park in north-

western Bexar County, strongly backed city ordinances designating major city highways as scenic corridors and regularly opposed such notions as a Corps of Engineers plan to replace a natural section of San Pedro Creek with a concrete culvert and a Southwestern Bell proposal for a 150-foot communications tower in a near-downtown neighborhood. (Minutes, D-Dec. 12, 1990, 2; D-Dec. 9, 1992, 4; D-May 19, 1993, 5–6; D-Jun. 9, 1993, 3; D-Feb. 17, 1993, 2; D-Aug. 18, 1993, 4.) Of the 30 specific-interest organizations to which the Conservation Society belongs, one-third are historically oriented state and national groups and another third target common interests in the natural environment. A similar proportion of the 41 community organizations monitored concern the environment, from the Edwards Aquifer Authority to the Salado Creek Foundation to the city's Open Space Advisory Committee. (*1994–95 Conservation Society Yearbook*, 13–14.)

89. Libby Willis, Texas/New Mexico Regional Director, National Trust for Historic Preservation, telephone interview with Lewis F. Fisher, Jun. 6, 1995.

90. Sally Buchanan OHT, May 31, 1994, 48. All chairmen of the 41 standing committees are appointed by the president and serve on the board, along with 5 other directors appointed by the president, 8 elected officers, 30 directors elected by the membership and all past presidents maintaining good board attendance. (Regardless of sex, the head of a committee is still always a "chairman," never a "chair.") Eligible to vote and hold office are active members, limited to 650 and chosen from recommended associate members who have belonged for at least two years. Given the president's ability to appoint directors, direction of the Conservation Society can change markedly every two years. (*1994–95 Conservation Society Yearbook*, 57–103.)

91. "In the Mailbox," *San Antonio Light*, Nov. 17, 1953, 22. The Texas Historical and Landmarks Society disbanded a few years after her death.

92. Minutes, G-Mar. 22, 1962.

93. Minutes, D-Mar. 22, 1965.

94. Minutes, D-Jun. 8, 1960; D-May 25, 1964. Other survivors of early days were being honored and mourned as well. Elizabeth Graham died in 1969. John M. Bennett Sr. was honored on his 95th birthday in 1973 for having signed the society charter 48 years before. Ethel Harris died in 1984 at the age of 91. Craftsman Henry C. Wedemeyer, who was present at the Conservation Society's organizational meeting, died in 1991, leaving Emily Edwards's niece, Floy Fontaine Jordan, as the last survivor of the session. (Minutes, D-Mar. 25, 1963, 2; D-Jun. 23, 1969, 1, 5; G-Mar. 22, 1973; D-Nov. 19, 1986, 2, 5–6; D-Jun. 19, 1991.)

95. Letters to the Editor, *San Antonio Express,* Nov. 7, 1978.

96. Emily Edwards to Doris Irby, Aug., 1979, in SACS Library.

15

Arsenal to Ursuline

As the national historic preservation movement grew, landmarks began to be seen not as isolated monuments but as part of a larger landscape in which the whole was greater than the sum of its parts. Preservation of landmark groupings "marked a new sophistication for the United States," noted preservation historian Charles Hosmer. "Americans were learning to define history in a new way; it was to be a part of their living environment, not merely a museum exhibit that somehow should inspire patriotism through a connection with a particular great person or event." Of the components of an historic neighborhood, "only a handful of the protected structures could serve as museum houses; the great majority added to a sense of continuity, beauty and tradition marking a settled community that had grown slowly."[1]

As America's first publicly preserved landmark outside New England and the deep South was in San Antonio, so more than a century later did establishment of the King William Historic District, first in the city and in the state, put San Antonio in the vanguard of establishing zoned historic districts outside those same regions. The King William district was formed in 1968, following passage in the fractious summer of 1967 of a city ordinance providing for historic zoning districts. The lead in passing the ordinance was taken by the independent King William Street Conservation Society, which coalesced by 1949 and shared many members with the San Antonio Conservation Society.

The King William Street neighborhood suffered from the long decline which most neighborhoods on the edges of America's downtowns also experienced. Verandas and galleries were enclosed for kitchens and bathrooms. Fire escapes cluttered deteriorating facades for the safety of tenants living in the Victorian mansions-turned-rooming houses. But there was no wholesale destruction in what had been San Antonio's most elegant neighborhood in the last quarter of the nineteenth century; San Antonio's development went

Above: The monumental cut limestone 401 King William Street home begun in 1876 by Russel Norton and added to five years later by Edward Polk was purchased in 1967 and restored by Walter N. Mathis, a year before it became a centerpiece of the state's first district protected by historic zoning. San Antonio Conservation Society.

Left above: Fire escapes and enclosed porches for apartments covered original features of many King William Street homes, including this one built by George Kalteyer in 1892, until the area became the state's first zoned historic district in 1968. Sidney J. Francis II.

Left below: Restoration revealed the Kalteyer home's original polychromed arches and other Romanesque Revival features, designed by James Riely Gordon, after the house was purchased in 1973 and restored by Sidney J. Francis II. San Antonio Conservation Society.

north of downtown rather than south. Of the fifty homes along the five-block King William Street, forty-three were judged as "contributing" to the nineteenth-century character of the street. Nearby Madison, Washington and Guenther streets—as well as others—had homes similarly significant.[2]

The core of remaining old families, determined to preserve the spirit of what survived, kept businesses away and blocked construction of a funeral home at the corner of King William and South St. Mary's streets, but permitted

In 1971, the Josiah Pancoast House was purchased by Walter Mathis and restored to its original design, which followed that of Henry Wadsworth Longfellow's home in Cambridge, Massachusetts. San Antonio Conservation Society.

The 1878 frame home built and enlarged by Josiah Pancoast had fallen into decay typical along King William Street before the area's revival. San Antonio Conservation Society.

architect O'Neil Ford to adapt an 1881 house at the end of the street as his office.[3] In a serendipitous result of the North Expressway project, in 1967 Walter N. Mathis, displaced from his home by the expressway route, purchased the rundown two-story Norton-Polk home begun in 1873 at 401 King William Street and meticulously restored the home and grounds. He also began purchasing a dozen additional decaying homes in the neighborhood, carefully restoring each and reselling most of them to individual families.

As the neighborhood pulled itself up by its bootstraps, the wheels of protective zoning ground slowly. Aided by O'Neil Ford's city planning associate Sam Zisman, by the late 1950s the City Planning Department was moving toward the historic zoning concept, with a push from newspaper editorials.[4] In 1966 the San Antonio Conservation Society officially joined the Texas State Historical Survey Committee to support forming the King William Historic District, and went on to urge making La Villita an historic district as well.[5] An ordinance to permit such districts passed city council in 1967. The next year the King William Area Conservation Society and the San Antonio Conservation Society jointly applied for a King William Street Historic District designation, and residents' petitions followed. On May 9, 1968, its boundaries were approved by city council by a vote of seven to one.[6]

La Villita was approved in October of 1969 as the city's second historic district, with the help of one of its few private landowners, the San Antonio Conservation Society.[7] In 1975, at the society's continued urging, La Villita Historic District boundaries were expanded to include the west side of South Presa Street.[8]

A longtime target of La Villita expansionists had been the obsolete power plant of the City Public Service Board beside the river at the northeast corner of Villita and South Presa streets, at the western entrance to La Villita. It was seen as a natural site for a badly needed convention facility. In 1956 O'Neil Ford designed for the utility company not a domed convention building which would dominate the area but a two-level, 25,000 square-foot circular, flat-roofed brick building eliminating the obstructing corner of the street and not competing with the smaller, square buildings of La Villita itself.[9] Villita Assembly Hall opened in the spring of 1959.

Extension of the HemisFair urban renewal area across South Alamo Street became the biggest boon to La Villita since its initial restoration in 1939. It was supervised by architect William Parrish and financed by the City Parks Department and by federal urban renewal funds. The original area of La Villita around Juarez Plaza was more than doubled in size, extending south past Bolivar Hall to Nueva Street and east to the newly widened South Alamo Street, taking in, across Villita Street from Conservation Corner, the two-story limestone building built in 1854 by F.W. McAllister, grandfather of the mayor.[10]

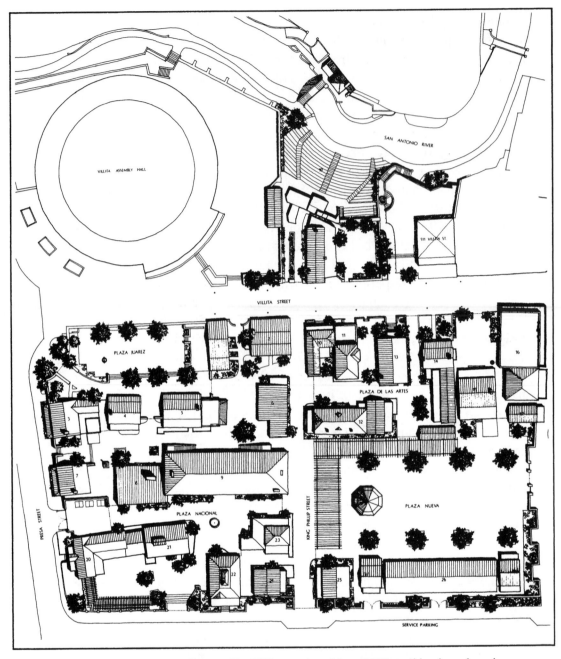

Expansion of restored areas of La Villita continued from 1939 until land purchases in conjunction with the 1968 HemisFair urban renewal project to the east added Plaza Nueva—renamed Maverick Plaza—and a section nearby. Associated Architects, Saldana Williams & Schubert, Ford, Powell & Carson Inc.

Villita Street became the long-sought pedestrian mall.[11] Curbs were eliminated and eighteen "Georgetown-style" mercury vapor lamps were installed along what was renamed Paseo de La Villita.[12] Fulfilling HemisFair urban renewal area goals, La Villita was expanded to fill the remainder of the city block. At its southeast corner, latter-day commercial buildings were cleared to form Nueva Plaza, renamed Maverick Plaza in 1984 in memory of the mayor who rescued La Villita nearly a half century earlier. A smaller area nearby was named O'Neil Ford Plaza in honor of La Villita's initial restoration architect. At the western edge of Nueva/Maverick Plaza, concrete block walls enclosing the rambling Joy Kist Candy Company building were thought to envelop three nineteenth century brick and frame homes. When stripped away they revealed five old homes, all then restored. The *palisado* Gissy House was brought from HemisFair Plaza and rebuilt at one corner, as promised. But the numbered stone blocks of the Frederick Groos House did not rise from their heap to be reassembled. After many were found to be broken or missing, there seemed nothing to do but haul the rest away.[13]

Included in the urban renewal expansion area was the area enclosed by South Alamo and Presa streets and, on the north and south, by Nueva Street and Durango Boulevard. It was divided into two blocks by the east-west Arciniega Street. In the block north of Arciniega Street was the first complex to be restored, the old German-English School, which became HemisFair headquarters and then office space for the City Planning Department. In the block south of Arciniega, three old homes were restored when the block was sold by the city for the 250-room Four Seasons Plaza Nacional Hotel. Opened in 1979, it was the first major new downtown hotel since the Hilton Palacio del Rio.[14]

Expanding the La Villita Historic District to include the western side of South Presa Street and to meet the King William district did not help the Conservation Society in its fifteen years of tortuous maneuverings with owners of two vintage homes in the newly added area.[15] The more significant target was the Manuel Yturri House at 337 South Presa Street, owned by a family of descendants of its original owner. The two-story portion at the rear dated from as early as 1817. Its one-story brick front, with distinctive Victorian gingerbread work, was an 1891 addition attributed to architect Alfred Giles.[16] After several years of working unsuccessfully with two brothers for the home's preservation, a sister in 1976 sold the Conservation Society her five percent interest for $5,000.[17] An appraisal put its value at $70,000, which the society offered the brothers. They refused, countering with a price of $240,000, or $15,000 for the society's interest. They filed for a demolition permit and began demolition.[18]

The Conservation Society and the City Preservation Officer got a restraining order on further destruction. But the order was set aside, and negotiations

The vacant 1811 Elmendorf-Taylor/Arciniega house stood at risk south of the La Villita restoration for more than a decade. San Antonio Conservation Society.

A swimming pool replaced the hard soil behind the Elmendorf-Taylor/Arciniega home after the block was purchased in 1979 for the Four Seasons/Plaza San Antonio Hotel, which incorporated that old home and two others nearby as dining or meeting facilities on the grounds. Lewis F. Fisher.

resumed.[19] In the spring of 1979 the case was postponed until summer, and the society was permitted to clean up the property.[20] On the basis of its minority ownership the society filed suit, but a judge in 1981 ordered the society to sell its interest back to the family, which still held the remaining ninety-five percent.[21] The family refused purchase offers and sued the society for $400,000 in damages.[22] As time passed, the landmark was further damaged by three fires, one of them conclusively ruled arson.[23] In 1987, all legal blockades exhausted, the ruins of the home were leveled to become a parking lot.[24]

The next historic district to be approved was a sixty-block area beyond the northern edge of downtown, the last of San Antonio's Gilded Age neighborhoods to retain its architectural integrity.[25] Sisters Emily Denman (Mrs. Charles) Thuss and Molly Denman (Mrs. James L.) Branton joined forces with Trinity University Professor Donald E. Everett and Conservation Society Administrative Director Conrad True after the old Denman family home on West French Place was razed and its spacious grounds filled with an apartment complex.[26] When nearly two years of efforts and the signatures of 1,600 property owners overcame protests and the Monte Vista Historic District gained the unanimous support of the city's Planning and Zoning Commission, "cheers and a standing ovation from an ecstatic group of Monte Vista residents broke order in the overflowing city hall council room . . . ."[27] City council two months later agreed with the Planning and Zoning Commission by a vote of 7-1.[28]

While the Monte Vista Historic District, like King William before it, was formed primarily through the efforts of its own residents, downtown areas like La Villita and the thirteen-block Main and Military Plaza Historic District, also approved in 1975, required coordinated support from public and private sectors. The dozens of persons and officials who presented the case for Main and Military plazas reflected months of work by the Conservation Society, Historic Preservation Officer Pat Osborne, the Chamber of Commerce, the Texas Historical Commission, the local chapter of the American Institute of Architects and a host of other groups and individuals who steered the proposal through a gauntlet of property owners and business and church interests.[29]

Compromise became a well-honed skill of preservationists. One hurdle for the Main and Military Plaza District was overcome when San Antonio Savings Association President Walter W. McAllister III, whose headquarters building overlooked Main Plaza from the north, withdrew his protest in return for the Conservation Society's agreement not to oppose SASA's demolition on the east side of the plaza of two historic buildings stripped and rendered unusable by a previous owner.[30] South of the Governor's Palace, the Vogel Belt Building complex, once earmarked for demolition, was restored for city offices. The former Frost Bank building, its refurbished lobby then a Luby's

The "Sold" sign was good news for the row of late nineteenth century buildings adjoining the Spanish Governor's Palace on the west side of Military Plaza, once scheduled for demolition. San Antonio Conservation Society.

Buildings on the west side of Military Plaza across from city hall were purchased by the city in 1979 and restored for city offices. San Antonio Conservation Society.

The apse of the original mid-1700s San Fernando Cathedral was surrounded by a later addition at the rear of the cathedral. The Institute of Texan Cultures, San Antonio, Texas, courtesy Ann Russell.

Restoration of San Fernando Cathedral in 1971 included tearing off additions around the original Spanish apse and restoring it. San Antonio Conservation Society.

The three-story building built by merchant George Dullnig had elaborate cupolas on two corners and, on the southeast corner of Commerce and South Alamo Streets, the entrance to the Fifth National Bank. San Antonio Conservation Society.

With the widening of South Alamo Street about 1913, the Dullnig Building lost its east tower and corner entrance. San Antonio Conservation Society.

By the 1970s, minus both towers and apparently almost everything else, judging from the new facades and white paint, the Dullnig Building was ready to become a parking lot. San Antonio Express-News.

In a last-minute rescue, the Duncan-Smith Company purchased and restored the Dullnig Building, which reopened in 1981. A painted cornice substitutes for the original. San Antonio Conservation Society.

By 1980, the original second-floor iron balcony grillwork was the last shred of dignity for the Albert Maverick Building (1881), the oldest downtown building surviving on Houston Street. San Antonio Conservation Society.

Cafeteria, was purchased by the city for offices and renamed the Municipal Plaza Building.[31] Preservationists withdrew objections to demolition of two 1860s buildings west of the courthouse to permit a $7.1 million Bexar County administration building and parking garage.[32] San Fernando Cathedral was restored to reveal its original Spanish-built apse, and Trevino Street beside it was changed to a stone-paved, tree-lined walkway.

On the other side of the old Spanish city, of the fourteen nineteenth-century structures in the Alamo Plaza Historic District, formed in 1978, two were in need of quick rescue. Clearance for HemisFair of commercial buildings on the south side of the intersection of Commerce and South Alamo streets left the three-story Dullnig Building as the dominant surviving structure on the intersection's northwest corner. Built in 1883 for Austrian immigrant grocer George Dullnig, its facade was covered by false fronts, stucco and white paint which even blanked out the windows.[33] In 1976 the building's owners thought the site better suited for a parking lot, and applied for a demolition permit. But the city already had a temporary freeze on downtown demolition pending redevelopment planning, and, with support of the Conservation Society, turned the application down.[34] Nearly two years later, when the freeze expired, city council turned down a renewed request for demolition.[35]

After tenuous negotiations, the Albert Maverick Building was kept from becoming a parking lot and was restored in 1983, its elaborate cornice replicated in fiberglass. San Antonio Conservation Society.

Extended negotiations by the Conservation Society, however, resulted in the building's purchase by Duncan-Smith, an investment banking company, which began restoration. Old facades and coverings came off, revealing deep-red brick walls and ornate window treatments. Fiberglass reproduced details on cornices and capitals of cast-iron columns. In place of reconstructing the elaborate roof cornice, a stenciled representation was painted in its place. When completed in 1981, fast-food franchises jumped at the opportunity for the location—including McDonald's, its golden arches discreetly cast on signs conservatively mounted above street-level windows.[36]

Equally dramatic was the rescue at another corner of the Alamo Plaza Historic District of the two-story limestone block 1881 Albert Maverick Building, oldest downtown building remaining on East Houston Street.[37] Long shorn of its exuberant pediment, the 11,000 square-foot structure's original exterior retained only the small iron balconies at its second-floor windows. Worse, the building stood beside the six-story New Moore Building, built in 1904 at the corner of Houston Street and Broadway. In 1982 both buildings were purchased by Williams Realty Corporation of Tulsa,

Oklahoma, an investment firm which saw the Albert Maverick Building as an ideal site for Moore Building construction equipment and then for parking. The Historic Review Board granted a demolition permit.[38]

The Conservation Society twice submitted earnest money contracts to purchase the building for $275,000. Society President Lynn Osborne (Mrs. Calhoun) Bobbitt, developer Arthur "Hap" Veltman and attorney Lewis Tarver flew to Oklahoma City to meet with the owners, but both contracts were rejected.[39] With the city's Conservation Society-inspired Historic Structures Task Force beginning its review and recommendations in the wake of the Texas Theater debacle, however, city council backed preservationists and twice unanimously rejected demolition requests. That brought the Oklahomans to heel.[40] Both Williams Realty and the Conservation Society agreed to choose from a list of independent appraisers and to accept that appraisal as the price of the sale, made to developers who replicated the building's original pediment with fiberglass in their $500,000 restoration.[41] Williams Realty restored the New Moore Building, renamed 110 Broadway, to its original splendor in a $10 million project, which included stripping layers of white paint to reveal a beige brick facade with terra cotta ornamentation. In the ceremony marking its completion, Mayor Henry Cisneros was joined by Michael Ainslie, president of the National Trust for Historic Preservation.[42]

Two more historic districts were formed in cooperation with the San Antonio Development Agency in deteriorating commercial districts around turn-of-the-century railroad stations on either side of downtown. To the east, in 1978, the St. Paul Square Historic District was formed over thirty-six acres anchored by the 1902 Mission Revival style Southern Pacific Depot, still used by Amtrak. The district was named for the 1870s former St. Paul United Methodist Church. This was the entertainment center for the city's black community in the 1950s. With railroad passenger traffic virtually gone and the area cut off from the rest of downtown by Interstate 37, it was ripe for change.[43]

With federal funds available in 1975, however, the script did not follow urban renewal of the previous decade. Trying to escape the burden of its old image, the Urban Renewal Agency even changed its name, to the San Antonio Development Agency. Now the agency bought sixteen buildings on six acres and sought rehabilitation by new owners, who with help from a Chamber of Commerce Task force formed an historic district and gained tax deductions.[44] By 1979 more than $3.8 million in public funds were invested in St. Paul Square, encouraging an additional $3.5 million investment nearby in the Conservation Society-inspired renovation of the old San Antonio Machine and Supply Company building as a state office building.[45]

Similarly isolated on the opposite side of downtown, in this case by Interstate 10, was an area that finally came together as Cattleman Square,

A copper Indian shooting an arrow atop the former International & Great Northern/Missouri Pacific railroad depot's dome remains a neighborhood symbol in the Cattleman Square Historic District since the building's preservation in 1985. San Antonio Conservation Society.

named for its role as an embarkation point of the Chisolm Trail.[46] In 1985 five businessmen formed the Cattleman Square Association and, with the backing of the Mexican-American Unity Council, helped fund a feasibility study leading to the area's designation as an historic district in 1988.[47] As St. Paul Square centered around a railroad depot, so did Cattleman Square. Its deserted 1907 Mission Revival International and Great Northern/Missouri Pacific Depot had a copper Indian shooting an arrow atop its copper-sheathed cupola. The station was purchased in 1985 and rehabilitated as headquarters of the City Employees Credit Union in a $3.2 million project.[48] Nearby, the century-old Tellerico Building, lately Los Buddies Lounge, was restored and expanded as the $3 million headquarters of the Alamo Community College District.[49] Far to the west, the Tranchese Center on Guadalupe Avenida was

Downtown development was approaching the site of the historic Ursuline Academy when, in 1953, members of the Ursuline Order decided to sell. The academy's four acres, shown at lower left center looking northeast in 1959, were surrounded on three sides by streets and on the fourth by the San Antonio River. Dominating the complex of Gothic Revival buildings is a four-story classroom building. At lower right is the new National Bank of Commerce Building, the only major downtown building built between the Depression and HemisFair. At top right of center is Municipal Auditorium. Zintgraff Collection, The Institute of Texan Cultures.

also restored.[50] Near Woodlawn Lake, the four-story, twenty-six room house designed by James Riely Gordon in 1889 as the Protestant Home for Destitute Children was privately rescued and restored by John and Cecilia Forres.[51]

As historic district designations began to protect areas of landmarks under multiple ownership, by 1970 the San Antonio Conservation Society was seeking to preserve four historic landmark groupings on properties under single ownership: the old Ursuline Academy; HemisFair Plaza, the third historic district formed in 1975; the United States Arsenal; and Fort Sam Houston. A tentative private-public partnership developed between the Conservation Society and city officials on one of these, among the society's most ambitious and complicated projects to date—preservation of the original Ursuline Academy complex.

The San Antonio Conservation Society's ten-year odyssey of involvement at the old Ursuline Academy would prove practically as twisting and unpredictable as the society's earlier pursuit of the preservation of the San José Mission complex. There would be similar elements of disaster—fire, rather than collapse of a tower; of shady characters—a charlatan, rather than a bootlegger; and of piecemeal land acquisitions, likewise viewed as dubious by hardened businessmen. Too, there were bizarre property lines, anxious fund-raising appeals after the purchase, volunteer clean-up teams and help from the Catholic hierarchy.

In 1953, word was out that the Ursuline order of nuns planned to abandon its historic complex along the San Antonio River on the northwestern edge of downtown to build a new campus on the then-suburban fringe of northern San Antonio.[52] The order had occupied the site since founding sisters arrived from the Ursuline convent in New Orleans and opened a school for girls in 1851. The complex formed one of the finest landmark groupings in the city. Primarily in a unique Gothic Revival ecclesiastical style, they ranged from the plain but well-proportioned two-story first academy building of 1851 to the two-story dormitory of 1866, the 1870 chapel, 1882 Priests' House and the four-story classroom building of 1910–12. Beside the river at the opposite end of the property stood a one-and-a-half-story plain rock building with a narrow ell. Built in the 1850s, it was renovated in 1910 as a laundry building.[53] Beyond its architectural significance, the Ursuline Academy held great senti-mental value for Conservation Society members as well. When the Mother Superior invited the society to meet at the academy in 1934, so many members reminisced about their student days there that it was "like a happy alumni meeting."[54]

The academy's 4.3-acre site had been eyed for other development as early as 1929, when it was one of seven sites considered for a new post office and federal building.[55] With developers stirring once again, withdrawal of the Ursuline sisters from the location was bound to create new speculation. Wanda Ford told society directors in 1953 she had learned that the price for the property was $2.5 million. She was already seeking potential buyers who might save the buildings.[56]

When plans were announced in 1961 for a 300-room, twenty-one-story luxury apartment complex on the site, the Conservation Society sent the developer a resolution requesting assurance that the Jules Poinsard stone house on the site would in fact be saved, as the developer had informally indicated he would do.[57] The developer, honored by the Conservation Society at a dinner at the Menger Hotel, announced that his redesigned Poinsard Square complex would also preserve "most of the historic buildings" on the site and also provide an office for the Conservation Society.[58]

However, the developer, a dentist from Washington, D.C., was sentenced to two years in federal prison on charges of fraud, leaving San Antonio associates in the lurch.[59] His plans were picked up by Dallas-based investors who, rather than promising to preserve all historic structures, gave the Conservation Society a one-year option on part of the property contingent on their completion of the purchase.[60] As expiration of the option drew near, the society negotiated a price of $250,000 for 37,000 square feet of property, including the Ursuline chapel and part of the adjoining 1866 dormitory building crowned by the clock tower plus the Poinsard House, Priests' House and fifty feet of river frontage.[61]

Directors termed the intensive week of March 1, 1965 "The Week of the Ursuline." On Tuesday, the Conservation Society's executive committee met on the nineteenth floor of the National Bank of Commerce Building, where members could get a good perspective of the Ursuline below. On Wednesday, the executive committee and the Ursuline committee toured buildings on the site with architects and an engineer and concluded that the former laundry building at the east end had to be included in their purchase.[62] On Thursday morning, Society President Lillian Maverick Padgitt and the executive committee agreed to make an offer. It was presented at three that afternoon. At four, society members met with the sellers' representative for more discussion of the contract, which he finally accepted. It was signed the next day.[63]

At this point the situation began to unravel, not to be resolved for another six months. Not all investors would agree to the terms accepted by their local representative. Two investors, Thomas Stanley and Link Cowen, asked that the terms be changed. They said they could sell only portions of dormitory and academy buildings, which would require new walls to be built to close the buildings once the ends were torn off. But they would, in return, sell an additional fifty feet of river frontage. After negotiating for an additional ten feet, two society committees agreed, only to have their decision overruled four days later when the board of directors, by a vote of 17-14 with 5 abstentions, decided to hold fast to the original agreement.[64]

By now the society's original contract technically had expired. But its existence, thought the society's attorney, still clouded the title. The Tobin Foundation warned the society that its commitment for a contribution would also soon expire. And the developers' own contract with the Ursuline sisters was about to expire as well, complicated by the withdrawal of all investors except Link Cowen. However, after a series of negotiations between the society and various representatives, the original deal went through after all, minus portions of the two dormitory buildings.[65] The sisters changed their mind about taking the clock tower and offered it to the Conservation Society for $2,000. Donors provided the funds, although the society still did not own the building beneath the clock.[66]

In a ceremony and open house at the old academy on the afternoon of October 24, 1965, Bexar County Historical Survey Committee Chairman Henry Guerra unveiled an historical marker and the Ursulines' Rev. Mother Mary Joseph formally presented the keys to Peggy Tobin, the Conservation Society's new president.[67] The "real transfer" of keys took place on a different afternoon. Remembered Mrs. Tobin: "I drove downtown—probably with

In the complicated piecemeal purchase of the Ursuline Academy property, the San Antonio Conservation Society and the Southwest Craft Center bought all of some buildings and portions of others. In 1965 the Conservation Society purchased the academy's clock tower, although it did not yet own the building beneath, shown during later restoration. Ford, Powell & Carson Inc., photo: Rick Gardner.

kids in the back of the car—to meet Rev. Mother Mary Joseph, who was loading a station wagon with such household chattel as brooms, mops and cans of Ajax, literally moving [the order] out of the convent after more than a century. She wiped her hands on her apron and handed me a heavy, clanking ring of keys. It was a very poignant moment, the only true moment in Texas history of which I was a part."[68]

Ownership of the main portion of the Ursuline property was only the beginning. Estimates of restoration cost had already been placed at $500,000.[69] Eight months after the purchase, donations averaging $1,000 a month plus a few larger gifts helped reduce the $200,000 note to $155,000.[70] Selling symbolic property deeds at one dollar per square inch brought in more than $1,100.[71] Tenants for the buildings were also being sought.[72] An art gallery was proposed.[73]

Adding urgency to the situation was the difficulty in guarding the derelict complex, which the society had to continually resecure to keep out transients.[74] "It was a maze," remembered Nelle Lee Weincek, the society officer in charge of keeping an eye on the property and seeing that it stayed boarded up. "Really, you could get lost in that place. You have never . . . outside of a locksmith shop seen so many keys. Boxes and boxes and boxes of keys!"[75] "Ursel," the young German Shepherd guard dog stationed on the site by the Conservation Society, was stolen, and his brother had to be donated as a replacement.[76]

Despite all efforts, vagrants trying to keep warm were suspected as the cause of a spectacular five-alarm fire which destroyed Cowen's four-story 1910-12 wing of the academy in mid-February of 1967. Miraculously, the adjacent historic buildings were saved. Peggy Tobin presented two fire chiefs with a special historic preservation award for their successful efforts in supervising thirty-five companies of 275 firemen, who used three million gallons of water to fight the blaze.[77]

Then Cowen put his 151,361 square feet of Ursuline property up for sale for some $10 a foot, or $1,057,000.[78] Beleaguered by fund-raising to restore the Ursuline property it already owned and by burgeoning controversies over the North Expressway, HemisFair and the tax situation, the Conservation Society was anxious to find others who could make good use of the buildings.[79] The San Antonio Housing Authority wanted to discuss housing the elderly.[80] But as time went on, the Conservation Society reconsidered buying the remaining property. Cowen came down on his price by nearly a third, to $732,500, and was willing to finance half that amount over seven years.[81] The society took a ninety-day option while President Pinkie Martin, Ursuline Committee Chairman Vivian Hamlin (Terrett) and Urban Renewal Agency Director Winston Martin went before city council to seek the entire property's inclusion in the Del Alamo Urban Renewal Area and to try for federal historic preservation funds as well.[82]

But the purchase option expired and the price went back up, causing members simply to go about cleaning up and restoring what they had.[83] Ursuline alumni cooperated by getting Scout groups and other teenagers to spend weekends washing windows and cleaning the yard.[84] Porches, roofs, floors and plumbing needed repair, a major electrical rewiring project was completed and ceramist Mary Green designed light fixtures to replace the fluorescent ones as interior restoration began in the chapel.[85] Installed in the new restrooms were pink marble washbasins salvaged from the 1870s Jefferson Hotel, being razed for a parking lot at Jefferson and Houston streets.[86]

The Conservation Society planned to use its property as an arts and crafts center, with society offices upstairs in the Poinsard House, and as an alternate site to La Villita for A Night in Old San Antonio.[87] By the fall of 1970, negotiations were under way with the Southwest Craft Center, which operated a gallery in La Villita but needed classroom space and wanted a crafts museum as well. The Southwest Craft Center would make no architectural changes in the buildings, and would seek to purchase the rest of the property from Cowen.[88] In January of 1971 the Craft Center moved in rent-free. It was soon joined by the 250-member Ballet Folklorico and the San Antonio Independent School District's Saturday Discovery Program in the Arts.[89]

By this time Link Cowen had died. His estate dropped the price of the Ursuline property to $4.25 a square foot or about $650,000, down from $1 million, and the Conservation Society decided to take a serious look.[90] For just under $100,000, two-thirds of it bank-financed, the society purchased another 23,000 square feet, including the rest of the Academy building. Its holdings came to 1.4 acres.[91] The Craft Center, under the leadership of Magaret (Mrs. Donald) Saunders (Block), purchased the rest of the dormitory building not totally owned by the Conservation Society, giving the Craft Center .4 acres. The remaining 2.5 acres were purchased by parking magnate W.J. Appedole, who leased the old laundry building to the Craft Center as a ceramics studio and put a parking lot in the open space.[92]

As these transactions occurred, the Conservation Society concentrated on preparing a $14.3 million proposal to make the complex and nearby area a cultural and educational center for the entire downtown area in cooperation with the Southwest Craft Center and with the San Antonio River Authority, one of four public agencies to be housed in a ten-story office building on the northern portion of the site.[93] The project was included in the adjacent Del Alamo urban renewal project, dubbed the "New Town in Town" to distinguish it from the San Antonio Ranch New Town project being planned in northwestern Bexar County.[94] In June of 1972 the Ursuline project and application for $13 million in federal funds was approved by the San Antonio City Council.[95] Three months later, however, the U.S. Department of Housing and Urban Development (HUD) turned down the request on the grounds that it did not meet the department's criteria "for research and demonstration funding."[96]

Since the Conservation Society had already invested just over $354,000 in the Ursuline, its next general membership session was devoted to summing up the situation and pledging renewed effort to undertake the project.[97] Some 250 members turned out for the evening meeting in the Ursuline chapel to hear a panel of fifteen community leaders, from the mayor to the county judge

The shaded courtyard leading to the old Ursuline Academy chapel and surrounding buildings reflects the charm of one of San Antonio's major restoration projects, which took a decade to complete. Ford, Powell & Carson Inc., photo: Rick Gardner.

to private investors, who by their presence gave testimony to the scope of the effort and to the new stature of the San Antonio Conservation Society in the city's power structure.[98]

While feelers went out for private capital instead of public funds, Nancy Negley (Wellin) led a delegation to Washington to plead with HUD officials, two Senators and three Congressmen for at least $4.3 million for the Ursuline buildings themselves.[99] Mayor John Gatti wrote HUD Secretary George Romney.[100] Although HUD turned down the project for good in January of 1973, the Department of Commerce gave the San Antonio Conservation Society the first-ever federal Economic Development Administration historic preservation grant—$136,000, to be matched by $34,000 from the society— toward restoration of the Ursuline complex.[101] As others began to express interest in the remaining property, Appedole said he would sell the southern part of his property, along the river and including the old laundry building, for $500,000 to the Conservation Society, which still owed more than $130,000 on its earlier purchases.[102]

Then there was the problem of the property line dividing the 1866 dormitory building between the Conservation Society and the Southwest Craft Center, now that the end was no longer to be cut off but preserved by the Craft Center. The Society's settlement offer in retrospect seems quite bizarre. In San Antonio historic preservation annals, it is approached only by the society's purchase four decades earlier of portions of the San José Granary from different owners.

Terms suggested by the Conservation Society on the Ursuline were:

> That a triangular section of the easterly most room in such building owned by the Society be traded to the Craft Center for a triangular area in the northeast corner of the room of the building owned by the Craft Center; the acquisition by the Society from the Craft Center of the fee title to that portion of the hallway of such building immediately adjacent to the room of such building, with suitable arrangements made for the granting of access rights to the Craft Center of ingress and egress through such hallway into the remainder of the building; and, that suitable arrangement be made with the Craft Center for the use, by the Center, of the center room of such building should the same be converted into a kitchen by the Society.[103]

The Craft Center, however, did not entirely like the proposal to ungerry-mander the property lines. "They did not want to sell the hallway," Nancy Negley (Wellin) reported, "but would exchange the two triangles to square up the lines. They will give us access to the hallway, and will reconsider the location of the air-conditioning units."[104]

Considerably more significant was the news that Carolyn Brown (Mrs. William) Negley had herself arranged purchase of the remaining property from Appedole for nearly $1 million.[105] She proposed a fifteen-year occupancy by the Southwest Craft Center of all space but the chapel, which would be shared with the Conservation Society. Restoration would be undertaken jointly. The Conservation Society was happy to agree.[106] From there it was a short step to outright purchase of the Ursuline complex by the Craft Center. When the letter of intent came, the Conservation Society set a price of $300,000.[107] The Craft Center ultimately assumed the society's remaining $81,792 indebtedness plus paid $100,000, made possible by a gift to the Craft Center from Adele (Mrs. Jack) Frost.[108] The property was turned over at the end of January 1975, when the Conservation Society's Economic Development Administration restoration project was completed.[109]

In 1975 the San Antonio Conservation Society sold its Ursuline Academy property to the Southwest Craft Center, in an agreement which ended more than twenty years of uncertainty over the future of the historic complex. Present at the signing were, seated from left, Jane Slavens, Conservation Society President Nancy Negley (Wellin), attorney Ed Kliewer and, representing the Southwest Craft Center, attorney Wayne Weber, Craft Center President Evelyn (Mrs. Tom) Berg and Margaret Saunders (Block). Standing are Conservation Society Administrative Director Conrad True and the Craft Center's Edith (Mrs. Walter W., Jr.) McAllister. San Antonio Conservation Society.

Society members were philosophical about the low selling price. They had already invested some $500,000 in the Ursuline property, and were getting back only twenty percent of that amount. But the society's purpose was to save such structures, members were reminded, and the Craft Center promised to be ideal for appropriate adaptive use. Moreover, much restoration remained to be done, and the Craft Center needed all available additional funds for that purpose.[110] Nor was the Conservation Society disappointed. In 1977, through a gift of Elizabeth Huth (Mrs. Samuel) Maddux, the chapel complex was completely restored and opened with a grand ball, reception and gourmet dinner, its menu planned by Julia Child.[111] The Craft Center paid off its mortgage four years later.[112] With pottery studios moving to quarters nearby, the old laundry building along the river was restored and enlarged into the elegant Club Giraud, its profits earmarked for the support of the Craft Center in the same manner as profits of the Argyle Club in the restored Argyle Hotel in Alamo Heights went to support the Southwest Foundation for Biomedical Research.

A second area under single ownership, HemisFair Plaza, faced historic preservation problems of a quite different nature. A month after the fair

The Ursuline Academy's chapel was restored for receptions and dinners by the Southwest Craft Center in 1977. Ford, Powell & Carson Inc., photo: Rick Gardner.

opened in April of 1968, the HemisFair Re-Use Committee began its work. In the hurry to get the fairgrounds ready, little thought was given to what would happen afterward—with the notable exceptions of the Convention Center complex, the Institute of Texan Cultures and the Tower of the Americas, with its revolving restaurant in the tophouse. The Re-Use Committee made its preliminary recommendations on August 1, two months before the fair closed: A single management body should be created to supervise the entire site. A third of its land should be devoted to educational and cultural purposes. The four-year state university long sought for San Antonio should be located on the fairgrounds. The HemisFair monorail should be extended to provide transportation as far as King William Street, the Alamo and Municipal Auditorium. Existing plazas needed to be redesigned and identified with particular countries.[113]

The HemisFair Re-Use Committee's recommendations, however, proved to be only the first in a long and wide-ranging succession of plans, most doomed to be clucked over and then ignored. What followed was a scenario that could not have been played with greater commotion and confusion by the Keystone Cops.

HemisFair Plaza got its own director, former Fair Executive Director Jim Gaines. The newly created University of Texas at San Antonio (UTSA) leased land and headquarters space in the old La Maison Blanche French restaurant and began its first classes nearby, only to move away all but a small branch when the new UTSA campus was completed in far northwestern San Antonio. The monorail was taken down and sold, and the plazas languished without being redesigned. The University of Mexico, on the other hand, opened an extension campus nearby and the Witte Museum moved its Transportation Museum into the old Spanish Pavilion, but suffered some damage to its collections after a small fire. An effort was made to keep the old Goliad Food Cluster open by leasing small restaurant spaces.[114]

Beyond that, late in the summer of 1969 the Chamber of Commerce appropriated $25,000 for the Southwest Research Institute to study how to turn forty-three acres of HemisFair Plaza into a park like Tivoli Gardens in Copenhagen. One year and several trips to Denmark later, cost estimates for the project came in at $10.3 million, and city council turned thumbs down.[115]

City Manager Jerry Henckel led an effort to have the plaza split by a four-lane roadway that would be part of the proposed Inner Loop and also help bring business to the Tower, which he thought was built in the wrong place.[116] The HemisFair Plaza Advisory Committee recommended several improvements to celebrate the bicentennial on July 4, 1976, and came up with the idea that the City Planning Department should be called in. From the viewpoint of another city agency, the Traffic and Transportation Department, the solution was, predictably, to cut up the plaza with more streets and build more parking lots. A UTSA team looked things over and decided there was too much parking space already.[117]

While these and other elaborate and conflicting plans were being offered, city officials admitted that parts of the plaza looked "like a ghost town," and confessed that the city was losing money on plaza operations. They blamed the dearth of tenants on unattractive short-term leases and on summer air conditioning costs which often exceeded the monthly rent.[118] The Conservation Society resolved that, whatever happened, all historic buildings in the HemisFair area should be saved, and set about getting markers for them.[119] The San Antonio Bicentennial Committee recommended that city council designate HemisFair Plaza an historic district.[120]

When the Conservation Society committee went to see about placing its plaques, however, two of the houses could not be found.[121] One missing "HemisHouse" was the Heinrich House, a one-story frame Victorian "little jewel" which the Conservation Society had paid to move from the site of the Institute of Texan Cultures. Investigators discovered it had been torn apart eight months before by a crew building the nearby City Water Board office.[122]

A check of the HemisFair grounds revealed more unreported atrocities. The preserved cupola of the old synagogue torn down for the fair had been run into by a truck and hauled off. Three fountains were seriously damaged, some perhaps beyond repair. The legs of one statue had been broken, causing it to be put into storage. And the entire seventeen-foot-high iron sculpture

Decay at a previously restored HemisFair Plaza house is inspected in 1972 by, from left, two Conservation Society representatives, President Vivian Hamlin (Terrett) and Pat Osborne, soon to become the city's first Historic Preservation Officer, and Plaza Director Jim Gaines, previously HemisFair's executive director. The San Antonio Express-News *Collection, The Institute of Texan Cultures.*

"Asterikos" was missing. Cast by New York sculptor Tony Smith and donated to the city by San Antonian Henry Catto, Jr., future U.S. Ambassador to Great Britain, and his wife, the sculpture had been placed on a site near the Convention Center. It was finally located, cut into pieces, in a city junkyard.[123] Sculptor Smith had kept the forms for "Asterikos," which was recast and safely donated this time to the McNay Art Museum.

But HemisFair Plaza itself could not be resurrected as easily. Only piecemeal efforts were addressing a solution for the site of a fair which, as predicted, left an enormously beneficial legacy for the city through construction of a major convention center and the consequent boost to the city's hotel and convention industry.[124] Nearly twenty years after HemisFair opened, one plan to combine ten unused acres of HemisFair Plaza with La Villita into a festival marketplace was advanced by Enterprise Development Co., headed by James W. Rouse, who had completed such developments elsewhere in the nation. A massive circular fountain in the center of South Alamo Street would link a German beer garden surrounded by retail shops on HemisFair Plaza with another upscale retail area encompassing several historic buildings in La Villita. A stairway through the Conservation Society's Casa Villita property was to link the development to the San Antonio River.[125]

The $25 million project's proposed transformation of La Villita, however, drew immediate opposition from the Conservation Society. It formed a

The United States Arsenal complex, shown looking southeast in 1929, was vacated by the Army after World War II and later set for at least partial demolition. San Antonio Conservation Society, U.S. Army Air Service photograph.

coalition named Amigos de La Villita joining tenants of La Villita, residents of nearby King William Street and members of the League of United Latin-American Citizens. A meeting of A Night In Old San Antonio workers at River House erupted in cheers when Society President Liz Davies announced that continued opposition and a lack of sufficient public funding had just caused Mayor Henry Cisneros to declare the project officially dead. The unused area was to be relandscaped and named HemisFair Park.[126]

Another group of historic buildings of increasing concern was the U.S. Arsenal, since 1859 south of downtown and across the river from King William Street. When Main Avenue was extended south past the courthouse in 1929, the city planned to cut the street on through the Arsenal, though that took another twenty years to accomplish.[127] Of the six major historic buildings on the site, four were west of the proposed Main Avenue: the limestone Office Building (1858–60) one of the first permanent federal government buildings in Texas; the Commanding Officer's Quarters, originally the home of Dr. James M. Devine and rebuilt in 1883; the Servants' Quarters, also predating the Arsenal; and the two-story masonry Storehouse (1883). East were the Magazine, its four-foot-thick limestone walls and barrel vault ceiling begun by the U.S. Army in 1860 and completed for the Confederate Army, and the masonry Stable (1858–60). Several large office/warehouse buildings were added later.

When the Army left in the mid-1940s, the Arsenal became a Federal Center under the jurisdiction of the General Services Administration (GSA).[128] Space was insufficient, however, and the government leased 188,700 additional square feet in at least eight other locations throughout the city.[129] In 1962 the Conservation Society heard that the GSA might raze the arsenal buildings to consolidate its offices in a Federal Center on the western portion of the Arsenal site. The society asked that at least the old Commanding General's Home be spared for a military museum.[130] In its announcement in 1963, however, the GSA announced intent to raze four buildings, including the Commanding General's House, for the $7.7 million center, which would include a new federal court house and a regional post office. The Conservation Society swung into action.[131]

"We're not in the way of progress," President Vivian Hamlin (Terrett) told the press, "but if those people in Washington don't have an architect who can plan their new building without tearing down the old general's headquarters, we do have one and we'll offer his services."[132] Soon the GSA was hearing from U.S. Senator John Tower, who got behind the Conservation Society's effort.[133]

As time passed, the Downtown Association and the Urban Renewal Agency began to complain that the facility should be closer to downtown.[134] When developer Perry Kallison criticized those trying to move the federal building site as a "selfish interest group," association spokesman Irving Mathews defended the association's position and warned that a federal building on the arsenal site would interfere with the expressway now being proposed through the arsenal. If it were constructed and blocked the proposed path of the expressway, he warned, the expressway would have to be re-routed through the King William area.[135]

In the meantime, a victory for preservation seemed to have been won by Vivian Hamlin (Terrett), by then a member of the board of the National Trust for Historic Preservation. At the National Trust's annual meeting in Washington, D.C. in the fall of 1966 she tackled one of the speakers—GSA Administrator Lawson B. Knott, Jr. himself. Knott checked into the Arsenal situation and wrote that he thought demolition of the Commanding Officer's Residence could be avoided.[136] In 1970 the Arsenal got further protection when it was placed on the National Register of Historic Places.[137]

Soon the Arsenal became the site of neither federal building nor expressway. In 1971 the GSA suggested to the City of San Antonio that they simply swap the federally owned 7.5 acre western portion of the Arsenal for 3.5 acres of city-owned HemisFair property adjoining the 4.5-acre grounds of the former United States Pavilion, plus two acres across Durango Boulevard for parking. The United States pavilion could become the federal courthouse and an eight-story federal office building could be built nearby. The regional post office would then be built not on the Arsenal property but at a suburban site on Perrin-Beitel Road. The Arsenal buildings could be used for privately developed housing, and at least some National Register protection would remain.[138]

The city took the GSA up on its proposal. After consultation with the Conservation Society, the GSA declared the western portion of the Arsenal, including the Commander's residence, as surplus and transferred it to the city, which planned to renovate three buildings as headquarters for the Parks and Recreation Department.[139] Buildings on the remaining twelve acres of Arsenal property, covering a six-block area east of Main Avenue to the San Antonio River, were to become housing for the elderly.[140]

But proposals to raze the eastern portion of the historic arsenal complex for a new federal building, bulldoze through it for an expressway or convert it into public housing for the elderly all failed, and the property, declared a city landmark in 1975, was put up for sale. The Conservation Society bid for a portion for A Night In Old San Antonio warehouse space.[141] In 1977 the entire site went to the San Antonio International Trade Center Ltd. for a distribution point for goods from Mexico and Central and South America, but reverted to the General Services Administration the next year when Canadian backers ran out of money.[142] The GSA planned to break it up into separate tracts, one for a GSA motor pool, another for residential development and a third for a San Antonio Independent School District food warehouse. Complex negotiations for the city to buy land elsewhere for the motor pool and warehouse site, then purchase the Arsenal property and resell it for residential development, were undone when Councilman Bernardo Eureste led a move which deleted appropriated funding.[143] A renewed effort for the school food warehouse collapsed after an uproar from members of the King William Association and other neighboring residents.[144]

The *deus ex machina* proved to be the H.E.B. Grocery Co. In 1982 H.E.B. purchased ten of the Arsenal's twelve acres for a $12 million, campus-style headquarters for its 450 corporate employees. Its headquarters would move from Corpus Christi when the new location was completed. "The place looked awful," recalled H.E.B. President Charles Butt, who bought and moved into the 1880 Carl Groos House on King William Street. One writer described the Arsenal as "like a war zone. Debris was scattered everywhere, and the half dozen buildings themselves reflected decades of neglect."[145] Under the architectural firms of Hartman-Cox of Washington, D.C. and Chumney/ Urrutia of San Antonio and of landscape architect James Keeter, the historic powder magazine and stable buildings were restored, three of the newer buildings were removed, three huge 1920s warehouse buildings were adapted and one new structure was built.

Accents of native limestone and wood combined with the tan stucco of the buildings and dark blue-gray of woodwork and metal windows to provide a unifying effect, as did the central plaza onto which the buildings fronted. The

The ten-acre main portion of the United States Aresenal was saved from an uncertain fate in 1982, when it was purchased by the H.E.B. Grocery Company and restored as its corporate headquarters. The two-story limestone block building at right center was built in 1858-60 as a stable. The San Antonio Light *Collection, The Institute of Texan Cultures.*

city landscaped the riverbank along the eastern 900-foot boundary. To make sure it stayed attractive, H.E.B. donated a thirty-year scenic easement to the San Antonio Conservation Society. In 1990, H.E.B. completed its nationally acclaimed complex by acquiring the remaining two acres of the Arsenal to the south and, to the north, of the U.S. Postal Service's vacant three-story Guilbeau substation, which the company razed for a landscaped parking lot.[146]

Meanwhile, preservation concerns were also surfacing about an historic military complex newer and much larger than the Arsenal, one which had gained great identity with San Antonio—Fort Sam Houston. Begun in 1876 as Post San Antonio on the open spaces of Government Hill beyond what then were the northeastern limits of San Antonio, Fort Sam Houston now encompassed more than three thousand acres and contained some 1,800 buildings, several hundred of which could be considered historic. Its initial

Among several hundred historic buildings at Fort Sam Houston is the 1881 residence of the United States Fifth Army commanding general, once the home of Gen. John Pershing. San Antonio Conservation Society, U.S. Army photograph, 41-133-1493-1/AF 77.

mission was to be headquarters for the Army's Department of Texas, provide a supply depot for troops putting down Indian uprisings on the distant frontier and to support patrols on the Mexican border. At its heart was the Quadrangle, enclosed by two-story limestone buildings on three sides and by a limestone wall on the fourth, with a landmark watch/water/clocktower of limestone blocks at its center.

Virtually intact, in addition to the Quadrangle, were several complexes of later buildings designed around separate parade grounds. Staff Post included fifteen sets of officers' quarters and a hospital, all designed by Alfred Giles. Infantry Post had Giles-designed barracks and support buildings of the 1880s to garrison infantry and cavalry troops. There were also the pre-World War I Artillery and Cavalry posts on opposite sides of Arthur MacArthur Field, birthplace of military aviation, which was flanked on its central and north-eastern sections by Spanish Colonial Revival buildings. At its eastern end stood the Art Deco complex of Brooke Army Medical Center.

Thousands of soldiers have passed through Fort Sam Houston, some of their names fixed permanently on the pages of history: General of the Armies John J. Pershing; the Pacific campaign's Sixth Army commander, Gen. Walter Krueger; Lt. Gen. Joseph W. "Vinegar Joe" Stilwell, commander of U.S. troops in Burma; pioneer military pilot Benjamin Foulois; and, assigned twice to Fort Sam, Dwight D. Eisenhower. The Apache chief Geronimo was held

Awaiting final preservation funding at Fort Sam Houston is the Band Barrack (1893), the only building of its type in the Department of Defense inventory. Newly replaced is the third-story belvedere where the band once played for soldiers marching on the facing field. Lewis F. Fisher.

there after his capture in 1886. But unlike the Ursuline Academy, HemisFair Plaza and the Arsenal, no new use was being sought for Fort Sam Houston.

In 1963, the San Antonio Conservation Society urged the visiting National Park Service historian to help make Fort Sam Houston's Quadrangle and Staff Post a National Historic Site.[147] Later, the Society for the Preservation of Fort Sam Houston rescued the Stilwell House from clearance and turned it into a military museum. In the summer of 1974 the Conservation Society learned more buildings were endangered, and an effort which began in 1976 got more than five hundred acres of the post designated a National Landmark.[148] Successful resolution of additional threats of demolition, however, would have to wait several years until reinforcements could mass for a final assault on the issue.

In the spring of 1978, extensive demolition again threatened Infantry Post. The Conservation Society tried persuasion through military as well as civilian channels.[149] Two years later, the Conservation Society joined with the Department of the Interior to split payment for the salary of an employee to spend two months documenting twenty-two historic buildings on the post.[150] In 1987, however, the Texas Historical Commission formally blasted Fort Sam Houston officials for altering the character of historic structures and abandoning "landmark buildings . . . to the perils of deterioration and vandalism."[151]

Conservation Society attention soon refocused on the post's landmark problems, in particular that of the unique Band Barrack, designed by Alfred Giles and the only building of its type in the Department of Defense inventory. Seriously damaged by fire, by 1990 it was on the State Preservation Office's list of the twenty-five most endangered buildings in Texas. Its third-story belvedere which once sheltered band members playing for parades on the facing field was gone. Lobbying by the San Antonio Conservation Society, however, helped secure $270,000 Department of Defense Legacy Resource Management Program funding, administered by the National Park Service, to help restore the building and permit documentation of all of the post's historic structures as well.[152] By the end of 1991 the Conservation Society's Fort Sam Houston Task Force could report completion of a memorandum of agreement involving five organizations in the study and management of "cultural and historical resources" at Fort Sam Houston: the Department of the Army, President's Advisory Council on Historic Preservation, the City of San Antonio, Texas Historical Commission and the San Antonio Conservation Society.[154]

First target was the Quadrangle, which the Texas Historical Commission ranked in statewide importance behind only the Alamo and the State Capitol. On the entire post, 934 historic buildings were counted, more than at West Point. In 1992, a $100.3 million project began. Interior surfaces were repaired, buildings restored and rerooffed, temporary buildings replaced.[155] In 1993 came completion of a $1.2 million restoration of the Gift Chapel, dedicated in 1909 by President William Howard Taft.[156] In a ceremony unveiling the 1888 Stilwell House's restored formal parlor, a project funded by the Conservation Society, former Texas Historical Commission Chairman T.R. Fehrenbach presented Lt. Gen. Tom Jaco, Fifth Army Commander, with the Texas Award for Historic Preservation. The five year-old Society for the Preservation of Historic Fort Sam Houston announced a $1 million campaign to complete restoration of the house.[157]

"We had allowed the infrastructure to decay and it was time to fix it," said Jaco of the overall project at Fort Sam Houston. "All of a sudden it just dawns on you that not only is it the right thing to do to preserve this place, it's the responsible thing to do."[158]

Notes

1. Hosmer, *Preservation Comes of Age*, 375, 377.

2. Notes the nomination form of the district to the National Register of Historic Places: "Three mansions on King William Street would be architecturally significant even isolated from the district: the eclectic Renaissance-derived Polk Mansion [at 401]; the Groos House [at 335], 1880, with elaborate Victorian tracery on its galleries and an Italianate cupola; and the Steves Homestead [at 509], 1876, another eclectic mix with French Renaissance touches on a sturdy symmetrical two-story house." Also cited was the Newton Mitchell/Ogé House, "an imposing two-story late Greek Revival residence built for the Commanding Officer's Quarters for the nearby San Antonio Arsenal in 1860." (National Register of Historic Places Inventory-Nomination Form, King William Historic District, Sept. 7, 1971, copy in SACS Library.)

3. Minutes, G-Feb. 24, 1949, 2; G-Nov. 17, 1949; G-Oct. 26, 1950; G-Dec. 21, 1950; D-May 24, 1954. In 1951 San Antonio Conservation Society board member Mrs. George Wurzbach was elected president of the King William group, and its president was later made an ex-officio member of the San Antonio Conservation Society board. (Minutes, D-Jun. 1, 1951; D-Nov. 22, 1954; D-Sept. 19, 1955.)

4. "Historic District Zoning Urged for San Antonio," *San Antonio News,* May 20, 1957, 4-A; Minutes, D-Mar. 24, 1958, 2; D-Mar. 25, 1963, 3. In 1965 the offices of Ford, Powell and Carson expanded into a nearby 1886 home on East Guenther Street.

5. Minutes D-May 23, 1966, 3; D-Sept. 8, 1966; D-Sept. 19, 1966, 2–3.

6. "Formal Application for Planning & Zoning," Oct. 30, 1967, copy in SACS Library; "City Sets boundaries of King William Area," *San Antonio News,* May 9, 1968.

7. Two of its members were placed on the La Villita board in 1953. (Minutes, D-Jun. 24, 1953.)

8. Minutes, D-Jan. 15, 1975, 4; G-Jan. 22, 1975; D-Feb. 26, 1975, 2; D-Mar. 19, 1975, 3. At 225 South Presa St. across from La Villita, the Conservation Society in 1976 purchased the Louis Gresser House, the last remaining on that side of the block. Called the Gresser-Hays House until archeological analysis determined that it had been constructed in the 1870s—too late to have been lived in by the legendary Texas Ranger Jack Hays—it was restored under the guidance of architect William Parrish and leased initially to restaurateur Frank Phelps. (Minutes, D-Jul. 21, 1976, 1, 2; D-Jan. 19, 1977; D-Oct. 18, 1978, 3; D-Mar. 21, 1979, 4; D-Aug. 1, 1979, 1–3; D-Oct. 17, 1979, 2.)

9. "Convention Hall-Civic Center Proposed for La Villita Area," *San Antonio Express,* Jul. 26, 1956; "Roundhouse Up," *San Antonio News,* Nov. 28, 1958, 14-A;

George, *O'Neil Ford,* 143. Enthusiastic Conservation Society directors endorsed the plan. (Minutes, D-Jun. 24, 1953, 1–2; D-Sept. 24, 1956.)

10. Minutes, D-Nov. 20, 1979. The Conservation Society's mortgage on Conservation Corner at the eastern end was paid off in 1979.

11. Minutes, D-Jun. 24, 1953; D-Sept. 23, 1957, 2.

12. Lloyd Larrabee, "Villita Project Bids Pondered by URA," *San Antonio Light,* Jun. 25, 1968. Conservation Society members were not totally pleased with the work, including style of light fixtures along Villita Street. (Minutes, D-Mar. 20, 1967, 3; D-Oct. 20, 1969, 4–5.)

13. Minutes, D-May 18, 1972, 1–2; Deborah Weser, "Old Candy Factory In La Villita Was Cocoon for Homes," *San Antonio Express-News,* Oct. 6, 1974, 10-B.

14. Deborah Weser, "Council OKs Hotel Project," *San Antonio Express-News,* Oct. 7, 1975; David Hendricks, "New hotel has grand opening," *San Antonio Express,* Apr. 17, 1979. Facing Presa Street on the hotel grounds is the 1870s Anton Phillip/Staffel House, a bar known as Victoria's Indiscretion. At the corner with Arciniega Street is the 1840s Diaz House, housing a reception and meeting area. Near the pool is the 1811 Elmendorf-Taylor/Arciniega House, the Restoration Bar and Grill. A fourth home on the site, next to the Staffel House, was quietly razed by the city in 1970, despite historic district covenants. (Lewis Fisher, "La Villita's Future: Uncertain," *San Antonio Express-News,* Dec. 20, 1970, 2-H.) Another feature in the hotel's courtyard is a century-old anaqua tree, successfully moved 40 feet from the path of construction. The hotel later changed hands and was renamed the Plaza San Antonio.

15. Minutes, D-Jan. 22, 1975; D-Feb. 26, 1975, 2; D-Mar. 19, 1975, 3.

16. Jutson, *Alfred Giles,* 24–25. A one-story historic home owned by the family on an adjacent site to the north was razed one weekend in 1977 without a permit. (Ralph Winingham and Bruce Davidson, "Fire threat warnings claimed ignored," *San Antonio Express-News,* Aug. 4, 1983.)

17. Minutes, D-Nov. 16, 1972, 2; "Historical structure's fate hangs," *San Antonio Express-News,* Feb. 24, 1987.

18. Ben King, Jr., "City loses battle on historic house," *San Antonio Express,* Feb. 23, 1977, 3-A.; Minutes, D-Jan. 19, 1977, 4; G-Mar. 23, 1977; D-Aug. 31, 1977; D-Nov. 15, 1978, 2.

19. King, "City loses battle;" Minutes, D-Jun. 14, 1978; D-Sept. 20, 1978.

20. Minutes, D-Apr. 11, 1979, 3.

21. Ibid.; "Historical structure's fate hangs," *San Antonio Express-News,* Feb. 24, 1987.

22. Minutes, D-Feb. 18, 1981, 2; D-Jul. 18, 1984, 2.

23. Ralph Winingham and Bruce Davidson, "Fire threat warnings claimed ignored," *San Antonio Express,* Aug. 4, 1983.

24. "Historical structure's fate hangs," *San Antonio Express-News.*

25. Donald E. Everett, *Monte Vista: The Gilded Age of an Historic District,* (San Antonio: *North San Antonio Times* and *Alamo Heights Recorder-Times,* 1987), 2. Dr. Everett dates the Gilded Age in San Antonio at 1890–1930, a somewhat later period than elsewhere in the nation.

26. Ibid., 57.

27. Nancy Scott Jones, *North San Antonio Times,* May 22, 1975, 1.

28. Reporter Nancy Scott Jones described the scene: "The council chambers at the outset looked more like the beginnings of an early afternoon garden party. Tanned mothers tucked the skirts of their sundresses under them and sat on the floor to hear the lengthy discussion. Elderly women peered from under their summer straw hats at the eight councilmen. Several men had taken the afternoon off from work to attend the session, and a few children were on hand to see city government in operation." (Nancy Scott Jones, "Monte Vista Zoning Approved," *North San Antonio Times*, Jul. 24, 1975, 1.)

29. "Conservation Society President Mrs. Alfred W. Negley to Friends," Sept. 22, 1975, copy in SACS Library.

30. Minutes, D-Sept. 2, 1975, 2; D-Oct. 15, 1975, 2; D-Nov. 5, 1975, 2.

31. David Anthony Richelieu, "Civic Center plans a legacy of leadership," *San Antonio Express-News*, Jan. 29, 1995. Also done at the time of the Municipal Plaza Building work was $3.2 million in restoration and repair work on city hall. (Minutes, D-Dec. 9, 1992, 2.)

32. "Society lets Bexar take old buildings," *San Antonio Express*, Apr. 14, 1978. The Conservation Society was particularly reluctant to give up on the 1862 limestone and brick building housing radio station KEDA, home of the *San Antonio Herald* from 1862 to 1877 and of the German newspaper *Texas Freie Presse fuer Texas* from 1865 to 1930. The society was assured by county officials that there was no way to incorporate the historic buildings into the new plans and that their facades had been destroyed in any event, although an on-site inspection for the society by architectural historian Eugene George suggested otherwise—correctly, it turned out, as the intact facades were revealed during demolition. Fears for the 19th-century three-story Artes Graficas building at 115 Camaron St., with original limestone walls and 15-foot ceilings, were relieved when it was saved by the city and restored by Williams, Shubert & Saldana Architects in 1978. (Minutes, D-Jun. 14, 1978, 2; D-Jul. 19, 1978, 3; D-Aug. 16, 1978, 2; "Sold," *San Antonio Light*, Sept. 5, 1985, H-2; Lynn Osborne Bobbitt to Mrs. James N. Castleberry, Jr., May 2, 1978, in SACS Library; "Conservation Society Opposes Demolition of Historic Main Plaza Building," statement of Jun. 19, 1978 in SACS Library.)

33. Larry Paul Fuller, "The Dullnig Block," *Texas Architect*, Jan.–Feb. 1982, 52–53. The east facade of the building was set back 16 feet when Alamo Street was widened, causing removal of the southeast tower. The second tower and the mansard roof were removed later.

34. "Society wants building to stay," *San Antonio Express*, Dec. 17, 1976; Deborah Weser, "Zoning director junks razing authorization," *San Antonio Express*, undated clipping in SACS Library.

35. Wade Roberts, "Council: Dullnig Building to stay," *San Antonio Express*, Jul. 14, 1978, 18-A. Declared an annoyed Councilman Glen Hartman: "The city and federal government are putting millions of dollars into the Alamo Plaza area—and here comes someone who wants to tear down a building and put up another parking lot."

36. Uma Pemmaraju, "Banking firm takes option on Alamo Plaza building," *San Antonio Express*, Aug. 29, 1978, 4-A; Fuller, "The Dullnig Block."

37. "Maverick Building Saved," *SACS Newsletter*, May–June 1983, 1; Anne Pearson, "Downtown site gets new life," *San Antonio Express*, Oct. 15, 1983. The

building was built by Albert Maverick, father of onetime Mayor Maury Maverick and brother of George M. Maverick, who built the onetime Maverick Bank Building across the street and, farther down, the French-style Maverick Hotel, razed to widen North Presa Street. The high-rise Maverick Building which replaced the hotel was planned, in 1995, for renovation for downtown apartments.

38. Ibid.

39. Ibid.; Minutes, D-Oct. 20, 1982, 2; D-Apr. 21, 1983.

40. "Maverick Building Saved," *SACS Newsletter*, May–June 1983, 1. Two dozen members of the Maverick family contributed more than $8,000 toward costs of saving the building. The Historic Structures Task Force, suggested to Mayor Henry Cisneros by Conservation Society President Lynn Bobbitt, met weekly for more than three years to revise and strengthen the city's historic preservation ordinance. The society covered expenses for opinions of a preservation lawyer.

41. Minutes, D-Feb. 16, 1983; D-Mar. 25, 1983; Pearson, "Downtown site gets new life."

42. Ibid.

43. Mary A.C. Fallon, "St. Paul Square area renovation work to begin next month," *North San Antonio Times*, Jan. 5, 1978, 1.

44. Ibid. The district in 1980 drew the architectural firm of Ford, Powell and Carson, which moved from crowded quarters in the King William area to a renovated two-story building at 1138 East Commerce St. (George, *O'Neil Ford, 216.*)

45. City Preservation Officer Pat Osborne denied the request of the State Board of Control to demolish the building, and the Conservation Society hired O'Neil Ford to make drawings of a renovated structure. President Mary Ann Castleberry showed them to State Representative Lou Nelle Sutton, who agreed with their potential as plans for a state office building, dedicated in 1982 and named in memory of her husband, long-time east side political leader G.W. Sutton. Rehabilitation rather than demolition and rebuilding was found to save more than $1 million. (Minutes, D-Oct. 19, 1977, 2; D-Aug. 16, 1978; D-Sept. 20, 1978; Richard Erickson, "Downtown faces east," *San Antonio Express-News*, Feb. 11, 1979; "Conservation Society dedicates old office complex," *North San Antonio Times*, Dec. 16, 1982.)

46. Irene Abrego, "Even in this part of town," *San Antonio Light*, AA-13.

47. Minutes, D-Mar. 18, 1985, 8. The association's first president was Charles Toudouze.

48. Mike Greenberg, "Mo-Pac depot back on the right track," *San Antonio Express-News*, May 15, 1988, 1-H. The derelict condition of the depot caused the Conservation Society to study purchase of the building in 1982. Three years later, when negotiations with the original developer-owner failed, the society planned to offer up to $600,000 at a foreclosure sale if necessary to save the building. (Minutes, D-Feb. 17, 1982, 2; D-Apr. 14, 1982, 2; D-May 29, 1985; D-May 30, 1985.)

49. Minutes, D-Mar. 19, 1975, 2; "ACCD's new administrative offices readied," *San Antonio Express-News*, Mar. 4, 1984, 5-B.

50. Minutes, D-Sept. 21, 1983; D-Nov. 16, 1983. The Conservation Society later donated $8,000 to the Avenida Guadalupe Association to help in a historical and cultural resources survey. (Minutes, Apr. 9, 1986.)

51. Stephanie Glass, "This old house is here to stay," *San Antonio Light*, Jul. 6, 1989, 1-C.

52. The new campus was on a shaded hilltop on Vance-Jackson Road beyond Loop 410, but enrollment gradually declined and the Ursuline Academy closed in 1993.

53. The first academy building (1851) is frequently hailed as a unique example of French architecture in Texas. But the Ursuline Academy's nomination to the National Register of Historic Places points out: "Whether the building may be considered a work of 'French' architecture is conjectural. It was erected by a French Bishop for French Ursulines by a French architect and was built in a French method of construction. Its plainness of style, however, makes it difficult to assess this building as showing significant Old World influence." (National Register nomination, Nov. 25, 1969, copy in SACS Library.)

54. Minutes, G-Apr. 26, 1934. The society was welcomed there again by Archbishop Robert E. Lucey on its Founders' Day in 1956, when the city's early religious leaders were being honored. (Minutes, G-Mar. 22, 1956.)

55. "7 Sites for San Antonio's New Post Office Inspected," *San Antonio Express*, Oct. 9, 1929, 5.

56. Minutes, D-Aug. 21, 1953.

57. "$9 Million Downtown Apartments Planned," *San Antonio Express*, May 5, 1961; Minutes, D-May 22, 1961, 3; G-May 25, 1961, 1–2.

58. Minutes, D-Jun. 30, 1961, 3; "Ursuline to Be Site of $11 Million Apartment Complex," *San Antonio Light*, Aug. 12, 1962, 1-B; Ann Goldsmith, "History of the Southwest Craft Center-Part III," *Southwest Craft Center Newsletter*, Jan.–Feb., 1981, 5.

59. Goldsmith, "History," *SWCC Newsletter*.

60. Minutes, D-Jun. 22, 1964; D-Sept. 21, 1964, 1-2; D-Nov. 23, 1964; D-May 14, 1965; "Option to Buy Signed," *San Antonio Light*, Mar. 6, 1965.

61. Minutes, D-Jan. 25, 1965; D-Feb. 22, 1965, 2. The society earmarked $50,000 for the purchase. Through Ursuline Committee Chairman Margaret Batts (Mrs. Edgar) Tobin, $25,000 was already offered by the Tobin Foundation.

62. Minutes, E-Mar. 5, 1965. The meeting was in the office of attorney William B. McMillan.

63. Ibid; "Option to Buy Signed," *San Antonio Light*, Mar. 6, 1965.

64. Minutes, E-Apr. 29, 1965; D-May 3, 1965.

65. Minutes, D-May 14, 1965, 1–2; D-May 24, 1965, 2; D-Jun. 8, 1965, 1–2; D-Jun. 21, 1965, 1–2; D-Sept. 20, 1965. Cowen lived in Shawnee, Oklahoma, complicating arrangements.

66. Minutes, D-Sept. 20, 1965; "Historic Clock Given Society," *San Antonio News*, Oct. 19, 1965. The funds were donated by Henry B. Dielmann, first dean of the St. Mary's University Law School, and his wife. The society later bought the contents of the chapel for $2,500. (Minutes, G-Sept. 23, 1965, 2.)

67. "Conservation Society Gets Academy Site," *San Antonio News*, Oct. 25, 1965.

68. Tobin to MacDougal, 2.

69. Minutes, D-Jun. 21, 1965.

70. Minutes, D-Jan. 24, 1966; D-Feb. 21, 1966; G-May 26, 1966; D-Jun. 31, 1969, 3.

71. Minutes, D-Dec. 16, 1968, 4.

72. Minutes, D-May 23, 1966, 1–2.

73. Minutes, D-Feb. 26, 1968, 2.

74. Minutes, D-Feb. 20, 1967.

75. Nelle Lee Weincek OHT, Feb. 12, 1987, 18.

76. Minutes, D-Oct. 20, 1969, 3; D-Nov. 24, 1969, 2.

77. Ann Goldsmith, "History," *SWCC Newsletter;* Minutes, D-Feb. 20, 1967. Most preservation plans had not included that building in any event. On the day of the fire, the San Juan acequia was reopened following completion of the River Authority's reconfigured waterflow plan. Water used to fight the Ursuline fire drained into the nearby San Antonio River and was considered to be the cause of flooding downstream and in the reopened acequia. (Minutes, G-Mar. 23, 1967.)

78. Minutes, D-Apr. 4, 1966; D-Mar. 20, 1967. Cowen paid $4.33 per foot—just over $650,000—for the property, before property taxes, legal fees and other expenses began. (Minutes, E-Jan. 22, 1968.) The Conservation Society paid approximately $6.75 a foot—$250,000—for its first parcel.

79. Minutes, D-Feb. 20, 1967, 2; D-Mar. 20, 1967.

80. Minutes, D-Apr. 3, 1967.

81. Minutes, D-Jun. 13, 1969, 3.

82. Minutes, D-Jul. 17, 1969, 1–2; D-Oct. 20, 1969, 3.

83. Minutes, F-May 25, 1970.

84. Minutes, D-Mar. 18, 1968; D-Jun. 23, 1969, 2.

85. Minutes, D-Jun. 23, 1969, 12; D-Apr. 13, 1970, 5; F-Sept. 21, 1970, 2.

86. Minutes, D-Oct. 21, 1971, 3.

87. Minutes, F-May 25, 1970.

88. Minutes, F-Sept. 9, 1970, 1–5.

89. Old Ursuline Academy Grant Application, May 1972, 8, copy in SACS Library. Terms for a long-term agreement were finally proposed at the end of 1971. (Minutes, F-Nov. 18, 1971, 1, 3–6.)

90. Minutes, F-Mar. 22, 1971.

91. Minutes, F-May 24, 1971, 1–2.

92. Minutes, Nov. 18, 1971; Old Ursuline Academy Grant Application, May 1972, 8.

93. Minutes, D-Sept. 23, 1971; F-Nov. 18, 1971, 1–2; F-May 18, 1972; D-Aug. 8, 1972; G-Oct. 25, 1972. The River Authority agreed to be the "public body" required for the grant application. Other tenants were to be the Alamo Area Council of Governments, San Antonio Development Agency (formerly the Urban Renewal Agency) and the San Antonio Housing Authority.

94. Minutes, F-Nov. 18, 1971, 1–2. Lou Rosenberg was named project director, architect Cyrus Wagner and other representatives went to lobby in Washington, Department of Housing and Urban Development representatives came to San Antonio and a host of city agencies had input. (Minutes, F-Jan. 20, 1972, 2; F-Feb. 17, 1972, 2; F-Mar. 16, 1972.)

95. Minutes, D-Jun. 22, 1972.

96. Ann B. Robinson, "$13 Million Ursuline Bid Nixed," *San Antonio Express,* Sept. 29, 1972.

97. Recent major gifts for the Ursuline project included $10,000 for restoration from the Brown Foundation of Houston, $11,000 from the Texas Historical Survey Committee toward purchase of the first Academy addition and $3,481 from the John Sheerin family for restoration of the chapel's stained glass windows, which were being damaged. One 1880 stained glass window was stolen but later recovered. (Minutes, F-Sept. 21, 1972, 2; F-Oct. 19, 1972, 1–2; F-Nov. 16, 1972, 2; D-Sept. 20, 1973, 3.)

98. Minutes, G-Oct. 25, 1972, 1–3.

99. Minutes, F-Oct. 19, 1972, 2; F-Nov. 16, 1972.

100. Minutes, F-Nov. 16, 1972.

101. Joe Faulkner, "U.S. Funds Will Help Restore Ursuline," *San Antonio Light,* Mar. 3, 1973. An earlier grant having been frozen by the Nixon administration, the EDA grant was engineered in large part by Beverly Blount (-Hemphill) to provide work for the unemployed. Workmen followed architect Brooks Martin's instructions carefully until the laying of the courtyard's flagstones, which were installed—and remain—upside down, on their rough side. (Pat Osborne OHT, Feb. 22, 1993, 16–17.)

102. Minutes, F-Jan. 18, 1973, 2–3.

103. Ibid., 2.

104. Minutes, F-Feb. 15, 1973.

105. Ibid; "Dream comes true for Ursuline Academy," *San Antonio Express-News,* Feb. 14, 1981, 6-A. Nancy Brown Negley and Carolyn Brown Negley were married to cousins, but despite their same maiden names were otherwise unrelated.

106. Minutes, F-Mar. 15, 1973, 1–2. The Craft Center's opening of its restored dormitory building occurred on Oct. 3, 1973. Boat access from the River Bend to the Ursuline complex had just been made possible by removal of gates blocking the River Bend. (Minutes, G-Jun. 28, 1973; G-Oct. 25, 1973, 4.)

107. Minutes, F-Feb. 21, 1974; D-Mar. 28, 1974, 2; F-Aug. 21, 1974.

108. Minutes, D-Sept. 20, 1974; G-Sept. 25, 1974; "Ball, picnic will reopen 1867 chapel," *San Antonio Express-News,* Mar. 13, 1977, 1-E. Should the Craft Center ever plan to dispose of the property, the Conservation Society retained the option to repurchase it at the original price.

109. "Historic academy sold to Craft Center," *San Antonio Express-News,* Jan. 4, 1975, 3-A. The parking lot remained in Carolyn Negley's possession until the Craft Center—with the aid of the Conservation Society—launched a drive for its purchase in 1979, and bought it the next year. (Minutes, D-Feb. 21, 1979; Goldsmith, "History," *SWCC Newsletter.*)

110. Minutes, G-Sept. 25, 1974.

111. "Ball, picnic will reopen 1867 chapel," *San Antonio Express-News,* Mar. 13, 1977, 1-E.

112. "Dream comes true for Ursuline Academy, *San Antonio Express-News,* Feb. 14, 1981, 6-A.

113. Diana Tamez, ed., *Hemisfair Plaza: A Background Study,* University of Texas at San Antonio Division of Environmental Studies (San Antonio, 1980), 4.

114. Ibid; "Council approves UTSA aid measure," *San Antonio Express-News.* The Transportation Museum was later closed and its collection auctioned off by the financially troubled San Antonio Museum Association.

115. Ibid., 4–5; Ed Castillo, "$8 Million HemisFair Plaza Plan Studied," *San Antonio Light*, Dec. 11, 1969.

116. Jeff Duffield, "Roadway Through HemisPlaza Urged," *San Antonio Express*, Nov. 21, 1969, 14-A; "A New HemisPlaza Controversy," *San Antonio Light*, Nov. 28, 1971.

117. *Hemisfair Plaza: A Background Study*, 6–7. A week after city council voted to pave HemisFair Lake for more parking anyway, the Centro 21 task force reported receiving a proposal to build a large HemisFair Plaza swimming pool "complete with wave machines, sandy beaches and secluded sections for nude swimming and sunning." (Ibid., 12.)

118. Jeff Duffield, "Roadway Through HemisPlaza Urged."

119. Minutes, D-Nov. 18, 1968, 2; D-Apr. 13, 1970, 3.

120. *Hemisfair Plaza: A Background Study*, 8.

121. Minutes, D-Feb. 22, 1971, 2.

122. Lewis Fisher, "Now it's whole HemisHouse gone," *San Antonio News*, Aug. 27, 1970, 1. Along Commerce Street on the other side of its new building, the City Water Board was determined to demolish another historic HemisFair house—the classic century-old Schroeder/Yturri House, its walls of solid limestone and its interior preserved much the same as when it was built. Officials wished to use the space for parking and the rock in landscaping the Market Street side of their property, and continued to ignore registered letters on the subject from the Conservation Society. Society President Beverly Blount (-Hemphill) was authorized to file an injunction against the Water Board if actual demolition began. Water Board officials relented and restored the structure only after the Conservation Society mounted a strong appeal to their boss—city council. The Conservation Society gave the Water Board a special award when restoration was completed. (Minutes, D-Sept. 20, 1971, 1–2; D-Aug. 21, 1974, 2; D-Sept. 20, 1974; D-Nov. 20, 1974, 2; D-Dec. 18, 1974; D-Jun. 16, 1976, 3.)

123. Ibid.; "Trinity prof to catalog S.A.-owned art," *San Antonio News*, Aug. 28, 1970, 2-A.

124. The Convention Center's arena—removed in 1995–96 to allow convention center expansion—provided the home to attract the National Basketball Association Spurs franchise, the Institute of Texan Cultures fostered a new statewide pride in ethnic origins, the new federal complex coincidentally helped solve the problem of the Arsenal and the Tower of the Americas gave the city a new municipal symbol. A 500-room Marriott Hotel, joined in 1988 by the neighboring 1,000-room Marriott Rivercenter Hotel and the innovative four-story Rivercenter Mall, would line Hemis-Fair Plaza's northern perimeter. In 1975 the San Antonio Conservation Society joined the River Walk Commission in opposing plans for a hotel to be built nearby over the river. (Minutes, D-Apr. 9, 1975, 3.)

125. Jim Wood and Wilfredo Ramirez, "Mayor: HemisFair plan dead," *San Antonio Express-News*, Mar. 18, 1988, 1-A.

126. Ibid.

Arsenal to Ursuline : 415

127. "Main Ave. to Be Extended Across Plaza to Arsenal," *San Antonio Express,* Oct. 2, 1927, 13; "Street Through Arsenal Urged," *San Antonio Express,* Apr. 14, 1929, 1-A; *San Antonio Express,* Mar. 25, 1930, 4; *San Antonio Express,* Apr. 5, 1930, 3. In extending past the west side of the courthouse, the new street set off the courthouse in its own block. A proposal that the street cut off two courtrooms protruding from the main part of the building was rebuffed by county commissioners, and the route was moved slightly west.

128. Ronald F. Lee to Ethel Harris, Jun. 3, 1953, in SACS Library.

129. "Conservationists Take On the GSA," *San Antonio News,* Feb. 15, 1963, 2-B.

130. Minutes, D-Jun. 25, 1962, 3; D-Sept. 24, 1962, 3.

131. "Conservationists Take On the GSA," *San Antonio News,* Feb. 15, 1963, 2-B; "Arsenal Site Said Still Plan," *San Antonio Express,* May 12, 1966.

132. "Conservationists Take On the GSA," *San Antonio News,* Feb. 15, 1963, 2-B.

133. "Tower Helps On Museum," *San Antonio Express,* Mar. 6, 1963, 4-D. Unlike Senator Tower—who did not live in San Antonio—Congressman Henry B. Gonzalez refused to take sides in the dispute. ("Arsenal Site Said Still Plan," *San Antonio Express,* May 12, 1966.)

134. "GSA Intends To Locate New Federal Building on Arsenal Site," *San Antonio News,* Mar. 2, 1966, 4-A.

135. "Kallison's Proposal Claimed Speculation," *San Antonio Light,* Jun. 23, 1966. One participant at the press conference drew chuckles when he observed of the proposed expressway, "You know what we'd have on our hands with the good ladies of the Conservation Society if we tried to go through the King William area."

136. Lawson B. Knott Jr. to Mrs. Winfield Scott Hamlin, Oct. 19, 1966, in SACS Library.

137. Minutes, D-Feb. 23, 1970, 6.

138. Norma Reed, "Federal Building Plans Set," *San Antonio Light,* Sept. 15, 1971; "Courthouse land swap is studied for Arsenal," *San Antonio News,* Feb. 23, 1972.

139. Minutes, D-Apr. 7, 1972; "S.A. Handed Deed To Old Arsenal Site," *San Antonio Express,* Jul. 20, 1972, 2-A.

140. Minutes, D-Feb. 26, 1975, 2.

141. Minutes, D-Oct. 20, 1976, 3.

142. "Trade zone board will break contract for Arsenal center," *San Antonio Express-News,* Oct. 15, 1978, 11-A.

143. Jim Wood, "Undoing plan for arsenal may cost city," *San Antonio Express,* Apr. 23, 1979.

144. Ibid.; Cecil Clift, "New site eyed for food facility," *San Antonio Express,* Jun. 19, 1979, 7-A. The Arsenal property situation was at the top of the list of items discussed by Joanna Parrish, the society's second vice president, at a meeting in Washington, D.C. with the President's Advisory Council on Historic Preservation's executive director. Former Society President Eleanor Bennett was named to the Advisory Council in 1972. (Minutes, D-Apr. 7, 1972, 2; D-Jun. 20, 1979, 2.)

145. Jonathan Walters, "Battle Plan for a Texas Arsenal," *Historic Preservation,* Jul.-Aug. 1986, 54–55.

146. Ibid.; Minutes, D-Mar. 16, 1983, 2; Leonard Lane, "H.E.B. Pulls Out The Artillery For Its Supermarket Offices," *Texas Architect,* Nov.–Dec. 1985, 104–09; "H.E.B. Moves To San Antonio," *San Antonio Light,* Dec. 29, 1985; David Anthony Richelieu, "H.E.B. to expand headquarters," *San Antonio Express-News,* May 22, 1990. A minor tussle at the outset was resolved when the National Park Service overruled the state preservation office's blocking of demolition of the three "very ordinary industrial buildings." Another problem had been removed long before. After the 1847 Guilbeau House's razing, efforts were made to transfer the aura of Guilbeau's association with saving the French wine industry to the nondescript two-story structure remaining nearby. In 1952 the outbuilding was "definitely confirmed" as having been the original Guilbeau home. It was later identified as having instead been everything from the servants' quarters to the slave quarters to the kitchen to the wine cellar, and efforts were made to restore it. However, a 1968 study by National Park Service architectural historian John C. Garner Jr. found no documentary evidence nor architectural merit about it, concluding its only value was in having been associated in some way with Guilbeau. The building, whatever it was, was razed that year when widening of Durango Boulevard nearby gave the parking lot in which it stood less parking space, and more was needed for Hemisfair crowds. (Minutes, G-Dec. 4, 1952, 2; G-Nov. 24, 1958, 2; D-Jan. 3, 1968, 2–4; John C. Garner Jr., "Preliminary Research Report on the old Guilbeau House," 1968, copy in SACS Library.)

147. Minutes, G-Sept. 26, 1963.

148. Minutes, D-Jun. 19, 1974, 4; D-Jul. 17, 1974, 3; D-Jan. 15, 1975, 4; D-Mar. 19, 1975, 3; D-Nov. 17, 1976, 3.

149. Minutes, D-Mar. 15, 1978, 2.

150. Minutes, D-Mar. 19, 1980.

151. James Coburn, "Fort Sam building work is saluted," *San Antonio Express-News,* Oct. 17, 1993, 1-B.

152. Minutes, D-Apr. 13, 1988, 2; D-Sept. 21, 1988, 4; James Coburn, "Fort Sam undergoing $100.3 million face lift," *San Antonio Express-News,* Jul. 6, 1993, 8-A; Schooler OHT, 10.

153. Minutes, D-Nov. 20, 1991, 1–2. Representatives of the five signatories were to meet annually to review the agreement and preservation progress on the post. (Ibid.; Minutes, D-May 20, 1992, 2.)

154. James Coburn, "Fort Sam undergoing $100.3 million face lift."

155. Ibid.

156. Minutes, D-Sept. 21, 1988, 4; James Coburn, "Stilwell House bears fruits of restoration," *San Antonio Express-News,* Nov. 19, 1993, 2-B. While Fort Sam Houston, Fort Bliss and Fort Hood were commended for their preservation projects by the President's Advisory Council on Historic Preservation, Randolph Air Force Base was criticized for inappropriate renovations to its historic structures. At Kelly Air Force Base, the Base Office of History rallied preservationists to beat back federally planned demolition of the base's 17-house Bungalow Colony of the 1920s. (Minutes, D-Dec. 12, 1990, 2–3; D-Oct. 9, 1991; D-Jan. 22, 1992; D-Dec. 9, 1992, 2; Coburn, "Fort Sam building work is saluted.")

157. Ibid.

16

No Shows at the Texas, None X-Rated at the Aztec

 In the topsy-turvy world of San Antonio preservation, the earlier antagonism between city hall under Mayor Walter McAllister and the Conservation Society seemed to melt altogether under the persuasive charms of Councilman and then Mayor Henry Cisneros, who became a successful negotiator for preservation in several high-profile causes. As San Antonio emerged from the 1960s, the city itself began officially engaging in historic preservation, aiding implementation of new preservation techniques, routing federal funding toward urban renewal preservation projects and helping the number of historic districts to proliferate. In 1974, when the city also passed a revised historic districts and landmarks ordinance, Conservation Society stalwart Pat Osborne was hired by the City of San Antonio as the first Historic Preservation Planner for the Planning and Community Development Department, one of the first such posts in the nation.[1]

Restoration even won out over demolition in the case of one of San Antonio's greatest civic landmarks—the 1926 Spanish Colonial Revival Municipal Auditorium, its interior and its structural steel roof frame critically damaged in a four-alarm fire as repairs were being completed in January of 1979.[2] The Conservation Society decided "to pursue any means feasible" to encourage its restoration, including committing its own funds if necessary.[3] As officials tried to decide whether repairs were worth the expense, attachment felt by San Antonians who had attended high school graduations, concerts and other events in the auditorium during the past half-century created a groundswell of support for its restoration. In the face of organized opposition from the San Antonio Taxpayers League, the Conservation Society hired an

The 1913 Rand Building was to become the site of a parking garage until the Conservation Society in 1981 purchased and resold the building for renovation as first-class office space. San Antonio Conservation Society.

advertising agency to help promote a $9.1 million auditorium restoration bond issue, which passed by a two-to-one margin in April of 1981.[4]

As San Antonio's post-World War I prosperity culminated in the downtown building boom of the late 1920s, so did energy sparked by HemisFair development culminate in the downtown building boom of the early 1980s. Fortuitously, tax incentives for adaptive reuse were enacted about the same time, giving preservationists a potent incentive in urging developers to preserve older structures. The net result gave downtown San Antonio an unusual mingling of modern steel and glass high-rise buildings and stone and frame lower structures from the past.[5]

Construction of Frost National Bank's building on Main Plaza in 1922 had been an early indicator of the larger boom which soon followed. So, a half century later, was Frost Bank's new twenty-one-story Houston Street headquarters in the block to the north in 1971 a harbinger of what was to come. This time, Frost Bank itself took the lead in developing the northwestern sector of downtown. The bank acquired the entire block across Houston Street north of its new building, and announced plans for a $70 million Two Frost Tower on the site.[6] A parking garage was to go west of Two Frost Tower. Another was to go east of the 1971 Frost Tower, one of two parking garages in the area to be built by the city. That site was already jointly owned by Frost Bank and Macro Investments, which was gutting the former San Antonio Savings Association building, originally built by the National Bank of Commerce, and expanding it into twenty stories of first-class office space.

There were several major physical obstacles to the entire plan. One was the Stowers Building, one of the city's early skyscrapers, in the heart of the Two Frost Tower site. Beside it, on the proposed site of one parking garage, were several smaller structures, among them the remaining shell of the 1860s First Presbyterian Church. Worse, on the parking garage site across from the first Frost Tower was the 1913 Rand Building, its eight stories mostly vacant since the Wolff & Marx department store moved to North Star Mall in 1965. It was designed of red brick with white terra cotta work on the top floor by the Fort Worth firm of Sanguinet and Staats, the state's premiere skyscraper designer of the time. The Rand Building's large fixed plate-glass windows were flanked by sash windows in a style similar to Louis Sullivan's landmark Carson-Pirie Scott department store in Chicago. Observed one critic: "Compared to the neighboring Frost Bank Tower, whose heavy gray concrete piers and dark recessed window bands spread gloom for blocks, the Rand Building is cheerful, delicate and inviting."[7]

The Rand Building, already on the National Register of Historic Places, became a *cause célèbre*. Early in the century, few persons were bothered when the Garza House, the largest remaining Spanish residence in San Antonio and a onetime Spanish mint, was torn down to make way for the Rand Building. But six decades later the aging Rand building was within the Main and Military Plaza Historic District. City, state and federal legal requirements were on the books, a preservation office was an official arm of city hall and independent preservation organizations were ready to go on alert once the alarm was sounded.

That alarm went off at the close of 1980, when Conservation Society President Joanna Parrish formally advised city council of the value of the Rand Building.[8] But before plans had a chance to become widely known and discussed, San Antonio City Council voted 8-3 to erect in its place an $8 million eight-story garage with 855 parking spaces. Hastily mobilized preservationists were unable to delay council action for thirty days so the Conservation Society could find a buyer and an alternate use.[9] "It is unfortunate that the Rand Building has outlived its economic usefulness," one Frost Bank official stated flatly. A prominent real estate broker added that studies showed its restoration to be unfeasible.[10]

Others, however, began coming forward with different opinions. One architect revealed he did a study for another real estate broker two years earlier and found the building suitable for first-class office space. Two more reported their studies found it suitable for apartments and offices, and for retail space on the street level. Frost Bank officials didn't agree, and vowed to tear down the Rand Building whether or not the city built a parking garage there.[11]

With the battle lines clearly drawn, San Antonio Conservation Society directors under newly elected President Peggy (Mrs. Harvey) Penshorn voted

to seek an injunction prohibiting demolition of the Rand Building, and prepared to take out newspaper advertising to explain their position.[12] In August, they decided to submit an earnest money contract of up to $100,000 to buy the Rand Building outright.[13] Although the bank responded with terms "so restrictive as to be unacceptable," within a few intensive days society attorney Robert Moore of Galveston—no San Antonio attorney could be found to take on Frost Bank—engineered a compromise.[14] Mayor Henry Cisneros persuaded bank officials to listen to the Conservation Society, which then obtained a purchase option from Frost Bank and a grace period in which to find a developer.[15]

As the deal worked out on November 5, 1981, the Conservation Society exercised its option to purchase the Rand Building and immediately sold it to Houston's Spaw-Glass Co., located by former Conservation Society president Beverly Blount (-Hemphill), which would renovate the building for first-class office space. Tenants were allotted up to 200 parking places in a 600-space garage between the Rand Building and Macro Investments' building. Church's Fried Chicken, with its long-term lease, would remain in its corner in the Rand Building. The Conservation Society, in turn, agreed not to oppose Frost Bank's demolition of the Stowers Building, and could coordinate removal of its artifacts if removal costs were paid. Frost Bank could take down the shell of the old Presbyterian Church, but promised to incorporate the stones in walls for a small park nearby. Frost Bank also agreed to protect smaller nearby landmarks and to pay for moving the two-story stone August Stuemke Barn, first built behind the Stowers Building at North Flores and Travis streets in 1867. The barn ended up reassembled on the grounds of the Conservation Society's Wulff House.[16]

On a Sunday morning three months and three days after the Rand Building agreement was signed, an Oklahoma demolition firm placed 250 pounds of explosives throughout the Stowers Building. They were timed to detonate in twelve half-second intervals. In six seconds, the ten-story Stowers Building imploded into a twenty-foot pile of rubble and dust.[17]

Mayor Henry Cisneros was called upon again in an upcoming crisis involving the formidable RepublicBank of Dallas which had an elaborate San Antonio expansion plan of its own, one involving the fate of a landmark which would deeply divide San Antonio preservationists and their allies. RepublicBank in 1978 acquired Bexar County National Bank, based for forty-four years in nondescript quarters at the corner of Travis and St. Mary's streets. In

Left: As part of the deal which saved the Rand Building, visible at top left beside Frost Bank in the first picture, the 1867 Steumke Barn's blocks were numbered and then disassembled at the original site, then moved at the expense of Frost Bank. The blocks were arranged by number and put back together on the grounds of the Conservation Society's Wulff House headquarters on King William Street. San Antonio Conservation Society.

1974, Bexar County National Bank had bought the last parcel of property in an entire block bounded by Houston, St. Mary's Travis and Soledad streets, a block divided by the San Antonio River.[18]

Two blocks away, Republic's rival InterFirst Bank, in the San Antonio market since acquiring George W. Brackenridge's old First National Bank, was planning its own architectural tour-de-force, a postmodern twenty-one-story showpiece of red granite and glass designed by Skidmore, Owings and Merrill that would pick up motifs of the city's earlier skyline.[19] With the largest locally owned bank's Two Frost Tower on the drawing boards and the second-largest National Bank of Commerce also planning a new landmark headquarters tower in the neighborhood, RepublicBank was not to be outdone.

In 1981, RepublicBank's plans took the shape of a three-building, one million square-foot, $125 million Republic of Texas Plaza opening onto the San Antonio River. A thirty-story office tower was to anchor the plaza and a six-story banking building would face Travis Street to the west. A fifteen-story office building was planned to the south, at the traditional central downtown corner of Houston and St. Mary's streets on the site of the Gunter Building, longtime home of Hertzberg's Jewelers.[20] The landmark cast iron seventeen-foot Hertzberg Clock was to remain on the corner, under ownership of the Conservation Society.[21] Razed in addition to the Gunter Building was to be the 3,000-seat 1926 Spanish Revival-style Texas Theater, one of 127 movie palaces designed by the Kansas City architectural firm of Robert Otto Boller.[22]

RepublicBank and the Conservation Society seemed mutually dismayed by the ensuing uproar. Conservation Society officials had met with Bexar County National Bank officials early in 1977. The bank said there were no immediate plans for the Texas Theater, and promised to keep in touch on the matter when the Conservation Society informed the bank of its opposition to demolition.[23] After RepublicBank took over, however, its officials claimed to have "no evidence" of any such prior contact between Bexar County Bank and the Conservation Society. "Already," concluded a subsequent newspaper analysis, "the threads of miscommunication were being woven between the community group and the bank, with one side believing it was delivering its message and the other side hearing no message at all."[24]

Bank officials later said they waited for suggestions on what conservationists would like to see done after the Conservation Society toured the unused theater in 1979, but got instead only a letter of thanks. They said they took this as a signal that the theater was not important to the society. When there were reports that the theater would be torn down for a parking lot, "We were asked specifically if we were going to make it a parking lot," remembered the new RepublicBank president, "and we answered specifically that we were not."[25] RepublicBank hired the firm of Ford, Powell and Carson to present

Timed explosives caused the landmark ten-story Stowers Building to collapse into a twenty-foot pile of rubble in six seconds. The demolition was part of a deal with Frost National Bank, in background, which saved the Rand Building nearby. San Antonio Express-News.

a preliminary plan for the site, with Boone Powell as project architect. In mid-1981 the land-use plan recommended razing all of the Texas Theater but its facade, which would be incorporated into the facade of the fifteen-story office building.

When plans were made public in December, Conservation Society leaders reacted positively.[26] But later that month, Conservation Society directors voted to "actively oppose" demolition of the theater.[27] Hostilities escalated.

The Texas, one of downtown San Antonio's great movie palaces, was the scene in 1927 for the nation's premiere of Wings, *the locally filmed movie which won the first Academy Award for Best Picture. Zintgraff Collection, The Institute of Texan Cultures.*

In a strategy session, directors decided to write the RepublicBank board and send copies to city council members and newspapers.[28] Two months later they sponsored "Save the Texas Theater" displays at shopping malls and at a National Preservation Week reception.[29] The Conservation Society also tried an outright purchase of the Texas Theater from the bank.[30]

Next, the Historic Review Board denied the bank's application for a demolition permit. As the bank was preparing to seek a city council override of the denial, Conservation Society directors in special session asked for an injunction to block demolition while "all applicable historic preservation laws" were exercised.[31] The result was an Agreed Temporary Order, signed with Mayor Henry Cisneros acting as mediator. The bank agreed not to begin demolition for sixty days while the Conservation Society developed an alternate plan, which the bank was under no obligation to accept. The plan could include an offer for purchase by the society of the entire block. Both sides were barred from talking to the press.[32]

The Conservation Society turned to architect Alex Caragonne of Rayna/Caragonne Architects, who called in Princeton University's noted postmodern architect Michael Graves. The Chicago firm of Schlaes & Company was retained for the financial analysis and feasibility study.[33] Those

Postmodern architect Michael Graves proposed a plan to save the Texas Theater by building beside it four high-rise towers of pink granite and limestone, topped with truncated penthouse pyramids. The model shows how air space lost above the theater by its preservation is offset by large adjacent towers. San Antonio Express-News.

hoping for an innovative design that would preserve the Texas Theater while still providing the required one million square feet of usable office space were hardly disappointed. Graves came up with what one observer termed "a Beaux Arts vision of a Mesopotamian palace."[34] Its facade featured four high-rise towers, each with the first seven floors of pink granite and upper floors of natural limestone broken in the center by a column of deep sea-green tiles. The truncated penthouse pyramids capping each tower were to be pale blue.[35] Lynn Osborne Bobbitt's first meeting as incoming Conservation Society president was the emergency session called on Friday, July 9, to plan a press conference for the following Monday—the last day possible under the court order—to present the finished plans, which cost the society more than $123,000.[36]

Graves's bold design polarized public opinion. Some called it "a monstrosity." Even some proponents called it "bizarre." After studying the plan for a week, RepublicBank simply called it impractical. Costs were too high, it would take longer to build and was not oriented well to the river, officials said.[37] The bank also rejected the Conservation Society's offer to buy the entire block for

Ultimately, only the Texas Theater's ornamental facade was saved, to be incorporated in one building of the failed RepublicBank's unfinished Republic of Texas Plaza. The San Antonio Light *Collection, The Institute of Texan Cultures.*

$12.2 million.[38] Demolition of all but the ornamental facade of the Texas Theater began.

Rejection of the Michael Graves proposal in favor of the Ford, Powell and Carson plan satisfied O'Neil Ford, who had jested in his personal journal that the Graves design showed "not one indication of whether it was to be built—or extruded or fashioned by a pastry cook."[39] But satisfaction did not overcome dismay at the feeling of so many conservationists that Ford, the lifelong supporter and practitioner of enlightened historic preservation, had lost the faith by a desire to keep a big client.[40] "The Texas Theater is no jewel—never was anything but a mishmash of Italian-Spanish stuff," he wrote, "but so were hundreds of other theaters of that period."[41]

At 76, Ford, who eight years earlier had the distinction of being designated a National Historic Landmark by the National Council on the Arts, had a serious heart condition. He died on July 20, 1982, hours after receiving a triple coronary bypass. "Perhaps it was inevitable that the scrappy fighter would depart in the middle of a donnybrook," wrote his biographer. In a eulogy that preceded a feast at Willow Way, an event described as "a combination of an Irish wake, a New Orleans jazz funeral and a Mexican fiesta," Maury Maverick, Jr. quoted a definition of "the enemy" as one "who daily defiles the beauty that surrounds him and makes vulgar the tragedy." Said Maverick: "In his life and in his architecture, O'Neil stood up to those who would destroy beauty, who would make vulgar the tragedy."[42]

While San Antonio's two largest locally based banks planned their high-rise headquarters battles with two interloping bank conglomerates, what was once San Antonio's third-largest bank—Alamo National, by then a branch of MBank—was still happily ensconced in its Art Deco tower. MBank, however, found itself in the landmark demolition business by default.

MBank Alamo became the owner of the Blue Bonnet Hotel after its mortgagees were unsuccessful following a 1978 renovation. Designed by Paul Silber and opened at 426 North St. Mary's Street in 1928, the twelve-story, 220-room hotel had decorative Spanish Mission Revival style stonework.[43] It stood among a cluster of contemporary skyscrapers forming an impressive urban vista, or an urban canyon, depending on one's point of view. Studios in the Blue Bonnet made it a pioneer recording center for a host of western swing and cowboy singers, blues musicians and Hispanic vocalists and players. Best known was the legendary black Mississippi delta singer and guitarist Robert Johnson, who cut his first record at Radio Station KONO's recording facility in the Blue Bonnet Hotel in 1936.[44] The bank leased the hotel to new managers, who also fell behind in their payments and were foreclosed on early in 1985. The bank announced plans to close the hotel.[45] Next it applied for a permit to raze the building for a small park, awaiting the site's use for a high-rise office building.[46]

But the city's historic preservation ordinance had just been toughened, and things became more complicated. Previously, a building could be razed simply by waiting 120 days after the Historic Review Board had denied a demolition permit. Now demolition would be considered only after severe economic hardship had been proven and when definite plans had been shown for appropriate development of the site. There was no more waiting period after which demolition could proceed, but appeals could be made to city council. The Blue Bonnet case was seen as a test of the new ordinance.[47] But its companion four-year study by the city's Historic Sites and Structures Task Force was not yet complete. The Historic Review Board designated the Blue Bonnet as "significant" in advance of consideration of the other 1,400 buildings studied.[48] When the designation got to the City Zoning Commission, however, it was rejected. Amid objections to "the manner in which

Use of a telephoto lens enlarges the relative size of the distinctive 30-story Smith-Young Tower/Tower Life building, shown looming over the urban canyon of South St. Mary's Street. This 1960s view changed with a bank's demolition of the Blue Bonnet Hotel, its site promised to remain a park—until the failed bank's property was taken over by developers who turned the park into a parking lot. The Institute of Texan Cultures, courtesy San Antonio Development Agency.

MBank had gone about influencing the Zoning Commission," Conservation Society directors voted to withdraw the society's deposits from MBank in protest and to commission their own cost study for rehabilitating the Blue Bonnet.[49]

Next MBank appealed the Historic Review Board's designation to city council. The Conservation Society thought city council's support of its own ordinance to be "of vital importance to the whole preservation effort," and hired former City Attorney Lloyd Denton to present its case to the council.[50] It thought the hotel ideal for renovation for middle-income apartments.[51] At the city council meeting at the end of September, 1988, MBank Chairman Bob Davis declared that the council needed to support the bank in "a costly, dangerous and unattractive situation that needs to be remedied right away." Preservation proponents warned that if city council did not follow its own process, their action would be "a dangerous precedent." By a vote of four in favor, three opposed and two abstentions, with two members absent, the designation fell short of a majority. MBank was free to demolish the Blue Bonnet Hotel.[52]

But the Conservation Society was not ready to give up. After deciding there were insufficient grounds for a lawsuit, Society President Liz Davies got Mayor Cisneros, who voted with the preservationists, to agree to meet with bank officials to seek a city lease of the hotel for downtown housing.[53] Nothing materialized. When the United States Comptroller of the Currency replied to an inquiry of the Texas Historical Commission that no federal funds were being used to demolish the building, hope of preservation was lost.[54] The Blue Bonnet came down and the bank, as promised, landscaped the site as a park, awaiting construction of a high-rise office building.[55]

The next use of the Blue Bonnet site, however, was not for a high-rise office building. Nor, a decade after the Rand Building and Texas Theater imbroglios, did three of the four banks racing to the sky ever occupy the main buildings they had planned so boldly. Soon after the dust of the Stowers Building settled, Frost National Bank planted grass and wildflowers on the vacant site of the unbuilt Two Frost Tower, and became the only one of the ten largest banks in Texas to escape the fruit basket turnover of the state banking industry as key elements of the Texas economy collapsed.[56] RepublicBank incorporated the facade of the Texas Theater into a thirteen-story office building and put up the second, eight-story building on the opposite corner.[57] The struggling Republic and InterFirst banks first merged and consolidated San Antonio operations in the InterFirst Building, then failed altogether. The pieces were picked up by what became NationsBank—except for the unfinished Republic of Texas Plaza, foreclosed upon on the courthouse steps, its thirty-story tower unbuilt.[58] Likewise, in assuming the wreckage of MBank, Bank One did not pick up MBank's Blue Bonnet Hotel site. That

site was sold by the Federal Deposit Insurance Corp. to others, who bulldozed the new park not for an office building but for a parking lot.[59]

San Antonio may have lost the Texas Theater, but three other major downtown movie palaces remained—the Majestic on East Houston Street; the Empire, abutting the Majestic building but facing South St. Mary's Street; and, a block south, the Aztec, in 1988 the only downtown motion picture theater still operating in a major Texas city.[60] Exteriors of the three remaining theaters were undistinguished. It was, after all, the interiors which were more important "in conveying an exotic fairy tale environment."[61]

The interior of the shuttered 1,700-seat Empire, opened in 1916, had "a serenely elegant post-Victorian space," its architectural highlighting done originally in a half-dozen shades of gold.[62] The 3,000-seat 1926 Aztec Theater, which remained open, had "the grandest Meso-American interior in Texas."[63] Exuberant abstractions in geometrically patterned brickwork, relief carvings, step-back zigurrat masses, vibrant colors and hieroglyphs featured stone-faced mask of Coyclaxiuhqui capping each column of the grand lobby, while colorful deity masks flanked a great sun disk in the center of the proscenium arch.[64] The 3,700-seat Majestic Theater's 1929 atmosphere of baroque fantasy represented the peak of theater designer John Eberson's career.[65] Indoors, past the Moorish-style ticket office, the asymmetrical Spanish-garden design had a ruffled proscenium arch balancing cathedral bell towers on one side and, on the other, a Moorish castle "abandoned except for a few doves and some Texas turkeys."[66]

In the mid-1970s, the Arts Council of San Antonio envisioned a downtown theater district which would include all three theaters.[67] Its attention focused on the Majestic, in 1974 the first of the three to close. The concept attracted a group of local investors, who in 1978 refurbished and reopened the theater as the Majestic Music Hall. An opening series of thirty stage performances began with comedian Milton Berle's tribute to show business.[68]

While the short-lived music hall operation buoyed hopes for the Majestic, plans also surfaced for the Aztec. One developer wanted to alter its interior as part of a festival market place, although another, inevitably, proposed to raze the building for a parking garage.[69] In 1983, the San Antonio Conservation Society decided to help rescue the Aztec Theater by giving a boost to downtown developer Arthur P. "Hap" Veltman, who planned a $31 million effort to transform it as home of the San Antonio Symphony, then dividing its concerts between Trinity University's Laurie Auditorium and the convention center's Theater for the Performing Arts, where scheduling conflicts with conventions were increasing. Retail space would go on the lower levels and upstairs would be condominiums.[70] The Conservation Society advanced $240,000 for a purchase option, another $150,000 for consulting and legal fees and offered a $1 million subsidy to Veltman's Aztec Development Partnership.[71] The symphony board voted to move in, and the Target '90 Performing Arts District Task Force in 1986 proposed, unsuccessfully, a municipal bond issue to buy both the Majestic and the Aztec.[72]

By 1987, evolving plans for the Aztec saw it instead as a performing arts hall for an arts high school to be housed in the adjoining Karotkin Building, to be renovated under overall sponsorship of the San Antonio Independent School District.[73] But the economic slowdown hampered private financing, and concern for the Aztec's ownership increased. As the Texas economy worsened, the price dropped by more than two-thirds. Sensing that the theater's value would return long-term and that the time was right to make a good deal to assure its preservation, at a special two-hour meeting on July 13, 1988, directors under the leadership of President Liz Davies voted to buy the Aztec Building for the Conservation Society itself.[74]

The Conservation Society's saving of the Aztec Theater was the catalyst for accomplishing what came next, according to the chairman of the newly formed Las Casas Foundation, Joci (Mrs. Joe Jr.) Straus, in the midst of a $21.1 million project to rescue the Majestic and Empire theaters.[75] Encouraged by saving of the Aztec, within three months city council increased its year-old Majestic project commitment to $6.8 million. Priority was designated to the Majestic so it could open as the new home of the San Antonio Symphony a year later, the symphony's fiftieth anniversary.[76] To complete first-phase financing of $2.6 million, the Conservation Society pledged to loan Las Casas $500,000 if necessary.[77] As cost estimates of the Majestic's first-phase restoration rose to $4.4 million, the society replaced the pledge with an outright gift of $250,000.[78] The magnificently restored Majestic Theater opened on schedule in October of 1989.

Back at the Aztec, the San Antonio Conservation Society had found itself in the unlikely role of operating a downtown movie theater.[79] Or, to be precise, three downtown movie theaters, since the Aztec's balcony had been

Movies like Red Sonja *could be seen during the year the San Antonio Conservation Society operated its newly purchased three-screen Aztec Theater as a commercial movie house. San Antonio Conservation Society.*

separated from the downstairs auditorium and divided into two additional, smaller theaters. All showed first-run action-adventure and horror films, such as "Gates of Hell," "Sister-Sister" and "Murder on Elm Street." It was expected that previous owner Maurice Braha would continue operating the three-screen complex.[80] Scarcely a month after the sale closed in the fall of 1988, however, Braha phoned to say he would shut down the theaters the next week, citing poor health. If the Conservation Society wanted the inventory and projection equipment, the price was $20,000.[81]

The building was better cared for if occupied rather than vacant, society directors decided. And, they rationalized, while the fare may not be the best, at least films were not pornographic—"'R' maybe, but not 'X.'"[82] Rather than have a film management company operate the theater, directors formed a for-profit subsidiary named Aztec Conservation Inc. to try operating it themselves for forty-five days.[83] They hoped to improve quality of the films "on at least one screen," but soon realized that suppliers had to be "persuaded" to furnish better movies.[84] Then came the revelation that such films, even on a first-run basis in the summer, required a prepaid guarantee of some $5,000 each. Aztec Conservation Inc. decided to bid for June films only.[85] Nor was it easy to publicize even then what was being shown; President Davies protested to the publisher of the *Light* that a local theater chain got preferred advertising placement over independent theaters like the Aztec.[86]

Then came other joys of building management. Repairs had to bring the building up to code requirements. Short of tenants for the upper floors, the society fixed the first two floors and closed the top floors altogether.[87] There was haggling with a departing tenant wanting to use his security deposit as his last month's rent, and with another who wanted to stay but couldn't afford the insurance. The building's previous owner lost his copy of the promissory note, which caused some legal problems.[88] An electrical fire in the basement required the society to come up with temporary electrical service.[89]

The biggest frustration was shared with other downtown businesses in struggling through a massive downtown street and utility upgrade program. Construction crews broke a cellar skylight unit in the Aztec sidewalk, a $10,000 problem the society asked the construction company to fix.[90] Five new light poles on the Commerce Street side were said to require drilling through the pavement into the boiler room and basement. That raised fears of water seepage, and the society's lawyer was instructed to say that neither the drilling nor replacement of the sidewalks was acceptable.[91] Next came news that paving St. Mary's Street past the theater would take two and a half months, certain to reduce movie attendance—as would work on the sidewalk, which construction workers had just carefully cleaned but would now replace. Access difficulties at least solved the cost problem of first-run movies; until construction work was finished, Aztec Conservation Inc. would show just second-run movies at reduced admission, but still no X-rated films.[92]

During the Conservation Society's first two weeks in the commercial movie theater business, daily attendance averaged 175, then jumped to 236 during the first two weeks of October. The net income of $4,500, however, was wiped out by the mid-October payroll.[93] By February, Aztec Conservation Inc.'s losses of nearly $23,000 were covered by a loan from the Conservation Society.[94] April's net profit of $225 did not go far toward offsetting another $12,000 in losses, however, and soon operations were reviewed on a month-to-month basis.[95] By October, the last office and retail tenants moved out and the Aztec was considered an empty building. Monthly insurance rates more than tripled to $17,000.[96] With monthly operating losses still averaging $11,000, directors voted to close the entire building, including the theater.[97] In February of 1990, three months after the theater closed, Aztec Conservation Inc. was dissolved.[98]

By this time, the Conservation Society planned to sell the Aztec Building for $2 million cash as part of a package which included using the adjacent Karotkin Building as a hotel. A hotel tower would go above Crockett Street, and shops would be entered at river level. The theater itself would be owned by the Conservation Society.[99] After one prospective purchaser failed to come up with earnest money, a Dallas-based entertainment company did, but then, after two years of extensions, was unable to get financing.[100] A San Antonio Community Development Council Inc. proposal to buy the office portion of the building for a $2.14 million fifty-unit, federally funded apartment project was rejected.[101] In May of 1992, the Conservation Society was approached by restaurateur Thierry Burkle, who wanted to turn the theater into a dinner theater with laser and electronic shows and live performances and to use the rest of the building for apartments and a river-level restaurant and shops.[102] The project was approved by the Historic Design and Review Commission and by city council. The sale closed in August of 1993.[103]

Meanwhile, things were going well at the two nearby theaters. The Majestic was the site of a dinner hosted by President George Bush for six heads of state visiting San Antonio for a hemisphere economic summit conference.[104] Fifteen of the eighty-nine apartments being renovated in the Majestic Building were leased sight unseen.[105] A Las Casas survey of arts organizations pointed to the Empire's destiny as a theater for smaller events, its 1,700 seats to be configured into more open seating for 900.[106] In the summer of 1991, Las Casas began a $300,000 phase of a $5 million Empire Theater restoration project. The mother-daughter team of Conservation Society members Cisi (Mrs. Lloyd) Jary and Pam Rosser painstakingly revealed and restored ornately colored interior architectural highlights and stenciling.[107] Layers of orange and white paint and plaster were peeled back as original colors of eggshell, light brown and greens covered in gold leaf and gold powder paint were restored.[108]

A fourth major theater awaited attention—the 3,000-seat Alameda Theater (1949) on West Houston Street at the western fringe of downtown, with its trademark 86-foot illuminated sign atop its marquee. Designed in the late Art Moderne style by local architect N. Straus Nayfach for Mexican vaudeville acts and Spanish-language movies, the Alameda's curving side walls featured brightly colored murals of sights and symbols, those of Texas on one side and those of Mexico on the other.[109] Unlike the Majestic Theater or the San Pedro Playhouse, both owned by the city, no private foundations were ready to supplement public funds and assure appropriate restoration, and Conservation Society assets were still tied up in the Aztec. So in 1994 the Alameda was purchased for preservation as a Mexican-American performing arts center by the City of San Antonio, in an action 180-degrees from preservation-blind decades of yore.

Notes

1. Minutes, F-Feb. 22, 1973; G-Jan. 24, 1974.

2. Safety of the Indiana limestone auditorium was a political issue at the time of its completion, during the colorful gubernatorial campaign between Miriam "Ma" Ferguson, wife of former Governor James Ferguson, and Daniel Moody. In a letter to San Antonio Mayor John W. Tobin, a Moody partisan, former governor Ferguson demanded that Tobin not "continue to publicly abuse me and my good wife." He accused Tobin, a prime backer of the auditorium's construction, of "waste of the people's money in building a fire-trap auditorium." In introducing the ultimately successful Moody in a rally at the east front of the new auditorium, Tobin read Ferguson's letter and responded by declaring furiously, among other things: "I could burn a carload of hay in this building without having to turn in a fire alarm. It would be as hard to burn it as it would be to burn the Rock of Gibraltar." ("Tobin Reveals Ferguson Challenge," *San Antonio Express*, Aug. 21, 1926, 1.)

3. Minutes, D-Dec. 5, 1980.

4. Don Walden, "Voters approve Muni Auditorium bonds 2–1," *San Antonio Express-News*, Apr. 5, 1981, 1. Coordinating the society's effort was its fourth vice president-public relations, Marlene (Mrs. Martin W.) Gordon. The vote was 75,675 to 43,811. Another $3.9 million in public funds brought total restoration costs to $13 million. On Veteran's Day in 1984, city officials rededicated the completed auditorium to the memory of servicemen who died during World War I. ("Rededication of auditorium is scheduled," *San Antonio Light*, Nov, 9, 1984, B-1.)

5. Mike Greenberg, "San Antonio Grows: Coping With Prosperity In The Alamo City," *Texas Architect*, Sept.-Oct. 1983, 34.

6. "$70 million tower due," *San Antonio Express*, Jun. 30, 1981, 1.

7. Mike Greenberg, "A randy ending for a grand old building," *San Antonio Express-News*, Jun. 21, 1981, 10-H.

8. "Society asks Rand Building be preserved," *San Antonio Express*, Dec. 10, 1980, 8-B.

9. Deborah Weser, "Council clears way for 2 more garages," *San Antonio Light*, May 29, 1981, 2-A. The garage on the Rand Building site, dubbed the Banking Corridor Garage, was to be one in a series of downtown garages. All were to be above ground and operated not by a lessee but by the city. The Marina Garage built for HemisFair was joined in the 1970s by the River Bend Garage at Market and Presa streets. The Banking Corridor Garage was approved at the same time as the Mid-City Garage, built at Houston and Navarro streets beside the Majestic Theater.

10. Mike Greenberg, "Battle shaping up on fate of Rand Building," *San Antonio Express-News*, May 24, 1981, 1-D.

11. Ibid.

12. Minutes, D-Jul. 7, 1981; D-Jul. 15, 1981, 2.

13. Minutes, D-Aug. 19, 1981, 2.

14. Minutes, D-Sept. 16, 1981, 2; D-Sept. 21, 1981; "Rand Building ownership transferred," *San Antonio Light*, Nov. 6, 1981.

15. "Rand Building ownership transferred," *San Antonio Light*, Nov. 6, 1981.

16. Minutes, D-Sept. 21, 1981; D-Oct. 21, 1981, 3; D-Oct. 30, 1981; D-Nov. 18, 1981; D-Jan. 20, 1982, 2; D-May 19, 1982, 2; Deborah Weser, "Rand deal in closing stages," *San Antonio Light*, Nov. 5, 1981; "Rand Building ownership transferred," *San Antonio Light*, Nov. 6, 1981. Directing the Steumke Barn project was architect Lewis S. Fisher. Curtis Hunt, Jr. was the master stonemason in charge of dismantling and reassembling the building. Frost Bank, ironically, ended up leasing space in the restored Rand Building for its own offices so it could rent premium space in its own building at the market rate.

17. Susan Lindee, "Noted demolition expert to raze downtown building," *San Antonio Express*, Jan. 28, 1982; Gordon Dillow, "12 blasts bring Stowers Building crumbling down," *San Antonio Light*, Feb. 8, 1982, 1. This was the second downtown building destroyed with timed explosives. The first went down in 1978, when the eight-story Elks Building, built in 1912 at the corner of Pecan and Navarro streets as the private Travis Club, was imploded with 250 pounds of nitroglycerine-based dynamite. "My grandson had wanted me to buy him a toy called 'The Liquidator,' where you just point and make believe you destroy something," said Leroy G. Denman, Jr., chairman of San Antonio Bank & Trust Co., which wanted the Elks Building site for a parking lot. When he pressed the button, "That's what I felt like—a liquidator. Just point and the building is gone." Conservationists were regretful but did not object to demolition of the building, which survives in drawings on boxes of San Antonio's Finck Cigar Company's Travis Club Cigars. (Minutes, D-Apr. 5, 1978; "Destruction of building is approved," *San Antonio Express*, May 19, 1978, 9-A; Alan Bailey, "Downtown Elks Building blown to bits," *San Antonio Express*, Jun. 19, 1978, 1; "Travis Club will live on," *San Antonio Express*, Jun. 19, 1978, 3-A.)

18. Mike Greenberg, "Battle shaping up on fate of Rand building," *San Antonio Express-News*, May 24, 1981, 1-D; Richard Erickson, "Now showing at the Texas: 'The Great Bank Holdup,'" *San Antonio Express-News*, Jul. 4, 1982, 1-G.

19. Conservation Society directors commended InterFirst for the building being "compatible and sensitive to the architectural charm of San Antonio." (Minutes, D-Jun. 15, 1983, 2.)

20. Mike Greenberg, "Design grows out of location problems," *San Antonio Express-News*, Dec. 13, 1981, 1-B; Erickson, "Now showing at the Texas."

21. Manufactured by E. Howard Co. of Boston, the same firm which manufactured the clock for San Antonio's city hall tower, the clock has an eight-day movement and is hand wound. It was installed at the original Hertzberg location on Commerce Street in 1878 and moved with the store to its new location in 1910. It was donated in 1982 by Hertzberg heirs to the Conservation Society, which dedicated the restored clock in 1990. ("Official Clock Winder Regrets," *San Antonio Express*, May 22, 1927, 8; Doris Irby, "Hertzberg Clock Home Again," *SACS News*, Jan.–Feb., 1991.) A suburban artifact was preserved by the Conservation Society when it was granted guardianship of the neon sign of the flying red horse added atop the 1920s Magnolia Oil Company's Spanish Colonial service station at Broadway and Austin Highway in Alamo Heights when Magnolia was acquired by Mobil Oil. (Minutes, D-Jun. 17, 1986; D-Aug. 20, 1986; Henry, *Architecture in Texas*, 185.)

22. George, *O'Neil Ford*, 217.

23. Minutes, D-Feb. 16, 1977, 2.

24. Erickson, "Now showing at the Texas."

25. Ibid.

26. Ibid.; Jan Jarboe, "O'Neil Ford," *San Antonio Express-News*, Aug. 15, 1982, 1-H. In January of 1982, the society newsletter praised the bank "for preserving the important facade of the Texas Theatre." ("the president's report," *SACS Newsletter*, Jan. 1982, 2.)

27. Minutes, D-Jan. 20, 1982.

28. Minutes, D-Feb. 3, 1982.

29. Minutes, D-Apr. 14, 1982.

30. Ibid.

31. Minutes, D-Apr. 22, 1982. This was to give time for the National Register of Historic Places listing process, which would deny any use of federal funds for the building's demolition. In May, the Texas Historical Commission unanimously voted to put the Texas Theater on the National Register. (George, *O'Neil Ford*, 217.)

32. Minutes, D-Apr. 29, 1982; D-May 19, 1982, 2; D-Jul. 9, 1982; George, *O'Neil Ford*, 218; Erickson, "Now showing at the Texas."

33. Minutes, G-May 26, 1982; Jon Thompson, "Graves Designs Alternative in RepublicBank, Texas Theater Imbroglio," *Texas Architect*, Sept.-Oct., 1982, 13–14.

34. Thompson, "Graves Designs Alternative."

35. Ibid.

36. Minutes, D-Jul. 9, 1982; D-Jul. 21, 1982. Lynn Osborne Bobbitt is the daughter of Pat Osborne, San Antonio's first Historic Preservation Officer.

37. Thompson, "Graves Designs Alternative."

38. George, *O'Neil Ford*, 219.

39. Ibid., 218–19.

40. Jarboe, "O'Neil Ford."

41. Ibid.

42. George, *O'Neil Ford, Architect*, 211, 219, 222.

43. "Bluebonnet Hotel," summary in SACS Library.

44. Stephen Cicchetti, "Blues wizard's S.A. legacy," *San Antonio Express-News*, Nov. 30, 1986, 1-J.

45. Mike Davis, "Hotel to close," *San Antonio Express-News*, Feb. 16, 1985.

46. David Anthony Richelieu, "Battle lines drawn on hotel demolition," *San Antonio Express-News*, Jun. 21, 1988, 5-A.

47. Ibid.

48. David Anthony Richelieu, "Recording facilities may net special designation for hotel," *San Antonio Express-News*, Jun. 28, 1988, 14-A; Minutes, D-Jul. 20, 1988, 2, 6.

49. Minutes, D-Aug. 17, 1988, 1, 3; D-Sept. 28, 1988, 2.

50. Minutes, G-Sept. 28, 1988.

51. David Anthony Richelieu, "Recording facilities may net special designation for hotel."

52. Patrick Canty, "Council fails to designate Blue Bonnet a historic site," *San Antonio Light*, Sept. 30, 1988.

53. Minutes, D-Oct. 5, 1988; D-Oct. 19, 1988, 2.

54. Mike Greenberg, "Blue Bonnet's last chance for survival fails," *San Antonio Express-News*, Jan. 4, 1989.

55. David Bennett, "Parking lot to replace private park," *San Antonio Express-News*, Jul. 31, 1991.

56. In 1989 Frost Bank built a 12-lane motor bank with walls of stone from the old church. (Minutes, D-Mar. 15, 1989, 2–3.)

57. Richard Erickson, "RepublicBank downtown construction under way," *San Antonio Express-News*, Apr. 2, 1983.

58. Rob Liebold, "476 properties foreclosed on July 4th," *San Antonio Express-News*, Jul. 5, 1989. Three years later, the office building with the Texas Theater facade was leased by Southwestern Bell (later SBC) for its corporate headquarters, newly moved from St. Louis. (T.D. Honeycutt, "S.W. Bell's move to boost downtown," *San Antonio Light*, Oct. 1, 1992, 7-B.)

59. David Bennett, "Parking lot to replace private park," *San Antonio Express-News*, Jul. 31, 1991. The 32-story building being built by the National Bank of Commerce before its demise was later named Weston Tower.

60. David Anthony Richelieu, "Society completes Aztec Theater sale," *San Antonio Express-News*, Aug. 17, 1988. The original Majestic Theater in the Stowers Building continued as the State Theater, while the Princess Theater across the street from the new Majestic was razed for the Frost Brothers department store. The Depression cut short the theater building boom in San Antonio as it did the boom in everything else. Never built was the million-dollar Travis Street Theater, "not quite so elaborate as the Texas" but still having a capacity of 3,000 persons. To face Travis Street directly behind the Texas, it was designed by Texas Theater architect Robert Boller of Kansas City in 1929. ("City Will Get New Theater," *San Antonio Express*, Oct. 6, 1929, 1-A.)

61. Henry, *Architecture in Texas*, 308.

62. Karen Moser, "Restorative Powers," *Southern Accents*, Nov.–Dec. 1994, 240-DD; David Anthony Richelieu, "Empire to be gilt spectacle," *San Antonio Express-News*, Jul. 22, 1993, 1-B.

63. Henry, *Architecture in Texas*, 308. Its design is attributed to Mey and Hollyer and to local architects Robert Kelly and R.O. Koenig.

64. David Naylor, *Great American Movie Theaters* (Washington: The Preservation Press, 1987), 193; National Register of Historic Places Nomination Form, 1990. Reported *House and Garden* magazine: "As solemn and ecclesiastical in its way as the cathedral at Chartres, the Aztec's grandiose lobby seems lost in some mystical Mesoamerican twilight, its massively articulated faux stone walls groaning with ornament and sighing under a dusky patina meant to suggest the smoke from a thousand sacrificial fires." (Alison Cook, "Mayan Revival Revival," *HG*, Jan. 1990, 30–31.)

65. Ibid., 194.

66. Ibid.

67. David Anthony Richelieu, "Society negotiating to obtain Aztec Building," *San Antonio Express-News*, Jul. 21, 1988, 1-A.

68. David Hendricks, "Majestic Theater reborn as music hall," *San Antonio Express*, Sept. 8, 1978.

69. Richelieu, "Society negotiating."

70. Richelieu, "Society negotiating."

71. Ibid.; Minutes, D-Jul. 20, 1983, 2; D-May 16, 1984, 2; D-Oct. 12, 1984; D-Jan. 16, 1985, 4; D-Apr. 15, 1985; D-Jun. 1, 1988; D-Jul. 13, 1988. Promise of $150,000 from the Conservation Society to help match a federal Economic Development Administration grant had, however, permitted construction on the river level below the Aztec of arches as planned by Robert Hugman for an arcade. It was hoped the arches would become the entrance from the River Walk beneath Crockett Street into new basement-level shops in the Aztec Building. (Minutes, D-Jul. 16, 1988; David Anthony Richelieu, "Society has contract to buy Aztec building," *San Antonio Express-News*, Jul. 22, 1988, 1-A.)

72. Minutes, D-May 9, 1986; Richelieu, "Society negotiating."

73. Susie Phillips, "Majestic bought for Symphony," *San Antonio Express-News*, Sept. 30, 1988, 1-D.

74. Minutes, D-Jul. 13, 1988, 1–3. Confidentiality of the price was a condition of the sale. The society saved interest and paid off the note early at the end of 1992. (Minutes, D-Jul. 20, 1988; D-Aug. 21, 1992, 2; D-Jan. 15, 1992, 2; D-Nov. 18, 1992.)

75. Phillips, "Majestic bought for Symphony;" Minutes, D-Nov. 16, 1988, 3.

76. Phillips, "Majestic bought for Symphony." The city would lease the theaters for $1 a year to Las Casas, an acronym for the Foundation for Cultural Arts in San Antonio. The independent Majestic Development Co. financed residential and commercial development for the rest of the Majestic Building, completed prior to start of work on the Brady Building which housed the Empire Theater.

77. Minutes, D-Jun. 1, 1988; D-Nov. 16, 1988, 3, 14. As fund-raising progressed, the pledge was to be reduced by an amount equal to one-fourth of all pledges made within the next two years, and to be eliminated altogether if additional pledges totaled $2 million by that time. (Minutes, D-Nov. 16, 1988, 3, 10, 16–17.)

78. Minutes, D-Aug. 4, 1989, 1, 4. The donated amount represented prepayment of the remainder of the society's declining pledge to Las Casas, which had already received $850,000 in other pledges. The Conservation Society held a reception for a Las Casas fund-raiser the next month in conjunction with the society's annual awards presentation held in the Majestic Theater. (Minutes, D-May 16, 1990, 3.)

79. Richelieu, "Society completes Aztec Theater sale."

80. David Anthony Richelieu, "Society completes Aztec Theater sale;" Minutes, G-Sept. 28, 1988.

81. Minutes, D-Sept. 21, 1988.

82. Minutes, G-Sept. 28, 1988.

83. Ibid., 1–2.

84. Ibid., 2; D-Nov. 16, 1988, 2.

85. Minutes, D-Apr. 26, 1989.

86. Minutes, D-Mar. 15, 1989, 10.

87. Minutes, D-Nov. 16, 1988, 2.

88. Minutes, D-Jan. 18, 1989, 2.

89. Minutes, D-Nov. 18, 1992; D-Dec. 9, 1992

90. Minutes, D-Feb. 15, 1989, 3; D-Mar. 15, 1989.

91. Minutes, D-Apr. 26, 1989, 1–2; D-Jun. 21, 1989, 2; D-Jul. 19, 1989.

92. Minutes, D-Apr. 26, 1989; D-May 17, 1989, 4.

93. Minutes, D-Oct. 19, 1988, 3.

94. Minutes, D-Feb. 15, 1989, 1–2. The vote to approve the loan was 35–19.

95. Minutes, D-May 17, 1989, 11; D-Aug. 16, 1989.

96. Minutes, D-Oct. 18, 1989, 2. Four months earlier, monthly rent from commercial tenants was nearly $3,000. (Minutes, D-Jun. 21, 1989, 2.)

97. Ibid.

98. Minutes, D-Nov. 15, 1989, 2; D-Feb. 21, 1990, 2.

99. Minutes, D-Jan. 18, 1989, 2, 10; D-Mar. 15, 1989, 3, 12. Tours of the theater at the time of the San Antonio Museum of Art's four-month "Splendors of Mexico" exhibit in 1991 drew more than 700 persons. (Minutes, D-Feb. 20, 1991, 2; D-Jul. 17, 1991, 2.)

100. Minutes, D-Aug. 4, 1989; D-Oct. 3, 1989; D-Jun. 20, 1990; D-Nov. 14, 1990, 2; D-Dec. 12, 1990; D-May 15, 1991, 2.

101. Minutes, D-Jul. 17, 1991; D-Jul. 22, 1991, 1–2; D-Jul. 31, 1991; Rolando Martinez, "Conservation Society nixes plan," *San Antonio Express-News*, Aug. 1, 1991, 14-A.

102. Minutes, D-May 20, 1992, 2–3; G-May 27, 1992; Susie Phillips Gonzalez, "Aztec Theater's sale to developer finally finished," *San Antonio Express-News*, Aug. 25, 1993, 1-B.

103. Minutes, D-Oct. 5, 1992; D-Mar. 17, 1993, 2; D-Jun. 9, 1993, 1–2; D-Jun. 18, 1993; D-Sept. 15, 1993. Historic interior surfaces and other significant features were protected by preservation covenants and approval by the State Historic Preservation Office was required of all renovation plans. (Gonzalez, "Aztec Theater's sale.")

104. Stefanie Scott, "Sources: Majestic to be site of state dinner," *San Antonio Express-News*, Feb. 15, 1992, 1.

105. Ashley Blaker, "Majestic models opened up," *San Antonio Light*, Nov. 19, 1992.

106. Linda McCann, "Theater district plan backed," *San Antonio Light*, Mar. 1, 1990, C-1; Mike Greenberg, "Empire Strikes Back," *San Antonio Express-News*, May 7, 1991, 13-A.

107. Richelieu, "Empire to be gilt spectacle;" Greenberg, "Empire Strikes Back;" Karen Moser, "Restorative Powers," *Southern Accents*, Nov.–Dec. 1994, 240 CC-FF. Longtime Conservation Society volunteer Cisi Jary, who with her daughter formed Restoration Associates of San Antonio, also worked on restorations of the Grand Opera House in Galveston, the Steves Homestead and the State Capitol in Austin.

108. "The Golden Empire," *The San Antonio Cultural Arts District News, The Publication of Las Casas Foundation*, Sept.–Oct. 1993, 1.

109. Naylor, *Great American Movie Theaters*, 192; Bruce MacDougal, "Viewpoints," *San Antonio Conservation Society News*, Jan. 1995, 3.

17

Hits and Misses

As new downtown landmarks were thrust into the familiar San Antonio skyline dating from the 1920s, preservationists found themselves facing crises caused not only by city government, individuals and private developers but also problems created by a bewildering array of civic and cultural institutions with which preservationists once felt comfortable: two Baptist churches and an order of nuns, a private university, a research institute, a non-profit retirement home, a women's volunteer organization and three of the state's largest banks.

Despite concerted efforts to preserve landmarks wholesale in clusters, saving isolated landmarks was still very much in order. Several successes happened easily, by donation directly to the Conservation Society. The first, in 1961, was the adobe Yturri-Edmunds House, on Mission Parkway north of Concepción Mission. Most of its original contents remained. Bequeathed by Ernestine Edmunds, a longtime teacher in the Harlandale and Alamo Heights school districts, it was built between 1840 and 1860 by her grandfather, Manuel Yturri Castillo. Underbrush was cleared with the help of workmen and garden club volunteers and the house was restored, with the aid of architectural artifacts scrounged from urban renewal sites. Ernst Schuchard, who helped restore the San José mill years before, and architect Marvin Eickenroht directed construction of the adjacent 1820 Concepción Acequia-powered grist mill and outside water wheel. The 1881 Ogé Carriage House, a two-story board-and-batten structure needing to be removed for river widening near King William Street, was purchased and taken to the Yturri-Edmunds property. It was restored for a caretaker's apartment upstairs, a meeting room downstairs and, briefly, for light lunches served on Tuesdays by volunteer retired teachers.[1]

In 1965 the Conservation Society was given another King William Street landmark, the Ike West House. Built in 1888, the three-story brick home had a turreted entrance, elaborate wooden balustrades and decorative iron grillwork

At the beginning of Mission Parkway north of Concepción Mission is the adobe 1840-60 Yturri-Edmunds House, bequeathed to the Conservation Society in 1961, restored and maintained as a house museum. San Antonio Conservation Society.

around the rooflines. After renting it out for eight years, the society sold the house with deed restrictions requiring that internal and external architectural integrity be preserved.[2] In 1968 the Charles A. Zilker estate donated the two-story rock 1870 Heidgen-Zilker House at Elm and Starr streets, northeast of the HemisFair grounds. The only area home with walls still connecting with the Alamo acequia, it had a frame exterior porch and stairway across the front, and needed extensive work. It was donated in 1970 to the Alamo Council of Camp Fire Girls for restoration as its headquarters.[3]

Another target for divestiture was the Navarro House, one of the society's hard-won successes. Its ongoing operation was not as easy as that of the Steves Homestead, which had the advantages of being grander, less isolated and in an area already attractive to tourists. In 1967, the paid curator at the Navarro House was replaced by a volunteer staff.[4] In the fall of 1973, members opened Cocina Navarro in the courtyard, serving buñuelos and coffee in midmorning and then hot lunches prepared in the new kitchen. Councilwoman Lila Cockrell officiated at its opening.[5] The first profits came a year later, but were not consistent. Cocina Navarro was closed in the spring of 1975.[6] The society decided to declare victory at the Navarro House and withdraw. The complex was donated to the Texas Parks and Wildlife Commission, with covenants that

The 1880 Ike West House on King William Street, left to the Conservation Society in 1965, was resold, with deed restrictions, eight years later. San Antonio Conservation Society.

it be operated as a museum and could still be used by the Conservation Society on special occasions.[7]

Among the acres of dilapidated but antique structures doomed by urban renewal on the near west side was another, in addition to the Navarro House, which the Conservation Society tagged for special attention in the early 1960s: the remaining portion of the Rivas House, built in 1832 on the corner of West Houston and Laredo streets across from the Alameda Theater, in the Rosa Verde Urban Renewal Area three blocks north of the Navarro House. Even though truncated in an early widening of Houston Street, it was an increasingly rare survival of structures built during the Mexican rule of San Antonio. Conservation Society officials insisted it did not seriously interfere with the site and could be saved, but Urban Renewal officials insisted that the new property owners, the Santa Rosa Development Corp., planned a medical office building on the entire property and wanted the Rivas House removed. When Urban Renewal employees pried the Texas historical medallion off the front of the building, Conservation Society President Vivian Hamlin (Terrett) and others hoped fund-raising could offer an alternative.[8] Five days later, however, the Rivas House was abruptly bulldozed into a pile of rubble.

In the ensuing commotion, San Antonio State Representative Jake Johnson, co-author of the 1969 Texas Antiquities Act, charged that not only was the demolition illegal, the agency was guilty of "bulldozing the Mexican-American heritage of San Antonio." Urban Renewal Agency Director Winston Martin countered that the agency was simply following orders and had, in any event, "never heard anything about the historic value of the structure

The remaining portion of the 1832 Mexican-era Rivas House, a Texas historical marker beside its entrance, was one of San Antonio's few structures left from the time of Mexican rule. Institute of Texan Cultures, San Antonio, Texas, courtesy of San Antonio Development Agency.

Below: The Rivas House was abruptly bulldozed in 1971 by the Urban Renewal Agency as preservationists worked to save it. The historic Alameda Theater across the street remained. The San Antonio Express-News *Collection, The Institute of Texan Cultures.*

until the private developers took over," presence of the historical medallion on the front of the building for the previous nine years notwithstanding.[9] At the Conservation Society's meeting the next day, Old Buildings Committee Chairman Pat Osborne urged members to pick up new bumper stickers emblazoned "Remember the Rivas House," adding that it "exemplifies what we hope will not happen again."[10]

Soon the same scenario seemed to be unfolding a few blocks away on the western banks of San Pedro Creek, where urban renewal demolition of surrounding buildings revealed the old San Antonio Soap Works, built by Johann Nicholas Simon Menger. Its rough-hewn limestone blocks allowed for a high ceiling and tall windows for ventilation of the suet, lye and acids that boiled in San Pedro Creek water in vats on the flagstone floor. It was considered the oldest industrial building in San Antonio and one of the oldest in the Southwest. But none of the bids for the land considered the building's preservation, and Urban Renewal Agency officials were making unsettlingly familiar statements about it facing a short future.[11]

Vowing that the building would not be demolished like the Rivas House, ten days after the Rivas House went down Conservation Society President Vivian Hamlin (Terrett) was in federal court getting an injunction barring demolition of the Menger Soap Works by the Urban Renewal Agency or its director, Winston Martin; by property developer Robert Callaway or his company; or by Housing and Urban Development Secretary George Romney or HUD's Urban Renewal Demonstration Program Division director. The Texas Historical Survey Committee in Austin recommended the building for the National Register.[12] Surprised Urban Renewal Agency officials responded that the Soap Works was not scheduled for demolition and asked that the suit be dismissed.[13] Callaway announced plans to restore the building with the aid of a Texas Historical Commission grant as the office of what became the 262-unit Soap Works Apartments, completed under the lead of developers Seymour Dreyfus, Bernard Lifshutz, and Stanley Hammer.[14]

Five blocks south, a reinvigorated Market Square, completed in 1976, preserved for use as restaurants and shops the commercial buildings lining two blocks of a pedestrian mall known as Produce Row, once part of Commerce Street. Its 1938 Municipal Market House, on the site of the ornate 1899 Alfred Giles–designed Market House, was renovated to house thirty shops with an atmosphere resembling the covered markets of Mexico.[15] Among buildings razed east of Market Square was the brick two-story F.A. Chapa Drug Co., with its two French-style, overhanging second-floor wooden window bays and its unusual wooden cupola. In 1894 newly arrived pharmacist Frank L. Chapa painted on the corner building's west wall a six- by ten-foot symbol of the pharmacy for which he had worked in Monterrey, Mexico—a framed golden lion on a field of green. Regular repainting kept the larger-than-life symbol fresh until the building made way, in 1970, for the northbound lane of Santa Rosa Avenue.[16]

In the Rivas House affair, city officials used with great effect their long-time excuse that "the conservation interests" should present the city with a master reference list of historic structures "instead of waiting until a crisis like this one."[17] The charge seemed proof of a city hall viewpoint that "conservation interests" were not among the proper interests of city government, even though in the case of San Antonio's sister "unique" city of New Orleans it

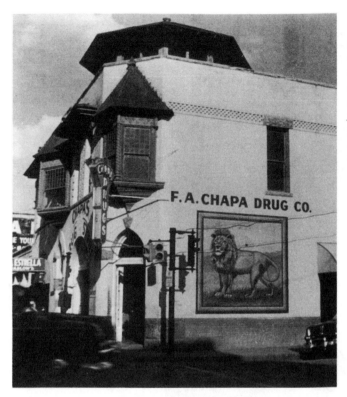

Left above: In the wake of the Rivas House bulldozing, the Urban Renewal Agency was barred by court order from destroying the Menger Soap Works beside San Pedro Creek, one of the earliest industrial buildings in San Antonio. San Antonio Conservation Society.

Left below: The Menger Soap Works was restored by developer Robert Callaway as offices for his adjoining new Soap Works Apartments complex. Lewis F. Fisher.

was city government itself which initiated and put through an Urban Renewal Demonstration grant for a multivolume study of downtown landmarks in the French Quarter, completed in 1968.[18]

One quasi-public agency in San Antonio which did grasp practical advantages of historic preservation was the newly reorganized U.S. Postal Service, which needed to vacate its Federal Building offices on Alamo Plaza in 1972. Postal Service District Director E.C. Stevenson had to look only a block east to the empty three-story, mansard-roofed Turner Halle on Bonham Street. Designed by James Wahrenberger in 1891 for a German community group, it was still coated in a bilious green from its days as a USO. Stevenson, not colorblind but seeing the intrinsic value of the building, decided against another coat of paint. Supervised by the Postal Service's district engineer, employees volunteered their spare time to fix up the interior and restore the exterior as well. Their sandblasting revealed a multicolored facade of dark red Chicago pressed brick, Kerrville limestone and polished granite columns. Side

New Postal Service District Director R.E. McCoy stands in front of the 1891 landmark restored by Postal Service volunteers in 1972 as the Postal Service's new district headquarters. San Antonio Conservation Society.

walls turned out to be of cream-colored Calavares brick, with dark red brick alternating in the window arches and scrolls carved into the sills. Postal Service officials estimated the cost of restoration was a third the cost of building or leasing quarters elsewhere.[19]

Elsewhere, official interest or disinterest notwithstanding, thorough inventories were done by private preservation groups themselves, as in Charleston, South Carolina, and Providence, Rhode Island. In San Antonio, however, the Conservation Society still seemed "long on inspiration" but "short on research."[20] At least, unlike local city government at the time, the Conservation Society was willing to accept some responsibility and take the initiative. The HemisFair crisis, reviving the Conservation Society's on-again, off-again attempts to catalog historic buildings, put architect Henry Steimbomer to work in 1962 on an Historic Index, an effort revitalized in 1967.[21] That joint effort with the Bexar County Historical Survey Committee and the National Park Service's Historic American Buildings Survey was undertaken "in light of the unusually great demolition of historic buildings in San Antonio."[22]

Established in 1933 as a public relief project for architects and draftsmen, the first phase of the Historic American Buildings Survey (HABS) lasted three months and recorded 882 buildings. The most extensive records produced were of the San Antonio missions, among the 242 buildings recorded in Texas under the direction of Marvin Eickenroht. Reestablished in 1957, work resumed in San Antonio in 1961 with HABS measurements of the Alamo by architect Eugene George. Once full-scale work resumed in Texas in 1966, architectural historian John C. Garner, Jr., who had been working on a survey of 1,000 buildings in Galveston under the sponsorship of the Galveston Historical Foundation, was loaned to San Antonio for an expanded HABS project.[23]

In San Antonio, three entities each paid a third of the $50,000 cost of the project. The Conservation Society contracted with Garner, who prepared inventory forms and photo-data books. The Bexar County Historic Survey Committee covered costs of measured drawings. The Historic American Building Survey paid for administrative support, including a task force of two architects and four student draftsmen, and for records for the Library of Congress. The San Antonio Chapter of the American Institute of Architects lent "professional guidance and advice" on the project, which studied nearly two hundred buildings.[24] The Texas State Historical Survey Committee completed a more detailed initial survey of buildings in the central city in 1971. The next year the City of San Antonio came up with $14,000 to start its own survey of historic sites under architect Andrew Perez, coordinated by the Conservation Society's Historic Buildings chairman, Pat Osborne, to avoid duplication.[25] After three years of looking at more than 3,000 downtown buildings, the city's Historic Resources Inventory listed 1,194 landmarks, 350 of them deemed vital to the city's character.[26]

Even though documentation provided an important defense for landmarks, those threatening San Antonio's landmarks had their own new ammunition, literally. Not only could lawyers often outflank new legal barriers or suggest that it would be easier to bulldoze a landmark on a weekend when no one was watching, new technology permitted landmarks simply to be dynamited—as the Stowers and Elks Club buildings were, in full view of spectators and television crews. Helpful though historic districts were in bringing order to neighborhood evolution and in allowing early detection of preservation problems, vast areas of moldering buildings were still unprotected. Unlike the cases of undefended landmarks in the booming 1920s, however, neither individuals nor businesses nor respected institutions in these latter-day prosperous times could count on anonymity or benign inattention when they placed a landmark at risk.

The Conservation Society, for example, did not hesitate when it found itself on a collision course with old allies from North Expressway days—the Sisters of Charity of the Incarnate Word. At issue was the distinctive Mother House on the Incarnate Word College campus at Broadway and Hildebrand Avenue.

Designed in 1899 by Alfred Giles, the red brick Mother House had a dramatic marble and granite stepped portico and peaked fourth-story bays along the front. The Sisters planned to remove it for a $15 million nursing home and health care facility, and had an engineering study showing that foundation work needed on the old structure would make its replacement more economical. San Antonio restoration architect Killis Almond disagreed, and came up with preliminary figures showing savings of $1 million if the building were simply restored. The Conservation Society offered to pay for a formal study, but the Sisters refused the offer.[27] The Texas Historical Commission, chaired by nearby resident T.R. Fehrenbach, also asked the Sisters to reconsider.[28]

Frustrated but unwilling to give up, the Conservation Society in mid-1986 launched a public relations campaign which included a "Save The Mother House" banner strung across Broadway within view of the building.[29] Public attention helped get the sisters and their architects to a Conservation Society board meeting for a presentation and question-and-answer session, but it was to no avail.[30] When the archbishop refused to get involved, Conservation Society President Janet (Mrs. Sidney J. II) Francis wrote Pope John Paul II and asked, unsuccessfully, for an audience on the subject during his upcoming visit to San Antonio.[31] Soon the building went down, and on January 6, 1989 a new one was dedicated on the site. Architect John Kell kept the new building in a similar style, replaced the original entry portico and replicated the original peaked fourth-floor bays, their windows vacant since the new building was only three stories.[32]

Downtown, in mid-1985 the Historic Review Board unanimously denied First Baptist Church's request to demolish the two-story Fourth Street Inn across the street. The 1880s frame building may have been the last remaining Victorian-era grocery store downtown.[33] As had the Incarnate Word Sisters, the Baptists refused Conservation Society offers of technical assistance, razed the building and replaced it with one they said was similar, but which Conservation Society President Janet Francis declared had only "vague references" to the original structure.[34]

The newly organized Monte Vista Historical Association in 1974 beat back an attempt by the nonprofit Morningside Manor Inc. to erect a high-rise convalescent facility in place of the turn-of-the-century West French Place home of financier E.B. Chandler. Morningside Manor instead restored the home and added a smaller facility to the rear.[35] A decade later, however, along Mulberry Avenue in the eastern part of the Monte Vista District Trinity Baptist Church sought to level a block of houses across from the church for parking. After a legal battle with the Monte Vista Association, the church succeeded.[36] Soon after, Trinity University sought to enlarge its playing fields and athletic facilities down the hill by removing houses it purchased along the southern edge of the campus. After opposition from the Monte Vista Association—

The 1891 Queen Anne shingle-style Thomas Franklin House on the campus of San Antonio Academy was the target of a $388,000 restoration project, completed in 1988. San Antonio Conservation Society.

backed by the Conservation Society—the university agreed to leave "exceptional or significant" homes in place, to help pay moving costs of others and to keep new open space available to neighbors.[37]

Other nonprofit institutions had trouble facing restoration costs for historic homes on their properties. At the western edge of San Antonio, the Southwest Research Institute grew up on the onetime 8,700-acre ranch of Rock Island Railroad President Philander Lathrop Cable, who built an elaborate two-story Victorian Eastlake-style ranch house there in 1883. Southwest Research officials in 1979 declared an estimated $200,000 in restoration costs to be impractical. They played down any importance of the house, but allowed the Conservation Society to find a buyer who would move it. But no buyer could be found. After a year and a half, the house was demolished.[38] Nearer downtown, in 1986 the Junior League of San Antonio also insisted on demolishing an extraneous building on its property—the 1880 stone and frame home built by Joseph Hermann, a blacksmith born in Alsace-Lorraine. The Hermann House stood behind headquarters of the Junior League, since

The city-owned water works pumping station in Brackenridge Park was later used as a studio by Gutzon Borglum, who designed his Mount Rushmore sculpture there, and was restored for architects' offices in 1984. Lewis F. Fisher.

The reassembled 1896 Sullivan Carriage House opened in 1995 at the entrance to the San Antonio Botanical Center. Lewis F. Fisher.

One critic described the former Lone Star Brewery-turned-San Antonio Museum of Art complex as being "done up with turrets and battlements the way Mad King Ludwig of Bavaria might have done it, had he been a St. Louis beer brewer." San Antonio Express-News.

The old Lone Star Brewery's high ceilings made ideal gallery space for the new San Antonio Museum of Art. The main building opened in 1981. San Antonio Express-News.

1929 headquartered, ironically, in the carefully restored, Alfred Giles-designed Claudius King stone house at 819 Augusta Street. A $100,000 fund-raising proposal by several Conservation Society members who were also active in the Junior League was rejected by a majority of Junior League members, and the Hermann House was demolished.[39]

Back in Monte Vista, however, San Antonio Academy accepted the Conservation Society's help with the Thomas H. Franklin House (1891) and its carriage house, both in great need of repair. The academy had already razed a lesser landmark home for a playground, over the protests of preservationists.[40] Built on East French Place and designed by J. Riely Gordon, Franklin's three-story house had become a rare example of Queen Anne shingle-style residential architecture. It had been added in 1923 to the adjoining campus of Saint Mary's Hall, a girls' school which moved and sold its campus twenty-five years later to the boys' San Antonio Academy.[41] In 1982 the Conservation Society donated $4,000 toward initial work and preparation of a feasibility study, and a contractor was hired to begin immediate repairs.[42] The Friends of the Franklin House raised funds.[43] A 1988 open house showcased the restoration, which cost $388,000, three-fourths of it contributed by the Conservation Society.[44] During the project, Franklin House restoration architect Joe Stubblefield and associate Richard Mogas also restored as their offices the deteriorated city-owned 1885 water works pumping station in Brackenridge Park rented by Gutzon Borglum as his studio. In it, Borglum, who lived in San Antonio between 1924 and 1937, designed schematics for his sculptures on Mount Rushmore.[45]

Landmarks were actively sought by two institutions—the San Antonio Museum Association and the San Antonio Botanical Society. Fate of the gabled limestone Sullivan Carriage House, built downtown by banker Daniel Sullivan in 1896, had concerned preservationists since 1971, when the Hearst Corporation, owner of the adjoining *San Antonio Light*, removed the landmark Sullivan House itself for a parking lot.[46] The Conservation Society sought preservation of the carriage house on its original site, then reluctantly agreed to its being moved.[47] Hearst gave the carriage house to the Witte Museum. When fund-raising to move and restore it fell short, the museum gave the building to the San Antonio Botanical Center. In 1988, the 7,675 square-foot reassembled carriage house was dedicated in the San Antonio Botanical Center above Mahncke Park. Of the $325,000 moving and reassembly costs, $100,000 was donated by the Conservation Society, $50,000 by the Meadows Foundation of Dallas and the rest by more than three hundred persons.[48] Following interior restoration, it opened in mid-1995 at the Botanical Center entrance. Its lower level became a gift shop and tearoom—tables were set in the former horse stalls—and the upper level a lecture hall.[49]

Construction of the Hyatt Regency Hotel included a water garden circulating water from the San Antonio River through the lobby upward to a new opening facing the Alamo. Ford, Powell & Carson Inc.; Thompson, Ventullet and Stainback; Associated Architects; photo: Hursley/Lark/Hursley.

A spectacular restoration project was the vacant Lone Star Brewery complex just north of downtown, which became the San Antonio Museum of Art.[50] Built in 1904 by Anheuser-Busch of St. Louis, it was saved under the leadership of Conservation Society activist Nancy Negley (Wellin) and Jack McGregor, director of the San Antonio Museum Association that included the Witte Museum. High ceilings for brewing vats offered ideal gallery space. As a $7.2 million fund-raising drive got under way, planning and design was begun by Cambridge Seven Associates of Cambridge, Massachusetts, assisted by the local firm of Chumney, Jones and Kell. Interior iron columns and washboard-vault ceilings were preserved. Glass-walled elevators with chrome-plated machinery were encased in glass shafts in the main brick building's two towers, connected at an upper level by a glass-enclosed walkway looking out on the downtown skyline. The 80,000 square-foot main building opened in 1981, while smaller buildings awaited renovation.[51] As he praised the result, architectural critic Wolf Von Eckardt wrote in the *Washington Post* that the buildings were "done up with turrets and battlements the way Mad King Ludwig of Bavaria might have done it, had he been a St. Louis beer brewer."[52]

Crises and opportunities on the edges of downtown and in suburban areas for the most part, however, did not face the array of diverse factors nor require the same intensity of attention as did those brewing in the caldron of downtown itself. There, during the boom years of the early 1980s, preservation of existing buildings was given a powerful antidote to the routine destruction of earlier construction booms—tax breaks.

In mid-1980, with the backing of the Conservation Society, city council passed a tax abatement program giving qualifying commercial property a 100 percent abatement for five years, and a 50 percent abatement for the next five. Based on a state law passed in 1975, qualifying residential property got a full break for ten years and added federal benefits the following year. Under the Economic Recovery Tax Act of 1981, investors got an historic rehabilitation federal tax credit of 25 percent with no limit on investor income, plus a credit of 20 percent on capital gains at the time of sale. Five years later, however, the Tax Reform Act of 1986 drastically scaled credits back. The rehabilitation tax credit dropped to 20 percent. Worse, investors with an annual income greater than $250,000 were no longer eligible, and a sharp drop in the number of historic preservation projects resulted. Other tax changes coupled with plummeting oil prices and the bad Texas economy sent San Antonio's downtown development into virtual hibernation for more than five years. In the meantime, great things had been done.[53]

Typical of the successful sagas is that of the adjoining three-story Staacke Brothers and John J. Stevens buildings designed in 1891 and 1894 by J. Riely Gordon on the north side of Commerce Street, which had escaped the turn-of-the-century widening on the south side of the street. Across the river to the north was the landmark high-rise Nix Hospital. The Nix lost badly needed parking space to construction around the River Bend of the sixteen-story Hyatt Regency Hotel, which extended the river in the form of a water garden through its lobby and on upward to Alamo Plaza, spurring restoration of the century-old Crockett Block.[54] In 1978, the Nix Hospital Trust took an option on the central portion of the block across the river to its south to demolish the Staacke and Stevens buildings for surface parking.[55] A false front covered the white granite pilasters on the ground level of Stevens Building and, above, the polished marble columns on either side of curved windows. The Staacke Building had a Renaissance Revival facade of red sandstone and red granite, and inset bowed windows on its second level.[56]

In November of 1978, the Nix Hospital Trust successfully applied for a demolition permit for the two buildings. The Conservation Society protested, and voted to seek to purchase the buildings and then sell them, with protective covenants.[57] As the 120-day waiting period after the demolition permit wore on, Society President Mary Ann Castleberry and Joanna Parrish suggested that the rear of the two buildings be razed for parking, and that would-be

Complicated negotiations by the San Antonio Conservation Society preserved the 1890s Staacke and Stevens buildings for restoration by others. San Antonio Conservation Society.

parking space taken up by the remainder be replaced by the adjoining lot owned by Groos National Bank.[58] The Nix Trust, however, rejected all proposals, and negotiations broke down by mid-April.[59] At that point, City Councilman Henry Cisneros offered to help negotiate a solution. As a result, the Conservation Society purchased the Groos Bank lot as well as an adjoining corner property, then exchanged most of the parcels with the Nix Trust for the front 97 feet of the Staacke and Stevens buildings. The remainder of the rear portions of the buildings were removed for parking spaces, and new back walls were built.[60] Thanks to the enticement of preservation tax credits, the Conservation Society sold the Staacke Building in 1980 for a restaurant and offices, and sold the Stevens Building in 1982.[61]

Nowhere, however, did the sinister forces of a collapsing financial structure and of political expediency collide more dramatically with the carefully crafted legal defenses of preservationists than in the case of an isolated landmark standing practically alone in the newly cleared reaches of the Vista Verde urban renewal area west of Interstate 35, at the edge of the Cattleman Square Historic District. Nor was such a collision more swiftly, if indirectly, avenged.

The late nineteenth-century brick and stone Woeltz Building in the shadow of the two-level expressway was first a grocery and saloon, then was used for manufacturing or storing cigars, primarily by the Finck Cigar Co. A designated city landmark, in early 1991 it stood, empty and damaged by vandals, not far from the former Hood Elementary School. The three-acre site also included the Vista Verde Joint Venture's new and nearly empty five-story Vista Verde Plaza office building. The half dozen politically connected owners faced foreclosure by the successor of the failed bank which made the construction loan, until the note was assumed by an unnamed party before the foreclosure deadline. The building became more attractive once county commissioners decided the county needed more office space somewhere. Commissioners voted 3–2 to buy Vista Verde Plaza's entire three acres for $3.1 million—which would more than pay off the note—but only if the two historic buildings were already gone. The demolition could eventually occur even under the city's newly tightened historic preservation laws, but the new foreclosure deadline was too soon for the legal process to play out.[62]

At 7:45 AM on Sunday, February 18, a contractor arrived at the site without a permit, unloaded a bulldozer and front-end loader and began to demolish the Woeltz/Finck Building. Assistant City Manager Rolando Bono, passing by on his way to city hall, saw what was going on. He called police and City Director of Building Inspections Gene Camargo on his car phone.[63] By the time Camargo arrived at the site forty-five minutes later, only part of one wall was still standing. "It was pretty bizarre," said Camargo. Said City Preservation Officer Pat Osborne, who arrived about the same time: "I've never been so disgusted in my life."[64] Not surprisingly, owners of the office building said they had no idea who hired the contractor, nor even who was about to foreclose on the property. Their attorney would not talk. One owner finally said he thought the foreclosure was threatened by a relative of another owner. Mayor Lila Cockrell asked for a full report. The next day the city filed charges against the contractor for demolition without a permit, which carried a fine of $1,000.[65]

Ten years earlier, another Sunday morning demolition, of the onetime Kung Tong Chinese Masonic Lodge on East Nueva Street within the Main and Military Plaza Historic District and on the National Register of Historic Places, netted little more. That demolition company was warned not to proceed without a permit when it started wrecking the interior the previous week. A permit to repair the roof was posted at the time the entire building was demolished soon after. The company was charged with seven violations, each carrying a maximum penalty of $200, and nothing further happened.[66]

By the time of the Woeltz/Finck Building's demolition, however, preservationists were better prepared to retaliate. Conservation Society President Jane Foster offered city council legal support to help enforce its historic preservation ordinance, and urged it to proceed with civil action.[67] Instead, by an 8–3 vote San Antonio City Council approved sale of the Vista Verde urban renewal site to the county in exchange for $25,000 from the developers, which—with $40,000 in back taxes—was to go toward rebuilding the Woeltz/Finck Building and restoring the Hood School building. One newspaper editorial called the sum "laughably short of the amount needed to do the job." But demanding the $200,000 needed to rebuild the building, the council majority was told, would drive the Vista Verde Joint Venture into bankruptcy.[68] Among minority voters on the council was Nelson Wolff, who was challenging Mayor Lila Cockrell for her position. He charged Mrs. Cockrell, who voted with the majority, with lack of leadership in enforcing the historic preservation ordinance.[69] He picked Historic Preservation Week as an opportunity to stand beside the rubble of the Woeltz/Finck Building and promise that if elected mayor, as he was, he would press for "the full measure of damages" in any such demolition case.[70]

The Woeltz/Finck Building was not rebuilt, but its loss was not in vain. As another indication of the acceptance and effectiveness achieved by historic preservation proponents, in June of 1991 Governor Ann Richards signed into law Senate Bill 923, which imposed strict penalties on those who illegally tore down any registered historic structure. Sponsored by San Antonio legislators State Senator Frank Tejeda and Representative Frank Madla because of the Woeltz/Finck Building's destruction, the law required responsible parties to pay full rebuilding costs.[71] Conservation Society volunteers helped a title search firm qualify 1,200 of San Antonio's historic structures for protection under the Tejeda Bill.[72]

While developers renovated the interior of the Reuter Building on Alamo Plaza, the San Antonio Conservation Society was given its facade for restoration and continued ownership by the society. Removal of the covering hiding the old facade was a highlight of Historic Preservation Week activities in 1978. San Antonio Conservation Society.

By now, new ordinances and codes and many drills seemed to have ritualized preservation battles into the mechanical strategies and tactics of Napoleonic warfare. The Conservation Society gained a seat on the city's Master Plan Task Force, maintaining official awareness of preservation and landscape issues while increasingly having to deal with issues having no easy solution. One ongoing struggle that seemed to be leading nowhere was the decade-long effort to preserve the vacant ten-story 1922 Robert E. Lee Hotel, isolated in an empty area on the western edge of downtown. The Conservation Society had to come up with "money and court orders and everything else" to block owners who periodically started to tear it down. In 1995 developer and Conservation Society member Milton Zaiontz came up with a successful $5.5 million plan to convert the Robert E. Lee into a housing project for the elderly, and preservationists breathed a collective sigh of relief.[73]

As solutions to problems involving lower-profile landmarks became increasingly sophisticated, so did solutions to such general challenges as encroachments on parks and place names changes require patience and imagination. In 1986 a concessionaire began building a carousel in the pastoral reaches of what was commonly called Brackenridge Park. But the project was, more particularly, on adjacent parkland donated by brewer Otto Koehler. Construction was halted when it was found that no building permit had been issued. Koehler heir Margaret Pace (Mrs. Robert) Willson sued the city, charging that operation of a carousel was contrary to terms of the land's donation. From Mrs. Willson the Conservation Society obtained a reversionary legal interest in the park, then charged that the carousel would transform the area into an amusement park. A judge ordered work to stop.[74] City council, however, passed a clarification of the concessionaire's license and moved the carousel site a short distance away onto Brackenridge Park land, removing the Conservation Society's legal standing, and the carousel was completed.[75] Conservationists did get city council to specify that no additional amusement rides would be permitted in either Brackenridge or Koehler parks.[76]

Nor were continually changing times keeping traditional names out of harm's way. In 1983, new chain owners of the St. Anthony Hotel announced plans to rename it the San Antonio Inter-Continental Hotel. Dropping the Spanish name of the city's patron saint from San Antonio's historically premier hotel did not sit well with the media or with the public in general, but out-of-state corporate owners provided a difficult target.[77] The Conservation Society praised the corporation for its "sensitive restoration" of the hotel but left the perpetrators no doubt that "regardless of legal title, citizens of this unique city feel that they 'own' certain of its institutions."[78] Officials acquiesced. The hotel was named the St. Anthony Inter-Continental San Antonio.[79]

Notes

1. Minutes, G-Dec. 7, 1961, 1–2; D-Jan. 22, 1962, 4; D-Oct. 28, 1963; D-Jan. 25, 1965; D-Sept. 20, 1965, 3; G-Sept. 23, 1973, 2; Minnie Campbell OHT, May 12, 1991, 11–17; Nelle Lee Weincek OHT, 23. In 1985 the small Christof Postert House, built of caliche block and stone rubble at 1604 S. Flores St. about 1855, was rebuilt behind the carriage house through a gift from Floy Fontaine Jordan in memory of her grandfather, Frank Mudge Edwards.

2. Minutes, D-Sept. 20, 1965, 5; D-Oct. 19, 1972, 2; D-Nov. 16, 1972, 3; D-Feb. 15, 1973, 2; D-Nov. 29, 1973; D-Aug. 8, 1975.

3. Minutes, D-Dec. 16, 1968, 1–2; D-Jun. 23, 1969, 4; D-Nov. 12, 1969, 1–3, 6–8; D-Nov. 24, 1969, 4; D-Jan. 19, 1970, 2, 8; D-Feb. 23, 1970, 2; D-Aug. 24, 1973. In view of the property tax dispute still going on with the city, the gift of the Heidgen-Zilker House was made in consultation with the Internal Revenue Service

and, like the Ike West House, was subject to restrictions and to ongoing inspection. After the initial restoration, some later alterations were required to be changed. The house reverted to the society in 1987 and was resold—with the same covenants—three years later.

4. Minutes, D-Jul. 17, 1967.

5. Minutes, F-Aug. 24, 1973; D-Oct. 25, 1973, 4; D-Nov. 15, 1973, 2.

6. Minutes, D-Nov. 20, 1974; D-May 28, 1975, 2.

7. Minutes, F-Mar. 19, 1975; D-May 28, 1975, 2.

8. Minutes, D-Nov. 19, 1962; Barry Browne, "Standoff in Historic Duel," *San Antonio Light,* Sept. 18, 1971.

9. "Rivas House Torn Down," *San Antonio Express,* Sept. 23, 1971, 2-A; Deborah Weser, "End to Rivas House Triggers Dispute," *San Antonio Express-News,* Sept. 26, 1971. Director Martin denied that his agency was bulldozing the city's Mexican-American heritage, stating that the building was only a portion of the original Rivas House "and the remnant had none of the architectural character of the original structure." Mrs. Weser's article quoted President Richard M. Nixon's 1971 Environmental Message to Congress: "Too often, we think of environment only as our natural surroundings. But for most of us, the urban environment is the one in which we spend our daily lives. America's cities, from Boston and Washington to Charleston, New Orleans, San Antonio, Denver and San Francisco, reflect in the architecture of their buildings a uniqueness of character that is too rapidly disappearing under the bulldozer."

10. "Rivas House Pieces Saved," *San Antonio Express,* Sept. 24, 1971.

11. Lewis Fisher, "First Soap Factory in S.A. May Be Doomed by Progress," *San Antonio Express-News,* Mar. 15, 1970, 4-B; Lewis Fisher, "Historic S.A. Building May Be Destroyed," *San Antonio Express-News,* May 17, 1970, 18-A. The Bexar County Historical Survey Commission had been quick to urge its preservation. ("Move Urged To Preserve Old Soap Works Building," *San Antonio Express,* Mar. 20, 1970, 2-A.) In addition to its significance for San Antonio, architectural historian John C. Garner, Jr. termed the Soap Works a significant example of "vernacular industrial architecture," a field which was only recently gaining attention from architects at the national level.

12. Deborah Weser, "Conservationists Fear for Soap Works," *San Antonio Express,* Sept. 29, 1971; Deborah Weser, "Old Soap Works Demolition Barred," *San Antonio Express-News,* Oct. 2, 1971. Society Attorney Phillip D. Hardberger's charge that the Urban Renewal Agency destroyed the Rivas House even though it knew fund-raising efforts to save it were under way was sufficient evidence for the judge to grant the restraining order pending a full hearing. "If the past is to be sterilized from the minds of our citizens," the petition to the court stated, "then sterility shall certainly be the fate of our children."

13. "URA Seeking Suit Dismissal," *San Antonio Express,* Nov. 28, 1971.

14. Minutes, D-Nov. 15, 1973; G-Sept. 25, 1974; D-Mar. 19, 1975, 2. Similarly orphaned in empty stretches of urban renewal clearance was the mid-1800s Ximenes Chapel or Chapel of the Miracles at 113 Ruiz St., several blocks northwest of the Soap Works. Believed to be the last remaining example in the city of a private chapel building detached from a main residence, it remained privately owned but open to

the public and still revered by many Mexican-American families. Although other buildings were leveled for blocks around, the chapel was never threatened despite its proximity to the expanded Interstate 10 right-of-way. (Minutes, D-Sept. 20, 1974.)

15. The Market Square project was sponsored by area merchants and by the San Antonio Chamber of Commerce, City of San Antonio and the Urban Renewal Agency. Included in the shops was the Botica Guadalupana, opened in 1893 and the city's oldest continually operated pharmacy. At the western end, rooftop parking opened on the new Farmers' Market building. ("Market Square," City of San Antonio Market Square Dept., 1994, 1–4.)

16. Lewis Fisher, "Fading color of city adds the old lion," *San Antonio News,* Sept. 2, 1970, 15-A. The drug store, officially known as La Botica del Leon, and the physicians upstairs were patronized after the turn of the century by Miguel Quiroga, Emiliano Zapata and many of the other Mexican revolutionaries who sought refuge in San Antonio, according to Chapa's son. Other landmarks razed in this ethnically diverse neighborhood included the Teatro Nacional, Paletta's Italian grocery and the old meeting hall of a Chinese Tong society.

17. Deborah Weser, "End to Rivas House Triggers Dispute," *San Antonio Express-News,* Sept. 26, 1971.

18. New Orleans Bureau of Governmental Research, *Plan and Program for the Preservation of the Vieux Carré,* (New Orleans, 1968), 1.

19. Lewis Fisher, "U.S. Postal Service rescues landmark," *North San Antonio Times,* Nov. 9, 1972, 1.

20. Caught again with its research down when the suddenly appreciated Baron de Bastrop House was leveled on the future HemisFair grounds, for example, the Conservation Society was left to sputter in a formal statement, "On the very day of its demolition, the Bexar County Archivist . . . verified the fact that the Baron de Bastrop purchased the property on December 20, 1816, from Miguel Arciniega." That the razing came "on the very day" that a new historical fact was discovered was hardly the sort of news destined to send practical city officials into rigors of remorse. (San Antonio Conservation Society statement, Jun. 3, 1968, copy in SACS Library.)

21. Minutes, D-Nov. 23, 1964; D-Jun. 25, 1962, 3; D-Nov. 19, 1962. The work was picked up after Steinbomer's death two years later by Marvin Eickenroht. In 1970 the society's Old Buildings Committee under Esther MacMillan divided downtown into four parts, and had two committee members in each quadrant adding to Steinbomer's and Eickenroht's earlier work. A Fine Arts Commission established by the city to provide guidance in such matters was proving to be ineffective. (Minutes, D-Nov. 19, 1962, 2; G-Jan. 28, 1965; D-Oct. 19, 1970, 2.)

22. Minutes, D-Jul. 17, 1967, 2; D-Sept. 25, 1967, 2–3.

23. Paul Goeldner, comp., *Texas Catalog, Historic American Buildings Survey* (San Antonio: Trinity University Press, 1975), 1–30; Eugene George to Lewis F. Fisher, Nov. 1, 1995.)

24. Minutes, D-Sept. 25, 1967, 2–3; D-Oct. 25, 1967, 2. Much of the basic research was to be done by Bexar County Archivist Richard Santos and by Mrs. Val Luckett, chairman of the Conservation Society's Old Buildings Committee. Headquartered in the old Ursuline Academy, by the end of a year the HABS program produced 9 sets of drawings totaling 62 sheets for 18 separate buildings, more than

150 pages of reports on more than 40 buildings, 100 photographs of 20 buildings and brief reports on another 100 buildings. (Minutes, D-Jul. 24, 1968, 2; D-Sept. 23, 1968; D-Dec. 16, 1968, 2.)

25. Minutes, D-Mar. 22, 1971, 2; D-May 18, 1972.

26. David Anthony Richelieu, "Downtown makes history," *San Antonio Express-News*, Nov. 24, 1985, 1-J.

27. Charles E. Gallatin, *Texas Architect*, Sept.-Oct. 1987, 10–11. The Mother House was within the city limits of Alamo Heights, which had no historic preservation ordinance and thus escaped the surveys and National Register enrollment drives within San Antonio city limits.

28. "THC joins fight to save Mother House," *North San Antonio Times*, Nov. 12, 1987.

29. Minutes, D-Jun. 17, 1986; D-Oct. 21, 1986; D-Nov. 19, 1986.

30. Minutes, D-Feb. 18, 1987.

31. Robert Goetz, SACS wants to talk to pope," *North San Antonio Times*, Jul. 9, 1987; "SACS asks pope to save IWC house," *San Antonio Express-News*, Jul. 12, 1987, 2-B.

32. Virginia Gonzalez, "New Motherhouse ready for dedication," *San Antonio Express-News Sunday Magazine*, 2. When the Texas Society of Architects gave the project an award, the Conservation Society sent a letter of protest to the society. (Minutes, D-Nov.14, 1990, 1–2.)

33. David Anthony Richelieu, "First Baptist Church asks to demolish Fourth Street Inn," *San Antonio Express-News*, Jun. 11, 1985, 4-D. The church had been cited the previous year for illegal demolition of a house nearby.

34. Mrs. Sidney J. Francis II, Letter to the Editor, "Demolition was not restoration," *San Antonio Express-News*, Dec. 1986. As part of a $1.64 million land deal two years earlier, First Baptist Church acquired the 1889 home of onetime merchant Saul Wolfson at 415 Broadway, a block east of the church. The ornate two-story late Victorian brick house had already been restored, and was not altered in its new function as an education center. (E.J. Slayman, "First Baptist makes land deal," *San Antonio Light*, Nov. 8, 1984.)

35. Minutes, D-May 16, 1974.

36. Minutes, D-Aug. 21, 1985, 3, 4; D-Dec. 17, 1985, 3. In 1985 the San Antonio Conservation Society contributed $5,000 to the Monte Vista Association's legal fund.

37. Minutes, D-Jul. 15, 1987, 3; D-Apr. 13, 1988, 2, 3.

38. Deborah Weser, Historic House To Be Razed," *San Antonio Light*, Jun. 16, 1979; "Cable House to be razed," *San Antonio Express*, May 21, 1980. One candidate was former Governor John Connally, who considered moving the Cable House to his ranch near Floresville. The Cable Ranch was originally stocked with the first Aberdeen Angus imported from Scotland to Texas. The Cable House arbor, manufactured by Alamo Iron Works, and its stone carriage step were donated to the Conservation Society for use at the Wulff House. (Minutes, D-Jan. 16, 1980, 2.)

39. Rosanne Doyle Fohn, "Vote seals fate of historic Hermann house," *North San Antonio Times*, Jun. 5, 1986; David Anthony Richelieu, "House stirs battle in Junior League," *San Antonio Express-News*, Jun. 9, 1986, 1-C; Jutson, *Alfred Giles, Architect*, 37.

40. David Hendricks, "Demolition to begin on Stevens Home," *San Antonio Express*, Apr. 3, 1980. Franklin, coincidentally, had been the attorney to whom Rena Maverick Green and Emily Edwards first went for advice on how to organize the Conservation Society.

41. Dorothy McKinley and Mary Everett, "National Register of Historic Places Inventory-Nomination Form," 1980.

42. Minutes, D-Jul. 21, 1982, 2; D-Nov. 17, 1982.

43. Minutes, D-Feb. 20, 1985, 3; Blair Corning, "A look inside," *San Antonio Express-News*, Feb. 8, 1988, 11-A.

44. Corning, "A look inside."

45. Sally Boothe-Meredith, "Architects restore Borglum Studio," *San Antonio Express*, Aug. 26, 1984, 1-J.

46. Minutes, D-Oct. 21, 1971, 2. The carriage house was designed by Alfred Giles.

47. Minutes, D-Apr. 9, 1980, 2; D-May 21, 1980, 3; D-Mar. 16, 1983, 2.

48. Sally Slade, "Sullivan Carriage House Adds 'Touch of Tradition' to Botanical Center," *SACS Newsletter*, Sept.–Oct. 1988.

49. "Sullivan Carriage House to Open!," *News from the Botanical Gardens*, San Antonio Botanical Gardens Society, Summer 1995, 1. A smaller carriage house adapted on its original site is the two-story Queen Anne style brick structure designed in 1908 by Atlee Ayres for rancher Alfred Gage behind his home on West French Place, in what became the Monte Vista Historic District. Gage's home was torn down for parking space by nearby Christ Episcopal Church, but the church preserved the carriage house and renovated it for classroom use in 1961. (Lewis F. Fisher, *Christ Episcopal Church: The First Seventy-Five Years*, San Antonio: Christ Episcopal Church, 1986, 98–100.)

50. With Prohibition the complex became the Lone Star Cotton Mills. It was unrelated to the later Lone Star Brewery south of downtown.

51. Michael Benedikt, "San Antonio Museum of Art," *Texas Architect*, Jul.–Aug. 1981, 76–79. The building won a *Progressive Architecture* design award in 1979. The San Antonio Museum of Art, Witte Museum and the short-lived San Antonio Transportation Museum operated jointly as the San Antonio Museum Association. The Museum Association dissolved in 1994, and the Witte Museum and the San Antonio Museum of Art began operating independently. Art Museum funding included a $2.5 million Economic Development Administration restoration grant. (Minutes, D-Jul. 20, 1977.)

52. "Art critic looks at San Antonio," *San Antonio Express*, Nov. 23, 1980.

53. *Preservation Tax Incentives for Historic Buildings*, U.S. Department of the Interior-National Park Service and National Conference of State Historic Preservation Officers (Washington, D.C., 1987), 4–24. In 1995, U.S. Housing and Urban Development Secretary Henry Cisneros, who as San Antonio's mayor had seen the benefits of historic preservation, was seeking to reincorporate historic preservation in HUD programs. ("Making Up," *Historic Preservation*, Jul.–Aug. 1995, 18.)

54. Minutes, G-Mar. 28, 1979, 2. The publicly funded Alamo Plaza linkage was proposed earlier by the city's Centro 21 task force, and was endorsed by the Conservation Society. (Minutes, D-Nov. 17, 1976.) The Staacke Building stood on

the site of the adobe building used by the Presbyterian Rev. John N. McCullough to open San Antonio's first Protestant church in 1846.

55. Ibid.

56. David Anthony Richelieu, "S.A. Conservation Society, Nix at impasse on old buildings," *San Antonio Express*, Apr. 25, 1979, 5-A; Elizabeth A. Goodman and Tom Schuver, "Stevens Building National Register of Historic Places Inventory-Nomination Form," 1981; Lynn Osborne Bobbitt, "Staacke Brothers Building National Register of Historic Places Inventory-Nomination Form," 1980. Copies in SACS Library.

57. Minutes, D-Jan. 17, 1979, 2; Richelieu, "S.A. Conservation Society, Nix at impasse."

58. Minutes, D-Feb. 21, 1979, 2; D-Mar. 21, 1979; G-Mar. 28, 1979; D-Apr. 3, 1979.

59. Richelieu, "S.A. Conservation Society, Nix at impasse." "I don't understand what all the ruckus is about," a Nix attorney told a reporter early in the discussions. "I think these buildings look pretty awful, don't you?" (Ibid.; "Setting it Straight," *San Antonio Express-News*, Apr. 28, 1979.)

60. David Anthony Richelieu, "Conservation society saves two landmarks," *San Antonio Express*, May 17, 1979, 12-A. The society kept the front 97.5 feet of the Groos Bank's old lot and leased it to the Nix Hospital for parking. Net cost for the entire project was $566,000, with $140,000 financed by using the two buildings as collateral. (Minutes, D-May 16, 1979, 1, 6–10; D-Jul. 18, 1979, 2–3.)

61. Minutes, G-Oct. 24, 1979; D-Jan. 16, 1980.

62. Don Driver, "Finck Cigar building razed," *San Antonio Express-News*, Feb. 18, 1991, 9-A; Gloria Padilla, "Building razing called surprise," *San Antonio Express-News*, Feb. 19, 1991, 9-A; Kim Webre and Gloria Padilla, "Charges filed in Finck razing," *San Antonio Express-News*, Feb. 20, 1991, 7-A. The removal requirement was the county's effort to shield itself from the landmark demolition business, since the county said it could not afford restoration of the two buildings and the developers told the county they couldn't, either. (Dan Kelly, "State to lower boom on razing historic sites," *San Antonio Light*, Jun. 17, 1991.)

63. Patricia Osborne OHT, 20.

64. Driver, "Finck Cigar building razed."

65. Ibid.; Webre and Padilla, "Charges filed." Owners of the building—incorporated as the Vista Verde Joint Venture—were reported as Bernard Lifshutz, Frank Sepulveda, Phil Sheridan and Lawrence J. Gibbons. (Gloria Padilla, "County officials ask city to alter historic site label," *San Antonio Express-News*, Mar. 10, 1994, 1-B.)

66. Alan Bailey and Deborah Weser, "City probes razing of historic building," *San Antonio Light*, Sept. 21, 1981, 1; Danny Garcia, Gordon Dillow and Deborah Weser, "Seven complaints filed in historic destruction," *San Antonio Light*, Sept. 23, 1981, 1. An Hispanic landmark listed on the National Register of Historic Places, the vacant Martinez Tamalina Mill, thought to be the first masa mill in the United States, was a victim of arson. Built at 701 S. Leona St. in 1903 to grind corn for masa, the main ingredient in tortillas and tamales, it was destroyed by fire one Monday afternoon in 1986. (Rick Gonzales, "Hispanic landmark destroyed in fire," *San Antonio Light*. Jul. 29, 1986; "Arson ruled in blaze at historic site," *San Antonio Light*, Jul. 30, 1986.)

67. Minutes, D-Feb. 20, 1991; D-Apr. 10, 1991, 2. The situation involved the city's right to prosecute its own laws; the Conservation Society had no legal standing to file suit itself. (Conservation Society President Jane Foster, Letter to the Editor, *San Antonio Express-News*, May 19, 1991.)

68. "Council action guts own law," *San Antonio Light*, Apr. 20, 1991, B-6.

69. Bruce Davidson, "Familiar themes resurface in Cockrell-Wolff skirmishes," *San Antonio Express-News*, May 1, 1991, 11-A.

70. James Coburn, "Wolff: Demolish building, pay price," *San Antonio Express-News*, May 15, 1991, 11-A.

71. Dan Kelly, "State to lower boom on razing of historic sites," *San Antonio Light*, Jun. 17, 1991. To be prepared for such an eventuality, the Conservation Society appropriated $5,000 for legal information on ownership of the 1,200 designated landmarks in San Antonio. The nearby fire-ravaged Hood School was ultimately razed by the county—legally, and over the strong objections of the Conservation Society. (Minutes, D-Apr. 8, 1992, 2; D-Aug. 19, 1992, 2–3; D-Dec. 9, 1992, 3; Gloria Padilla, "County officials ask city to alter historic site label," *San Antonio Express-News*, Mar. 10, 1994.)

72. Inell Schooler OHT, Jun. 6, 1995, 5.

73. Ibid., 18–22, 26; Cindy Tumiel, "Celebration marks Lee Hotel's rebirth," *San Antonio Express-News*, Mar. 16, 1995, 1-E. Another building of that era, the Calcasieu Building on Broadway at Travis Street, was the target of a $2.4 million similar rehabilitation project. (Patricia Konstam, "Calcasieu Building to become apartments," *San Antonio Express-News*, Mar. 22, 1995, 1-C.)

74. Deborah Weser, "Crew ordered to halt work on carousel site," *San Antonio Light*, Nov. 13, 1986; "Judge: No more work on carousel," *San Antonio Express*, Nov. 14, 1986.

75. "The Great Carousel Caper," *SACS Newsletter*, May-June, 1987.

76. Susie Phillips, "City Council vetoes Riverbend Garage art project," *San Antonio Express-News*, Sept. 8, 1989. The exception did not include the San Antonio Zoo in Brackenridge Park.

77. Jan Jarboe, "St. Anthony's bandwagon," *San Antonio News*, Jan. 28, 1983, 4-A.

78. Minutes, D-Jan. 19, 1983; D-Feb. 16, 1983.

79. Ibid.; "St. Anthony's Name Remains," *San Antonio Light*, Feb. 11, 1983, 1A. Another major downtown hotel, the Gunter, was restored without a name change, and in 1986 new owners of the six-story Crockett Hotel behind the Alamo decided to keep the original name of their restored seventy-seven year-old hotel after receiving a Conservation Society resolution on the subject. Dillard's could not be dissuaded from changing the name of its newly acquired Joske's Department Store on Alamo Plaza to Dillard's, resolutions, petitions and advertising protesting the change notwithstanding. The society was pleased, however, with change of the official name of Main Plaza to Plaza de las Islas and of the Chinese Sunken Gardens in Brackenridge Park back to Japanese Gardens, as they were known prior to World War II. (Minutes, D-Oct. 17, 1984; D-Jul. 16,1986, 2; D-May 20, 1987; D-Jun. 2, 1987; D-Jun 17, 1987, 2.)

18

The Case of the
Fairmount Hotel

Newspaper readers in Oslo, Norway were greeted one Tuesday in April of 1985 with the headline, "Hotell på flyttefot i Texas." Beneath it was pictured a crowd in front of an old three-story brick building bannered "Fairmount Hotel," and sitting on a huge platform in the middle of a street. The vehicles in front were pulling the building down the street, the caption explained, in San Antonio.[1]

Westward across the North Sea in Great Britain, television viewers followed the Fairmount Hotel's journey on the BBC. Behind what was then the Iron Curtain, listeners heard about it on the Voice of America. In the United States, television crews broadcast news of its progress from San Antonio on NBC, CBS, ABC and CNN.[2]

Two days before, reported the *Washington Post*, the Fairmount had been waiting in the intersection of Bowie and Market streets, "needing to hang a right." The *Post* found the building's chief mover needing to find a phone to call Las Vegas, where, he said, bookmakers at Caesars Palace had dropped the odds against the move's success from 5 to 1 down to 7 to 3.[3]

The object of all the attention was simply a thirty-room "salesmen's hotel," built halfway between the Southern Pacific Railroad depot and Alamo Plaza in 1906 as prosperity from the railroad transformed a neighborhood of small stone and wooden buildings. Its undistinguished Italianate Victorian design was typical of the city's commercial architecture of the time. As for its importance, those assessing its significance felt obliged to note, "the inhabitants, the owners and the managers of the Fairmount Hotel made no real historical impact."[4] The Fairmount fell vacant in 1968. Then it had the misfortune of being in the way of a mall and hotel project. As a writer for an architectural magazine observed, "If the Fairmount had been torn down, few would have missed it." Therefore, "The importance of the project lies in the fact that it occurred at all."[5]

Marveled the move's project director: "You know, I've worked in cities big and small all over the country on these kinds of projects. I've never been any place before where so many people want to save a building so much. The whole city government is just doing everything it can to help us out and tell us things we need to know. It's just amazing. This is quite a place. I've really never seen anything like it."[6]

The Fairmount Hotel's five-year odyssey from obscurity to the *Guinness Book of World Records* began in June of 1980, when developers announced plans to build a $250 million downtown shopping mall and hotel complex near San Antonio's convention center. One partner was Allied Department Stores, which would make its downtown Joske's subsidiary the western anchor building. The other partner was Edward J. DeBartolo Corp. of Youngstown, Ohio, the fabled shopping mall developer, which would build an adjoining multistory mall around a new extension of the San Antonio River. At its eastern end would be a thousand-room Marriott Hotel, which at forty-two stories would become San Antonio's tallest building. Most of the land for the project was already used only for parking—except, at the far southeast corner, for the site of the derelict Fairmount Hotel.[7]

The Fairmount was in double jeopardy, for it also partially blocked the widening of Bowie Street, which would have more traffic. To be saved, the Fairmount would have to move at least forty-five feet west toward the new development. But developers were not at all certain that the Fairmount should play any part in their plans.

Despite the Fairmount's humble standing, it had managed to make the list of the city's historically significant structures. That fact was pointed out to DeBartolo himself the day after the project's announcement by Joanna Parrish, president of the San Antonio Conservation Society. The society would like to meet with company officials, wrote Mrs. Parrish, and discuss the possibility of incorporating the Fairmount into the mall. There were, she reminded him, tax incentives for rehabilitating historic structures.[8]

After receiving the letter, DeBartolo checked out the Conservation Society. He concluded that it was no ephemeral group but did wield some power and had his local attorney set up an introductory meeting with society representatives.[9] But as weeks passed, there were no substantive discussions. Developers and preservationists seemed headed for a traditional confrontation: the Historic Review Board declined to approve DeBartolo's request for a permit to demolish the Fairmount and Conservation Society directors decided that the old hotel should be kept in its existing location or, as a last resort, be moved to some site nearby.[10]

A preliminary meeting between DeBartolo's attorney and the Conservation Society indicated that the Fairmount would not be demolished at least until federal funding was approved, but preservationists were not impressed. They

The Fairmount was a "salesmen's hotel" of little distinction when it was built on Commerce Street between the Southern Pacific Railroad depot and downtown in 1906. The Institute of Texan Cultures.

had heard that before from developers who precipitously cleared away land-marks only to have the sites remain vacant as their projects were never built. The Conservation Society asked DeBartolo to post a bond to assure the Fairmount would not be torn down until his project actually began.[11]

Rejection by the Historic Review Board compounded by the attitude of the San Antonio Conservation Society gave DeBartolo an immediate problem. His July 31 application deadline for $30 million in federal funding was very close. He needed a demolition permit for the Fairmount in hand to show that the entire site was in fact available for development. The Review Board's decision could be overruled by city council. But there was not enough time to regroup if the Conservation Society swayed the council into approving the Review Board's decision.

And so, on July 17, an extraordinary agreement was made. To assuage fears of premature demolition, DeBartolo agreed to pay the Conservation Society $50,000, guaranteed by a letter of credit, if the Fairmount happened to be demolished before financing was approved. In that eventuality DeBartolo would also donate $50,000 to the city's Historic Facade Restoration Fund. Barring this, when financing did go through DeBartolo would have ten days to decide whether to use the Fairmount or to move it elsewhere himself. If he did neither, the Conservation Society would have sixty days to move it, with the help of a $50,000 donation from DeBartolo. Once off the site, the Conservation Society would take title to the building.[12] In consideration for all this, Conservation Society President Joanna Parrish agreed to appear before city council and endorse DeBartolo's pro forma request for a demolition permit for the Fairmount.[13]

The Fairmount turned into a case of hurry-up-and-wait. Nearly four years elapsed before financing for the mall/hotel project was in place. With plans moving again in 1984, developers said they did not want the Fairmount at all and gave the Conservation Society until spring to move it off the site, with assurances that the original agreement still stood. So, as owner of the building once it was off the site and with the guarantee of $50,000 to start the job, the Conservation Society went out looking for a customer and for a suitable site. Both were eventually found.[14]

The Conservation Society was not intimidated by what lay ahead. It hadn't been easy either, seventy years earlier, when the new five-story Alamo National Bank Building was rolled back for the widening of Commerce Street. Masonry buildings were moved in Galveston when land was raised following the Great Storm of 1900, and far heavier buildings had been moved on rails and rollers. In Aberdeen, South Dakota, a 4,000-ton, sixty-five room hospital was rolled eleven and a half blocks during seven months in 1940-41. A few years earlier, the 15,000 ton Indiana Telephone Company was moved diagonally across the block in twenty-six days, while operators handled calls inside.[15]

A study commissioned by DeBartolo found the Fairmount quite capable of being moved. Its thick brick exterior walls were augmented by load-bearing cast-iron columns on the first floor and by load-bearing corridor walls on the upper two stories. The obvious new site was one block east, on land owned by the City Water Board, and moving the Fairmount there should not be terribly difficult. For $250,000, steel beams could be placed beneath load-bearing points and the building lifted onto train wheels and rolled on rails down the block. On its new site, the study noted, the Fairmount would provide "a spectacular transition" between the San Antonio River extension and the new mall. Best of all, tax breaks for historic structures would make relocation and rehabilitation costs competitive with the cost of new construction.[16]

City Water Board trustees, however, would not go along. They wanted to expand their parking lot rather than give up space to the Fairmount. The Conservation Society found that to compensate with a four-level, 440-car parking garage on part of the site would be too expensive. Another place had to be found.[17]

With Mayor Henry Cisneros supporting the project behind the scenes, local downtown developer C. Thomas Wright and attorney Virginia Kazen (Mrs.

Gus) Van Steenberg signed up to take on a larger project. They were joined by a third investor, King Ranch heir Belton K. Johnson, part-owner of San Antonio's new Hyatt Regency Hotel.[18] Once they were given the Fairmount by the Conservation Society, the developers estimated it would take $3 million to rehabilitate the building and double its size to become San Antonio's first small luxury hotel, with thirty-seven guest rooms.[19] It would have an "easy ambiance" like the Mansion on Turtle Creek, which launched the Texas trend toward intimate hotels when it opened in a Moorish-style building in Dallas in 1980.[20]

Logistics, already formidable, were complicated further by the danger of crossing downtown bridges. No site further than eight blocks away could be risked.[21] In January of 1985, city council offered a thirty-year lease on the closest site that could be found—a city-owned parking lot at the southwest corner of South Alamo and Nueva streets at the edge of the La Villita Historic District. The trek was six blocks from the original site, but across a bridge over an extension of the San Antonio River.[22] To take it there, the Conservation Society located a moving company in Portland, Oregon, Emmert International, which said it would do the move for $530,000.[23]

The project's attraction for developers was a substantial federal tax incentive for historic preservation. "You might say I'm moving a tax break six blocks," co-owner Thomas Wright told the *Washington Post*.[24] Success of the deal was assured when the Conservation Society loaned developers $260,000 to cover initial operating shortfalls.[25]

The job would be supervised by Terry Emmert, assisted by the company's prior owner, Peter Friesen. The company had already set records with moves ranging from churches to oil drilling rigs to a 450-ton brick railroad depot, racking up the industry's top safety awards in the process.[26] A plan was devised to have the Fairmount strapped with tubular steel around its outside walls and held together inside by a spiderweb of cables. Windows and doors would be reinforced with cross-bracing.[27] Once steel beams were inserted under key points, jacks would perform what Emmert called the only risky part—lifting the building and separating it from the original basement foundation and piers. Then more than 7,000 railroad ties and timbers, weighing 400 tons, and a 280-ton network of more than fifty steel beams would make a temporary foundation platform as the Fairmount was inched up eight feet above the ground.[28]

Nothing approaching the size of the Fairmount had ever been moved for such a distance on the tires which would be the key to the entire move. Thirty-six specially designed dollies would each have a set of eight fifteen-inch tires and their own hydraulic lifts and disc brakes. They were linked with hoses to permit hydraulic fluid to move from one to another and balance the load to keep the building level at all times. Used normally in mines, the dollies were

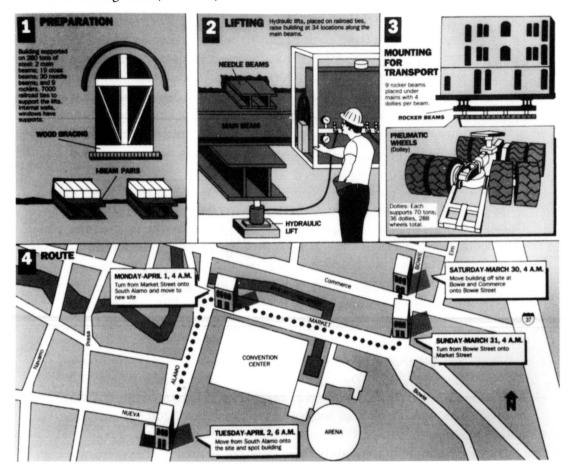

The move of the Fairmount Hotel got under way eleven hours behind schedule and was completed two days later than planned, but not a single brick was lost in transit. San Antonio Light, San Antonio Express-News.

valued at more than $30,000 apiece. A pulley and cable system would allow cranes with heavy-duty transmissions to pull the building at a speed of up to four miles an hour. In front, seven dump trucks fully loaded with sand would be tied in with cables to serve as counter-weights.[29]

All utility poles and wires, traffic signals, parking meters, waste containers, newspaper boxes and bus benches would have to be removed and then replaced in the hotel's wake. Since the Fairmount was ten feet wider than the streets, it would overhang sidewalks on each side by five feet, the dollies riding two feet inside each curb. The building would make two right-angle turns and cross the bridge before being turned ninety degrees to be moved back onto its new foundations. Each turn was expected to take seven hours, as the front axles of all dollies had to be straight for each maneuver.[30]

While Emmert International started preliminary work and the city's Department of Public Works began its operations plan, the next immediate obstacle turned out to have nothing to do with moving a three-story hotel six blocks. It had to do with who controlled its new site, a question raised at once by owners of the six-year-old Plaza Nacional Four Seasons Hotel, later Marriott's Plaza San Antonio, a block away. The Four Seasons went to court for an injunction to block the move. Its attorney claimed that the Fairmount was too large for the original urban renewal concept of the site, violated a city ordinance on minimum lot size for a hotel and, besides, would be on property that the city had already leased to the Four Seasons.[31] Nonsense, said the city, which had considered such legal problems before giving the go-ahead; the Four Seasons had known for a long time that its lease on adjacent property did not include the corner lot, even though the Four Seasons used it for parking.[32] City workers mounted a 3 AM expedition to the site with chains, barricades and signs declaring it to be city property.[33]

Although Mayor Cisneros had doubted there were enough votes to approve a thirty-year lease of the site to the Fairmount, two weeks later city council emerged from executive session to grant the lease unanimously.[34] But Four Seasons owners got a temporary restraining order, halting initial foundation work.[35] The order had little immediate effect, since the move had been delayed a week to allow archeologists to finish their survey.[36] But DeBartolo wanted the Fairmount gone by the end of March, and the city wanted the hotel off the streets five days later to accommodate Easter weekend traffic.[37] When the injunction was lifted on March 4, the Fairmount was nearly ready to be raised from its original foundations.[38]

After being postponed again when heavy rains made hotel grounds too muddy to support heavy equipment, the first major step came on Wednesday, March 20. City department heads, two dozen assistants and representatives of the San Antonio Conservation Society and the city's Historic Preservation Office gathered with hotel owners to watch the initial lift. As the hotel gradually rose four inches, a jagged gap appeared at ground level as mortar and the foundation walls separated. What the mover called "the only risky part" had come off without a hitch.[39]

As workers continued to lift the hotel eight feet at the rate of one foot a day, and to arrange underpinnings, the city's Department of Public Works finished a ten-page plan worthy of a military operation. A command post was set up in the Convention Center, midway along the route. Three teams were formed, each led by a Public Works official directing some twenty representatives of city branches from the police and fire departments to Building Inspections, Parks & Recreation, Risk Management, Public Information and utility agencies, plus those from such outside groups as Southwestern Bell, the San Antonio Conservation Society and Fairmount owners, architects, movers and insurers. Developers would reimburse the city for all costs.[40]

Catholic Auxiliary Bishop Bernard Popp blessed the newly raised Fairmount Hotel the afternoon before it began its journey. San Antonio Express-News.

The Control Team, headed by Public Works Director Frank Kiolbassa assisted by Project Coordinator Frank Perry, was to assemble at a Convention Center command post each morning at 5:30 to oversee the public portion of the move and direct any repairs. The Operations Team would supervise relocation and protection of public facilities, crowd control and traffic. The Assessment Team would inspect the route immediately before and after the move, taking field notes and photographs of any damage. The Operations and Assessment teams would also meet at points designated in the daily operations calendar. More than two hundred city workers would be involved.[41] Work itself was to begin each day at 4 AM with removal of traffic lights, utility poles and other obstructions. Steel plates laid on the street would distribute the building's weight evenly. The San Antonio River would have to be drained beneath the Market Street bridge so the bridge could be shored up from below.[42]

As moving day approached and the intensity of media coverage increased, a local television news crew reported that new cracks in the building would delay the move. Workmen refused to go back inside the Fairmount the next morning until they were repeatedly assured by architects and contractors that while minor cracks may have appeared, the building was safe and the television report was "absolutely not true." Fairmount owners took early profits from the sale of T-shirts emblazoned with the hotel logo and the proclamation, "I shared in a moving experience." A breakfast was set for members of city council and the press in a parking garage near the hotel.[43]

The Fairmount Hotel was the largest building of its type yet moved on pneumatic tires, which required careful alignment. San Antonio Express-News.

As developers held their third general coordinating session at city hall one week before the actual move was to begin, a more ominous risk resurfaced in the courthouse. Four Seasons Hotel owners made good on their threat to take their case to trial. Pleadings on ownership of the Fairmount's destination site were set for April 1, when the hotel was to have been on its way for two days. Attorneys for the city and the Fairmount asked for more time to prepare. The trial was delayed until June. In the meantime, the hotel was free to move.[44] "The delay doesn't really change things as a matter of law," said the Four Seasons attorney, "but we just wish the hotel weren't going to be on the new site when the trial begins."[45]

On its journey, the Fairmount would be under the special care of San Antonio's patron saint, St. Anthony of Padua, who was given the assignment by Roman Catholic Auxiliary Bishop Bernard Popp in an ecumenical ceremony at the old hotel the afternoon before it was to start. The responsibility was not a light one. The three dozen moving engineers who gathered in San Antonio from around the country to watch were well aware of an incident in Miami only four months before, when the third section of a coral stone mansion being moved in three pieces toppled into a pile of rubble only two hundred feet from its destination.[46]

The move was to start at 6 AM on Saturday, March 30. At 4 AM, the street was closed, traffic signals were removed and the three Public Works teams

With the Tower of the Americas in the background, the Fairmount is readied to turn the corner onto Market Street. San Antonio Express-News.

met for a last-minute briefing. But when the crane intended to move the hotel started up, the hotel did not budge. A second and then a third crane were hooked up. Finally, at 3 PM, the Fairmount began to inch onto Commerce Street, to the delight of thousands of onlookers, including co-owner Virginia Van Steenberg, who clutched her St. Jude medal. Moving in fits and starts, by nightfall the Fairmount was back on schedule, ready to turn from Bowie Street onto Market Street in the morning.[47]

Turning the corner ended up taking less than four hours, nearly half the time expected. But the hotel stopped short of the Market Street bridge, and celebrants at a Sunday night street party at Market and South Alamo streets had to view the hotel from farther away than planned.[48]

At 9 AM Monday, inspectors took a final look at the maze of steel supports and reinforcements finally completed under the bridge. Two Lone Star longneck beer bottles were placed between supporting timbers and the bridge wall as warning devices. If any weight shift or vibration caused the supports to bend, the bottles would crack and shatter, providing time to halt the moving building before it was too late. A large crowd, including viewers on balconies of the nearby Marriott Riverwalk Hotel, "held its collective breath" as the hotel rolled slowly onto the bridge.[49]

Turning the corner from Bowie Street onto Market Street took the Fairmount less than four hours, half the time expected. San Antonio Express-News.

In nine minutes, the 3.2 million-pound hotel was across. Steel plates laid down had shifted the load directly to the bridge's framework and temporary supports, which bore the full weight of the building for only about four minutes. The bottles were unharmed, proving that the bridge did not move or vibrate. The crowd burst into applause and cheers. Owners of the construction company that did the bracing, brothers Cosmo and Tom Guido, headed to St. Joseph's Catholic Church nearby for "a little prayer of thanks." At the late afternoon press briefing, the control team leader could report that the day's total damage was only a few broken tree limbs, some squashed traffic buttons and one cracked manhole cover, which turned out to have been damaged long before and was already scheduled for repair.[50]

While there were no immediate reports from Las Vegas on how the successful crossing had affected odds on the move, some of the 2,000

Having safely turned onto South Alamo Street, the Fairmount Hotel is pulled over steel plates protecting the street as it passes the Hilton Palacio del Rio Hotel at the left. San Antonio Express-News.

delegates attending a petroleum refiners' convention indoors at the Convention Center did react. Said one delegate from Brussels who stepped outside to watch the move: "It's a lot more interesting than our business sessions."[51] In his greetings, Mayor Henry Cisneros told delegates, "We've always wanted more hotels on the river. We may end up with a hotel *in* the river if this move does not go well."[52] Tennessee's former U.S. Senator Howard Baker told convention-goers who stayed to hear him speak: "Thank you for being here. I thought I had lost out for the first time in my career to a moving hotel."[53]

Once past the bridge, it took three quick pulls to roll the hotel to the tricky Alamo Street turn, where layers of sand as well as steel plates were spread out to contend with a center median. That turn took only two hours. By 7 PM, after working in the rain for an hour, movers had the Fairmount past the

The Fairmount is prepared to be backed onto its new site over a network of 7,000 railroad ties and timbers before being lowered onto the waiting foundations. HemisFair Plaza's Beethoven Hall is partly visible at the far right. San Antonio Express-News.

Hilton Palacio del Rio on South Alamo Street to the entrance of La Villita, and called it quits after a thirteen-hour day.[54]

By dawn Tuesday the skies were clear but it was unseasonably cool, in the low 40s.[55] As mid-morning temperatures headed toward the upper 70s and spectators shed some of their wraps, the hotel was under way again. Now it was barely one block from its new home. But the thousands of timbers from the old site were not all yet moved to the new site, and the Fairmount had to spend the night in the street.[56]

While its basement framework was finished, movers on Wednesday worked on pivoting the hotel so it could be backed onto the site, a task made even more perilous by the danger of hitting the USO Building on HemisFair Plaza across the street. Turning such an immense object ninety degrees with no forward movement had never been done before, and gripped the attention of visiting movers. "It is literally going to turn on a dime," predicted the chief mover. He was right. The city's Public Works director thought the tortuous pivot, which began at 11 AM and took five hours, was one of the most fascinating parts of the entire move.[57]

For the new wing of the Fairmount Hotel, Alamo Architects reversed colors of the original building's brick and trim and stepped the addition back and down to lessen competition with the old portion and with the former German-English School building at left. San Antonio Conservation Society.

The Fairmount spent Wednesday night, too, in the street, to the discomfiture of city officials worried about traffic snarls with Easter weekend approaching. The next morning, as cranes began to tug the Fairmount to its new foundations, a reinforcement bar installed in the basement as a hold for the pulleys broke. Then while the hotel was being pulled over the South Alamo Street median a cable snapped, and the building lurched backward. Soon a dolly got disconnected and flipped up. But by 3 PM everything was fixed, and the hotel began to roll haltingly out of the street. By sundown the task was done, two days behind schedule but without a single major complication. There were no accidents or injuries, and not a brick had fallen off.[58]

Plaudits flew in every direction. "What was incredible to me was how the various city departments worked so well together," said Conservation Society President Bebe (Mrs. Sherwood) Inkley. "You sometimes think in your city that nobody cooperates with each other, . . . but this was a wonderful example of everybody working together to attain a major goal."[59] The Brick Institute of Texas decided the successful move provided yet "another splendid example of the strength and durability of brick structures."[60] Word arrived from the publishers that the Fairmount would make the next *Guinness Book of World Records* as the heaviest building ever moved on pneumatic wheels.[61]

Architects pronounced the Fairmount perfectly poised above its new foundations. Relieved utility workers began replacing poles, lights and signals for Good Friday traffic. Moving crews took a short vacation, then returned for the two-week job of slowly lowering the Fairmount to its final height so the

Before the Fairmount Hotel arrived at its new site, a team of archeologists organized by the University of Texas at San Antonio made one of the great archeological discoveries in the city: the first military post ever found of Santa Anna's army during the siege of the Alamo. This view looking west shows St. John's Lutheran Church in the background. Center for Archaeological Research, The University of Texas at San Antonio.

basement could be built up to meet it. The job was finished on May 9. The bill from the city came to $61,843. Total relocation costs were $1.2 million.[62]

Once the threat of a trial over rights to the site evaporated, Alamo Architects could focus on the $3.1 million renovation and expansion. The original hotel had thirty rooms, including two suites, but only four bathrooms. This was addressed by sectioning corridors into new bathrooms, which could then link several original rooms to form suites. Although the newly enlarged hotel was twice as big, it had only seven more rooms, but these included seventeen suites plus two private function areas, staff offices, a landscaped courtyard and a restaurant and bar.[63]

A greater challenge was design of the three-story addition, which the Fine Arts Commission and the Historic Review Board finally approved. The new wing was set back from the original facade and its height stairstepped down so its mass would not compete with the original building nor, immediately to the south, with the historic two-story German-English School. The Fairmount's original exterior colors, once revealed beneath layers of paint, were reversed on the addition, with cream-colored brick for the new wing and red brick for its trim. Iron porches reconstructed on the original facade were extended around to part of the wing, where they were adapted into the porte cochere of the new main entrance.[64]

On Friday evening, September 6, 1986, Mayor Henry Cisneros presided over dedication ceremonies of the resurrected hotel. "San Antonio is one of the most unique and interesting cities in this country because of the unique nooks and crannies it possesses," Cisneros told those present. "The Fairmount Hotel is yet another of these."[65] The previous evening, legendary trumpeter Dizzy Gillespie joined San Antonio's Happy Jazz Band at a preopening event which spilled across Nueva Street into La Villita's Maverick Plaza. It honored the Conservation Society and benefited the University of Texas at San Antonio's Center for Archaeological Research, still restoring artifacts uncovered during excavations at the hotel site the year before.[66]

The sort of sophisticated deal-making which accomplished the move had been filtered through the prism of the city's historic preservation movement, polished by the growing appeal of the ambiance so precariously preserved during the previous hundred years. Moreover, as the Fairmount crept across a bridge of the uniquely preserved river and captured the imaginations of nearby convention-goers, it headed toward a site not only dating from the birth of the city, but newly discovered as a key location in the legendary battle which first made San Antonio known to the world.

The Fairmount's destination at the edge of La Villita was a lot cleared by the city for parking for HemisFair. Earlier it was the site of a two-story commercial building and a gas station, built after an 1860s home was removed during street widening in the booming 1920s. It had first been part of the lands of Mission San Antonio de Valero—the Alamo—the founding of which in 1718 marked the beginning of the City of San Antonio.[67] During the siege of the Alamo in 1836, the area was occupied by the Mexican Army. Mexican artillery earthworks were long known to have been somewhere in the area, but no archeological evidence of the trenches had ever been found. On the Fairmount's small plot, nothing special was expected to turn up.[68] The sudden appearance of military artifacts came as a thunderbolt.

As personnel from the University of Texas at San Antonio's Center for Archaeological Research stood by, two bulldozers in mid-February of 1985 began removing soil in six-inch strips to make it easier to spot artifacts. Three feet down, a "linear ashen feature" was exposed that predated known residential occupation of the site. Bulldozing stopped, and shovel tests defined limits of the material.[69]

A quickly assembled team of sixty-three archeologists, ten of them on the UTSA staff and the rest students and amateurs, began work, a twenty-five foot square tent shielding them from winter rains. Soon an outline appeared of an L-shaped trench some thirty feet long and between three and nine feet wide. A rare bronze howitzer shell turned up and the fragment of another, then an iron cannon ball, bayonets, grape shot, musket balls and musket parts. A cooking area was uncovered at one end, with an iron knife blade. All items were typical of those used by the Mexican Army in 1836.[70]

The first military post ever found of Santa Anna's army during the siege of the Alamo had been discovered. The UTSA's Center for Archaeological Research director called the project one of the "top two or three digs" in San Antonio's history.[71]

Daily excavations lasted twelve hours. They were extended two days past the original deadline, until February 28. Once formal excavations and screening ceased at 9 PM on the last day, workers spent more than three more hours shoveling artifact-laden soil into buckets, developers providing an electric generator and lights plus food for the workers. The next morning, a bulldozer removed designated remaining soil. Some of it was loaded into three dump trucks and taken to the UTSA campus to be screened for additional artifacts as laboratory analysis and further study began. The collection was designated a State Archeological Landmark.[72]

In the epic journey to its future, the Fairmount Hotel had arrived on a hearthstone of the beginnings of San Antonio.

Notes

1. *Oslo Aftenpostens*, Apr. 2, 1985.
2. David Anthony Richelieu, "Fairmount Hotel to make '86 record book," *San Antonio Express*, Aug. 7, 1985, 2-H.
3. Paul Taylor, "San Antonio Hotel Makes Its Move," *The Washington Post*, Apr. 1, 1985, A-3. The reporter mistakenly wrote "Bowie and Commerce streets," but he was not the first visitor confused by the city's streets.
4. *Historical & Architectural Assessment, La Plaza del Rio UDAG Development Project, Fairmount Portion*, 1982. Veronica Felix, widow of Theodore Felix, ventured into a man's world to complete the hotel after her husband died in 1903, with most of its planning completed. Architect for the hotel was Leo M.J. Dielmann. (Kym Fox, "That's his granddad's dream they're moving," *San Antonio Express-News*, Apr. 1, 1985.)

5. Leonard Lane, "A Moving Experience for the Fairmount Hotel in San Antonio," *Texas Architect*, Jan.–Feb., 1987, 47.

6. David Anthony Richelieu, "Fairmount not just any old job for project boss," *San Antonio Express-News*, Mar. 29, 1985. Project director was Rusty Gorman.

7. Mike Greenberg, "The guardians of good old S.A.," *San Antonio Express-News*, Aug. 24, 1980, 1-H. The two partners were later joined by a third, Williams Realty of Tulsa, Oklahoma.

8. Greenberg, "The guardians of good old S.A."

9. Ibid.

10. Minutes, D-Jul. 16, 1980; David Anthony Richelieu, "Street plans for mall create controversy," *San Antonio Express*, Jul. 24, 1980.

11. Ibid.

12. "Mall planners agree to save hotel," *San Antonio Express*, Jul. 25, 1980, 2-A; Greenberg, "The guardians of good old S.A."

13. Greenberg, "The guardians of good old S.A." There were some who didn't get the message. After the demolition permit sailed through city council and City Manager Tom Huebner headed for Washington to lobby for funds, one thoroughly puzzled councilman said of Conservation Society members, "I can't imagine why they have taken such an interest in that building." (Ibid.; Deborah Weser, "Huebner Off to D.C. In Pitch for Mall $s," *San Antonio Light*, Jul. 25, 1980, 8-B.)

14. Minutes, D-Jul. 18, 1984, 2; D-Oct. 18, 1984; Jim Wood, "Fairmount Hotel denied new site," *San Antonio Express*, Aug. 21, 1984.

15. J. Michael Parker, "Report: Hotel not heaviest building moved," *San Antonio Express-News*, Apr. 3, 1985, 7-A; "Fairmount a record-setting move," *San Antonio Express-News*, Apr. 4, 1985, 10-A.

16. Killis Almond, Jr., "Feasibility of the Relocation of the Fairmount Hotel," 1–3, copy in SACS Library; SACS President Mrs. Sidney J. Francis II to National Trust for Historic Preservation, May 8, 1987, copy in SACS Library.

17. Mike Greenberg, "Fairmount still breathing," *San Antonio Express*, Sept. 16, 1984; David Hawkings, "City Water Board agrees to check into moving of old hotel," *San Antonio Light*, Sept. 19, 1984, C-1; Minutes, D-Oct. 12, 1984; SACS President Bebe Inkley, May 30, 1985, remarks to Arlington, Tex., Rotary Club, 5, script in SACS Library.

18. Minutes, D-Nov. 2, 1984; D-Feb. 20, 1985, 8; Patricia Osborne OHT, 15. Mall developers required the Conservation Society to promise not to sue them if the society's proposed removal plans fell through. (Minutes, D-Nov. 14, 1984.)

19. "Fairmount Hotel dedication held," *San Antonio Express-News*, Sept. 6, 1986; Alamo Architects, "The Fairmount Hotel," SACS 1987 Awards Nomination form in SACS Library. Partners in the firm were Irby Hightower, Michael Lanford and Michael McGlone.

20. Mark Seal, "Texas Feuds Now Fought Over Hotels," *The New York Times*, Mar. 18, 1987, C-1.

21. Inkley, "Remarks to Rotary Club," 4.

22. Susie Phillips, "Historic Fairmount to be moved to city property," *San Antonio Express-News*, Jan. 18, 1985; "Historic hotel's owners given 30-year lease," *San Antonio Express-News*, Feb. 22, 1985, 8-C.

23. Bebe Inkley OHT, Mar. 4, 1991, 12–13; Mike Davis, "Small Hotel Makes It Big," *San Antonio Express-News*, Jun. 19, 1988, 7-K.

24. Taylor, "San Antonio Hotel Makes Its Move."

25. Ibid., Bebe Inkley, "Remarks to Rotary Club," 8–9; Minutes, D-Sept. 16, 1987, 3–4.

26. David Anthony Richelieu, "Greatest move on wheels," *San Antonio Express-News*, Feb. 10, 1985, 1-H. Advance Moving Contractors of West Chicago, Ill., was subcontracted by Emmert to help.

27. Ibid.; David Anthony Richelieu, "Hotel to be blessed before tricky move," *San Antonio Express-News*, Mar. 29, 1985; Taylor, "San Antonio Hotel Makes Its Move;" Nancy Scott Jones, "Fairmount Hotel Fact Sheet," copy in SACS Library.

28. Ibid.

29. Ibid.; David Anthony Richelieu, "Dramatic hotel move begins this weekend," *San Antonio Express-News*, Mar. 28, 1985 and "It's moving, it's moving!," *San Antonio Express-News*, Mar. 31, 1985, 1-A; Jones, "Fairmount Hotel Fact Sheet."

30. Ibid.; Joseph Treml, "West Chicago firm is on a roll," *Aurora (IL) Beacon-News*, Apr. 5, 1985.

31. "Hotel move may spark suit," *San Antonio Express-News*, Jan. 26, 1985, 7-B; "Four Seasons claims it leases Fairmount's new land," *San Antonio Express-News*, Feb. 26, 1985.

32. "Fate of hotel still in limbo," *San Antonio Express-News*, Jan. 11, 1985; "Attorney: Hotel owners knew tract was divided," *San Antonio Express-News*, Feb. 27, 1985.

33. "Pre-dawn land visit described," *San Antonio Express-News*, Mar. 1, 1985, 3-B.

34. "Historic hotel's owners given 30-year lease," *San Antonio Express-News*, Feb. 22, 1985, 8-C.

35. "Four Seasons claims it leases Fairmount's new land," *San Antonio Express-News*, Feb. 26, 1985.

36. Jones, "Fairmount Hotel Fact Sheet," 2.

37. "Hotel's still in limbo," *San Antonio Express-News*, Mar. 2, 1985.

38. "Developers get green light to move Fairmount Hotel," *San Antonio Express-News*, Mar. 5, 1985.

39. David Anthony Richelieu, "Fairmount Hotel hoisted," *San Antonio Express-News*, Mar. 21, 1985.

40. City of San Antonio Department of Public Works, "Operations Plan for Moving the Fairmount Hotel," Mar. 22, 1985 (rev.).

41. Ibid.; David Anthony Richelieu, "Owners to pay moving costs," *San Antonio Express-News*, Apr. 2, 1985, 6-A.

42. "Preparing for Fairmount Move," *San Antonio Express-News*, Mar. 29,1985; Jones, "Fairmount Hotel Fact Sheet," 2; David Anthony Richelieu, "It's moving, it's moving!," *San Antonio Express-News*, Mar. 31, 1985, 1-A.

43. David Anthony Richelieu and Susie Phillips, "Hotel still in one piece," *San Antonio Express-News*, Mar. 23, 1985, 1-A.

44. Ibid.

45. Ibid. Four Seaons attorney was William T. Kaufman.

46. David Anthony Richelieu, "Fairmount blessed, ready to hit the road," *San Antonio Express-News*, Mar. 30, 1985, 1-A; Richelieu, "Hotel nears home," *San Antonio Express-News*, Apr. 2, 1985, 1-A. Blessings were also bestowed by Rabbi Samuel Stahl of Temple Beth-El and by the Rev. T.J. Youngblood of Central Christian Church.

47. Richelieu, "It's moving!"

48. Kym Fox, "That's his granddad's dream they're moving;" "Operations Plan," 7.

49. David Anthony Richelieu, "Hotel nears home," *San Antonio Express-News*, Apr. 2, 1985, 1-A; Treml, "West Chicago firm is on a roll."

50. Ibid.; Robert Cahill and Deborah Weser, "The Fairmount's almost home," *San Antonio Light*, Apr. 2, 1985, A-1; David Anthony Richelieu, "Mobile hotel ready to settle down," *San Antonio Express-News*, Apr. 3, 1985, 1-A.

51. Ibid.

52. "Hotel gives competition," *San Antonio Express-News*, Apr. 7, 1985, 4-D. Leaders of the American Petroleum Refiners Association, captivated by the convention sideshow, asked to string a banner across the hotel for a publicity photo and reserved the entire Fairmount Hotel for a meeting the next year. (David Anthony Richelieu, "Fairmount ready to settle into new home," *San Antonio Express-News*, Apr. 3, 1985, 1-A.)

53. "Hotel gives competition."

54. Richelieu, "Hotel nears home."

55. Cahill and Weser, "The Fairmount's almost home."

56. David Anthony Richelieu, "Fairmount ready to settle into new home," *San Antonio Express-News*, Apr. 3, 1985, 1-A; Deborah Weser, "Fairmount movers told to get it off the street," *San Antonio Light*, Apr. 4, 1985, A-1.

57. David Anthony Richelieu, "Few see moving miracle," *San Antonio Express-News*, Apr. 4, 1985, 1-A.

58. David Anthony Richelieu, "Fairmount placed over new foundation," *San Antonio Express-News*, Apr. 5, 1985; Richelieu, "Hotel's in place at last," *San Antonio Express-News*, May 10, 1985.

59. Bebe Inkley OHT, 15.

60. "Six-block move of historic San Antonio hotel," *Brickline '86, Newsletter of the Brick Institute of Texas*, Feb. 1986, 1.

61. David Anthony Richelieu, "Fairmount Hotel move to make '86 record book," *San Antonio Express-News*, Aug. 7, 1985, 2-H.

62. Richelieu, "Fairmount placed over new foundation;" Richelieu, "Hotel's in place at last;" Alamo Architects, "The Fairmount Hotel," Feb. 2, 1987, copy in SACS Library. The city's bill included loss of two days' revenue at the Marina Parking Garage near the start of the journey. Traffic control was by off-duty police officers hired under private contract. (Arthur Moczygemba, "City bills Fairmount $61,843," *San Antonio Express-News*, May 11, 1985, 1-B.)

63. "Fairmount Hotel dedication held," *San Antonio Express-News*, Sept. 6, 1986.

64. David Anthony Richelieu, "Historic board approves Fairmount renovation plans," *San Antonio Express-News*, Nov. 5, 1985, 5-D; "Discord surfaces over Fairmount's design," *San Antonio Express-News*, Nov. 9, 1985, 11-A; "Fairmount Hotel dedication held," *San Antonio Express-News*, Sept. 6, 1986; Lane, "A Moving

Experience," 26, 47; Alamo Architects, "The Fairmount Hotel." Concern that the Fairmount would overshadow surroundings in its new site caused the Fine Arts Commission at first to disapprove the proposal by a vote of five to three, with two abstentions. (Nancy Perdue and Steve Schlather, "Group tries to stop Fairmount Hotel move," *San Antonio Light*, Feb. 9, 1985.)

65. "Fairmount Hotel dedication held," *San Antonio Express-News*, Sept. 6, 1986. The hotel opened under the management of a Dallas-based company composed of several former personnel of the similarly appointed Mansion on Turtle Creek in Dallas. (Steven H. Lee, *The Dallas Morning News*, Sept. 8, 1986.)

66. Ibid.

67. Joseph H. Labadie, comp., *La Villita Earthworks, A Preliminary Report of Investigations of Mexican Siege Works at the Battle of the Alamo,* Center for Archaeological Research, University of Texas at San Antonio, Archaeological Survey Report No. 159 (1986), 12–21; Katherine Cruse, "Preliminary Report, Nueva and S. Alamo Streets," 1985, 1, typescript copy in SACS Library.

68. Labadie, *La Villita Earthworks*, vi, 2–6; Cruse, "Preliminary Report," 3–5.

69. Labadie, *La Villita Earthworks*, 2–3.

70. Ibid., 6–8; "Diggers given extra time at Fairmount site," *San Antonio Express-News*, Feb. 27, 1985; "Fact Sheet, UTSA Excavations at La Villita (Fairmount Relocation Site)," University of Texas at San Antonio Center for Archaeological Research, 1985, 2.

71. "Fact Sheet, UTSA Excavations," 1; Tim Griffin, "Scientists hail 'treasures,'" *San Antonio Express-News*, Mar. 2, 1985; Griffin, "Dig site yields artifacts of Santa Anna's army," *San Antonio Express-News*, Mar. 7, 1985, 1-A. Director of the UTSA center was Dr. Thomas Hester. Project director was Joe Labadie.

72. "Fact Sheet, UTSA Excavations," 2; Labadie, *La Villita Earthworks*, vi, 8. Since the artifacts were found on city-owned land, under the Texas Antiquities Act they reverted to state ownership. Archeological testing of the southern part of the site four months later found nothing of significance. (Joseph H. Labadie, "Additional Archaeological And Historical Studies For The Fairmount Hotel Project," Center for Archaeological Research, The University of Texas at San Antonio Archaeological Survey Report No. 160 [1986], 25.)

Toward San Antonio's

Fourth Century

(since 1996)

19

Smartphones to the Rescue

The thirty-story Smith-Young/Transit/Tower Life Building, built in 1928, remained the tallest building in San Antonio for sixty years. It was reported that in no other major American city in modern times had a tallest building kept such a title for so long. Because of San Antonio's arrested development, by the early 1960s San Antonio had more buildings surviving from the nineteenth century than did any other city in Texas or in most of the United States.[1]

During the adversarial 1960s, however, while the Conservation Society was diverted in mortal combat with city hall over an expressway, two-thirds of the city's most significant vintage buildings were destroyed. National Park Service architectural historian John C. Garner, Jr. estimated that in 1960 San Antonio had one thousand buildings "of historic and vintage character." But when he oversaw completion of the city's Historic American Buildings Survey at the end of the decade, he counted no more than three hundred.[2]

San Antonio's landmark destruction, euphemistically called "urban renewal," was greater in the 1960s than during the city's wholesale street widenings earlier in the century. Vast historic areas in the western downtown core were bulldozed to await redevelopment while other picturesque neighborhoods dwindled by default. Just outside central La Villita, in 1963 twenty-four historic homes lined the two blocks of South Presa Street from Villita Street to Durango Boulevard. Seven years later only thirteen remained, four of them boarded up. Critics charged that in La Villita itself, new changes overseen by the recreation-oriented Parks Department seriously damaged its vaunted ambience.[3] Elsewhere, historic buildings next to the Spanish Governor's Palace were threatened with destruction as landmarks elsewhere continued to vanish.[4]

On the other hand, conservationists had been able to mount a few successful rear guard actions, and backers of urban renewal–supported HemisFair

The River Walk helped draw people to downtown San Antonio with developments like Rivercenter Mall (1988), which opened beside a River Walk extension next to the new forty-two-story Marriott Rivercenter Hotel. Lewis F. Fisher.

'68 did jolt downtown San Antonio out of its slumber. The convention center built for the fair became the cornerstone of a mushrooming $13 billion hospitality industry, the city's second largest. The adjoining arena provided the initial home for the city's first major league sports team, the National Basketball Association's Spurs. The Tower of the Americas gave the city a new symbol. The new arm of the River Bend created for the fair was itself extended in 1988 to reach the unique new Rivercenter Mall and the city's new tallest building—the thousand-room, forty-two-story Marriott Rivercenter Hotel—and in 2001 was extended again into an expanded convention center.

It was too much to hope that the start of new cooperation between city government and conservationists could bring immediate consensus and well-planned development. The two decades between HemisFair and the Marriott Rivercenter Hotel were ones of uneven achievement and not infrequent regression. Although Unique San Antonio posters went up in travel agencies across the country once the fair was over, most of the two dozen historic buildings which visitors thought made HemisFair unique among world's fairs stood derelict while city hall was distracted by indecision over what to do with the grounds. The chronically understaffed City Planning Department had to work on routine growth and could be of no help. Official committees looking into such matters were ignored.[5] The San Antonio Convention and Visitors Bureau was so underfunded it could not implement plans for a downtown walking tour for visitors once they arrived. Of America's other "unique cities," in 1970 San Francisco had a $1 million annual tourist promotion budget, New Orleans $250,000 and Boston $150,000. San Antonio had $80,000. "Even Corpus Christi spends $150,000 a year," lamented one bureau worker.[6]

Nevertheless, as time went on city government and preservationists came to respect mutual strengths and the value of each other's goals. Resources were more evenly allocated, and cooperation improved. Building on their accomplishments of earlier years, latter-day preservationists took on all comers. Already they had helped an old three-story, three-million-pound hotel roll down the street out of harm's way, bought a historic theater—and found themselves in the motion picture business, and implemented a grant program for local preservation projects. They financed it all through a four-night annual Fiesta extravaganza that drew tens of thousands of celebrants to La Villita, setting a national record for preservation fund-raising events and helping vault the San Antonio Conservation Society into a unique position among the nation's preservation organizations.

There was growing awareness that "a building does not have to be an important work of architecture to become a first-rate landmark," as the architectural critic Herbert Muschamp once put it. "The essential feature of a landmark is not its design but the place it holds in a city's memory." And the city's Office of Historic Preservation quoted British planner Graeme Shankland as saying, "A city without old buildings is like a man without a memory." Aided by such observations, appreciation grew beyond understanding the importance of saving only landmarks with notable links to history, like the Alamo and the Spanish missions. Realization spread that distinctive and familiar longtime streetscapes and tumbledown cantinas once considered mundane and insignificant could also be important to local identity and to proclaiming San Antonio's unique place in the world.[7]

But city government in general and historic preservation in particular kept getting more complicated for San Antonians as the population spiraled ever upward, from 1.1 million in the mid-1990s to 1.5 million by the mid-2010s. While the eighteen fulltime staff members of the city's Office of Historic Preservation tried to ride herd on developing and enforcing official protections, a vigilant San Antonio Conservation Society, still trying to preserve a broad spectrum of the city's heritage, had to be everywhere at once. Its fifteen fulltime staff and 1,700 members backed up city staff with new information and sent volunteers to monitor meetings to detect sleights-of-hand by self-interested developers and uncaring citizens.

The burgeoning burden of rules and regulations required ever more sophisticated efforts to navigate the historic preservation process. Gone were days like those when preservationists could simply sweep into the ruined compound of Mission San José, fence off land nobody seemed to own and claim it for the cause. Now threatened sites had to be considered by an eleven-member Historic and Design Review Commission that parsed details carefully calibrated within stringent parameters—though its decisions carried the ever-present possibility of being overruled by city council. To help keep procedures straight, in 2009 city council adopted a 128-page Strategic Historic Preservation Plan that codified goals and synthesized city preservation planning, zoning and economic development strategies along with methods of implementation.[8]

Dealing with the forum of public opinion also became more complicated. Press releases alone no longer sufficed. Information output had to be supplemented on well-designed websites that were easy to navigate. Social media postings had to be maintained. Parties and dinners needed to honor achievers, and awards had to be presented. New funding had to supplement the prodigious annual yield of A Night In Old San Antonio. In 2008 the Conservation Society formed the Capital Club to draw larger donors in support of education programs in particular. Soon it was garnering more than $100,000 a year in new funds. The familiar run of black-tie charity galas was joined in 2012 by the PROM—the Preservation PROMenade—sponsored by the new Power of Preservation Foundation to benefit Office of Historic Preservation programs. The event was held in major endangered or newly rescued landmarks, settings sure to draw media coverage.[9]

An ongoing frustration was identifying landmarks before problems arose. More than 60,000 structures and locations newly defined as historic had been noted within the city's original thirty-six square miles. Of these, more than 10,000 gained a degree of protection through designation as city landmarks or by being included in a historic district. In addition, distinctive views along the San Antonio River and at the Alamo were protected by viewshed regulations approved by city council in 2002. The identification effort went back decades but still included less than half the estimated number. It was a highly labor intensive, tedious process. To help, the Office of Historic Preservation enlisted new technology.[10]

"Take out your smartphones," Shanon Shea Miller, the city's historic preservation officer, told citizens in 2016 as she launched the ScoutSA campaign, an effort to engage residents in landmark designation. Then, she explained, go to SApreservation.com and use the new data collection tool to report places important to you. GIS technology would automatically put the site on a map. Her office would take it from there, using the new data in decision making about potential landmark and historic district designations. The process could add archives of whole city blocks.

Next, Miller—who also chaired the executive committee of Washington, DC-based Preservation Action—called up reinforcements for homeowners trying to restore their homes at a reasonable cost. "People are doing projects all over our historic districts," she said, "but they're kind of going it alone." The new Rehabber Club would build an online support group of carpenters, craftsmen and others to aid do-it-yourselfers in revitalizing neighborhoods through regular meetings and events. The Office of Historic Preservation already administered an online program allowing residents to report vacant and underutilized vintage buildings in danger of being demolished by neglect.[11]

The growing number of designated historic districts helped define significant historic neighborhoods and added a structure of consistent and enforceable guidelines. Since the King William Historic District became the first in San Antonio—and in Texas—in 1968, the number of locally designated historic districts had risen to twenty-seven, protecting structures within from hasty demolition or inappropriate exterior change. Several held dual recognition as National Historic Districts, selected through a process managed by the National Park Service—which also managed prestigious selection of National Historic Landmarks, a designation that conveyed federal tax benefits but offered no local zoning or legal protections.[12]

City-designated historic districts could be perceived as cumbersome to organize, as they first required consent from at least 51 percent of residents. Some residents complained that once district designation was approved, property owners might have to hire an architect to negotiate changes during the review process. Others feared that gentrification could follow and cause taxes to rise to the point that some would have to move out of the district.[13]

To ease requirements on distinctive neighborhoods not wishing to deal with full historic district status while still providing stability so homeowners "don't have to worry about someone down the street doing something that hurts the value of the neighborhood," as Mayor Howard Peak put it, preservationists came up with Neighborhood Conservation Districts. These would offer design guidelines fitting the character of the neighborhood and regulation of new construction, additions and some alterations but would not address demolition. Ann McGlone, then City Historic Preservation Officer, liked their flexibility, observing that "sometimes they are a buffer zone around a historic district and sometimes they act as a baby historic district." In 1998, with the aid of Dallas consultants funded by the Conservation Society, McGlone and Society President Paula Piper set to work. An enabling ordinance for Neighborhood Conservation Districts was passed two years later. By 2015 the city had nine.[14]

The process, however, was not always smooth. The Mahncke Park neighborhood, some forty-five blocks of increasingly well kept Craftsman-style bungalows east of Broadway between Fort Sam Houston and Alamo Heights, became a Neighborhood Conservation District peacefully enough in 2008. An application was in place to upgrade to a historic district when, in 2012, city

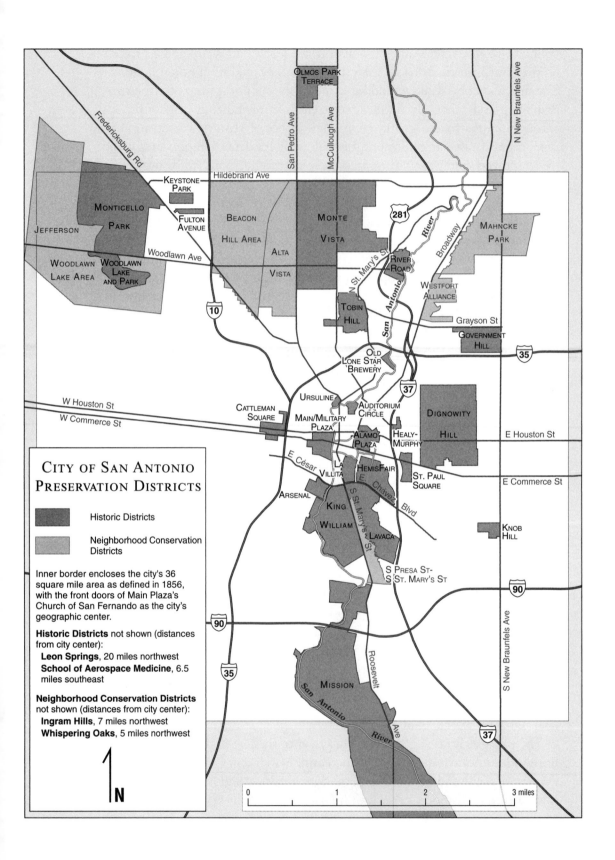

OLMOS PARK TERRACE

San Pedro Ave

McCullough Ave

N New Braunfels Ave

Fredericksburg Rd

KEYSTONE PARK

Hildebrand Ave

MONTICELLO PARK

FULTON AVENUE

BEACON HILL AREA

MONTE VISTA

281

River

Broadway

MAHNCKE PARK

JEFFERSON

Woodlawn Ave

ALTA

VISTA

N St. Mary's St

RIVER ROAD

WOODLAWN LAKE AREA

WOODLAWN LAKE AND PARK

10

San Antonio

WESTFORT ALLIANCE

Grayson St

GOVERNMENT HILL

35

TOBIN HILL

OLD LONE STAR BREWERY

37

W Houston St

W Commerce St

URSULINE

AUDITORIUM CIRCLE

DIGNOWITY HILL

E Houston St

CATTLEMAN SQUARE

MAIN/MILITARY PLAZA

ALAMO PLAZA

HEALY-MURPHY

CITY OF SAN ANTONIO PRESERVATION DISTRICTS

Historic Districts

Neighborhood Conservation Districts

Inner border encloses the city's 36 square mile area as defined in 1856, with the front doors of Main Plaza's Church of San Fernando as the city's geographic center.

Historic Districts not shown (distances from city center):
 Leon Springs, 20 miles northwest
 School of Aerospace Medicine, 6.5 miles southeast

Neighborhood Conservation Districts not shown (distances from city center):
 Ingram Hills, 7 miles northwest
 Whispering Oaks, 5 miles northwest

LA VILLITA

HEMISFAIR

St. Paul Square

E Commerce St

ARSENAL

KING WILLIAM

LAVACA

E César Chávez Blvd

S St. Mary's St

KNOB HILL

90

S PRESA ST-S ST. MARY'S ST

90

35

MISSION

Roosevelt

San Antonio

River

S New Braunfels Ave

37

N

0   1   2   3 miles

council changed the rules. Previously, the designation process could not go forward if 51 percent of residents were opposed. Then city policy changed to permit the process to go forward if 30 percent of property owners approved. The rationale was that it was hard to get enough people to vote for anything, but many did not see it that way. Mahncke Park erupted.[15]

Black and white yard signs proclaiming "NO HISTORIC" sprung up throughout the neighborhood, and the message adorned tee shirts as well. Why, asked the new Property Rights Coalition of Mahncke Park, should 30 percent be able to tell everyone else what to do, especially if the coalition could claim signatures from 55 percent who opposed the designation? Neighborhood Association President Daniel Lazarine personally favored the designation, but although the association itself remained neutral, yard signs began to mysteriously disappear, and discussion turned into "a very nasty dialogue." Some originally supporting petitioners disavowed their signatures. The Office of Historic Preservation scheduled public meetings. Director Shanon Miller said fears were an "exaggeration" and that "misinformation and misunderstanding" had distorted the process of providing an added level of protection to keep neighborhood changes "safe and appropriate." But the application for historic district status, though technically still active, was placed on hold, and Mahncke Park remained a Neighborhood Conservation District.[16]

Nevertheless, designated districts have provided a helpful framework for targeting preservation projects. Since 1998 the Conservation Society has given more than $1.5 million in community grants to help owners improve historic residential and commercial properties, their chances of selection enhanced if they are within a designated district. In 2010 the Office of Historic Preservation began twice a year producing and equipping teams of undergraduate and graduate architecture students to make minor home repairs for selected homeowners within historic districts under S.T.A.R.—Students Together Achieving Revitalization. The program was a partnership of the Office of Historic Preservation, San Antonio College, the University of Texas at San Antonio student Historic Preservation Association and UTSA's College of Architecture, Construction and Planning.[17]

S.T.A.R. began in 2010 when a "nice little house" in Dignowity Hill was marked for demolition partly because the owner wasn't in town to object when the ruling was made. Shanon Miller thought some simple repairs could prevent demolition and asked UTSA's College of Architecture, Construction and Planning for help. Architect and senior lecturer Sue Ann Pemberton—a future Conservation Society president—took it on. More than 250 UTSA students contributed two weekends that November, saving the flagged house from demolition and also doing exterior repairs and maintenance projects from yard maintenance to window repair, woodwork and exterior painting on a dozen nearby homes.[18]

While student volunteer repair teams have since rotated twice a year in different districts, Dignowity Hill remained a difficult case. First developed in the mid-nineteenth century and then separated from downtown by the Southern Pacific Railroad, its seventy-block mix of distinctive Victorian homes and later Craftsman bungalows were already suffering from abandonment and decay when it was made a historic district in 1983. Though by 2014 Dignowity Hill had become home to both Mayor Ivy Taylor and Conservation Society President Sue Ann Pemberton, many restored homes still stood beside derelict structures not easily rescued. One obdurate owner of two houses, built on Nolan Street in 1873 and in 1912, had a yearlong standoff with neighbors and preservationists over whether the homes were salvageable and whose rehabilitation cost estimates were more realistic. The Historic and Design Review Commission denied the owner's request for demolition but was overruled by the city's Building Standards Board, which, tired of waiting, decided the two houses were too far gone to be saved.[19]

Preservationists' relationships with institutions could be as smooth or as fraught as those with individuals. Things went well with the San Antonio Independent School District, which in 1997 asked the Conservation Society to survey its pre–World War II educational facilities and identify notable architecture worth saving in upcoming renovations. Things did not go well three years later with the Roman Catholic Archdiocese of San Antonio over the fate of Mary Catherine Hall, a three-story Colonial Revival brick dormitory near Woodlawn Lake designed in 1922 by noted Adams & Adams, Architects. The last surviving building on the former Westmoorland College/University of San Antonio/Trinity University campus, and newly vacated by the Mexican American Cultural Center, it had been sold to the Archdiocese in 1952. The Archdiocese thought the building too costly to upgrade and applied for a demolition permit. Mary Catherine Hall had not been named a city landmark, but Historic Preservation Officer Ann McGlone put a two-week hold on the permit request so its merits could be evaluated.[20]

When McGlone and two members of the Historic and Design Review Commission arrived to inspect the site, however, they were astonished to find demolition well under way. Doors and windows had been removed, the interior gutted, plumbing taken out. They called a building inspector, who determined that indeed no demolition permit had been given and immediately issued a stop-work order. The next day the Historic and Design Review Commission unanimously rejected the permit application and declared the building historically significant, the first step toward landmark designation. Archdiocesan officials pleaded little knowledge of the building's history. "We would simply like to remove it until we get ready for a future expansion," ex-

Preservationists had to deal with unsympathetic institutions like the Roman Catholic Archdiocese, which began demolition of a historic Spanish Colonial Revival dormitory without a permit. Rivard Report.

plained Msgr. Lawrence Stuebben. Although Conservation Society President Loyce Ince thought the building remained "structurally sound and architecturally receptive to adaptive reuse," the archdiocese was ultimately allowed to complete its demolition. The Conservation Society vowed to help head off such incidents in the future by contributing $50,000 toward the city's historic structures survey."[21]

Then preservationists found themselves in a series of contretemps with the

University of the Incarnate Word over land in Brackenridge Park south of Hildebrand Avenue, across the street from the university's crowded campus.

First to flare up was a title issue over Miraflores Park, fifteen acres at the southeast corner of the San Antonio River and Hildebrand Avenue that had been made into a sculpture garden in 1921 by Dr. Aureliano Urrutia, a noted physician and refugee from the Mexican Revolution. Incarnate Word thought its receipt of the land as a gift gave it clear title and planned development, but its Spanish land grant origins were murky. At the urging of Conservation Society President Barbara Johnson, the city sued for title to the land. Incarnate Word settled in 2005 by exchanging its claim on Miraflores for ownership of city-owned land up the hill at the corner of Devine Road, where it built a pharmacy school.

Five years later, on the opposite side of the river, the Parks Department had moved out of its offices in the Donkey Barn, built in 1920 to store hay for donkeys used in rides in the park. An Alamo-like stone facade was added in 1956. The surrounding maintenance area was vacated as well. A Brackenridge Park Master Plan adopted by the city in 1980 marked the 2.5-acre area for expansion by the adjacent San Antonio Zoo, which was expecting to take it over. But when Incarnate Word President Lou Agnese looked down from a university building he saw "a very ugly site. Period." The university offered to contribute $1.1 million to a park restoration fund in exchange for a fifty-year lease on the site. A $20 million fine arts center and fencing studio would be built there, with an eighty-eight-car parking lot nearby. The Donkey Barn could be restored as an art gallery. Agnese also made another pass at taking over nearby Miraflores Park, where city restoration had stalled from lack of funds.

San Antonio Zoo Director Stephen McCusker was "frankly, shocked," adding that "we didn't know we would be competing for that space." Leilah Powell, director of the private Brackenridge Park Conservancy, formed in 2008 by the Conservation Society and the Parks Department, was "flabbergasted." Conservation Society President Rollette Schreckenghost said: "That is our zoo; that is our park. UIW is a wonderful university, but it does not belong to the people of San Antonio." Deputy City Manager A. J. Rodriguez said he knew nothing of the area being intended for the zoo—"the master plan is thirty years old"—and that the city's main consideration would be "a plan with the greatest public use and benefit." Mayor Julián Castro parried, observing, "Park land is quite precious." Use of the site ultimately remained with the park.[22]

Scarcely six years later, in January 2016, Brackenridge Park supporters were dumbfounded to learn of the University of the Incarnate Word's approach to the San Antonio Independent School District to lease 2.4 acres the district owned in an isolated upper corner of the park, near the corner of Hildebrand Avenue and US 281 across from the university campus. The San Antonio

Zoo thought it had a tentative deal with the district to use the site for a badly needed 600-space public parking garage and had started construction planning. The parking garage was included in a new park master plan to be considered by city council that summer. Hours before a school district board meeting, however, a proposed memorandum of understanding signed by Incarnate Word's vice president for business and finance was emailed to trustees. It would provide the university a ninety-nine-year lease on the same property and allow it to build a twelve-story building. The upper half would be a student dormitory and the lower half a 646-space parking garage, with a third of those spaces available for public use.[23]

News of Incarnate Word's plan had broken the day before. An outraged crowd descended on the school board meeting. Twenty-one speakers opposed the Incarnate Word plan, ranging from former Mayor Lila Cockrell to Zoo Director Tim Morrow, Conservation Society President Janet Dietel and Brackenridge Park Conservancy Director Lynn Bobbitt, a former Conservation Society president. Afterward trustees went into a lengthy executive session. A week later trustees approved the original park plan by a vote of 6-0. Incarnate Word President Lou Agnese angrily denied having had any knowledge of the dormitory/garage proposal submitted by his vice president.[24]

Trinity University was also under scrutiny from the society with a watchful eye emblazoned on its seal. The Conservation Society joined the Monte Vista Historical Association, the Office of Historic Preservation and the Historic and Design Review Commission in crying foul to Trinity President Dennis Ahlburg for the university's unauthorized changes in converting four Monte Vista Historic District landmark homes on Oakmont Court from residential to faculty office use. In an eight-page agreement signed in 2012 after thirteen hours of mediation, the Monte Vista association agreed not to oppose Trinity's use of the four houses as faculty offices, and Trinity agreed not to seek any zoning changes for the next twenty-two and a half years on any properties it owned or acquired in the historic district.[25]

Two miles away, the McNay Art Museum wanted to be rid of the 1910 Queen Anne farm cottage that had been the home of Marion Koogler McNay while her home next door, which later became the museum, was built. In 1954 it had become the home of John Leeper, the McNay's first director, and his family. Conservation Society President Jill Souter saw its potential for visitor reception at the new Mitchell Lake Audubon Center south of the city. The original section of the Leeper House was moved there in 2003 and restored.[26]

Beyond caring for landmarks and public spaces, preservationists maintained vigilance in protecting other elements of the city's culture. In defense of the city's 1881 naming of streets for cities in Mexico, the Conservation Society kept a section of Laredo Street from being renamed Goodwill Way in 2005 and prevented a name change for El Paso Street in 2012. Society

Among some 1,500 gas stations in various stages of repair surveyed by preservationists was this one built in Alamo Heights by the Magnolia Oil Company (1930), which gained the familiar Pegasus neon sign when it was acquired by Mobil Oil. The Conservation Society holds a protective guardianship of the sign. Lewis F. Fisher.

opposition in 2003 led city council to reverse its decision to rename Durango Boulevard in honor of the late Judge Hipolito Garcia, making that an honorary designation instead. But in 2011 the council renamed Durango Boulevard again, this time in honor of the late labor leader César Chávez, whose name had been unsuccessfully proposed for Commerce Street in 1999. The Conservation Society sued in protest but withdrew in exchange for an amended city policy requiring name change proposals to be heard by the Historic and Design Review Commission when they involved major thoroughfares or were within historic districts, or were within—or emanated from—the city's original thirty-six square miles.[27]

Visual pollution by billboards had been a concern in San Antonio since reformers first targeted an oversupply in 1911. When digital billboards emerged in 2007 to the dismay of preservationists, Conservation Society President Marcie Ince formed a Digital Billboards Task Force to address safety, energy and aesthetic issues. Despite numerous benefits of digital billboards cited by San Antonio–based Clear Channel Outdoor, which owned twelve of the city's thirteen digital billboards erected under a city-approved test program, the city banned additional digital billboards and required removal of existing ones if they were damaged beyond half their value.[28]

Even the lowly gas station found its place in the preservation spectrum.

Called "filling stations" from 1910 to 1920, "gas stations" for the next twenty years and then "service stations," many were built by major oil companies in their own distinctive styles while locally owned stations were built according to operators' sometimes eccentric tastes. In 1983 Conservation Society member Kitty Massey led the gathering of photos and reports on stations within original city limits that could be located in city directories from 1910 to 1940. Nearly three decades later member Frederica Kushner's new Historic Gas Station Survey Committee scanned the old photos, extended the survey to 1970 and posted 1,500 images and reports on the society's website. By 2016 six gas stations had been named city landmarks and another three dozen had been nominated for the title. When completed, it was estimated that the number of stations surveyed and dating from 1910 to 1970 would to reach 2,000.[29]

Notes

1. Minutes, D-Apr. 5, 1965, 2. The statement was made by architectural historian John C. Garner, Jr.

2. Lewis Fisher, "Dwindling Heritage," *San Antonio Express-News,* Mar. 29, 1970, 1-H. Many more old buildings of less interest or "vintage" age did, of course, remain.

3. La Villita nevertheless remained popular. In 1970 the Parks Department rented its buildings and plazas for some 300 events (including A Night In Old San Antonio) which drew nearly 320,000 persons. (Lewis Fisher, "La Villita's Future: Uncertain," *San Antonio Express-News*, Dec. 20, 1970, 2-H.)

4. Lewis Fisher, "Unique San Antonio . . . How Long Will It Be That Way?" *San Antonio Express-News,* Feb. 1, 1970, 1–2-H.

5. Ibid.

6. Ibid.

7. "Why Is Preservation Important?" accessed Feb. 6, 2016, at www.sanantonio.gov/historic/information.aspx.

8. The Strategic Historic Preservation Plan summarized six months of interview sessions with various groups of stakeholders by the Lakota Group, a Chicago-based firm specializing in planning, urban design, landscape architecture, historic preservation and community relations. The plan included recommendations with short-, mid- and long-term outcomes during the next fifteen years in planning, zoning, economic development, historic resources, incentives and education and advocacy. ("Strategic Historic Preservation Plan," accessed Feb. 4, 2016, at www.sanantonio.gov/historic/Docs/Strategic-His toric-Plan_Final-8-2009.pdf.)

9. Galas have been held at the Mission Road Power Plant, the Inter-Continental Motors Building beside Brackenridge Park, the Woman's Pavilion at HemisFair Park and Stinson Municipal Airport.

10. In 2002 the Office of Historic Preservation and the Conservation Society had accelerated efforts to expand existing identifications of historic resources within the thirty-six-square-mile city limits as defined in 1856.

11. Scott Huddleston, "City seeks to save historic San Antonio," *San Antonio Express-News*, Jan. 27, 2016. Miller, who succeeded Ann Benson McGlone as San Antonio's preservation officer in 2008, said such technology was already in use studying blighted neighborhoods in Detroit. The Vacant Building Initiative was approved by city council in 2014.

12. National Historic Districts in San Antonio include Alamo Plaza, Blue Star Street Industrial, Bungalow Colony, Fort Sam Houston, Kelly Field, King William, La Villita, Lavaca, Main and Military Plazas, Monte Vista, Randolph Field, San Antonio City Cemeteries (Old), San Antonio Missions National Historical Park, Source of the River, South Alamo Street–South St. Mary's Street, Southern Pacific Depot, U.S. San Antonio Arsenal and Voelker Farmstead. (Accessed Mar. 30, 2016, at www.nationalregisterofhistoricplaces.com/tx/bexar/districts.html.) More than 130 individual San Antonio landmarks were also listed on the National Register of Historic Places, administered by the National Park Service.

City-designated historic districts include Alamo Plaza (formed in 1978), commercial blocks surrounding the Alamo; Arsenal (1975), a core complex of six buildings established west of downtown as a U.S. Arsenal in

1859 and renovated as H-E-B grocery corporate headquarters; Auditorium Circle/ Veterans Memorial Plaza (2006), four Spanish mission–style landmarks on the northern edge of downtown; Cattleman Square (1985), a late-nineteenth- and early twentieth-century commercial and industrial district around the former International & Great Northern/Missouri Pacific depot west of downtown; Dignowity Hill (1983), a neighborhood of distinctive small Victorian homes and Craftsman bungalows east of downtown; Fulton Avenue (2001), several blocks of 1920s Spanish Eclectic homes east of the intersection of Fredericksburg Road and North Zarzamora Street; Government Hill (2002), an eclectic residential neighborhood developed south of Fort Sam Houston after the post opened in 1879; Healy-Murphy (1978), surrounding a late-nineteenth-century African American hospital and school east of downtown; HemisFair Park (1975), grounds and surviving buildings of the 1968 World's Fair; Keystone Park (2009), two blocks of 1920s Tudor Revival homes east of the intersection of Fredericksburg Road and West Avenue; King William (1968), where German families built elegant homes southwest of downtown in the latter nineteenth century; Knob Hill (2010), four blocks of early twentieth-century Craftsman bungalows and Classical Revival homes east of South New Braunfels Avenue and south of Iowa Street; La Villita (1969), its mid-nineteenth-century downtown rock homes comprising an arts center; Lavaca (2001–4), a surviving neighborhood of eclectic homes south of HemisFair Plaza dating from the mid-nineteenth century; Leon Springs (2003), at a former stagecoach stop northwest of the city; Main and Military Plaza (1975), two downtown Spanish plazas laid out in the early eighteenth century; Mission (1977), encompassing the four Spanish missions neighborhoods in San Antonio Missions National Historical Park; Monte Vista (1975), 100 blocks of homes two miles north of downtown nearly intact from the city's Gilded Age of the late nineteenth and early twentieth centuries; Monticello Park (1975–2010), a residential neighborhood developed in the second quarter of the twentieth century northwest of downtown around Jefferson High School; Old Lone Star Brewery (1980), a turn-of-the-twentieth-century brewery complex north of downtown renovated as the San Antonio

Museum of Art; Olmos Park Terrace (2007–10), a 1930s subdivision of English stone cottages and small traditional homes northwest of Olmos Park; River Road (2010), a secluded neighborhood from the second quarter of the twentieth century between the Brackenridge Park Golf Course and the San Antonio River; St. Paul Square (1978), a late-nineteenth- and early twentieth-century commercial area around the former Southern Pacific depot east of downtown; School of Aerospace Medicine (2003), site of U.S. Air Force scientific research from 1959 to 1970 at the former Brooks Air Force Base at the southern edge of San Antonio; Tobin Hill (2007–8), an urban neighborhood dating from the late nineteenth century between downtown and Monte Vista; Ursuline Academy (1975), a mid-nineteenth-century girl's school campus north of downtown that became home to the Southwest School of Art; and Woodlawn Lake and Park (2000), a scenic residential district from the late nineteenth century northwest of downtown. ("Local Historic Districts," accessed Feb. 6, 2016 at www.sanantonio.gov/historic/Districts.aspx; Shanon Miller to Lewis F. Fisher, Feb. 5, 2016.)

13. To address residents' concerns, in 2012 the city adopted an illustrated set of historic district guidelines and three years later *released Historic Preservation: Essential to the Economy and Quality of Life in San Antonio*, an in-depth study by preservation economist Donovan Rypkema highlighting economic and social benefits of historic districts.

14. Amy Dorsett, "Ordinance about conservation districts," *San Antonio Express-News*, Sept. 30, 1998; J. M. Scott, "Potential historic districts," *San Antonio Express-News*, Sept. 1, 2015, accessed Feb. 13, 2016, at www.mysanantonio.com/news/local/slideshow/Virtually-historic-districts-in-San-Antonio-116189/photo-8565347.ph.

Neighborhood Conservation Districts include Alta Vista (2003), a fifty-six-block early twentieth-century neighborhood primarily north of San Pedro Park between San Pedro Avenue and the Union Pacific Railroad; Beacon Hill (2005), a mixed 520-acre neighborhood dominated by Craftsman homes between Fredericksburg Road and West Hildebrand Avenue east of IH-10 and west of the Union Pacific Railroad; Ingram Hills (2004), a post–World War II neighborhood east and south of Callaghan and Babcock roads and north of Ingram Road; Jefferson (2009), a 475-acre suburban neighborhood built before and after World War II between St. Cloud Road and Wilson Street south of Babcock Road and north of West Woodlawn Avenue; Mahncke Park (2008), a 445-acre neighborhood between Broadway and North New Braunfels Avenue south of East Hildebrand Avenue and dominated by Craftsman bungalows; South Presa Street/ South St. Mary's Street (2002), a narrow twelve-block late-nineteenth-century neighborhood east of South St. Mary's Street to just past South Presa Street northwest of the Southern Pacific Railroad; Westfort Alliance (2011), an eighty-acre neighborhood of one- and two-story mainly Craftsman early twentieth-century homes between Fort Sam Houston and Broadway; Whispering Oaks (2005), a 1960s neighborhood between Lockhill-Selma Road and the Union Pacific Railroad west of Dreamland Drive and east of Wurzbach Road; and Woodlawn Lake Area (2010), a 527-acre neighborhood of primarily Craftsman-style homes between Bandera Road and North Zarzamora Street south of West Woodlawn Avenue and north of Culebra Road. ("Neighborhood Conservation District," accessed Feb. 5, 2016, at www.sanantonio.gov/CitySearchResults .aspx?q=neighborhood%20conservation%20district.)

15. Edmond Ortiz, "Mahncke Park residents at odds," *San Antonio Express-News*, July 23, 2014.

16. Edmond Ortiz, "Historic district process," *San Antonio Express-News*, Aug. 13, 2014; Josh Brodesky, "Dispute roils Mahncke Park," *San Antonio Express-News*, Aug. 22, 2014.

17. "Community Grants," accessed Feb. 5, 2016, at www.saconservation.org/pres ervationprograms/grants.aspx; "S.T.A.R. Program," accessed Feb. 5, 2016, at www.san antonio.gov/historic/STAR.aspx; "Historic Preservation Association," accessed Feb. 5, 2016, at http://cacp.utsa.edu/students/historic-preservation-association.

18. Nicole Chavez, "Students Together Achieving Revitalization," accessed Feb. 5, 2016, at http://cacp.utsa.edu/news/students-together-achieving-revitalization-s.t.a.r.

19. Vianna Davila and Benjamin Olivo, "Despite objections," *San Antonio Express-News*, Mar. 13, 2015.

20. David Anthony Richelieu, "A 'historic' battle," *San Antonio Express-News*, Aug. 11, 2000, 1-A; Paula Allen, "Dorm switched," *San Antonio Express-News*, May 1, 2016, A-4. In 1937 the two-year Westmoorland College became the four-year University of San Antonio. It merged with Trinity University five years later when Trinity moved to San Antonio and onto the University of San Antonio campus. Trinity remained until its new campus was completed in 1952, when Mary Catherine Hall became a dormitory for nearby Assumption Seminary. A decade later the building became the Mexican American Cultural Center, which moved into new quarters nearby in 2000.

21. David Anthony Richelieu, "Demolition permit rejected," *San Antonio Express-News*, Aug. 18, 2000, 7-B.

22. Melissa Ludwig and Tracy Idell Hamilton, "UIW, Zoo want slice of Brackenridge Park," *San Antonio Express-News*, Mar. 6, 2010.

23. Robert Rivard, "Brackenridge Park: The Public Interest," *Rivard Report*, accessed Feb. 16, 2016, at http://therivardreport.com/brackenridge-park-the-public-interest-vs -uiw-expansion; Robert Rivard, "UIW Sought to Influence," *Rivard Report*, Jan. 14, 2016, accessed Feb. 16, 2016, at http://therivardreport.com/uiw-sought-to-influence -saisd-trustees-on-day-of-board-meeting.

24. Beckah McNeel, "SAISD Board Hears Public Support," *Rivard Report*, Jan. 12, 2016, accessed Feb. 16, 2016, at http://therivardreport.com/saisd-board-makes-no-decis ion-on-brackenridge-park-land; Brian Chasnoff, "University's sneak attack falls flat," *San Antonio Express-News*, Jan. 13, 2016; Beckah McNeel, "SAISD Board and San Antonio Zoo Reach Agreement, *Rivard Report*, Jan. 19, 2016, accessed Feb. 16, 2016, at http:// therivardreport.com/saisd-board-san-antonio-zoo-reach-agreement. In support of park-land elsewhere, in 1994 the Conservation Society swung behind a neighborhood group and helped gain an $800,000 city council appropriation to preserve eighty threatened acres in northeast San Antonio as Comanche Lookout Park. (Susie Phillips Gonzalez, "Council to buy land for new park," *San Antonio Express-News,* June 3, 1994, 5-C.)

25. Scott Huddleston, "Old country house," *San Antonio Express-News*, Jan. 7, 2012; Huddleston, "Trinity, Monte Vista settle," *San Antonio Express-News*, Mar. 29, 2012.

26. "Leeper House," *San Antonio Conservation Society Journal* 39:6, June 2003, 8; Anne and Cecile Parrish, "Leeper House Finds a New Home," *San Antonio Conservation Society Journal* 40:2, Winter 2005, 6. In addition to the McNay Art Museum and the

Conservation Society, the move was aided by architectural restoration plans drawn up by future Conservation Society President Sue Ann Pemberton and by efforts of the Office of Historic Preservation, the San Antonio Water System and the Mitchell Lake Wetlands Society. The Mitchell Lake Audubon Center planned bird tours of the grounds of the remains of the historic Hot Wells Hotel, halfway between the center and downtown. Hotel ruins had been purchased in 2015 from developer and Blue Star Arts complex owner James Lifschutz by Bexar County, which planned to turn the area into a park under Bexar Heritage and Parks Department Director Betty Beuché. (Jackie Calvert, "Hot Wells Conservancy," *Rivard Report*, July 9, 2014, accessed Feb. 16, 2016, at http:// therivardreport.com/chillin-history-hot-wells-conservancy-unveiled; Adolph Pesquera, "Preservation Plans," *Rivard Report*, Dec. 16, 2015, accessed Feb. 16, 2016, at www .virtualbx.com/construction-preview/23538-preservation-plans-for-hot-wells-ruins-fast -tracked.html.)

27. Josh Baugh, "Durango name change," *San Antonio Express-News*, May 19, 2011. Baugh, "Conservation society settles," *San Antonio Express-News*, Dec. 15, 2011.

28. Fisher, *American Venice*, 28; "Digital Billboards Have Not Proven to be Safe," Nov. 30, 2007, position paper in SACS files; David Hendricks, "No permits for new digital billboards," *San Antonio Express-News*, Mar. 29, 2010.

29. Frederica Kushner, "Filling Stations Survey," *San Antonio Conservation Society Advocate* 49:1, Fall 2012, 1; "San Antonio Historic Gas Stations," accessed Feb. 16, 2016, at http://gasstationsurvey.omeka.net/about.

20

The Core City Crucible

Preservationists had roamed far in the wake of the city's growth as new neighborhoods matured and became historic, but downtown San Antonio's concentration of diverse landmarks kept it a crucible for historic preservation. Alamo Plaza, HemisFair Plaza and Houston Street all suffered from chronic preservation issues that demanded regular attention. Long-term solutions seemed to dangle barely out of reach, while other problems kept surfacing nearby.

As vexing as any were the challenges reflected by the two San Antonio landmarks on a new Preservation Texas list of Most Endangered Places: the John H. Wood Jr. Courthouse (1968) on HemisFair Plaza and the Woolworth Building (1920) on Alamo Plaza, where saving the Alamo in 1883 had made the plaza the birthplace of publicly funded historic preservation in the western United States.[1]

The Woolworth Building, a civil rights landmark, anchored a key corner on the inner western edge of the Alamo's original Spanish mission plaza. On March 16, 1960, its lunch counter was the first that Woolworth's opened in the South to African Americans. Other places in town immediately followed suit, making San Antonio—where a sit-in had been held three days earlier—the first large southern city to integrate its lunch counters. It was a major victory for the integration movement. It helped put San Antonio on a peaceful integration track and avoid the racial violence that plagued other cities.[2]

The three-story Woolworth Building and two beside it were purchased in 2015 by the State of Texas, though the General Land Office said little about intentions for them. Some thought the Woolworth Building should be renovated for interpretive use rather than continuing to house the sort of carnival-style emporiums of wonder that lined the west side of the plaza. Others called for the building to be razed in an effort to re-create the appearance of the area at the time of the 1836 battle. They proposed removing along with it neighboring landmarks like the Alfred Giles–designed Crockett Block (1882)

Three buildings facing the Alamo to the east were purchased for an Alamo Plaza restoration project, including the Crockett Block (1882) at left and, at far right, the Woolworth Building (1920), a civil rights landmark. They could be used for interpretive purposes or razed to return the plaza to its appearance at the time of the 1836 battle, an effort that would also require removing the Alamo's roof and iconic gabled parapet. Lewis F. Fisher.

and the Romanesque U.S. Post Office and Courthouse (1937), and other structures like the Express-News Building (1929). Restoring the scene to the time of the battle would also require removing the Alamo's latter-day roof and the signature gabled parapet atop its facade, added years later by the U.S. Army.[3]

Where should change and clearance stop? Or should it start at all and leave visual documentation of the plaza's historic evolution in place? "We want to keep those buildings as they are," said Conservation Society President Janet Dietel. "They are part of that place."[4]

Similar questions had arisen in 1936, after the state purchased land directly behind the state-owned Alamo church. The Conservation Society had clashed with the Daughters of the Republic of Texas—entrusted by the state with the Alamo's guardianship since 1905—over what would become of the historic buildings erected behind the Alamo in the century since the battle. The Daughters, unheeding, cleared the antique structures for a greensward to enhance the site as a shrine. But disagreements had not gone away, in particular regarding memorials. How to suitably honor the battle's dead culminated in the bitterly debated erection in 1940 of a cenotaph, designed by the noted sculptor Pompeo Coppini. In 1994 a dispute over where or whether to place a memorial to pioneer Alamo preservationist Adina De Zavala, expelled from the Daughters after falling out with Clara Driscoll so long before, divided local Daughters and caused the Bexar County Historical Commission to stop meeting for more than a year. The latest solicitation of plans for a reunified Alamo mission plaza, to be chosen in an international design competition, stalled in 1995 for lack of funds.[5]

The Texas General Land Office cancelled the Daughters' longtime guardianship in 2011 and four years later removed them from any management role at the Alamo, citing financial, maintenance and administrative infractions. The state readied plans to spend $5 million on repairs. To address comprehensive issues in partnership with the state, the city in early 2014 appointed a twenty-one-member Alamo Plaza Advisory Committee, chaired by City Councilman Diego Bernal, Witte Museum President Marise McDermott and Conservation Society President Sue Ann Pemberton. A planning firm selected in a city-sponsored national competition was about to be hired the next year when the process was taken over by the General Land Office and the private Alamo Endowment. They announced plans to "assemble the dream team" of consultants themselves, in consultation with the city.[6]

Pent-up frustration also swirled around HemisFair Plaza, where patchwork changes had given the plaza no coherence in the nearly fifty years since the World's Fair. The plaza's northern sector was gradually taken over by the Convention Center, which opened a seven-year, $325 million cavernous expansion to the east in 2016. It was the city's single largest capital project to date, and it permitted the convention center's outdated original section, completed in 1968, to be razed for a park. Elsewhere on the plaza, historic homes saved for the fair were being restored as sixty-eight acres were replanned by the Hemisfair Park Area Redevelopment Corporation, established by the city in 2009 and on track at last toward a solution that would reach a high level of urban design. Half of that land would be reserved for open spaces, the rest for mixed-use development. Much of the prefair street grid would be restored.[7]

HemisFair Plaza's endangered John H. Wood Jr. Courthouse had been built as the fair's United States Pavilion. Once a new courthouse was constructed elsewhere the former pavilion would be vacated. Many considered the circular concrete colonnaded, glassed structure an icon of both the World's Fair and of midcentury architecture. Others considered it too large to fit well in the smaller-scale redevelopment and its repair costs prohibitive. The Conservation Society opposed demolition.[8]

A block south down Alamo Street, a 1924 Spanish Colonial Revival fire station was renovated as "an old-school style Italian steakhouse" to become part of the culinary scene of Southtown. That two-square-mile area spread southward through the King William Historic District, beyond the former

A building boom in the two-square-mile Southtown neighborhood includes adaptive reuse of the former Big Tex Grain Co. elevators in an apartment complex. Rivard Report.

warehouse district transformed as the Blue Star Arts Complex and into once deteriorating commercial and residential neighborhoods being reborn for chic residential, office and business use. Southtown's revitalization was implemented through a variety of neighborhood organizations and also gained support, in 1995, as one of the National Trust for Historic Preservation's first Urban Main Street Projects.[9]

A third major mix in the downtown crucible was Houston Street, San Antonio's thriving commercial heart during the middle half of the twentieth century and the premier shopping destination for South Texas and northern Mexico. Top local and national architects had lined the street with landmark retail buildings. As shopping shifted to suburban malls, its pedestrian traffic was partly replaced by restored theaters and adaptive apartments and offices, though many storefronts became vacant. But a fast-growing convention industry and a vibrant River Walk helped keep San Antonio's historic city core from becoming deserted and gave it the opportunity to be reshaped with hotels, retail centers and condominium and apartment towers. In 1998 a Maryland developer—Federal Realty Investment Trust—bought eleven properties and retail rights to a twelfth along three key blocks of Houston Street. It would be a $100 million project. Preservationists worked with Federal Realty on developing design guidelines.[10]

A priority for Federal Realty was building a twelve-story, 213-room hotel

Developers of Houston Street's Valencia Hotel preserved a landmark 1898 core city corner building and set back the hotel tower. Lewis F. Fisher.

on the south side of Houston Street between the River Walk and South St. Mary's Street, a section occupied by a row of century-old commercial buildings erected by George M. Maverick. They were nondescript with two exceptions: a vaguely Chinese-style concrete balcony over the River Walk at one end and, at the other, an 1898 corner building designed by Alfred Giles, though it had been stripped of its original second-story bay windows and architectural embellishments. When Conservation Society members sensed a double-cross on promises that the Giles-designed building would be saved, they called a news conference at the corner.[11]

"We are not against the [overall] project," Conservation Society President Loyce Ince told reporters and television crews. But, she said, after a Federal Realty presentation made no mention of razing the building, "we were stunned to hear from other sources, two days later, that the building was to be demolished." Another speaker, architect Lloyd Jary, chided the Maryland developers: "This isn't just anywhere, this is San Antonio." Within an hour the developer's project manager called Ince to say that it was all a mistake and they had always planned to save the building and would revise their presentation to prove it.[12]

When the stylish Hotel Valencia opened in 2003, its tower was set back from the corner to allow the Giles-designed building—bay windows and embellishments restored—its separate identity. At the riverside end of the hotel, negotiations with the city's Historic and Design Review Commission had required the high-rise structure to maintain the scale of the streetscape and be built back from the river. What by then was being called the Maverick Balcony had been removed from its demolished host building and redesigned at a lower level as an independent structure and focal point of the hotel's outdoor restaurant beside the River Walk.[13]

Two blocks east, Federal Realty sought to close South Presa Street just south of its Houston Street intersection for an outdoor market, turning its bridge over the River Walk into "a decorative appendage." The Conservation Society successfully advocated for a plan proposed by the city's historic preservation officer, Ann McGlone, that kept the bridge open and removed part of an adjacent sidewalk above for an elevator and an open stairway to bring light down to what had been one of the River Walk's darkest spaces. The new access also offered pedestrians a way to access Houston Street. Not as successful was the society's vocal opposition to Federal Realty's decision to raze the adjoining two-story Walgreens Building (circa 1885) and Stuart Building (1926). Both were replaced by one building in a vintage style, in what architect Lloyd Jary termed a choice between "historic restoration and historic fabrication." Across the street, regaining their luster were the 1890s Vogue Building's red brick and terra cotta exterior and the 1938 Kress Building's gleaming art deco facade of white glazed tile with twin towers and lighted red letters.[14]

Restoration of its facade of white glazed tiles and store name in projecting red rooftop letters made the 1938 Kress Building once again a Houston Street favorite. Rivard Report.

By the time Federal Realty sold its Houston Street properties to San Antonio–based GrayStreet Partners in 2015, the Valencia Hotel had been joined by extended-stay hotels in the renovated South Texas Building (1919) and the Neisner Building (1948). Office space was added, major restaurants opened and a new city-built parking garage was built nearby. But pedestrian traffic was inconsistent, and much retail space remained unfilled. GrayStreet pledged to invest some $200 million in its downtown properties to address the issues.[15]

Down Houston Street at the western edge of downtown, the Conservation Society's 1981 rescue of the Rand Building proved fortuitous when the eight-story structure became an anchor for San Antonio's burgeoning high-tech industry. Purchased in 2013 by Weston Urban LLC, the Rand housed Geek-dom, incubator space for small start-up technology companies and the home of Rackspace's Open Cloud Academy, which taught computer networking and coding. Less than three years later Geekdom expanded across the south side of Houston Street into the vacant three-story limestone landmark Sole-dad Block (1884) and University Block (1893), linked in 1912 as the Savoy Hotel.[16]

Nearby, preservationists had been keeping an eye out as one new hotel joined another along the River Walk. The Historic and Design Review Commission permitted the twelve-story Hotel Contessa (2005) on the southern leg of the river bend to remove one of the three distinctive concrete benches designed by River Walk architect Robert Hugman to make space for an entrance to the hotel. Without being required to, Contessa developers preserved the bench indoors as a centerpiece in the lounge. On the river bend's northern leg, developers of what became the ninety-nine-room Mokara Hotel & Spa were attempting to build within the shell of the six-story Frank Saddlery/Karotkin Building (1901) when one wall collapsed. The other walls were taken down and replicated in the building, which opened in 2005. Across the way, the exterior of the Atlee Ayres–designed six-story City Public Service Building (1921–27) was restored and its interior renovated as a Drury Inn.[17]

On Commerce Street, Drury extended the reach of another new hotel—in the twenty-four-story former Alamo National Building (1929)—a block west to the River Walk by cutting passages through its adjacent parking garage, which towered above the sheer concrete walls of the river's cutoff channel. A three-mile flood control tunnel completed in 1997 had lowered the estimated maximum flood flow through the surface cutoff channel. This permitted a river-level walkway to be built inside the channel's walls and gave the river bend a circular pedestrian flow by connecting the walkways that originally stopped at either end of the bend. The cutoff channel was also bridged to the far side, where part of the channel wall was removed to create a stepped portal to Main Plaza, one goal of the city's Historic Civic Center Master Plan.[18]

The Historic Civic Center, as defined, encompassed the heart of the old Spanish city from the river westward across Main and Military plazas to Market Square. Indicating the growing level of cooperation between city government and preservationists, Conservation Society representatives were brought in at the planning stage rather than being left to react once plans were unveiled.[19] Mayor Nelson Wolff accepted the plan proposed by Conservation Society President Inell Schooler, with backup design by architect Andrew Perez.[20] Envisioning the area as the center of city government, the plan's focal point was the 1993 renovation of the city's Municipal Plaza Building, originally Frost National Bank, for city offices. The former bank lobby-turned-Luby's Cafeteria was transformed into the city council's meeting chamber, with the aid of $30,000 from the Conservation Society to restore the decorative ceiling.[21] The society also spent nearly $10,000 to restore twenty-four portraits of mayors, placed in the society's custody in 1959, before they were hung in the new chamber's entryway.[22]

Next to the Municipal Plaza Building, in 2003 a $15 million project included restoration of San Fernando Cathedral and adding a two-story Cathedral Centre beside it on what had become a parking lot.[23] On the south side of the plaza, the $9.1 million restoration of the red granite and sandstone Bexar County Courthouse (1896), aided by $300,000 from the Conservation Society, was completed in 2015.[24]

Main Plaza itself got a $12 million facelift that finished in 2008, when a three-year effort spearheaded by Mayor Phil Hardberger but ultimately opposed by the Conservation Society closed north-south streets on either side of the old Spanish plaza, making it accessible only to pedestrians between San Fernando Cathedral and the River Walk. Added were new fountains, seating, three shade structures, new trees and a concession stand. In 2014 Main Plaza became the viewing area for the ten-year run of a twenty-four-minute video installation by French artist Xavier de Richemont that projected the city's history across the facade of San Fernando Cathedral four nights a week.[25]

During all of this, preservationists had no respite from crises and ambushes in far-flung parts of the city. On Guadalupe Street south of downtown, the 1830s Bergara-LeCompte House, one of San Antonio's few surviving early examples of adobe homes, was in danger of collapse after suffering from years of fires, heavy equipment vibration and strong rains. In 2005 it was rescued through two $15,000 grants—one from the Texas Historical Commission and the other from the Conservation Society—and a $35,000 grant from the city. On West Commerce Street in Prospect Hill, the Bill Miller Bar-B-Q restaurant chain was dissuaded in 2007 from tearing down the Queen Anne–style childhood home of Carol Burnett for a parking lot; in a 1985 visit, the actress and comedienne had found marks from her roller skates still embedded in the wooden floor. The one-story frame home was sliced into three pieces and moved eight blocks. There it was reassembled and restored as a learning center for American Sunrise, a nonprofit organization established by former mayor (and former U.S. Secretary of Housing and Urban Development) Henry Cisneros and his wife, Mary Alice, a former city council member.[26]

Nearly three miles south, H-E-B planned to replace its oldest operating grocery, opened in 1945 on Nogalitos Street, with a larger, two-level store bearing no resemblance to the original sleek, Moderne-style building. At the urging of the Conservation Society and with approval of the Historic and Design Review Commission, the new market, opened in 2014, incorporated part of the original's curved entrance, topped with horizontal bands of glass blocks and preserving the signature pylon with a neon outline of Texas. Not successful was preservationists' effort a decade earlier to prevent the demolition of a picturesque but vacant tourist court, built on Fredericksburg Road in 1928 in the days of the Old Spanish Trail promotions.[27]

In 2008 the outgoing city planning director "on his way out the door" abruptly signed a demolition permit for the two-story Jorrie Building (1929), a rare surviving vintage commercial structure on lower San Pedro Avenue at the northwestern edge of downtown. The building was promptly razed. Since the planning director was above the Historic and Design Review Board, which had yet to consider the case, infuriated preservationists were left sputtering. Later that year the city upgraded the Office of Historic Preservation, newly headed by Shanon Miller, putting it under oversight by the Office of

An iron conveyor bridge that once connected two towers of the old Lone Star Brewery was repurposed as a pedestrian bridge across the northern segment of the extended River Walk. San Antonio River Authority.

the City Manager, a post held by Sheryl Sculley, and removing it from oversight by the Department of Planning.[28]

Some crises were avoided when early warnings allowed the Conservation Society Foundation's revolving fund to directly purchase an endangered landmark. A typical low-profile success was the 1998 purchase of an endangered two-story Neoclassic Revival house on Carson Street in the future Government Hill Historic District. The house was resold for rehabilitation in accordance with the society's covenants. In 1998 the Conservation Society rescued a former commercial building known as the Alaskan Palace, sheathed in a 1940s Art Deco facade that masked two stone structures predating 1873. Isolated on the southern edge of downtown at Navarro and Nueva streets and, at the rear, adjoining the society-owned Gresser House, it was rehabilitated and leased by the society for commercial use.[29]

Preservationists had to expend little energy on expanding one of the city's marquee elements, the River Walk, already considered among the world's finest urban linear parks. The nine-year project captured the city's imagination as the River Walk grew from three to fifteen miles in length. When nearly completed in 2013 it had been extended south some eight miles from Alamo Street to Mission Espada, the farthest of the Spanish missions, as a hike-and-bike trail. Environmental restoration included removing a broad concrete flood channel and replicating the original curve of the stream, plus restor-

The renovated high-rise Brew House (1894) of the former Pearl Brewery opened in 2015 as the Hotel Emma, the centerpiece of a restaurant, retail and apartment complex along the newly extended northern River Walk. Rivard Report.

ing native trees and plants. To the north the River Walk was extended four miles beyond Lexington Street into Brackenridge Park. A new dam and lock structure permitted boats to go as far as the once derelict Pearl Brewery. That complex was dominated by a mansard-roofed brick brew house, the tallest building in San Antonio when completed in 1894.[30]

Silver Ventures Inc., the private equity firm of San Antonio's Christopher "Kit" Goldsbury that purchased the former brewery complex in 2001, expanded the brew house into the luxury 146-room Hotel Emma and surrounded the Pearl's other rehabilitated historic structures with new restaurant, retail and apartment buildings and a branch of the Culinary Institute of America. As venues in the complex opened and the hotel took its first guests in the fall of 2015, its effect on locals and outsiders seemed electric. *Condé Nast Traveler* joined the chorus by declaring the Emma "a steampunk-meets-Golden-Age charmer" and observing that the surrounding area had "the idealistic vibe of a college campus, but with bike-sharing and well-dressed thirtysomethings instead of Ultimate Frisbee and lounging co-eds."[31]

San Antonio preservationists were unaccustomed to seeing adaptive reuse unfold so tastefully on this scale without the familiar brinksmanship of alarms and crises. The San Antonio Conservation Society presented Goldsbury with its highest honor, the Amanda Cartwright Taylor Award, named for a pioneering society president.

Notes

1. Preservation Texas, "Most Endangered Places," accessed Feb. 20, 2016, at www
.preservationtexas.org/2016-texas-most-endangered-places.

2. Smith et. al., *Complete Encyclopedia of African American History*, 121; Debolt Baugess, *Encyclopedia of the Sixties: A Decade of Culture and Counterculture* I: 148; Alison Shay, "Remembering the San Antonio Sit-In," accessed Feb. 23, 2016, at https://lcrm.lib.unc
.edu/blog/index.php/2012/03/16/remembering-the-san-antonio-sit-in.

3. Iris Dimmick, "State Purchases Three Buildings," *Rivard Report*, Dec. 2, 2015, accessed Feb. 22, 2016, at http://therivardreport.com/state-purchases-buildings-across
-from-alamo-plaza; Scott Huddleston and Benjamin Olivo, "Alamo Plaza purchase," *San Antonio Express-News*, Oct. 10, 2015.

4. Scott Huddleston and Benjamin Olivo, "Alamo Plaza purchase," *San Antonio Express-News*, Oct. 10, 2015.

5. Rolando Martinez, "DRT tries to block honorary marker for Alamo 'savior,'" *San Antonio Express-News*, Jan. 28, 1994, 1-B; Christopher Anderson, "De Zavala's marker lies in basement," *San Antonio Express-News*, Sept. 5, 1995, 1-B; Christopher Anderson, "Historical panel tries to establish new path," *San Antonio Express-News*, Oct. 17, 1995, 1-B; Christopher Anderson, "Financial difficulties derail Alamo Plaza design competition," *San Antonio Express-News*, Aug. 19, 1995, 1. A plaque honoring Adina De Zavala was eventually placed near the Alamo cenotaph.

6. Beth Brown, "Control of Alamo," *Texas Tribune*, July 26, 2011, accessed Feb. 22, 2016, at www.texastribune.org/2011/07/26/alamo-responsibilities-shifting; Scott Huddleston, "Committee begins work," *San Antonio Express-News*, "Master plan RFQ," *Public Works*, Feb. 10, 2015, accessed Feb. 22, 2016, at www.pwmag.com/construction/
master-plan-rfq-deadline-is-march-3_t.aspx; Iris Dimmick, "City Council Unanimously Approves," *Rivard Report*, Oct. 15, 2015; Scott Huddleston, "Alamo work," *San Antonio Express-News*, Feb. 21, 2016.

7. Iris Dimmick, "Photo Gallery," *Rivard Report*, Jan. 27, 2016, accessed Feb. 22, 2016, at http://therivardreport.com/san-antonios-convention-center-unveiled-to-an-eager
-market.

8. Benjamin Olivo, "Conservation Society opposes," *Express-News Downtown Blog*, Apr. 18, 2012, accessed Feb. 22, 2016, at http://blog.mysanantonio.com/down
town/2012/04/conservation-society-takes-stand-on-institute-of-texan-cultures-wood
-courthouse-demolition.

9. Richard Webner, "San Antonio restaurateur," *San Antonio Express-News*, Feb. 8, 2016.

10. Mike Greenberg, "Heart of the City," *San Antonio Express-News*, July 22, 2001, 1-H. In 2015 new owners of the Aztec Building, its theater being used as a live music venue, received city financing incentives for converting the Aztec's upper floors into forty-one apartments. (Benjamin Olivo, "Majority of Aztec," *San Antonio Express-News*, Sept. 23, 2015.)

11. The street-level balcony was added in 1918 so diners at the Riverside Restaurant could view the newly landscaped banks of the River Park below. It was considered San

Antonio's first new construction to specifically address a beautified river. (Fisher, *American Venice*, 45.)

12. David Anthony Richelieu, "Historic building rescued," *San Antonio Express-News*, Dec. 15, 1999, 1-B.

13. Fisher, *American Venice*, 160; Jeffrey Fetzer, "River commission," *San Antonio Express-News*, Feb. 10, 2006, 9-B.

14. Elizabeth Allen, "Downtown Rebirth," *San Antonio Express-News*, July 13, 2000; Mike Greenberg, "Houston Street's transformation," *San Antonio Express-News*, July 22, 2001, 1-H; Mike Greenberg, "River 'flows' up," *San Antonio Express-News*, May 5, 2002, 5-H. The bridge project was one of those benefiting from funding from the Houston Street Tax Increment Reinvestment Zone created by city council at the time of Federal Realty's arrival in December 1999. (Benjamin Olivo, "Downtown Dispatches," *San Antonio Express-News*, Dec. 29, 2012.)

15. Benjamin Olivo, "Downtown Dispatches," *San Antonio Express-News*, Dec. 29, 2012; Benjamin Olivo, "Local developer purchases," *San Antonio Express-News*, Apr. 27, 2015; Benjamin Olivo, "Once vibrant Houston Street," *San Antonio Express-News*, May 2, 2015. Two blocks north of Houston Street, the Conservation Society settled its lawsuit in 2012 with Bexar County and the Bexar County Performing Arts Foundation over the redesign of Municipal Auditorium (1926) into the Tobin Center for the Performing Arts, which was demolishing all but the auditorium's iconic facade. Demolition would continue, but the center would be required to preserve the auditorium's original wooden front doors and the style of lettering on the front, and to pay $80,000 in grants and attorneys' fees. Society President Nancy Avellar termed the settlement "a small silver lining out of the whole thing." (Jennifer Hiller, "Lawsuit over auditorium," *San Antonio Express-News*, July. 31, 2012.)

16. Robert Rivard, "Weston Urban Purchases," *Rivard Report*, Feb. 25 2016, accessed Feb. 25, 2016, at http://therivardreport.com/weston-urban-purchases-historic-savoy-building.

17. Fisher, *American Venice*, 160.

18. Fisher, *American Venice*, 170–71; Lisa Sandberg, "New park links River Walk," *San Antonio Express-News*, Oct. 1, 2001, 3-B. The $3 million entrance, dubbed Portal San Fernando, was designed by Lake/Flato Architects using 200 tons of limestone in a landscaped descent from Main Plaza and its San Fernando Cathedral, with water features symbolizing the city's original acequia system.

19. Minutes, D-Dec. 9, 1992, 2; D-Jan. 20, 1993, 3; D-Jan. 27, 1993, 2. Perhaps inevitably, fires still had to be put out. The head of the city's Code Compliance Department was suspected of conspiring with the mayor to bypass the Historic Preservation Office in seeking demolition of "dangerous premises." Conservationists, excluded from initial consideration, were once again left with the disadvantage of having to react negatively once they were tipped off. (Minutes, D-Jan. 19, 1994; D-Feb. 16, 1994, 1, 4.)

20. Inell Schooler OHT, 13–14. A piece of the civic center implementation plan to benefit tourism fell into place in 1999, when attorney David Carter spearheaded the effort to move the O. Henry House—saved and moved south to the Lone Star Brewery by the Conservation Society forty years earlier—from the newly shuttered brewery to the corner of Laredo and Dolorosa streets, between Military Plaza and Market Square. (David Uhler, "O. Henry House reopens," *San Antonio Express-News*, May 26, 1999,

1-B.) Carter also restored Main Plaza's 1880s Wolfson mercantile building, which incorporated part of the once famed White Elephant Saloon and Gambling House. After the building burned in 2011, the site was sold for yet another hotel.

21. Minutes, D-Oct. 20, 1993. A request for $66,000 to restore the council chamber's footed reflective lights was not approved. The historic Municipal Plaza, Plaza de Armas and Continental Hotel buildings were purchased by the city for office space for $21 million in time to take advantage of historic preservation tax credits ending at the close of 1986. With interest, the cost was $38.6 million, compared with the estimated cost of $56 million to lease similar space for twenty years. (Susie Phillips, "Council moves to purchase buildings; legal battles rage," *San Antonio Express-News,* Dec. 19, 1986, 1-A.)

22. Minutes, D-Sept. 18, 1991, 3; D-Aug. 19, 1992; D-Sept. 16, 1992, 3.

23. The apse of San Fernando's original church (1738–55) was preserved when the rest of the church building was removed for expansion in a Gothic Revival style (1868–1902). A $2.6 million restoration of San Antonio's oldest Protestant church building, St. Mark's Episcopal Church on Travis Park, was completed in 2013. St. Mark's is one of the few buildings west of the Mississippi designed by Richard Upjohn, one of the nation's great church architects of the nineteenth century. (Fisher, *Chili Queens*, 57, 67; Fisher, *St. Mark's*, 10; Abe Levy, "St. Mark's recaptures," *San Antonio Express-News*, Jan. 11, 2013.)

24. John W. Gonzalez, "Bexar courtroom," *San Antonio Express-News*, Jan. 6, 2015; Joan Vinson, "Bexar County courthouse," *Rivard Report*, accessed Feb. 6, 2016, at http://therivardreport.com/bexar-county-courthouse-rededicated-after-restoration-project. The original lower west side of the courthouse was restored when windowless additions made in 1963 and 1972 were declared structurally unsound and removed. Interior restoration included removal of a floor to help return an 1896 courtroom to its original two-story vaulting appearance. Private funding was through the Hidalgo Foundation, headed by Tracy Wolff. Another $300,000 Conservation Society grant, in 1994, harked back to the society's founding. That grant was to restore the deteriorating San Pedro Playhouse, leased by the city to the San Antonio Little Theater. Its facade design had been inspired by the lost Market House, the cause that sparked organization of the society.

The continuing sweep of the Conservation Society's Community Grants program is indicated by $10,000 in grants approved in mid-1992: interpretive markers for La Villita, $3,250; Roosevelt Park, $1,000; administrative expenses for the Southtown Urban Main Street Program, $3,250; reroofing the original St. Anthony Shrine, $2,500; and the gift of a park bench for the Riverside Neighborhood. A year later, nearly $22,000 was awarded: $5,000 to the Society for the Preservation of Historic Fort Sam Houston toward restoring the Stilwell House; $3,000 to two individuals for exterior restoration of 910 South Alamo St.; $2,500 to the Alamo Area Council of Governments for quarterly conservation workshops; $2,400 to the Main Street Alliance for educational programs at Bonham Elementary and Brackenridge High schools; $500 toward rehabilitation of the Torres Building at 1012-1032 South Presa St.; $5,000 to the San Antonio Coalition of Neighborhood Associations for fund-raising work; and $3,500 to the city's Arts and Cultural Affairs Department for a downtown outdoor sculpture walking tour brochure. Among other grants were $67,145 to the city in 1999 for construction of iron fences around city cemeteries on East Commerce Street and $10,000 to the Witte Museum in 2004 for Hertzberg Circus Collection preservation.

25. Josh Baugh, "Main Plaza wins," *San Antonio Express-News*, Oct. 14, 2010.

26. Alex De La Garza, "Bergara-LeCompte House," *San Antonio Conservation Society Journal* 41:4, Fall 2005, 7; Carol Burnett's childhood home," Feb. 11, 2010, accessed Feb. 12, 2016, at https://urbanspotlight.wordpress.com/2010/02/11/carol-burnetts -childhood-home.

27. Neal Morton, "H-E-B wins formal support," *San Antonio Express-News*, Mar. 19, 2014; Scott Huddleston, "Crumbling motel to be fenced as wrecker's ball looms large," *San Antonio Express-News,* July 19, 1995, 1-B.

28. Elaine Wolff, "Out with the old," *San Antonio Current*, June 4, 2008; Bruce Mac-Dougal, "Major Changes," *SACS Preservation Advocate* 44:1, Fall 2008, 2. Office of Historic Preservation Director Ann McGlone said the developer had not expressed interest in adaptive reuse for the building and hired a lobbyist, who approached the departing planning director, Emil Moncivais.

29. "Society Properties, Gresser–Foutrel Complex," accessed Feb. 12, 2016, at www.saconservation.org/OurHistory/PropertiesPurchased/SocietyProperties/tabid/153/ArticleID/55/ArtMID/526/Gresser---Foutrel-Complex-.aspx.

30. Fisher, *American Venice*, 177–99. The city's Office of Historic Preservation hosted meetings to help finalize redesign of $175 million in improvement projects on long neglected San Pedro Creek through western downtown in time for San Antonio's tricentennial celebrations in 2018. (Lea Thompson, "Rapid-Fire Public Input," *Rivard Report*, Feb. 11, 2016, accessed Feb. 12, 2016, at http://therivardreport.com/rapid-fire-public -input-meetings-set-for-san-pedro-creek-project.)

31. Paul Brady, "Pearl District: The San Antonio Neighborhood You Need to Visit," *Condé Nast Traveler*, Oct. 14, 2015, accessed Feb. 12, 2016, at www.cntraveler.com/stories/2015-10-14/pearl-district-the-san-antonio-neighborhood-you-need-to-visit.

21

Defending Cultural Heritage

 Endangered landmarks known less for architectural distinction than for reflecting cultural heritage were drawing broader concern as the twenty-first century dawned. One dramatic case was that of La Gloria, a corner gas station with a rooftop dance floor built at Laredo and Brazos streets in 1928.

La Gloria had been a popular gathering spot that many believed was the first local venue to feature Tejano music. It held fond memories for many neighbors and for others beyond. The graffiti-plagued vacant building became a cause célèbre in 2002 when it was to be razed for a vehicle repair shop. Neighborhood preservationists won a temporary restraining order, but that was reversed.

The Esperanza Peace and Justice Center, San Anto Cultural Arts Center and San Antonio Conservation Society huddled and were ready to sign a contract for the original asking price of $239,000. With demolition about to begin, two neighbors went to the site to present the owner with a check but were restrained by police. Owner Tony Limon said he did not know whether the check was good, and, after four months, "I feel like I gave them more than enough time." A backhoe knocked down La Gloria as Limon watched from his seat on the tailgate of a pickup truck. "I am shocked," said Conservation Society President Jill Souter, whose group had pledged $50,000. "We worked on this all weekend. It was just a matter of pulling all of the money together."[1]

Office of Historic Preservation Director Ann McGlone saw a silver lining in the outcome. "The going down of La Gloria was not good," she said, but the debacle had "galvanized" those who cared about the west side's history. Their newfound enthusiasm would help prevent future problems, though this landmark had been lost. "Unfortunately," she added, "that's how historic preservation works."[2]

Indeed, the loss of La Gloria led to the organization, in 2009, of the Westside Preservation Alliance, a collaborative group soon with more than

(above and opposite) Demonstrators may not have prevented destruction in 2002 of La Gloria (1928), a favorite neighborhood landmark at Laredo and Brazos streets, but the common cause they found led to formation of the Westside Preservation Alliance. San Antonio Conservation Society.

a hundred members. McGlone's successor, Shanon Miller, began a Westside Cultural Resource Survey two years later, a combined effort of the Office of Historic Preservation, the Westside Preservation Alliance and the San Antonio Conservation Society. Within two years more than ninety potential landmarks had been identified. The growing intensity of this interest was abruptly revealed in a controversy that drew national attention. It found the Historic and Design Review Commission and the Office of Historic Preservation on opposite sides of the barricades from the Conservation Society and from preservationists elsewhere.[3]

A South Carolina–based real estate management company named Greystar in 2013 was purchasing a prime location on César Chávez Boulevard between the San Antonio River and South St. Mary's Street, directly behind and across the street from the Conservation Society's King William Street headquarters. It planned a 350-unit riverside apartment complex to replace the recently vacated studios of KWEX-TV, the nation's first Spanish-language television station. KWEX had been founded in 1955 as KCOR-TV by Raoul Cortez, who sold it in 1961 to his son-in-law Emilio Nicolas and others. The next year the new owners joined the station with their new KMEX-TV in Los Angeles and formed Univision, which by 2013 was the nation's largest Spanish-language television network. The two-story KWEX Building (1955) was replete with vintage broadcast equipment but was being lauded by preservationists for its role in Hispanic culture and as an early local example of Midcentury Modern architecture, with its "clean lines, lack of traditional or-

nament and bands of windows." A former Univision reporter termed it "the birthplace of Hispanic broadcast journalism in the United States." Others saw it as a plain, uninteresting structure badly needing repair. Unfortunately for preservationists, the building had not yet been listed on the National Register of Historic Places and had no landmark safeguards at all.[4]

In May 2013 the Historic and Design Review Commission unanimously approved conceptual plans for the apartment project and for demolition of the KWEX Building. That also got the Office of Historic Preservation's support. But the San Antonio Conservation Society and the Texas Historical Commission countered that the building was worthy of listing on the National Register even if the owner—Univision—and the developer didn't want it listed. The National Trust for Historic Preservation's senior field officer in Houston declared that the building's national role in Spanish-language television development "cannot be overstated," and that preserving the building would provide "this important piece of Latino heritage to teach future generations to celebrate the cultural diversity evident in our nation's history."[5]

After the HDRC voted 5 to 3 to deny the Conservation Society's request to grant the building local landmark status, a dozen Westside Preservation Alliance members and other Latino preservation advocates protested with a news conference at the site. The Conservation Society appealed to the Board

The Midcentury Modern studios of KWEX-TV (1955), destroyed in 2013, were considered the birthplace of Hispanic journalism in the United States. San Antonio Conservation Society.

of Adjustment, which ruled that it had no jurisdiction in the case. Demolition, however, had already begun. The Conservation Society found a judge who issued a temporary restraining order against further demolition, but that order was soon dissolved. As razing resumed, eight Latino protestors ranging in age from 22 to 71 scaled fences onto the site. They were arrested for trespassing but freed when the developer declined to press charges.[6]

Once the building was gone, Conservation Society President Sue Ann Pemberton said the process in place to consider the building's merits was "violated." Office of Historic Preservation Director Shanon Miller believed the building's significance could be "recognized in different ways," such as with a historical marker, without the structure needing to be preserved. Greystar spokesman Bill Kaufman thought the HDRC had given the case a fair hearing and "that should've been the end of it."[7]

The clash illuminated preservationists' difficulties in playing catch-up in identifying cultural landmarks of the city's cultural groups and was valuable in raising general awareness of issues involved and in lessons learned about the process. Three months later, Westside Preservation Alliance members spoke before the Historic and Design Review Commission as it considered designation for two dozen cultural landmarks. These ranged from a former Pig Stand to an Asian bungalow being used as a bank to the former print shop of political sage Ruben Munguia. Preservation Alliance member Claudia Guerra noted that the Office of Historic Preservation's selection survey had been "a very respectful process," compared with the abruptness and arrests of the KWEX affray. "Social progress can be made when organizations work together," she said. In 2014 Guerra became the Office of Historic Preservation's first cultural historian.[8]

Few west side icons were clustered as closely as the six landmarks in the Guadalupe Cultural Arts Center area, which included the Guadalupe Theater (1942) and a plaza fronting Our Lady of Guadalupe Church (1921). Nor were many as architecturally distinctive as the towering Basilica of the National Shrine of the Little Flower (1931), a national historic landmark on North Zarzamora Street. More typical was Lerma's Nite Club, an Art Deco hangout built down Zarzamora Street in 1942. For more than a half century Lerma's hosted the top names in conjunto, the distinctive South Texas sound fusing Czech, German and Mexican musical traditions. It was the longest-running live conjunto venue in the region and, by default, in the world. "People expect conjunto at Lerma's," said Gilbert Garcia, who had purchased the place from the son of its original owner, Pablo Lerma. "Button accordion, bajo sexto, bass and drums—that's all they want."[9]

But a surprise visit from city code inspectors in mid-2010 turned up so many violations that Lerma's and its adjacent strip center were ordered evacuated immediately. The city's Dangerous Structure Determination Board ordered demolition. Lerma's owner Gilbert Garcia, however, showed up at the board meeting with so many supporters that he was granted sixty days—and, later, six more months—to come up with a plan for repairs. The Conservation Society persuaded the National Trust for Historic Preservation to pay for a structural engineer to prepare an assessment. The society pledged a $15,000 reimbursable grant toward the work. Society President Rollette Schreckenghost called the cultural history of the club "unparalleled." Juan Tejeda, director of the conjunto music program at Palo Alto College, said the club literally helped its neighbors survive. "People went there to dance, have a good time and get charged up so they could go back to work for another week," he said. "It was an important meeting place for people. We went there to reinforce our friendships, our culture and our identity."[10]

Restoration stalled due to lack of funds, but there was no shortage of other support. Lerma's gained a listing on the National Register of Historic Places. Conservation Society Executive Director Bruce MacDougal used a branding and development strategic plan for Lerma's as part of a case study in the historic preservation course he taught at the University of Texas at San Antonio. In 2012 the property was purchased by the Esperanza Peace and Justice Center, which began efforts to raise $2.1 million to turn Lerma's and adjacent space into a 10,000 square-foot multiuse community space.[11]

Farther down Zarzamora Street stood the two-story Basila Frocks Building, designed by a noted local architectural firm in 1929 for Syrian immigrants who made early ready-to-wear dresses during San Antonio's years as a

The two-story former Beacon Light Lodge building anchors the restored Ellis Alley enclave, the only remnant of San Antonio's earliest African American neighborhood. Lewis F. Fisher.

garment manufacturing center. Its owners at the time of the cultural resources survey opposed official historic designation. New owners, who said they were unaware the building had been flagged as historic, planned to raze it. The Westside Preservation Alliance, Conservation Society and local chapter of the American Institute of Architects rushed to the defense of area residents who thought it historic and sought historic designation status from the Historic and Design Review Commission, while the new owners' representative, Bill Kaufman, stated that "our position is that it is not historic" and cited high costs of restoration.[12]

Three miles east, on the opposite side of downtown, San Antonio's African American community had an anchor on North Hackberry Street with the Carver Community Cultural Center, a restored Art Deco building built in 1929 as the Colored Branch of the San Antonio Library and Auditorium. Five blocks to its west, between the Union Pacific Railroad and IH 37 and spanning East Commerce Street, was St. Paul Square Historic District. It included the Mission Revival Southern Pacific Depot (1902), restored as the center-piece of an entertainment complex, and the former St. Paul African Methodist Episcopal Church (1884), successor to a frame church built in 1866 by newly freed slaves.[13]

Up Chestnut Street from St. Paul Square at Ellis Alley, in 1995 the Conservation Society identified five buildings that formed the only surviving remnant of the city's earliest African American neighborhood. Two houses were adequately maintained, but three other small frame homes dating from the 1880s were in precarious condition. So was the two-story frame building facing Chestnut Street that in 1909 had become the Beacon Light Lodge. It had provided meeting space for the Odd Fellows and for the Star Tom Lodge of Free and Accepted Masons.[14]

In 1997 VIA Metropolitan Transit purchased a broad swath of the Ellis Alley area for a Park and Ride facility and a customer service office. It was also intended as a bicycle transportation hub, based on its proximity to the vintage two-span iron truss Hays Street Bridge that crossed the Union Pacific rail yards separating the east side from downtown. Closed to traffic since 1982, the bridge was earmarked for restoration for pedestrians and bicycles. A Conservation Society grant of $50,000 in 2001 helped encourage a $2.9 million enhancement grant from the Texas Department of Transportation the next year, and the bridge finally reopened in 2010.[15]

Early planning to restore the Ellis Alley neighborhood collapsed during a VIA dispute with a developer and from the declining economy. Resolution came in 2009 with a new developer in place and with VIA agreeing to no longer consider demolition on the site. In exchange for a $1 lease on the three key buildings, the Conservation Society would make in-kind contributions valued at $32,000 while overseeing restoration. The Ellis Alley buildings would be maintained and operated under VIA ownership. Funding was finalized in 2012. Two years later—with the aid of drawings by Conservation Society President Sue Ann Pemberton, the first architect to lead the society—restoration of the enclave was complete. The Beacon Light Building became the offices of San Antonio for Growth on the Eastside, an economic development nonprofit known as SAGE.[16]

As San Antonio sprawled more than twelve times beyond its historic city limits, it seemed only a matter of a short time before Bexar County's remaining seven hundred rural square miles would be covered as well. Unlike counties in states to the east and north with more fertile land, most Texas counties were so sparsely settled that other than one or two towns the counties included few communities larger than a couple of homes and perhaps a church or store. Even those could be hard to spot, for they were often scattered amid farm and ranch acreage down rutted lanes connected only by a rough caliche-topped county road. The occasional appearance in the distance of some cluster of low farm buildings or a small home gave only a hint of the rich variety of farm and ranch homesteads. In heavily populated Bexar County, it was easy to think that the state's wealth of rural diversity was all somewhere else.

The nagging awareness that there was more to rural Bexar County than most people thought caused former Conservation Society president Joanna Parrish in 2001 to recruit another former president, Loretta Huddleston, and, with the aid of City Archeologist Kay Hindes, set out to determine what was out there before it was too late. By 2005 two dozen historic farm and ranch complexes had been found and documented, a few already swallowed within San Antonio city limits. Many were abandoned and overgrown by vegetation and hard to reach from county roads, even if landowners would grant permis-

*The Von Plehwe family built this home in the
1850s in northern Bexar County, part of the scores
of isolated farm and ranch complexes documented by
a Conservation Society survey begun in 2001. San
Antonio Conservation Society.*

sion for access. But micro-level fieldwork indicated enough potential in the
hunt for President Barbara Johnson to form a Farm and Ranch Committee
and, in 2006, to hire Prewitt and Associates, Austin-based cultural resources
services consultants, to analyze findings and prepare a thorough study with
broad historical perspective. Four years later, a ninety-six-page nomination
brief documented eighty-five farms and ranches deemed worthy of a multi-
ple-property listing on the National Register of Historic Places, and many
more were being researched further.[17]

The survey revealed a cultural kaleidoscope of vernacular farm and ranch
complexes built throughout Bexar County by immigrants from England
(Presnall-Watson House, 1854, Neal Road), Germany (Von Plehwe complex, 1850s, Boerne Stage Road), Ireland (Jenney House, 1877, Somerset),
Mexico (Blas–Herrera Ranch, 1830s, Old Somerset Road), Poland (Kiolbassa
House, 1850, east of La Vernia), Scotland (Marnoch House, 1850, Helotes)
and the southeastern United States (Trueheart-De La Garza complex, 1858,
Blue Wing Road, on which the Conservation Society gained a five-acre protective easement in 2010). Also being studied were farmsteads of immigrants
from Belgium, Hungary, Italy, France and Sweden. Often built in styles of
their owners' native countries, construction techniques ranged from frame
and sophisticated stone masonry to German-style brick nogging, tongue and
groove planks, horizontal logs and vertical pole palisado construction, the
poles chinked with stone and mud and roofed with straw.[18]

Although landmark designation drew attention to their significance, survival of many of the scattered structures was feared tenuous due to their ease of being bulldozed, unseen, for subdivisions or of simply collapsing in isolation. But some were located fortuitously, like the two-story limestone Huebner-Onion Homestead, built off Bandera Road above Leon Creek in 1862. The home, outbuildings and cemetery had been vandalized as the northwestern suburb of Leon Valley grew up around them. In 1999 the derelict complex was to be bulldozed by a hotel chain. The suburb's more than 10,000 residents, however, realized that this was their only historic landmark. The owner agreed to donate the house to the Leon Valley Historical Society if the City of Leon Valley would buy the adjoining property for $350,000. The city did. In 2002 the San Antonio Conservation Society donated $25,000 to the project—following up with a smaller grant two years later—and the Texas Historical Commission donated $15,000. A series of fundraisers launched the homestead's restoration as centerpiece of a thirty-six-acre natural area.[19]

In southern Bexar County, two buildings from the 1850s Walsh Ranch complex were disassembled in 2005 at the construction site of a Toyota truck manufacturing plant and rebuilt nearby at the Land Heritage Institute, which preserved 1,200 archeologically rich acres once set for inundation by the controversial and never constructed Applewhite Reservoir and then donated to the institute by the San Antonio Water System. There the two buildings joined the 1854 stone Presnall-Watson House and its barn, smokehouse, water tank and tool shed to become the Land Heritage Institute's Presnall-Watson Living History Farm Museum.[20]

What amounted to a military subculture in San Antonio dated from the city's founding. The city's oldest military complex, the ten-acre U.S. Arsenal (1859) near downtown, had been split when the Arsenal was declared surplus property and Main Avenue was cut through in 1949. The city closed that section of Main Avenue in 2015 at the request of H-E-B Grocery Company, so the former Arsenal buildings comprising its corporate headquarters would no longer be divided by the street. The landmark Commander's House remained a city-owned center for senior citizens.[21]

Succeeding rounds of military base closings nationally had a mixed impact on San Antonio and on historic preservation as well. A host of Fort Sam Houston's landmarks were upgraded as base facilities expanded to accommodate units arriving from bases closed or downsized elsewhere. The abandoned Alfred Giles–designed Long Barracks, built in 1887 to house eight companies of troops, got a $23.8 million restoration under National Historic Preservation Act guidelines to house Mission and Installation Contracting Command offices. The former Brooke General Hospital (1938), its eight-

Among the landmarks on San Antonio's current or former military installations is Hangar 9 (1918), the nation's oldest surviving frame military aviation hangar, on the former Brooks Air Force Base. Mike Osborne.

story Spanish Baroque exterior restored during renovation by a private developer using federal tax incentives, became headquarters for U.S. Army South. The Spanish Colonial Revival Fort Sam Houston Theatre (1935) underwent a $16.9 million restoration and enlargement by the U.S. Army Corps of Engineers for an Army command's entertainment division being relocated from Fort Belvoir, Virginia. Historic staff homes facing parade grounds were restored as well.[22]

Brooks Air Force Base southeast of downtown San Antonio, however, was closed and turned over for private development. In doubt was the fate of the deteriorating Hangar 9 (1918), the nation's oldest surviving frame military aviation hangar, among sixteen World War I–era hangars built at Brooks for flight training. All three still standing in 1969 were scheduled for destruction when Hangar 9 was singled out for preservation through efforts of a group led by Lone Star Brewery President Harry Jersig and aviation pioneer and inventor Col. Carl J. Crane, who at the age of ten had witnessed Capt. Benjamin Foulois's first flight at Fort Sam Houston. In 2012 the Conservation Society nominated Hangar 9 for the National Trust for Historic Preservation's list of the nation's eleven most endangered historic sites. Three years later, $2.5 million was found to begin restoring the hangar and rebuild its giant sliding doors, long frozen shut as the framework settled. Incorporated nearby in a historic district in 2003, after Brooks closed, were fifteen buildings of the former U.S. Air Force School of Aerospace Medicine, its dedication in 1963 one of the last official acts of President John F. Kennedy.[23]

Some two miles west, Stinson Municipal Airport, established in 1915 as a flying school by Marjorie, Katherine and Eddie Stinson, was used for Army Air Corps flight training before being returned to civilian use. Its Art Deco terminal (1936) was marked for replacement by a larger building until preservationists helped reverse the decision. The terminal reopened in 2010, restored and flanked by modern wings.[24]

In western San Antonio, Kelly Air Force Base, the city's largest employer, was closed in 2001 and converted to an industrial park known as Kelly USA and then as Port San Antonio, capitalizing on its runway, rail and highway connections and retaining a major aircraft maintenance function. Kelly's remaining significant historic feature was its Bungalow Colony, sixteen officers' homes dating from 1917 and built in large part from scrap lumber. Virginia Hudnell, widow of Maj. Gen. William T. Hudnell, remembered of her former bungalow home that "when a wall was torn down, a wooden plank that had been part of an airplane crate bore the words 'Manila to San Antonio' and a World War I Army officer's name in black military stencil." The Bungalow Colony was listed on the National Register of Historic Places in 2003, but, with personnel no longer living on the former base, its preservation would remain a long-term effort.[25]

Notes

1. Any Dorsett, "Time Runs Out," *San Antonio Express-News*, Apr. 2, 2002, 1-A.

2. Amy Dorsett, "Out of ashes: preservation," *San Antonio Express-News*, Apr. 8, 2002, 1-A.

3. Scott Huddleston, "Protection sought," *San Antonio Express-News*, Jan. 18, 2013; Scott Huddleston, "West Side landmarks," *San Antonio Express-News*, Nov. 21, 2013. Four Westside Preservation Alliance members participated in the organization in May 2015 of the national organization Latinos in Heritage Conservation. (Elaine Ayala, "S.A. represented," *San Antonio Express-News*, Jun. 14, 2015.)

4. Texas Historical Commission Director Mark Wolfe to Conservation Society President Nancy Avellar, June 5, 2013, letter in SACS files; Scott Huddleston, "Move to save TV building," *San Antonio Express-News*, Aug. 28, 2013; Scott Huddleston, "Old Univision building," *San Antonio Express-News*, Sept. 11, 2013; "Eight Arrested," Texas

Public Radio transcript Nov. 13, 2013, accessed Feb. 10, 2016, at http://tpr.org/post/eight-arrested-trying-halt-kwex-univision-building-demolition#stream.

5. Scott Huddleston, "Move to save TV building," *San Antonio Express-News*, Aug. 28, 2013; Joey Palacios and Lauren Walser, "Lost: Univision Building," National Trust for Historic Preservation, Nov. 20, 2013, accessed Feb. 10, 2016, at https://savingplaces.org/stories/lost-univision-building-demolished-in-san-antonio.

6. Scott Huddleston, "Pending Destruction," *San Antonio Express-News*, Sept. 30, 2013; Joey Palacios, "Eight Arrested," Texas Public Radio transcript, Nov. 13, 2013, accessed Feb. 10, 2016, at http://tpr.org/post/eight-arrested-trying-halt-kwex-univision-building-demolition#stream; Scott Huddleston, "'Univision 8,'" *San Antonio Express-News*, Nov. 14, 2013.

7. Scott Huddleston, "Old Univision building," *San Antonio Express-News*, Sept. 11, 2013; Huddleston, "'Univision 8,'" *San Antonio Express-News*, Nov. 14, 2013. In a post-mortem, *Express-News* urban affairs writer Benjamin Olivo outlined HDRC members' dilemma in factoring economic development into a preservation decision, quoting two who chose economic benefit over landmark designation but were "on the fence." Pemberton was quoted, on the other hand, as saying, "I don't know that that really is the question. The question is whether the building should be designated." Concluded Olivo: "She's absolutely right. The building should [have been] saved and incorporated into the development." (Benjamin Olivo, "Univision postmortem," *Express-News Downtown Blog*, accessed Mar. 9, 2016, at http://blog.mysanantonio.com/downtown/2013/09/unvision-postmortem-explaining-hdrcs-double-bind.)

In another defeat, in 2001, the Conservation Society had been unable to prevent the short-lived Museo Americano from gaining permission to demolish the original arches of the 1922 city-owned Centro de Artes Building in Market Square. Museo Americano, whose other names included Museo Alameda, opened as an affiliate of the Smithsonian Institution to display Latin American art. After the museum closed in 2012 the building was taken over by Texas A&M University-San Antonio as its Educational Cultural Center. (Elda Silva, "A&M-San Antonio center," *San Antonio Express-News*, Mar. 10, 2015.)

8. Scott Huddleston, "West Side landmarks Proposed," *San Antonio Express-News*, Nov. 21, 2013.

9. Nicole Chavez, "Save Lerma's," *San Antonio Current*, Dec. 15–21, 2010, 12.

10. Ibid.

11. Hector Saldaña, "$2.1 million plan," *San Antonio Express-News*, Sept. 3, 2015.

12. Scott Huddleston, "Battle over W. Side building," *San Antonio Express-News*, Mar. 26, 2016.

13. Abe Levy, "St. Paul working," *San Antonio Express-News*, Feb. 5, 2011; Tyler White, "St. Paul United Methodist Church," *San Antonio Express-News*, Dec. 11, 2015. In 1922 the congregation moved three blocks east to its current home where, as St. Paul United Methodist Church, it was named a city landmark in 2015.

14. "Statewide Transportation Enhancement Program Nomination Form 2009," SACS files.

15. Amy Dorsett, "Historic bridge given new life," *San Antonio Express-News*, Feb. 1, 2002, 1-B; S. Patrick Sparks, "Rehabilitation of the Historic Hays Street Viaduct,"

American Society of Civil Engineers Library, accessed Feb. 18, 2016, at http://dx.doi .org/10.1061/41031(341)37. Named a city landmark in 1987 and a Texas Civil Engineering Landmark in 2001, the bridge was built in 1881 as a railway bridge over the Nueces River. In 1910 it was moved to San Antonio and reconstructed to carry vehicular traffic above the rail yards. It was abandoned as unsafe and close to being taken down when preservationists, spearheaded by retired civil engineer Douglas Steadman, mounted a long-term effort to save it.

16. Vianna Davila, "City OKs money," *San Antonio Express-News*, Mar. 9, 2012; Drew Joseph, "Refurbishment project," *San Antonio Express-News*, Nov. 27, 2014; "Statewide Transportation Enhancement Program Nomination Form 2009," SACS files.

17. A survey in 1973 by the Alamo Area Council of Governments had identified nearly 200 historic properties in the county, but the survey's original negatives and photographs had been lost and only the text survived. Bruce MacDougal, "Preserving Pioneer Settlers' Houses," *San Antonio Conservation Society Journal* 41:4, Fall 2005, 1; Amy E. Dase et. al., "Historic Farms and Ranches of Bexar County," 65–69, accessed Feb. 19, 2016, at www.sanantonio.gov/historic/Docs/Hist_Farm_Ranh_Context_NR.pdf. In 2004 Barbara Blount Johnson, daughter of former Conservation Society president Beverly Blount-Hemphill, became the third society president's daughter to lead the organization, after Wanda Graham Ford and Lynn Osborne Bobbitt. Marcie Ince, daughter-in-law of former president Loyce Ince, was elected president in 2007.

18. Ibid; "Trueheart-De La Garza Complex," accessed Feb. 20, 2016, at www.sacon servation.org/PreservationPrograms/Easements/tabid/138/ArticleID/58/ArtMID/515/ Trueheart---De-La-Garza-Complex.aspx.

19. "Huebner-Onion Homestead timeline," *San Antonio Express-News*, Oct. 16, 2012.

20. "Land Heritage Institute Chronology," accessed Feb. 20, 2016, at http://land heritageinstitute.org/History.html; "Development Plan," accessed Feb. 20, 2016, at http://landheritageinstitute.org/gpaged.html. The move was aided by a grant from the Conservation Society.

21. Benjamin Olivo, "Council likely to approve," *Express-News Downtown Blog*, Dec. 5, 2013, accessed Feb. 20, 2016, at http://blog.mysanantonio.com/downtown/2013/12/ council-likely-to-approve-h-e-bs-proposal; Neal Morton, "City starts preparing," Feb. 11, 2015, *S.A. Shop Talk*, accessed Feb. 20, 2016, at http://blog.mysanantonio.com/ sashoptalk/2015/02/city-starts-preparing-for-main-avenue-closure. The project received Conservation Society support.

22. Jason Buch, "Renovation planned," *San Antonio Express-News*, Mar. 9, 2010; Sig Christenson, "Long Barracks gets new mission," *San Antonio Express-News*, May 19, 2011. To facilitate management of the post's historic properties, a joint agreement was signed in 2011 with the Texas Historical Commission, San Antonio Conservation Society and the Society for the Preservation of Historic Fort Sam Houston, headed by Joan Gaither. (Lori Newman, "Conservation, preservation," *Fort Sam Houston News Leader*, May 19, 2011.)

23. Amy Dorsett, "Brooks history honored," *San Antonio Express-News*, May 15, 2002; Scott Huddleston, "Brooks' Hangar 9 nominated," *San Antonio Express-News*, Apr. 7, 2012; Scott Huddleston, "Brooks marks milestone," *San Antonio Express-News*, Dec.

6, 2015; "Historic Hangar 9," *San Antonio Express-News*, Mar. 30, 2016; "Carl Joseph Crane," accessed Mar. 31, 2016, at https://tshaonline.org/handbook/online/articles/fcr56.

24. "Stinson Municipal Airport," accessed Feb. 24, 2016, at www.beatypalmer.com/projects/stinson-municipal-airport-administration-building.

25. Scott Huddleston, "Kelly history lives," *San Antonio Express-News*, Oct. 21, 1996, 9-A.

22

A World Heritage Site

San Antonio preservationists' ability to deal with a myriad of alarms and fire bells in the night showed an effectiveness typical of many of the nation's preservation groups in responding to a range of crises.

Few preservation organizations, however, enjoy a more dramatic sweep of achievement than the San Antonio Conservation Society's nearly century-long odyssey in advancing one of its founding goals—preservation of San Antonio's crumbling Spanish colonial missions. Generations of Conservation Society members have wound their way through increasingly complex mazes to reach first local, then state, then national tiers of preservation status. Ultimately they successfully launched pursuit of the highest level of international recognition—United Nations Educational, Scientific and Cultural Organization (UNESCO) designation as a World Heritage Site, bestowed in 2015.

In 1978 extended negotiations between the Catholic Church, the State of Texas and the National Park Service had culminated in an agreement to turn the hard-won San José Mission State Park into a centerpiece of a San Antonio Missions National Historical Park. That took an inspired overnight national lobbying effort by San Antonio preservationists, who found themselves at the critical moment in a Chicago hotel, to get enabling legislation through Congress.

The National Park Service in 1961 had deemed the Mission San José grounds that early preservationists had so struggled over to be well kept. Poor historical interpretation of the site was the major problem, but there was little hope that state finances would permit replacing assorted objects—many irrelevant, badly labeled and displayed in outdated cases—with professional exhibits.[1] San José's situation looked worse when the Conservation Society learned that the Texas State Parks Board expected no funds to repair or improve things for another ten years. If the site were operated by the National

The unfinished church of Mission San Antonio de Valero, later known as the Alamo, was roofed and gained its iconic gabled parapet after the battle in 1836. Mike Osborne.

Park Service, however, federal funding would be available much sooner. The State Parks Board was loath to transfer San José but knew it was the only hope for adequate funding. The San José Mission Board, chaired by Conservation Society veteran Amanda Taylor, requested the transfer, backed up by a society resolution.[2] In 1967 Congressman Abraham "Chick" Kazen, whose district included the missions, introduced a bill to create a Missions National Historical Park. It got nowhere.[3]

Simply finding all the missions remained a challenge for visitors. During the previous century, a grid pattern of streets had developed more for needs of residents than for convenience of tourists, and it bore little relationship to the course of the winding river the missions had been built along. Tourists faced numerous unmarked street turns best navigated by a guide. With friction increasing between the Conservation Society and city hall on other issues, progress on a coherent roadway connecting the missions bogged down as well.[4] "We can't wait for the millennium," Henry Guerra, the Chamber of Commerce Mission Road Committee chair, told officials during a bus tour in 1969. "We want this right now for tourists. It is the kind of package that would bring the type of tourist volume they have in California." The thousands who visited the San Antonio missions during the record year of Hemis-Fair didn't come close, he added, to the half million or more visiting the Cal-

The church of Mission Concepción, unreconstructed since its completion, has much of its convento remaining, at right. Mike Osborne.

ifornia missions each year.[5] Federal, state and local funding gradually came through during the next twenty-five years, but clarity of the route remained elusive.[6]

In 1970 another assault was mounted for a National Historical Park.[7] After endorsements in 1973 by the Conservation Society and the Catholic Archdiocese, San Antonio's city council endorsed it as well. To help consolidate a future property transfer to the federal government, city council accepted the society's donation of Acequia Park, which an earlier council had refused during the tax fracas of 1968.[8] The society's ownership of Espada Aqueduct land, named the Elizabeth O. Graham Conservation Park, was likewise transferred to the city.[9] The Conservation Society lobbied heavily in Austin to get the Parks and Wildlife Department to surrender the park and stopped leasing the society's Texas State Historical Theater at San José so that it, too, could be transferred.[10] The Archdiocese agreed to donate its mission lands to the National Park Service, but Archbishop Francis Furey was adamant that the church buildings remain functioning parishes under church ownership. "I do not want a repetition of the Alamo," he said of the mission church that was sold and became a tourist attraction with scant regard for its religious origins.[11]

The National Park Service Advisory Council backed the plan. By 1975 it

Spanish Baroque features of the church of Mission San José include its ornate entrance and the window of its 1777 sacristy, lower right. Mike Osborne.

was ready to present to Congress, along with a bill seeking $1.7 million to strengthen the missions' acequia system.[12] The next year Congressman Kazen again introduced a bill to create a Missions National Historical Park.[13] This time, however, it got entangled in the issue of separation of church and state: Did federal financial aid to a complex surrounding Catholic-owed missions consecrated as churches violate first amendment rights regarding establish-

A distinctive feature of Mission San Juan's 1750s chapel is its espadaña with three bells. Mike Osborne.

ment of religion? The Department of the Interior's legal staff thought the only significant challenge regarded management issues between the Catholic Archdiocese and the National Park Service and concluded that careful legal structuring could avoid both constitutional and operational conflict.[14]

By spring 1978 a $1.4 billion parks bill included $10.5 million for development, renovations and new property for a 450-acre San Antonio Missions National Historical Park. Reported out of the Interior Committee of the U.S. House of Representative in midsummer, it passed the house 341–61.[15] Then missions park authorization ran into trouble in the Senate. The society's administrative director, Conrad True, went to Washington to get to the bottom of things. A flurry of phone calls, letters and telegrams went to Washington as well.[16] "We lobbied in Washington, we lobbied everywhere," recalled Mary Ann Castleberry, Conservation Society president at the time.[17]

The problem turned out to be a misunderstanding within the Office of Management and Budget, which thought the mission churches were to be owned by the federal government rather than by the Catholic Church.[18] Once that was cleared up, the parks bill passed the Senate in early October.[19] But when it reached the House in the wee hours on Sunday morning, October 15, the day Congress was to adjourn, two controversial last-minute attachments seemed to doom the bill. The news reached Conservation Society leaders

Mission Espada's 1750s chapel is noted for the irregularly placed stones of its arched entry. Mike Osborne.

shortly after 1 a.m. at the Drake Hotel in Chicago, where they were attending the annual meeting of the National Trust for Historic Preservation.[20]

San Antonio conservationists fanned out to fellow preservationists throughout the hotel, "down in the hotel lobbies and bars and everywhere, saying, do you know anyone in Congress who could help us? Who could vote with us? Do you know of a bill that we can attach to?"[21] In the hotel bar at 1:30 a.m., a preservationist from Missouri watched another from Illinois come in looking for a Republican from Virginia to help save the bill for the missions in Texas.[22] National Trust Chairman Carlisle Humelsine joined the telephone campaign. National Trust Advisory Council Director Bob Garvey gave advice on how to reach senators and congressmen in the cloakrooms.[23]

At 2 a.m. Conservation Society member Pat Osborne, headquartered in Room 202 of the Drake, got through to San Antonio Congressman Bob Krueger, also the Democratic nominee for the U.S. Senate. Krueger was told that his Republican opponent, Senator John Tower, was in Texas campaigning for reelection and was unavailable. Could Krueger help?[24]

Krueger walked over to the Senate side and ran into Senate Majority Leader Robert Byrd, who went onto the Senate floor to find the missions bill. Congressman Kazen joined Kreuger, and the two huddled with Texas Senator Lloyd Bentsen. At 3 a.m. Krueger and Kazen returned to the House floor to enlist support. The parks bill floor manager, Congressman Phil Burton of California, suggested that Krueger attach the missions park authorization to a bill authorizing redevelopment of Pennsylvania Avenue between the White House and the Capitol. That was one of President Jimmy Carter's pet projects and had to be passed and signed, he said, since construction had already started. At 5:30 a.m. Krueger went back to confer with Henry Jackson, the Senate Interior Committee chair. Idaho Senator Frank Church, sitting nearby, promised his support if a project involving the Grand Tetons was added.[25]

At 7:30 Sunday morning, under the guiding hand of Lloyd Bentsen, the Senate passed the Pennsylvania Avenue/San Antonio Missions bill, with the Grand Tetons project tacked on. But now unanimous consent of the House was needed, and by noon one Florida congressman was still a holdout; he wanted a park in his district and there was none in the bill. Kazen promised the congressman he would support the Florida project when the new Congress convened in January and got others to call him.[26] Texas Congressman Jim Wright, the House Majority leader, kept the House from adjourning. Congressman Henry B. Gonzalez assisted on the House floor.[27] Finally, at 2 p.m. Sunday, twelve hours after the Conservation Society got on the case, the House passed the bill by unanimous consent.[28] Mary Ann Castleberry said that when Congressman Kazen called to tell her the bill had passed, "I just screamed."[29] The Conservation Society called the President's signature on the bill on November 10 "the culmination of a dream come true." Senator Lloyd Bentsen called it "a major step in historical and cultural preservation."[30]

But euphoria was short-lived. A week later it was clear that the bill was signed simply because of the Pennsylvania Avenue redevelopment. In a memo to the Secretary of the Interior, President Carter blocked funding for the park because it "would result in significant federal expenditures on active churches that are inconsistent with appropriate church-state relationships." Carter said his administration would consider federal participation only if the mission churches were no longer used as active parish churches.[31]

Archbishop Francis Furey was "surprised, dumbfounded and flabbergasted."[32] He called the move a "plain, unadulterated double-cross."[33] The Interior Department tried to put the best spin on the situation for the government by saying that preliminary estimates of $500,000 to restore the physical missions could be inaccurate and that "it could cost all the way up to $40 million—a substantial sum to give to an active church."[34]

Four months later, the Department of the Interior's associate solicitor suggested in a sixteen-page opinion that President Carter's memorandum be considered a statement of administration policy rather than a ruling on the constitutionality of the San Antonio missions legislation. He concluded that repairs had a secular purpose—historic preservation—and would have a primarily secular effect. Thus any benefit to religion was incidental, and restoration funds did not amount to "excessive entanglement" between church and state. Similarly, he wrote, federal assistance for Boston's Old North Church because of its association with Paul Revere's ride served "a secular government purpose, even though the church may remain an active place of worship.[35]

In an effort to remove the church-state issue altogether, the nonprofit Bexar County Historical Foundation was organized to raise restoration funds for the mission churches to avoid any appearance of need for federal contributions for the churches.[36] Representatives of the Archdiocese, Bexar County, the City of San Antonio and the Conservation Society met in San Antonio with the associate director of the Office of Management and Budget and formally requested, at the end of June 1979, that a National Park Advisory Commission be established for the park, as normally required within six months of enabling legislation.[37] Two months later President Carter signaled his satisfaction with the new arrangement by approving the commission.[38]

Nearly a year after the long-sought legislation passed, implementation began. The National Park Service director arrived in San Antonio to announce that $700,000 in federal funds would be available shortly, that National Park Service liaison officer José Cisneros would become the park's first superintendent and that, although the Moody Foundation had already donated $250,000 to the Bexar County Historical Foundation for restoration of the mission churches, the door was not necessarily closed on future federal funding for the church buildings.[39] Preliminary studies began. An industrial development planned near the park was beaten back as plans were made for transfer of title to the federal government.

Suddenly the Texas Parks and Wildlife Department became possessive.[40] Officially, the agency still planned to transfer the San José Mission State Park title to the national government. Unofficially, however, Parks and Wildlife officials broached the idea that they might keep the title and continue to op-

San Antonio's Roman Catholic archbishop, the Most Rev. Patrick Flores, addresses the gathering in 1983 at the signing of the agreement creating San Antonio Missions National Historical Park. Others shown are, from left, Bishop Charles Graham, San Antonio Conservation Society President Lynn Bobbitt, Missions Advisory Commission Chairwoman Patsy Light, San Antonio City Councilwoman Helen Dutmer and National Park Service Assistant Mary Lou Grier. The group is seated by the Rose Window of the sacristy of Mission San José's church. San Antonio Conservation Society.

erate the park, or just keep the title and let the National Park Service run it. The Department of the Interior, horrified, put a hold on acquiring new land.[41] Parks and Wildlife officials said they weren't sure that the Archdiocese, which in 1941 had been slow in agreeing to create the state park in the first place, would really transfer title to its property around the churches to the National Park Service. Another explanation was that state officials wanted to stay in charge because "they probably now realize that it's the best historical site they've got in the state."[42]

After taking heat from the public and facing heavy legislative lobbying by the Conservation Society, the Parks and Wildlife Department overcame its case of seller's remorse and signed.[43] To the strains of mariachi music on the last Sunday afternoon in February 1983, Texas Parks and Wildlife Department Director James Bell joined Archbishop Patrick Flores and San Antonio Conservation Society President Lynn Bobbitt beside the Rose Window at San José Mission to sign agreements establishing the park.[44] On March 31 the final documents were signed at San José, and Bell formally presented the iron key to San José to José Cisneros, the San Antonio Missions National Historical Park Superintendent. Successive ribbon cuttings took place at each of the four missions on April 1.[45]

Spurred by the missions' elevation to National Historical Park status, the number of visitors rose to nearly 2 million annually. Congress appropriated more than $1 million for improvements, parkland was expanded to 850 acres and in 1989 the street passing in front of Mission Concepción's church was rerouted around the far edge of the old mission plaza. Planning began for a 12,000 square-foot, $9 million visitors' center near Mission San José, which finally received federal funding and opened in 1996. In 1984 six individuals and families, three corporations and the San Antonio Conservation Society pledged $25,000 each to form a private support group named Los Compadres de San Antonio Missions, for projects lacking government funding.[46]

An early Los Compadres project funded restoration of surviving frescoes in rooms of Mission Concepción's convento. In 1988 the International Council of Monuments and Sites and the International Center for the Study of Preservation of Restoration of Cultural Property directed a team of conservators from San Antonio, New York and Italy, some of whom had worked on ceiling restoration in the Vatican's Sistine Chapel. In addition to uncovering wall designs and frescoes framing doorways, conservators removed layers of salt deposited from leaks through a barrel-vaulted stone ceiling to reveal that what had previously been seen as a single "Eye of God" was actually part of a round mestizo face. Its moustache, goatee and halo with radiating sunlike rays showed a mixture of traditional native motifs and European artistic tradition that linked the Christian concept of a single omnipotent God with the familiar power of the sun.[47]

Since accidental discovery of its 1790s site in 1933 and subsequent reconstruction, the grist mill outside San José's north mission wall had been a static structure, with no water flowing to power its wheel. Los Compadres funded excavation of a section of the acequia and of its lateral ditch that fed the mill. By recirculating water in that length of the acequia, visitors could see the mill in full operation grinding grain. In August 2001 the completed project was dedicated during a visit by President and Mrs. George W. Bush.[48]

Architectural restoration and preservation planning began for each of the missions by Ford, Powell and Carson Inc., under the direction of first O'Neil Ford and then Carolyn Peterson. But work on the mission churches and chapels, owned by the Catholic Church, was still ineligible for federal funding. They had urgent needs, from shifting foundations to drainage to rising damp, a condition where ground moisture rises into limestone walls and weakens the rock. To meet such challenges the Archdiocese formed Old Spanish Missions Inc., headed first by Rev. Msgr. Balthasar Janacek and, after his death in 2007, by Rev. David Garcia. In October 2003 the group launched a $15.5 million campaign, $9 million for restoration and enhancements and the remainder for a church-run endowment for ongoing maintenance. Under Garcia's "persistent if not zealous" fundraising, the goal was reached in 2010.[49]

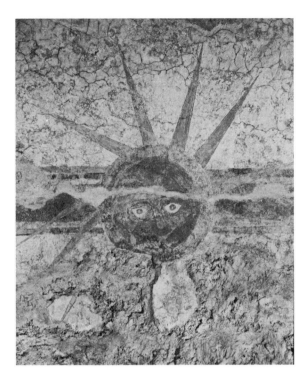

An international team of conservators restoring frescoes in 1988 in Mission Concepción's convento removed ceiling salt deposits that had covered a round mestizo face mixing native motifs and European artistic traditions. Lewis F. Fisher.

Already the Archdiocese had repaired and restored walls in Concepción's baptismal and confessional rooms and sacristy, revealing new swaths of frescoes. Restoration of the church's interior would be the fund campaign's first major project. In six months it was transformed from stark white to the original rich earthtone hues found in fragments long hidden beneath the whitewash.[50]

A year and a half later, in August 2011, the church at Mission San José reopened to a similar transformation. The $2.2 million undertaking included restoration of its distinctive Baroque frontispiece, what Boston-based master stonemason Ivan Myjer termed "one of the most spectacular Spanish colonial art treasures in the United States." Myjer had to deal with subtle repairs not true to Spanish Colonial times, such as those by an Art Deco–influenced Italian stone carver who worked on the facade in the 1930s and replaced the head on the statue of San José. "I stared and stared at San José's 'new head,' wondering what made it so different," said Myjer. "Then I realized it wasn't just the Art Deco triangularity of the face. San José has no ears."[51]

Restoration of the church stopped short of re-covering exterior walls with plaster and repainting that with bright designs. "I believe passionately that the limestone plaster should go back on," said Myjer, whose credits included work at the White House and New York's Cathedral of St. John the Divine. "If you don't put it back on, you will eventually lose these stone walls. The stone wasn't meant to be exposed. It's like building a wood house and not painting

Mission San Juan's acequia was reopened in 2011, as U.S. Senator Kay Bailey Hutchison opened a rebuilt irrigation gate. Onlookers included Bexar County Judge Nelson Wolff and San Antonio Mayor Julián Castro and his twin brother Joaquin, soon elected to Congress. National Park Service.

it." Father David Garcia, however, was not optimistic about getting that approved by regulatory agencies, since so little original painted plaster remained on which to base an authentic restoration. He saw a "stronger case for doing Mission Concepción, because so much more of the old painted plaster was found." Restoration efforts moved on to the Espada and San Juan chapels. San Juan's 6.7-mile acequia, severed from the river in a 1950s flood control project, was ceremoniously reopened in September 2011 to irrigate a mission demonstration farm.[52]

At the same time came a groundswell of hope that the missions could attain UNESCO designation as a World Heritage Site, joining manmade and natural treasures from the Taj Mahal to Stonehenge to the Grand Canyon. Ownership status would not change, but the imprimatur would focus international attention to help dissuade interference with the well-being of the sites and to increase the number of visitors. There were nearly 1,000 such designated sites in the world. Fewer than two dozen were in the United States, none in Texas.

The spark for nomination came in 2006 when San Antonio Conservation Society Director Bruce MacDougal heard from a friend, Cuban-born preservation architect Gustavo Araoz, then in Washington, D.C., as director of the U.S. office of the Paris-based International Council on Monuments and Sites, which advises the UNESCO committee on World Heritage Site selection. Why didn't the Conservation Society nominate the missions, Araoz asked

MacDougal. MacDougal shared the suggestion with Conservation Society President Virginia Nicholas, who quickly appointed a committee to study a nomination.[53]

Competition for the crown was fierce. Despite the odds, the Conservation Society began to build momentum to get the missions on the Department of the Interior's tentative list for nomination. Timing was good for demonstrating worthiness, good management and community support, all required to assure sites' ongoing character and integrity. Four of the five missions already formed a well-established National Historical Park. Their community support group, Los Compadres, headed by Susan Chandoha, had a broad base of 800 members. Also, the Catholic Archdiocese was at work on its $15.5 million campaign to restore the churches and chapels.

One wrinkle was that the fifth mission, the Alamo in downtown San Antonio, would have to be part of the World Heritage Site. The State of Texas owned the Alamo church and the City of San Antonio owned most of the old mission plaza, rimmed by a range of tourist emporiums. Both the city and, eventually, the state were agreeable, though there was as yet little consensus on how the plaza and its perimeter would be changed and there was concern that the uncertainty could impact the committee's final decision. Still, advocates went ahead, although by mid-2011 U.S. Secretary of the Interior Ken Salazar's list had climbed to a dozen potential nominees. But during a mid-2011 visit to dedicate a park near Mission Concepción, Salazar, involved at the behest of Henry Muñoz, surprised the group by declaring of a missions nomination, "I'm ready to sign off today."[54]

That informal endorsement intensified local efforts. Los Compadres and the Conservation Society came up with $50,000 to help complete the nomination. Bexar County appropriated $10,000 for an economic impact study. Chief preparer of the nomination would be San Antonio historian Paul T. Ringenbach, working through Los Compadres and aided by World Heritage Coordinator Susan Snow, archeologist with San Antonio Missions National Historical Park.[55]

As preparations went forward, in April 2012 San Antonio preservation groups convened a "Meeting of National and International Experts" to evaluate worthiness of the nomination. The twenty attendees issued a stirring endorsement that could be included in the formal nomination. Another boost came from Gustavo Araoz, who in 2006 had first urged the Conservation Society to consider the nomination. He had since risen to become the first American elected president of the UNESCO advisory International Council on Monuments and Sites. Though prevented by ethics policy from being directly involved in consideration of an American site, Araoz volunteered to help San Antonio prepare "the strongest possible nomination."[56]

The resulting nomination, dated January 2014, was an exemplary work.

Softbound and printed on high-quality letter-size coated enamel stock, with dramatic but restrained use of color photography plus maps, diagrams and a 15-page bibliography, its 344 pages were expertly designed and chockablock with carefully outlined documentation and analyses of the missions' history. Seven pages of charts compared the San Antonio missions with conditions of 13 surviving Spanish Colonial mission "ensembles" and 117 individual Spanish colonial mission churches in North and South America and the Philippines, from a database prepared by University of Texas at San Antonio architectural graduate students of William A. Dupont, who held the San Antonio Conservation Society Endowed Professorship in Memory of Mary Ann Blocker Castleberry.

The conclusion was that San Antonio's formed "the most complete and intact example of the Spanish Crown's efforts to colonize, evangelize and defend the northern frontier of New Spain during the period when Spain controlled the largest empire in the world." Outlined were the missions' more than fifty standing masonry structures, ranging from a functioning irrigation aqueduct to a mill, kilns and granaries to ruins in the National Park Service–owned ninety-nine-acre core of Mission Espada's ranch, Rancho de las Cabras, thirty-seven miles southeast near Floresville. All told, the form stated, "these attributes are unmatched in number and diversity among surviving Spanish colonial missions." The work pointed out that the World Heritage List "does not yet include any mission complexes in North America, one of the primary territorial interests of the Spanish Crown."[57]

Though the nomination was formally submitted to the World Heritage committee in February 2014, not all perceived threats had been stamped out. New ones would keep the city suffering from an extended case of the jitters.

One potential problem had come up the year before, when owners of the vacant Joske's Building that dominated the south end of Alamo Plaza proposed adding a hotel higher than twenty stories atop the existing five-story building. A structure "so imposing and so enormous" looming over the nearby Alamo "could only be prejudicial" to the World Heritage Site proposal, warned Conservation Society President Nancy Avellar that May. Although the Historic and Design Review Commission rejected the plan, city officials, who leaned toward the developers, could reverse that decision. In June the U.S. National Park Service director informed Mayor Julián Castro that such a hotel tower could in fact jeopardize the nomination. Elected officials were well aware that losing the designation would mean forfeiting a multitude of new visitors, plus losing a projected $105 million in new revenues and 1,100 new jobs. Two months later, the developers withdrew their application.[58]

Concern over World Heritage status was also cited in a mission neighborhood uprising that caused another developer to withdraw plans for a 144-unit apartment complex some thought too close to Mission San José. Zoning regulations approved in October 2014 provided buffer zones and protected views around the five missions to "enhance the pending nomination," said the city's historic preservation officer, Shanon Miller. UNESCO's World Heritage Site Committee could be shown hope for curing Alamo Plaza's chronic tourism shortcomings by the city's formation of an Alamo Plaza Advisory Committee and by the state's new interest in restoration work at the Alamo. Passage of an Alamo preservation bill by the Texas legislature, thought the bill's sponsor, State Rep. Ryan Guillen, should "show the panel how serious Texans are about the Alamo."[59]

Some Texans, however, were so deeply emotional about the Alamo that officials could not convince them that the UNESCO designation would not mean that the United Nations would control the shrine. One conservative leader blogged that Texans should refuse to allow the Alamo to be influenced or managed by "any foreign interest." As fears spread through social media that "a blue U.N. flag may fly above the historic shrine of Texas liberty once it falls under U.N. control," State Senator Donna Campbell of New Braunfels, whose district included much of San Antonio, swung in. She asserted that the Alamo was where "Texas first stood her ground to be free, and the U.N. doesn't have any business there." She introduced a bill to prohibit the state from entering any agreement permitting an "entity formed under the laws of another country" to own, operate or manage the state-owned shrine. Senator Campbell received little support. Texas Land Commissioner Jerry Patterson dismissed the effort as "horse hockey."[60]

The sideshow did not deter a major boost in May 2015, an endorsement by the influential International Council on Monuments and Sites, two months before UNESCO's World Heritage Committee was to meet in Bonn, Germany. A bevy of ten optimistic San Antonians, including County Judge Nelson Wolff and Mayor Ivy Taylor, made plans to attend the July 5 session. They were not disappointed. Quipped the first delegate to speak, Khalil Karam of Lebanon: "I am of the generation that has Davy Crockett as a hero. Now we know that the Alamo has these other missions."[61]

After twenty-three minutes of presentations and comments, San Antonio's missions were named a UNESCO World Heritage Site by acclamation.

Two days later, Judge Wolff and Mayor Taylor were back in San Antonio to preside over a public celebration in front of the Alamo. Another memorable observance came two months later at Mission Concepción, where a celebratory crowd of 300 people gathered in front of the mission church as the sun set. At dark, projectors programmed with colors based on fragments revealed during restoration bathed the facade in the long-lost bright red, green and yellow geometrical patterns painted on in 1755, restoring the original facade by light.[62]

The UNESCO designation had been nine years in the making. It had been

In one celebration after San Antonio's five missions were named a UNESCO World Heritage Site, Mission Concepción's church gained a "restoration by light," as a nighttime crowd watched projectors cast on its exterior the original geometric patterns and colors long faded away after the church was completed in 1755. Rivard Report.

thirty-two years since Congress approved San Antonio Missions National Historical Park; forty-eight years since national park legislation was first introduced; seventy-four years since the Catholic Church, Bexar County and the San Antonio Conservation Society created San José Mission State Park; ninety years since the Conservation Society first considered seeking national park status; and one hundred thirteen years since Adina DeZavala gathered supplies on Alamo Plaza, hitched up a horse and wagon and headed south to begin the long journey to restore Mission San José.

Treacherous twists and turns like those of this epic journey still lurk in the precarious quest to preserve and interpret what yet remains at risk throughout historic San Antonio. If the thrust of their record is any indication, San Antonio's preservationists will forge on with gusto, tempered by the trials of the past and adapting to the demands of the present, relentless in their pursuit of saving San Antonio.

Notes

1. Erik K. Reed, "Report 10a7 on San José Mission National Historic Site," 1962, 1-3, copy in SACS Library. As for the two smaller missions south of San José, Reed

was pleased with the recent work directed by architect Harvey Smith and funded by the Catholic archdiocesan missions fund, augmented by the church's share of admissions receipts at San José. Smith died in 1964. Restoration at San Juan four years later under architect Carolyn (Mrs. Jack) Peterson was "not to take it back to the way it looked at one particular era or age, but to be a restoration of the life of the mission over all the ages." (Minutes, G-Oct. 24, 1968.)

2. Minutes, D-June 19, 1961, 2. A heated minority dissent on the Texas State Parks Board came from Frank D. Quinn, who as chairman of the board in 1941 helped engineer naming of San José as a National Historic Site. "Something I cannot understand is the fact that your Society would even *think* of taking the San José Mission away from the jurisdiction of the Texas State Parks Board and turn it over to the National Park Service," Quinn wrote the Conservation Society. He believed that of the state parks, San José was "a rose among many thorns." Quinn sensed he had been purposely circumvented, thinking the proposal went straight to the board because Site Manager Ethel Harris knew he would oppose it; this was "the first move she has made without advance notice and discussion with me." (Frank D. Quinn to Mrs. James V. Graves, June 28, 1961; Frank D. Quinn to Mrs. Ethel W. Harris, July 29, 1961; Frank D. Quinn to Mrs. Winfield S. Hamlin, July 31, 1961. Letters in SACS Library.)

3. Mary Ann Castleberry, "President's Report," *SACS Newsletter,* Oct.–Nov., 1978.

4. Ibid.

5. Lloyd Larrabee, "Mission Loop Urged," *San Antonio Light,* Feb. 28, 1969. After the Conservation Society complained to the mayor that creating a coherent roadway to link all the missions had been delayed far too long, new planning sessions began with City Manager Jack Shelley and a Chamber of Commerce committee. (Minutes, G-Feb. 22, 1962.) By January 1963, seven miles of new pavement from Roosevelt Park to Espada Mission established a single road to all of the missions, twisting and ill-marked though it may have been. (Minutes, D-May 21, 1962, 2; D-Sept. 24, 1962, 3; G-Sept. 27, 1962, 2; G-Oct. 25, 1962; D-Jan. 21, 1963, 5.) Further development of Mission Parkway was approved in a 1964 bond issue. (Minutes, D-Oct. 25, 1965, 3.) In January the Conservation Society asked that at least $150,000 in bond issue funds be earmarked for the Mission Parkway. Federal funds for historic parkways were used with bond issue funds primarily for right-of-way acquisition. (Minutes, D-Jan. 20, 1964; D-Nov. 21, 1966; G-June 22, 1972.) Things were soon back on track, with the City Planning Department working on a master plan and the Conservation Society ready to take legal action to prevent inappropriate industrial zoning changes in the parkway's vicinity. (Minutes, D-Apr. 12, 1973, 1, 2; D-July 2, 1975.)

6. Roadway land acquisition was boosted in 1973 as the city, having reached a détente with preservationists, earmarked $300,000 in federal funds for the project. Twenty years later the city's Mission Parkway Steering Committee hired a consulting firm for help. The next year the Mission Parkway project got $14.1 million from the Texas Department of Transportation. Matching funds were approved in a city bond issue. ("S.A. to get funds," *San Antonio Express-News,* June 29, 1976; Minutes, D-Apr. 14, 1993, 4, 6; Minutes, D-May 18, 1994.) Federal funding was through the Community Development Act.

The Conservation Society did not at first have a seat on the Mission Parkway Steering Committee. Said Inell Schooler: "I had to make kind of a scene at a [public] meeting one night . . . that the Society had worked on this for 60 years, and that if anybody had a right to be part of this planning process the Conservation Society did .... Maybe out of embarrassment or maybe to shut me up. . . . we were automatically put on the steering committee." (Inell Schooler OHT, 24–25.)

7. Minutes, D-Sept. 9, 1970, 2; G-Oct. 25, 1973; G-Mar. 26, 1975, 2.

8. Minutes, D-Oct. 28, 1968, 2; D-Dec. 16, 1968, 2; G-June 24, 1971, 2; G-Feb. 24, 1972; D-May 24, 1973; D-May 18, 1977.

9. Minutes, D-July 17, 1974, 4; G-Sept. 25, 1974. It was assumed that while the Conservation Society owned the land, ownership of the aqueduct itself had devolved on the Espada Ditch Co., established in 1895 by owners of property adjoining the acequia. The aqueduct turned out to be publicly owned, by either the city or the state. A two-hour meeting in Washington in 1975 between Conservation Society President Beverly Blount (-Hemphill) and officials of the U.S. Army Corps of Engineers followed by the help of Senator Ralph Yarborough got funding passed by both houses of Congress the next year for an overflow channel to protect the aqueduct from damage during flooding. (Minutes, D-Feb. 26, 1975, 2; F-Mar. 19, 1975; F-May 21, 1975, 2; G-May 28, 1975, 3; D-July 21, 1976, 2; G-Sept. 22, 1976, 2.)

10. "Council Sponsors Missions," *San Antonio Express-News,* Mar. 1, 1974, 12; Minutes, D-Mar. 19, 1975, 2; D-May 18, 1977, 2; Mary Ann Castleberry OHT, Sept. 21, 1990, 15. Renovation to accommodate 1,600 persons was completed in 1975 in time for the bicentennial play *Winds of Freedom* the next year. (Minutes, G-Mar. 26, 1975, 3.)

11. Helen Parmley, "Bentsen appeals for park," *Dallas Morning News,* Dec. 23, 1978, 20-A.

12. 24. Minutes, D-Aug. 8, 1975, 2; D-Nov. 5, 1975, 3.

13. David Hendricks, "Mission park plan advanced," *San Antonio Express-News,* June 26, 1977. A hearing on Kazen's bill was held in San Antonio in December 1976. Senate investigation took the form of a visit to San Antonio the next summer by a delegation headed by Senator James Abourezk of South Dakota.

14. James D. Webb, U.S. Department of the Interior Associate Solicitor, "Memorandum to Legislative Council," Aug. 31, 1977, copy in SACS Library. Assistant Solicitor David A. Watts concurred that the proposal did not violate first amendment rights "provided these buildings are being preserved for the benefit of the general public." (David A. Watts, U.S. Department of the Interior Office of the Solicitor, "Memorandum to National Park Service Director," Oct. 7, 1977, copy in SACS Library.)

15. Minutes, D-May 17, 1978, 3; July 19, 1978, 2; "House passes bill containing Missions park," *San Antonio Express-News,* July 13, 1978, 7-B; Jan Jarboe, "Missions Park Bill Approved," *San Antonio Light,* Oct. 16, 1978, 1.

16. Minutes, D-Aug. 16, 1978, 2; G-Sept. 27, 1978. A rebellion of mission area homeowners was put down when the number of families to be displaced by land acquisition was cut from 60 to 4. ("Mission Park Plan Trimmed," *San Antonio Light,* Apr. 26, 1978.)

17. Mary Ann Castleberry OHT, 14.

18. Mrs. James N. Castleberry, Jr. to Secretary of the Interior Cecil Andrus, Sept. 22, 1978, copy in SACS Library.

19. Jarboe, "Missions Park Bill Approved."

20. Mary Ann Castleberry, "President's Report."

21. Patricia Osborne OHT, 15. Conservation Society members leading the charge in Chicago were President Mary Ann Castleberry, Lynn Bobbitt, Joanna Parrish, Pat Osborne and Administrative Director Conrad True. (Castleberry, "President's Report.")

22. Castleberry, "President's Report." The Republican from Virginia was being sought to help reverse opposition of Virginia's Republican Senator William Scott, who was objecting vigorously to the missions bill because it included a Manassas battlefield project which he opposed. (Jarboe, "Missions Park Bill Approved"; Kemper Diehl, "Missions park up to Carter," *San Antonio Express-News,* Oct. 16, 1978, 1.)

23. Castleberry, "President's Report." Also credited with a key role in saving the missions bill was Preservation Action's Nellie Longsworth.

24. Jarboe, "Missions Park Bill Approved"; Diehl, "Missions park up to Carter."

25. Ibid.

26. Ibid.

27. Castleberry, "President's Report."

28. Jarboe, "Missions Park Bill Approved"; Diehl, "Missions park up to Carter."

29. Castleberry, "President's Report"; Castleberry OHT, 16; "President's Report." As they marshaled support from Chicago, Conservation Society leaders ran up a phone tab of $1,000.

30. Don Warden, "Parks bill signed," *San Antonio Express-News,* Nov. 11, 1978, 1. Had the President not signed the bill at that time, it would have died by a pocket veto.

31. Helen Parmley, "Bentsen appeals for park," *Dallas Morning News,* Dec. 23, 1978, 20-A.

32. Ibid.

33. Wade Roberts, "Mission park funds frozen," *San Antonio Express-News,* Jan. 13, 1979, 2-A.

34. Ibid.

35. Webb, "Memorandum," 1, 3, 5, 12.

36. The Bexar County Historical Foundation was formed by Bexar County Historic Survey Committee Chairman Maj. Gen. William Harris, Henry Guerra and Gilbert Denman Jr., who was honored with the papal Benemerenti Medal in 1994 for raising more than $750,000 for the foundation's work. The Conservation Society provided the foundation with administrative support. (Minutes, D-July 18, 1979, 2; J. Michael Parker, "Episcopal layman receives papal medal for helping S.A. missions," *San Antonio Express-News,* Feb. 26, 1994, 27-A.)

37. Parmley, "Bentsen appeals for park"; Rev. Msgr. Charles Grahmann, Bexar County Judge Albert Bustamante, San Antonio City Councilwoman Helen Dutmer and San Antonio Conservation Society President Mrs. William E. Parrish to Eliot R. Cutler, June 29, 1979, copy in SACS Library; "Missions Park gets Carter boost," *San Antonio Express-News,* Sept. 5, 1979.

38. "Missions Park gets Carter boost," *San Antonio Express-News.*

39. David McLemore, "Missions Park squabble ends," *San Antonio Express-News,* Sept. 21, 1979, 8-A; "Mission Park Gets $694,000," *San Antonio Light,* Sept. 21, 1979.

40. Ed Castillo, "Historic Park's Future Bright," *San Antonio Light,* July 24, 1980; "Groups beat back industrial plans," *San Antonio Express-News,* July 24, 1980; Dick Merkel, "Legislators move to transfer mission park tide," *San Antonio Express-News,* Feb.

28, 1981; Tom Nelson, "Missions Park plans in danger," *San Antonio Express-News,* Feb. 24, 1982, 1.

41. Nelson, "Missions Park plans in danger."

42. Ibid.

43. Castleberry OHT, 15.

44. Karen Kennedy, "New park protects missions," *San Antonio Express-News,* Feb. 28, 1983, 1.

45. "U.S. gets key to missions," *San Antonio Express-News,* Apr. 1, 1983, 6-A; Ralph Winingham, "Missions now park," *San Antonio Express-News,* Apr. 2, 1983.

46. "Los Compadres to honor its founders," *San Antonio Light*, Oct. 24, 1984; "SACS is 'Founder' in Los Compadres," SACS Newsletter, Nov.–Dec. 1984, 2; J. Michael Parker, "Mission exhibit center groundbreaking held," *San Antonio Express-News*, July 7, 1989, 1-C; Mark Smith, "House approves more than $1 million to upgrade missions, *San Antonio Express-News*, July 13, 1989; Don Driver, "Plan review set for park expansion," *San Antonio Express-News*, May 29, 1994, 3-B; "New mission facility," *San Antonio Express-News*, Nov. 29, 1994, 1. In 1989 Los Compadres funded a small visitors' station at Mission Concepción.

47. Fisher, *The Spanish Missions of San Antonio*, 42, 50.

48. Gary Martin and Jaime Castillo, "Bush defends tax cut," *San Antonio Express-News*, Aug. 30, 2001, 1.

49. Mike Greenberg, "Fund-raising party to mark 10 years of Los Compadres," *San Antonio Express-News*, Apr. 3, 1994, 5-J; Vianna Davila, "Missions fundraising goal complete," *San Antonio Express-News*, May 19, 2010, 1-B; Catholic News Agency, "San Antonio Catholics donate $1M to Spanish mission churches," accessed Jan. 26, 2016, at www. catholicnewsagency.com/news/san_antonio_catholics_donate_1m_to_spanish_mission _churches. The Archdiocese's Old Spanish Missions Inc. replaced the fundraising function for church properties first filled in 1979 by the private Bexar County Historical Foundation, which was dissolved in 2004.

50. Amy Dorsett, "Exposing the past," *San Antonio Express-News*, June 11, 2002, 1-B; Vianna Davila, "After six-month renovation," *San Antonio Express-News*, Mar. 21, 2010; Abe Levy, "Revitalized San José," *San Antonio Express-News*, Aug. 20, 2011.

51. Robert Rivard, "Artists at Work: Restoring Frontispiece to Masterpiece at Mission San Jose," *Rivard Report*, Mar. 29, 2012, accessed Jan. 26, 2016, at http://therivard report.com/artists-at-work-restoring-frontispiece-to-masterpiece-at-mission-san-jose. Some stonework in the restoration came from rock from St. Michael's Catholic Church dumped in a ravine near Mission San Juan after St. Michael's was razed for the HemisFair site.

52. Robert Rivard, "Artists at Work," *Rivard Report*, Mar. 29, 2012, accessed Jan. 27, 2016, at http://therivardreport.com/artists-at-work-restoring-frontispiece-to-master piece-at-mission-san-jose; Elaine Ayala, "San Juan Acequia flows again," *San Antonio Express-News*, Sept. 28, 2011. In 2014 the Conservation Society pledged $100,000 to establish an endowment fund for the demonstration farm.

53. Bruce MacDougal to Lewis F. Fisher, Feb. 3, 2016, email copy in SACS files.

54. Tracy Idell Hamilton, "S.A. missions could be on international stage," *San Antonio Express-News*, July 7, 2011; Robert Rivard, "San Antonio Missions and Alamo Now

a World Heritage Site," *Rivard Report*, July 6, 2015, accessed Jan. 26, 2016, at http://therivardreport.com/san-antonio-missions-alamo-now-a-world-heritage-site.

55. John W. Gonzalez, "Bexar backs bid," *San Antonio Express-News*, Sept. 28, 2011.

56. Ringenbach, *San Antonio Missions*, 342–43; Scott Huddleston, " 'A crown jewel' strives," *San Antonio Express-News*, June 2, 2012.

57. Ringenbach, *San Antonio Missions*, 158, 170.

58. Benjamin Olivo, "Sculley backs Joske's concept," *San Antonio Express-News*, May 11, 2013; Neal Morton and Benjamin Olivo, "Joske's owner is axing tower for hotel," *San Antonio Express-News*, Aug. 20, 2013; Jeremy T. Gerlach, "Missions still have strong economic impact," *San Antonio Express-News*, Apr. 22, 2014.

59. Steve Bennett, "Board backs plan," *San Antonio Express-News*, Aug. 20, 2014; Katherine Nickas, "Alamo Plaza Committee," *Rivard Report*, Aug. 25, 2014, accessed Jan. 27, 2016, at http://therivardreport.com/alamo-plaza-advisory-committee-public-meeting; Robert Rivard, "Mission Overlay Districts," *Rivard Report*, Sept. 18, 2014, accessed Jan. 27, 2016, at http://therivardreport.com/mission-overlay-districts-strengthen-world-heritage-bid; Rivard, "San Antonio Missions Get New Zoning Protections," *Rivard Report*, accessed Jan. 27, 2016, at http://therivardreport.com/historic-missions-now-protected-encroaching-development; http://therivardreport.com/mission-overlay-districts-strengthen-world-heritage-bid; Jeremy T. Gerlach, "Trio of developments," *San Antonio Express-News*, July 21, 2015; Nicole Cobler, "Could DRT still play a role," *San Antonio Express-News*, May 26, 2015; Nicole Cobler, "Abbott signs," *San Antonio Express-News*, June 12, 2015. An unfounded fear far easier for officials to tamp down was that refusal of the United States to pay its UNESCO dues would affect site selection.

60. Scott Huddleston, "Officials bash rumors," *San Antonio Express-News*, Oct. 3, 2013; Eva Hershaw, "Sen. Campbell Wants to Ban Foreign Control of Alamo," *Texas Tribune*, Jan. 30, 2015, accessed Jan. 26, 2016, at www.texastribune.org/2015/01/30/donna-campbell-looks-ban-foreign-ownership-alamo; Nicole Cobler, "Senators question need for bill," *San Antonio Express-News*, Feb 24, 2015. The post sparking the concerns was by George Rodriguez, former president of the San Antonio Tea Party. He later hedged by terming his article "a cautionary piece," adding that "I'm constantly saying 'may' or 'might.' I'm never once saying this is going to happen. We need to be aware."

61. Scott Huddleston, "Missions' World Heritage bid," *San Antonio Express-News*, May 6, 2015; Robert Rivard, "San Antonio Missions and Alamo Now a World Heritage Site," *Rivard Report*, Jul. 6, 2015, accessed Jan. 26, 2016, at http://therivardreport.com/san-antonio-missions-alamo-now-a-world-heritage-site. A last-minute negative surfaced during the meeting when the representative from Portugal held up a letter he received that he said expressed concern that HemisFair Park, not far from the Alamo but not included within the site's proposed boundaries, was being developed over indigenous burial grounds, a claim not supported in the archeological record. Committee Chair Maria Böhmer of Germany did not respond directly, and nothing further was heard of it.

62. Joan Vinson, "Mission Concepción Restored by Light," *Rivard Report*, Oct. 16, 2015, accessed Jan. 27, 2016, at http://therivardreport.com/mission-concepcion-restored-by-light.

Afterword

San Antonio's communal glow from the missions' elevation to the rarified rank of World Heritage Site was not about to fade. The city launched a series of World Heritage Symposiums to explore implications of the selection and to use it as "a catalyst for socio-economic change, with increased visitation and tourist spending," said City Manager Sheryl Sculley. The discussions would "set the framework for the next steps for a comprehensive planning effort," not just to aid mission neighborhoods, which had long lacked attention, but also to help upgrade the entire city. Soon the city hired a World Heritage Director—Colleen Swain—to develop and implement a comprehensive plan to capitalize on the designation.[1]

Already World Heritage Site status had helped *Lonely Planet* place the city eighth in the category "unexpectedly exciting sites to see in the United States." *Travel & Leisure* magazine listed San Antonio eighteenth among fifty world destinations worth visiting and called the Pearl's Hotel Emma one of the "49 best new hotels on the planet." The *Rivard Report* believed "San Antonio is on the cusp of extraordinary opportunity."[2]

"Many of San Antonio's attractions are unique and provide an ambience that is difficult, if not impossible, to recreate elsewhere," concluded an Urban Land Institute analysis.[3] While other groups and newer city agencies have been helpful, it is apparent that overall the long-term, broad role of the San Antonio Conservation Society is most responsible for having preserved the setting that sustains San Antonio's vital $13 billion tourism industry, among the city's largest. It is a record unique in the nation.

Many state and regional preservation organizations have impressive accomplishments—the pioneering Society for the Preservation of New England Antiquities, the Society for the Preservation of Virginia Antiquities, the Landmarks Preservation Council of Illinois, the Georgia Trust for Historic Preservation, the Landmarks Club of California. Many private organizations are responsible for reclaiming local historic ambience and the consequent economic health of smaller cities: Historic Annapolis, the Historic Charleston Foundation, the Historic Savannah Foundation, the Galveston Historical Foundation, all in cities a tenth the size of San Antonio but with achievements proportionately heroic to those of their counterparts in cities of any size.

In the nation's largest cities, however, the preservation playing field becomes not only larger but also more confusing, and harder for any single group to deal with. There is a bewildering array of conflicting urban issues and a host of special interest groups to consider. Game plans become more complicated. End runs must be more circuitous. Duplicity is easier to conceal.

Preservation in Boston, Philadelphia and other of the nation's oldest major cities was accomplished for the most part by groups focusing on specific targets. Likewise, recently formed preservation organizations in some newer cities first focused on single targets: Historic Denver conquered the odds and saved Larimer Square, and the Foundation for San Francisco's Architectural Heritage achieved passage of a municipal preservation plan that is a national model. In a few cases, enlightened municipal governments played a lead role: the Vieux Carré Commission in New Orleans and Historic Seattle were both formed as governmental entities.

The major private metropolitan preservation organization that seems to have the most in common with the San Antonio Conservation Society, in terms of origin and achievement, is in Pittsburgh, a city with a French heritage going back almost as far as San Antonio's Spanish heritage. The Pittsburgh History and Landmarks Foundation was organized in 1964 to take on an entire business and political establishment, as had the San Antonio Conservation Society. The Pittsburgh group's immediate target was impending federally funded urban renewal destruction of "all historic neighborhoods in the city."[4]

The Pittsburgh foundation rescued a downtown railroad station as a focal point for preserved landmarks in a fifty-two-acre section of the urban triangle created where the Allegheny and Monongahela rivers join to form the Ohio. By focusing on preservation aspects of "what people like as opposed to what planners think they ought to like," the group also inspired $3.75 billion in private and public investments to rehabilitate and preserve thirty-three significant nineteenth-century neighborhoods, most in Pittsburgh's inner city, at a time when comparable neighborhoods in near-western San Antonio and on HemisFair Plaza were being swept away.[5]

In downtown Pittsburgh, the restored Fort Pitt blockhouse of 1764 guards the tip of that city's renewed Golden Triangle, much as San Antonio's restored Spanish Governor's Palace of 1728 enhances Military Plaza.[6] The restored Station Square draws a third of downtown Pittsburgh's 10 million annual visitors and ranks among the top attractions in Pittsburgh's $5.6 billion tourism industry. That tally, however, is less than half the amount produced by tourism in San Antonio, where tourism is among the city's largest industries.[7]

Conservation Society leaders are careful not to take all the credit for San Antonio's progress in preserving its heritage. When Bruce MacDougal retired as the society's executive director in 2016, he observed that at the time of his arrival twenty-five years before, "basically, we were the main game in town." But as "conservation literacy and education" advanced and with the increasing aid of city government, "it's collaboration with volunteers and [other] organizations that has made the progress that we've seen."[8]

Yet the San Antonio Conservation Society's record stands. In none of America's other largest cities can the basis of a $13 billion industry so critical to that city's economy be credited so directly to the work of a single private historic preservation organization.

Notes

1. Joan Vinson, "City Convenes First World Heritage Symposium," *Rivard Report*, Nov. 1, 2015.

2. Syd Kearney, "Hotel Emma one of the best," *San Antonio Express-News*, Feb. 4, 2016; Robert Rivard, "Getting real," *Rivard Report*, Feb. 15, 2016.

3. *An Evaluation of Expansion Opportunities for the Henry B. Gonzalez Convention Center* (Washington, D.C.: Urban Land Institute, 1995), 8, 12, 13, 18. The study also noted: "Historic preservation is built into the culture of San Antonio, which has retained an entertaining sequence of buildings from three centuries mixed with new buildings subjected to a high standard of design review. . . . Visitors and residents delight in San Antonio's downtown area, with its retail operations, businesses, entertainment offerings, cultural/historical attractions and restaurants all within walking distance of one another and linked by the most exotic pedestrian environment in the Southwest—the River Walk."

4. The appraisal of the Pittsburgh History and Landmarks Foundation's work is by co-founder Arthur Ziegler. By the time of its founding there was no need for it to focus on the natural environment, since a land conservancy was in place. Pittsburgh men played a key role in organizing the Pittsburgh History and Landmarks Foundation and comprised half its 2,500 members in the mid-1990s. (Arthur Ziegler to Lewis F. Fisher, telephone interview, June 15, 1995.)

5. Arthur Ziegler to Lewis F. Fisher, telephone interview, June 15, 1995.

6. As efforts to save the Governor's Palace were begun by the Texas Historical and Landmarks Association in the decade prior to organization of the Conservation Society, so was the Fort Pitt blockhouse saved by the local Daughters of the American Revolution in the decade prior to formation of the Pittsburgh History and Landmarks Foundation.

7. "Station Square," retrieved Feb. 20, 2016, at www.stationsquare.com/mimages/StationSquareDemographics.pdf; "Tourism Impact," retrieved Feb. 20, 2016, at www.visitpittsburgh.com/about-us/tourism-impact.

8. Camille Garcia, "Conservation Society Leader Bruce MacDougal to Retire," *Rivard Report*, accessed Jan. 26, 2016, at http://therivardreport.com/san-antonio-historical-conservation-leader-to-retire.

Chronology of
Historic Preservation
in San Antonio

1879
Alamo Monument Association chartered to build a memorial to Alamo heroes
and preserve the Alamo.

1883
Alamo church purchased by the State of Texas, first historic structure west of
the Mississippi officially preserved as a landmark. Custody given to City of San
Antonio.

1887
Adina De Zavala gathers a group of "patriotic women" in San Antonio to
promote interest in Texas history.

1891
De Zavala Chapter of Daughters of the Republic of Texas (DRT) formed in
San Antonio by Adina De Zavala with special purpose of studying local
landmarks.

1897
City of San Antonio faces its first legal action over an historic building when
it seeks demolition of Veramendi Palace, city's finest Spanish colonial residence.

1901
Tablet on Alamo is first of two dozen markers placed on landmarks during
coming decades under leadership of Adina De Zavala.

1902
In agreements with Catholic Church, DRT's De Zavala Chapter does stabi-
lization work on San José Mission church ruins and gets five-year lease on San
Juan Mission.

1903

Clara Driscoll becomes treasurer of DRT De Zavala Chapter, then engaged in nationwide fund-raising to purchase convento property beside Alamo church and prevent hotel developers from having convento torn down for a park.

1904

Clara Driscoll advances nearly $60,000 in personal funds to cover DRT fund-raising shortfall and purchase Alamo convento and grounds.

1905

Texas Legislature reimburses Clara Driscoll, removes Alamo church custody from City of San Antonio, gives both church and convento custody to DRT.

1908

Adina De Zavala draws national attention by barricading herself inside Alamo convento for three days to prevent its rumored desecration.

1910

As debate rages over appropriate historic preservation at the Alamo, DRT's new Alamo Chapter wins Alamo custody battle with De Zavala Chapter.

City razes Veramendi Palace to widen Soledad Street.

1912

Spanish colonial Garza House complex razed for eight-story Rand Building.

Upper walls of Alamo convento removed so they do not overshadow Alamo church.

Texas Historical and Landmarks Association formed by Adina De Zavala from membership of DRT's De Zavala Chapter, which ceases to exist.

1915

Widening of Commerce Street becomes largest street widening project removing landmarks.

Texas Historical and Landmarks Association begins efforts to save Spanish Governor's Palace.

1917

Catholic Church under leadership of Rev. William W. Hume stabilizes walls at San José Mission church using rocks from collapsed dome, reopens sacristy next year.

1920

Chamber of Commerce, Old Spanish Trail Association and Real Estate Board assert desire to save places of historical interest to aid city's appeal to tourists.

1921

Flooding San Antonio River inundates downtown, showing need to build Olmos Dam and straighten riverbed to prevent future floods.

1924

Men's Technical Club proposes S.O.S. (Save Old San Antonio) effort to deal with landmarks management.

Artists Rena Maverick Green and Emily Edwards organize San Antonio Conservation Society to save 1859 Market House and the city's cultural heritage, Emily Edwards elected president. Conservation Society may be first group in nation to seek preservation of both the historic built environment and the natural environment.

Conservation Society seeks option on lands around all missions for parks under leadership of Rena Maverick Green.

Conservation Society stresses need for city to establish a planning department.

1925

City razes 1859 Market House for street widening, San Antonio River flood-control channel planned through site.

Conservation Society and DRT Alamo Chapter co-sponsor public meeting seeking purchase of remaining privately owned property adjoining Alamo church.

1926

Witte Museum, city's first public museum, opens with backing of Conservation Society.

Last original doors of San José Mission Granary become Conservation Society's first property.

1927

Anna Ellis, then Margaret Lewis, elected Conservation Society president.

1928

Catholic Church restores San José Mission church tower following its collapse.

Proposal to fill downtown River Bend for development is defeated.

1929

City bond issue funds purchase of Spanish Governor's Palace. Rena Green named chairman of restoration committee composed of six organizations' representatives.

Proposal to extend Losoya Street above portion of River Bend is defeated.

Conservation Society endorses Robert Hugman's river beautification plan.

Conservation Society begins purchasing San José Mission Granary property.

New San Pedro Playhouse preserves facade design of razed Market House.

1931
Restored Spanish Governor's Palace dedicated on 200th anniversary of arrival of Spanish immigrants from Canary Islands.

Conservation Society completes purchase of San José Mission granary and begins restoration.

Franciscans return to San José Mission after absence of 107 years.

Amanda Cartwright Taylor elected Conservation Society president.

1933
Rena Maverick Green elected Conservation Society president.

First Historic American Buildings Survey documents major San Antonio landmarks.

San José Mission granary restoration completed.

1935
San Antonio Congressman Maury Maverick introduces Historic Sites Act in House of Representatives. It passes Congress, giving U.S. its first national policy on historic preservation.

Congressman Maury Maverick seeks designation of San José Mission as national park.

Elizabeth Orynski Graham elected Conservation Society president.

1936
State purchases remaining private land around Alamo church.

Restored San José Mission compound dedicated, City Public Service Company begins tour bus service.

Conservation Society purchases Espada Mission acequia aqueduct.

Conservation Society holds first Indian Harvest Festival, precursor of A Night In Old San Antonio, on San José Mission Plaza.

1937
Catholic Church dedicates restored San José Mission church.

Lee Upson Palfrey elected Conservation Society president.

1939

Mayor Maury Maverick begins federally funded La Villita restoration project.

Federally funded work begins on Robert Hugman's River Bend beautification plans.

Amanda Taylor elected Conservation Society president for second time.

1940

Annual Indian Harvest Festival moved from San José to San Antonio River as a Jubilee promoting River Bend project.

Menger Hotel kept from becoming parking lot.

1941

Conservation Society, Bexar County and Catholic Church cooperate in transfer of San José Mission compound property except church to State of Texas as state park. San José Mission is designated National Historic Site.

Martha Camp elected Conservation Society president.

River Bend Project dedicated, Conservation Society celebrates with River Festival.

La Villita restoration dedicated.

Twohig House becomes first of three historic homes moved to Witte Museum grounds with aid of Historic Buildings Foundation.

1942

Conservation Society purchases Dashiell House at 511 Villita Street.

1946

Conservation Society's annual fall River Festival moved to spring for Fiesta Week, later named A Night In Old San Antonio.

1947

Blum Street neighborhood razed for parking.

Mary Kenney elected Conservation Society president.

1948

Conservation Society begins annual preservation awards program.

San Pedro Park kept from becoming junior college campus.

Agnes Virginia Temple elected Conservation Society president.

1949

Conservation Society purchases Bombach building at Villita and South Alamo streets.

Floy Edwards Fontaine elected Conservation Society president.

King William Street Conservation Society formed.

1951

Ethel Wilson Harris elected Conservation Society president.

Texas Under Six Flags theme used for Conservation Society master plan to save endangered landmarks.

German-English School placed under Conservation Society custody.

1952

French-style Guilbeau House (1847) sold by city and razed, despite earlier promises to save it as museum.

Outcry fails to prevent razing of 1859 Vance House, deemed one of state's finest buildings, for Federal Reserve branch bank.

Steves Homestead on King William Street donated to Conservation Society.

1953

Conservation Society begins eight years of Arbor Day tree sales.

Conservation Society begins campaign to save José Antonio Navarro House complex.

Eleanor Freeborn Bennett elected Conservation Society president.

City plans underground parking garages beneath Travis Park, Main Plaza, Alamo Plaza and part of La Villita. Conservation Society backs suit filed by Maverick heirs to void 1,100-car Travis Park garage contract.

Texas Historic Survey Committee formed.

1954

Restored Steves Homestead opens to public as house museum.

Second night added to A Night In Old San Antonio in La Villita.

1955

Court rules against Conservation Society-backed Travis Park suit, but Good Government League sweeps to city hall victory and Travis Park garage contract is voided.

A Night In Old San Antonio attendance exceeds 10,000.

Wanda Graham Ford elected Conservation Society president.

1956

Third night added to A Night In Old San Antonio.

1957

Texas Supreme Court rules Travis Park garage contract illegal under city charter, ending threat of garages beneath city parks.

Conservation Society purchases 25 acres near Espada dam for Acequia Park.

Helen Bechtel elected Conservation Society president.

1958

Fourth night added to A Night in Old San Antonio.

1959

Conservation Society helps defeat multi-story city tourist information center planned in Alamo Plaza.

Lois Graves elected Conservation Society president.

Conservation Society purchases O. Henry House, sells it to be moved to Lone Star Brewery grounds.

1960

Conservation Society leads opposition in defeating city highway bond issue including North Expressway through Olmos Basin floodplain.

1961

Resubmitted North Expressway city bond issue passes. Conservation Society joins Sisters of Charity of the Incarnate Word in lawsuit to stop expressway.

Vivian Hamlin (Terrett) elected Conservation Society president.

Yturri-Edmunds House on Mission Road donated to Conservation Society.

1962

North Expressway right-of-way acquisition begins as litigation continues.

A Night In Old San Antonio annual profits for historic preservation first exceed $100,000.

1963

Lillian Maverick Padgitt elected Conservation Society president.

World's fair site chosen on property to be developed with urban renewal funds.

Mission Road improvements link Spanish missions.

1964

German-English School restored as HemisFair headquarters.

Conservation Society, other San Juan acequia property owners win court battle with San Antonio River Authority to restore water flow in San Juan acequia.

Restored Navarro House complex opened to public.

1965

Sisters of Charity of the Incarnate Word drop North Expressway litigation with city, Conservation Society votes to carry on alone.

Conservation Society begins purchase of old Ursuline Academy complex.

Peggy Tobin elected Conservation Society president.

City establishes Fine Arts Commission.

1966

Humble/Exxon is first HemisFair exhibitor to restore historic structure as its pavilion.

U.S. Senator Ralph Yarborough gets amendment to block unreasonable transfer of parkland for expressways, another to require maximum preservation of historic HemisFair site structures. U.S. Department of Commerce chooses Conservation Society to oversee preservation of HemisFair sites.

1967

Conservation Society sues to halt North Expressway project.

City of San Antonio sues Conservation Society for unpaid property taxes.

Lorraine Reaney elected Conservation Society president.

City of San Antonio adopts its first historic zoning ordinance.

First San Antonio Missions National Historical Park legislation introduced in Congress.

1968

Restored buildings on grounds draw wide praise during six-month HemisFair, which also provides city with modern convention center.

La Villita territory enlarged as part of HemisFair urban renewal project.

Lita Price elected Conservation Society president.

A Night In Old San Antonio presented at second American Folklife Festival on Capitol Mall in Washington.

King William Historic District formed, first historic zoning district in Texas.

1969
Pinkie Martin elected Conservation Society president.

La Villita Historic District formed.

Two-year Historic American Buildings Survey of San Antonio landmarks is completed.

1970
San Antonio Conservation Society Foundation established to own and manage society properties.

Conservation Society drops litigation against North Expressway, which opens eight years later as McAllister Freeway.

1971
City settles property tax issue with Conservation Society.

Conservation Society holds its first historic preservation seminar.

Vivian Hamlin (Terrett) elected Conservation Society president for second time.

Rivas House abruptly leveled by Urban Renewal Agency. Conservation Society gets injunction to prevent agency from doing same to endangered Menger Soap Works, later restored by developer.

1972
City trades HemisFair pavilion site to federal government for new U.S. courthouse in exchange for western portion of near-downtown U.S. Arsenal.

Yturri-Edmunds Mill reconstruction completed.

1973
Beverly Blount (-Hemphill) elected Conservation Society president.

1974
City revises historic districts and landmarks ordinances, hires Pat Osborne as city's first Historic Preservation Officer.

Nation's first federal grant for historic preservation given for Ursuline Academy restoration.

Conservation Society moves headquarters from La Villita into newly restored Wulff House on King William Street.

1975
Nancy Negley (Wellin) elected Conservation Society president.

Conservation Society sells its Ursuline Academy property to former minority owner Southwest Craft Center, which begins restoration.

Monte Vista, Main and Military Plaza and HemisFair historic districts formed.

Conservation Society transfers Acequia Park to city, deeds Navarro House complex to Texas Parks and Wildlife Commission.

1976
Attendance first reaches 100,000 during four-night A Night In Old San Antonio, nation's largest single historic preservation fund-raising event.

National landmark status attained for 500 acres of Fort Sam Houston.

City's completed Market Square renovation includes historic structures.

Conservation Society purchases Gresser House in La Villita Historic District.

Conservation Society transfers Espada Aqueduct property to city.

Ursuline Historic District formed.

Second San Antonio Missions National Park bill introduced in Congress.

1977
Mission Historic District formed.

National Trust for Historic Preservation presents Crowninshield Award to San Antonio Conservation Society for national impact on historic preservation activities.

Mary Ann Blocker Castleberry elected Conservation Society president.

Restoration of San Fernando Cathedral reveals mid-1700s apse.

1978
Reuter Building facade is first facade donated to Conservation Society Foundation and restored.

St. Paul Square, Alamo Plaza, and Healy-Murphy historic districts formed.

San Antonio Missions National Historical Park approved following last-minute lobbying by Conservation Society members.

1979
Purchase and preservation of Staacke and Stevens buildings on Commerce Street is negotiated.

Joanna Parrish elected Conservation Society president.

1980

Old Lone Star Brewery Historic District formed.

1981

Narrowly rescued Dullnig building opens in Alamo Plaza Historic District.

San Antonio Museum of Art opens in restored original Lone Star Brewery complex.

Peggy Penshorn elected Conservation Society president.

Conservation Society negotiates Rand Building purchase and resale for preservation. As part of agreement, Steumke Barn is relocated to Wulff House grounds and ten-story Stowers Building is dynamited.

1982

Hertzberg Clock at Houston and St. Mary's streets donated to Conservation Society.

Lynn Osborne Bobbitt elected Conservation Society president.

Only facade of Texas Theater remains in RepublicBank building project, despite preservationists' pleas.

1983

San Antonio Missions National Historical Park formed.

Albert Maverick Building, oldest on Houston Street downtown, saved.

1984

Dignowity Hill and Alamo Plaza historic districts formed.

City rededicates Municipal Auditorium, restored with bond issue funds after fire.

Bebe Canales Inkley elected Conservation Society president.

Los Compadres support group formed for San Antonio Missions National Historical Park.

1985

Cattleman Square Historic District formed.

Three-story brick Fairmount Hotel moved six blocks to new site near La Villita.

A Night In Old San Antonio annual profits for historic preservation first exceed $500,000.

Janet Wheat Francis elected Conservation Society president.

Missouri Pacific Depot in Cattleman Square restored by City Employees Credit Union.

1986
Restored and enlarged Fairmount Hotel dedicated.

1987
Liz Davies elected Conservation Society president.

1988
City preservation ordinances strengthened.

Blue Bonnet Hotel razed.

Restored Franklin House dedicated on San Antonio Academy campus.

Aztec Theater purchased by Conservation Society.

Arsenal, Auditorium Circle, South Alamo/South St. Mary's Street, El Mercado historic districts formed.

Paseo del Rio River District formed.

1989
Majestic Theater reopens as home of San Antonio Symphony, restoration by Las Casas Foundation aided by $250,000 from Conservation Society.

Jane Foster elected Conservation Society president.

1990
City's plan to eliminate its Historic Preservation Office is defeated.

Restored eastern U.S. Arsenal complex dedicated as H.E.B. Grocery Co. corporate headquarters.

1991
Sunday morning demolition of Finck Building inspires Tejeda Bill, toughening state laws on illegal demolition of historic structures.

Inell Schooler elected Conservation Society president.

1992
Fort Sam Houston quadrangle restored, followed by start of $100.3 million program to restore post's 934 historic buildings.

1993
City's master plan includes historic preservation requirements.

Marianna Jones elected Conservation Society president.

City restores Municipal Plaza Building for city offices, council chamber.

Conservation Society sells Aztec Theater with restoration covenants.

1994

Conservation Society pledges $300,000 to San Pedro Playhouse restoration.

City bonds, state funding to upgrade Mission Parkway.

San Antonio Missions National Historical Park begins San José Mission Visitor Center construction.

City purchases Alameda Theater to restore as Mexican American performing arts center.

1995

Robert E. Lee Hotel renovation begins for downtown housing.

Relocated Sullivan Carriage House dedicated at San Antonio Botanical Center.

Conservation Society $100,000 grant establishes Mary Ann Blocker Castleberry graduate chair for historic preservation in University of Texas at San Antonio architecture program.

Sally Matthews Buchanan elected Conservation Society president.

Southtown revitalization made an Urban Main Street Project by National Trust for Historic Preservation.

1997

Paula D. Piper elected Conservation Society president.

Conservation Society completes historic facilities survey for San Antonio Independent School District.

1998

Federal Realty Investment Trust launches Houston Street revitalization project.

1999

O. Henry House moved from Lone Star Brewery to downtown site.

Loyce Ince elected Conservation Society president.

New Hotel Valencia preserves Alfred Giles–designed building and Maverick Balcony by River Walk.

2000

Assumption Seminary's demolition of Mary Catherine Hall spurs survey of historic structures.

City authorizes Neighborhood Conservation Districts.

Huebner-Onion House saved for Leon Valley Historical Society.

2001

Jill Harrison Souter elected Conservation Society president.

Restored Mission San José gristmill dedicated by President George W. Bush.

Silver Ventures Inc. purchases former Pearl Brewery complex for historic restoration/redevelopment.

Conservation Society begins Bexar County historic farms and ranches survey.

2002

City ordinance protects viewsheds along San Antonio River and at the Alamo.

La Gloria razing leads to increased survey of west side cultural landmarks.

2003

San Fernando Cathedral restoration completed.

Leeper House moved to Mitchell Lake Audubon Center.

Loretta Huddleston elected Conservation Society president.

Former Brooks Air Force Base U.S. Air Force School of Aerospace Medicine preserved in historic district.

Bungalow Colony on former Kelly Air Force Base named to National Register of Historic Places.

2004

Barbara Johnson elected Conservation Society president.

2005

City establishes ownership title to Miraflores Park.

2006

Presnall-Watson House moved from Toyota plant site to nearby Land Heritage Institute.

Virginia S. Nicholas elected Conservation Society president.

Conservation Society begins UNESCO World Heritage Site nomination process for city's Spanish missions.

Walgreens and Stuart buildings on Houston Street demolished.

2007

Marcie Ince elected Conservation Society president.

Carol Burnett's childhood home moved to safety.

2008

Brackenridge Park Conservancy formed by Parks Department and Conservation Society.

Shanon Shea Miller named director of city's Office of Historic Preservation.

City's Office of Historic Preservation upgraded from Planning Department to Office of City Manager.

Main Plaza renovation completed.

2009

Westside Preservation Alliance organized.

Rollette Schreckenghost elected Conservation Society president.

City adopts Strategic Historic Preservation Plan.

City establishes Hemisfair Park Area Redevelopment Corporation.

2010

Hays Street Bridge opens for hike-and-bike use.

City prohibits additional digital billboards.

University of the Incarnate Word expansion plan into Brackenridge Park defeated.

City's Office of Historic Preservation begins neighborhood upgrades through Students Together Achieving Revitalization (S.T.A.R.) and the University of Texas at San Antonio's College of Architecture, Construction and Planning.

Old Spanish Missions Inc. reaches $15.5 million goal for missions restoration, completes restoration of Mission Concepción church.

Restored Stinson Municipal Airport terminal reopens.

2011

Fort Sam Houston's Long Barracks restoration highlight of post preservation projects.

Nancy Avellar elected Conservation Society president.

Protested renaming of Durango Boulevard as César Chávez Boulevard results in tighter street name change ordinance.

State retakes Alamo guardianship from the Daughters of the Republic of Texas.

Mission San José church restoration completed.

Mission San Juan's acequia reopened.

2012

Conservation Society expands historic gas stations survey.

Rescued Lerma's Nite Club purchased by Esperanza Peace and Justice Center for community center.

2013

River Walk expansion from three to fifteen miles completed.

Proposal defeated for twenty-story Alamo Plaza hotel tower atop former Joske's Building.

Hispanic broadcast landmark KWEX-TV Building razed for apartments.

Sue Ann Pemberton elected Conservation Society president.

2014

City Vacant Building Initiative seeks to avoid demolition by neglect.

Ellis Alley enclave restoration completed.

City appoints twenty-one-member Alamo Plaza Advisory Committee.

Video art presentation of San Antonio history by Xavier de Richemont begins four nights weekly on San Fernando Cathedral facade.

2015

Bexar County Courthouse restoration completed with aid of $300,000 Conservation Society grant.

Janet Dietel elected Conservation Society president.

UNESCO names San Antonio's Spanish missions a World Heritage Site.

2016

Preservationists block University of the Incarnate Word attempt to build dormitory/parking garage in Brackenridge Park.

Office of Historic Preservation launches ScoutSA program for smartphones to aid historic buildings survey.

Texas General Land Office and Alamo Endowment take over Alamo Plaza master planning.

Preservation Texas adds HemisFair Plaza's John H. Wood Jr. Courthouse and Alamo Plaza's Woolworth Building to Most Endangered Places list.

Selected Bibliography

Listed below are major sources consulted in the preparation of this book. Not included for reasons of space but also contributing to the text were several dozen letters, reports and interviews and more than 650 articles from the *San Antonio Express, San Antonio News, San Antonio Express-News, San Antonio Light, Christian Science Monitor, Dallas Morning News, New York Times, North San Antonio Times, Rivard Report, Wall Street Journal, Washington Post* and a number of other daily and nondaily newspapers, newsletters and websites. These sources are identified in the appropriate endnotes.

Ables, Luther Robert. "The Second Battle of the Alamo." *Southwestern Historical Quarterly* 70, no. 3 (January 1967): 372–413.

———. "The Work of Adina De Zavala." Master's thesis, Mexico City College, 1955.

Ahlborn, Richard Eighme. *The San Antonio Missions: Edward Everett and the American Occupation, 1847.* Fort Worth: Amon Carter Museum, 1985.

Almaráz, Félix D. Jr., and Gilbert R Cruz. "The San Antonio Missions after Secularization, 1800–1983." San Antonio Missions National Historical Park, 1994. Photocopy.

Baumbach, Richard O. Jr., and William E. Borah. *The Second Battle of New Orleans: A History of the Vieux Carré Expressway.* Tuscaloosa: University of Alabama Press for the Preservation Press, 1981.

Beckelman, Laurie, and Anthony Robins. "Coping with History, Cultural Landmarks and the Future of Preservation," *Historic Preservation Forum* (May–June 1994): 11–17.

Benedikt, Michael. "The Lone Star Brewery's Canny Conversion." *Texas Architect* (July–August 1981): 76–79.

Bennett, John M. *Those Who Made It: The Story of the Men and Women of the National Bank of Commerce of San Antonio.* San Antonio: n.p., 1978.

Black, Sinclair. "San Antonio's Linear Paradise." *AIA Journal* (July 1979): 30–38.

Brear, Holly Beachley. *Inherit the Alamo: Ritual and Myth at an American Shrine.* Austin: University of Texas Press, 1995.

Broussard, Ray F. *San Antonio during the Texas Republic: A City in Transition.* El Paso: Texas Western Press, 1967.

Brown, Louis D., et al. *Plan and Program for the Preservation of the Vieux Carré*. 4 volumes. New Orleans: City of New Orleans Bureau of Governmental Research, 1968.

Burkholder, Mary V. *The King William Area: A History and Guide to the Houses*. San Antonio: King William Association, 1973.

Bushick, Frank H. *Glamorous Days*. San Antonio: Naylor Co., 1934.

Carson, Chris, and William McDonald, eds. *A Guide to San Antonio Architecture*. AIA San Antonio, 1986.

Chabot, Frederick C. Papers. Center for American History, University of Texas at Austin.

——. *Presidio de Texas at the Place Called San Antonio*. San Antonio: n.p., 1929.

——. *With the Makers of San Antonio*. San Antonio: n.p., 1937.

Chipman, Donald E. *Spanish Texas, 1519–1821*. Austin: University of Texas Press, 1992.

Cook, Alison. "Mayan Revival Revival." *House and Garden* (January 1990): 30–31.

Coppini, Pompeo. *From Dawn to Sunset*. San Antonio: Naylor Co., 1949.

Corner, William. *San Antonio de Bexar*. San Antonio: Bainbridge & Corner, 1890.

Crawford, Ann Fears, and Crystal Sasse Ragsdale. *Women in Texas*. Austin: State House Press, 1992.

Dase, Amy E., and Summer Chandler, Stephanie Katauskas and Céline Finney. "Historic Farms and Ranches of Bexar County, Texas." National Register of Historic Places Multiple Property Documentation Form, 2010.

Davies, Wallace Evans. *Patriotism on Parade: The Story of Veterans' and Hereditary Organizations in America*. Cambridge: Harvard University Press, 1955.

Davis, J. Frank. *San Antonio: A History and Guide, Compiled by Workers of the Writers' Program of the Work Projects Administration in the State of Texas*. Revised edition. San Antonio: Clegg Co., 1941.

Davis, John L. *San Antonio: A Historical Portrait*. Austin: Encino Press, 1978.

de la Teja, Jesús F. *San Antonio: A Community on New Spain's Frontier*. Albuquerque: University of New Mexico Press, 1995.

De Zavala, Adina. *History and Legends of the Alamo and Other Missions in and around San Antonio*. San Antonio: n.p., 1917.

——. Papers. Center for American History, University of Texas at Austin.

——. Papers. St. Pius X Library, University of the Incarnate Word, San Antonio.

Debolt, Abbe A., and James S. Baugess, eds. *Encyclopedia of the Sixties: A Decade of Culture and Counterculture*. Santa Barbara, California: Greenwood, 2012

[Edwards, Emily]. *Conservation in San Antonio since 1924*. San Antonio Conservation Society, 1970.

Elliot, Keith. "The First Downtown World's Fair." *Saturday Review* (March 9, 1968): 46–47.

Everett, Donald E. Collection. Coates Library, Trinity University, San Antonio.

——. *Monte Vista: The Gilded Age of an Historic District, 1890–1930*. North San Antonio Times, 1988.

——. *San Antonio: The Flavor of its Past, 1845–1898*. San Antonio: Trinity University Press, 1975.

——. "San Antonio Welcomes the 'Sunset'–1877." *Southwestern Historical Quarterly* 65, no. 1 (July 1961): 47–60.

Everett, Richard. "Things In and About San Antonio," *Frank Leslie's Illustrated Newspaper* 7 (January 15, 1859): 1.

Fehrenbach, T. R. *Lone Star: A History of Texas and the Texans*. New York: Macmillan, 1968.

——. *The San Antonio Story*. Tulsa: Continental Heritage Press, 1978.

Fisher, Lewis F. *American Venice: The Epic Story of San Antonio's River*. San Antonio: Trinity University Press, 2015.

——. *Chili Queens, Hay Wagons and Fandangos: The Spanish Plazas in Frontier San Antonio*. San Antonio: Maverick Publishing Co., 2014.

——. *Saint Mark's Episcopal Church: 150 Years of Ministry in Downtown San Antonio, 1858–2008*. San Antonio: Maverick Publishing Co., 2008.

——. *The Spanish Missions of San Antonio*. San Antonio: Maverick Publishing Co., 1998.

Fisher, Lewis F., and Maria Watson Pfeiffer. *San Antonio Architecture: Traditions and Visions*. AIA San Antonio, 2007.

Fisher, Mary Maverick McMillan. "San Antonio I–The Hoover Era." In *Texas Cities and the Great Depression*. Austin: Texas Memorial Museum, 1973.

Fox, Anne A. *Archaeological Investigations at the United States Arsenal Site (41 BX 622), San Antonio, Texas*. Archaeological Survey Report No. 137. Center for Archaeological Research, University of Texas at San Antonio, 1986.

——. *The Archaeology and History of the Spanish Governor's Palace Park*. Archaeological Survey Report No. 31. Center for Archaeological Research, University of Texas at San Antonio, 1977.

Fox, Daniel E. *Traces of Texas History*. San Antonio: Corona Publishing Co., 1983.

Frazier, Irvin. *The Family of John Lewis, Pioneer*. San Antonio: Fisher Publications Inc., 1985.

Freed, Elaine. *Preserving the Great Plains and Rocky Mountains*. Albuquerque: University of New Mexico Press, 1992.

Frost, Susan Toomey. "San José and Miz Harrie." *Tile Heritage* 2 (fall 1995): 19–25.

Fuller, Larry Paul. "The Dullnig Block." *Texas Architect* (January–February 1982): 52–53.

Gallatin, Charles E. "A Clash of Causes in the River City." *Texas Architect* (September–October 1987): 10–11.

Garner, John C. Jr. *Historic American Buildings Survey, San Antonio*. San Antonio: n.p., 1969.

Garvin, Alexander. *The American City: What Works, What Doesn't*. New York: McGraw–Hill, 1996.

George, Eugene. "The Hispanic Touch," *Discovery* (summer 1984): 8–10.

George, Mary Carolyn Hollers. *O'Neil Ford, Architect*. College Station: Texas A&M University Press, 1992.

Gideon, Samuel E. Papers. Center for American History, University of Texas at Austin.

Glick, Thomas F. *The Old World Background of the Irrigation System of San Antonio, Texas*. Southwestern Studies, no. 35. El Paso: University of Texas at El Paso, 1972.

Goeldner, Paul, comp. *Texas Catalog: Historic American Buildings Survey*. San Antonio: Trinity University Press, 1975.

Gomez, Arthur R. *Espada Dam: A Preliminary Historical Report*. San Antonio Missions National Historical Park, 1990.

Green, Rena Maverick. Letters to Lola Maverick Lloyd. Schwimmer–Lloyd Collection, New York Public Library.

——. Papers. Private collection of Anne L. Fenstermaker, Boerne, Texas.

———, ed. *Memoirs of Mary A. Maverick*. Lincoln: University of Nebraska Press, 1989. Reprint of 1921 edition.

Green, William Elton. "Historical Preservation in Texas: A Chronology." Canyon, Texas: William Elton Green, 1995. Photocopy.

———. "Remembering the Alamo." Canyon, Texas: William Elton Green, 1990. Photocopy.

Greenberg, Mike. "San Antonio Grows: Coping with Prosperity in the Alamo City," *Texas Architect* (September–October 1983): 34–43.

Gruen Associates. *San Antonio North Expressway Study*. Washington: U.S. Dept. of Transportation Federal Highway Administration, 1971.

Guerra, Mary Ann Noonan. *The History of San Antonio's Market Square*. San Antonio: Alamo Press, 1988.

———. *The San Antonio River*. San Antonio: Alamo Press, 1987.

Habig, Marion A. *The Alamo Chain of Missions*. Chicago: Franciscan Herald Press, 1968.

———. *San Antonio's Mission San José*. San Antonio: Naylor Co., 1968.

Haley, James L. *Texas: From the Frontier to Spindletop*. New York: St. Martin's Press, 1986.

———. *Texas: From Spindletop through World War II*. New York: St. Martin's Press, 1986.

Henderson, Richard B. *Maury Maverick: A Political Biography*. Austin: University of Texas Press, 1970.

Henry, Jay C. *Architecture in Texas 1895–1945*. Austin: University of Texas Press, 1993.

Heusinger, Edward W. *A Chronology of Events in San Antonio*. San Antonio: Standard Printing, 1951.

Hosmer, Charles J. *The Presence of the Past*. New York: G. P. Putnam's Sons, 1965.

———. *Preservation Comes of Age, from Williamsburg to the National Trust, 1926–1949*. 2 volumes. Charlottesville: University of Virginia Press for the Preservation Press, 1981.

Howard, Pearl. "Southern Personalities: Adina De Zavala, Patriot-Historian." *Holland's Magazine* 64 (December 1935): 36.

Hyman, Sidney, et al. *With Heritage So Rich*. New York: Random House, 1966.

Johnson, David R, John A. Booth and Richard J. Harris, eds. *The Politics of San Antonio*. Lincoln: University of Nebraska Press, 1983.

Johnson Fain, et al. *Hemisfair: Transforming San Antonio, Framework and Master Plan*. San Antonio: Hemisfair Park Area Redevelopment Corp., 2012.

Jutson, Mary Carolyn Hollers. *Alfred Giles: An English Architect in Texas and Mexico*. San Antonio: Trinity University Press, 1972.

Knippa, Lyndon Gayle. "San Antonio II: The Early New Deal." In *Texas Cities and the Great Depression*. Austin: Texas Memorial Museum, 1973.

Labadie, Joseph H., comp. *La Villita Earthworks: A Preliminary Report of Investigations of Mexican Siege Works at the Battle of the Alamo*. University of Texas at San Antonio Center for Archaeological Research, 1986.

Lakota Group. *Strategic Historic Preservation Plan, San Antonio, Texas*. City of San Antonio, 2009.

Lane, Leonard. "A Moving Experience for the Fairmount Hotel in San Antonio," *Texas Architect* (January–February 1987): 16–26.

——. "H.E.B. Pulls Out the Artillery for Its Supermarket Offices." *Texas Architect* (November–December 1985): 104–109.

Lochbaum, Jerry, ed. *Old San Antonio: 250 Years in Pictures.* San Antonio: Express Publishing Co., 1968.

Marks, Paula Mitchell. *Turn Your Eyes toward Texas: Pioneers Sam and Mary Maverick.* College Station: Texas A&M University Press, 1989.

Matovina, Timothy M. *Tejano Religion and Ethnicity, San Antonio 1821–1860.* Austin: University of Texas Press, 1995.

McComb, David G. *Texas: A Modern History.* Austin: University of Texas Press, 1989.

McLemore, David. *A Place in Time: A Pictorial View of San Antonio's Past.* San Antonio: Express-News Corp., 1980.

Miller, Char, and Heywood T. Sanders, eds. *Urban Texas: Politics and Development.* College Station: Texas A&M University Press, 1990.

Minor, Joseph E., and Malcolm L. Steinberg. *The Acequias of San Antonio.* San Antonio Branch of the Texas Section of the American Society of Civil Engineers, 1968.

Minter, Jeffrey A., ed. *An Evaluation of Expansion Opportunities for the Henry B. Gonzalez Convention Center.* Washington: Urban Land Institute, 1995.

Montgomery, Roger. "HemisFair '68: Prologue to Renewal." *Architectural Forum* (October 1968): 86–88.

Morfi, Juan Agustín. *History of Texas, 1673–1779.* 2 volumes. Albuquerque: Quivera Society, 1935.

Moser, Karen. "Restorative Powers." *Southern Accents* (November–December 1994): 240 CC–FF.

Mulloy, Elizabeth D. *The History of the National Trust for Historic Preservation.* Washington: Preservation Press, 1976.

Murphy, Jim. "La Villita, San Antonio: Little Town." *Progressive Architecture* (November 1983): 108–13.

Murtagh, William J. *Keeping Time: The History and Theory of Preservation in America.* Pittstown, New Jersey: Main Street Press, 1988.

Naylor, David. *Great American Movie Theaters.* Washington: Preservation Press, 1987.

Newcomb, Pearson. *The Alamo City.* San Antonio: n.p., 1926.

Olmsted, Frederick Law. *A Journey through Texas.* New York: Dix, Edwards & Co., 1857.

Osborne, Mike. *San Antonio Portrait.* San Antonio: Maverick Publishing Co., 2005.

——. *San Antonio's Missions: A Portrait.* San Antonio: Maverick Publishing Co., 2010.

Pisano, Marina. "The Conservation Society." *SA: The Magazine of San Antonio* 3 (April 1979): 24–33.

Poyo, Gerald E., and Gilberto M. Hinojosa, *Tejano Origins in Eighteenth-Century San Antonio.* Austin: University of Texas Press for the University of Texas Institute of Texan Cultures at San Antonio, 1991.

Ragsdale, Kenneth B. *Centennial '36: The Year America Discovered Texas.* College Station: Texas A&M University Press, 1987.

Ramsdell, Charles. *San Antonio: A Historical and Pictorial Guide.* Austin: University of Texas Press, 1959.

Reps, John W. *Cities of the American West: A History of Frontier Urban Planning.* Princeton University Press, 1979.

[Ringenbach, Paul D., prep.]. *San Antonio Missions: Nomination for Inscription on the World Heritage List.* [Washington, DC: U.S. National Park Service], 2014.

San Antonio, City of. Commissioners Minutes, 1924–1930. San Antonio: City Clerk's Office.

——. *Downtown Neighborhood Plan.* City of San Antonio in cooperation with the Downtown Advisory Board and the Downtown Alliance, 1999.

——. *Houston Street Tax Increment Reinvestment Zone Number Nine, Final Project Plan.* Revised edition. City of San Antonio, 2010.

——. *San Antonio Historic Resource Data Cards.* 2 volumes. San Antonio Community Renewal Program, a Division of the San Antonio City Planning Department, 1972.

San Antonio Conservation Society. Minutes, 1924–1926, 1930–1995. San Antonio Conservation Society Library.

——. Oral History Transcripts. San Antonio Conservation Society Library.

——. *Yearbooks.* San Antonio Conservation Society.

San Antonio Federation of Women's Clubs. Minutes, 1927–1930. San Antonio Public Library.

Scheutz, Mardith K., et al. *San Antonio in the Eighteenth Century.* San Antonio Bicentennial Heritage Committee, 1976.

Schoelwer, Susan Prendergast. *Alamo Images, Changing Perceptions of a Texas Experience.* Dallas: DeGolyer Library and Southern Methodist University Press, 1985.

Sibley, Marilyn McAdams. *George W. Brackenridge: Maverick Philanthropist.* Austin: University of Texas Press, 1973.

——. *Travelers in Texas, 1761–1860.* Austin: University of Texas Press, 1967.

Simons, Helen, and Cathryn A. Hoyt. *Hispanic Texas: A Historical Guide.* Austin: University of Texas Press, 1992.

Smallwood, James M., ed. *Will Rogers' Weekly Articles. Vol. 2, The Coolidge Years, 1925–1927.* Stillwater: University of Oklahoma Press, 1980.

Smith, Jessie Carney, and Lean'tin Brack and Linda T. Wyne. *The Complete Encyclopedia of African American History.* Canton, Michigan: Visible Ink Press, 2014

Steinfeldt, Cecilia. *Art for History's Sake: The Texas Collection of the Witte Museum.* Austin: Texas State Historical Association for the Witte Museum, 1993.

——. *San Antonio Was: Seen through a Magic Lantern.* San Antonio Museum Association, 1978.

Tamez, Diana, ed. *Hemisfair Plaza: A Background Study.* Division of Environmental Studies, University of Texas at San Antonio, 1980.

Texas Historical Commission. *Historic Preservation in Texas.* 2 volumes. Austin: Texas Historical Commission and U.S. Department of the Interior Office of Archeology and Historic Preservation, 1973.

Thompson, Jon. "Graves Designs Alternative in RepublicBank, Texas Theater." *Texas Architect* (September–October 1982): 13–14.

Thurber, Marlys Bush, et al. *Of Various Magnificence: The Architectural History of the San Antonio Missions in the Colonial Period and the Nineteenth Century.* 2 volumes. Santa Fe: National Parks Service Southwest Regional Office Southwest Cultural Resources Center, 1993.

——. "Building the Missions of San Antonio." *Texas Architect* (May–June 1986): 54–58.

Thurber, Marlys Franc, and Richard W. Sellars. *Proposed San Antonio Missions Na-*

tional Historic Park: Alternatives for Implementation. Santa Fe: National Park Service Southwest Regional Office Division of Cultural Resources, 1975.

Tranchese, Carmelo, trans. *Los Pastores.* San Antonio, n.p., 1949.

Turner, Martha Anne. *Clara Driscoll: An American Tradition.* Austin: Madrona Press, 1979.

U.S. Department of the Interior National Park Service and National Conference of State Preservation Officers. *Preservation Tax Incentives for Historic Buildings.* Washington: U.S. Department of the Interior National Park Service and National Conference of State Preservation Officers, n.d.

Walters, Jonathan. "Battle Plan for a Texas Arsenal." *Historic Preservation* (July–August 1986): 54–55.

Webb, Walter Prescott, and Eldon Stephen Branda, eds. *The Handbook of Texas.* 3 volumes. Austin: Texas State Historical Association, 1952–1976.

Weber, David J. *The Mexican Frontier, 1821–1846.* Albuquerque: University of New Mexico Press, 1982.

———. *The Spanish Frontier in America.* Hartford: Yale University Press, 1992.

Woolford, Bess Carroll, and Ellen Schulz Quillin. *The Story of the Witte Memorial Museum, 1922–1960.* San Antonio: n.p., 1966.

Zunker, Vernon G. *A Dream Come True: Robert Hugman and San Antonio's River Walk.* Revised edition. San Antonio: n.p., 1994.

Index

LEWIS F. FISHER is the author of *American Venice: The Epic Story of San Antonio's River; San Antonio: Outpost of Empires; The Spanish Missions of San Antonio; Chili Queens, Hay Wagons and Fandangos: The Spanish Plazas in Frontier San Antonio;* and *No Cause of Offence: A Virginia Family of Union Loyalists Confronts the Civil War.* He has received numerous local, state and national writing awards and was named a Texas Preservation Hero by the San Antonio Conservation Society in 2014. He lives in San Antonio.